Personality in Intimate Relationships
Socialization and Psychopathology

Library of Congress Cataloging-in-Publication Data

L'Abate, Luciano, 1928–
  Personality in intimate relationships : socialization and psychopathology /
  Luciano L'Abate.
      p. cm.
  Includes bibliographical references and index.
  ISBN 0-387-22605-2
      1. Family—Psychological aspects. 2. Interpersonal relations—Psychological
  aspects. 3. Personality development. 4. Personality. 5. Socialization. 6. Psychology,
  Pathological. 7. Intimacy (Psychology)   I. Title.

  RC455.4.F3L3327 2005
  158.2′4—dc22   2004061909

ISBN 0-387-22605-2   e-ISBN 0-387-22607-9   Printed on acid-free paper.

Printed in the United States of America.

9 8 7 6 5 4 3 2 1

springeronline.com

To Peggy, my beautiful wife, best friend, amusing muse, faithful companion, competent collaborator, articulate colleague, unwavering and adamant supporter, and fearless critic, whose nurturing love gave ample space to my work in more ways than one.

Preface

"Under whatever disciplinary flag, however, someone will always ask how individuals are different from each other, how behavior changes, how people perceive, think, and plan, how people experience reality, and even what might be going on in the regions of the mind usually hidden from view. The basic questions of personality psychology will simply not go away (Funder, 2001, p. 216)."

The purpose of this work is to update, expand, examine, and evaluate a developmental, relational, and contextual theory of personality socialization and psychopathology in intimate and nonintimate relationships, family, friends, and other settings, namely: home, school/work, and surplus/leisure time activities (L'Abate, 1976, 1986, 1990, 1994, 1997, 2002, 2003a; L'Abate & De Giacomo, 2003). By intimate is meant relationships that are close, committed, interdependent, and prolonged. By close is meant relationships that are bound by emotional, physical, financial, legal, generational, and practical ties. By committed is meant a belief that the relationship will survive and that both partners and family members are involved in it reciprocally and mutually. By interdependent is meant that members of the unit, whatever that unit may be, have to depend on each other for survival and enjoyment. By prolonged is meant relationships that have been preserved and have survived the passage and test of time.

By the same token, nonintimate relationships are distant, spatially and temporally, uncommitted, by blood, or by any other means, short-lived and superficial, where other relationships are available to satisfy dependency needs. Closeness, commitment, interdependence, and prolongation in no way imply the level of functionality in a relationship. Satisfaction in a relationship may well be independent from those four characteristics. One could be close, committed, and interdependent for a prolonged period of time and feel perfectly miserable in the relationship or the relationship itself could be eminently dysfunctional. As we shall find out in the course of this work, other factors account for the level of functionality in a relationship (Le & Agnew, 2003).

In the past, the family has been thought of as the major context for socialization in the development of functionality and dysfunctionality. As Phares (1996) has amply demonstrated in her monumental review, the level of functionality in fathers, and, by the same token, in mothers, relates (dares one to say causes?) to functionality and dysfunctionality in their offspring. With exceptions, functional parents or caretakers tend to produce functionality in their children. With exceptions, dysfunctionality in parents or caretakers tends to produce dysfunctionality in their children. Here, dysfunctionality will be viewed on a continuum ranging from levels of functionality, to levels of semifunctionality, as in personality disorders, and to levels of psychopathology, as in dissociation, severe depression, bipolar disorder, criminality, and psychopathology.

Following a theoretical framework close to the Diagnostic and Statistical Manual-IV (DSM-IV; American Psychiatric Association, 1994), however, the classification used here will show continuity and contiguity between superior functionality and severe psychopathology. The discrete categories of the DSM-IV will be expressed into continuous, and when possible, relational dimensions, using prototypes to define extremes of each dimension (Kirmayer & Young, 1999), with functionality in the middle of each dimension. Criminality, dysfunctionality, and psychopathology may arise from genetic and hereditary factors. However, here the influence of socialization in intimate relationships will be stressed, even though there is no denying the influence of earlier factors.

The concept of intimate relationships instead of "family" is used here because the family as an intact unit or system is no longer tenable. Only circa 25% of domiciles in the United States are composed of a traditionally intact family, two long-married parents and two children. The rest are composed of single individuals, single parents, remarried couples and step-families, same sex couples, children raised by grandparents and by foster parents. Even though some units can be called "families" because its members all live under the same roof, this term has become relative. Although the term "family" might sometimes be used in this work, one should understand that family could also stand for "alternative" or "substitute" intimate relationships of the type mentioned above.

Indeed, in the past generation, the role of close friendships has taken over emotional and practical roles that were heretofore allocated to the family (Fehr, 1996). These relationships do have in common, in varying degrees and in varying qualities, some degree of closeness, some degree of commitment, some degree of interdependence, and some degree of prolongation. Whether these four characteristics are necessary and sufficient remains to be seen throughout the pages of this work. Instead of the nuclear family as traditionally conceived, many alternatives and substitutes have assumed the same function, perhaps with a much greater degree of choice and freedom than may have existed in the past. In some cases, such as grandparents taking care of grandchildren, this is not a choice but a forced duty fostered by the inadequacy or absence of parental caretakers. Nonetheless, these alternatives indicate how important intimate relationships are, regardless of legal or traditional blood ties.

This theory can be evaluated through systematic administration of paper-and-pencil, self-report tests in the laboratory, enrichment programs in primary prevention, self-help, mental health workbooks in secondary prevention, and specific, theory-derived tasks and prescriptions in tertiary prevention or psychotherapy. Previous works cited above and various papers and chapters reviewed and summarized the nature of this theory with the evidence to support its validity and usefulness current at the time. However, more evidence needs to be added to expand and update the theory. Unless necessary, previous publications will not be mentioned again in this work. Serious limitations of space reduced significantly the number of primary references (originally over 2,000!) used to support most statements made in the course of this work. Many references supporting each statement had to be erased. They are retained when there could be a challenge to statements made here. In spite of necessary selectivity in choosing references, the most significant and recent ones are cited.

The major feature of this version is to focus in greater detail on the nature of models derived from the theory. Hence, this work deals with links between personality and intimate relationships, not in opposition but, if valid, in continuity with evidence gathered from contrived, short-lived, and superficial laboratory findings and applications of models of the theory in evaluation, and primary, secondary, and tertiary prevention approaches. To support the validity of theoretical models, in addition to self-report, paper-and-pencils tests, and preventive interventions, a great many references have been used way beyond what might be required. The main reason for such an inordinate number of references is to bolster the validity of each model and its allocation and placement within the DSM-IV framework. One could say that the theory attempts to provide a conceptual framework for a psychiatric classification found in the DSM-IV that, as a whole, lacks one. Consequently, it is crucial to summarize as much evidence as one can find to support such an allocation and placement, showing how the theory is isomorphic with the reality of functionality in continuity with dysfunctionality, criminality, and psychopathology, as viewed by the DSM-IV and its successors.

This theory has also been called "developmental competence theory" in past versions. Linking theory with evaluation and with specific interventions is difficult if not impossible to achieve when interventions take place verbally. This link is much easier to achieve when repeatable operations derived directly from the theory itself, through writing in the laboratory, with paper-and-pencil, self-report tests, or through repeatable interventions in three prevention approaches, primary, secondary, and tertiary. This link is relatively easier to obtain if the theory is evaluated with test instruments derived directly from the theory as well as by test instruments or interventions indirectly or independently related to the theory itself. A unique characteristic of this theory, for instance, is to suggest and show how self-help workbooks are and can become a way of evaluating models of the theory. Consequently, in addition to workbooks derived from previous versions of this theory, the whole theory is summarized into a parenting workbook available online with other workbooks (L'Abate, 1996). Workbooks can be used alone or in conjunction with primary, secondary, and tertiary prevention approaches. In preventive settings, models of the theory can be evaluated through structured enrichments programs in primary prevention, self-administered workbooks in secondary prevention, and therapeutic tasks in tertiary prevention. All of the above is in writing and it is reproducible, and therefore, replicable. This process cannot be achieved as easily through talk.

This theory proposes that hurt feelings and their avoidance are at the bottom of personality socialization in intimate relationships. Most, if not all, hurt feelings are produced within the context of intimate relationships. Even though other contexts (school/work, surplus leisure time) are important, *how* hurt feelings are experienced and expressed throughout the life cycle depends a great deal on how we learn to experience and to express them from our families of origin and past intimate relationships. Hurt feelings, however, are like the heart of an artichoke. One needs to peel off all the leaves and the choke (of anger and rage!) before getting to its heart, where hurt feelings are kept, and oftentimes remain, jealously and rigidly, unexpressed. Consequently, one needs to examine and to evaluate the validity and usefulness of looking at hurt feelings as being basic to personality socialization in functional and dysfunctional relationships.

Hurt feelings are still a taboo topic that has been bypassed or even ignored by many personality theorists, personal relationships experts, as well as by many therapists. Synonymous circumlocutions, like "distress," "trauma," "grief," or "negative feelings," have been used instead. Intimacy, the sharing of hurts and of fears to being hurt, has not been considered in many theoretical and therapeutic treatises until recently, thanks to the work of Pennebaker (2001) on expressive writing.

To support the isomorphy between theory and psychiatric classification, another feature of this book consists of using prototypes of personality disorders, as well as criminality and severe psychopathology to illustrate extremes that define dimensions related to specific models. For instance, an extreme of approach in a dimension of distance and the ability to love (Ch. 7) would be dependent and symbiotic personalities from Axis II, Cluster C. Gradual increases in the opposite side of avoidance in the same dimension of distance would be procrastination, social anxiety, social phobia, and in the extreme, the avoidant personality.

The extreme in the dimension of control (Ch. 8) and the ability to negotiate, bargain, and problem-solve (Ch. 17) would be discharge, as exhibited by impulsive and acting out personalities in Axis II, Cluster B. At the other extreme of delay in the same dimension, one could place the personality disorders from Axis II, Cluster C. Thus, an attempt will be made to illustrate each theory-derived dimension by prototypic examples of how that dimension is defined at opposite ends, initially by gradual extremes in personality disorders, and eventually, those disorders will be related to severe psychopathology, depression, bipolar disorder, and schizophrenia (Ch. 12).

OVERVIEW OF THE BOOK

The introductory Chapter 1 reviews critically the nature of a theory and the fragmentation among diverse fields of personality, social psychology, personal relationships, developmental psychology, family therapy, and sociology of the family as far as intimate relationships are concerned. In their fragmentation from each other, they are continually ignoring deviant relationships, criminality, and psychopathology, as well as preventive and therapeutic applications to help change those very deviant relationships. Deviant relationships and preventive and therapeutic applications will be reviewed in their relevance to each model of the theory, summarized in one table.

Part I is devoted to the two necessary and possibly sufficient requirements for this or any theory. Chapter 2 focuses on one requirement for a theory of this nature, that is, reducibility from known, usually monadic psychological to relational constructs, proffering the thesis that most constructs dealing with relationships are already present in the extant psychological literature. However, they need to be viewed within the context of relationships rather than individually. Rather than using intrapsychic, mentalistic concepts or external behavioral concepts in a vacuum from their natural contexts, intimate and nonintimate relationships are the focus of this work. Intimate relationships, as already defined above, are usually called "communal." These ties, however, are not found in usually short-lived, superficial, nonintimate, commercial, i.e., "exchange," relationships. Emphasis is placed on "relationships" rather than on "mind" or even "behavior," since behavior is the outcome of relationships among individuals as well as between individuals and objects in various settings and specific contexts.

Chapter 3 expands on the empiricist's credo that it is better to be specific and be *found* wrong or inaccurate on the basis of evidence gathered by those who are external to the theory, rather than being generally vague and claim to be right without evidence or, on faith, personal opinion, or on opportunistic whim or will. This position focuses on accountability as the second *conditio sine qua non* for developing a theory of personality in its natural contexts, the family, intimate relationships, and other settings. The theory, however, is broken down into models to make it more specific and more verifiable.

Part II summarizes the three metatheoretical assumptions of the theory, that is, assumptions that go above and beyond the theory itself, representing and summarizing past theories and views. Chapter 4 covers the horizontality of relationships according to their width, following an information processing model that includes five component resources of Emotionality, Rationality, Activity, Awareness, and Context (the ERAAwC Model[1]). Chapter 5 covers verticality, the depth dimension of relationships according to descriptive and explanatory levels and sublevels. Chapter 6 reviews the nature of settings according to a classification that distinguishes where intimate relationships take place, mostly in the home. Nonintimate relationships take place in school/work and leisure or surplus time settings necessary for survival as well as in settings that are not only necessary for survival but also for enjoyment.

Part III covers the two assumptions of the theory proper through two *processes*: the ability to love, and the ability to negotiate. An extra postulate about contents that mediate assumptions with the models of the theory proper is necessary. Chapter 7 stresses the ability to love, where space deals with *distance*, how close or how far people are and stay from each other. Here is where prototypes from Cluster C (in the DSM-IV) will be used to define extreme ends of this dimension. Chapter 8 covers time as viewed in the dimension of *control* basic to the ability to negotiate, how fast or how slow people respond to or with each other. Here is where prototypes from Cluster B will be used to define extremes of this dimension. Chapter 9 is the extra postulate necessary to deal with the *contents* of what is being exchanged, the three modalities of Being, Doing, and Having. Prototypes from both Clusters B and C will be used here. However, some prototypes not included in either cluster or even the DSM-IV classification will be added to demonstrate the continuity of each dimension rather than discrete categories without continuity or contiguity.

Part IV covers four major models derived from the metatheoretical assumptions as well as the two assumptions and postulate of the theory proper. Chapter 10 expands on the developmental continuum of likeness that was not as developed in past writings as it is here. This chapter shows how this continuum is basic to identity formation and differentiation, as it develops from the assumptions of the theory. Chapter 11 covers three major relational styles that derive directly from the likeness continuum and that describe intimate relationships, a functional one, two semifunctional, and a dysfunctional. Chapter 12 expands on the major model of the theory, selfhood, with its four personality propensities. The major implication of this model lies in its classification of functional intimate relationships seen in contiguity and continuity with dysfunctional ones, such as criminality, affective, psychosomatic, and addictive disorders as well as more extreme psychopathologies. Therefore, this chapter elaborates on this comprehensive (some would call it grandiose!) classification to detail even further how mental and behavioral disorders (listed in the DSM-IV) can be viewed as extremes of this model, along two orthogonal dimensions: (1) vertically, functionalities/dysfunctionalities, and (2) horizontally, externalizations/internalizations. Chapter 13 deals with priorities, a construct that derives from the assumption of importance basic to emotional and economical survival and enjoyment. One cannot love and negotiate without being well differentiated in identity and selfhood and having functional rather than dysfunctional priorities (self, partner, children, parents, etc.).

Part V includes chapters that are direct derivations and applications from the previous four chapters. For instance, Chapter 14 is an expansion of Chapter 7 to show how we regulate distance to avoid confronting hurt feelings. Chapter 15 is an expansion of previous models in Chapters 10 and 11 that cover the universal triad of Savior, Persecutor, and Victim as the beginning of dysfunctional relationships. Chapter 16 is an expansion of Chapter 12 to cover intimacy as the sharing of joys and hurts and of fears of being hurt, arguing that we are all needy, fallible, and vulnerable to hurt feelings, either in producing or in receiving them from loved ones. Chapter 17 deals with the structure and process of negotiation and problem solving, as derived from previous models, and especially the ERAAwC Model[1] in Chapter 4. Chapter 18 included a grand model including and integrating all the previous models, proposing also a comparison of the selfhood model from Chapter 12 with other models independent of the theory.

In the concluding Part VI, Chapter 19 summarizes up-to-date evidence to support models of the theory, while Chapter 20 prognosticates about how this theory may supersede traditional, *in vacuum* theories that have considered personality development and socialization as taking place apart from relationships with intimates, other human beings, or even objects.

Separate appendices available online (L'Abate, 1996) contain information necessary to support the theory. Appendix A contains a list of workbooks designed to evaluate various models of the theory in an interactive fashion. Appendix B contains items and scoring information to administer the Relational Answers Questionnaire (RAQ), developed by Mario Cusinato and his students at the University of Padua, to measure components of the ERAAwC model (Ch. 4). Appendix C contains a way to measure Likeness in intimate relationships (Ch. 10). Appendix D contains a Planned Parenting workbook, completely derived from the theory itself, available to evaluate the theory in clinics as well as in interactive laboratory and Internet applications.

INTENDED AUDIENCE FOR THIS BOOK

Who would be interested in a book of this kind? Hopefully, graduate courses in personality development and abnormal psychology classes should be interested in a more relational, contextual theory that is testable not only in the laboratory, but also in clinical and nonclinical settings. Mental health professionals, either preventers or therapists, as well as researchers, will be able to apply a theory with nonclinical and clinical applications by making the theory isomorphic with the DSM-IV. Since the theory links individuals with intimate relationships as well as with settings in which they live, individual, couple, and family therapists might be interested in a theory of this kind. This theory no longer looks at personality development in *a vacuum*, as personality has been viewed traditionally, but where it matters, in intimate relationships and in specific settings.

This theory breaks new theoretical, preventive, and therapeutic grounds that were not present in existing theories or therapies, that is: connecting theory with practice and developing specific and replicable ways and means to evaluate the theory and its outcome on hurting and troubled people. In the laboratory, the theory has been tested through paper-and-pencil, self-report tests (available in previous publications) that have been developed directly from the theory over the past 20 years of my academic tenure and retirement, as well as by my major collaborator, Mario Cusinato from the University of Padua, and his students. These instruments can be used as before-after measures to evaluate the outcome of theory-related or theory-independent interventions in primary, secondary, and tertiary prevention approaches (L'Abate, 1996).

Luciano L'Abate
May 7, 2004

Acknowledgments

Among many friends and colleagues who helped throughout the writing of this book, I need to mention my very first and most recent editor, who rekindled my energy (and my theory), keeping both alive since her editing my very first book with Grune and Stratton, and who is now responsible for the publication of this book: Sharon Panulla, senior editor at Springer. Her belief in my work helped me surmount years of frustrations, when I was told by quite a few editors that: "Theories do not sell." Let us see whether this does.

I am grateful to Jim Pate for his help with Chapter 4, and to Leslie L. Bowden for typing hundreds of references at the time I had been left months behind by an unexpected blow-out in the hard drive of a previous typist's computer. I am especially grateful to Mrs. Karon S. Wilson, whose technical computer expertise and competence with thousand of references, and her goodwill in a time of crisis, allowed me to complete a job I could not have ever completed by myself. To the folks at AIS Computers, I am grateful for helping me with unexpected emergencies and formatting problems well beyond my simple word processing knowledge that allowed me to complete this job: Joel Crawford, David Reynolds, Michael Solberg, and Jabari Williams. I am also grateful to Benjamin Scott, librarian at Georgia State University for the hurried, last minute retrieval of a few still missing references. I am grateful to Gabriel Kuperminc for updating me about the work of his former mentor and my fellow postdoctoral fellow at Michael Reese Hospital in Chicago years before either one published any book, Sidney J. Blatt.

The following publishers have graciously allowed printing of figures, tables, and quotes used throughout this book. American Psychiatric Association for criteria 100, 90, and 80 from their Diagnostic and Statistical Manual-IV. Annual Reviews for the quote from Funder (2001). Greenwood

Publications for Figure 12.4, and Figures 16.1 and 16.2, as well as Tables 18.1 and 18.2 from L'Abate and De Giacomo (2003). Guilford Publications for the quote from Cummings, Davies, and Campbell (2000). Lawrence Earlbaum Associates for quotes from Burleson (2003), Canary (2003), and Onorato and Turner (2002), MIT Press for the quote from Gibbs (2001). Sage Publications for the list of criteria for theory construction in Chapter 3 from Klein and While (1996). John Wiley & Sons Publishers for the quote from Greenfield (2000).

Atlanta, GA
May 7, 2004

Contents

Chapter 1

Background for a Theory of Personality Socialization in Intimate Relationships and Psychopathology

"The creation of models is a mainstay of the scientific mind-set.... The idea is to capture the critical feature or essence of an otherwise slippery or complex phenomenon ... the overall picture of a system (Greenfield, 2000, p. 21)."

"Intimate relationships are intense interactions, by definition, with emotions weaving through each interaction and often contributing heat to any light that cognition may shed (Sinnott, 2002, p. 229)."

The purpose of this chapter is to consider and review the background for a theory of personality socialization in intimate relationships, the family, and other settings. This background also includes a review of the considerable fragmentation that exists among various theoretical frameworks about personality socialization, a summary of the theory with past efforts to evaluate it in the laboratory and other settings, and look at workbooks as vehicles of theory/model evaluation.

THE ROLE OF THEORY IN MODEL CONSTRUCTION

American psychological literature, especially most peer-reviewed publications sanctioned and supported by the American Psychological Association, is either devoid of theory or theory takes a second place to emphasis on small, repeatable experimental designs that bypass or ignore theory testing and discourage theory building (Omer & Dar, 1992). At best modest models are created without relationship to a larger, more encompassing theory. One does not receive a Ph.D. degree or obtain research grants to develop a theory. Both degrees and grants are given on the basis of empirical evidence or the need to obtain results based on some kind of evidence around small, researchable topics. Hence, theory construction, unless based on empirical evidence, is relegated to a secondary position, if not ignored altogether. As discussed further in Chapter 3, small and specific models can be evaluated. Large and vague theories are difficult if not impossible to evaluate. This is the reason why this theory has been broken down into smaller, more manageable models, each with its own matching way to evaluate itself.

Research without Theory

This conclusion is too important and relevant to leave without some support. In the first place, the same charge has been made by Baumeister and Tice (2001) in their criticism of the literature on sex research. While theory was paramount to psychological science, that no longer seems the case. Schore (2003), for instance, agrees with the foregoing conclusion: "In the life sciences, there has been almost an aversion to overarching theoretical schemas (p. xv)."

In the second place, Bergman, Magnusson, and El-Khourn (2003) commented on the same conclusion in developmental science:

> "Too often, developmental research is caught in the prison of piecemeal theories and/or sophisticated statistical models and methods, without the necessary reference to proper analysis of the phenomena at the appropriate level.... The remedy of this situation is the acceptance and application of research strategies in which empirical studies on specific developmental issues are planned, implemented, and interpreted with explicit reference to an overriding, common theoretical framework (p. 6)."

In the third place, Omer and Dar (1992) reviewed 252 empirical studies of psychotherapy published in the *Journal of Consulting and Clinical Psychology* in the years 1967/1968, 1977/1978, and 1987/1988. Articles were rated on their theoretical relevance, clinical validity, and methodology. These authors found that the major trend over the period of time was a decline in theory-guided and a rise in pragmatic, clinically oriented research. After highlighting the disadvantages of a purely empirical approach to psychotherapy research, Omen and Dar distinguished between the different purposes of pragmatic versus theory-driven research. The former is oriented toward the solution of immediate human problems. The latter is oriented toward understanding the complexity of human problems before attempting to solve them. Jensen (1999) stressed the need for linking practice with theory and research, adding:

> "Evolving theories of behavior have several characteristics in common; namely: that they are developmental, transactional, contextual, malaptational, multilevel, and multidetermined (p. 553)."

Hopefully, this theory will join other theories in sharing the common characteristics listed by Jensen. What this theory will not join lies in his stress on intimate "relationships" rather than "behavior."

As we shall see below, the strategy of this work is to link theoretical models to *replicable* operations, such as: (1) specific paper-and-pencil, self-report tests; (2) to written-down enrichment programs for couples and families in primary prevention (L'Abate & Weinstein, 1987; L'Abate & Young, 1987); or (3) self-help workbooks in secondary prevention, and (4) specific therapeutic tasks. To be replicable, an operation must be written down for ease of application, as in the case of all the methods listed above.

In the fourth place, most textbooks on personality and personality theories are stuck in reporting and reviewing the old, tired, sometimes tried, and questionably true, monadic and a-contextual theories of personality, repeatedly from one textbook to another, the individual without or outside the context of intimate relationships (Cervone & Mischel, 2002; Feist & Feist, 2002; Hogan, Johnson, & Briggs, 1997; Mischel, 2004; Pervin & John, 1999). The sole exception to this conclusion is Bowlby's attachment model (Kenny & Barton, 2002; Schore, 2003), that has dominated a great deal of the psychological literature in the past decade. However, this model has not yet filtered down to most textbooks on personality theory cited above, or even couple evaluation treatises (Sperry, 2004). Again, all that is required is comparing two or more personality theories texts and the reader can evaluate whether this conclusion is valid or not, as well as explore current, refereed psychological journals and find whether this conclusion is valid or not. Instead of theories, models are modest and confined interpretations of specific relationships, as elaborated below.

Confusion between Theories and Models

Oftentimes, theories are confused with models and are made synonymous with models. Attachment theory, for instance, is but one example of a model that is called a theory, perhaps because it was derived from object relations theory (L'Abate & De Giacomo, 2003). Nonetheless, no matter what attachment theory is called, it still consists of one model that has produced a plethora of studies around the world. Yet, in spite of being a model, it is still called a theory, demonstrating the synonymous use of both terms.

In addition to attachment theory, another example of a synonymous match between model and theory is found in social comparison theory, where the same charge could be leveled and has been leveled (L'Abate & De Giacomo, 2003). In spite of its fruitfulness as a model based originally on Fenstinger's social behavior theory, it still remains a model about a specific topic, and nothing else. It is a model but it is called a theory, as will be considered in Chapter 8. Relational models theory (Haslam, 2004) is an another example of a model that has been called a theory.

In this work, the terms theory and model are not used synonymously. This theory is composed of many models, as shall be shown throughout this work. A model is part of a theory. Without such a link, how can any model survive isolated from theory or from other models? As Cummings, Davies, and Campbell (2000) commented on this issue:

> "Theory-driven research on both prevention and treatment, while time-consuming and difficult to conduct, is really one of the only ways we have to test models that may identify etiological factors and causal pathways leading from early developmental risk to later maladjustment and diagnosable disorder (p. 414)."

Consequently, the result of this emphasis on research at the expense of theory has been the production of small, verifiable models that remain the province of a close-knit group of dedicated researchers. Their time and energy is spent to evaluate various implications of each model, oftentimes separate from other models or theories. There is a great deal to commend in model-building by knowing more and more about detailed aspects of any model. This is truly the experimental method at its best, as discussed further in Chapter 3. Yet, the issue remains: after a variety of models have been constructed and validated how are they going to be linked together? Who is going to do it, at the cost of being called "grandiose" or "irrelevant"? What happens after all these models have been built and tested? How and who is going to put them together into one overarching theory?

An example of this state of affairs is found in the work edited by Liddle, Santisteban, Levant, and Bray (2000). They stressed the importance of empirically based methods of treatment, presenting a variety of theoretical models unrelated with each other. More importantly, the models were unrelated to empirically based treatment approaches! Hence, the criterion of empirically based treatment models, amply supported in this work, needs to be paired with another criterion not considered by Liddle et al., as well as by many researchers who profess allegiance to empirically based treatments, and that is: *theory-derived, empirically replicable psychological interventions* (L'Abate, 2003a). Psychological models, therefore, not only need to be empirically verifiable, as will be discussed in Chapter 3, they must also be theory-derived or at least, theory-related. Otherwise, many empirically based treatments would be free-standing, without any rationale behind them. This criterion will be discussed in greater detail later in this chapter.

Another way to understand the weak link between theory and research would be the emphasis on testable empirical studies and models as being ahead of theory. As Barnett and Hyde (2001) have indicated, previous theories are irrelevant to present day conditions. Hence, one could say that theory has to catch up to research results and model-building. A theory has to be up-to-date with research in order to be viable. That means that a theory must be comprehensive enough to include as much as empirical evidence is available to support it. Past theories may not have been used by researchers because they may have found them irrelevant or inapplicable to present day evidence and models. In this regard, Dahlstrom (1995) argued that:

> "...contemporary theorizing about the nature of personality has neglected typological formulations. Instead, reliance has been placed on multidimensional geometric models that fail to capture the crucial configural nature of personality structure and functioning. As a result, there has been little progress in the development of a comprehensive taxonomy of human personalities or in the establishment of a personological systematics. Reasons for this neglect...are related to a general aversion to 'pigeon-holing' people and the risk of applying stereotypes rather than theorotypes....Potential benefits for the science and art of personality assessment...(can) be gained from a comprehensive personological taxonomy...(p. 3)."

Whether this theory will live up to Dahlstrom's standards remains to be seen. However, robust links among theory, research, and practice would enable elaboration of a treatment framework that is practical in its development, effective in its methods, and compelling in its rationale (L'Abate & De Giacomo, 2003). All of the above is quite consistent with the aims and thesis of this work, except to express a repeated skepticism that few changes will occur as long as psychological interventions are based on talk (L'Abate, 1999b).

FRAGMENTATION IN PSYCHOLOGICAL THEORIES AND MODELS

This section will argue that the considerable fragmentation among theories and models of personality socialization, developmental, social, and adult psychology, as well as personal relationships makes it necessary to develop a theory that will attempt to integrate these specializations in a consistent framework.

Personalities without Intimate Relationships

Before beginning with the theory proper, however, it is important to consider the current status of personality theories, at least in the United States, to introduce a conceptual background that would allow comparing and contrasting this relatively new theory with existing personality theories. Most personality theories not only are a-contextual and nonrelational, but they also ignore intimate relationships as a basic unit for personality socialization, its development, and psychopathology. I have documented this frequently in the past but it needs further elucidation. Barnett and Hyde (2001), for instance, argued that in terms of all the changes in women's roles, past theories of personality are "obsolete." Further evidence will be presented here to support that conclusion. Most personality theories cited above or models of adult development (Demick & Andreotti, 2002) make few references to marriage and the family, as if individuals grew up suddenly as adults without any nurturing socialization from parents, siblings, relatives, and extended family, friends, foes, or lovers.

Personality development is still seen as a matter of internal factors, like genes and temperament, rather than an interaction between hereditary and family-derived factors. A survey (L'Abate & Dunne, 1979) of textbooks on personality, exceptional children, and developmental psychology found that to be true in 15% of developmental psychology textbooks to less than 1% of references on family-related topics (family, father, marriage, mother, parents, siblings) in theories of personality textbooks. The same survey repeated years later (1994), only with theories of personality textbooks, showed only .05% of references linked to family-related topics. A recent survey of personality theories gives two pages to the family constellation and no pages to other family concepts, like marriage, parenting, parent-child or sibling-sibling relationships (L'Abate & De Giacomo, 2003).

Ditto for social psychology, adults are considered as having never grown up developmentally. They are suddenly adults without any historical antecedents, no parents, no siblings, no relatives, and no extended family, or intimate relationships (Chaiken & Trope, 1999; Higgins & Kruglanski, 1996).

The field of personal relationships does consider intimate relationships at developmental stages in the life cycles, rather than focusing on contrived, short-lived, and superficial laboratory studies or paper-and-pencil reports with college sophomores. In all fairness, a treatise on personal relationships (Duck, 1988) did have seven pages (out of 702) devoted to family systems, 12 pages and seven footnotes devoted to marital distress, interaction, quality, satisfaction, therapy, and types, with one page and three footnotes devoted to parent-child relationships. A more recent text (Harvey & Weber, 2002), however, dedicated four pages (out of 249) to family and 19 pages to marriage, but none to parent-child relationships, leading to the conclusion that this discipline is slightly more interested in intimate relationships than personality or social psychology, but in a selective, non-systematic fashion.

Developmental psychology does indeed acknowledge the importance of parents, siblings, relatives, and the extended family. However, it does stop short of adulthood, leaving theorizing and empirical studies to the other fields of personality and social psychology. Hence, we need a theory of personality socialization in intimate relationships that covers various stages of individual lifespan and family life cycles, functionalities and dysfunctionalities, as well as reproducible ways to prevent and treat the latter (Cummings et al., 2000).

Intimate Relationships without Personalities

In spite of sociologist Burgess's 1927 dictum (Loukas, Twitchell, Piejak, Fitzgerald, & Zucker, 1998) about the family as "a unity of interacting personalities," systems theory, one of the many fads in family theories "dismissed the importance of individual functioning and history (Lebow, 2001)." Family therapists and sociologists refer to the family without consideration of the personalities involved (Klein & White, 1996). Misleading or unnecessary dichotomies between psychological and sociological theories prolong the myth that there are indeed distinctions between the two types of theories. This dichotomy would lead to greater fragmentation: theories for individuals, theories for couples, and theories for families, leading to misguided and unnecessary chaos and confusion. The fact that there are separate textbooks for the assessment of individuals, couples, and families attests to this fragmentation in practice as well as in theory. This outcome would make it difficult to verify any model of intimate relationships.

In pursuing the conclusion of intimate relationships without personalities, an old hobby-horse of family therapists, that is, systems thinking, is appealing and seductive but not testable. It is a paradigm or metatheory rather than a theory. It is indeed focused on the family rather than on the individual personalities within the family. Furthermore, it is separate in concepts, constructs, and methodology (if any) from psychology as a science and as a profession. Hence the creation and existence of family psychology as a discipline dedicated to study individuals in the family, rather than the family qua family as in sociology and in family therapy, or personalities without intimate relationships, as already discussed.

Finally, all of the fields surveyed above ignore deviant relationships, leaving out from their considerations the most intense of all relationships, those that lead to death, suicide, incarceration, and hospitalization, that is: criminality and psychopathology. All one has to do to verify this conclusion is to check contents and indices for the texts cited above and verify whether this conclusion is valid or not.

Additionally, as Bradbury (2002) has pointed out, not without controversy (Hendrick, 2002; Muehlhoff & Wood, 2002; Reis, 2002), all of the above theoretical frameworks have one characteristic in common, that is they all lack practical applications beyond self-report, paper-and-pencil tests and contrived laboratory experiments. None of them leads or has lead to preventive or therapeutic advances. The present theory aims at correcting such a shortcoming.

Integrating the Fragmentation

More recently, there is a movement afoot to add a new category of "Relational Diagnosis" to the DSM-IV, after early suggestions about its irrelevance to family therapy (Frances, Clarkin, & Perry, 1984). This step indicates the need to view psychopathology from the "outside" or "among and between individuals" rather than just "inside" the individual. This view results from how individuals relate specifically in certain intimate relationships, rather than how they behave in an interpersonal vacuum. This position is supported, among others, by what Hendriks-Jansen (1996) has called "interactive emergence," that relationships are the outcome of emergent interactions between two or more individuals, or between individuals and objects, a position championed years ago by J. R. Kantor's "inter-behavioral field." What here are called "relationships" have characteristics of their own that need to be evaluated in their own rights, as L'Abate and De Giacomo (2003), besides others (Gibbs, 2001) have proposed. Fiske and Haslam (1996) put it this way:

> "Social scientists may concern themselves with two kinds of variables when making sense of social relations. On the one hand, they may refer to the attributions of individuals, such as their genders, races, ages, and personalities. All of these attributes inhere in persons, or are socially constructed as inhering in them. These attributes are features of individuals. Some characteristics, on the other hand, cannot be ascribed to individuals, but only to the relations between them. Whereas individual attributes define kinds of people, these other characteristics define kinds of relationships (p. 141)."

Consequently, intimate relationships are the outcome of interactions between and among individuals who are emotionally close, committed to maintain the relationship over time, and interdependent in sharing common responsibilities. These relationships transcend the individual personalities of partners and members in functional cases. However, in dysfunctional cases, personality disorders and individual psychopathology may be the products and producers of relationships that fail to work over time. Indeed, intimate relationships have become the focus of what is now called "relationship science" (Reis, Collins, & Berscheid, 2000).

REQUIREMENTS FOR A RELATIONAL THEORY OF PERSONALITY

Hence, this work will show how it is possible to link theory with practice not just in psychotherapy, i.e., tertiary prevention, but also in the laboratory and in primary and secondary prevention. To achieve this goal, one will need to expand on a theory of developmental, relational competence that has attempted to develop this link. Additional requirements for this theory concern its reducibility to known psychological constructs (Ch. 2), and its verifiability and accountability (Ch. 3).

Relational

In the first place, the theory must be relational, stressing the nature of intimate relations as functions of individual characteristics in transactions with demand characteristics of intimate others and of various settings across generations (Bergman et al., 2003; Gergen, 1994). This requirement means seeing both functional and dysfunctional relationships as being transmitted over generational lines. Furthermore, one cannot have a theory about how individuals behave separately from how they behave with their partners, parents, children, siblings, relatives, friends, neighbors, co-workers, and occasional salespersons. By the same token, nor can one have a theory of couples without considering their families. Furthermore, the breakdown of the traditional family (L'Abate, 2004c) has produced subgroups and alliances that were either minimal or ignored in the past, such as same-sex parents, adoptive or step-parents, grandparent-grandchild dyads, singles, or co-habiting couples. How can one have different theories for each of these subgroups? Perhaps models for each of these subgroups may be the answer. However, any attempt of this kind would be met by frustration and failure since no current theory could encompass them.

This theory, therefore, stresses relationships between and among intimate others, rather than having separate theories (or models!) for individuals, separate theories for couples, subgroups, or separate theories for families. Individuals are products and producers of the very relationships they live in, in a process of continuous and reciprocal exchange, giving and taking. What is exchanged? This is the crucial question attempted in vein by systems theories but never satisfactorily answered. What and how one learns to behave in intimate relationships tends to generalize to other settings. This link between intimate relationships and other settings is especially visible in explanatory styles of optimism versus pessimism (Buchanan & Seligman, 1995; Seligman & Csikszentmihalyi, 2000). Functional intimate relationships are optimistic. Dysfunctional intimate relationships are pessimistic, producing individuals who, very likely behave likewise.

Contextual

In the second place, the theory must be contextually ecological, relating to events within each setting and relationships among various settings: residence, school/work, and surplus time settings. We take our intimate relationships of origin and of procreation along with us and keep them inside everywhere we go in how we behave toward other intimates and non-intimates. Nonetheless, besides the family or its substitute system, other settings do influence personality socialization. Normatively speaking, intimate relationships may be primary, with other settings being secondary. However, in some individuals, secondary settings may become primary, as in the case of workaholics or Type A personalities. For instance, the latter are consumed by their work. Extreme athletes are consumed by their sport. Hoarders are consumed by amassing things, or tycoons are consumed by accumulating money.

Developmental

In the third place, this theory must be developmental. It must be applicable to most if not all major stages of the life cycle: (1) dependence in early childhood; (2) denial of dependence in adolescence; (3) interdependence-autonomy in adulthood; and (4) return to dependence in old age. By developmental is meant to also include various stages of the individual-family life cycle, i.e., getting married, having children, seeing them leave to produce their own families, retirement, death and its aftermath on the family.

This theory acknowledges the importance of specific developmental competencies as a function of interactions with specific people and settings. Acquisition of personal and interpersonal competence is a socialization process that acknowledges the importance of specificities peculiar to given people and to a given setting. These personal specificities are abilities and skills particular to the interaction between specific task characteristics and specific demands of settings and other individuals. Given a grocery store, for instance, one needs to know rules of entrance, layout of goods, their nature in comparison to similar goods, prices, and exit rules relating to check-out and payments. As discussed in Chapter 6, each setting has its own task demands that change from one setting to another. By the same token, intimate relationships have their own explicit, spoken rules and rituals, and implicit, unspoken ones for entry and exit. These rules and rituals may well be transferred to the next generation without any awareness from those who practice them.

Applicable

In the fourth place, this theory must be applicable to a continuum of care presented in past publications, using all three media of communication—verbal, nonverbal, and written—rather than just the verbal. Included in this continuum, in addition to the laboratory, would be clinical (clinics, hospitals), criminal (jails, penitentiaries), and nonclinical, educational institutions (schools, colleges, universities). For instance, a recent review of principles regulating effective prevention programs (Nation et al., 2003, p. 452) found that programs for risky sexual behavior were "theory driven" in 73% of the cases reviewed. Substance abuse was theory driven in 58% of the cases. Delinquency was theory driven in 29%, while school failure was found to be theory driven in 0%. These percentages support the view that theory is inconsistently or weakly used to develop and apply preventive programs. This shortcoming will be addressed in this work. Interventions need to be theory derived and replicable to allow verification of the models of the theory, not only in the laboratory but also in schools, clinics, hospitals, and in the offices of private practitioners.

Encompassing Functional and Dysfunctional Relationships

In the fifth place, this theory must be sufficiently wide to encompass functional and dysfunctional aspects of personality socialization in intimate relationships. This width includes relationships more relevant to the administration of self-help workbooks, that is, functionality, externalizations, internalizations, and psychopathology. Severe psychopathologies consist of inconsistent and contradictorily extreme combinations of internalizations and externalizations (Ch. 12). For instance, Krueger (1999) found two factors basic to mental disorders: (1) externalizations, reflecting alcohol, drug dependence, and antisocial personality disorders; (2) internalizations included two components: (a) anxious misery, reflecting major depression, dysthymia, and generalized anxiety disorders, and (b) a fear component comprising social and simple phobia, agoraphobia, and panic disorders. Bradley (2000) also differentiated among internalizations, externalization, and psychopathologies. Here, more than one model in this theory shows how deviant patterns are continuous and contiguous with functional personality propensities, and how this theory may be isomorphic, in many ways, with the DSM-IV.

What theory or model of personality will describe, "explain," or predict these four factors, functionality on one hand, and three different types and severities in internalizations, externalizations, and psychopathologies, on the other hand? Certainly, attachment theory achieves this purpose. However, its relationship to a selfhood model of personality, discussed in previous publications and evaluated by L'Abate et al. (2001), demonstrates the overlap between the two models. If these characteristics, functionalities and dysfunctionalities are not predicted by a model, above and beyond what is claimed rather than what is verified, what kind of specificity is then achieved? Without such specificity how can we intervene effectively? This writer prefers for the theory or any of its models to be specific and run the risk to be found empirically "wrong," rather than being vaguely general and claiming to be "right." Specificity can be evaluated. Vague generalities of the kind proffered by systems thinking or psychoanalysis, for instance, are difficult if not impossible to verify. Hence, the existence of models inside and outside this theory.

Verifiable

This theory, therefore, attempts to meet at least three requirements, to: (1) define and refine personality according to relational, ecological, developmental, and contextual concepts, including functionalities and dysfunctionalities, (2) reduce these concepts to known and accepted psychological constructs, and (3) verify these concepts empirically as well as applicatively. From the viewpoint of comprehensiveness and integration, this theory is admittedly quite ambitious in attempting to integrate earlier theories as well as the full range of functionalities and dysfunctionalities. However, it is quite simple in its structure and concrete in its stress on visible and measurable constructs.

This theory stresses individual *relational* characteristics that in turn are developed from the family of origin or past intimate relationships. Two individuals start a family by conceiving children and, hopefully, living under the same roof. Both individuals are the products of their respective families of origin. Both partners carry influences, positive and negative, from their families of origin into their new families of procreation. Individual characteristics must adapt to and adopt new demands from different settings, which in turn influence the functioning of their offspring.

This theory, therefore, straddles individual/couple/family perspectives by viewing individual socialization in the context of intimate relationships. This goal requires keeping the importance of the intimate relationships context primary, relating individual determinants to the functioning of those relationships, and using relational rather than inferred or hypothetical intrapsychic or systems language. If the family, or its alternatives, is a unit(y) of interacting personalities, as Burgess wrote long ago, then we need to define personality within its various contexts, as in different settings (Ch. 6). How one behaves at home does not necessarily predict how one is going to behave at work. Thus, this theory defines socialization and functioning in intimate relationships as a set of competencies in diverse settings. Personality socialization and psychological theory have been strongly influenced by what has been called "interactionism" (Bergman et al., 2003; Magnusson, 1999), with personality being the product or outcome of a personality × situation interaction. Since both terms are quite vague and are usually left unspecified, it will be useful later on to break down a definition of personality into specific competencies × settings interactions.

THE FUNCTIONS OF THIS THEORY

Emphasis on contrived and detailed experimentation and development of "models," therefore, have left out "grand theorizing," that would integrate some, not all, existing models. Models are produced at an ever increasing rate. However, these models lack integration into a "overarching" theoretical framework. Even family psychology, for instance, lacks an integrative theoretical framework, even though a great many disconnected models are presented (Liddle et al., 2002), among others. We need to evaluate this theory in applied, clinical and nonclinical settings, through its applications where it matters, with intimates and nonintimates.

A Theory for Intimate Relationships

As argued throughout this work, we cannot have theories or models for individuals, however, that do not apply to couples anymore than we need theories or models for couples that are not valid for families. Nor can we have theories for individuals who live by themselves, for couples who live in same sex relationships, for grandparent/grandchild dyads, and so on. It would be impossible to develop theories or models that would encompass all of these alternative relationships. We need models of relationships among intimates and nonintimates. Hence, we need a theory that will deal with intimate (close, committed, interdependent, and prolonged) relationships, not just individuals, couples or families, since even single individuals live in relationships, no matter where they live. We are indeed the products and producers of relationships, intimate or otherwise.

The Functions of Any Theory

There are at least four functions performed by a theory, or at least this theory, as a: (1) map to describe the territory to be explored, i.e., personal relationships, however, as Korzybski (1949) was fond of assuring us: "A map is not a territory"; (2) compass to give direction in our search and letting us know whether we are headed in the right direction or not; (3) clothes-hanger in which we can put all sorts of disparate models into one single place; and (4) strait-jacket that might limit us in looking at parts of the map that might be discovered were we free of intellectual and conceptual biases and constraints.

In additions to serving as maps, theories also function as compasses to direct, understand, predict, and prescribe relationships. For instance, once a territory like "intimate relationships" is staked out as being part of the theory or the theory itself, compasses, in the form of probe bodies or test instruments, allow us to consider whether the map covers the territory adequately, or whether one is going in the wrong direction and being mislead into a territory outside the map. It would be an extra bonus if this theory were also applied to maps of similar territories. Test instruments calibrated in the laboratory can be validated on their own, in terms of concurrent and criterion validities, but now they can also be validated prescriptively through workbooks, as shown elsewhere and discussed below.

This theory serves also as a clothes-hanger, in which parts and pieces of this and similar, annexed, theories, theorettes, and models have been hung according to some systematic order. For instance, there are models of the theory that relate with and are similar to other models or other theories. By the same token, a theory may also become a strait-jacket, not allowing one to look outside of it, restricting one's vision to just one theory and that one alone, without paying attention to other theories, as in the case of psychoanalysis, or cognitive-behavioral theory, among others. This is the reason for always comparing a theory with others, lest one becomes so enamored of a theory to the point of making it into a religion rather than a fallible map vulnerable to faulty compasses. There is no perfect theory, just like there are no perfect maps. They are just condensed approximations awaiting improvements. They are never the territory itself. There is no way they can ever be.

Functions of This Theory

This theory, therefore, attempts to fulfill three functions that are common to any science, namely: understanding, predicting, and controlling individuals in their intimate relationships and other settings.

Understanding Individuals in Intimate Relationships

The purpose of this theory is to understand how individuals learn to socialize in intimate, prolonged, close, interdependent, and committed relationships, usually but not always, found in families or family substitutes. This is the purpose of family psychology in contrast to family sociology. The latter wants to understand families as wholes and not as parts. Since psychology is devoted to the study and understanding of individuals, alone and in groups, family psychology, by the same token, studies and tries to understand the individual in intimate relationships.

Predicting What Individuals Will Do in Intimate Relationships

Prediction is a test of how understanding translates itself into the accuracy of predictions. If our understanding is general, vague, and not verifiable, then one's predictions, without evidence, will be usually thought to be correct, at least qualitatively. If our understanding is specific enough, then predictions will tend to be specific as well, and, if verifiable, found to be either valid or not. One example is found in the preliminary evaluation of L'Abate, L'Abate, and Maino (in press) about the use of workbooks in psychotherapy with individuals, couples, and families. Against frequent claims of cost-effectiveness for self-help, mental health workbooks, for instance, were tentatively found to prolong rather than shorten the number of psychotherapy sessions. L'Abate's "clinical," qualitative, impressionistic judgment was completely wrong, at least in this exploratory study.

Controlling What Individuals Will Do in Intimate Relationships to Improve Them

There are sciences that can understand and predict but cannot control, like astronomy. Psychology, however, does want to improve the human condition, and therefore needs to control relationships that have been lead by or lead to both functionality and dysfunctionality. Control, in this book will be achieved through the administration of self-help workbooks, administered at a distance rather than traditional talk and face-to-face (f2f) contact between a professional helper and people in trouble, as discussed at greater length below. This new paradigm aims to add or substitute distance writing for the old one instead of f2f talk.

SUMMARY OF THE THEORY

The purpose of this section is to preview the theory summarized in Table 1.1. A concluding Chapter 19 will explicate this table, that at first blush

Table 1.1. Summary of a Theory of Personality Socialization in Intimate Relationships and Other Settings#

A. Requirements
1. Reducibility to Psychological Constructs (Chapter 2)
2. Verifiability
3. Accountability in the Laboratory, in Primary (Enrichment), Secondary (Workbooks), and Tertiary (Psychotherapy) Prevention (Tasks)

Models	Tests	Enrichment	Workbooks	Tasks

B. Metatheoretical Assumptions

1. Horizontality in Relationships

Models	Tests	Enrichment	Workbooks	Tasks
ERAAwC[1]	RAQ*	Negotiation Potential	Negotiation	

2. Verticality of Relationships Levels of Observation/Interpretation[2] in Relationships to be evaluated
3. Settings[3] (home, school/work, leisure time, transit, and transitory). Time estimates objectively and semantic differential subjectively.

C. Theoretical Assumptions

Models	Tests	Enrichment	Workbooks	Tasks
4. Ability to Love[4]	WATMTIAW?**			
5. Ability to Negotiate[5 & 6]	WATMTIAW?**	Negotiation Potential	Negotiation	
6. Modalities[7]			Assignment in Negotiation	

D. Theoretical Models

Models	Tests	Enrichment	Workbooks	Tasks
7. Likeness: Model[8]	Likeness Scale Likeness Grid WATMTIAW?** Likeness Questionnaire (Appendix C)		Who Am I?	
8. Styles in Relation-ships[9]	PIRS***	Negotiation Potential	Negotiation assignment	f2f interviews
9. Selfhood[10]	SOPC+ PIRS*** DRT++		Self-Other Codependency	Drawing lines
10. Priorities[11]	Grid, Inventory	Negotiation Potential	Negotiation assignment	

E. Applications of Theoretial Models

Models	Tests	Enrichment	Workbooks	Tasks
11. Distance Regulation[12]			Depression assignment	3HC
12. Drama Triangle[13]			Depression assignment	

(Continued)

Table 1.1. (*Continued*)

13. Intimacy[14]	SOHS+++		Intimacy	Sharing hurts
14. Negotiation[15]		Helpfulness	Negotiation	
15. Toward a Classification of Relationships: Model[16]	Difficult to evaluate unless one were to develop a workbook based on the diagnostic instrument			
16. Integration of Selfhood with other models[17]	Partially evaluated			

*From L'Abate and De Giacomo, 2003. Reprinted with permission.
*Relational Answers Questionnaire (Appendix A).
**What Applies To Me That I Agree With? (L'Abate & De Giacomo, 2003).
***Self-Other Profile Chart (L'Abate, 1992, 1994, 2001, 2002, L'Abate & De Giacomo, 2003).
+Problems in Relationships Scale and Matching Assignments (L'Abate, 1992, 1996, McMahan & L'Abate, 2001).
++Dyadic Relationships Test (Cusinato & L'Abate, 2003, 2004).
+++Sharing of Hurts Scale (Stevens & L'Abate, 1989).

may seem like a very complex array of a completely new framework. Briefly, the theory consists of two requirements, reducibility to psychological constructs (Ch. 2) and verifiability and accountability in the laboratory as well as in applied and clinical settings, primary through enrichment programs, secondary, through self-help workbooks, and tertiary prevention, through prescriptive tasks (Ch. 3).

Three metatheoretical assumptions attempt to integrate past psychological theories in ways that will allow us to relate the present theory to past ones that form the basis for this model. As discussed at great length in Chapter 4, the first model views relationships along a horizontal axis in terms of their width. Here, a model is a simplified, usually visual, summary simplification and representation of more complex concepts or patterns derived from the assumptions and postulates of the theory. For instance, the two assumptions of the theory, space and time, become more concrete and visible when distance and regulation with their respective polarities are visualized as two orthogonal dimensions, making them into a first model. By the same token, the three modalities of Being, Doing, and Having can be visualized as an equilateral triangle with Presence at the bottom, Performance on the left, and Production on the right, making them also into a second model.

Using an information processing approach, this model includes *E*motionality, *R*ationality, *A*ctivity, *A*wareness, and *C*ontext (ERAAwC). It can be evaluated with the Relational Answers Questionnaire (RAQ), a Negotiation Potential enrichment program (L'Abate & Weinstein, 1987; L'Abate & Young, 1987), and a Negotiation workbook (L'Abate, 1996).

A second metatheoretical assumption deals with the depth or verticality of relationships according to two levels of observation/interpretation, descriptive and explanatory, as discussed in Chapter 5. Description of relationships occurs at two sublevels, presentational/public and phenotypical/private. Explanation of relationships occurs at two sublevels, genotypical/hypothetical, and historical/developmental. These levels can be evaluated through tests genotypically, and intergenerationally and developmentally through family and individual history.

A third model (Ch. 6) deals with settings that define Context in the ERAAwC model, composed of: home, school/work, leisure settings, transit, and transitory. They can be evaluated through time analyses objectively and through the semantic differential subjectively.

The theory itself is composed of two assumptions about the ability to love (Ch. 7) and to negotiate (Ch. 8) processibly with modalities about how these processes are exchanged and through contents and modalities of Being, Doing, and Having, the Triangle of Life (Ch. 9).

Models of the theory proper include self-differentiation according to a likeness continuum (Ch. 10), which has been evaluated with the Likeness Grid, Likeness Inventory, and the method developed by Scilletta (2002). This model is also contained in two assignments of the parenting workbook in Appendix A. Styles in intimate relationships (Ch. 11) can be evaluated through the Problems in Relationships Scale and program, where partners' discrepancy scores in conflict areas are matched with specific, written homework assignments. A selfhood model (Ch. 12) has been evaluated most frequently with the Self-Other Profile Chart, the Problems-in-Relationships Scale (PIRS) (McMahan & L'Abate, 2001), and the Dyadic Relationships Test (Cusinato & L'Abate, 2003), as well as a workbook matching the two dimensions of the test, self and intimate others. A Priorities model (Ch. 13) has been evaluated with the Priorities Grid and Priorities Inventory (L'Abate, 1994), while distance regulation (Ch. 14), the drama triangle (Ch. 15), intimacy (Ch. 16), and negotiation and problem-solving (Ch. 17), can be evaluated through couple and family enrichment programs and workbooks. The theory concludes with a chapter (18) integrating all the models of the theory into a comprehensive model, and comparing the selfhood model (Ch. 12) with relational models extraneous to the theory itself but that contain common characteristics inviting invidious comparisons.

WORKBOOKS AS INSTRUMENTS OF THEORY TESTING

Control of deviant and troubled behavior has been established in the past century through f2f, talk-based psychotherapy, while prevention of deviant and troubled behavior has been established through a variety of structured programs devoted to parenting, assertiveness training, marriage preparation, and so forth. However, it is my opinion that both the fields of psychotherapy and prevention will not advance as long as they rely on f2f talk between professionals and respondents. Why? Because f2f talk is both difficult and expensive to record and replicate. Furthermore, as long as psychological interventions are based and dependent on talk, a great many troubled people will not be able to be helped, especially in the case of children (Kataoka, Zhang, & Wells, 2002). Talk is nonspecific, extremely variable, and uncontrollable (L'Abate, 1999b). Hence, all attempts, including those I have previously made to make psychotherapy and prevention into separate sciences are bound to take a great deal of time and expense. Furthermore, research about psychotherapy and its process as well as prevention will remain in the hands of few researchers who qualify for grants. Research will be out of reach from Main Street professionals. Recording, transcribing, and classifying psychotherapy or prevention audio recordings are very time-consuming jobs left in a handful of grant-supported researchers.

Hence, there is no way advances can take place unless the whole process of psychotherapy and prevention occurs through the writing medium between professionals and respondents. Why? Because only through writing one can keep records of the process about what is going on between professionals and respondents. Instead of talk, respondents should be required to rely as much as possible on their writings rather than just on talk, as done by Gould (2001) with thousands of patients for years. Written protocols can be completed by respondents at home and sent to professionals through the Internet or fax (Esterling, L'Abate, Murray, & Pennebaker, 1999; Lepore & Smyth, 2003).

Science, law, industry, medicine, architecture, and most fields of endeavor rely on the written record to serve as a background from the past and an advance for the future of each field. Skyscrapers are not built on talk. They are built on solid blueprints based on mechanical, scientific bases. It is difficult if not impossible to improve the human condition as long as talk remains the main or sole medium of healing. To attempt to help and heal all the people who hurt through f2f talk is simply impossible. Psychotherapy and prevention are the last remaining fields of endeavor where only f2f talk is required. The outcome is a veritable Tower of Babel, where extreme, unproven, and even ridiculous remedies are administered by duly licensed professionals who, for whatever reason, have forgotten and left behind their scientific heritages.

As a result, the only record of what has happened between professionals and their respondents is found in the notes of professionals. These notes are kept private and there is no way one can find how accurate or complete these notes are. They cannot be used to prove whether improvement in respondents has taken place or not. They are naturally self-serving and not shared by being kept in the professional's private office. There is no way that those notes are going to be used to improve one's professional practices. Furthermore, there is no way to find out how self-serving those notes are, even if they supposedly document process and progress in psychotherapy or prevention.

Consequently, only through research it is possible to advance the fields of psychotherapy and prevention in the hands of university-affiliated researchers whose findings are usually ignored by professionals on Main Street. Who can forget decades ago clinicians claiming that evaluation would interfere with the process of therapy? By how many years has that unfounded claim delayed and derailed linking evaluation with intervention? As a result, research and practice in psychotherapy remain and are destined to remain separate fields of endeavor, with no hope of being united and integrated for the betterment of humanity's ills. Through writing it will be possible to keep records of what professionals and respondents feel, think, and do. This conclusion does not mean that f2f talk should be eliminated from the process of healing. It would be impossible. It means than an additional medium should be added to f2f talk in a way that will increase synergistically the power of both media, f2f talk and distance writing. In most cases, however, in the not too distant future, writing, instead of just supplementing f2f talk, will most likely supplant it, especially in preventive interventions.

Writing varies along four levels of structure: (1) *open-ended*, as in journals and diaries; (2) *focused*, as in the expressive writing paradigm of Pennebaker (2001) about one's undisclosed past traumas or autobiography; (3) *guided*, written questions to be answered in writing, and (4) *programmed*, as in self-help workbooks (L'Abate, 1996). Among the four structures, the most amenable to research is programmed writing.

Rather than rely solely on paper-and-pencil, self-report tests that, as indicated above, abound in this theory, one unique and additional way in which this theory can be evaluated is through self-help, mental health workbooks that derive directly from the theory, as shown in a parenting workbook, among others. A workbook consists of a series of written homework assignments around a specific topic to be answered in writing by respondents. Workbooks supposedly are cost-effective, mass-producible, versatile, and specific enough to allow evaluation of the theory or model from which they were derived. However, recent results, already mentioned, raise serious questions about the cost-effectiveness of workbooks in psychotherapy (L'Abate, L'Abate, & Maino, in press). Instead of shortening the number of psychotherapy sessions with individuals, couples, and families, workbooks were found to lengthen it significantly. Hence, one can no longer claim that they are cost-effective, even though much more research will be needed to reach a definite conclusion on this matter. Whether the increased number of psychotherapy sessions would lead to greater efficacy is an open question that could not be answered in that research.

Mass-orientation for workbooks is a given, because questions asked on a piece of paper or on a computer through the Internet are a much cheaper approach than if the same questions were asked by a professional helper. Professional time and expertise are a hundred times more expensive and less replicable than one or two pages of questions. Versatility means being used under different conditions in different settings. For instance, workbooks can be used f2f as structured interviews between professionals-in-training and respondents, in spite of their cost. They can be used at a distance from respondents when assigned as homework in addition to f2f talk-based sessions for children, youth, adults, couples, and families. They can be used in prevention, where mass-orientation and cost-effectiveness are important criteria to consider. They can be used solely or in conjunction with psychotherapeutic practices or medication (L'Abate, 2004a, 2004b).

There is no way that current preventive (Weinberg, Kumpfer, & Seligman, 2003) and psychotherapeutic practices based on f2f talk are going to meet all the mental health needs of this or any other nation. Interventions will need to occur with a minimum of professional contact and time (Stevenson, Stevenson, & Whitmont, 2003). An evolutionary shift from talking to writing media will allow expansions to populations that were heretofore unreachable through f2f talk but that become reachable once writing, computers, and the Internet become the vehicles of delivery and possible healing (Ritterband et al., 2003; X Day & Schneider, 2002).

The specificity of workbooks is achieved by their matching a referral question, a test profile, or a test score with a diagnostic label or a reason for referral. Given the diagnosis of depression, for instance, there are at least half a dozen workbooks designed to deal with such a diagnosis. There is now a workbook for practically any known clinical and nonclinical condition for children, youth, adults, couples, and families (L'Abate, 1996, 2004a). This specificity allows us to fulfill a major desideratum of mental health practices, and that is: matching treatment with diagnosis in a way that cannot be reached and will not be reached when f2f talk is the sole medium of exchange between professionals and respondents. If and when that match is reached, as noted repeatedly, it is due to grants to few researchers whose findings are usually irrelevant to practicing clinicians.

Finally, one way in which workbooks become interactive instruments of theory testing is through the construction of workbooks directly from test instruments. This link is achieved through a very simple, easy device. One can take all the items from any test or from any list of factorially- or research-derived items and transform them into a workbook. This transformation is obtained easily by asking respondents to define (in writing, of course!) each item in the list and give two examples for each item. After completing this task, respondents are asked to rank-order the items according to how much each item applies to them, from a great deal to nonapplicable. The rank-order is then used to administer all the subsequent assignments according to a standard format. This format is the same from one assignment to another, but with a different title for each assignment that follows the original sequence of rank-ordered items. Since all the tests used were copy-written, special permission (and fees!) was required to convert them into workbooks (L'Abate, 2002).

In this fashion, therefore, workbooks can be nomothetic as well as idiographic. They can fulfill research functions in the sense that all respondents can answer the same number of assignments, usually no more than six. They are also idiographic, in the sense that the sequence of homework assignments follows specifically what individual, couple, or family respondents have deemed as applying uniquely to them. For example, one can take and use all the rating scales, symptom checklists for adults, checklists for children and adolescents, functional impairment or disability, and quality of life or psychological well-being, to evaluate social anxiety disorder (Feldman, & Rivas-Vazquez, 2003, p. 402). By the same token, workbooks could be developed from a whole list of test instruments available to evaluate risk in sex offenders (Beech, Fisher, & Thornton, 2003, p. 346).

Consequently, one can then transform most tests into active and interactive vehicles of theory-testing from a relatively inert, static, and passive collection of paper-and-pencil, self- or other-report instruments, as already done for both single or multiple score tests (L'Abate, 1996). Once a workbook has been derived from a theoretical or empirical model, it becomes a direct instrument of theory- or model-testing. This advantage adds to the versatility of workbooks.

Hence, through workbooks, the link between evaluation and intervention is straightforward and direct, in a way that would be difficult if not impossible to achieve f2f verbally. If a workbook is derived from a validated list of items defining depression, as in the case of the Beck Depression Inventory or Hamilton Depression Scale, for instance, they are now directly linked to the diagnostic label of depression. Therapists would not need to demonstrate that, verbally or through therapy notes, they have followed a treatment plan that derives from the original diagnosis. The workbook itself will fulfill this function, allowing direct demonstration and documentation that there is indeed a direct link between evaluation and intervention. No wonder that the market for self-help workbooks has increased exponentially in the past decade (L'Abate, 1996, 2004a).

There is another clinical advantage implicit into this transformation from statically inert tests into interactive workbooks. By administering a list of items defining any psychological construct or symptom, and asking respondents to define them and give two examples, one seems able to bridge the considerable semantic gap between professionals and respondents (L'Abate, 2004d). Instead of giving a diagnostic label with serious and likely threatening connotations, i.e., depression, anxiety, or even bipolar or schizophrenic disorder, the administration of a workbook constructed from test items or any other list of items would allow respondents to know exactly what is meant by labels or diagnoses assigned to them by professionals. This process would demythologize a great deal of the professional jargon that keeps respondents distant from professionals in a one-down position. The use of diagnostic labels ascribes the professional attributes and powers that respondents likely do not have (L'Abate, 2004b).

Furthermore, instead of just one feedback change loop from professionals to respondents through f2f talk, workbooks increase the number of feedback change loops available to respondents. They now have to answer questions that may have never been asked before. This process could be conceived as a form of self-monitoring, especially if it takes place at specific, predetermined times and places as homework (Craske & Tsao, 1999). Respondents now have to think on their own about how to answer each question, rather than talking to a professional. If they have partners or family members who are answering the same set of questions, partners or family members can set appointment times to exchange, compare, contrast, and discuss their answers with those of others. Even if respondents have no one to discuss their answers, like single adults or single parents, their completed assignments can become grist for discussions with professionals who administered the workbook, as would be the case with couples and parents (Appendix D).

In this regard, evidence to support or invalidate the models of this theory will be broken down into three possible levels between evidence and theory. Workbooks have been developed from: (1) constructs, concepts, tests, or evaluative instruments that are conceptually similar but completely independent from the models of the theory, as, for instance, those on depression or anxiety, among many others; (2) constructs or concepts that are conceptually similar and somewhat related to the models of the theory, as, for instance, codependency, and (3) constructs or concepts that are completely and directly derived, i.e., driven from models of the theory itself, as seen in the Depression, Negotiation, and Intimacy workbooks (L'Abate, 1986), and in the Planned Parenting workbook (Appendix D). Consequently, there are workbooks that are independent of the theory but that are deemed to be conceptually similar to some of its models. There are workbooks that are in some way related to the models of the theory. There are workbooks that are completely and directly derived or driven from models of the theory.

In this way, workbooks become another, interactive way to verify the validity of theoretical models, in addition, of course, to relatively static and inert paper and pencil, self-report tests. Consequently, under these three levels, workbooks can and are active and interactive vehicles of validation for models of the theory, as shown throughout this work.

CONCLUSION

Personality development, as conceived by some theorists (in the United States) is strictly physical, internal growth based on genetic and physiological variables. Personality socialization, on the other hand, consists of all the interactions with intimates over time who matter and who furnish and receive nurturance emotionally, physically, financially, and materially. Consequently, the purpose of this book is to present a theoretical framework that integrates personality socialization in functional and dysfunctional intimate relationships, along the whole individual and family life cycles, in continuity with evidence generated from sources internal and external to the framework.

Part I

Requirements for
the Theory

*"Family development theory is not to be confused with theories about
individual development, such as those offered by psychologists
(e.g., Erikson, Freud, Piaget). Although family development theorists
acknowledge the importance of individual development, the
development of the family as a* group *of interacting individuals and
organized by social norms is their major focus* (Klein & White, 1996,
p. 120)."

The purpose of this section is to consider three major requirements for a theory of personality socialization in intimate relationships and other settings, including psychopathology: reducibility to known psychological constructs (Ch. 2), verifiability, and accountability (Ch. 3). This theory is primarily a theory about visible, repeatable, recordable, and measurable *relationships* among intimates rather than about inferred or hypothetical internal states and traits in isolated individuals void of relationships with intimates.

Chapter 2

Reducibility to Known Psychological Constructs

"There is an urgent need for more complex and sophisticated models for understanding how individuals develop.... models that consider the operation of multiple factors and their interaction over time, and that identify the causal process(es) that underlie relations between experiential events and child development (Cummings, Davies, & Campbell, 2000, pp. 35–36)."

The purpose of this chapter it to relate most concepts and constructs used in this theory to known psychological constructs by expanding them into their relational rather than their monadic meaning. Many psychological constructs do have relational meaning (except for self-esteem and self-efficacy among others!). However, they have not been used relationally. For instance, sex and sexuality may be considered as separate from relationships and may be studied in vacuum, as a function of hormones or other internal physiological functions. However, these terms acquire meaning when applied to relationships between partners, as shown below. Terms of the personality circumplex (friendly/hostile, dominant/submissive), let alone those defining attachment styles (secure/insecure, dismissing, preoccupied, and disorganized) only have meaning in interactions with others, not just in paper-and-pencil, self-report tests or laboratory experiments with college sophomores.

By the same token, many internal personality traits that are used a-contextually, such as extroversion, acquire meaning when a so-called extroverted individual meets with someone else in an intimate encounter. Depending on the characteristics of the other, the meeting could result in a positive, neutral, or negative outcome. The meaning of a trait or any other internal, hypothetical, or inferred personality characteristic is acquired within the context of relationships. It is not acquired in the short-lived, contrived, and artificial vacuum of a self-report, paper-and-pencil test. Nor can this meaning be acquired in contrived, artificial laboratory situations, or in superficial or occasional encounters with sales persons, bank tellers, counter clerks, no matter how rigorous, replicable, and replicated findings from such sources may be. That meaning is acquired within the context of intimate relationships, as defined here.

DEVELOPMENT VERSUS SOCIALIZATION

Originally (L'Abate, 1994) this theory was called "personality development" even though it was conceived as "personality socialization." Hence, the term "development" was a misnomer because, as a whole in the psychological literature, development is considered a coming from the "inside" of the individual, be that inside genetic, hereditary, or temperamental. Hence, the appropriate term for this theory instead of development was changed to socialization (L'Abate, 1997). However, rather than an either/or position, where one negates or denies the importance of the other, the both/and position is taken. Personality development from the inside interacts in multiple ways with socialization from the "outside." Development may give us the cards to play with but socialization teaches us how to play them.

Two Different Viewpoints or Two Sides of the Same Coin?

Furthermore, one could argue that development cannot take place unless there is sustenance and nurturance from the outside. That nurturance could just be extremely concrete, like food or water, or could be emotional, affective, and physical, as in caresses, hugs, soothing words, etc. Without these external resources, no matter how physically healthy an infant may be initially at birth, that infant is bound to die. Given an unhealthy baby, appropriate medical treatment as well as emotional support as defined above may allow that baby to grow into a fairly healthy adult. Consequently, the dual process of development and socialization takes place along two parallel tracks, joined together by multiple ties. Development is enhanced by socialization from the outside. Growth from the inside determines how that child will respond to the outside. The two tracks are intrinsically united throughout the whole life cycle.

Linking the Theory with Psychological Constructs

This theory is linked with psychological constructs in many different ways, as already indicated in previous writings. New links are added here. One link is found in the emphasis on constructs such as self or personality, that, although derived from individual psychology, will be redefined here according to relational and interrelational concepts (e.g., love and negotiation). Self here will be given a specific meaning in a relational selfhood model (Ch. 12), rather than as an internal state or trait. Consequently, self is just one component of personality. It takes more than a self to make up a supraordinate construct like personality, especially when that term is given a specific, relation meaning.

Second, recording and applying the six resource classes from exchange theory (really a model!) in social psychology (Foa, Converse, Tornblom, & Foa, 1993) has brought some changes in the names of those classes. For instance, "status" in the original theory was changed to "importance" leading to a selfhood model of relationships (Ch. 12). "Love" was changed to "intimacy" (Chs. 7 and 16). These constructs are relational to the extent that they imply consistent and persistent interactions either with people or with objects, or with both.

Third, another link is found in the spatial assumption of approach-avoidance and the development of dependencies and interdependencies in the ability to love (Ch. 7). A comparative, already established model, attachment theory, is part of that dimension.

Fourth, a link is found in the construct of control, defined by extremes in discharge-delay functions (Ch. 8) and in the ability to negotiate (Ch. 17). Control here represents how one controls oneself in relationship to others, not in a vacuum, void of other persons or objects. Addicts exhibit little control over their substances, just as angry individuals become angry in relationship to others, not just themselves.

Fifth, a link is found in sex and sexuality, which are two of the biologically evolutionary and social bases for the formation and development of the family. Yet, sex without partners may lead to masturbation, but as a solitary activity, does little to improve relationships with intimates. This link will be developed in greater detail in Chapter 9.

Finally, a link is found in the emphasis on individual differences, especially gender differences, that differentiate at least two strategies for dealing with stress, one presence-related and the other performance- or production-related (Ch. 9). These differences, as related to a selfhood model (Ch. 12), will be highlighted throughout this work.

There are many other links throughout this work that will expand on the foregoing list. Many psychological terms and constructs have a relational meaning, even though they have not been used heretofore relationally.

"RELATIONSHIPS" RATHER THAN "MIND" OR "BEHAVIOR"

The focus of this work, therefore, is neither on "*mind*" nor on "*behavior*" but on "*relationships*." This focus is not just on relationships in general or even vague "interpersonal relationships," but specifically on intimate relationships. Emphasis on *relationships*, rather than on "mind" or on "behavior," is the outcome of historical developments in human thinking: from (1) *magical*, in ancient mythology ("The devil made me do it."), to (2) *reactive*, in the Middle Ages, as a function of internal factors ("He is stupid or intelligent."), to (3) *interactive*, in the 19th century ("It takes two to tango."), and, finally (4) *transactive*, in the 20th and 21st centuries (my watching an interaction) changes the nature of that interaction, making it into a transaction, since as an observer I have intervened in it. This fourth stage incorporates what is known as the Heisenberg Principle, observing an interaction changes its nature or process.

Psychology historically, i.e., before the past century, was the science of the "Mind." This stage is similar to the magical stage in human thought, when behavior and events were made a function of unexplained, unexplainable, and mythical factors, like "God's will," imaginary beings ("Angels, ghosts, the devil"), which were eventually metamorphosized into inferred and hypothetical internal dimensions, states and traits, like ego, superego, and id, self-esteem, extroversion-introversion, or similar traits or states.

After John Watson, at the beginning of the past century, psychology became the science of "behavior," usually without a context. This stage is similar to the reactive stage in human thought, where behavior is still seen as stemming from internal sources or causes, as in the "the bed seed" view, a view that is still rampant in many psychological quarters. These quarters are still looking for ubiquitous genes as internal causes of everything that happens in mental health and in mental disorders. The term behavior per se has no meaning, because it fails to define under what external context that behavior has been elicited, let alone what consequences it will have.

Finally, psychology has become the science of "relationships," between and among intimates and nonintimates and between individuals, settings, and objects. This stage represents two separate phases in human thought: an interactive one, where relationships are the result of interactions among human beings, and a second one between human beings with settings and objects. Heisenberg's Principle in physics, however, heralded a later stage in which interactions, when observed, become transactions because the process of observation disturbs and changes the interaction itself.

Hence, we are products and producers of relationships. Even an IQ score is the result of an interaction between an individual and an examiner or between an individual and a paper-and-pencil test. Even responding to a self-report, paper-and-pancil test or questionnaire constitutes an interaction, i.e., a relationship between the respondent and a piece of paper. This interaction becomes a transaction whenever the score is interpreted and related to other measures of intellectual or emotional functioning. Its interpretation constitutes a transaction, because the interpreter cannot help inject his or her own predilections and biases. All psychological measures, therefore, are the outcome of relationships. Relationships are the result of interactions (X) between both internal, endogenous, and/or of external, exogenous, circumstances.

Consequently, we are not interested in just relationships (X) in short-lived, contrived, artificial, and superficial laboratory studies, which may or may not be relevant, but we are interested in intimate (close, prolonged, interdependent, and committed) "real life" relationships, which may or may not be consistent with contrived laboratory observations. Intimate relationships (X) between one individual and another individual, that is, intimates (family, friends, neighbors, teachers, etc.) constitute our "community" where mostly *communal* relationship are paramount. Inside that community there are inevitable exchanges of goods and money. However, most business exchanges take place outside of the immediate context of intimate relationships.

Superficial, short-lived, temporary relationships composed of business *exchanges* between nonintimate individuals and their surrounding settings constitute our "environment." Settings are composed of objects, material nutriments, like clothes, food, furnishings, house, cars, etc. However, throughout this work, objects in settings will be identified with specific disturbances, like addictions or extremes in performance or production, as well as with new technology, that is, self-help workbooks, in a completely new environment, computers and the Internet, as already discussed in Chapter 1.

Kurt Lewin (1935) stressed the contextual formula that "Behavior is a function of Person X Environment ($B = f(PXE)$." Bronfenbrenner (1979), among others, developed the E side of the formula, while the purpose of this work is to look at, enlarge, and stress the importance of all three parts of the formula, namely ($IR = f(PSXE)$, where IR stands for intimate relationships, PS stands for Personality Socialization, and E is specified as "intimate relationships in the family and other settings." X stands for the interaction between PS and E. Others, Cervone and Mischel (2002) among them, for instance, developed the P without X or without E. Context (family, family substitutes, intimate relationships, and community) has been ignored even though vague and general terms like "situation," "culture," or "society" have been used quite often. Furthermore, the X in Lewin's formula can be expanded arithmetically into five different and more specific types of relationships: ×, +, 0, − , and /:

1. Multiplicative (×), when interactions between two or more intimately related people tend to produce a multiplicative and integrative growth, something that is creative as a result of the relationship. These individuals, couples, and families are not only creative within the context of their immediate relationships, but are also creative in settings outside the family. Hence, the need to include and specify what settings are necessary to the expansion of creativity in relationships (Ch. 6).
2. Additive (+), interactions between two or more intimately related people could be additional growth, but not multiplicative, there is positive change but it is not creative as in multiplicative relationships. There is satisfaction but there may not be a creative integration at higher levels both inside and outside the home.
3. Static, equal to 0 (=), interaction between two or more intimately related people could be repetitively the same, without change one way or another, neither party profits by the relationship and the relationship remains the same over time, unchanged, neither improving nor deteriorating.
4. Subtractive (−), when negative and reactive interactions between two or more intimately related people take away from each partner or family members, sometimes remaining static, sometimes leading toward the fifth possibility, deteriorating slowly until a break within an individual member or within the relationship between partners or among family members occurs.
5. Divisive (/), when very negative, chronically abusive-apathetic interactions between two or more intimately related people could produce a split or a break, either inside the individual or between or among individuals involved in the interaction, as in divorce, psychosis, murder, or suicide.

The major issue with this expansion deals with what personality characteristics lead to which outcome in intimate relationships. An answer to this question will be provided throughout this work.

CAUSALITY AND PERSONALITY SOCIALIZATION

One cannot build a theory of intimate relationships without including causes for how these relationships develop. Haynes (1992) considered causal

Table 2.1. Models of Causality: Linear and Nonlinear

Linear, ideal unipotentiality:
One cause leads to a corresponding effect as in astronomy, physics, chemistry,
  organic and physiological diseases, etc.
Nonlinear, real:
One cause leads to a variety of many effects = equipotentiality or multipotentiality.
Various causes lead to the same effect = equifinality.
Various causes lead to various effects = multifinality (orderly/chaotic complexity)

---

relationsips as: probabilistic, nonexclusive, bidirectional, always conditional,
dynamic, varying in degrees of modifiability, nonlinear and discontinuous.
The simplified summary (Table 2.1) does not give justice to the complexity of the issues as addressed admirably by Haynes. Relationships (X) are
governed by four principles about causality:

1. *Unipotentiality*: one cause may produce a specific outcome, as seen
   in biological (genetic) and neuropsychological determinism, but not
   in relational probabilism or pluralism where it is impossible to detect one cause as being the only antecedent of a psychological
   relationship between two or more human beings.
2. *Equipotentiality*: one cause may produce multiple and different outcomes. For instance, incest may lead to promiscuous sexual behavior later on in the victim's life, or lead to complete sexual abstinence,
   or addictions of various kinds. Intergenerational transmission of
   abuse may produce different types of abuse, but the pattern of
   abuse may remain the same.
3. *Equifinality*: different causes may lead to the same outcome. For
   instance, depression may be the outcome of temperamental factors,
   modeling with a valued caretaker, poor self-concept, past traumas,
   or peer rejection.
4. *Multifinality*: many produce many different outcomes, such as the
   need for a holistic, multidetermined, and multidimensional view
   of relationships, functional and otherwise (Cummings et al., 2000).
   This is the reality of most intimate relationships. Even though now
   we can statistically tease out what antecedent variables may have
   influenced a particular personality characteristic, it is now possible
   to assess the amount of influence a given variable may have in
   comparison to the amount of influence of other variables from more
   than one person.

CONCLUSION

Personality socialization, therefore, is the study of communal and exchange relationships between and among intimates and nonintimates in specific settings. Most psychological terms or constructs do have relational meaning once it is understood that even internal, intrapsychic constructs have definite relational outcomes. This meaning will be expanded in all the subsequent chapters of this book.

Chapter 3

Verifiability and Accountability
Applications to Nonclinical and Clinical Populations

"A formal program, in which practitioners plan in advance to use specific evidence-based clinical interventions is probably the best way to treat. . . . Indeed, formally planned programs are probably best when treating most problems (Kassinove & Tafrate, 2002, p. 77)."

The purpose of this chapter is to explain why verifiability is required as a sine qua non condition for theory construction, and to expect accountability for clinical and nonclinical applications derived from models of the theory. Without both requirements, verification and accountability, psychological interventions would fall back to the early stages of magical thinking and reactivity. Under those conditions, these fields would rely on wishful or magical thinking, without planning and without checking on whether clinical applications stem directly from a theory or are independent and free from any theory. Without both required constraints, theory derivation and empirical support, psychological interventions will remain the Tower of Babel that they are now. Without constraints, some professionals will feel free to inject reactively their unique "creativity" without any explanation, rationale, or empirical bases on why and what they used—just personal intuition.

This would make psychological interventions a catch-as-you-can process controlled by immediacy and reactivity. Some professionals would feel free to mindlessly do whatever pleases them without any consideration about the welfare of respondents, paying attention only to their own needs "to help" without any considerations that they act as artists rather than as scientists. Indeed, many pride themselves as being artists rather than scientists. If and when the explanation is given, it lacks rational or empirical evidence. We expect more from veterinarians who treat our pets than we expect from some mental health professionals who treat human beings.

VERIFIABILITY AS THE FIRST REQUIREMENT
OF THE THEORY

Throughout the construction of this theory, attempts have been made to ensure that each model would be phrased in such a way as to make it suitable to evaluation. Hence, the major criterion has been to calibrate some of the measures and applications derived from its models from the outset of the theory construction (L'Abate, 2003a; L'Abate & Wagner, 1985, 1989). As the theory developed, additional or alternative laboratory measures, as well as enrichment programs, workbooks, and therapeutic tasks were developed (see Table 1.1).

There are two aspects of its verifiability that are relevant to this theory. A dialectical aspect may be verifiable qualitatively/impressionistically. A second aspect is demonstrability, what is verifiable quantitatively. Both aspects, dialectics (rhetoric and qualification), and demonstrability (data, evidence, and quantification), are necessary for scientific and applied enterprises (L'Abate, 1986, 1994, 1997). Dialectics relies on generating hypotheses. Demonstrability relies on testing the validity of those hypotheses (McGuire, 1997). These two aspects are equivalent to two aspects of f2f talk in prevention and psychotherapy, as traditionally practiced: (1) the individual *style* of the professional helper is personal, unique, and difficult if not impossible to replicate, and (2) the *method*, a sequence of supposedly replicable steps, if any, that the professional follows or claims to follow (L'Abate, 1986).

Of course, seven types of validity typically used in one way or another in psychological evaluations need to be included here from the outset. The first type is *face* validity: Is what the theory claims to explain relevant to the individual reader? For instance, can readers see themselves in models of the theory? The second type is *construct* validity, that is, are the constructs underlying the models of the theory valid or are they bogus? For instance, are constructs like "love," or "negotiation," valid? The third type of validity is *concurrent*. Are measures developed from models of the theory correlated to other established measures of the same construct? For instance, is a measure of intimacy correlated to other measures of intimacy developed by other investigators? The measure used to evaluate an important model of the theory, selfhood (Ch. 12), the Self-Other Profile Chart was found to correlate with a measure of attachment (L'Abate, 2003a; L'Abate & De Giacomo, 2003; L'Abate, De Giacomo, McCarty, De Giacomo, & Verrastro, 2000). A fourth type is *discriminant* validity. Will constructs from the theory be reliably different from other constructs that measure different variables? For instance, a measure of intimacy should correlate positively with measures of functionality but negatively with measures of couple conflict or dysfunctionality. The fifth type is *content* validity. Are the contents of the theory relevant or do they need changing? For instance, the construct of "intimacy" was substituted for the construct of "love" (Chs. 7, 9) in the original version of Foa and Foa's (1974) social exchange model, while their construct of "status" was changed to "importance" (Ch. 12). The name was changed, but does it matter if the change produces different predictions from the original versions? The sixth type is *predictive* validity, the ability to foretell the nature, course, and outcome of certain relationships. For instance, would intimacy be more likely to occur in functional than in dysfunctional relationships? The seventh type, added some time ago (L'Abate, 1990) is *prescriptive* validity, the equivalent of being able to control certain relationships by determining their course. This validity is found in matching a particular workbook with a matching diagnosis or problem. When the workbook is based on a test that evaluates a particular clinical label, then one is able to prescribe which workbook will match which particular diagnosis, as noted in Chapter 1.

Thus far, most of the attempts of verification for models of the theory were directed toward evaluating the validity and reliability of measures developed to operationalize constructs, like the ERAAwC model (Ch. 4) with the Relational Answers Questionnaire (RAQ) the continuum of likeness (Ch. 10) with the Likeness Chart; the selfhood model (Ch. 12) with at least three different paper-and-pencil tests; the priorities model (Ch. 13); the intimacy model (Ch. 16); and the negotiation model (Ch. 18). Research and evidence to support or invalidate each model will be included in the relevant chapters. Where evidence to support a specific model is not yet available, either in the laboratory, or in primary, secondary, or tertiary prevention, suggestions will be given on how that model could be evaluated.

The Three Levels of Evidence

As already suggested earlier (Ch. 1), this work brings the theory up to date conceptually as well as empirically. In evaluating the validity of this theory one needs to consider three levels of evidence: (1) *independent* of the theory but conceptually similar to it, (2) *indirectly* related to the theory from theories and models that were used to derive models of the theory, and (3) *directly* derived from models of the theory evaluated according to four

different sources of evidence: (a) laboratory evaluation, (b) primary prevention, (c) secondary prevention, and (d) tertiary prevention or psychotherapy.

Independent evidence can be epistemologically similar in contents with
concepts to specific models of the theory. Conceptually independent but
similar theories include such constructs as love (Ch. 7), negotiation (Ch. 8),
or both, among other models, using constructs that seem similar to this theory, i.e., face validity. Love and the ability to love (Ch. 7) as well as control
and the ability to negotiate (Ch. 8) have been considered in a plethora of
theoretical sources. The four-partite classification of insecure, dismissing,
preoccupied, and fearful types drawn from the attachment model (Sanford,
1997) resembles the four personality propensities of the selfhood model
with selffulness, selfishness, selflessness, and no-self respectively (Ch. 12).
Correlations between a measure of attachment and a measure of selfhood
showed that there were significant correlations between the two measures
as well as some gender differences contrary to those predicted by the selfhood model (L'Abate, 2003a; L'Abate & De Giacomo, 2003; L'Abate et al.,
2000). Hence, what seemed prima facie conceptual independence, since
the attachment model derives from a completely different theory, became
similarity on the basis of empirical evidence. Sources that are conceptually
independent could support specific models of the theory empirically.

A theory can be evaluated also indirectly, when some of its constructs
are derived from another theory very similar to it. For instance, selfhood, a
major model of the theory, is derived from the resource exchange model
(Foa & Foa, 1974; Foa et al., 1993). Hence, any evaluation about the validity
of the resource exchange model would indirectly enhance the validity of
the selfhood model. Indirect evidence would include results from resource
exchange constructs and methodology, and from Clark, Pataki, and Carver's
(1996) elaboration of Bakan's (1968) highly cited distinction between agentic
and communal relationships. The latter would relate to the ability to love
(Ch. 7), while agentic processes would relate to the ability to negotiate
(Ch. 8).

A third way to test a theory is directly, that is, through test instruments,
workbooks, therapeutic tasks, and operations derived directly from the theory (see Table 1.1). Direct evidence is whatever results are obtained from
procedures derived from models originating from the theory itself. This evidence is reviewed below and summarized in Table 1.1 to illustrate how this
theory can be evaluated in four settings: laboratory, primary, secondary, and
tertiary prevention.

For instance, the ERAAwC model (Ch. 4) has been evaluated with the
RAQ (Appendix B). Identity-differentiation (Ch. 10) has been evaluated in
Italy with an earlier version of the Cusinato-Maino-Scilletta (CMS) Like-
ness Questionnaire (Appendix C). The selfhood model referred to earlier

(Ch. 12) has been evaluated in its psychometric properties through the Self-Other Profile Chart (SOPC; L'Abate, 1992, 1997), the Problems in Relationships Scale and Workbook (L'Abate, 1992; McMahan & L'Abate, 2001), the Dyadic Relations Test (Cusinato & L'Abate, 2003, 2004). Intimacy (Ch. 16) has been evaluated with the Sharing of Hurts Scale (Stevens & L'Abate, 1989).

If some models of the theory have not been verified as yet, as indeed is the case, attempts were made to couch them in ways that make them amenable to verification. Even better, some forms of verification could be suggested. For instance, in Chapter 6, settings can be evaluated objectively according to time analyses, how long does one spend in a particular setting. However, the subjective meaning of a setting cannot be evaluated by time analysis alone. One could spend a great deal of time at work, but hate it, while regretting so little time spent with family because of work demands. That meaning, for instance, could be measured by the semantic differential, among others.

I suggest a method of evaluation for a model of this theory, propose others, and develop ways and means to evaluate each model. However, I may not have had the opportunity to evaluate them all. Furthermore, it would suspicious if I attempted to evaluate all models myself. It is much better for the evaluation to occur by someone else who is extraneous to the theory or even unfriendly to it.

Criteria for Theory Construction

Klein and White (1996, p. 259) listed and commented on 13 criteria for construction and validation of a theory. These criteria can be applied to this theory as well. In some ways they have guided the construction of this theory from its outset, even though they may have not been followed literally.

1. Internal consistency with no contradictions among parts of the theory, as would be among models of this theory. Again, its author can attempt to impart as much internal consistency among the models of the theory. However, someone else, not so involved with this theory, needs to evaluate whether this consistency exists here, and if it does, to what extent it does.

2. Clarity or explicitness, unambiguous and explicated where necessary, as attempted in each chapter of this book. An author can strived to achieve as much clarity and explicitness as possible, especially in making workbooks one method of theory evaluation. Nonetheless, the ultimate judgment about clarity and explicitness must come from sources external to this writer, the readers.

3. Explanatory power is related to validity, it explains what it is intended to explain, in this case, intimate relationships. In addition, explanatory power relates also to prediction and control, that is, predicting how people behave in intimate relationships and prescribing what they should do to improve them when they are wanting.

4. Coherence, key concepts are integrated and interconnected avoiding loose ends, as hopefully attempted in the rest of this work. Each model of the theory is connected to all the other models, not only conceptually, but also empirically. For instance, certain scales of the RAQ (Ch. 4) correlate significantly with a measure of selfhood (Ch. 12).

5. Understanding as a comprehensible sense of the whole phenomenon being examined, that is, between and among individuals involved in intimate and nonintimate relationships with each other and with objects, and settings, i.e., context and environment.

6. Empirical fit, confirmed by observations, controlled or otherwise, which in this case applies to the laboratory evaluation, and to primary, secondary, and tertiary prevention (see Table 1.1).

7. Testability, to be empirically supported or refuted, as already reported in previous publications of this theory as well as in this version.

8. Heuristic value, generating research and intellectual curiosity (debate and controversy), as taking place mostly at the University of Padua under the direction of Mario Cusinato, where a major research effort to evaluate and create instruments to evaluate models of the theory is occurring. Approximately 50 dissertations have evaluated various models of the theory. Half of them were devoted to evaluating the Dyadic Relations Test (DRT) (Cusinato & L'Abate, 2003, 2004).

9. Groundedness is built from detailed information about events and processes. Even though attempts to follow this criterion were made, it remains to external observers to judge whether it was followed correctly.

10. Contextualization means stressing social and historical contexts affecting or being affected by key concepts or constructs, as in the case of intimate relationships, and especially in the ERAAwC model (Ch. 4), a depth model (Ch. 5), and in settings (Ch. 6).

11. Interpretive sensitivity as felt by experiences practiced and felt by those to which it is applied (face validity). Indeed, an Italian student (Dr. Claudia Scilletta, personal communication, June 23, 2003), who was familiar with the theory, commented on the fact that students who studied it had to learn it to pass an examination but not to understand it. Another senior lay-person, who had been present when this theory was in its inception in 1988, when I was visiting professor

at the University of Padua, recently (June 26, 2003) commented that one needs to be old to understand this theory. One needs to be old to write about it as well!

12. Predictive power, predicting successfully what will take place after the prediction is made, a process that is yet to occur. Yet, this theory attempts to go beyond prediction by stressing prescription by matching one workbook with a referral reason, a test score, or a test profile. If one respondent claims to be depressed, shows instances of depression, scores high on measures of depression, then one could administer one of the many depression workbooks available commercially (L'Abate, 1996, 2004a).

13. Practical utility. This statement applies readily to social problems and programs of action in prevention, like enrichment programs (see Table 1.1), secondary prevention, like workbooks, and tertiary prevention or therapy, as in prescribed tasks (Table 1.1; Ch. 18).

Other Ways to Evaluate a Theory

Gurman (1997) proposed an even more specific classification of evaluative methods, distinguishing between "traditional" versus "modern" perspectives and "soft" versus "hard" methodology. Soft methodology and traditional perspective include ethnography, grounded theory, phenomenology, and case studies. Soft methodology and modern perspective include critical theory, conversation analysis, feminist theory, and focus groups. Hard methodology and traditional perspective includes quantitative methods like scale development, program evaluation, experimental research, cost-effectiveness, surveys, and predictive methods.

Hard methodology–modern perspective include metaanalysis, structural equation modeling, Delphi methods, and event-based analysis. One is inclined to include in this category theory-building and theory-testing with prescriptive therapeutic tasks. Both traditional-modern perspectives and soft-hard methodologies are necessary for theoretical and therapeutic purposes. One perspective or one methodology cannot be pursued solely at the expense of its counterpart (Rennie, 1998). Both dialectics and demonstrability are two sides of the same coin. F2f talk in prevention and psychotherapy is based on dialectics. Workbooks are based on demonstrability because being based on the written word makes them replicable *ad infinitum*.

L'Abate (2004b) suggested a continuum of verifiability that starts from the least empirical and ends with the most empirical bases, as in: (1) anecdotal, impressionistic, and subjective evidence, as in case studies, (2) consumer satisfaction surveys, as in the case of the controversial *Consumer Reports* (1995) survey on the effectiveness of psychotherapy; (3) pre-post evaluation of outcome through objective, self-report, paper-and-pencil tests, compared with a control group, or (4) ratings from external observers or behavior samples, (5) combination of steps $2 + 3$ or $2 + 4$ or $3 + 4$, or $2 + 3 + 4$, (6) comparative evaluation of different approaches aimed at and claiming to treat the same condition, as in the case of evaluating three different workbooks, all claiming to deal with depression (L'Abate, Boyce, Fraizer, & Russ, 1992) or long-term effects of workbook administration, (7) experimental (active and controlled) manipulation of variables, as in working at a distance from respondents through workbooks versus f2f psychotherapy, or workbooks versus physical exercise, workbooks versus therapists' manuals, as in a review of 25 years of private practice (L'Abate, L'Abate, & Maino, in press) with and without workbooks to evaluate whether they are cost-effective in shortening the number of therapy sessions (they do not, they seem to prolong it!), (8) metaanalyses of studies, as performed, for instance, by Smyth and L'Abate (2001) about the effectiveness of workbooks, and (9) metaanalyses of metaanalyses.

Verifiability and Circumplex Models

Some verifiable theories can be expanded to clinical applications and some cannot. For instance, Olson's circumplex model (Gorall & Olson, 1995) has lead to the creation of preventive and therapeutic applications. By the same token, many monadic theories of personality and psychopathology based on the circumplex were verified in the laboratory (Kiesler, 1996; Plutchik & Conte, 1997). However, they failed to develop direct conceptual and empirical applications and links with couple, or family functioning/dysfunctioning or with prevention or psychotherapy, perpetuating the individual in a vacuum view of personality. Hence, as in the case of a great many psychological tests, the personality circumplex remains inert and limited in its applications strictly to the laboratory.

Verifiability and the Attachment Model

Attachment theory, on the other hand, through its strange situation, the Attachment Story Completion Task (ASCT; Bretherton, Ridgeway, & Cassidy, 1990), structured, semistructured interviews, and rating scales, has been verified in laboratories around the globe. Its direct and indirect preventive and therapeutic implications have been widespread (Slade, 1999). However, most of these applications still rely on f2f talk, making it difficult to evaluate whether the talk stemmed directly from the model. Nonetheless, that is a beginning.

As far as I know, there has been at least one direct (i.e, theory-derived or model-driven) clinical application of the attachment model that is verifiable or that could be verified in its preventive or psychotherapeutic applications (Stosney, 1995). This contribution to "attachment abuse," in spouses, does rely on written homework assignments and "worksheets," making it a veritable, verifiable workbook. However, no data were given to demonstrate the usefulness of this workbook approach. How much these assignments and worksheets derive directly from the attachment model is up to someone else to evaluate. The term "attachment" could have become a catch-all for all kinds of relationships with no direct links with the original model.

Furthermore, what information would this model add to a clinical population? When people ask for professional help, it is assumed that they are "insecure," that is, either fearful, dismissing, or preoccupied. If they were secure would they ask for help? What would be relevant pertains to identifying which type of insecurity is present. Given that identification, however, one needs to demonstrate that different therapeutic approaches were used to match each specific insecurity, rather than a vague, nonspecific, pall-mall approach. As far as I know, this matching has not taken place because, as long as words are used in the process of intervening, it will be difficult if not impossible to prove that that match did occur.

Hence, some of the most verified models of this time, personality circumplex and attachment, are found wanting in terms of their clinical and preventive applications to either individuals, couples, or families. Of course, there are treatises about clinical applications of attachment theory (Erdman & Caffery, 2003; Shane, Shane, & Gales, 1997), but, with the exception of Stosney (1995), they seem based on wishful thinking and words rather than on repeatable operations. As Bradbury (2003) concluded, most evaluative laboratory measures have not lead to preventive or psychotherapeutic applications.

On the Nature of Evidence to Evaluate a Theory: An Empiricist's Credo

In addition to the criteria already considered above, one addition is necessary. Here, I must state my beliefs as an empiricist, even though some would dispute the validity of such a label on himself, suggesting, perhaps correctly, that he may be more of a soft-hearted clinician than a hard-boiled researcher. This empiricist's credo is as follows: "I prefer to be specific and be found wanting, wrong, or incorrect, rather than be generally vague and claim to be right or correct." The validity of understanding, predicting, and prescribing changes in intimate relationships stands on their specificity, not on their generality. This is why research, as considered in Chapter 1, is about relatively small, specific models rather than about general, vague theoretical notions. Specific predictions can be verified. Vague and general predictions are difficult if not impossible to verify at all. As Millon (2003) commented on this issue:

"Unfortunately, the formal structure of most clinical theories of the past has been haphazard and unsystematic; concepts often were vague, and procedures by which empirical consequences could be derived were tenuous, at best. Instead of presenting an orderly arrangement of concepts and propositions by which hypotheses could be clearly derived, most theorists presented a loosely formulated pastiche of opinions, analogies, and speculation (p. 952)."

This credo, therefore, lies in between three different polarities about the validity of theoretical statements that abound in this theory.

1. *Finding versus claiming*: Finding means an active search for ways and means to evaluate models of the theory, without claiming any validity before it is "found." This approach means proffering hypotheses and create an active manipulation of variables involved. Claiming means talking about the validity of any theory or model, as it was the case for decades for psychoanalysis, without any empirical evidence.

2. *Correct versus incorrect*: Correction must come from external sources to whomever claims correctedness of one's statements. The source could be evidence generated by the claimant, in the form of controlled studies, or from someone else who is not making the same claim but who provides evidence to either support or invalidate the claim. In science, as well as in law, validity of any statement needs corroboration from at least two independent sources that are not related to each other. This is why it is always difficult to believe evidence obtained by someone who has a stake in the validity of a claim. It is better for an external, independent source to validate any claim.

   The author of the theory may develop ways and means to evaluate models of the theory, but ultimately, the burden of proof lies in evidence gathered by someone else who is not the author. For instance, I have claimed for years the cost-effectiveness of workbooks (L'Abate, 1992, 2001, 2002; L'Abate & De Giacomo, 2003), in the sense that they would shortened the number of therapy session. As noted earlier, when this claim was evaluated (L'Abate, L'Abate, & Maino, in press), it was found to be completely wrong. Workbooks significantly increased the number of therapy sessions in individuals, couples, and families. Whether this increase meant higher levels of involvement, and therefore, effectiveness, remains to be seen.

3. *Specific versus nonspecific*: The more specific a prediction is the better, because the more general a prediction the more difficult it is to verify it. This is why f2f talk is difficult to use in verifying any

theory or preventive or therapeutic approach (L'Abate, 1999). The written record can be replicated *ad infinitum* (L'Abate, 2003b). Talk is difficult and expensive if not impossible to replicate. This is why workbooks (Ch. 1) are used to evaluate some models of this theory. Words won't cut it.

Evaluating a theory of this kind and magnitude cannot be performed by a single author. One can develop as many *replicable* model-derived methods of evaluation as possible in the hope that someone else will perform the task of evaluating their validity.

ACCOUNTABILITY AS A SECOND CRITERION FOR THEORY EVALUATION

In addition to verifiability, however, this theory, to be applied to clinical or preventive settings, should produce results in both prevention and therapy, thus fulfilling a second criterion of accountability: does it produce results in the applied arena? As Stricker (1997) suggested: ". . . for science and practice to be commensurable, the same theoretical matrix must generate both science and practice activities (p. 442)."

Accountability and verifiability, however, are independent of each other. We need verifiability in theory-building and theory-evaluation, but the criterion of accountability is more relevant to preventive and therapeutic outcomes than to theory construction and testing (L'Abate, 1986). Producing results, however, is no longer a sufficient criterion both in prevention and in psychotherapy with either individuals, couples, or families. The current movement for evidence-based interventions speaks well to the requirement of accountability, results-based outcome. However, in its frenzy and fashion to apply only empirically based treatments, theory has been completely forgotten. No reference has been made, as far as I know, about the need for *both* theory-derivation and empirically based treatments (L'Abate, 2003a).

If a theory or a technique is useful to a practicing clinician, is that all that is necessary? For instance, some very appealing theories of therapy may produce impressionistic results in spite of their inherent unverifiability, as it used to be (in part) the case with psychoanalysis in its early stages and is still the case with systems theory. At least in psychotherapy, a theory could conceivably account for a positive outcome on a post hoc basis, but remain unverifiable otherwise. Apparently, many therapists work on the basis of this assumption. Theories be dammed. Results are all that matters. If at all, theories are used post-facto to explain but never to predict, because, as I have stressed repeatedly, what people, professionals as well as respondents, *say* is impossible to predict and even less possible to control. Only the written record allows such predictability because it can be controlled from its outset, when it is administered, and to its end, when respondents complete it, as in the case of workbooks (Ch. 1).

To take into account both criteria, therefore, this theory needs to be verifiable as well as accountable. Verifiability and accountability, of course, are relative and a matter of degree. Both criteria depend on the peculiar predilections of preventers and of therapists. Accountability may be necessary in therapy but insufficient in theory, just as verifiability may be necessary in theory but insufficient in therapy. Both criteria are necessary and sufficient to verify a theory in the laboratory if the theory is to be applied also in clinical and preventive settings (Nation et al., 2003; Wandersman & Florin, 2003).

Theory and Accountability in Interventions

Accountability, therefore, deals with how people change and how we professionals help them change. Hence, accountability and change are two sides of the same coin. After defining what is meant by verifiability, this section argues that five minimally necessary and possibly insufficient conditions necessary for change are: (1) admission of problematic issues, problems, or symptoms that are not changing for the better; (2) allowing for external intervention to help change existing dysfunctional patterns; (3) receiving positive, direct, and indirect communications about one's sense of importance and about the importance and severity of the referral problem; (4) achieving hope that change is possible and that it can take place, if one wants it and works for it, and (5) establishing a sense of control where controls have been either defective or missing.

Change here does not only mean change just for respondents. It also means change for the profession of psychotherapy. Psychotherapists want to help people change, but can they help change themselves as professionals? We cannot forget that "Them" is "Us" (L'Abate, 1997). How do psychotherapists change themselves as persons and as professionals? They supposedly know how to change themselves as persons by putting themselves in the role of respondents and making the psychotherapeutic experience part of their training. However, how many psychotherapists put themselves in that position? Furthermore, even if they change as persons, how do psychotherapists change as professionals? How does a profession change its practices, if that change is at all possible? This argument begs the question of "How is this change to take place?" In this section, various hypotheses will be advanced about helping respondents change and bringing about change in the profession of psychotherapy. If change is good for respondents should not change be good for the psychotherapy profession? On the other hand, could it be that the field of psychotherapy is as deeply and rigidly entrenched as most dysfunctional people are, to the point of even denying its dysfunctionality?

Years ago, Rogers (1957) considered three necessary and sufficient conditions for change: empathy, warmth, and unconditional regard. Rogers's original considerations, however, need further expansion by bringing up additional, also necessary, and probably insufficient, conditions for personal and professional change that he had not considered. His original conditions may have been necessary then from a monadic, humanistic viewpoint, but they seem rather insufficient now in view of further developments in the field of psychotherapy that stress attention to contextual factors. The three sine qua non conditions stressed by Rogers may be necessary and sufficient for certain individuals, i.e., University of Chicago undergraduates, but seem rather limited and limiting in view of further developments in marital and family therapy, and work with character or personality disorders. They may be necessary, but they are definitely insufficient in helping severely dysfunctioning individuals, deeply entrenched, conflictful couples, and dysfunctional families (L'Abate, 1986; Liddle, 1992). With personality disorders, for instance, these qualities may be counterproductive. These individuals may be suspicious of these qualities as being too seductive and too manipulative. We know, of course, that these stylistic qualities do not work at all with schizophrenics.

Rogers's conditions refer to the style of the therapist, but have little if anything to say about structuring skills in psychotherapy. Style may represent those relationship skills that are fundamental in starting the process of therapy. Structuring represents the method that is necessary to help people change, independent of the therapist's style (Table 3.2). Both skills may be necessary to help people change, especially couples and families. Hence, professional change will mean not only reconsidering style as a necessary but insufficient condition for psychotherapeutic change, but also reconsidering method as another necessary but insufficient condition to obtain change. Whether style and method together become sufficient to deal with human problems remains to be seen. We and our respondents need both, style and method, to obtain results. While issues of style are so personal that they remain outside of the purpose of this section, issues of theory and method will be considered as being important for personal and professional change.

Shortcomings in the Profession of Psychotherapy

As traditionally practiced through the spoken medium, there are many shortcomings in the profession of psychotherapy that are either denied or are swept under the rug of avoidance and even arrogance. Among the ones that come to mind are: (1) proliferation of therapeutic approaches, a plethora ranging into the hundreds; (2) immediate denial of negative feedback, whoever is foolish enough to raise criticisms about the status of the psychotherapy profession (i.e., negative feedback) is either ignored, or personally criticized for whatever arguments are used to bolster such criticisms; (3) entrenchment and rigidity in its practices, because of their undeniable and evident success—if a good living is to be made in this practice—why change it?; (4) conflicts, splits, disagreements, and divisions: (a) among theoretical positions, many of them with mutually antagonistic clinical practices, (b) in the failure of evaluation to direct practice, where most research on diagnostic and evaluative instruments takes place without treatment, and where treatment takes place without evaluation; (c) in the failure of theory and research to direct evaluation and practice; (d) between research and practice, through avoidance of evaluation of outcome as standard operating procedures in private practices; (e) in the unbridled and uncritical acceptance of untested and untestable therapeutic gimmicks and gurus; (f) in the adoption of techniques on the basis of their seductive appeal or the charismatic influence of their leader rather than their proven usefulness; (g) in the avoidance of joining and integrating psychotherapy with preventive and psychoeducatonal approaches; (h) in an obsessive avoidance of empirical verifiability and professional accountability; (i) in the traditional overreliance on the verbal medium with parallel underreliance on both nonverbal and written media; (j) overreliance on individual approaches rather than using groups, couples, and families, making therapy more expensive than it needs to be; and (k) inability to define minimal or average levels of professional competence, a deficit that may be resolved, in part, by Drum and Hall's (1993) recommendations.

The best example of the denial of reality that surrounds the profession of psychotherapy is the trend toward skyrocketing costs in physical and mental health care, with little attention by the profession to deal with cost-effectiveness and accountability in treatment. If these trends persist, and there is no evidence that they will not, ultimately, psychotherapeutic practices, as presently existing, will be insufficient in dealing with the many human ills of our society and provide adequate services for those who need them. Considering the millions of people needing help, half a million therapists and counselors will not be sufficient to deal with them. Psychotherapy based on the spoken medium is a drop in the mental health bucket, and an expensive drop at that!

Furthermore, as long as we limit ourselves to the spoken medium and fail to use the other two media available to us, we will fail to find out which medium is best for which condition or for which type of person. For instance, middle-class, educated, depressed, or anxious individuals do well in f2f talk psychotherapy. However, thousands of individuals in jails and reformatories cannot and will not be changed by talk alone. As a result, our clinical practices are destined to remain static and unchanging (L'Abate, 1999). Yes, we are a much-needed profession well-established in the mainstream of American culture. If psychotherapists can add to the tremendous strides made in the past quarter century with computers and the Internet, we will increase the relevance of psychotherapy manifold over what has been accomplished thus far.

The Challenge of Managed Care

Managed care in mental health care is here to stay, whether therapists like it or not. Therapists are being questioned about their practices, demonstrating their results, and defending their fees (Winegar, 1992). The issue of effectiveness and especially cost-effectiveness is now becoming paramount: "Clearly, the ability to measure the clinical effectiveness of psychotherapy is emerging as an important marketing tool for both medical care companies and therapists (Ridgewood Finantial Institute, 1993, p. 34)." Cost-containment and continuous quality improvement will become standard criteria of evaluation. Therapists will need to ". . . establish standard clinical problem-solving methods that can be measured against treatment outcomes (p. 34)."

As Goodman et al. (1992) summarized these issues:

" 'Private practice' is becoming an endangered species. Unless mental healthcare practitioners can articulate what they are doing for their patients and also convincingly explain why they are doing it, purchasers and providers [of mental health insurance] are going to be increasingly unwilling to pay for their services. If mental healthcare services are too subjective to quantify, they 'may well be too subjective to pay for.' . . . Practitioners are being asked to articulate their clinical rationale for the recommended treatment, and, for the first time, to provide the supportive, convincing clinical evidence that is the basis for that treatment decision—what is known as 'articulating the process of care.' Clinicians are not systematically educated about the value of articulating and documenting their own (usually intuitively accurate and preconscious) thought processes. Instead, they are trained to make the expedient, though tunneled, leap from diagnosis to treatment with nary a glance into the chasm of treatment choices and alternative care options that have become the focus of today's external reviewers (p. 15)."

Winegar (1992) warned therapists who fail to heed the call for managed care for cost-containment and cost-effectiveness:

"Those professionals who fail to understand these revolutionary changes will see their ability to provide services to their clients and to control their professional futures greatly diminished. Those who do understand these changes, and understand that all practitioners in the coming years will be involved in this revolution, will not only exercise more control over their practices and professional lives, but prosper and grow in this era of change (p. 1)."

The foregoing quotes indicate that these changes are being mandated from outside the profession, leaving no choice to psychotherapists but to change if they want to survive. Thus, the dreaded danger of external coercion, demands for accountability, scorned by most therapists in the past, and emphasis on pragmatic demonstrability rather than dialectical aesthetics will stress the role of the therapist as a scientist rather than as an artist. Style alone will no longer be sufficient to demonstrate results. What method(s) are used and what results are obtained, in addition to style, will be the bottom line of clinical practice. Therapists will have no choice but to use additional media of communication, like writing and computers, and more cost-effective group compositions. This conclusion also means that therapists will have to start using objective evaluations on a pre- or post-treatment basis, learning to rely on writing as a cost-effective medium of communication, not only with their clients, but also with their insurance providers.

Why Change Psychotherapeutic Practices?

Why should change take place when it is not wanted? There are reluctant respondents who do not want change even though other family members and professionals see the need. Why should the field of psychotherapy change when it sees no need for it? One needs to deal with denial from the outset as the major defense against change. How do psychotherapists deal with denial in their respondents? The answer, of course, is: "In various ways." They first look at the roots and rationale for the denial. What prompted this individual, couple, or family to deny the referral problem, and, by extension, possibly the reality and painfulness of the situation? Underneath the denial there may be fear of the unknown, hopelessness, threat to feelings of self-worth, esteem, and inadequacy. The process of denial, then, has little to do with any rational basis, but it has a great deal to do with an emotional one (L'Abate, 1997, 1999).

By the same token, the fear of change in the psychotherapy profession is no different from the same fear of change in respondents. We are not dealing with rationality. We are dealing with emotionality, an aspect that cannot be solely dealt with rationally, as cognitive-behavioral therapists well know. However, if professional change does not take place from the inside the psychotherapy profession, eventually, it will be forced from the outside. Change is now being mandated through a variety if mechanisms, like reduction and restrictions in insurance and third-party payments, managed care, and even elimination of mental health benefits if deemed too expensive and too inefficient.

Wanting to Change

Hence, we have to ask ourselves: "How does change come about?"; "Why and when do people want change?" There are at least three reasons for people to want change. The first reason is *necessity*. Change is wanted when the costs of staying the same are higher than the costs of changing. When one is faced by alternative choices like hospitalization, incarceration, divorce, financial or emotional bankruptcy for self or for loved ones, and there are no other alternatives except therapy, then one may accept the inevitable choice that seems less costly than others. In spite of this argument, of course, many dysfunctional people still refuse help, no matter how serious the consequences may be for themselves and for their loved ones.

The second reason is *conflict*. When conflict, either internal or external, is too high and, again too costly, then one will consider cheaper alternatives. As Averill and Nunley (1992) concluded: ". . . of all the sources of novelty, perhaps none is more important than conflict (p. 242)." Whether change in therapy can be equated to novelty remains to be seen. However, the psychotherapy profession will not change unless there is sufficient conflict, both internal and external to the profession, to warrant a more effective course of action. The issue here, of course, is what that course of action should be.

The last reason for change is *coercion*. Although none of us, as persons and as professionals, consider coercion in positive terms, if change does not take place from inside a profession, then it may be mandated by the outside. This coercion is already taking place. Many insurance companies demand an accounting of treatment and severely limit the number of sessions available to their (our) clients. Mental health benefits, seen as too expensive by many insurance companies, are being written off from other health benefits. How can psychotherapists help when clients tell them from the outset that their insurance contracts limit the number of therapy sessions available? Should psychotherapists send clients away or should they consider more cost-effective, helpful strategies?

Psychotherapists will have to learn to rely on group techniques more than on individual ones. The latter will become the luxury of those who can afford them, regardless of insurance benefits. Furthermore, in addition to learning to rely more on group techniques and less on individual ones, psychotherapists will need to enlarge their professional repertoire to include new ways of helping. They will have to use two other media of intervention that, thus far, have been given short shrift by the psychotherapeutic community, that is, the written and nonverbal (see Table 1.1). Is that enlargement to other media too painful to consider? Are psychotherapists so rigid and entrenched in their practices that they cannot add a few new skills to their traditional (mostly verbal) repertoires?

What Does Change Mean?

If we have learned anything about changing in the past generation of practice and research in the field of psychotherapy (Ehrenwald, 1991; Freedheim, 1992), then we should summarize what change means. For change to take place, four minimum factors seem necessary. They may well be insufficient. Change takes place when there is a new response that is also positive and strong enough to be incorporated in one's repertoire by making a distinct difference and giving direction to one's life (Prochaska, DiClemente, & Norcross, 1992). Thus, novelty, positiveness, strength, and direction describe, at least in part, the qualities necessary to the process of change. A new experience becomes positive to the extent that the professional helper affirms the client's individual worth directly and indirectly, by, among others, listening and complimenting efforts to change. Meeting regularly with a professional listener and helper is a new and positive experience that becomes strong enough in its weekly repetition.

The first component of newness or novelty is defined by any experienced attitude, feeling, or behavior that was not previously present in the past and that becomes presently available in one's emotional, cognitive, and behavioral repertoire. This new experience is therefore different from past ones or, even if potentially available, it has not been used heretofore. This is a new experience for those who have not been listened to in their past relationships. Talking about oneself to someone who listens and who seems to care by responding to one's inner feelings is a new, positive, and exciting experience, in a way that may not have occurred in past experiences. In the client's past, feelings and subjective perceptions may have been discounted and even punished.

The second component of change requires a new response to be of a positive nature, defined as self-enhancing and rewarding behavior that does not damage anyone else. After all, one can change for the worst by either doing nothing or using negative means. Any new positive behavior helps one feel "good," enhanced, and whole as a human being, to the extent that no one gets hurt by this behavior. This sense of positivity is achieved through: (1) hearing someone in authority affirming the validity of one's perceptions as determined by attendant feelings; and (2) affirmation of the validity and importance of past, painful experiences that have been negatively influential in one's life. These two aspects (regularity of meetings and talking), in and by themselves, may be sufficient enough to make a difference in one's life.

Positive affirmation and reframing can be a new experience where negativity may have been the hallmark of past experiences. As Cantor and Kihlstrom (1987) suggest, effecting change is based on avoiding what they called "old scripts" and learning new ones (pp. 227–234), while persisting in change efforts, and reflecting on the self. Persistence means frequent repetition, practice, and rehearsal that may increase the habitual preeminence of this new behavior, a third component of change characterized by strength. This quality of strength is added when one's perceptions and experiences are affirmed and validated repeatedly. By strength is also meant any behavior that is forceful, intense, and powerful enough to make a difference in how one is going to live the rest of one's life. This difference is seen in Rogers's (1957) "corrective emotional experience," so-called peak experiences, or even in routine repetition and repetitive practice of new and positive behaviors.

These three components of change can be reframed as being based on frequency and duration of appointments and positive affirmations, and on intensity in the emotional experience of meeting with someone to share intense and painful feelings and emotions. A fourth component of direction is necessary to find out how we learn from past experiences to change our lives toward more rewarding and realistic goals. One can have novelty, positivity, and strength, but without direction in how to use these factors, one could go around in circles, like in a maze, without being able to direct one's energy and efforts toward rewarding goals.

Thus, the psychotherapeutic experience allows for the acquisition and emission of new responses that were not experienced or present in one's past repertoire, either emotively, cognitively, or behaviorally. For instance, preset appointments help achieve some sense of regularity, predictability, and stability, where none was present in the past. This regularity is important to establish or reestablish a sense of control where controls, in the past, were either not present or, at best, weak, too strong, or inadequate.

Given these components of change, why are so many people (professionals are people too!) afraid of it? Among the many possibilities that come to mind the following are derived from clinical practice: (1) change so defined is too demanding of one's limited resources, thus; (2) change is a threat that may prove one's "badness," "craziness," or inadequacy, with the threat of possible banishment and hospitalization; (3) inability to change in general is a lifelong pattern that has in itself produced and propounded the problem, as seen in addictions, borderline cases, and psychoses; (4) rejection of treatment as a pattern of overall denial of dependency and proclamation of "independence" without consideration that the human condition is characterized by interdependence—so-called "independence" does not exist because we are all, in one way or another, interdependent on one another; and (5) loss of power, especially in dyadic and family relationships, where the one who has the most power with little on no responsibility, stereotypically the man, sees change as a threat to that position. No wonder that men are the ones who are most threatened by change and find it difficult to accept psychotherapy as a benign process. Fortunately, this pattern seems to have changed in the past generation.

Hence, change is no different from other behavioral dimensions of: (1) *duration*, as seen in the length of a therapy session and a sequence, however short or long, of sessions, (2) *frequency* of positive experiences, the peak experiences that take place inside and outside the therapist's office, or rate of appointments, if these can be equated to frequency of positive experiences, (3) *intensity* of depth and strength in the experience, and (4) *direction*, which is just as important as any other component. All four components intermingle in the therapeutic experience. However, they can be enhanced when the structured written medium, as in regular and systematic written homework assignments, is an integral part of the process of change.

The Necessary (but Insufficient) Conditions for Change

The foregoing definition of change, a process characterized by novel, positive, frequent, intense, and focused relationships between an individual, couple, or family seeking help from a professional, is independent from the process necessary to obtain change. If we have learned anything from systems thinking, it is that the first condition necessary for change in any system, be it physical, human (individual, dyadic, or multirelational, like a family), philosophical, or otherwise, is to admit that it needs external intervention. It can no longer cope or survive with its existing resources. Calling a professional and asking for help is the first step in producing change. Sometimes this step may be all that is necessary. The admission in itself may provoke a critical reexamination of the system's assets and liabilities that may prompt and provoke a change.

Many therapists are aware of potential clients who have called for help and who, when called back for their failure to follow through with the initial call, indicated how they no longer needed the sought-after help. After the initial call, apparently they came up with some new conclusion about or solution for their problem. These people may be a minority. Nevertheless, they suggest how the admission of the problem is the first step toward its solution. Admission of one's weakness, as indicated even by a simple phone call, takes a lot of strength and may lead toward a reexamination of one's way of living. Very dysfunctional systems may be too weak and unable to ask for help, as in the case of addictive, borderline, criminal, and psychotic relationships.

Thus, a necessary condition for change in a failing, dysfunctional system is to ask for and obtain external intervention. In most frequent and functional conditions this intervention may consist of talking with a friend or family member, reading a self-help book, going to a concert, meditating and reflecting, taking a trip, or attending a lecture. What happens when we are confronted by more dysfunctional conditions? Here we need to differentiate among degrees of dysfunctionality. For instance, most shy individuals could learn from an assertiveness training workshop or similar social skill training. Shy but also withdrawn and fearful individuals, however, will need more than preventive, psychoeducational interventions (De Maria, 2003). Shy, withdrawn, and fearful individuals without a job may need therapeutic interventions in their various available compositions (individual, group, marital, or family).

The second condition necessary for change in any system is for intervention to take place from outside that system. As much as we may dislike mechanical metaphors or analogies, just as any malfunctioning machine or motor needs a mechanic and a possible change or realignment or replacement of defective parts, so too do human systems. We all need outside intervention to change. Even a small cut, if unwashed and unkempt, may fester and deteriorate into a dangerous infection, just as a dysfunctioning motor or machine may finally break down if no outside mechanic intervenes. Why should we think that human systems are any different from or better than physical systems to the extent that both need external intervention to change? We readily admit to a machine needing an external replacement or adjustment to keep on working. However, we are not willing to admit the same principle for ourselves. For instance, clichés like "Marriages are made in heaven" and many other of the same ilk, testify to the same kind of fatalistic and optimistic thinking. Somehow, no matter how terrible things are, relationships (and individuals) will fix themselves by themselves and without external intervention. Behind this thinking there is apathy, helplessness, and tremendous fear of change and confrontation of the unknown ("The devil I know is better than the devil I don't know!").

There is no dysfunctional system, whether physical or human, abstract or concrete, that can adjust, fix itself, and survive from the inside. We may not like the analogy of human systems with physical ones. However, we may need to ask what makes us think that human systems are any better than physical ones? What evidence do we have that dysfunctioning human systems have a greater or different ability to fix themselves than physical systems? A great deal of this thesis lies on the nature of what constitutes external intervention. It would not need to be only psychotherapy. Any kind of positive, external intervention or service of sufficient intensity and regularity may produce change. This change may take place provided that it matches the immediate and transcendent needs of clients and that clients themselves are able and willing to absorb and assimilate it for the better.

This optimal match has been the golden fleece of psychotherapy theory and research since its very outset.

The third necessary condition is to give our clients a sense of importance, as expanded in Chapter 12. This sense of importance is basic to the establishment of and exchanges within intimate human relationships. Without the establishment of this sense of importance, it would be difficult to help people who want our help. How is this sense of importance communicated? It is communicated both directly and indirectly, verbally and nonverbally. It is communicated directly by: (1) listening to someone problems and plight; (2) affirming the validity of someone perceptions; and (3) asserting the seriousness of the problem as perceived by the one reporting it. It is communicated verbally by reframing positively the request for help ("Only people who care for themselves ask for help"; "You must care a lot about yourself (or each other) if you were strong enough to ask for help"; "You must be very strong because mostly strong people ask for help, weak people are too weak to ask"). It is communicated indirectly nonverbally, by our relating with them as if they were guests in our offices and accepting their plight as if it were ours.

The fourth condition necessary for change is to give a sense of hope that through appropriate help change for the better can and will take place. Thus, one needs to be reassured that admission of a problem, asking for help, and the importance of the problem for the system, regardless of the objective seriousness of the problem, are relevant and important to the professional helper. Furthermore, the subjective estimation of the seriousness of the problem itself, rather that its objective outcome, is necessary to give reassurance that the problem can be solved and that change will bring about such a solution ("This is a very serious problem, but with your help, I think we can work on it").

The fifth necessary condition for change is to give respondents a sense of control and mastery over their lives. People want help because their lives or someone in their lives is out of control. However, how is a sense of control and mastery to be achieved? References cited in previous publications concerning this topic focused on dialectical or empirical aspects of control. They do not give any hint or suggestion on how to help people establish or reestablish a sense of control and mastery over their lives. Past behavioral positions have simplistically stressed the importance of immediate consequences and contingent reinforcements. However, these positions have been shown to be practically, philosophically, and empirically limited in helping complex human systems. We are controlled by external reinforcements as well as by internal emotional attitudes and cognitions that direct our behavior above and beyond immediate and concrete reinforcements. Many people work for internal and abstract, if not transcendental, reasons (L'Abate, 1986, 1994). Behavioral positions deal strictly with the output of intimate relationships, not with their input or their processes, and, in that regard, remain incomplete and wanting. Control is achieved when access, input, and the beginning of any relational sequence, as well as the process, exit, output, and end of that sequence are regulated. It is just as important to help people establish a sense of control at the input side, from the beginning of undesirable behavior ("If you want to stop it, start it!") as well as at the output, its end side (L'Abate, 1986, 1994; Weeks & L'Abate, 1982).

How is control established in real life? In actual, everyday reality, control consists of beginning a behavior, like going to work at a certain, predetermined time and exiting from work at a given, preestablished time. Employers control their employees by requiring them to show up at an established time and to leave the place of work at another, already predetermined time. If employees are late, they better come up with a good excuse, and if they want to leave earlier, they also have to come up with a good reason. In certain cases, employees are penalized for any deviation from the agreed-upon norm of preestablished starting and ending times. Thus, control is established through regulation of inputs (entrances, beginnings, accesses), interviewing processes, as well as outputs (exits and endings). Rules of entry and exit vary from one setting to another, as discussed in Chapter 6.

This real life analogy is also a rationale for establishing controls during the process of psychotherapy. We give our clients a preset time where the appointment time and duration is established in a predictable, regular, and repeatable sequence. Sometimes, this sequence may not be sufficient, or it may be too expensive, chancy, and lengthy. Consequently, it is necessary to require a parallel process of homework meetings and written assignments at preset, prearranged times, to increase repetitive predictability and establish regularity (L'Abate, 1986, 1992). The quality of regularity, just as brushing our teeth every day three times a day, having three square meals daily, and going to work everyday at the same time and coming home from work at the same time, helps establish a sense of control. The establishment of regularity over beginning, process, and end of any behavioral or relational sequence, plus directions over what should happen in between, is control. Very likely, without a sense of repetitive regularity, such a sense of control would not be established.

The repetitive regularity of therapy appointments has a great deal to do with helping establish or reestablish a sense of mastery and control over one's life. Regularity of therapy appointments is doubled by requiring clients to have regular home meetings to match and parallel the frequency of therapy sessions. The practice of regular home meetings, although based on personal impressions, whether required of individuals, couples, or families, seems to produce a faster increase in a sense of mastery than just the regularity of therapy sessions alone (Kazantzis, Deane, Ronan, & L'Abate, in press). Once this double regularity (at home and therapist's office) is accepted and agreed upon from the outset of the therapeutic relationship (through a written contract), it is incumbent for the therapist to administer sufficient written homework to make sure that the therapy hour is even more effective and productive by enlarging and strengthening the sphere of therapeutic influence from the therapy office to the home, i.e., generalization from the office to the home (L'Abate, 1986, 1990, 1992).

The Context of Change: The Magical Number Three

Once we define what change consists of and we specify the conditions necessary for change, we beg the question of where is change to take place? An answer to this question can be found, in part, in intimate relationships. As soon as we answer in this fashion, however, we have to define what these relationships consist of. We assume without questioning that change needs to take place within intimate relationships and within individuals who determine these relationships. Furthermore, we need to specify that change should be in relationships that matter, that is, those enduring, committed, close, and prolonged ones based on interdependence. This specification is not sufficient because these relationships are embedded into a cultural context that needs specification as well. Contextually, dysfunctionality takes place at various individual, dyadic, or multirelational levels, especially in the family as a whole unit of interacting personalities. One cannot change at the individual level without impinging and influencing change in those who live close by or who are related by blood, legal, or emotional ties.

A more comprehensive viewpoint, summarized in Table 3.1, above and beyond interdependent relationships, would need to pinpoint where change is to take place, once we consider "larger interactional systems" as representing the context for change. Once we break down the rather general and encompassing term "context" into three specific settings, we obtain a matrix of three "larger interactional systems," which would include: (1) communication media through exchange resources, either nonverbal, verbal, and written; (2) settings; and (3) resource modalities.

Communication Media

The three media of communication are fairly well defined inside and outside the therapy office. Ideally, there should be an isomorphic process going on between the therapist's office and the other three settings: home, work,

Table 3.1. Media of Communication and Functions of
Intervention Settings

Medium of Communication	Therapist's Office	
	Inside	Outside
(1) Verbal	Evaluation Direction of treatment Emotional support Confrontation of issues Motivation for change Generalization to outside	Dialogues with: self, partner, relatives and family of origin, friends, children, and coworkers
(2) Nonverbal	Awareness exercises Nonverbal communication Calistenics, aerobics Dance, art, play Biofeedback Kinesiology	Sports and exercise Nutrition-diet Vitamins Meditation Relaxation
(3) Written	Distance Writing Outside the Therapist's Office	

Structure	*Specificity*	*Content*	*Goal*	*Abstraction*
Open-ended Focused Guided Programmed	General versus specific	Traumatic versus trivial	Cathartic versus prescriptive	High versus low

and leisure. As Table 3.1 shows, thus far therapists have used one third
of the three available communication media. The traditional overreliance
on the verbal medium at the expense of the other two has severely curtailed
the options available to us and to our clients. In the future, change for
therapists will include learning how to use judiciously the other two media
of communication, nonverbal and written, in addition to the verbal. Once
these two media are added to the therapeutic armamentarium, the other
change will consist of decreasing the number of individual sessions and
increasing group, couple, and family sessions. Once these two changes are
in place, it will be easier to help more people for one unit of therapist's
time than ever before. In addition to the three media mentioned here, there
is the kinesthetic medium that is just as important as the other three media,
but which is included in the nonverbal medium.

Settings

As far as settings are concerned, we may assume that intimate relationships
are the primary setting, but that is not necessarily the only setting impinging

on us. Those relationships may be the most immediate and major focus of therapy. However, there are other settings, each with its own peculiar and specific task demands, that influence our lives. There is work and surplus time activities, for instance, that have a great deal of influence and, in some cases, more influence than either family or intimate relationships. Witness the influence of religion, for instance, and sport addictions, like running, that in some cases, are stronger in their influence than either family or work settings (Yates, 1991). By surplus time is meant whatever time is left after taking care of home and work responsibilities. This time includes transitory settings, like banks, bars, beauty salons, churches, grocery stores, hospitals, libraries, schools, stadiums, sport arenas, and shopping malls. These settings are necessary for enjoyment and survival, but they do not have the permanency and primary survival value of home and work. Surplus time also includes transit time that is necessary to go from one setting to another. These settings include airports, buses, bus stations, cars, highways, roads, trains, and hotels (Ch. 6).

Resource Modalities

Although the number of three communication media and three settings may be obvious, the three modalities mentioned here may not be as explicit. From this vantage point, then, therapy means helping individuals, couples, and families change from their concerns with performance and production to concerns about presence and the ability to love. Admittedly performance and production are necessary for survival, but they are not sufficient for full enjoyment as well as survival (Ch. 9). Dysfunctional individuals need help to increase their presence, that is, becoming more emotionally available to themselves and to important others. Changes need to be introduced in how clients prioritize the relative values of media, modalities, and settings. By changing one part, change may reverberate to other parts of the context thus defined, producing the so-called ripple effect so dear to systems thinking.

Given three communication media, three settings where exchanges take place, and three exchange modalities, we now obtain a framework of "larger interactional systems" that defines the overall context of change. Once we have this definition of context, then we can specify in greater detail one of the major maxims of systems thinking, namely, that change in one part of this context may affect other parts of the same context. Interconnectedness and wholeness are useful systems concepts which are represented concretely by the analogy of the ripple effect. However, compared to the rest of systems thinking, this proposal shows some advantages over traditional systems thinking that were not possible heretofore.

For instance, this proposal includes manageably finite and limited processes rather than infinite and unlimited ones. Consequently, these processes are more specific and detailed in comparison with rather general, undefined, and vague concepts of systems thinking. It is also more concrete than the abstract notions of systems thinking. Consequently, because of these characteristics, finiteness, specificity, and concreteness, this proposal is more verifiable than systems thinking, which, as a whole, is difficult to evaluate and verify.

Change from Respondents to Professionals

The process of change for our clients should possess the same components for psychotherapists. We psychotherapists, however, are as resistant to change as some of the very clients we want to help, if not more. For instance, how does the principle of external intervention apply when the hailing system is an organization, or even at a higher supra-ordinate level, a whole profession? What will it take for the whole profession of psychotherapy to acknowledge the need for external intervention? The first necessary step for external intervention to take place, of course, lies in the profession itself acknowledging and admitting the need for change. Without this initial acknowledgment and admission there would not be room or reason for external intervention to take place. The admission of needing external help, however, can only take place if and when the profession admits to the need for change, but "What change?"

Professional change will take place when psychotherapists will start practicing new, positive practices with sufficient intensity, regularity, and strength to make a difference for themselves and for their clients. The major change might take place in terms of cost-effectiveness, that is, greater effectiveness in clinical procedures, more clients per unit of therapist's time, and, consequently, smaller costs for clients. This is a direction quite different from existing practices, where cost-effectiveness and accountability, among other criteria, are not even addressed and, have been, in fact avoided if not scorned. This change, of course, implies using frequently new, positive, and powerful practices that have not been used in the past, as suggested earlier.

Admitting that the field of psychotherapy may need change, a position many therapists would not be willing to accept, what would this change consist of? How can this change take place if the therapeutic community denies that it, indeed, needs change? It takes conflict and pain to ask for change and help from the outside. After all, the field of psychotherapy is by now: (1) well institutionalized to the point of being a tax-deductible item in the formal IRS tax returns; (2) quite successful in providing a fairly good living and important status for most of its competent practitioners; (3) fairly organized in various large and growing professional mental health organizations and disciplines; (4) largely spread out and still growing among various mental health disciplines, and (5) sufficiently pervasive at all private and public levels of human enterprise. With all these positive qualities, how can one argue for dysfunctionality and need for change?

One would need to make the unpopular and questionable case for change as one would make it for any change-resistant human system that is receiving rewards for its dysfunctionality. Addicts, for instance, strongly deny their need for therapy because they do not want change to take place. As long as their addiction gives them immediate pleasures that they would not receive otherwise, why should they change? By the same token, the psychotherapeutic community would resist and attack any position that would speak to its supposedly sick or seemingly unhealthy condition, when so many positive, immediate qualities and rewards, listed above, are available.

What are the characteristics of an unhealthy organization? How can one make the case for dysfunctionality in what seems an otherwise very healthy, successful, and well-functioning profession? Whoever is willing to make this case runs the risk of professional retribution, even rejection and banishment. In spite of possibly nefarious consequences, a proposal for change at the professional level will be suggested. This proposal derives from what we know about changing clients, whether this knowledge is relevant to changing a profession or not. As Liddle (1992) noted:

"For clinicians to change their personal practice model in a way that would incorporate empirical values requires not only new information, examples to learn from, and new modes of thinking but also a way of dealing with the emotional aspects of a change of this nature (p. 256)."

Research, however, is not, and it is very doubtful whether it will ever be, a characteristic of a profession, including the mental health professions. Research is mostly an academic pursuit based on transcendental determinism and objective, public, and intersubjective demonstrability. A profession is usually based on dialectical immediacy and private, personal profitability (L'Abate, 1986; Stricker, 1992). Hence, we are faced by two quite different value systems (L'Abate, 2004b). The sooner we accept them as being almost mutually exclusive the better off we will be. There may be a few professionals who are able to balance and integrate both value systems. However, these few may not be greater than 3% to 5% of the whole psychotherapy profession. How can a small minority influence change for the majority? That task is clearly unrealistic and bound to fail.

If we change our traditional clinical and professional practices, and the analogy of a ripple effect mentioned above is valid, then we should be able to change ourselves as persons at home, at work, and in leisure time activities. If flexibility (rather than rigidity) is the characteristic of a functional system, should this quality reflect itself in everything we are, do, or have? If we are indeed open to change, should psychotherapists not be more amenable to change than even their clients? By enlarging personal and professional repertoires should psychotherapists not be able to help a wider number of clients? If psychotherapists do not change, how can they expect their clients to change? One of the few examples of professional change over time, derived from self-critical feedback, is the one illustrated by the work of Selvini-Palazzoli, Cirillo, Selvini, and Sorrentino (1989). Of course, there may be other examples I am not aware of.

SHOULD MANUALS BE FOR CLINICIANS OR FOR RESPONDENTS?

Manuals for therapists have become the most recent hobby horse of empirically minded psychologists who want to decrease the therapist's variability and increase accountability in psychotherapy. Although these goals fit into an empirical agenda, they are not sufficient to increase accountability for the following arguments. Manuals, in my opinion, used as part of the psychotherapeutic process, tend to preserve the status quo in psychotherapy for the following reasons: (1) manuals leave responsibility solely on the shoulders of psychotherapists; (2) manuals help to avoid or minimize interactive involvement from respondents; (3) the process obtained from manuals is just as expensive to record, transcribe, and code as the process obtained from psychotherapy without manuals; (4) psychotherapy with manuals is no more researchable or more efficient than psychotherapy without manuals; (5) manuals completely ignore prevention of psychological disorders. Since manuals and workbooks present many similarities, they should be compared to evaluate as to which approach is more cost-effective.

Manuals offer no solution to issues about replicable and researchable applications in psychotherapy. At the cost of antagonizing clinical psychology colleagues who, for all too long have argued about their pros and cons (Westen, 2000), one respectfully disagrees about their alleged advantages. Manuals do not improve the research quality of psychotherapy process and outcome, nor do they indicate how psychotherapy should be conducted in the future. Indeed, they tend to prolong the status quo in psychotherapy.

In considering past and present papers on the subject, too many to cite here, one cannot help but feel that their supporters present and represent them as the only hope for improving how to intervene positively in troubled people's lives, as if there were no other alternative to improve the human condition. Fortunately for clinical psychologists and not necessarily for psychotherapists, there are other alternatives that are even more reproducible, researchable, and, in comparison, more cost-effective, versatile, and mass-administered than manuals, as argued earlier, workbooks.

Arguments against the use of manuals in psychotherapy are made the on grounds that may have not been covered sufficiently or strongly enough in past and present controversies about their clinical and research uses. The final conclusion, however, is that manuals, in their current usage, tend to perpetuate psychotherapy as the sole means of helping and healing, perhaps bypassing more cost-effective ways to prevent and intervene in troubled people's lives.

Manuals Leave Responsibility Solely on Therapists

Manuals continue to put the onus and responsibility for the outcome of treatment on the shoulders of psychotherapists rather than on the shoulders of respondents, where the responsibility belongs, as Bohart and Tallman (1999), among the few, have argued. In taking on such a responsibility, psychotherapists who use manuals tend to perpetuate the image of all-knowing dispensers of health in one-up position over poor, ignorant, and helpless respondents. As long as psychotherapists dispense what manuals tell them should be said and done to respondents, actually manuals are responsible for the outcome of treatment, not the therapist. This, admittedly, is one step forward to traditional, noncomparable and unrepeatable practices of most therapists in the past and in the present. Respondents, however, do not know this and must assume that what therapists say or do comes directly from the therapists themselves and from no one else, especially a manual! Even if an informed consent does explain the manual-derived nature of the treatment, ultimately that treatment still comes from the mouth of a therapist, making the therapist legally, ethically, and professionally responsible for the outcome.

Manuals Avoid or Minimize Interactive Involvement with and from Respondents

Because responsibility rests on the shoulders of therapists, respondents may indeed feel that they are not in a position to actively interact with anyone except the therapist. If and when homework assignments are administered, they play a secondary role to the two major vehicles of treatment, f2f contact and talk. If writing is used in homework assignments, it does not have a prominent position in the whole treatment framework. The two traditional mainstays of psychotherapy still remain f2f and talk. F2f still remains inevitably a two-way street. Talk is reciprocal as well. However, when talk flows from the therapist, i.e., manuals, to respondents, it carries the burden of implying and producing change. Respondents take whatever has been said by the therapist and think it over, without direct request or assignments for skill practice that would produce interactive actions on their part. The variance for the effects of homework assignments from manuals, as far as I know, has not been studied separately from the overall treatment outcome.

Manuals Are Expensive to Record, Transcribe, and Code

Manuals do not decrease by one iota the length and costs of psychotherapy, or at least there is no evidence that they do. If such evidence does exist, I would apologize for this ignorance. One could even wonder whether they lengthen the process. Nonetheless, the process of recording, transcribing, and coding psychotherapy transcripts from manually administered treatment is no less expensive or time-consuming than when the same process is applied to transcripts from psychotherapy without manuals. Costs, therefore, remain the same, and there is no progress here.

Manuals Are No More Researchable or More Efficient than Psychotherapy without Manuals

Consequently, because manuals are the basis for therapeutic talk, they do not make the process of therapy any more researchable than psychotherapy without manuals. Sessions need to be recorded, transcribed, and coded, as argued above, a process that, as Gottman (1979) reported years ago, takes up to 27 hours of technical time for each hour of therapy. Hence, only researchers competent enough to qualify for grants can enter this process of analysis. Certainly, psychotherapists on Main Street cannot compete or even add to the process. Manuals, therefore, are not going to be part of the main stream of most psychotherapists because they are still equated with research and with practices that are outside of most therapists' interests or skills.

Manuals Ignore Completely Prevention of Many Psychological Disorders

Manuals are still part of the psychotherapy mythology that remains completely ignorant or uninterested in preventive approaches. If one considers that for every respondent, whether individual, couple, or family, seen in psychotherapy, there are 4 to 10 respondents who need some kind of help, not necessarily psychotherapeutic, then, psychotherapy, whether practiced with or without manuals, remains a drop in the bucket in the delivery of mental health services, as indicated by the report of the surgeon general (U.S. Department of Health and Human Services, 1999).

Manuals, as used by most researchers, have not shown, as far as I know, a public health orientation. They are still limited to psychotherapeutic practices. As long as they are based on f2f talk, they will remain the province of few professionals who are not interested in helping anyone except those fortunate enough to obtain professional help as part of a research project. Those who are not that lucky will have to rely on public health facilities that are notoriously understaffed and not able to reach all potential respondents in need of help. Manuals have not yet entered the public health arena, nor have they made any substantial contribution to preventive mental health practices.

Manuals Help Keep the Status Quo in Psychotherapy

If the above criticisms are valid, they indicate that manuals, still based on f2f and talk, continue to maintain the status quo in psychotherapy. By relying solely on f2f talk, rather than on the other two media of treatment—nonverbal and writing—manuals are not in any way changing the process of psychotherapy. Indeed, they keep it as it is, in the illusion or delusion that manuals will make a difference in how psychotherapy is going to be practiced in this century. As long as the effectiveness and efficiency of f2f talk are not challenged directly (L'Abate, 1999a), psychotherapy is condemned to remain as it is, keeping the status quo, with no changes in its practices. Paradoxically, no change will take place in a profession whose stated mission is to help others change for the better!

Manuals as Workbooks

Change will take place when the traditional paradigm of f2f talk is challenged and perhaps changed for interventions based on writing and working at a distance from respondents, without even seeing them or seeing them as little as possible (L'Abate, 1999b, 2003a, 2004b). Reliance on writing, whether expressive (Lepore & Smyth, 2002; Levy & Randsdell, 1996; Pennebaker, 2001) or programmed (L'Abate, 2001, 2002), will allow psychologists to reach respondents who up until now were unwilling or unable to ask for professional help based on f2f talk. The written medium: (1) is more cost-effective and much more researchable than talk (Esterling et al., 1999); (2) is more cost-efficient than talk because it bypasses at least three time-consuming and, therefore, expensive steps in the process of research considered above; (3) records what is being said; (4) can be transcribed and recorded; and (5) after transcription can be classified and coded. As indicated above, these processes can only take place with the help of research grants, which are not available to most practicing psychotherapists.

Programmed writing in the form of systematically written homework assignments designed around one specific topic are called workbooks. As already argued in Chapter 1, they are reproducible *ad infinitum*, costing only the paper in which they are printed, making comparative research easy to conduct. They are cost-effective whenever f2f, talk-based contacts are minimized or eliminated. They are versatile in both f2f or distance on-line treatment. They maximize the involvement of respondents by making them responsible for whatever change may occur rather than leaving this responsibility solely on the shoulders of the therapist (L'Abate, 2002, 2004b).

There are now around 300 workbooks available for children, adolescents, single adults, couples, and families to choose from, covering any imaginable clinical, semiclinical, or nonclinical condition (L'Abate, 2004a). The first metaanalysis of mental and physical health workbooks (Smyth & L'Abate, 2001) found estimated size effects of 44% for mental health and of 25% for physical health workbooks.

Workbooks cover the whole range of clinical and nonclinical conditions that do not require either recording, transcribing, or coding. More important, any clinical or nonclinical condition can be matched with a treatment in a *much more specific fashion* than manuals. In addition to being the software for computer-assisted and online interventions (Fogg, 2003), workbooks represent to psychological interventions what medications represent to psychiatric interventions. Even though their dosage is admittedly limited, it would be difficult to administer the same workbook twice; there are quite a few different workbooks to deal with the same condition, just as there are quite a few medications to treat a psychological or physical disorder. For example, depression or anxiety, for that matter, can be treated with quite a few workbooks that differ in format, theoretical or empirical origin, and price. They can be used by themselves as self-administered help in prevention and synergistically with f2f talk psychotherapy and/or medication.

Of course, their use does open a whole new set of possible professional and ethical issues, especially if administered at a distance online (Fogg, 2003; L'Abate, 2001, 2002). To evaluate their *real* effectiveness, free from therapist's influences, manuals themselves should be administered without the therapist's presence and personal involvement, and administered as written homework assignments, converting them into workbooks. Workbooks do not share manuals' disadvantages and should be compared with manuals to see which is more cost-effective and efficient than the other.

Workbooks enlarge preventive and therapeutic practices to underserved populations because they can be administered online or through the mail for those who do not have access to computers or the Internet. However, public libraries and churches, in addition to clinics and hospitals, will have computers available for those who do not have access to them, if not now, than certainly in the future.

Conclusion

Given the many advantages of workbooks and the disadvantages of manuals, why are research-oriented clinical psychologists so involved with manuals? Rather than just argue about manuals as the only solution to most mental health problems, manuals need to be administered as workbooks, with a minimum of f2f talk, and compared with workbooks treating the same condition to see which of the two is more effective and cost-efficient. Given two methods of treatment producing the same results, one chooses the least expensive.

A PROPOSAL FOR PROFESSIONAL CHANGE

Among the many cost-effective possibilities that will be considered here, change in the psychotherapy profession can and will take place by: (1) enlarging psychotherapeutic practices from overreliance on the spoken word and adding the two nonverbal and written media to our mostly verbal interventions, as shown in Table 3.1; (2) enlarging composition to include individuals in groups, couples, and families, and less time in individual f2f contact; (3) requiring evaluation at the outset and reevaluation at the end of the treatment process as standard operating procedure, a process that clinical psychologists were trained to do but that was forgotten in the immediate need to help clients and making a living; and (4) submitting our results to the scrutiny of professional peers or review boards.

These are four practices that the psychotherapy profession will be strongly resistant to on the basis of a variety of relevant and irrelevant arguments. Ultimately, as discussed above, the decision to change and to incorporate new or more cost-effective practices might be mandated by health providers, since change in current therapeutic practices will not take place otherwise. Initial resistance to the use of writing in psychotherapy practice, either by itself or conjoined with verbal and nonverbal media, is inevitable. Reliance on the nonverbal and written media as additions or as alternatives to the spoken medium is going to increase slowly but inevitably. The nonverbal medium includes so many techniques (Table 3.1) that it makes it difficult to compare it to the other two media. The spoken and written media have been compared in terms of their respective advantages and disadvantages so often that it would be redundant to repeat them here. Although both verbal and nonverbal media may require direct, f2f contact with a therapist or trainer, writing does not require this contact. It allows us to work at a distance, a practice that may have its advantages and disadvantages, as already considered in previous publications.

Enlarging Psychotherapeutic with Preventive Practices

By enlarging and expanding therapeutic practices we should be able to help a much wider range of problems than relying only on the spoken word. For instance, by introducing nonverbal approaches we may help individuals who are lower in their intellectual and educational functioning, and who are not as comfortable relying on the spoken word as we are. This population could include clients from lower socioeconomic status (SES) or personality disorders who are action- rather than introspection-oriented. We are so used to relying on the spoken word that we tend to forget that there are many other people who are not as comfortable in relying on it as we are.

In addition to the above changes, therapists may consider enlarging their practices by supervising selected middle-level professionals or lower level paraprofessionals in the use of psychoeducational, social skills training programs that, as a whole, have been used in preventive programs and not in psychotherapy as traditionally practiced (De Maria, 2003).

Cost-efficiency needs to include the group composition of our clients interacting with either one of the three media. For instance, group composition is much cheaper than individual composition for a unit of a professional helper's time. Nonverbal approaches would be more effective with groups than with individuals, because their use with individuals would be as expensive per unit of a professional helper's time as the verbal medium. Of the three media, the written medium may be the cheapest yet, while the verbal, especially with individuals, may definitely be the most expensive.

F2f contact with an individual client is the norm in traditional psychotherapeutic practices. It is also the most expensive because it essentially occupies the therapist's time. As soon as one adds another client in the therapy office, the cost of the therapy hour is halved. By adding a third client in the same office the cost is reduced by one third, and so on. Of course, some clients want the privacy and privilege of being seen individually, since they see themselves as losing face, or other characteristics, by being in a group. Yet, group therapy is certainly more cost-effective than individual psychotherapy. Insurance providers, therefore, will have to insist, and even demand, that clients will be reimbursed for group therapy, and only in exceptional cases for individual sessions (Gould, 2001). Standard insurance practices still reinforce the use of individual sessions, and only under special conditions, they reimburse marital and family therapies. In fact, many insurance companies do not reimburse either marital or family therapy, because an identified patient needs to be stigmatized with a diagnosis for reimbursement.

Not only are group sessions cheaper than individual sessions, but the use of written homework assignments in parallel with f2f group sessions may also decrease the number of sessions needed to achieve the desired outcome. Once we introduce these two factors into cost-effectiveness, more people can be helped for unit of professional's time.

Pre- and Postevaluation as a Standard Operating Procedure

The normative state of affairs in the mental health field consists of practitioners doing psychotherapy without evaluation and some researchers doing evaluation without psychotherapy. There is a great deal of research on evaluative instruments. One really does not need to proffer evidence to support this conclusion. A perusal of the majority of mental health and clinical psychological journals will support it. However, more often than not, research for evaluation instruments is performed without pairing it with psychotherapy process and outcome. As a result neither the field of evaluation nor the field of psychotherapy profit by the experience of the other. They are two completely separate fields of endeavor with little if any feedback from one to the other. Combinations of both into one process are few and far between. Usually, it takes a research grant to combine both. The use of writing can overcome this disadvantage, as discussed at length in Chapter 1, here, and elsewhere (L'Abate, 2003, 2004b).

Briefly, no matter how much we may justify and rationalize the importance of evaluation, an objective evaluation pre- and posttreatment has failed to be an integral part of psychotherapeutic practices. Most of us still rely on the interview and on the verbal medium to arrive at an understanding of what is going on in our clients' minds. One reason for this failure lies in the inadequacy of the spoken medium to direct treatment. As long as evaluation is based on the spoken word, treatment planning and treatment in general will be based on a catch-as-you-can basis and not on rationally or even empirically based grounds. Only if part of treatment is based on written homework assignments can evaluation be linked with treatment.

Furthermore, evaluation performed initially, before treatment, to meet external demands or routines is limited in its value unless performed again at the end of treatment. However, unless a contract to this effect is made at the very outset of therapy, with prepayment from the outset, many clients who quit prematurely will not be reexamined at the end. Is a rationale for reevaluation necessary? How can we assess whether we have been of help or not? How can we distinguish whether our clients have "improved" by feeling better or by negotiating a better lifestyle? How can we check on self-reported comfort when we cannot find out whether changes have taken place at different levels and parts of the context of change? Is the interview sufficient in suggesting treatment planning and predicting treatment progress? It is definitely necessary, but is it sufficient? Without some objective ways of verifying whether change has taken place, how can we document our competence?

A solution to this problem would be to charge clients for both pre- and posttreatment evaluation from the very beginning of therapy. If they drop out of treatment without reevaluation, they are going to lose the amount prepaid. Pre- and posttreatment evaluations, of course, would not be the only means of evaluating one's practice. One could use a number of sessions, drop-out rates, and no-shows, as well as regular self-reports of client's satisfaction, as other indicators of substantive professional practice.

Sharing Results with Colleagues or External Evaluators

Most war stories of psychotherapists focus on extreme and exotic examples of deviancy, reliance on a newfound gimmick, and claimed successes indicating the undisputed competence of the therapist. Thus far, no objective method has been found to document therapeutic competence. I have not yet found one therapist who doubted in any way his or her clinical and therapeutic competence. They were licensed, were they not? Most practicing therapists need to bolster their self-esteem or sense of importance by their successes. Very few therapists seem to focus on their failures or to learn from failures as much as it would be necessary. We learn from our failures not from our successes. Private practice, after all, is based on the marketplace. Supposedly competent therapists are sought after and those less competent have to make a living the best way they can by reducing their fees to accommodate a larger number of clients. Sharing our results with our peers? Who has ever heard of such a weird idea! It would require making our results available intersubjectively in a way that would violate all standards of accepted practice. Why should we?

If we were to evaluate our clients on a pre- and posttreatment basis as a standard operating procedure, perhaps this practice might obviate the need to make our procedures open to scrutiny and inspection from outsiders. Lacking this practice, however, we need to ask how we are credentialed by state agencies and how this credential allows us to practice within existing legal and ethical guidelines. These credentials have been granted on the basis of "paper" examinations and not on the basis of visible, observed "hands-on" practice, as done, for instance, in advanced certification for board examinations. Certainly, opening our files to external scrutiny would raise many questions about issues of confidentiality. On the other hand, without such a scrutiny, we would leave open and unanswered the whole issue of professional competence.

Preventive Practices

Preventive practices can be divided into primary, secondary, and tertiary.

Primary or Universal Prevention. Primary prevention consists of f2f psychoeducational methods (De Maria, 2003; McFalane, Dixon, Lukens, & Lucksted, 2003) for functioning or semifunctioning individuals, couples, and families who want and need to improve their relationships that are at risk for future breakdown (L'Abate, 1990). To improve couple and family functioning 50 structured enrichment programs were written with verbatim instructions for administration by paraprofesssional personnel (L'Abate & Weinstein, 1987; L'Abate & Young, 1987). These programs cover a variety of theory-independent topics, but also cover two major theory-derived topics: negotiation and intimacy. Their specific applications have been covered elsewhere (L'Abate, 2004b). However, because of their verbatim format theory-derived, theory-related, and theory-independent programs can be administered and evaluated (Ch. 19).

Secondary or Targeted Prevention. As detailed elsewhere (L'Abate, 1990), secondary prevention deals with people who not only are at risk but also need some kind of intervention, even though it may not be crisis intervention or psychotherapy. Writing, away from the presence of a clinician, as in written homework assignments is called "distance writing." As secondary prevention, distance writing can be applied both parapreventively and paratherapeutically, in the sense that it can be combined before, during, or after with either preventive or psychotherapeutic interventions (Esterling et al., 1999). Its structure, already considered in Chapter 1, can be divided into: (1) open-ended, as in diaries and journals, (2) guided, as in a series of written questions designed to be answered as written homework assignments ("I have read your autobiography and have written down some questions that I would like to have you answer in writing"), (3) focused, as in Pennebaker's (2001) assignment to write about past hurts, and (4) programmed

(L'Abate, 1992) as in workbooks ("I want you to answer in writing the first assignment of an anxiety program consisting of six assignments").

Many workbooks were derived from models of the theory. The first consisted of a depression workbook drawn isomorphically from a dyadic model of depression (L'Abate, 1986). When this program was compared with two other depression workbooks based on Beck's (1976) cognitive model and on an empirical definition of depression, respectively (L'Abate, 1992), this workbook produced significant results in undergraduates who scored high on both the Beck Depression Instrument and the Center for Epidemiological Research Depression scale (L'Abate et al., 1992).

The second was a negotiation workbook consisting of nine assignments that were derived isomorphically from its theoretical model consisting of homework assignments such as: Styles in Intimacy and the ARC model (L'Abate, 1986, pp. 268–269) reviewed in Chapter 11; Options in Responding (E, R, and A) (L'Abate, 1986, pp. 269–270), Aw, and C (L'Abate, 1986, pp. 271–272), reviewed in Chapter 4; Priorities (L'Abate, 1986, pp. 271–274), reviewed in Chapter 13; and Resources and Modalities Exchanged (L'Abate, 1986, pp. 274–276), reviewed in Chapter 9. Together with a third Intimacy program (L'Abate, 1986, pp. 281–290) that was also derived isomorphically from its theoretical model (reviewed in Ch. 16), both workbooks can be administered to: (1) verify the validity of their underlying models and (2) see whether they produce better results than similar workbooks derived from other theories or models. When both workbooks were administered to a group of undergraduate couples either in front of a "therapist" for 45 minutes or as homework assignments with a "therapist" standing at the office's door for 5 minutes, the former format of administration produced results that were significantly different from the latter (L'Abate, 1992, 2004d). When two workbooks or methods produce the same results, one should pick the one that is most economical.

A fourth workbook, called Social Training, was developed specifically to deal with "selfish" individuals, usually acting out juveniles or incarcerated felons. An addendum of this workbook, together with an anger program, attempts to enlarge the number of sessions needed to deal with externalizing individuals (L'Abate, 1996, 2002). A codependency workbook, isomorphic with a model developed from selflessness (L'Abate & Harrison, 1992), was administered to selfless individuals in clinical trials (Jordan & L'Abate, 1995; L'Abate, 2003a).

Programmed distance writing, as in workbooks, therefore, provides the software for computer-assisted training, where it is possible to reach populations that could not be reached through a f2f format (missionary and military families, hospitalized and incarcerated individuals, isolates and shut-ins). By the same token, all structured enrichment programs, because

Table 3.2. Differences between Unstructured and
Structured Psychological Interventions

Unstructured	Structured
Immediacy	Delay
Indeterminate	Determinate
Dependent on therapist	Independent of therapist
Nonreplicable	Replicable
Relationship-oriented	Symptom-oriented
Subjective, global	Objective, detailed
Perhaps necessary to start relationships	Necessary to produce changes
Impressionistic/anecdotal	Reductionistic/factual
Extremely variable	Variability reduced
Relatively unplanned	Completely planned
Reliance on office	Reliance on homework
Mainly reactive	Mainly proactive
Reliance on f2f talk	Reliance on distance writing
Reliance on therapist (nonrepeatable)	Reliance on method (repeatable through sequential steps)
Reputedly systematic	Systematic
Mainly idiographic	Mainly nomothetic but reducible to idiographic
Usually antiempirical	Mainly empirical

of their verbatim format, can be reduced to programmed distance writing
workbooks and thus also serve as software for computer-assisted training
(L'Abate, 2004d). Differences between unstructured practices based on talk
and those structured based on writing are summarized in Table 3.2.

Tertiary or Indicated Prevention—Prescriptive Tasks in Psychotherapy.
Tertiary prevention includes crisis interventions and psychotherapies designed to lower the level of distress and improve the functioning of people
who are in crisis, and are clinical, or chronic in their unhappiness to the
point of needing professional help. One way to deal with clinical conditions, in addition to distance writing, is to administer prescribed tasks to be
performed either in the therapist's office or at home. A task to be prescribed
in therapy needs to fulfill the following requirements in order to be called
"therapeutic": (1) The task is defined and identified clearly and precisely
in order to be replicated by other clinicians, (2) the identified patient (IP)
and his or her family are interested in solving the problem, (3) the task prescribed to deal with the problem is accurately chosen in view of the needs
of the IP and the family, (4) the task needs to be justified and explained
for its use to intimates, that is, it flows directly from the stated needs of the

IP and the desires of intimates to be together more often "without doing anything," and (5) the task needs to be straightforwardly simple, concrete, and easy to administer and to be followed by any group of intimates, regardless of ethnic background, education, socioeconomic level, and, in this case, (6) the task needs to be derived directly from a model of the theory.

Three tasks that fulfill the foregoing requirements have been applied in private practice derived from the theory. They need replication from other professionals to evaluate their clinical and therapeutic usefulness. The first task is the "sharing of hurts" exercise that has been used mainly with couples, but that could be used with individuals as well as families (L'Abate, 1986, 1994, 1997). In this task, administered strictly in the clinician's office and nowhere else, partners sit facing each other holding hands and keeping their eyes closed. If the patient has no partner, the therapist can assume the role of a partner or keep the role of therapist. Patients or partners are asked to concentrate on their internal bodily sensations, by first commenting on the feelings aroused by holding each other's hands. After this introduction, they are to concentrate on all the hurts that each has held inside for a long time. Once they become aware of these hurts, they have to share them by repeating: "I am hurting. I hurt." A variety of clinically useful patterns follows from this task (L'Abate, 2000). Predictably, many clinical men have difficulty not only crying but in empathizing with their partners, while most clinical women have no trouble disclosing and sharing their hurts, crying as a result of an expression of feelings that not always leads to its sharing with the partner.

The second prescriptive task derived from the theory consists of "Drawing Lines," which is actually one assignment in the codependency workbook mentioned earlier (Appendix A). It assumes that one of the most difficult tasks of most selfless individuals is "drawing lines" on what they will put up and will not put up with from their partners. These partners are usually "selfish" individuals who "push the limits" with most everyone. It consists of having codependent, i.e., "selfless," patients draw: (1) two horizontal parallel lines and writing "Yellow" in the middle; (2) two horizontal parallel lines with a break in the middle; (3) one segmented horizontal line, and (4) one dotted horizontal line. After drawing the client is asked: "What do these drawings remind you of?" Most clients recognize the similarity of these drawings with highway or road signs. Once the recognition is achieved, they are to label the first drawing as "nonnegotiable."

At home, they are to list what values or expectations they consider absolutes not to be broken under any condition, either by themselves or by their partners. The second drawing means what nonnegotiables can be broken just once, but never again. The third drawing includes a list of all the issues that need to be negotiated with the partner, and the fourth line includes issues between partners that do not need negotiation. Completion of these lists as homework assignments and sharing them with the therapist bring about a discussion of how one failed to make the self important by making their partners more important than themselves. This exercise is sometimes followed by instructions to write a "Bill of Rights" for codependents: how one deserves to be treated by everyone, intimates and nonintimates.

The third prescribed task, derived from the notion of presence, or being emotionally close and physically available among loved ones, consists of "being together." This tasks requires couples and families members to hug, hold, and huddle together at home, in the dark, without any interference from external sources (telephone, doorbell) for as long as 10 to 15 minutes, either every day for 1 or 2 weeks or every other day between therapy sessions (L'Abate, 2001; L'Abate & De Giacomo, 2003).

CONCLUSION

It is better to be humbly "wrong" or incorrect in the pursuit of specificity than being seemingly correct in the grandiose pursuit of being "right" while pursuing vagueness and generality. The answer to the initial question of how does a whole profession change, is: slowly, painfully, and, very likely from external pressure. One can no longer use stereotypically the monolithic term "psychotherapeutic community" as a homogeneous group. This community admittedly encompasses a variety of disciplines and organizations made up of professionals with very different value systems and practices, even within the same organization or discipline. Some therapists may find it difficult to practice according to new, cost-effective ways of helping people. Some will strongly deny the need for any change and continue in their own merry, traditional ways. Some undoubtedly and inevitably will attack the validity of the present thesis and recommendations for change, but will buckle down to face reality, at least as presented here. Therapists in the private sector, those who are doing well financially and who are not concerned about the public sector and about seemingly academic issues like costs, cost-effectiveness, accountability, verifiability, and outcome in large-scale preventive and therapeutic interventions, may well rebel against and reject vehemently what they perceive as a direct threat to their status quo.

Who will be ripe and ready for change? Very likely, therapists in the public sector may be ready to consider this proposal. Psychotherapists whose major professional identification is scientific, rather than the other way around "artistic" or "pure" psychotherapists whose major identification is as artists, may well be concerned about some of the issues mentioned here, and welcome change.

Part II

Metatheoretical
Assumptions

Before going into the theory proper, however, one needs to consider assumptions that go above and beyond the theory. Even though they could stand apart from the theory, because directly or indirectly they are shared with other theories, these metatheoretical assumptions are still related to the theory. They also lead to testable models relevant to the theory itself. These assumptions encapsulate past knowledge that cannot be ignored and that needs to be included not only in this theory but also in most theories of personality socialization and psychopathology.

The purpose of this section, therefore, is to consider three major assumptions that go above and beyond assumptions that belong to the theory proper. Each assumption, whether metatheoretical or theoretical, will be reduced to models that lend themselves to empirical verification. One could say that these metatheoretical assumptions summarize what is (selectively!) known up to now about relationships, integrating past theories and models into new models of their own.

A model is a simplified, usually visual summary of more complex concepts or patterns derived from assumptions of the theory. The three metatheoretical assumptions deal with: (1) the width of intimate relationships, horizontally, like on a flat surface, in Chapter 4; (2) their depth, vertically, below the appearance of superficial appearances or contrived laboratory experiments, to be considered in Chapter 5; and (3) settings, where relationships, whether intimate or nonintimate, occur, in Chapter 6.

Chapter 4

The Horizontality
of Relationships
A Width Model[1]

*"Research on women and work has reached a milestone. The
cumulative body of new findings on men's and women's roles at home
and at work has rendered current theories obsolete. A review of the field
reveals a disconnect between theories driving the literature, the
assumptions on which they were based, and the results of the research
of the past two decades* (Barnett & Hyde, 2001, p. 281)."

The purpose of this chapter is to view relationships and especially intimate
relationships along a horizontal surface or axis. This axis is defined according
to how information is received, processed, expressed, and reflected upon
in a relational context according to resources that are basic to personality
socialization in intimate relationships. This integrative model of relationships
among intimates and nonintimates lies along a horizontal, flat axis that is
observable and measurable.

HORIZONTALITY: THE EXPERIENCING-EXPRESSING
CONTINUUM AND THE ERAAwC MODEL[1]

Starting with how information is received to how it is expressed, this circular, comprehensive model, already introduced in previous publications,
but needing expansion, consists of five components resources or parts: *Emotionality, Rationality, Activity, Awareness,* and *Context* (ERAAwC) shown in

79

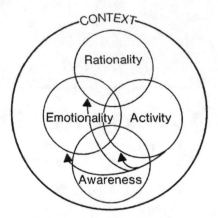

Figure 4.1. The ERAAwC model.

Figures 4.1 and 4.2. As these figures show, these five components vary in: (1) size, (2) strength of boundaries, and (3) amount of overlap among each other, producing completely different outcomes in intimate relationships.

This assumption deals with the width of relationships along a horizontal axis. This axis describes how relationships unfold from their inception, when information is received and experienced (input), to how this information is processed (throughput), and how and where it is eventually expressed (output) (Westen, Muderrisoglu, Fowler, Shedler, & Koren, 1997). Input that comes from external sources is usually emotional because neutral input would leave few if any traces inside the individual. We might respond to neutral information but it does not leave an internal imprint as much as emotional information does. Information of most value, at least among intimates (parents, partner, offspring, siblings, and friends), is usually emotional in nature. Thus, reception and experiencing of external, emotional information is classified under the rubric of (*E*) for Emotionality, the subjective side of this dimension. Once this information is received, whether it is approached and acknowledged or not, and whether it is seemingly avoided, suppressed, repressed, or processed, it does remain inside the organism. As we shall see, from *E* stem approach-avoidance, i.e., distance tendencies toward or away from intimates and nonintimates that develop over time into the ability to love (Ch. 7).

If the information is accepted emotionally, it is then processed cognitively in terms of appraising and evaluating it, deciding what kind of information it is, and how it should be responded to: "Is it dangerous? Threatening? Painful? Joyful? Pleasurable? To be acted upon immediately? To be delayed to a later date?" This processing requires the rational resources of the individual (*R*). Processing involves also deciding how to express that information: "Verbally? Nonverbally? In writing? Aggressively? Assertively? Passively? Nonexpressively?" From *R* stems discharge-delay, i.e., control tendencies that develop over time into the ability to negotiate (Table 4.1; Chs. 8 and 17). Expression, the objective side of this dimension, takes place through some kind of activity (*A*), either internal and invisible to the naked eye or external and visible to observers. *A*, in turn, leads to a feedback loop involving a corrective change, as found in reflection and *Aw*areness. After *A* one needs to be aware of the impact such an expression has had on a target, either self or others, its Context (*C*).

This model, to be sure, makes a strong distinction between receptive and expressive sides of emotionality. *Feelings* are what happens to us as we experience, perceive, and receive external events internally. In this regard, feelings vary along dimensions of pleasantness-unpleasantness, short-long duration, and strong-weak intensity. Hence the major issue here is whether these feelings are accessible and available to us (approach) or whether they are inaccessible and nonavailable to us (avoidance), as, for instance, in alexithymia. *Emotions* are how and what we express outwardly that has been felt, either positively or negatively, constructively or destructively, hurtfully or helpfully.

Assuming that the target is human, awareness (*Aw*) of and reflection about what has been said or done implies a corrective process whereby one becomes cognizant of the outcome of what was expressed: "Was it helpful? Was is hurtful? Was it pleasurable? Was it negative or positive? What were the reactions of those who received what was said or done?" *Aw*, therefore, is the corrective loop that leads to change, provided one reflects on the consequences of one's actions (*A*). Without reflection, that is *Aw*, either before or after *A*, there is little room for change. Furthermore, *Aw* not only involves internal reactions, but it involves external *Aw*areness of the context (*C*), as well as the impact of *E*, *R*, and *A* have had on the individual, intimates, and nonintimates. Appropriate replies to provocation, demands, requests, criticisms, or put-downs, most of the time, require an awareness, i.e., reflection of one's internal feelings (*E*), how to deal with the situation (*R*), and how to respond (*A*), as well as awareness of contextual factors (*C*) that need to be taken into consideration before responding. Context may be proximal, as in family relationships, or distal, as in culture (Mantovani, 2000). The family or intimates is the filter through which most cultural values are transmitted.

Any component part of this model can be avoided and therefore, short-circuited and reduced in its influence, leading to a lowering of functioning. For instance, if *E* is avoided (suppressed, repressed, denied), this avoidance may lead to obsessive rumination and compulsive behavior. If *R* is avoided in addition to E, it may lead to a magnification of A, as in the case of impulsivity, drivenness, or criminal behavior. Avoidance of E may lead to a restriction in Aw as well, the individual is unable to reflect on the consequences of A, as in the case of acting out individuals. A restriction in Aw may lead to a denial of C, or, in some cases, externalization on C. The external context (C) is blamed to avoid taking personal responsibility without reflecting on one's behavior and its outcome on others. Too much emphasis on the importance of C, on the other hand ("What will the neighbors think? Be sure to make a good impression!"), may be present in internalization disorders, where the individual pays so much attention to C that the other four components (E, R, A, Aw) are diminished. By the same token, one may be so preoccupied with A that the other four components of this model become restricted (Table 4.1).

This ERAAwC model, as we shall see, allows psychologists to evaluate and train couples and families in the step-wise process of negotiation (Chs. 8 and 17; Appendices A and D) as well as to classify theoretical and therapeutic schools (Table 4.2). In the latter instance, the humanistic school, stressing the importance of phenomenological experiencing and personal feelings, would be classified under E. Psychodynamic, rational-emotive, and reality-oriented, schools that stress the importance of logical, cognitive processes would be classified under R. Schools stressing activity and observation of external reinforcements, like behaviorism, would be classified under A. Schools stressing awareness, such as Gestalt, Eastern philosophies, or personal narratives would be classified under Aw. Most theories of personality and therapy involving family and community systems would be classified under C. The latter theories and therapies, in turn, can be classified under either E, R, A, or Aw (Hansen & L'Abate, 1982) in terms of their emphasis on anyone of the other four components. Hybrid schools, like the cognitive-behavioral school, for example, derive from the combination of two schools of thought, the cognitive (R) and the behavioral (A).

This model, therefore, includes five major component resources derived from five major schools of thought and therapy preeminent in the past century and even earlier. These schools, because of their importance, are still influential in this century and will be for some time to come. They can be considered as proposing which resources are available and exchanged in intimate and nonintimate relationships within self and with others.

Commonalities among Component Resources of the Model

These schools share common characteristics. Each school: (1) claims and pretends to be superior in wanting to reign hegemonic over the other four schools, producing heated controversies and conflicts among proponents of each school; (2) suggests that its own resource is a determinant of how we relate within ourselves and with others; (3) is responsible for a proliferation of subschools within itself, producing ample literature of its own as well as scientific and professional societies and journals devoted to promoting entirely its importance and its superiority over the other four schools; (4) has produced its own major therapeutic trend with all minor offshoots that are the outcome of proliferations of subschools, each proposing its own therapy as cure-all for many ills of humankind, producing a veritable Tower of Babel in that field; (5) claims to account for extreme deviations in its own resource, suggesting psychopathologies that derive directly from that component resource.

By the latter token, each component resource of the model, as supported by its own schools and subschools, can increase or decrease qualities in duration, intensity, rate, frequency, and direction. When there is an increase in one component resource, one needs to determine whether an increase or decrease is occurring in the other four component resources. For instance, if one resource becomes accentuated, will this increase produce an increase or decrease in the qualities of the other four resources?

Ít follows from the above, that by necessity, only exemplary, selected, and strictly representative publications can be cited here. Any exhaustive inclusion of publications devoted to each component resource, especially primary sources, would be impossible in a work of this nature or even in works of any other kind or size.

Definitions of Terms: Component Resources of the Model

The component resources of this model, therefore, are Emotionality (*E*), Rationality (*R*), Activity (*A*), Awareness (*Aw*), and Context (*C*). In information processing language, these components include input, throughput, output, feedback loops, and context respectively. In ordinary language (Table 4.1), these components are composed of structure, process, outcome, change

Table 4.1. Resources Necessary for Relationships

Ordinary Language	Information Processing	Combination of Ordinary Language and Information Processing	Language of Integrative Model
Structure	Input	Reception	Emotionality (*E*)
Process	Throughput	Processing	Rationality (*R*)
Outcome	Output	Expression	Activity (*A*)
Change	Feedback	Reflection	Awareness (*Aw*)
Context	Context	Context	Context (*C*)

Table 4.2. Selected Representatives of Past Theoretical Schools and Component Resources Derived from Them

Schools of Thought				
Humanism	Rationalism	Empiricism		Systems
Component Resources				
Emotionality (*E*)	Rationality (*R*)	Activity (*A*)	Awareness (*Aw*)	Context (*C*)
G. Berkeley	R. Descartes	G. Galilei	J. M. Baldwin	C. Darwin
F. Brentano	B. Spinoza	J. Locke	J. Piaget	W. James
G. W. Leibniz	I. Kant	W. Wundt	I. S. Vysotsky	J. Dewey
G. Hegel	D. Hume	I. Pavlov		A. Korsybski
E. Husserl	J. Bowlby	K. R. Popper		K. Lewin
S. Kirkegaard		G. Ryle		L. V. Bertalanffy
F. Nietzche				J. R. Kantor
J. P. Satre				G. Bateson
M. Heidegger				J. Ruesch
G. Marcel				J. Spiegel

mechanism, and context respectively. Combining both, one obtains reception, processing, expression, awareness, and context. Using language that is most common in psychological literature, these component resources represent ERAAwC.

Historically, selected representatives of the five schools underlining each resource are listed in Table 4.2. Some representatives could be placed as being influential in more than one school. For instance, empiricism was the predecessor to behaviorism, stressing measurable observables under controlled conditions. It was a judgment call to place selected representatives where they are placed here. Certainly, there could be some expected and understandable disagreement about these placements. By the same token, the most influential therapists (Table 4.3) could produce additional disagreements, even though their placements may seem clearer than those of past theorists.

Each resource will be considered here according to its: (1) developmental trajectory; (2) functionality; (3) dysfunctionality; (4) connections with other resources, and (5) its relevance to relationships.

Emotionality (E)

Only in the third part of the past century, *E* has finally achieved a position that views it as a basic resource for structuring the other four (Bradley, 2000; Lewis & Haviland-Jones, 2000; Mayne & Bonanno, 1998). *E* includes affect,

Table 4.3. Selected Representatives of Therapeutic Schools Derived from Components of the ERAAwC Model

Emotionality (E)	Rationality (R)	Activity (A)	Awareness (Aw)	Context (C)
Humanistic	Psychodynamic Cognitive	Behavioral	Awareness	Family
D. Snygg &	S. Freud	J. B. Watson	W. Kempler	H. S. Sullivan
H. W. Coombs	C. Jung	B. F. Skinner	F. Perls	P. Watzlawick
C. R. Rogers	O. Fenichel	J. Wolpe		S. Minuchin
R. May	H. Hartmann	H. Eysenk		M. Selvini
S. Jourard	K. Horney	G. Patterson		D. D. Jackson
A. H. Maslow	A. Ellis	N. Azrin		J. Haley
A. Mahrer	A. T. Beck	T. Ayllon		M. Bowen
L. Greenberg				C. Whitaker
S. Johnston				V. Satir

moods, and feelings subjectively experienced. Watson (2000) expanded on Thayer's (1989) original distinction between tense and energetic arousal by distinguishing between negative (fear, sadness, guilt, and hostility) and positive (joviality, self-assurance, and attentiveness) affects. Oftentimes, subjective, receptively experiencing aspects of *E* are not always differentiated from its expressive aspects that are objectively observable and measurable in expressed emotions (*A*). However, *E* is oftentimes (Watson, 2000) persistently divided into "negative" and "positive" affects, even though what is experienced varies along dimensions of arousal and pleasure (Watson & Tellegen, 1985). Watson's (2000, p. 19) contention that *E* constitutes the "primary, conscious, subjective experience," supports the assumption that *E* furnishes the primary structure, albeit fragile and variable, for the other four component resources (Bless & Forgas, 2000; Diener, 1999). Schore (2003) suggests that the right hemisphere of the brain is the location for most if not all *E*. If that suggestion is correct, then the left hemisphere would be more responsible for *R*. Hence, if talk in therapy is based predominantly on the right hemisphere, writing may be more related predominantly to the left hemisphere (McMahan & L'Abate, 2001).

Negative (adverse and threatening) events may evoke strong and rapid physiological, cognitive, emotional, and social responses. This organismic mobilization seems followed by physiological, cognitive, and behavioral responses that damp down, minimize, and even erase the impact of that event. This pattern of mobilization-minimization appears greater for negative events than for neutral or positive events (possibly producing a higher gradient of avoidance than approach). However, no single theoretical mechanism can explain this pattern, due possibly to disparately cause effects (Taylor, 1991). Taylor's conclusion would support the need for a multicomponent model to account for such a mobilization-minimization process.

Developmental Trajectory

The child is born in a world of *E*, becoming progressively socialized from contentment, interest, and distress proliferating and differentiating with age into self-conscious emotions, anger and hostility, sadness, and fear (Harris, 2000; Mascolo & Griffin, 1998; Lewis, 2000; Saarni, 1999; Schore, 2003). With age, these feelings become even more differentiated into controversial lists, ranging anywhere from five to 15 or more. These feelings may eventually become mixed, even confused, oftentime hidden, and at times avoided or covered up to meet personal or societal expectations, producing nonlinear gaps between what is experienced in *E* and what is expressed in *A* (Lewis & Haviland-Jones, 2000; Lewis & Michalson, 1983). This point will be elaborated in Chapter 16. Young children possess the potential for cognitive self-control of their own affective states and the effects on learning suggest that even transient mood states may produce lasting changes in behavior (Masters, Barden, & Ford, 1979).

Coping strategies to deal with sadness and anger in elementary school children seem to be predominantly behavioral, verbalized, and self-oriented. The most common strategy seems to engage in a distracting activity. Strategies used with parents may differ from those used with peers. Girls seems more reactive to sadness-inducing events than boys, especially in interacting with mothers (Franko, Powers, Zuroff, & Moskowitz, 1985).

The emotional development of the child is significantly affected by parental child-rearing practices, child-rearing attitudes, and personality (Agrawal & Saksena, 1977). Indeed, the emotional availability of parenting refers to several parental dimensions: sensitivity, structuring, nonintrusiveness, and nonhostility that interact with two child dimensions—responsiveness to parent and involvement of parent (Biringen, 2000). Consequently, it follows that intimate relationships appear as an important setting for learning about emotions and how to express them within a social context (Halberstadt, Cassidy, Stifter, & Parke, 1995).

Growth is facilitated when a strong, affective bond is established with an important other and when the inevitable disruptions of this bond is repaired. Personality maturation across the life span could be attributed to the internalization of admirable qualities of important others. Furthermore, interactional dynamics associated with internalization involve establishing a strong affective bond with an important other and repairing this bond's inevitable ruptures (Bahal & Sexena, 1978; Lewis, 2000).

Functionality

Functionality would imply positive *E* together with other positive aspects of the other four components. It is usually assumed that pleasurable *E* is functional while unpleasant or painful *E* is dysfunctional. Hence, individuals who share characteristics of positive affects a la Watson (2000), function more effectively than those who share negative characteristics, such as anger, hostility, anxiety, depression, or panic attacks (Lewis & Haviland-Jones, 2000). There are possible stages of affection and perhaps *E* in adolescence, first from parents to friends, then from one parent to another, and lastly from same-sex to opposite-sex friend (O'Donnell, 1979).

Dysfunctionality

Excessive *E*, that is, hyperarousal might imply hysterical, borderline, or histrionic personality disorders and even criminal and violence-prone personalities (Geiger & Crick, 2001; Schore, 2003), where *E*, in the form of anxiety, depression, and panic attacks, runs rampant, dominating whatever the individual says and does. Insufficient or even seemingly inexistent *E* would indicate alexithymia (Taylor, Bagby, & Luminet, 2000), where individuals are unable to experience and, therefore, express feelings, and in extreme cases, schizophrenia (Geiger & Crick, 2001). Schore (2003) contends that insufficient *E* leads to dissociation. Consequently, men may be more prone to hyperarousal, while women may be more prone to hypo-arousal and possibly dissociation. In spite of possible gender differences in reception and processing of *E*, there is no question that emotional inhibition may influence psychological functioning (Gross & Levenson, 1997).

A negative, relatively undifferentiated emotional structure seems significantly related to depressive symptomatology, independent of self-esteem and other variables (Goldston, Gara, & Woolfolk, 1992). Negative *E* would imply what Pennington (2002) calls disorders of motivation, that is: depression and dysthymia, anxiety and posttraumatic stress disorders (Brennan & Harvey, 2001; Hammen & Garber, 2001; McNally, Malcarne, & Hansdottir, 2001). The latter, together with Flack and Laird (1998), follow an intrapsychic, neurological orientation, ignoring the immediate, proximal, and distal context of psychopathology, and that is, intimate relationships (Bradley, 2000; Cummings et al., 2000; Fonagy, Target, Cottrell, Phillips, & Kurtz, 2002; Sameroff, Lewis, & Miller, 2000). Schore (2003) together with Lewis, Amini, and Lannon (2000) do incorporate caregivers and early attachments to physiological factors. Miller (2003) proposed a three-factor model composed of negative *E*, positive *E*, and constraint/inhibition to propose that high negative *E* "... is the primary personality risk factor for the development of

Post-Traumatic Stess Disorders (p. 373) . . . whereas low constraint/inhibition and low positive E serve as moderating factors in the extent of this disorder." The third factor, constraint/inhibition would be part of *A*, as discussed below.

Shame-proneness may be related to psychological maladjustment in general and to a depressogenic attributional style in particular (Tangney, Wagner, & Gramzow, 1992). Emotionality and extraversion seem to account for 25% of the variance in mental health. However, emotionality seems to account for most of the variance, with extraversion accounting only for 2%, supporting the construct of negative affectivity (Levenson, Aldwin, Bossé, & Spiro, 1988).

Alexithymia is an important disturbance that indicates what happens when we, mostly men, are unable to become aware of and use our feelings (Sifneos, 1996). Rather than one single condition, alexithymia may include different symptomatologies (Norton, 1989). For instance, in recently sober alcoholics, only one dimension, among others, associated with an inability to identify feelings and to distinguish them from bodily sensations, may be related to depressive symptoms (Haviland, Hendryx, Cummings, & Shaw, 1991).

This condition is observable in a wide range of medical and psychiatric disorders, including psychogenic pain, substance abuse, stress, and depression (Taylor, 1984). Individuals who have difficulty identifying and describing their feelings may show a combination of poor nonverbal expressivity and frequent self-directed patterns suggestive of anxiety and tension. Additionally, a tendency toward externally oriented thinking may be related to avoidance during f2f interviews (Troisi, Delle Chiaie, Russo, & Russo, 1996). Insecure, preoccupied, and fearful attachment styles may also be related to heightened levels of alexithymia. These results would suggest a role for early developmental factors in the etiology of alexithymia (Troisi, D'Argenio, Peracchio, & Petti, 2001). Men reporting greater gender role conflicts also may also acknowledge greater levels of alexithymia and fear of intimacy, even after controlling for socially desirable responding (Fischer & Good, 1997).

Alexithymia may not necessarily develop in response to a single traumatic event, but instead may result from repeated exposure to extreme stress, as a means of avoiding painful conflict (Zeitlin, McNally, & Cassidy, 1990). Emotional messages from one generation to another could be transmitted by means of subtle behavioral and symbolic forms of communication, as seen in generational vendettas in certain cultures, where one generation attempts to avenge and redress injustices, real or imagined, suffered by the previous generation (Rogers, 1976). Some adolescents, for instance, elicit the negative affective style that puts them at risk. That elicitation seems strongly linked to adolescents' expression of negative affect toward their parents (Cook, Kenny, & Goldstein, 1991). Panic disorders may constrict emotional experience thereby reducing the likelihood of experiencing physiological symptoms that accompany affect (Zeitlin & McNally, 1993).

Connections with Other Resources

It follows from this integrative model that no single component resource can be made responsible for a complete understanding and determination of either functional or dysfunctional, intimate and nonintimate, relationships. This statement can be repeated for all the other four resources, in spite of expectable objections from proponents of each resource. All five are important, no matter what champions of each resource may claim. The issue here is whether all five resources are equally important and, if they are, in what ways they are more important than the other four. It seems clear that each resource fulfills specific functions that cannot be allocated to the other four.

Relevance of E to Intimate Relationships

Some relationships that start as pleasurable *E* turn into the opposite, negative *E* over time, producing extremes in feelings and eventually determining breakups, divorces, murders, and suicides. *E* has been connected with social behavior (Clark, 1992), cognition (Clark & Fiske, 1992), social cognition (Forgas, 2001), health (Shaver, 1984), and personality (Magai & McFadden, 1995), among others.

Rationality (R)

Other terms related to *R* may be cognition, logic, thinking, emotional intelligence, and intellectualization.

Theoretical Background

R is defined as the ability to reason using logical, intellectual schemes, including constructs like cognition, intelligence, thinking, planning, and problem-solving (Bandura, 2001; Steinberg & Ben-Zeev, 2001). There are at least three major issues, among the many underlying this component resource, that need consideration here. The first deals with the distinction between intelligence, as a cognitive, purely intellectual ability, and emotional intelligence (Bar-On & Parker, 2000; Matthews, Zeidner, & Roberts, 2002). If *R* functions as a processing resource, receiving cognitive information, how does that information transform itself into *E* in dealing with relationships? Should emotional intelligence be considered under *E* or *R*? There may be at least two systems of reasoning. One system may be associative because its computations reflect similar structure and relations of temporal contiguity. The other system may be "rule based" because it operates on symbolic structures that have logical content and variables, because its computations have the properties that are usually assigned to rules. These systems serve complementary functions and can simultaneously generate different solutions to a reasoning problem. The rule-based system can suppress the associative system but not completely inhibit it (Sloman, 1996).

The second issue, which derives directly from the first one, and that of the relationship between *R* and *E*. How much does one component affect the other? Does *E* affect *R* or the other way around? For instance, unconscious and automatic thoughts can be effortless and uncontrollable, influenced by drugs and hormones, and irrevocable by deliberate efforts. Such types of *R* could be part of affective responses and can play a role in producing certain emotional qualities. This possibility would justify the use of cognitive therapies to treat affective disorders (Parrott & Sabini, 1989). The issue has produced a great many controversies that cannot be reviewed here. Suffice to say that one school of thought (forgive the pun!) supports the traditional position that affective judgments are postcognitive and they occur without extensive perceptual and cognitive encoding. The other school makes *E* primary in effecting *R* (Watts, 1983).

This controversy could be resolved if one were to consider the nature of the stimulus event. A sudden and unexpected loss may provoke an immediate emotional reaction, followed eventually by rational consideration of what to do to deal with the loss. An unexpected accident while driving may require immediate cognitive controls followed by a subsequent emotional reaction. Another solution to this issue could be found in the construct of cognitive-affective balance, the unique manner in which personalities coordinate and meet both the requirements of external stimuli/tasks and those of fantasies and affects (Santostefano & Rieder, 1984).

The third issue relates to control. Is *R* the seat of control? If inhibition and disinhibition define a dimension of control (Twenge & Baumeister, 2002), as assumed in Chapter 8, is control a major function of *R* or other resources, or of *R* combined with other resources? Is *R* a major determinant of control? How about *A*wareness and *C*ontext? If cognition is so difficult to evaluate, how can we assume that it is directly responsible not only for *E* but for whatever components of the model that follow (Clark, 1988)?

Developmental Trajectory

As the toddler grows from a world of *E*, the ability to think, plan, and choose according to *R* becomes increasingly stronger and eventually matures into the ability to plan ahead, negotiate, and limit extremes in either excessive or insufficient *R*. From a Piagetian early preoperational stage, the child moves on to concrete operations, culminating in formal and abstract thinking and postformal operations. This final stage means eventually assimilating and accommodating and integrating (both-and) seemingly opposite and mutually exclusive (either-or) ambiguity and uncertainty, irony, and contradiction. With input from other resources, abstract thinking may become more contextual and transactional in late adulthood and seniority in some but not all individuals (Grams, 2001).

Functionality

Proper functioning is possible when *R* is focused on positive aspects of relationships, directed toward realistic and appropriate goals, flexibly balanced with other resources and expectations. Family size and birth order may have important consequences on cognitive functioning and may partially explain different performances related to social class and ethnic origin. However, when individual variation is explored, the effects of family configuration may become relatively trivial, making confluence theory (Markus & Zajonc, 1977) that has claimed such influence, appear relatively untenable. Apparent effects of family size, for instance, far from explaining population differences, may be the result of group admixtures, whereas the small, residual birth-order effects may be the outcome of other variables (Page & Grandon, 1979), like SES, sibling variables, and family environment (Walberg & Marjoribanks, 1976). Indeed, the confluence model and parental occupation may be insufficient in accounting for racial difference in intelligence (Barnes, Fisher, & Palmer, 1979).

Dysfunctionality

Excessive *R* might imply disorders of thinking as found in autism and obsessive compulsive disorders, even though this latter disorder has been disregarded by Twenge and Baumeister (2002). Insufficient or low *R* would imply either educational underachievement, mental retardation, as well as dyslexia and other language disorders (Cummings et al., 2000; Ingram & Price, 2001; Pennington, 2002; Sameroff et al., 2000). Insufficient or low *R* coupled with negativity would also imply criminal and acting-out disorders, where no thought is given to the consequences of one's actions (*A*). Under the latter condition, individuals behave immediately and impulsively, especially when threatened or planning to perform criminal acts (Bradley, 2000). There is a school of thought (Grieger & Grieger, 1982) that makes incorrect or "irrational" thinking responsible for how one feels—*E*.

This school uses "rational-emotive," and "cognitive-behavioral" therapies (Table 4.3).

Thought suppression seems to produce a significant impact on the understanding of emotional disorders characterized by persistent, repetitive, and unwanted thoughts, but not on other affective disorders (Purdon, 1999). Cognitive biases related to anxiety in children are similar to those found in adults, and parents might play a role in influencing the degree of cognitive biases (Chorpita, Albano, & Barlow, 1996). Those biases may have some effects on the etiology of depression (Coyne & Gotlib, 1983).

Worry, or the repetitive reoccurrence of unwanted thoughts or thoughts about painful experiences has been the subject of a great deal of attention in the literature. Worry involves a predominance of verbal thought activity, functioning as a type of cognitive avoidance, and apparently inhibiting emotional processing. It produces both anxious and depressive experiences. Suppression of upsetting thoughts may not necessarily increase their intrusive quality, and thereby contribute to anxiety or depression (Mathews & Milroy, 1994).

This pattern seems developmentally connected to enmeshed childhood relationships with the primary caretaker and currently associated with significant interpersonal problems, especially those involving a tendency to be overly concerned with the welfare of others. Physiologically, worry could be characterized peripherally by parasympathetic deficiency and autonomic rigidity, and centrally by left-frontal activation (Berkovec, Ray, & Stober, 1998; Wells & Morrison, 1994). Worry seems more associated with relaxation than imagery (East & Watts, 1994). Goal interruption, failures of emotional processing, and information processing may lead to repetitive thoughts that increase negative mood states, including both anxiety and depression (Freeston, Dugas, & Ladouceur, 1996; Segerstrom, Tsao, Alden, & Craske, 2000).

Whether worry and obsession are consistent or inconsistent with self-definitions and expectations seems an important factor in understanding their nature (Langlois, Freeston, & Ladouceur, 2000). Where does worry end and obsession begin? Both occur in response to stress (Tallis & DeSilva, 1992), perhaps with worry being related to relationships with others, and obsession being related to relationships with objects?

An area that has produced a great deal of interest and research has been devoted to "expressed emotions" (EE) (Wearden, Tarrier, Barrowclough, & Zastowny, 2000). This pattern evolved in an effort to understand the impact of family and social environment on the vulnerability to relapse in schizophrenics (Gottschalk & Keatinge, 1993). This pattern came into being by the original finding that it predicted relapse in schizophrenic patients (Hinrichsen & Pollack, 1997). Nonetheless, its influence has not been limited to psychiatric patients, since it is present also in diabetic patients (Koenigsberg, Klausner, Pelino, & Rosnick, 1993).

Even though a complete review of the literature is impossible to undertake here, it is important to briefly review this area to examine the functions of EE in intimate relationships. EE comprises voiced criticisms, hostility, and emotional overinvolvement (Hooley & Richters, 1991). There are some questions on whether this pattern is limited to certain Western cultures and not present in other (Jenkins & Karno, 1992). What seems more significant may be an alternation of harsh and mild criticism than just overreliance on one or the other pattern (Valone, Norton, Goldstein, & Doane, 1983).

Little, however, seems known about the personality characteristics of high and low EE relatives of schizophrenics. Apparently, compared with low EE relatives, high EE relatives seem more conventional in favoring established norms and less satisfied with themselves and their lives, being also less flexible, less tolerant, and lower in empathy and achievement via independence than low EE relatives. Of all these characteristics, flexibility may be the most significant predictor of high EE use (Hooley & Hiller, 2000).

High EE relatives seem to spend more time talking and less in looking at the patients, while low EE relatives seem more prepared to remain silent. This pattern could suggest that high EE relatives may be more socially intrusive than low EE relatives who may be more supportive to schizophrenic patients (Kuipers, Sturgeon, Berkowitz, & Leff, 1983). Achievement orientation in mothers of disruptive and obsessive compulsive children seems related to high EE, as may be familial conflict and a high preponderance of psychiatric disorders in the parents of disturbed children in comparison to parents of controls (Hibbs, Hamburger, Kruesi, & Lenane, 1993).

Consequently, extremes in parental EE seem related to psychopathology in their offspring, supporting the importance of how feelings are experienced, expressed, and shared in intimate relationships, positively or negatively. This issue will be covered again in reviewing EE in families of schizophrenics (Ch. 12).

Connection with Other Resources

Bandura (2001) and Forgas (2001) connected R to A, Clark and Fiske (1992), Grieger and Grieger (1982), as well as Power and Dalgleish (1997) related R to E. Carroll and Payne (1976), among many others, related social behavior A to R. In all these connections, an assumption is explicit or implicit that either E or R, or both resources together, are determinants of A. Which is primary in relationship to A depends very likely on the nature of the interaction, its Context.

Relevance of R to Relationships

There are communal relationships based on *E*, mainly those among family members and friends (Clark, 1988). There are exchange relationships based on *R*, as in school/work settings and business. Nonetheless, even in prolonged exchange relationships, there may be an establishment of communal bonds, just as communal relationships may involve exchanges. Furthermore, there are definite differences among *E* and *R* due to hemispheric specializations that need to be taken into account (Joseph, 1992; Schore, 2003).

Activity or Action (A)

Terms related to this resource may be behavior, acts, doing, performance, performing, and talking. Activity preference, including the choice of jobs, learning institutions, and leisure-time activities, may be related to someones underlying personality structure and to satisfying various needs. For instance, extroverts seem to have a significantly different pattern of activity preferences from introverts (Furnham, 1981). Hence, activities/actions are not random, they follow definite trajectories that depend a great deal on who one is and does, and what he or she has, as discussed in Chapter 9.

Theoretical Background

Objectively observable and measurable relationships, what is said or done, passively or actively, has been the hobby horse of behaviorism since the beginning of the past century (Gollwitzer & Bargh, 1996). What is relevant here is whether to accept an orthodoxically simplistic position, negating the influence of internal determinants like *E* or *R*, or reject such a position as being theoretically and empirically untenable. Going beyond it, what is relevant to relationships is distance, whom and what to approach and whom or what to avoid (Elliott, 1997; Higgins, 2001), as discussed in Chapter 7. It would be easy to connect distance to the law of effect, we approach who or what we like and avoid who or what we do not like. However, in the real world, oftentimes we need to approach whom we do not like, like our boss, or a coworker, or a subordinate, let alone nasty relatives or noisy neighbors. Nonetheless, distance is still observable not only with people but in settings. We may dislike our job or our boss, but we need to approach them to survive. By the same token, we may like a great many luxuries while window-shopping, but we cannot afford them.

In *A* is where most feelings (*E*) are expressed verbally and nonverbally, rendering or transforming them into emotions. They can be positive or negative according to how helpful or hurtful they are. *E* can be avoided, kept inside, leaving it unexpressed and festering. However, expression of *E*, even in writing, if not verbally, does lead to observable and measurable behavior, *A* (Lepore & Smyth, 2002). Control of *A* (Twenge & Baumeister, 2002) is visible when *A* is delayed after the introduction of a stimulus event, i.e., avoided, inhibited, suppressed, or repressed. Thus, in relationships, *A* can be assessed by how close (approach) or distant (avoidance) one is from others, and by how actively fast (discharge) or how passively slow (delay) one responds to stimulus events or to goals and priorities, as discussed in Chapters 7 and 8. Issues of measurement have been discussed by Labouvie (1975). Simple rating scales to evaluate both behaviors (active/passive and approach/avoidance) have been developed by Beech, Fisher, and Thornton (2003) to evaluate sex offenders. Nonetheless, both scales can be used to evaluate other types of personalities, and can be used to develop isomorphic workbooks, as already discussed in Chapter 1. It would be useful to have available simple rating scales to evaluate discharge-delay functions as well.

Developmental Trajectory

With age, the behavioral repertoire (*A*) becomes more and more differentiated emotionally (*E*), intellectually (*R*), occupationally, relationally, and in leisure-time activities. Skills are acquired developmentally and progressively through education and experience. This acquisition does follow what Higgins (1997) has called promotion (approach) and prevention (withdrawal), to the point that usually, we approach helpful *A* and avoid hurtful *A*. Of course, the dimension of control, how actively fast or how passively slow we approach or avoid, intersects with distance. From an early stage of dependency in childhood to a denial of dependency in adolescence, adulthood implies interdependence, just as advanced seniority implies a relative return to dependency.

A child's activity level seems highly related to parent-child interactions. Parents of highly active children may tend to intrude physically and could be described as getting into power struggles and competition with their children. Impatience or hostility toward active children seems present in most parent-child dyads except father-son combinations. Interactions involving less active children might be generally more peaceful and harmonious (Buss, 1981).

Functionality

The more differentiated (flexible, positive, appropriate) one is in using *E*, *R*, and *A* the greater the likelihood of reaching functionality in relationships, even though one would need *Aw* and *C* and more to reach well-rounded functioning. This functioning may relate to how one defines oneself as in the concept of identity differentiation expanded in Chapter 10.

Dysfunctionality

Extremes in approach, leading to "overly close relationships" are found in borderline, histrionic, symbiotic, and dependent personality disorders (Ch. 7). Extremes in avoidance would lead to "distant/avoidant relationships," as found in obsessive-compulsive, paranoid, schizoid, schizotypal, and antisocial personality disorders (Ch. 12; Geiger & Crick, 2001, p. 60). Excessive A, that is, discharge, would imply drivenness, impulsivity, and immediacy in orientation that may lead to attention deficits, hyperactivity, conduct and externalization disorders, and addictions (Chassin, Collins, Ritter, & Shirley, 2001; Geiger & Crick, 2001). An example of driven, excessive, noncriminal A would be Type A behavior (Ch. 9) that may lead to coronary-prone personalities, as evaluated by the Jenkins Activity Survey (Hayano, Takeuchi, Yoshida, Jozuka et al., 1989; Yarnold, Bryant, & Grimm, 1987). Insufficient or inadequate A (delay), that is, passivity, procrastination, and inactivity, may be found in rigid or dependent personalities, internalization disorders, and in extreme cases, schizophreniacs (Pennington, 2002; Sameroff et al., 2000).

Thought-action fusion, the mixing of both R and A, seems related to at least two dimensions of Morality, the belief that unacceptable thoughts are morally equivalent to overt actions, and Likelihood, the belief that thinking of an unacceptable or disturbing situation will increase the chances that situation will actually occur. This fusion between R and A seems associated with symptoms of obsessive-compulsive disorder as well as with symptoms of anxiety and depression (Muris, Meesters, Rassin, & Merckelbach, 2001). This likelihood seems related to exaggerated beliefs about thoughts regarding the reduction of harm, that is, the more one thinks about it, the less the possibility of its occurrence (Amir, Freshman, Ramsey, & Neary, 2001). Both thought-action fusion and thought suppression seem associated with severe psychopathology (Rassin, Diepstraten, Marckelbach, & Muris, 2001).

Connection with Other Resources

It is no longer possible to view A as isolated from preceding or following resources. However, it is important to consider that when A is predominantly determined by E, without some influence from R, it may lead to impulsive, "thoughtless" behavior based on immediate discharge, i.e., disinhibition, as discussed in Chapter 8. On the other end of a control dimension, when A is delayed and limited, one needs to invoke excessive inhibitions, extremes supposedly stemming from excessive R and avoidance of E. Criminal, driven, or addictive *A*, for instance, would suggest a deficit in *R*, at least in what is considered as "emotional intelligence" or controls.

Relevance of A to Relationships

Here is where positivity and negativity come into being, whether one wants long-term, committed and close relationships requiring appropriately flexible, and positively balanced *A* with other resources, or whether limiting the quality of relationships by inappropriately rigid, and negatively unbalanced *A*, and relying either too much or too little on other resources.

Awareness (Aw)

The position taken here is that *Aw* takes place after *A* and includes a recognition of personal and interpersonal consequences of one's actions or words (Wilson & Dunn, 2004). *Aw*, defined as the ability to reflect on one's own *E*, *R*, *A*, or *C*, follows from *A* because one needs to act in order to reflect on the costs or rewards of what was said or done to change it "after the fact." This is the corrective feedback loop necessary for change to take place (Mayer, 2003). Baumeister (1998) conceives of self-awareness as the first basic function of a self, which leads to self-esteem, self-perception, and self-knowledge. Nonetheless, if a construct like insight were to be included as part of *Aw* (Miller & Baca, 2001), a larger and wider field of study could be reviewed, making it into a school of thought, overlapping mostly with psychodynamic and therapeutic literature.

The process of *Aw* is composed of at least three components, two positive ones, that is, reflection and insight about one's relationships, and a third one, brooding and ruminating about one's relationships (Papageorgiu & Wells, 2003; Thayer, Rossy, Ruiz-Padial, & Johnsen, 2003; Treynor, Gonzalez, & Nolen-Hoeksema, 2003). Reflection, when positive, may usually lead to insights about one's relationships and how they may need to be changed. Brooding and ruminating include a process of repetitious, focused thinking about one's relationships, usually negative, which does not lead to any insight or, worst, change. *Aw* may be directed toward the self, toward others, and toward the Context of how the self relates with others, as well about one's *E*, *R*, and *A*.

Theoretical Background

As noted in Table 4.2, historically, no real school of thought could be determined, except for the indirect influence of thinkers who could have been placed as well under the heading of humanism, rationalism, or empiricism. A major text on this topic, Ferrari and Sternberg (1998), for instance, failed to give historical information that would suggest *Aw* as a school in and by itself, as concluded about other resources. This is why the relevant heading in Table 4.2 is left blank. Reflection might bring about anxiety in some situations but, on the other hand, it may also deter the emergence of anxiety in other situations. The issue here, of course, is to find which situation will provoke anxiety and which will not.

Attention can be directed either inside or outside the self at any given moment. The extent to which one is self-aware has important cognitive and behavioral consequences. When attention is brought to bear on the body, one may become increasingly prone to focus on other aspects of the material, social, or even spiritual self. Once self-directed attention is initiated, one's focus then will flow toward whatever feature of the self is most salient, but not to the entire self. Once attention comes to bear on a specific aspect of the self, self-evaluation begins. The self comes into play primarily when attention is turned inward (Wicklund, 1979). In line with these hypotheses, increases in objective self-awareness may lead to a more individualized conceptions of self. This effect may be more pronounced in low self-monitoring respondents (Ickes, Layden, & Barnes, 1978).

Developmental Trajectory

One would espect for *Aw* to increase with age. Indeed, some theorists conceive of reflective thinking as being present in adulthood rather than in earlier stages of development (Commons & Richards, 2002; Fischer & Pruyne, 2002; Sinnott, 2002). These theorists have developed stages in reflective thinking that go above and beyond Piaget's early ones. However, development of *Aw* is too connected to other resources and to self and personality functioning (Bouffard & Vezeau, 1998; Mascolo & Fischer, 1998) to project its limits as well as its adaptive or corrective functions over time. Furthermore, where is *Aw* focused? On *E* (Harris, 2000), *R* (Lewis & Haviland-Jones, 2000), or *A*? If so-called wisdom increases with age, does it mean that this increase is due to an increment in *Aw* (Shedlock & Cornelius, 2002)? One would need to search for studies of *Aw* in senior citizens to answer these questions. Problem children, on the other hand, seem to lag behind functioning children in their awareness of a five-stage developmental sequence of awareness of interpersonal issues, such as trust in friendship and loyalty in peer group relations (Selman, Jaquette, & Lavin, 1977).

Functionality

Supposedly, the more *Aw* one possesses, the greater the possibility of functionality. On the other hand, one could argue that some individuals do have

Aw about their dysfunctionality, but are either unable or unwilling to change their behavior (Ferrari, 1998). Consequently, insight or *Aw* cannot always be linked to change, except in functioning individuals or, in some cases, individuals undergoing verbal, nonverbal body, or writing therapies (Lepore & Smyth, 2002). Indeed, awareness training though exercise and yoga seems to increase "body satisfaction" (Clance, 1980). Even a brief body-movement experience can enhance understanding and self-awareness among normal respondents (Schofield & Abbuhl, 1975).

Objective self-awareness a la Wicklund (1979), produced by introducing a mirror or a camera into the experimental situation, seems to increase compliance but with different gender effects. Males may tend to show traditional patterns of reactance and compliance. Women may become more compliant under high threat situations to freedom with low reactance under low degrees of threat (Swart, Ickes, & Morgenthaler, 1978). *Aw* may be limited because is may occur at subliminal or preconscious levels (Mogg, Bradley, & Williams, 1995). Self-efficacy may be related to self-awareness as defined by Wicklund (1979). Low-efficacy women, for instance, could be distinguished from high-efficacy women by engaging in a preservative self-evaluation process that ultimately may lead to social withdrawal (Alden, Teschuk, & Tee, 1992). Apparently, manipulation of self-focused attention or objective self-awareness may activate self-relevant thoughts (Geller & Shaver, 1976).

Dysfunctionality

Is there such a thing as excessive *Aw?* Conceivably, as noted above, one could be so overwhelmed by excessive *Aw* that no proper or corrective course of *A* could be undertaken, as in rumination. Defective or a inadequate *Aw* more frequently might lead to repetition of the same negative *A* because no reflection and correction for change are occurring. Dissociation, shell-shock, and split-identities seem to be the outcome of defective *Aw* (Stout, 2001). Restricted *Aw* would clearly limit how one's resources are considered and applied. This might be the case in individuals who are impulsive and who do not stop to reflect on the consequences of their behavior. Current suicidal intent seems highly related to increased self-awareness. In many schizophrenics, an insight-demoralization-depression-suicidality syndrome may be present (Schwartz, 2001), suggesting that, in some clinical cases, increases in self-awareness may produce deleterious effects. However, self-awareness seems limited in predicting or relating to alcoholic involvement in an adolescent with a family history of alcohol abuse (Chassin, Mann, & Sher, 1988). A severe deficit in self-awareness may constitute a distinguishing pathological characteristic in severe bipolar disorders (Pallanti, Quercioli, Pazzagli, & Rossi, 1999).

Connection with Other Resources

In spite of connections of *Aw* with all four of the other component resources (Figures 4.1 and 4.2), Lane (2000) focuses on "the role of emotional awareness in social cognition during social interactions (p. 185)." Consequently, *Aw* is connected to other resources, of course, in different amounts and qualities. The issue here is to discover how this connection does occur and to what degree.

Relevance of Aw to Relationships

Successful relationships supposedly are based on corrective feedback, that is, *Aw*, at the intraindividual, dyadic, or multirelational level. Supposedly, without corrective feedback, there is no possibility of improvement, in the sense that relationships would tend to remain static and stationary, where the *status quo* would reign supreme, and in time, become more dysfunctional. Can change take place without *Aw*? Of course, it might. However, if change occurs without *Aw*, one would have to posit various levels of *Aw* from immediate to delayed and from conscious to unconscious.

Context (C)

Context usually means where and how relationships occur in a house, a home, an office, school, building, neighborhood, community, environment, society, and culture. Here, the term *C*, however, is limited to the influence of intimate relationships and objects in specific settings (Ch. 6).

Theoretical Background

Contexts have been subdivided usually into dimensions of proximal (close and immediate) on one hand, to distal (spatially or temporally) on the other. They can be the laboratory setting (Capaldi & Proctor, 1999) or any other setting (Biglan, Glasgow, & Singer, 1990; Bronfenbrenner, 1979; Cohen & Siegel, 1991; Kinderman & Valsiner, 1995; Mehrabian, 1976; Tudge, Shanahan, & Valsiner, 1997). More often than not, context is understood to mean generally vague, seemingly distal and all-encompassing terms like "environment," "culture," or "situation." Can one be more specific? One needs to distinguish among objective, proximal settings, such as home, school/work, leisure-time activities, transitory (church, bars, grocery stores), and transit (roads, airports, hotels) settings (Ch. 6). All can be photographed and recorded objectively.

However, this objectivity bypasses the personal, subjective meaning that those settings may have for survival and enjoyment. A physical structure with walls, a roof, doors, and windows may be a house, but for someone living there, it is a "home," where one's family and loved ones live. It could be a source of respite from the stresses of work and the external world, or it may be in itself another source of stress (Lazarus & Folkman, 1984). Once settings are defined by their subjective meanings, interpreting them as contexts, they become related to other resources in ways that could no longer be considered solely objectively. By the same token, there are impersonal, transitory settings, like banks, grocery stores, or service stations, that may not possess the same meaning that a house, a school, an office, or a neighborhood may have, where one has spent a great deal of time, and where an emotional attachment has been formed.

Cummings et al. (2000) have rendered the most succinct definition of contextualism available in the extant literature:

> "... contextualism regards development as imbedded in series of nested, interconnected wholes or networks of activity at multiple levels of analysis, including the intra-individual subsystem (e.g., interplay between specific dimensions within a domain such as affect and cognition), the intra-individual system (e.g., interplay between biology, cognition, affect), the interpersonal (e.g., family or peer relationship quality), and ecological or socio-cultural system (e.g., community, subculture, culture). Thus, development regulates and is regulated by multiple factors, events, and processes at several levels that unfold over time (p. 24)."

Developmental Trajectory

It may take time to evaluate the meaning, emotional or otherwise, i.e., context, of a setting. It may take even longer to develop a sentimental attachment to a place, to a person, or even to a pet. Without a certain degree of stability over time, no emotional attachment to a setting may develop. *Aw* and *C* probably are even more connected with each other than with the other three resources because this connection implies at least four stages of development in human thought, already considered. Finer and more elaborate discriminations of these stages have been made by Commons and Richards (2002), Fischer and Pruyne (2003), and Sinnott (2002).

Functionality

Contexts conceived as subjective, emotional attachments to relationships with either persons, animals, settings, or objects are what individuals make them. They may become extremely functional or extremely dysfunctional according to their subjective meanings produced by what positive or negative experiences have occurred in the background of an individual.

Dysfunctionality

Using a criterion of personal usage, some contexts may become or be viewed as extremely toxic or extremely pleasurable and somewhere in between. A context may become dysfunctional when one can no longer use personal resources to make it function or its malfunctioning impacts the resources one has available to survive and enjoy life.

Connection with Other Resources

Like *Aw*, *C* is connected to other resources, as encompassing and surrounding them in ways that should be identified and quantified (Figures 4.1 and 4.2). Although all resources can be viewed as endogenous and residing inside individuals, settings are exogenous, external, and residing outside individuals. Their appraisal and interpretation as contexts, however, and as determinants of relationships are endogenous, as a component of the other four resources (Ch. 6). Consequently, to paraphrase Lewin (1935), $A = f(ERAwXC)$, relationships are the outcome of interactions among personal resources and personal interpretations of a setting.

Relevance of C to Relationships

Relationships in themselves may count as contexts as well. Hence, each relationship has its own unique context, be it physical (gym), intellectual (school), or emotional (home and loved ones). It matters whether relationships are intimately communal (close, prolonged, interdependent, and committed) or nonintimate exchanges (temporary, distal, commercial, and financial).

FUNCTIONS OF THE ERAAwC MODEL

There are at least five functions fulfilled by this model: (1) integrative; (2) constructive; (3) circular; (4) diagnostic, and (5) prescriptive.

Integration of Previous Schools of Thought

The creation of a supraordinate ERAAwC model forces all five component resources to become equally important and interdependent, to the point that no one resource can claim hegemonic superiority over the others. Each resource is important in its own rights, with its own specific characteristics and specific functions, including multidirectionality, that is, being affected by or affecting other resources as well. If this conclusion is valid, then it would follow that one cannot study one resource independently from others. This interdependence or overlap (Figure 4.2) would imply that all five resources together would provide optimal functioning when they are used appropriately, selectively, and positively. Dysfunctionality would occur when one resource is overused or underused at the expense of the other four.

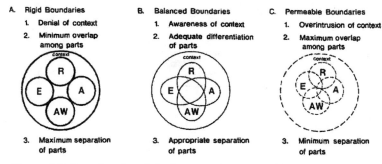

Figure 4.2. Functional and dysfunctional aspects of the ERAAwC model.

Construction of a Meta- or Pan-Theoretical Framework

The ERAAwC framework aims at going above and beyond campanolistic and parochial turf controversies about the superiority of one resource over others. In this regard, it could be conceived as being pan-theoretical. By uniting resources, this model is inclusively metatheoretical, to the extent that it includes specific theories underlying each resource.

Circularity

Besides being integrative and meta- or pan-theoretical, this model is also circular, as shown in Figure 4.1, through a loop emanating from Aw to other components. The circularity of this model is reflected in its sequence: from E to R to A to Aw and C. This sequence, however, does not imply linearity. One can skip from one resource to another without a linear sequence. After A, some people are able to reflect (Aw) about the quality of what they have said or done, others do not. On the basis of self-reflection and consideration (Aw) about personal and extra-personal contexts, some are able to change their behavior, some are not. It seems important at this juncture to discover who does and does not.

There are at least three variable factors that describe relationships among component resources: (1) size, (2) boundaries, and (3) overlap. Size means how large or small is each resource in relationship to others. Is $E > R$ or $A > Aw$? What happens when $E > R$, will the other resources shrink, and if they do, which one(s)? Is C so large that it looms over other resources, as shown graphically? Boundaries mean how strong and impermeable or weak and permable the limits are surrounding each resource. This factor is illustrated in Figure 4.2, where two extreme cases are shown with a functional possibility in the middle. Overlap describes how each resource merges or even melts with other resources, with almost no overlap on one extreme

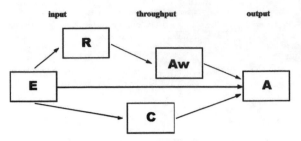

Figure 4.3. Formal nature of the ERAAwC model[1].

with denial of *C* and a great deal of overlap on the other, with overintrusion of *C* depending on the strength of boundaries in each resource.

When the model is simplified in terms of input, throughput, and output, its formal representation is shown in Figure 4.3, where *E* and *R* are part of input, *Aw* and *C* are part of throughput, and *A* is the output. This is the format through which the model will be evaluated.

Diagnostic

If this model could be measured, it would provide a ready source of information to pinpoint which resource is overused and which is not, which is functional and which is not. A correct diagnosis should direct matching prescriptions with missing, incomplete, or extreme resources. Descriptive labeling, i.e., diagnosis, would allow planned structured interventions designed specifically to either decrease an excessive resource or increase an insufficient one, as discussed below. For instance, if *E* were found wanting, workbooks about its development could be prescribed (Appendix A). If *E* were too excessive, then cognitively oriented workbooks could be described. The same process is described below.

Prescriptive

Constructive prescriptions are based on a proper diagnosis of which resource is missing, insufficient, or excessive. F2f psychotherapy is supposed to perform such a function. However, due to inherent inadequacies in the spoken medium (vagueness, lack of specificity, distortions, generalizations, and expense), matching diagnoses with prescriptions and treatment is chancy, difficult to achieve, and even harder to research. The introduction of writing, either expressive or programmed (Lepore & Smyth, 2002), instead of or in addition to f2f, talk-based psychotherapy, might improve the specificity necessary for prescriptions, because writing is more specifically efficient and more cost-effective than talk.

Simplistically, each resource has its own singly underlying prescription. For instance, in *E*, "If you were more in touch with your feelings, you would be much better." For *R*, "If you think correctly or less irrationally about your problems, you would be okay." For *A*, "'If you do right and say the right word, you would be okay." For *Aw*, "If you were more aware of your problems and how they were produced, you would be able to solve them." For *C*, "If you understood your circumstances or situation better, you would be able to solve whatever is a problem for you."

Of course, prescriptions are not as easy or simple as stated. Furthermore, very few people do follow prescriptive feedback, which might well be the very essence of functionality. Dysfunctionalities could be viewed as the inability to profit by constructive feedback, both internal or external. Constructive prescriptions are based on a proper diagnosis of which resource is missing, insufficient, or excessive. F2f psychotherapy is supposed to perform such a function. However, due to inherent inadequacies in the spoken medium (vagueness, lack of specificity, distortions, generalizations, and expense), matching diagnoses with prescriptions and treatment is chancy, difficult to achieve, and even harder to research (L'Abate, 1999b). The introduction of writing, either expressive or programmed (Lepore & Smyth, 2002), instead of or in addition to f2f, talk-based psychotherapy, might improve the specificity necessary for prescriptions, because writing may be more specifically efficient and more cost-effective than talk.

Another prescriptive function performed by this model, for instance, relates to the process of negotiation, considered in Chapters 8 and 17, and applied in a Planned Parenting Workbook (Appendix D, L'Abate, 1996).

Therapeutic

The issue of whether to intervene at the level of strengths or at the level of weaknesses in one's personality makeup can be settled clinically as well as empirically using the ERAAwC model. It can be performed impressionistically when the diagnosis is achieved through a f2f interview and a life history, or it can be achieved through the use of a battery of multiple tests, at least five, already existing on the market, to evaluate each of the component resources of the model. However, using different tests without comparative values among them would make it difficult, but certainly not impossible, to identify which resource is strong and which resource is weak. However, the battery could take some time in administration and scoring of the various tests. Would it be more efficient and practical to create an instrument that would include all five resources into one single source? That is the purpose of the next section.

Relationships among Component Resources

Proposals at the conceptual and studies at the empirical levels have been performed between component resources, as indicated selectively above. Relationships between two or, at best, three component resources have been presented (Izard, Kagan, & Zajonc, 1984). However, I am unaware of studies seeking to connect and link all five component resources. How can this study be performed if there is no underlying model? Thus, the purpose of the remainder of this chapter is to show how it is possible to connect empirically the five resources of this model.

MAJOR ISSUES WITH THE ERAAwC MODEL

Four major issues loom large in considering this model, learning more about: (1) the development of component resources over time, (2) sex differences, (3) psychopathology, and (4) relationship of the model with a supraordinate factor responsible for allocating how the resources are distributed and allocated. On the basis of the conclusions in the previous section, it is possible to make at least three predictions about interconnections among the five resources.

In the first place, developmentally, most individuals will learn to use all five components in an appropriately balanced and positively flexible manner. This prediction implies that, developmentally, adolescents and young people will not be using all five components until they reach maturity, somewhere between 30 and 40 years of age (Cummings et al., 2000; Ingram & Price, 2001; Sameroff et al., 2000; Scales & Leffert, 1999). Even then, resources may be differentiated between E, leading to communal, and R, leading to exchange relationships.

In the second place, there will be some gender differences that may follow stereotypical notions of women being more "emotional" and communal than men, who in turn will be more "rational" and exchange-oriented than women (Canary, Emmers-Sommer, & Faulkner, 1997). These differences become accentuated in psychopathology (Seeman, 1995). Of course, one could predict the same gender disparity in Aw and C, with women being more aware of themselves and of C than men.

In the third place, dysfunctional individuals at best will be overusing one or two resources at the expense of others, by either not using them or using them minimally or inappropriately, as noted earlier in regard to dysfunctionalities in each resource.

In the fourth place, this model requires the existence of an even higher, supraordinate mechanism regulating appropriate and positive balance among all five component resources. How are these five resources regulated? None can assume a hegemonic position or role over the other four. How can we use this model to go beyond it and find a higher regulative mechanism that will integrate this and other models? Is "personality" such a regulative mechanism? Should this regulating and allocating mechanism be located within E, R, A, Aw, or C? If there is an appropriate and positive balance among all five component resources, where does it come from, E, R, A, Aw, or C? Can a choice be made on the basis of empirical results? One cannot choose R, for instance, without promoting it to a different class from other resources.

Hence, one is stuck with having to include supraordinate constructs, like self or personality, as overarching regulating mechanisms (Mascolo & Fischer, 1998). They perform executive and organizational functions on how to relate self with others. This possibility may be acceptable, provided one were to consider that there is more to self and personality that just these five resources. This consideration involves aspects of self and personality, like identity differentiation (Ch. 10), style in intimate relationships (Ch. 11), selfhood (Ch. 12), and priorities (Ch. 13), among other models considered in the rest of this work. These aspects need integration with the resources of this model for appropriate regulation of distance, how to be close or distant from others, and control, whether to inhibit or disinhibit one's actions in relation to others. These issues, hopefully, will be answered in the rest of this book.

EVALUATION OF THE ERAAwC MODEL

The first part of this chapter explained the historical and theoretical underpinnings of an integrative model of component resources considered necessary for the establishment and perhaps maintenance of intimate and nonintimate relationships, communal or exchange. This model includes five primary component resources viewed from an information processing framework: Emotionality (E) for reception, Rationality (R) for processing, Activity (A) for expression, Awareness (Aw) for reflection and possible feedback functions, i.e., "the loop" in relationships; and Context (C) for surrounding, proximal, and distal factors both spatially and temporally. This model is summarized in short as ERAAwC.

This section presented evidence to evaluate and possibly support the validity of the ERAAwC model and its possible usefulness diagnostically, preventively, prescriptively, and therapeutically. Three major hypotheses derived directly from its characteristics: (1) developmentally, adults would use all five resources, while adolescents would only use some of them, and, by extension, children would use even less; (2) there would be gender differences according to stereotypical, socially derived roles, with women relying on E more than men, and men relying more on R than women; (3) psychopathologically, deviant populations would rely on one or two resources at the expense of the others, that is, the importance of one or two resources would be increased while the importance of the others would be decreased.

When the model is simplified in terms of input, throughput, and output, its formal representation is shown in Figure 4.3, where E and R are part of input, Aw and C are part of throughput, and A is part of the output. This is the format through which the model will be evaluated according to possible relationships among the five resources.

To evaluate this model, a self-report, paper-and-pencil questionnaire was developed over the past decade, the Relational Answers Questionnaire (RAQ) by Mario Cusinato and his students at the University of Padua (Appendix B).

The Relational Answers Questionnaire

The RAQ is a self-report, paper-and-pencil instrument constructed to evaluate the ERAAwC model. Its seventh and final revision is composed of 10 items for each resource. The RAQ was meant to fulfill at least five requirements: (1) items in each resource should possess satisfactory internal consistency; (2) items should be independent of each other to meet criteria set by Rasch's Simple Logistic Model, within the theory of latent traits (Bond & Fox, 2001); (3) respondents must evaluate items independently; (4) relational scores are generated from individual scores through dyadic comparisons within couples; and (5) a certain number of individuals can be considered as an aggregate insofar as they are participating in the same reality, giving well-defined answers in responce to the same dimensions, as proposed by Fisher et al. (1985). Alpha reliability coefficients for the five scales were: $E = .81$; $R = .85$; $A = .74$; $Aw = .64$; $C = .75$.

The seventh draft (Colombi, 2002) was administered to 515 nonclinical respondents from 14 to 60 years of age, which were not homogeneous for sex and age. From this sample, the following alpha values were obtained: $E = .81$; $R = 85$, $A = 74$; $Aw = 63$, and $C = .74$. Corsi (2002) administered the same revision to 480 respondents divided into 240 females and 240 males with 120 respondents in four age levels, 14–19, 20–30, 31–40, 41–60. All respondents were homogeneous for ethnic background (European), except for age, which is the basis for an analysis according to a developmental perspective. In this study, alpha values were as follows: $E = 81$; $R = .86$;

$A = .73$; $Aw = 64$; and $C = .75$. There was considerable difference in consistency according to the alpha values, in the subgroups, especially in the Aw scale: (1) sex, males $= .62$, females $= .65$; (2) age, 14–18 $= .52$, 20–30 $= .75$, 31–40 $= .57$, and 41–60 $= 69$. All these values are acceptable according to Rasch's analysis (Bond & Fox, 2001). Corsi's data are used to develop scoring standards and instructions for the RAQ in Appendix B.

Psychometric Properties of the RAQ

Administration of this final revision to 126 undergraduates juniors allowed researchers to verify an improvement in psychometric properties of this instrument, with acceptable consistency coefficients ranging from .71 to .85.

Fidelity

Results from this administration to 480 respondents divided equally for sex (240 women and 240 men), with four different subgroups divided according to age (14 to 19 years, $N = 120$; 20 to 30 years, $N = 120$; 31 to 40 years, 120; and 41 to 60 years, $N = 120$) showed that overall mean scores do not differ from those of previous administrations. Furthermore, contrary to results from a previous study, reliability analysis has been applied considering first sex and then age as independent variables. Men showed higher mean scores for internal consistency for E and A, while women showed higher scores for R, Aw, and C. Mean scores for the four age groups show a general increase in internal consistency with age for all five scales. The C scale is unique in showing a distinct increase in internal consistency scores in the older age group, 41 to 60 years of age.

Test-Retest Reliability

Consequently, a sample of 152 undergraduates was evaluated twice with the RAQ within a period from 8 to 15 days. Mean correlations between test and retest indicate acceptable high reliability for the RAQ with the following test-retest correlations for the five scales: $E = .85$; $R = .86$; $A = .77$; $Aw = .75$, and $C = .78$. The relatively and consistently low alpha value for Aw could be interpreted as representing a possible metacommunication of self-awareness, or a limited view of the multiple functions that Aw possesses in respect to the other four resources of the model. A further amplification of this scale, in terms of its multiple functions, is in progress (Mario Cusinato, personal communication, November 23, 2003).

Validity

The RAQ's validity was evaluated in its construct, content, concurrent, and discriminant validities applied to the sample of 480 respondents divided equally by sex and age.

Construct Validity. Correlation coefficients were all positive among E, A, C, and R, as well as between R, A, and Aw, between A and Aw ($r = .12$, $p < .01$), but were negative between A and C and between Aw and C. These correlations confirm the hypothesis of reciprocal, possibly circular influence among the five resources. Partial correlations showed that correlations between E and A vary when the other three variables are included. Of relevance is the partial correlation between E and C that suggests how the former is linked to external factors.

Content Validity. Item-scale correlation coefficients vary from .16 to .10 for Aw, while the higher scores are found for R, from .40 to .63, followed by E with scores between .26 to .61, A with scores between .24 to .53, and C with scores between .22 to .49. The lowest scores were for Aw, from .19 to .43. The latter scores are somewhat inconsistent with those found in previous studies.

Concurrent and Discriminant Validities. To evaluate these validities another paper-and-pencil, self-report test was used: the Self-Other Profile Chart (SOPC), evaluating a relational selfhood model based on attribution of importance to Self by self and by intimate Others (Ch. 12). This brief rating scale has already been validated in its statistical properties in a variety of studies reported in previous publications. A correlational analysis among scores on the RAQ and those on the SOPC showed that importance of Self is linked positively and significantly with R, A, C, and Aw, while importance of Others is linked positively to E and C, with the latter resource, C being present in both Self and Other importance.

The study of all other validities, except for the SOPC, was hampered by the lack of valid and reliable instruments that were not available in Italy where the RAQ was evaluated. Hence, further evaluations are necessary with English-speaking populations.

Empirical Verification of the ERAAwC Model

Once its statistical properties were established satisfactorily, the RAQ was administrated to 511 respondents from all walks of lives, mainly high school and college students, to see whether the predicted developmental changes would occur as a function of age and sex (Colombi, 2002). Four subjects were dropped for incomplete answers. There were 303 girls and women and 208 boys and men. They were divided by age into four groups: (1) between 14 and 19 years of age, $n = 135$; (2) between 20 and 30 years, $n = 130$; (3) between 31 and 40, $n = 120$; and (4) between 41 and 60, $n = 126$.

Data Analysis

The model was evaluated first through the analysis of partial correlations among dimensions for the whole sample. From this analysis, there is a direct relationship between E and C, filtered and elaborated by a circular process among R, Aw, and C. Correlations between E and A, E and C, R and C, R and A were all positive. Correlations between C and A and C and Aw were negative. Partial correlations varied significantly when the entire sample was subdivided into groups on the basis of age and sex. Through Linear Structural Relations (LISREL) analysis, various alternative models were evaluated sequentially, using different samples for sex and age, in order to verify their degree of closeness to empirical data. This analysis allows us to identify which model would be the best theoretical model. In the model produced by this analysis appear two endogenous, E and R, and three exogenous variables, A, Aw, and C.

The model, therefore, was evaluated through a multisample analysis, keeping sex and age in consideration. This procedure allows us to evaluate sequentially a series of hypotheses with different degrees of connection (Jöreskog & Sörbom, 1996), to verify successively the degree of fit between hypotheses and data, evaluating variance or invariance of the parameters involved. The outcome of such an evidentiary process was as follows:

1. There are no statistically significant differences for sex, therefore, parameter invariance between a model for males and a model for females can be assumed. Consequently, a model including the totality of respondents regardless of sex can be considered.
2. In regard to age, the invariance test of parameters was significant, implying a difference in the values of parameters among the four groups. Keeping in mind that regression coefficients were statistically significant, one needs to distinguish between the model for the entire sample from models based on age.

In considering the totality of the sample, these are the results: (1) both E and R influence A positively, while A is moderated slightly by C; (2) R strengthens Aw and the latter moderates C to a significant degree; (3) C is strengthened by both E and R, which in turn is moderated by Aw and moderates A.

As far as age is concerned: (1) departing from the two exogenous variables, E has a direct and positive influence on A for the 20 to 30 years group, while R explicitly influences A in respondents older that 30 years (groups 3 and 4); (2) R positively influences Aw in groups 1, 2, and 4, while in Group 3, between 30 and 40 years, Aw is essentially autonomous; (3) R strengthens positively C until 30 years of age; (4) E has a direct influence on C only in groups 2 and 4, while it shows an attenuating effect of Aw in group 3—consequently, it does not appear appropriate to advance hypotheses of relational significance based on these regression indices; (5) as far as the three exogenous variables are concerned, Aw, C, and A, the first result with a different value, the lowest coefficient is found in Group 1, while with age, the coefficient value reaches a peak in Group 2, decreasing successively, and eventually inverting the trend in Group 4. In regard to the three endogenous variables, there are two particular results. The first relates to the moderating influence of Aw on C for each age group, but with a different value. The lowest coefficient value is found in Group 1, with age development, there is a peak in Group 2, afterward the value decreases successively and at the end, reverses the trend in Group 4.

These results do provide a logical consistency, especially in regard to the influence of C on A. This influence, however, is relevant for Group 1, the youngest respondents who seem to be more influenced by environmental conditionings in comparison to older respondents.

Evaluation of RAQ with Deviant Populations

To evaluate the psychometric properties of the RAQ with deviant populations, in view of the hypothesis that these populations would rely mainly on one or two resources at the expense of the others, three different populations were administered the RAQ with other test instruments: (1) substance abusers; (2) parents of children with genetic malformations; and (3) parents of children with birth defects.

Substance Abusers

The experimental group included 102 male substance abusers between the ages of 17 to 60 (mean age 31) living in a communal residence of northern Italy (Franzoso, 2002). They could stay in this community as long as they participated in ongoing therapeutic modalities (group and individual). All clinical respondents were in the first phase of a 3-month treatment program. They were matched for age, sex, marital status, and educational level with a control, nonclinical group obtained from the same region. In addition to a test battery consisting of the RAQ, the SOPC, and the Minnesota Multiphasic

Personality Inventory-2 (MMPI-2), all respondents signed an informed consent form required by law. The MMPI-2 was also scored for two scales of relevance to an abusive population, the Addiction Potential Scale (APS) and the Addiction Admission Scale (AAS). Correlation coefficients between the *R* scale of the RAQ and AAS were significant ($r = .22$, $p < .05$), while the *C* scale correlated with both the two MMPI-2 scales ($r = .21$, $p < .05$ for the APS and $r = -.29$, $p < .01$ for the AAS).

Among abusers, there were significant correlations between self-importance and *E* ($r = .20$, $p < .05$), *R* ($r = .45$, $p < .01$), *A* ($r = .30$, $p < .01$) and *Aw* ($r = .29$, $p < .01$). Importance of Others correlated with *E* ($r = .23$, $p < .05$), *R* ($r = .36$, $p < .01$) and *A* ($r = .32$, $p < .01$). There were no significant correlations among the other variables. Hence, one can conclude that some resources in the ERAAwC model may relate to self and intimate others as measured by the SOPC.

Parents of Children with Malformation Syndrome and Birth Defects

To evaluate the model with deviant populations further, the RAQ was administered to parents in a hospital for handicapped children to evaluate: (1) the circularity of the theoretical model, attempting to identify which resource regulates the others; (2) the ability of the model to identify and discriminate family contexts that differ among themselves on the basis of presence/absence of a child with disability and according to which disability is involved (genetic versus nongenetic); and (3) within a family context, which component of the model is prevalently used and which is not (Maino, personal communication, Oct. 30, 2003).

To evaluate these three hypotheses, three different samples were evaluated with the RAQ: (1) an experimental sample of 40 couples with a child diagnosed with a malformation syndrome coupled with mental retardation between the ages of 1 to 16 years; (2) a second experimental sample of 15 couples with a child diagnosed with a nongenetic disability with mental retardation (e.g., cerebral palsy) between the ages of 1 to 15 years; (3) a control group of 40 couples—extracted from a larger sample of 247 couples—with healthy children, with at least one between 1 and 16 years of age.

All three samples were matched according to a modality of case-by-case to control for major sociodemographic variables. There were no differences for average *age*: (1) sample with a malformation syndrom, was 40.58 years old, (2) sample with a cerebral palsy child was 39.50 years old, and (3) control group was 39.56 years old ($F(2, 187) = .64$; $p = .53$); *education* ($X^2 (1, 4) = .80$; $p = .94$); *occupational level* ($X^2 (1, 6) = 3.25$; $p = .78$); average *years of marriage*, sample with a malformation syndrome 13.27 years, sample with a cerebral palsy child 12.40 years, control sample 13.45 years

$(F(2, 187) = .49; p = .61)$; *average age of first child*, 11.12 years for the sample with a malformation syndrome child, 10.80 years for the sample with a cerebral palsy child, and 10.33 for the control sample $(F(1, 187) = .48; p = .62)$; *average age for a second child*, sample with a malformation syndrome child, 5.47 years, sample with cerebral palsy child, 7.00 years, control sample, 5.33 $(F(1, 187) = 1.15; p = .32)$; *average age for a third child*, for sample with a malformation syndrome child, 1.02 years, for sample with a cerebral palsy child, 1.73 years, and for control sample, 1.02 years $(F(1, 187) = .89; p = .41)$. With this matching, the three samples differ only in the presence/absence of handicap and type of handicap (genetic versus nongenetic).

To verify connections among the five resources of the model, step-wise multiple regression analysis was used to consider one-by-one each scale of the RAQ as a dependent variable or criterion, while the other resources were considered as independent variables or predictors. This procedure was followed with the data collected from each sample.

Data analysis using a ISREL procedure yielded the following conclusions. The model derived from these analyses appears consistent with the theoretical assumptions of the model from which the RAQ is derived. According to these results, *Aw* functions as a feedback loop for the other resources. If this result is reliable, the more one is aware of self, of one's experience as well as of logical and cognitive processes and the context encompassing those processes, the more one is likely to express fully one's internal, but relational experiences. This expression possibly allows planning what needs to be done and regulating one's relationships according to overall, contextual influences of one's available resources.

In spite of this overall conclusion, it is important to highlight individual differences among the three samples. For instance, for the sample with a cerebral palsy child, a nongenetic handicap due to birth trauma, *E* does not seem influenced by any of the other resources, placing itself outside of possible regulation. Furthermore, *A* appears as strongly influencing *R* as well as *Aw*. If this conclusion is valid, it would seem that *E* might be a "free" resource, difficult to include in the overall functioning, while *A* seems predominant over *R*. If this is the case, as it appears also in the control group, *Aw* still retains as a corrective, feedback loop function over *R* and *A*.

One can interpret these results if one views parents of a cerebral palsy child who was healthy throughout the pregnancy but born with a handicap due to third party neglect or errors. Hence, *E* assumes a heightened proportion if one were to include in it anger, impotence, hurt, and depression. These feelings tend to linger long after the birth and are not expressed and do not reach *Aw*, remaining denied instead through increased

A and a continuous search to find rehabilitative cures that may "fix" the handicap.

Completely different is the case for parents of malformation syndrome children, a handicap of genetic origin. Here, Aw no longer functions as a feedback loop in relation to the other resources. Here, R dominates over Aw and is influenced, if not supported, by E. Apparently, a diagnosis of a genetic origin for the handicap taps R processes concerning understanding and integrating information about health, genetic laws, and probabilistic concepts usually not relevant to a functional population, and apparently not processed by parents with a cerebral palsy child. Oftentimes, a diagnosis of genetic malformation is reached during pregnancy, when parents find themselves in shock, not expecting to have a handicapped child. It is during this stage that these parents share the pain of an unexpected trauma, being thus able to rely on their rational resources to confront what is arriving at birth.

In sum, the present study verified the circularity of the theoretical model ERAAwC and its capacity to discriminate among different family contexts, identifying which resources are used according to circumstances prevailing at the time of the evaluation.

CONCLUSION

This model fulfills at least three functions. First, it serves as a basis for an understanding of socialization from E to C. It would take too much space to expand on this function, already explained in previous works. Second, this model serves to describe an almost invariant sequence of steps in the process of negotiation, as described in Chapter 17. Third, this model serves as a basis for a classification of theories of personality and therapy. Family therapies, as well as primary prevention programs, can be classified, in turn, according to the ERAAwC components of the model.

From the overall results of studies summarized above, one could conclude that the resource of R acts as a motor for activity in adult life phases. E shows a determinant influence in young adults, perhaps relevant to falling in love and the seeking of a stable partner. C plays a moderating role on A, especially during adolescence. Aw directly moderates E in middle age and continuously attempts to influence C. However, Aw is linked in turn in an almost continuous manner with R.

As noted from the outset, no one resource can claim hegemonic superiority over the other resources. All of them appear necessary to function at an adult level. The RAQ, used to evaluate the model, showed not only acceptable statistical strengths, but demonstrated further that it can be used as a diagnostic tool with functional and dysfunctional populations. If diagnoses reached by the RAQ are valid and reliable, specific preventive, prescriptive, and therapeutic interventions can be planned accordingly, through workbooks and specific therapeutic tasks that foster emotional availability through the sharing of hurts and being together through prolonged hugging, holding, huddling, and cuddling (Ch. 16).

Chapter 5

The Verticality of Relationships
A Depth Model[2]

*"There is an urgent need for more complex and sophisticated models
for understanding how individuals develop. . . . models that consider the
operation of multiple factors and their interaction over time, and that
identify the causal process(es) that underlie relations between
experiential events and child development* (Cummings et al., 2000,
pp. 35–36)."

The purpose of this chapter is to view relationships vertically in terms of
different levels of analysis, observation, and interpretation below the superficial, first-blush level of impression formation and management. This model
distinguishes among descriptive and explanatory levels and sublevels. It has
not been tested and is called metatheoretical because it goes above and beyond the theory itself, just like the preceding one. Furthermore. it belongs
to various theories, independent from this one, most reviewed in previous
works. This model pertains to levels of observation and interpretation, how
to look at relationships and how to make sense of them. Although relationships may be considered in their extensionality from internal to external, as
described in the previous model (Ch. 4), this model pertains more to the
deep, multilayered or multileveled dimension of relationships, intimate or
otherwise.

Levels of analysis/interpretation are helpful in understanding how people present themselves to others or to therapists, either to make a very
poor impression ("I am really sick") or to make a very positive impression

("I am ok ... I am normal. It's my partner or our child who is sick"). In addition, it is important to understand discrepancies among the various levels, i.e., how an addict may consider himself "good and healthy" while his codependent wife is "sick" because "she is depressed" and overdependent on the addict, who is not "depressed."

Levels of analysis, that is, the depth of behavior, or verticality, is interpreted through two descriptive and two explanatory levels. Descriptive levels include: (1) the presentational, external facade, how we manage to appear in public, and (2) the phenotypic, how we behave in the safety and privacy of our homes, away from external observation and possible judgment. An individual may want to appear as a "nice" guy with his superior but behaves like a sob with his subordinates or with his family members. A couple may appear lovey-dovey in public but fight like cats and dogs in the privacy of their home. Both levels can be observed and recorded, if we are allowed to observe them over time to make sense of them.

No formal, testable model has been derived or produced as yet from these levels of analysis/interpretation, perhaps because one might not be needed. However, there is no reason why these levels should not be formalized further in the future.

BEYOND AND BELOW IMPRESSION FORMATION AND MANAGEMENT

Model[2] discriminates among two major levels, descriptive and explanatory. Each level is divided into two other sublevels.

Description

Description of relationships means that both intimate and nonintimate relationships are visible to the naked eye and to the ear. It is based completely on Activity (*A*), talk and actions and no other component of Model[1] (ERAAwC). Relationships can be recorded or audio- or video-taped directly, without inferences or hypotheses. Description can either be public, including how a relationship is presented to outside observers ("I am a nice person with a nice marriage and nice children"), or more private, with *phenotypic* aspects that may be hidden from the self, from intimate others, and from public observation and even measurement. What really happens in the secrecy and privacy of one's residence? The publicly "nice" person may actually become a nasty partner privately, and a nasty parent with nasty children inside the home.

The public/presentational versus private/phenotypic distinction is supported in part by Hussong's (2000a, b, c) peer control model. She distinguished between overt versus covert behavioral and verbal controls. Evidence to support this distinction has been reviewed previously.

Presentational Sublevel

The first *descriptive* sublevel is *presentational*, what is visible and immediate, to the point of being photographed, audio-taped, or video-recorded. This sublevel is short-lived, superficial, public, and includes a social facade, consisting of impression formation and management (Burgoon & Bacue, 2003; Metts & Grohskopf, 2003). The aim of self-presentation is to behave according to socially desirable norms, where self-deception and impression management seem to be the two major components (Sabourin, Bourgeois, Gendreau, & Morval, 1989), supporting the social, interpersonal orientation of self-presentation, and in this case orientation in intimate relationships (Leary, 1979; Reis & Gruzen, 1976). Indeed, special characteristics of nonverbal behaviors are more difficult to suppress and are more accessible to observers than those who produce them. Consequently, the intention to produce a particular nonverbal expression for self-presentational purposes cannot always be successfully translated into the actual production of that expression (DePaulo, 1992). In spite of these difficulties, there is no question that this sublevel does exist even when some people desire to make the worst rather than the best possible impression.

Self-presentation implies that individuals are motivated to make a preferred impression on real or imagined audiences. Hence, cognitive rather than affective antecedents may be influential in trying to make "a good impression" (Himmelfarb, 1972; Schlenker & Leary, 1982). Indeed, another term used to describe self-presentation is "impression management," where strategies to make an impression on others and possibly influence their reactions could be subdivided into "defensive and assertive." The former or protective strategy, seeks to avoid blame or disapproval, while the latter attempts to gain approval, credit, or social power by approaching the relationship. Self-presentation may be related to social approval because of the material rewards contingent upon social approval and not because approval is inherently valuable (Jellison & Gentry, 1978). These strategies are similar to those advanced by Higgins (1997) in terms of promoting and protective strategies in approach-avoidance. Assertive strategies include supplication, ingratiation, self-promotion, and intimidation (Friedlander & Schwartz, 1985). Positive impression formation has been attributed repeatedly to physical attractiveness and, incorrectly, to sex-role stereotypes (Hill & Lando, 1976).

An important differentiation needs to be made between impression management and self-presentation. Although the literature ascribes or attributes conscious awareness of how one wants to impress others, self-presentation, as conceived in this model, also possesses aspects that are outside the realm of awareness, "unconscious" if you will. Many people are not aware of how they appear to others and others have no awareness of their motivation, especially in intimate relationships. As Leary and Kowalsky (1990) defined it, "Impression management, the process by which people control the impressions others form of them, plays an important role in interpersonal behavior (p. 34)." Here, one adds that this process has also an important role in intimate relations. Leary and Kowalsky conceptualized this process as being composed of two discrete subprocesses. The first component involves impression *motivation*, the extent in which we want to control how other see us in terms of goal-relevance, value of desired outcomes, and discrepancy between current and desired images. The second component involves impression *construction* in terms of self-concept, desired and undesired identity images, role restraints, target's values, and current social image.

Phenotypic Sublevel

This sublevel examines how we relate in private, under the stress of intimate relationships. This level is of great importance to this theory, this is where the "real" personality is shown and shared, in the heat of closeness, time, and commitment. This is the arena where this work is focused. Here is where positive, constructive as well as negative and destructive relationships take place, in the privacy of one's home, away from the public scrutiny, and safeguarded within the realms of personal and private. Even though some illustrations will be given here, additional sources will be included below, in the historical/developmental sublevel, and in Chapters 10, 11, and 12.

The connection between presentational and phenotypic sublevels can be minimal or completely reversed. What is presented publicly (outwardly) may be fairly consistent with what happens inside the privacy of one's home. Or else, this connection can be extremely inconsistent, for instance, nice on the outside publicly and nasty on the inside privately. By the same token, this connection, conceivably, could be reversed, nasty on the outside and nice on the inside, with all possible consistencies and inconsistencies in between the public and the private. For instance, Activity (doing and saying), in the ERAAwC model, is visible at the public level, while E is present but not always accessible at the presentational level. Indeed, the face ("Facework") may be the major source of information about how we present ourselves to others (Cupach & Metts, 1994).

Explanation

The explanatory level is what is used to make sense of both descriptive, pre-sentational and phenotypic levels, by stressing determinants of *A*. It includes the other four components of Model[1], ERAwC. They are the determinants, sometimes inferred, sometimes hypothetical, and sometimes attributed, of *A*.

The two explanatory levels are less visible, observable, and record-able than the presentational sublevel. The same applies to the phenotypical sublevel, even though it could be observable if hidden TV monitors were included in the home. They need to be inferred usually from self-report, paper-and-pencil tests rather than observed directly. Explanation is subdi-vided into genotypic and historic sublevels.

Genotypic Sublevel

The first, the genotypic level, involves how the individual sees him- or her-self, a process that involves self-concepts like self-esteem, internal working models, ego, etc. This level is not only inferred but it is also hypothetical, because, as far as one knows, no one has ever photographed or video-taped a person's self-esteem or similarly internal or intrapsychic constructs. We use paper-and-pencil, self-report tests to infer such traits. This is the level favored by most trait theorists (McCrae & Costa, 1997) that includes a variety of internal inferred conditions, like the Big Five Factors model, that supposedly "explain" the behavior of an individual at the two previous levels: "He killed his wife because he was extroverted, neurotic, posses-sive, insecure, etc." This sublevel includes hypothetical (id, ego, superego), attributed and ascribed needs (drive, motivation), or inferred traits (extrover-sion, open-mindedness, etc.), self-representations, and attributions (Forsyth, 1980; Harter, 1990; Safran, Segal, Hill, & Whiffen, 1990).

Various theorists have hypothesized a plethora of genotypic, explana-tory constructs, self-concept, self-esteem, identity, id, ego, superego, etc. Those with some empirical support will be considered below. Most geno-typic constructs consist of attributions we ask respondents to make about themselves, their self-worth, self-concept, and self-esteem, among other con-structs (Harvey & Galvin, 1984). Other explanatory constructs have been based on feelings. Which of these explanatory constructs will survive will be based on their relationships within a theoretical framework, the weight of empirical evidence, and the test of time.

Sources cited below cannot be considered exhaustive because a review of the literature on each of these constructs would require much more space than is possible here or anywhere else.

Self-Concept. The weak theoretical basis of this ubiquitous construct is bound to produce paradoxical results. For instance, highly creative males tend to give self-concept responses similar to those of minimally creative females, while highly creative females tend to have the lowest level of self-concept (Whiteside, 1977). This construct will be revisited in Chapter 10, where it will be equated with or renamed as identity differentiation.

Self-Efficacy. This construct relates more to expectations than solely to self-efficacy itself, which might be difficult to measure (Goldfried & Robins, 1982). Nonetheless, positive bonds with parents seem positively related with self-efficacy (Mallinckrodt, 1992).

Self-Esteem. I have criticized this construct in previous publications as being nonrelational, and not being part of any specific theory. Hence, it is ubiquitous theoretically, with no specific links to any given theory or model, and (worst!), it is nonrelational. In addition to those arguments, Baumeister, Smart, and Boden (1996) supported those arguments. Criminals have higher self-esteem than normals! Furthermore, we do not marry on the basis of one's self-esteem or the self-esteem of the spouse-to-be, even though when measured some correlations between levels of self-esteems in couples may be positive. We do not go to a funeral on the basis of our own or the deceased's self-esteem. Those choices, as argued in greater detail in Chapter 12, are made on the basis of how important we feel and how important to us our partner-to-be is or how important the deceased is to us. Nonetheless, self-esteem is the internalized representation of how important we feel relationally.

Apparently, self-esteem can be composed by two factors: a negative one, self-derogation, and a positive one, self-enhancement (Shahani, Dipboye, & Phillips, 1990). Supposedly, males score higher on self-esteem measures than females, but not significantly higher (Kling, Hyde, Showers, & Buswell, 1999; Wilson & Wilson, 1976). Greater parental support and milder punishments may be related to children's higher self-esteem, perhaps more in boys than in girls (Grown, 1980).

For instance, remitted bipolar patients scored the same as normals on a scale of self-esteem, suggesting that one cannot differentiate between normality and psychopathology on the basis of scores on such a self-report, paper-and-pencil test (Winters & Neale, 1985). Assertiveness, by the same token, bears no relationship to self-esteem (Pachman & Foy, 1978). Respondents low in confidence report significantly greater negative affect than respondents high in confidence (Lorr & Wunderlich, 1988). Self-esteem varies in different psychiatric conditions, being lowest in depression (Battle, 1978; Gardner & Oei, 1981), highest in anxiety, and as a whole lower than normals (Silverstone, 1991). Reports of depressive symptomatology increase as the number of prior questionnaires about self-esteem increases (Brody, Stoneman, Millar, McCoy, 1990). It is how individuals experience negative rather then positive characteristics that plays a determining role in the level of self-esteem (Christian, 1978). In spite of this contradictory evidence, measures of self-esteem do seem to correlate with measures of interpersonal behavior (Myhill & Lorr, 1988).

More relevant to intimate relationships, low self-esteem adolescents may view communication with parents as less facilitative than do high self-esteem adolescents (Matteson, 1974). Global self-esteem may be composed of two dimensions, self-liking, as in a sense of social worth, and self-competence, as in a sense of personal efficacy (Tafarodi & Swann, 1995).

Additionally, theorists and researchers in the area of self-perception have used the terms self-concept and self-esteem interachangeably. It is possible to distinguish between the two terms by refining the self-concept as descriptive and self-esteem as valuative (Beane & Lipka, 1980). This distinction is important because here the self-concept is equated with identity (Ch. 10), while self-esteem is the dimension possibly underlying a sense of self-importance (Ch. 12).

Hopelessness. This construct assumes that "latent" attributional diatheses combine with stressors to produce a specific subtype of depression characterized by a specific set of symptoms, and does not apply to depression in general (Spangler, Simons, Monroe, & Thase, 1993). This construct has received a great deal of theoretical and empirical attention, indicating that even children and adolescents scoring high on a scale of hopelessness might be at greater risk not only for suicide and depression but also for overall psychopathology (Kashani, Reid, & Rosenberg, 1989; Wetzel, Margulies, Davis, & Karam, 1980). The same results were found in groups of patients and prisoners, when hopelessness was associated with social desirability (Holden, Mendonca, & Serin, 1989).

A sense of general capability buffers the link of hopelessness to suicidal ideology. Hopelessness is uniquely associated both concurrently and prospectively with symptoms of depression but not anxiety. In spite of correlations with a variety of symptoms, hopelessness failed to predict sadness and low energy levels (Alloy & Clements, 1998). Nonetheless, there is the possibility that there may be two types (among many) of depression, one associated with hopelessness, and one without such association (Alloy, Abramson, Metalsky, & Hartlage, 1988; Metalsky & Joiner, 1997). Failure to support such a differentiation suggests the possibility of a continuum of hopelessness rather than a category or subtype of hopelessness (Whisman & Pinto, 1997). When hopelessness and self-esteem are combined to predict depressive states in respondents with negative explanatory styles, this combination seems to have greater predictive validity (Abela, 2002).

Learned Helplessness. This model maintains that a negative attributional style may be at the bottom of many psychopathological conditions, especially depression. Depressed respondents with low self-esteem scores make more internal characterlogical attributions for bad events than other groups. Nondepressed respondents make more internal behavioral attributions than depressed respondents (Stoltz & Galassi, 1989). Expectations of response ineffectiveness (Simkin, Lederer, & Seligman, 1983) or frustration theory (Levis, 1980) may mediate learned helplessness, even though doubts have been expressed about both explanations (McReynolds, 1980). This variable is associated with causal attributions and coping strategies (Mikulincer, 1989), and with vulnerability to depressed mood (Hunsley, 1989). Learned helpless explanatory style is associated with unpopularity in children (Aydin, 1988) with depressive symptoms who demonstrate an attributional style similar to depressed adults (Bodiford, Eisenstadt, Johnson, & Bradlyn, 1988). This model (called a theory by its author and others) has been seen as inadequate in accounting for evidence in the etiology of psychopathology and its generalization to other behaviors (Miller & Norman, 1979).

It is unfortunate that both hopelessness and helplessness models have been couched according to negative valences. It would have helped to expand both models in positive terms, like hopefulness and helpfulness and study the impact of both on fully functioning individuals in their intimate relationships.

Feelings. Confronting and dealing directly with feelings, and especially painful feelings, as discussed in Chapter 16, may have direct health promoting consequences. Just approaching and confronting what has been avoided (denied, repressed, and suppressed), i.e., exposure, may in itself produce changes in how those painful feelings are eventually perceived. The duration of exposure may in itself be a beneficial effect in well-functioning individuals, as shown by Pennebaker's writing paradigm (2001; Lepore & Smyth, 2002). In dysfunctional individuals, however, one needs to make sure that such confrontations occur under controlled conditions, providing well-rehearsed alternatives are precedently available to such exposure.

Among the many feelings (E) that have been postulated as determinants of relationships are guilt (Baumeister, Stillwell, & Heatherton, 1994), guilt and shame as predictors of dissociative tendencies (Irwin, 1998), "insecurity in search of security" (Karpman, 1996), and hurts (Ch. 16). A general but unspecified level of distress may be included among feelings (Coyne, 1994; Fincham, Beach, & Bradbury, 1989; Krain & Kendall, 2000; Pulakos, 1996).

Resiliency or the ability to withstand adversities and traumas (Bonanno, 2004) resides somewhere inside the individual, in order to literally fight illness and mortality (Ray, 2004). Whatever survival mechanisms, by whatever name, the ability to survive and to enjoy life with a sense of mastery over oneself seems the core of a positive genotype. Any other negative explanatory construct may well produce defective outcomes in relationships. Whether this genotype includes a sense of identity differentiation (Ch. 10) remains to be seen.

Another Viewpoint. A completely different position is taken here as far as the genotype is concerned. Instead of self-esteem, hopelessness, or helplessness, feelings, etc., one's hurt feelings (Ch. 16), as well as differentiation in identity (Ch. 10), styles in intimate relationships (Ch. 11) and one's sense of importance (Ch. 12) are responsible factors for how one behaves in intimate and nonintimate relationships. All the assumed genotypes plus all previous hypothetical traits or states listed above are related in one way or another to how one deals with hurt feelings, how one defines and differentiates self-identity, and how important one feels with or without intimate others. Here is where the analogy of personality as an artichoke, used in the Preface, seems useful to illustrate the point that underneath the leaves of the artichoke, that is, the presentational sublevel, styles in intimate relationships and selfhood at the phenotypic sublevel, and identity differentiation at the genotypic sublevel, one would also find how one deals with what is underneath the choke of sadness, anger, or rage, that is: hurt feelings (Ch. 16).

Historic: Intergenerational/Developmental/Situational Sublevel

The historic, explanatory sublevel consists of intergenerational, generational, and developmental events underlying the transmission of particular relationship styles or symptoms from one generation to another, including the present situation in the family of procreation (Seifer, Sameroff, Dickstein, & Keitner, 1996; Serbin & Karp, 2004).

This subordinate sublevel, not without controversy (Featherstone, 1979; Freeman, 1976; Wortman & Silver, 1989), "explains" the other three sublevels better than any observable relationships at the presentational and phenotypic sublevels or inferred traits or states at the genotypic sublevel. Here is where past, early traumas, illnesses, painful and joyful events help to explain how one relates with intimate others later on in life. A history of previous exposure (i.e., approach) to traumatic events, for instance, may be associated with greater risk for posttraumatic stress disorder (PTSD) later on in life (Breslau, Chilcoat, Kessler, & Davis, 1999). Maternal expectations may be translated into specific maternal behaviors that may become significant in a child's psychosocial adjustment (Nover, Shore, Timberlake, & Greenspan, 1984). Early family variables of life stress and child and maternal characteristics may be keys in subsequent child functioning, with spousal support playing a minor role (Abidin, Jenkins, & McGaughey, 1992). Even disorders in infancy, conceptualized as "relational psychopathologies," may be the outcome of parent-child-environment transactions (Cicchetti, 1987).

Crude rates of intergenerational transmission of child abuse suggest that one third of child victims grow up to continue a pattern of seriously inept, neglectful, or abusive rearing as parents. One-third do not. The other one-third remain vulnerable to the effects of social stress on the likelihood of their becoming abusive parents. Intrafamilial, rather than culturally condoned, factors appear to be the cause of personally directed child abuse. Broad social factors and some medical and psychiatric conditions may lower or raise thresholds in which family and personal vulnerabilities and propensities operate (Oliver, 1993).

More specifically, behavioral genetics suggests that the shared environment, including parental monitoring and discipline, may be important in the development and outcome of externalizing disorders (Ch. 8). Differential parental treatment of one sibling may be critical in the development and outcome of internalizing disorders (Ch. 7). Criticism, as measured by expressed emotions (Chs. 4 and 12) may be associated with poor outcome of many childhood medical and psychiatric disorders, and with difficulties in adhering to treatment. Chronic illness in a child may change the family dynamics toward becoming more structured and less emotionally warm and communicative. Families can cause problems. However, often these problems are in reaction to a child's problems (Wamboldt & Wamboldt, 2000).

The relationship among all four sublevels of analysis and interpretation can be illustrated, for instance, by the "impostor phenomenon," that is, an internal feeling of incompetence about deceiving others about one's abilities. Characteristically, individuals who present themselves with a need to look smart to others (presentational sublevel) report being more anxious and are considered introverted (phenotypic sublevel), with a propensity for shame about being an impostor (in spite of evidence to the contrary) at the genotypic sublevel. Most of them report a conflicted and nonsupportive family background (historical sublevel). This phenomenon may be the result of seeking self-esteem (self-importance in this theory) by trying to live up to an idealized self-image to compensate for feelings of insecurity and self-doubt at the genotypic sublevel (Langford & Clance, 1993).

Birth Order and Family Size. Here is where *Context*, in the ERAAwC model (Ch. 4), is omnipresent, as perceived and interpreted internally by respondents and externally by observers. Whether the family is the most important context in determining future behavior in the child depends on whether the family is still defined traditionally or nontraditionally, as well as culturally or otherwise (Uzoka, 1979). Yet, most of the evidence suggests that healthy families will tend to produce healthy offspring and that unhealthy families will tend to produce unhealthy offspring (Keitner, Ryan, Miller, & Kohn, 1995).

At the very least, the family apparently is partially responsible for the intellectual level achieved by its offspring (Berbaum & Moreland, 1980; Breland, 1977). However, this is still a controversial antecedent condition with inconsistent findings depending on the method of measurement; the family may well affect intellectual functioning more than any other personal characteristic (Majoribanks, 1976; Majoribanks & Walberg, 1975; Zajonc, 1976; Zajonc & Markus, 1975; Zajonc, Markus, & Markus, 1979). Birth order might be positively related to intellectual performance. Firstborns may be at lower risk than lastborns of being psychiatrically disturbed, and, regardless of any given family size, may tend to be least capable intellectually. Members of smaller families may tend to: (1) be more capable intellectually; (2) experience less school failure; and (3) be taller than children of larger family size. Only children do not seem to share these advantages (Belmont, 1978). Lastborns in large families, and especially males, may have a greater tendency to become alcoholics than firstborns (Blane & Barry, 1973).

Generational and Intergenerational Transmission. In spite of methodological difficulties in evaluating generational and intergenerational family reports and ratings (Brewin, Andrews, & Gotlib, 1993; Carpenter, 1984), it is possible to make comparisons between ethnic groups (Cromer, 1978), that evaluate generational gaps, indicating the importance of the perceived degree of mutual understanding, frequency and type of discussion, and restrictions versus freedom of expression. Of course, extra-familial stressors, like unemployment, low socioeconomic status, and ethnic origin may be considered as factors that affect the other three sublevels (Webster-Stratton, 1990a, 1990b). Psychopathology in men with multigenerational family histories of alcoholism is quite prevalent (Finn, Kleinman, & Pihl, 1990).

Child maltreatment is apparently transmitted generationally, suggesting also that women who were sexually abused as children would expose their children to molestation later in life. This equation, making the victim into a persecutor (Stanton, 1999), will be discussed in greater detail in Chapters 11 and 15. Families of schizophrenics, among others, fail to see generationally appropriate family relationships (Walsh, 1979).

Developmental Losses and Traumatic Childhood Experiences. Parental death and especially death of the mother in ones childhood is certainly one of the major antecedents of later psychopathology (Kendler, Neale, Kessler, & Heath, 1992; Ragan & McGlashan, 1986; Roy, 1985; Tennant, 1988). These traumas may include: visualized or otherwise repeatedly perceive memories of a past traumatic event, repetitive behaviors, trauma-specific fears, and changed attitudes toward people. Type I trauma includes full, detailed memories and misperceptions, while Type II trauma includes denial and numbing, self-hypnosis, and dissociation (Terr, 1991).

Even the death of grandparents or being adopted relates to some degree of pathology (Stasny et al., 1984; Yates, Fullerton, Goodrich, Heinssen et al., 1989). Whether the death of the father affects women more than men remains to be seen (Adams, Milner, & Schrepf, 1994; Lyon & Vanderberg, 1989). There is no question that the role of the father in the healthy development of the child has finally reached its due, after decades of stress on the role of the mother in that development (Marsilio, 1995). Children of schizophrenic mothers tend more so to breakdown after suffering the loss of their mother at an earlier age than children who do not breakdown. Those who broke down tended to also have mentally ill fathers as well as schizophrenic mothers (Mednick, 1973).

When asked to write about past, undisclosed traumas, even seemingly well functioning undergraduate respondents reported Type I or Type II traumas (Pennebaker, 2001). Hence, one can postulate that we all, in some degree or another, are vulnerable to traumas, admittedly in various degrees and forms. Without some painful experience acting as an antidote, we would be more vulnerable than people who would deny entirely such a possibility. Naturally, there is no doubt that some traumas affect and last a lifetime. Adults sexually abused as children, for instance, tend to demonstrate a much higher level of psychopathology than controls (Roesler & McKenzie, 1994). Positive appraisal by parents of their children in comparison to parents with negative appraisals has definite consequences on children (Pickett, Cook, Cohler, & Solomon, 1997). Again, this particular area will be reviewed in greater detail in Chapter 11.

Homeless men report poverty ("scarce family resources") and conflictual family relationships are part of their childhood experiences (Susser, Struening, & Conover, 1987). Depressed individuals are two and a half times more at risk than nondepressed individuals to develop severe psychopathology (Shrout, Link, Dohrenwend, Skodol, et al., 1989).

Sickness. Hypochondriac patients report being sick as children and missing school for health reasons more than nonhypochondriacs (Barsky, Wool, Barnett, & Cleary, 1994).

Parenting. This is an extremely complex construct that is difficult to measure and evaluate, because there are at least four factors that need consideration: (1) quality of the parent-child attachment; (2) ability of parents to perceive and respond to the needs of the child; (3) ability to transmit the values of the culture; and (4) overt and covert parental rejection (Steinhauer, 1983). The latter factors tend to support the levels of description and explanation of this model. A parent may seem to accept a child at one sublevel, either presentational or phenotypic, yet at a phenotypic sublevel wish that the child were never born.

Parental acceptance may have an effect as late as adolescence, when competence in boys may be predicted by paternal but not maternal acceptance, while the opposite pattern may exist in girls. Self-worth may significantly predict maternal and paternal acceptance for both boys and girls (Ohonnessian, Lerner, Lerner, & VonEye, 1998). Here is where parental practices impinge on the offspring genotype, such as self-worth.

Parental style could be conceived as the context that moderates the influence of specific parenting practices on the child (Darling & Steinberg, 1993). Whether this distinction has been followed in the literature remains to be seen. It may be meritorious if one were to distinguish between what parents think or say they do with their children, at the presentational sublevel, and what they really do at the phenotypic sublevel, let alone how they feel at the genotypic sublevel.

There is no doubt that parenting has a powerful effect on later development (de Figueiredo, Boerstler, & O'Connell, 1991). Because of its importance, it should not be assumed that we all can become parents without any preparation, only on the basis of what we have learned from our parents. Only to a modest degree do people learn to be parents directly from their parents (Gelso, Birk, & Powers, 1978). Unfortunately for our children and for our society, learning to drive a car is subjected to greater controls than learning to become a parent. Even feelings of parental caring may predict health status in midlife (Russek & Schwartz, 1997). However, perceptions of parenting received in childhood and the quality of current intimate relationships may become relevant only when there has been extreme deprivation of parental care. Only in that case, current intimate relationships in adults were more likely to be rated as "uncaring" (Parker, Barrett, & Hickie, 1992).

Parenting is composed of discipline and nurturance (Locke & Prinz, 2002), constructs that are similar to dimensions considered in Chapter 9 in terms of agency and communion respectively. Discipline relates to a dimension of power and agency, while nurturance relates to a dimension of communion. In psychotherapy both constructs can be related to dimensions of structuring (agency) and responsiveness (communion) (L'Abate, 1986). Communion will be considered in greater detail in Chapter 7, while agency will be considered in greater detail in Chapter 8. Both will be considered in Chapter 9.

Negative parenting, especially the father's, may be more predictive of PTSD when combined with relatively lower levels of combat exposure in grown children in the military (McCranie, Hyer, Boudewyns, & Woods, 1992). Whether parental socialization practices are different for boys or girls remains an open question according to the culture. In North America, for instance, the main socialization practice may consist of fostering sex-type activities. In other countries, physical punishment seems to be applied significantly more to boys than to girls (Lytton & Romney, 1991). Whether parental practices are related to temperamental, i.e., genetic or attitudinal factors derived from one's family of origin, is a possibility that needs further definition of "temperament" and "genetic influences" (Kendler, 1996), above and beyond what is generated from the immediate context.

More specifically: (1) extremely competent children are never the product of extremely noninvolved care taking; (2) instrumental competence is facilitated by firm parental control; (3) nonconforming parenting is associated with compliant and withdrawn behavior in offspring; (4) parental warmth is not directly related to instrumental competence; and (5) willingness to train the child cognitively (rather than emotionally or reactively) is highly associated with outstanding competence in the child (Baumrind, 1975).

Depending on a sequence of three practices (making rules, enforcing rules, and punishment) in parents of disturbed teenagers, four disciplinary configurations seem possible: (1) restrictive-loose-lenient; (2) permissive-tight-lenient; (3) restrictive-harsh-tight; and (4) undeveloped. Corresponding pathological behaviors in the teenagers that may relate to these configurations could be: (1) externalized-antisocial; (2) internalized-anti-self; (3) internalized-neurotic-symptomatic, and (4) withdrawn-reclusive (Singer, 1974). These four configurations will be expanded in Chapter 12 in relationship to a selfhood model based on one's sense of importance.

"Firm control" may suggest the child's willingness to obey rather than the parent's tendency to exercise control. The behavior of well-socialized children may be due to variables that accompany firm control rather than to firm control per se. Deleting firm control from authoritative parenting does not seem associated with less well-socialized behavior in the child (Lewis, 1981). Unfortunately, where does firm control end and overreactive/harsh parenting begin? Lax or permissive parenting may interact inconsistently with overreaction on the mother's side (Smith & O'Leary, 1995).

As discussed in greater detail in Chapter 10, socioeconomic status (SES) may be an important determinant of parenting. In economically deprived families, for instance, the mother alone may entail the highest risk for social maladjustment and psychological well-being in the child. However, the presence of significant other adults in the family, like a grandmother, in addition to a father or stepfather, may reduce this risk. Absence of the father may be less important than the aloneness of the mother in regard to subsequent risk in the child (Kellam, Ensminger, & Turner, 1978).

In addition to SES, ethnicity and gender may also determine the nature of parenting. Following Baumrind's (1980) influential classification of parental practices as autocratic, authoritative, permissive, and unengaged, which, parenthetically, could be related to the selfhood model mentioned above (L'Abate, 1997), as predicted from that model: authoritative parenting may yield best outcomes in children, while unengaged parenting may yield the worst outcomes, with permissive and autocratic parenting styles producing intermediate results, regardless of SES and ethnicity (Radziszewska, Richardson, Dent, & Flay, 1996).

Emotions may play an important part in whether parenting is going to results in positive or negative processes. When invested in the interests of children, emotions may organize sensitive, responsive parenting. Extreme inconsistencies in either too weak or too strong, or poorly matched to child-rearing tasks may undermine parenting. In harmonious relationships, positive emotions tend to allow parents to manage interactions in ways that both the parents' and the children's interests are promoted. In distressed relationships, chronic negative emotions may be both causes and consequences of interactions that undermine parental concerns and children's development (Dix, 1991).

The quality of parenting may leave a powerful imprint in the memory of many people, at least in women (Parker & Barnett, 1988). There is no question that parenting may be affected by the nature of the marital or caretaking couple relationship. Expressivity versus instrumentality (communion and agency by different names?) two major dimensions of parenting, may in themselves produce differences between parenting partners and the way parenting will take place (Klein & Shulman, 1980).

Marital Satisfaction. There are two hypotheses about the assumed link between marital satisfaction, parent-child behavior, and the child's behavior. A positive link would support a "spillover" hypothesis, while a negative linkage would support a "compensatory" hypothesis. A meta-analysis of 68 studies seems to support the spillover hypothesis, indicating that the link between marital and parent-child behavior is a "stable force" in determining the child's behavior in the future (Erel & Burman, 1995). Of course, parents' perceptions of their children's level of activity, persistence, and emotional intensity may be related to the child's adjustment (Brody, Stoneman, & Burke, 1988).

Once marital satisfaction is defined in terms of two orthogonal factors, positive interactions and negative sentiments, there may be marked differences on both dimensions over three generations, with the youngest generation highest on both positive and negative factors. The oldest generation may show moderately low levels of positive interaction but even lower scores on negative sentiment (Gilford & Bengston, 1979). Of course, marital satisfaction itself may be determined by personality patterns in both partners, determining in great part how parenting is going to occur (Abidin, 1992).

Absence of, Inadequate, or Abusive Parenting. Inadequate or abusive aspects of parenting will be considered in greater detail in Chapter 11. There is no question that paternal absence, either imagined or real, temporally or emotionally, has an adverse effect on children (Boss, 1977; Epstein & Radin, 1976; Henderson, 1980; Oshman & Manosevitz, 1976; Santrock, 1977).

Divorce. Separation and divorce can yield traumatic effects, particularly when children are at an early age and have already established emotional ties with their parents, especially if the father is the one who leaves the marriage (Hoyt, Cowen, Pedro-Carroll, & Alpert-Gillis, 1990). Negative effects of divorce are mediated by the overall adjustment level of the child (Kurdek, Blisk, & Siesky, 1981). If conflict between parents continues after the divorce, it will have an adverse effect on the children (Forehand, McCombs, Long, Brody, et al., 1988; Long, Slater, Forehand, & Fauber, 1988).

Body boundaries in prepubescent children of divorce tend to persist even years after the original family breakup (Spigelman & Spigelman, 1991). It is questionable whether divorce in and of itself may be solely responsible for the lower level of adjustment of children of divorce. Pre-divorce level of adjustment, perhaps due to predivorce parental conflicts, needs to be taken into consideration (Kelly, 2000), as well as the amount and kind of predivorce preparation do have an effect on the child (Jacobson, 1978). Whether boys are more negatively affected by the divorce than girls remains to be seen (Zaslow, 1988).

The failure of many fathers to remain involved with the children after the divorce is an important area to explore. Ihinger-Tallman, Pasley, and Buehler (1995) developed a model (actually called a theory!) to explain this failure to remain involved on the part of the father. Basic to this model is the sense of identity as a father. If this identity is salient over other identities (as a bread-winner, worker), many other variables being equal (which are usually not), the father may keep his parental role in spite of negative factors, like the former wife's interference, the number of children in the family, etc. This model is one of many that have been developed, once it was understood that the mother could not and should not be made responsible for all the ills of her children (Cath, Gurwitt, & Gunsberg, 1989).

The Sibling Bond. From a historical, explanatory sublevel viewpoint, this is the longest lasting relationship that can have profound influences at supraordinate levels of analysis and observation over a lifetime. Siblings may collude and align with each other at times when both resist the powerful influence of parents. Other sibling systems may serve to enmesh siblings even more with parents. Important sib-behavior patterns include: (1) death or departure of siblings; (2) interplay between the sibling subsystem and the parenting system; and (3) the roles that "well" siblings play in relationship to their "sick" siblings during family crises (Bank & Kahn, 1976). Competitive and reactive rivalry during childhood may transform itself into cooperative and loving involvement in adulthood and especially old age.

APPLICATIONS OF MODEL^2 TO LEVELS OF INDIVIDUAL RELATIONSHIPS

Hypothetical examples of relationships according to individual levels of functioning will be given below to illustrate how this model can be applied to nonclinical and clinical relationships.

Example of a Superior Individual

Descriptively, at the presentational sublevel, a superior individual is one who is considerate and respectful of intimate and nonintimate others, and is straight and honest in how he or she deals with them. This person would be functioning at a superior level not only in his or her family and work but also in other settings, as will be explained in the next chapter. He or she is optimistic about him- or herself and others and lives for the present and future (Vaughn, 2000). He or she has learned from past errors and has let go of painful, past experiences, using these experiences to improve the nature of his or her intimate relationships.

At the phenotypic sublevel, relationships with intimates would be characterized by the same style of consideration, respectfulness, cooperation, and intimacy with loved ones. Explanatorily, at the genotypic sublevel, this individual would feel sure of him- or herself, with clear articulate feelings, a positive sense of self, clear boundaries about who he or she is, considering him- or herself as hopeful and helpful. At the historical level, this individual grew up in a middle to upper-class family where loving, cooperative, and harmonious relationships were the norm, and where feelings, both positive and negative, were accepted as natural and necessary in their expression.

Example of a Semifunctional Individual

Descriptively, at the presentational sublevel, this individual could appear superficially to be jolly, gentle, sociable, and friendly in short-lived social encounters, trying hard to make a good impression on nonintimate others in the occupational arena. At the phenotypic sublevel, in the privacy of one's home, the social facade is gone to leave occasionally irritable and nasty behavior at home with family members. As an explanation, at the genotypic sublevel, this individual is anxious and fearful, slightly insecure with doubts about him- or herself. At the historical developmental level, he or she grew up in insecure family relations, the father frequently away from home, the mother slightly depressed with some sibling rivalry, dropping out at the high school level and unable to complete a college education, but becoming a blue-collar worker in spite of a higher educational level in the family of origin.

Example of a Clinical Individual

Descriptively, at the presentational sublevel, this individual was diagnosed in elementary school as having attention deficit disorder and was administered Ritalin on a routine basis. At the phenotypic sublevel, as an adult he or she learned to depend on intimate and nonintimate others, being unable to succeed educationally and occupationally, becoming a diagnosable dependent personality. At the genotypic sublevel, this individual may deny or suffer from an undiagnosed clinical or subclinical depression. At the historic-developmental sublevel, this individual grew up with a great deal of parental conflict, depression in one parent, drivenness in the other, a great deal of sibling rivalry, with many failures in the educational and occupational arenas.

Example of a Severely Clinical Individual

At the presentational sublevel, this individual tries to make the worst possible impression, possibly through drug addiction to self-medicate, contradictory and inconsistent extreme behaviors, as in bipolar disorder or schizophrenia, with frequent hospitalizations and/or incarcerations. At the phenotypical level, he or she is homeless, with no visible means of self-support, keeping distant from relatives and loved ones. At the genotypic sublevel there are extreme feelings of alienation, hopelessness, helplessness, with chaotic and confused feelings, thoughts, and ruminations. At the historic sublevel, this individual grew up with a father in prison and a mother drug-addicted and manic-depressed, siblings varied in their functioning from borderline to semifunctional, to completely dysfunctional.

IMPLICATIONS AND FUNCTIONS OF MODEL[2]

This model is integrative of past knowledge by presenting how intimate relationships are formed and consolidated: from a first, superficial impression in self-presentation to a more genuine phenotypic sublevel and on to deeper historic sublevels.

Diagnostically we need to ask about intimate relationships along various levels and sublevels of observation and interpretation. What we see is not always what we get, and what we get is not always what we are allowed to see.

Prescriptively, we need to consider what level of observation and interpretation needs to be addressed and prescribed. Therapeutically, again one needs to expand interventions not only at various levels and sublevels of observation and interpretation but also at the individual, dyadic, or familial level. There needs to be a climate where greater self-disclosure is encouraged until one shares one's history and one's family of origin, either verbally, f2f, or in writing at a distance.

CONCLUSION

Intimate relationships are not always what they seem or appear to be at the surface. They occur at various levels of analysis, observation, and interpretation. We need to look underneath them to find how and why we relate the way we do, positively, negatively, and in between. We may relate one way at one level but in another way at a lower level. The congruency of both levels may be determined by internal factors, that in turn are determined by our history, how we have been nurtured by our caretakers, and how we reacted to them.

Chapter 6

Settings as Contexts for Intimate Relationships
Model³

100. Superior functioning in a wide range of activities, life's problems never seem to get out of hand, is sought by others because of his or her many positive qualities. No symptoms.

90. Absent or minimal symptoms (e.g., mild anxiety before an exam) good functioning in all areas, interested in a wide range of activities, socially effective, generally satisfied with life, no more than everyday problems or concerns (e.g., an occasional argument with family members).

80. If symptoms are present, they are transient and expectable reactions to psychosocial stressors (e.g., difficulty concentrating after family argument), no more than slight impairment in social, occupational, or school functioning (e.g., temporarily falling behind in school work (American Psychiatric Association, 1994, p. 46)."

"*. . . understanding of developmental processes of individuals cannot be finally investigated and understood in isolation from its context* (Bergman, Magnusson, & El-Khouri, 2003, p. 17)."

This chapter will classify settings as contexts for personality socialization in intimate relationships and expand on the criteria for global assessment of functioning given in the DSM-IV above. This goal is achieved by presenting a model that allows a classification of settings as contexts for personality socialization in intimate relationships. In this chapter is where the *C* of the ERAAwC model (Ch. 4) is expanded. Settings are necessary to evaluate and understand personality and psychological functioning in its totality, not just in a vacuum or in the abstraction of a laboratory, but in the very settings that occupy our lives. One could be extremely successful in one setting and a failure in another, depending, of course, on what criteria are used to reach such a conclusion. A marvelous employee at work could be a failure at home. Without settings, personality and psychological functioning in intimate relationships would be evaluated and understood partially or piecemeal.

Furthermore, settings are necessary to evaluate and understand an individual's relationships with intimate and nonintimate others. The latter, like one's boss, may be responsible for the economical and physical well-being. Some bosses, however, and some coworkers could not be held responsible for one's emotional well-being. Psychological, self-report, paper-and-pencil tests are used to evaluate personality functioning in the abstract, how respondents see themselves. Ultimately, however, the major criterion for evaluation of functioning relies on how one acts and talks in various settings.

This model distinguishes among settings in two ways. First, it is possible to classify settings according to the major resource exchanged. For instance, importance (Ch. 12) and intimacy (Ch. 16) are more likely to be found at home than at work. Money is transacted in banks. Information is transacted in educational institutions, media, and libraries. Services are performed in most major settings, while goods are sold in malls and shops. Second, settings can be classified according to four major categories: (1) home, (2) school/work, and surplus time, which is divided into (3) transitory means settings that change over one's life cycle, such as schools, grocery stores, banks, barber shops, beauty salons, shopping malls, restaurants, churches, retail stores, sport arenas, and hotels; and (4) transit settings, used for transportation to move from one setting to another, to survive and to enjoy life, such as cars, buses, planes, trains, roads, highways, parking lots, airports, or train stations.

Settings are objective entities. They can be photographed, depicted, and recorded. Contexts represent the subjective interpretation, the emotional meaning, attachment, or dependency to a setting. Settings as objective entities are qualitatively and quantitatively different from contexts. The latter are differentially and subjectively perceived by multiple observers, self and others, within a given setting. The former are objectively observable and measurable. For instance, one can measure how long one spends on household chores, how long one spends in leisure activities, and so on. The meaning of these activities and settings represents the context as viewed by self and observers. Although one observer may discount the importance of housework, for instance, another may value it as an important contribution to the family well-being and functioning. By the same token, one may spend a great deal of time at work, but not consider it as important as other family activities. Settings as perceived contexts are less easily measured than settings.

Settings function at the macrolevel of observation. Contexts function at the microlevel of observation. This distinction, as well as the use of *Context* in the ERAAwC model, should not be confused as being part of or similar to the many schools of thought that advocate various brands of "contextualism" (Capaldi & Proctor, 1999). If contexts represent the subjective meaning of objective settings, then they can be evaluated as for their meaning to individuals, for instance, by using the semantic differential test, among other possibilities.

Another way to differentiate between settings and contexts can be achieved by considering settings as perceived cognitively, while contexts are perceived affectively. The latter can then be conceptualized according to a two-dimensional bipolar space defined by two major orthogonal axes: pleasant-unpleasant and arousing-sleepy or exciting-gloomy and distressing-relaxing. From these eight dimensions composing a circumplex model (Russell & Pratt, 1980), one could construct a semantic differential that would evaluate the affective-subjective meaning of many settings. However, one is inclined to add at least two other dimensions of warm-cold and important-unimportant to such an instrument.

THE NATURE OF SETTINGS MODEL[3]

The nature of settings needs specification to detail interaction with how individual competencies, abilities, and skills are manifested and used. As mentioned earlier, competence can be specified, even assessed, in a specific setting much more easily than through personality tests. Although personality seems to encompass a wide range of traits and states, most of them internal and difficult to measure, competence is limited to a definite number of settings. It may be a more restricted term than personality. However, it may also be easier to define and measure because, as suggested earlier, the interaction is more specific than person X situation. Person X setting interaction is more specific. For instance, there is a resource class (Ch. 9) X setting interaction to the extent that money, for example, as a resource class, is negotiated in banks, information in school, media, and libraries, services are provided in stores like hospitals and clinics (and now on the Internet), goods are sold in stores (and now on the Internet!), etc. Only in the family all resource classes of love, intimacy, money, information, services, and goods coalesce and supposedly differentiate.

The importance of settings in determining intimate and nonintimate relationships and their interactions has been stressed by ecological psychologists (Moen, Elder, & Luscher, 1995). Each setting has its own pe-culiar, explicit, or implicit rules, consistent or inconsistent, predictable or unpredictable regulations, peculiar requirements or task demands that are setting-specific and that differ from one setting to another. As indicated ear-lier, the three major settings where exchanges take place are: (a) residence; (b) school/work; and (c) surplus time. The latter is divided into survival and leisure time activities, i.e., survival versus enjoyment. All three settings interact and overlap with two other settings, transit and transitory. In some settings both dimensions overlap, as, for instance, in one's residence. Some people have fun at work. Others work very hard in settings that are sup-posed to produce enjoyment, like gyms, parks, and recreational facilities.

Contexts and Competencies

Competencies and abilities vary according to the task requirements of each setting. The number of settings is finite and objectively defined. In order of functional importance, they are, residence, school/work, surplus time (survival and enjoyment), transit and transitory. Of course, there may be overlaps among all five settings. For instance, leisure activities may take place in the home or, in some instances, in work settings as, for example, fitness rooms in workplaces. Competence in one setting does not necessarily predict and transfer to competence in another setting. One could be a terrific parent but a mediocre employee. By the same token, one could be a strong athlete during leisure hours but not function as well at work or at home.

Competence in various settings defines the level of functioning of an individual. Superior functioning, for instance, means being a caring and effective partner and parent, who excels in school or at work and enjoys leisure-time activities after successfully completing survival tasks. By the same token, settings can be used to discriminate adequate from mediocre and inadequate functioning. This differentiation will be elaborated further in Chapter 12.

Boundaries of Settings

In addition to the physical boundaries established by most settings, the space they occupy, there are other boundaries that determine rules of access, entry and exit, for any given setting. Settings vary in rules about their access and their exit. For instance, there may be least four different levels of access and exit;

1. *Completely Open*: Roads, streets, sidewalks, emergency rooms in hospital, and some grocery stores may be the most open or least restrictive of all settings. Yet, even roads, sidewalks, and grocery

stores have some restrictions in regard to acceptable behaviors. If one drives above the speed limit a speeding ticket may be issued. If one crosses the road outside of drawn limits, the jaywalker may get a ticket or become involved in an accident. Emergency rooms in hospitals may operate on a 24-hour, 7-day a week basis, accepting anyone who needs immediate medical attention and who can pay for it. Police stations and some business may operate on 24/7 schedules. Yet, each of them has rules about acceptable behaviors.

2. *Selective*, as in homes where only members of the family, without invitation, and guests with invitation, are allowed in the premises with exceptions for repairs and cleaning personnel, but by appointment only. Schools select students according to age and educational requirements. Some schools accept only students who can pay. Some accept any student who lives within certain geographical limits. Some schools accept only deaf or blind students.

3. *Limited*, as in institutions operating from a 9 to 5 time schedule or by set business hours, schools, banks, business office, etc.

4. *Completely Restricted*, as in penal, military, and certain government institutions that have restricted access, where entry and exit are rigorously controlled.

Settings provide social roles, defined by functions or tasks to be accomplished in each setting. Those functions and tasks are performed in one specific setting and nowhere else, as detailed below.

Residence

"A house is not a home." Where one lives is a physical structure and an address where one or more people lives but that structure and address do not necessarily make it a home. It is also the most private of all settings. One could live in a one-bedroom apartment all week to be close to work but leave on the weekend for what is called "home." A house or a dwelling does not a home make. Thus, by residence is understood a place where one lives most of the time. It may be called "home" if there are feelings attached to it, especially if loved ones live there also.

The household structure in terms of how many caretakers may be present to take care of children may reduce socialization pressures, to the point that more caretakers being present and available may reduce the stress on the major caretaker and give the child the experience of different models. The presence of adults besides the mother may tend to: (1) dilute specific parent-child interactions and demands on children by reducing the amount of exclusive parent-child interaction time; (2) curb a parent's child-directed emotional outbursts, providing some adult targets for relief of inner tensions; (3) allow a parent the choice between adults or children for interaction, and/or (4) provide a more efficient set of co-workers (Munroe & Munroe, 1980). The flip side of this almost idyllic portrayal must also be considered when there are conflicts and disagreements among present adult caretakers that may become violent and acrimonious in the presence of the child, subjecting the child to negative models of relating that may have a lifetime of negative influence.

This setting has task requirements that are related to the maintenance of a family as an emotional unit and to the home as a physical entity. Most responsibilities can be broken down into four specific roles: caretaker, provider, partner, and parent. Each role demands specific skills. For instance, the responsibilities of the *care-taking* role are of two kinds. One refers to the nurturing qualities that deal with love, being present, and emotionally available. The other refers to instrumental qualities that deal with the physical and material well-being of the home, such as cooking, cleaning, purchasing, repairing. The role of *provider* deals with the economic aspects of family living. Salary, income, credit rating, mortgages are aspects of this role. How much money comes into the home and how is it spent? Both caretaker and provider roles depend a great deal on the kind of person one is. How well one functions as a *partner* depends on a variety of personality competencies that will be summarized in the selfhood model to be presented in Chapter 12. In this role, abilities to love and to negotiate are necessary.

The fourth role—*parent*—is probably one of the most difficult and demanding in our lives, not without stress (Deater-Deckard, 1998). Often, this is the role for which we have received little if any training except for what we learned by watching our parents. Most of us perpetuate their errors and may forget their assets because the task requirements of today are different from those of preceding generations. The ability to love and to negotiate become crucial at this stage. Consequently, an appropriate developmental sequence requires first of all the development of personhood as being basic to partnership. Both personhood and partnership are basic to parenthood. Being able to be a partner is basic to being a parent, as discussed in greater detail in Chapter 13. Realistically, very few follow such an orderly sequence.

Childhood housework is an important area of family relationships that may provide many repercussions in later life. It may relate to the development of cooperative behavior, the fostering of responsibility, the nature of parental control or adult-guided learning, acquisition of gender roles, and its relation to SES. Its variability throughout social, cultural, and economic levels makes it difficult at the time to arrive at some definite conclusions about its presumptive values (Goodnow, 1988).

A family's health may well depend on its perception of its own paradigm, that is, the underlying assumptions, convictions, and beliefs that a family holds about its environment. This paradigm is conserved through routine application of pattern regulators, like rituals and ceremonials (Reiss, 1981). The relationship of this paradigm with a selfhood model of personality propensities will be presented in Chapter 18.

Educational Institutions

Schools, like work settings, require two separate but intertwined sets of skills. The first set consists of specific educational/occupational skills that are necessary to perform a job, such as reading, writing, arithmetic, filing, typing, drawing, writing, ditch digging, decision making, delegating, managing, etc. The second set of skills is extra-job, consisting of interpersonal skills to get along with schoolmates, peers, coworkers, superiors, subordinates, clients, or customers. This set of skills may require interpersonal sensitivity, political gamesmanship, and contextual awareness. It may have little to do with the substantive job skills necessary for success. Yet, these skills may make the difference between promotion, stagnation on the job, or being laid off!

Differences in school settings refer to private versus public and urban versus rural schools. Each of these settings includes different cultures and climates, some positive and some negatives. For instance, in the southwest United States, especially small rural schools may stress athletic abilities at the expense of academic ones.

At least in the Western culture, many people identify themselves according to their occupational roles. In fact, this role often may provide the main source of gratification (Axelrod, 1999). Therefore, it may require an investment of energy that would take away from other roles. If we tend to identify ourselves by what we *do* or what we *have* instead of who we *are* as persons, what happens to us when we lose our jobs or retire? Do we have any self left? How does this role (unemployed or retired) interfere with other roles?

Perceptions of a school climate, for instance, in keeping to the distinction between settings and context made above, were related to externalizing and internalizing problems, indicating that the most immediate context, the school, does affect a "broad range of student emotional and behavioral outcomes" (Kuperminc, Leadbeater, & Blatt, 2001; Kuperminc, Leadbeater, Emmons, & Blatt, 1997).

Work

The culture of work settings, especially the world of corporate and large businesses, has changed drastically during the past generation. Whereas in the past century loyalty between a company and its employees was valued, especially in its long-term functions, that loyalty no longer exists (Axelrod, 1999). Recent scandals in the corporate world, and especially the divide between salaries for top managers versus salaries for the "hired help," have reached increasingly extreme and almost ridiculous dimensions, widening the gap between the top echelon and bottom "hired help."

The change in loyalties, the extremely wide salary divide between top management and lower-level employees, recent scandals in white-collar crime, the subsequent loss of retirement income suffered by many employees of failed large business all have produced an increasingly stressful work environment, where no one is sure whether one will be working at the same job for the same company for longer than a year or so, certainly no longer for a lifetime, as in the past. This future perspective from the past is changed drastically now. One cannot plan beyond a few months rather than years as it used to be. The uncertainty in one's work position adds to stresses inherent in the job itself. Hence, the number of job-related casualties has increased noticeably in the past generation (Axelrod, 1999), producing self-help books that address some of the stresses and strains of work (Plas & Hoover-Dempsey, 1988).

Personal and environmental characteristics may lead to vocational choices and career achievements. The interaction of both characteristics may lead to stability/instability in the kind and level of work a person performs. Some people are able to make choices that are congruent with their vocational assessments. However, there are some people who do not (Holland & Gottfredson, 1975). Of course, vocational choices may well be related to personality factors. However, the evidence for this link is questionable (Gottfredson, Jones, & Holland, 1993). Satisfaction with various job characteristics rather than vocational choices may be related to how the quality of life is perceived (Evans, Pellizzari, Culbert, & Metzen, 1993). The work setting, therefore, may be more important in determining job satisfaction than elusive personality characteristics. Social resources, particularly marital status and SES, may well predict job satisfaction as well as adaptation to work or/and retirement (George & Maddox, 1977).

The importance of the home and work settings for healthy functioning have been supported, among many others, by McCubbin et al. (1992). On the basis of a discriminant analysis of responses by 117 women and 39 men to a health risk inventory, those investigators found six family and eight work factors in women that predicted health risk with 86.3% accuracy. For men, they found six family and four work factors that predicted health risk with 87.2% accuracy. Capacity to work in childhood may predict success even in underprivileged adult respondents. This factor may be even more powerful than social class, multiproblem-family membership, and all other childhood variables in predicting adult mental health and capacity for interpersonal relationships (Valliant & Valliant, 1981). Those conclusions may need specification in terms of gender differences, with women demonstrating significantly more psychological and physical manifestations of stress at work than men (Zappert & Weinstein, 1985).

Given such a climate, psychological separation and parental attachment may become important factors in how one commits to a given career in both genders. For women attachment to and conflictual independence from both parents may be positively related to progress in the commitment process and negatively related to the tendency to foreclose oneself from parents. For men, attachment to and attitudinal dependence on and conflictual independence from their fathers may predict progress in the commitment process (Bluestein, Walbridge, Friedlander, & Palladino, 1991).

There is the possibility that family dramas may be reenacted at work and that the meaning of a career change can be understood as a significant development of these dramas (Chusid & Cochran, 1989). As interesting as this hypothesis may be, it needs further evidence to be accepted as more than an interesting hypothesis, especially in linking family with work stresses. Strong work stress-strain and job satisfaction may be related and enhanced by negative affectivity (Decker & Borgen, 1993). Indeed, intrinsic satisfaction at work, such as meaningfulness of work, liking for it, and control over the pace of work may be correlated significantly with marital satisfaction in both partners. Extrinsic satisfaction of work, such as income, recognition, and job prestige, seems unrelated to marital satisfaction (Kemper & Reichler, 1976). Life satisfaction may well lead to job satisfaction not the reverse for both men and women (Smidt & Mellon, 1980).

Significant effects of work autonomy on the individual's sense of competence or self-efficacy are present. With work autonomy and other pertinent variables controlled, income, an indicator of extrinsic rewards and socioeconomic attainment, does not seem to enhance the self-concept over time. These results suggest a generalization model of adult socialization, in which adaptations to occupational activities and demands are conceptualized as major sources of personal change. A sense of competence, prior to labor force entry, may have significant implications for future income attainment and work autonomy (Mortimer & Lorence, 1979).

The acquisition of education and entrance in the workforce by women that occurred in the 19th century and progressed in the second part of the 20th century, has revolutionized the climate of many work settings, as well as the definition of feminine, supposedly expressive, and masculine, supposedly instrumental, roles (Mogul, 1979). These qualities can be specified and measured reliably (Alley, 1984).

Expressive/instrumental needs, work status, and attitudes toward women's roles seem significantly related to their parents' instrumental/expressive child-rearing practices, needs, and attitudes toward women's roles (Huth, 1978). Status inconsistencies and incompatibility between partners may be important variables for explaining life and marital dissatisfaction, especially if the wife is earning more than the husband or if she progresses in her career at a faster pace than her husband, even though these differences may depend on the achievement motivation of both partners (Hornung & McCullough, 1981).

For instance, women characterized as masculine may last in their jobs longer than women characterized as feminine. The more equalitarian the marriage, the more likely that women may continue their career participation after having children. However, regardless of employment status and equalitarianism in marriage, women report that they spend significantly more time alone with their children than their husbands do (Gaddy, Glass, & Arnkoff, 1983). Marital adjustment may be affected by dual-employment positively or negatively, depending on pro-feminist attitudes toward women and levels of education in both partners. However, family interests remain ranked as being more important than career interests (Hardesty & Betz, 1980).

Past maternal employment may be a more powerful predictor of children's academic performance and expectations than any amount of paternal involvement. Part-time maternal employment may be optimal for children's academic expectations (Williams & Radin, 1993). On the other hand, a high level of identification with fathers, at least in a rural setting, seems to predict higher levels of aspiration, more self-confidence, and greater satisfaction with school experiences (Jackson, Meara, & Arora, 1974). Women's attachment to their mothers and degree of family dysfunction combined may predict in part career search efficacy, while for men, only attachment to mother accounted partially for career choice efficacy (Ryan, Solberg, & Brown, 1996).

Axelrod (1999) has brought attention to disturbances in work roles, namely: work inhibitions or procrastinations, work compulsions, and chronic dissatisfaction with one's work. Compulsions describe the Type A personality, while dissatisfaction in one's work, according to Axelrod, is "...endemic to our time and is common in both normal work life and all forms of work disturbances (p. 55)." Certain work-related situations may be dangerously stressful for persons with a propensity for child abuse: (1) unemployed father caring for children at home; (2) working mothers overloaded with job and domestic obligations; (3) husbands, especially professionals, working so long and hard that they neglect their wives; and (4) traumatic experiences on the job resulting in undischarged tensions (Justice & Duncan, 1977).

Surplus Time: Survival versus Enjoyment

There are leftover skills that are neither home- nor school/work-related. Making fewer demands and having fewer requirements, these skills may be considered more discretionary than obligatory. These activities are divided into survival (paying bills, grocery shopping, buying clothes) and discretionary or enjoyment related. Survival skills are part of the roles reviewed under residence. Leisure activities, on the other hand, are discretionary, chosen freely by individuals on how to spend time after survival responsibilities have been fulfilled. In some cases these activities are pursued in spite of letting go of survival chores. They are sometimes spent at home, sometimes in other settings. Leisure time takes place in the company of others or it can be solitary. It can be active or sedentary, indoor or outdoor, oriented toward people or toward things. Working in one's basement on a hobby, participating in the Elks Club, watching TV, going to church, or running a marathon—all are examples of activities in this setting. Leisure activities are important for one's enjoyment of life and for personal socialization. They are an integral part of how we function as individuals. These activities specify the value we put on friends and relationships. Leisure settings require skills that are specific to the activity being performed in a particular setting as well as skills to develop and maintain relationships that are formed within each setting, whether partners, family members, relatives, friends, or just playmates.

Transit

These settings may not have been as important in the past as they are today, given our capacity to travel long distances in short periods of time. This capacity increases the number and variety of transit settings within which we interact each day (highways, airports, cars, buses). As perceptions about distance and time allotment change, the time and the activities spent in these settings may take on an identity of their own. Increased commuting time, for instance, requires the acquisition of the skills to commute and to make the best of it. But the ease of commuting within settings may also increase the chance of overlap among settings. For instance, having an office in one's home may reduce commuting time. However, it may produce conflicts in fulfilling responsibilities one might not be required to fulfill if one had an office away from home.

Transitory

These settings are temporary and vary in importance from one person to another and from one family to another. Purchasing goods and services, shopping in a mall, going to a beauty salon, or relaxing in a bar may require different time and energy requirements, depending on how important one considers that activity. There are purchasing geniuses who spend a great deal of time plotting how to use coupons to get a better bargain and comparing costs for the same merchandise sold in different stores. Getting the oil changed at the corner garage, waiting in an unemployment line, completing the requirements for automobile registration, buying a bottle of aspirin—each takes us to a different setting. Each setting has peculiar role demands and codes. Transitory settings may seem less important than other settings; yet, our ability to transact in these settings allows us to survive in the most important setting, the home.

Leisure

Leisure time is defined by whatever time is left after taking care of survival needs, work, and house chores. It can take place at work or anywhere else (Godin, Valois, Shephard, & Desharnais, 1987; Rosenthal, Montgomery, Shadish, & Lichstein, 1989). This time provides enjoyment or intrinsic satisfaction when it includes companionship, novelty, relaxation, aesthetic appreciation, and intimacy. By the same token, work provides external rewards through accomplishments, learning, and helping others (Tinsley, Hinson, Tinsley, & Holt, 1993). Even more, leisure activities can be classified according to agency, novelty, belongingness, service, sensual enjoyment, cognitive stimulation, self-expression, creativity, competition, vicarious competition, and relaxation (Dawis, 1995; Tinsley & Eldredge, 1995).

Perceived freedom, intrinsic motivation, facilitative arousal, and commitment are necessary but insufficient prerequisites for experiencing leisure. It would be necessary to add that the experience of leisure would result also in the absorption in the task at hand, lack of focus on self, feelings of freedom or lack of controls, enriched perception of objects and events, increased sensitivity to feelings, increased intensity of emotions, and decreased awareness of the passage of time (Baldwin & Tinsley, 1988). How leisure and work attitudes and activities are related to each other remains an important but open question (Tinsley, 1995).

The Importance of Play throughout the Personality Life Cycle

Lifelong play is an important component of both education and work as evaluated by how much time is dedicated to active versus passive play and leisure-time activities, vacations, and even doing nothing without requirements for performance, perfection, problem solving, or production. Two aspects of play could be physical exercise and love-making.

Play behavior has been the subject of a great deal of attention and speculation during the last third of the past century (L'Abate, 2004c). There is no question that play and playfulness are important activities related to personality development and functionality (Brown & Gottfried, 1985; Schwartzman, 1978), in spite of environmental constraints (Barnett, 1985). When play is coupled with laughter, rather than tears, definite developmental effects can be expected (Srofe & Waters, 1976).

Play, of course, is not limited to children but is extended throughout the whole personality life cycle. The major issue with playing lies in where it should take place, what settings are relevant to its promulgation and prolongation. In major urban centers there are various parks and for-pay activities. School yards are still open for children to play interactively and competitively. Adults have plenty of opportunities to access commercial exercise rooms, tennis courts, and golf courses. Yet, where are the equivalents of similar venues for children? In a recent visit to my childhood playgrounds in hometown of Florence (Italy not South Carolina!), I noticed the complete absence of children playing on those grounds. When asking the reason for this absence, the reply was: "They are at home playing games on their computers." If that conclusion is correct, it means that socialization suffers from restricted interactions, cooperatively as well as competitively, with peers. Socialization, then, may become a matter of computer games rather than close friendships with peers.

Research Supporting This Model

The relationship of this model with two previous metatheoretical assumptions and with the remainder of the models of the theory is considered below briefly. This model will be elaborated in one way or another in all the chapters of this book.

Evidence Independent but Conceptually Similar of the Model. Ecological psychology represents that background for this model. However, that field of study has failed (as far as I can tell) to distinquish among skills and abilities necessary to function in various settings. Nor has this field of study supported the position made by this model that settings represent one way to assess personality functioning and dysfunctioning. This differentiation will be addressed in greater detail in Chapter 12.

Evidence Indirectly but Somewhat Related to the Model. The major source of independent evidence to support this model comes from resource exchange theory (Foa et al., 1993) and relational models theory (Haslam, 2004).

Evidence Directly Derived from the Model. Except for suggesting evaluation of the meaning of each setting through the semantic differential, I
have failed to provide evidence to support this model except to offer possible ways to evaluate it.

Functions of This Model

This model, like others, fulfills a variety of functions:

Integration of Settings

This model allows settings to be an integral part of the theory to the extent
that it relates to the first metatheoretical model (Ch. 4) (ERAAwC) by expanding on the *C* of that model. It also includes the second model of levels of
observation (Ch. 5) by including not only the presentational level but also the
genotypic level: how one feels about a setting and how that setting becomes
a context for intimate relationships. In addition, as discussed in subsequent
chapters, and especially Chapter 12, settings allow us to evaluate levels of
personality functioning as defined by how one relates in various settings.

Diagnostic

By asking the question: "Where do you spend more of your time and energy?" one is able to evaluate objectively the personal involvement of an
individual. This evaluation should allow qualification that even though objectively one may spend a great deal of time at work, for instance, there are
corrections made for overinvolvement at work by spending a great deal of
time with the family on weekends and vacations. Even more important, one
needs to evaluate the emotional climate of the marital and family relationship to assess whether, in spite of overinvolvement with work, for instance,
there is enough love and devotion that reassures other intimates of their
importance to the major wage earner and his or her work involvement.

Preventive

There is a whole workbook (L'Abate, 1996) devoted to 15 abilities that allows respondents to deal with abilities that are basic to their survival and
enjoyment.

Prescriptive

It is very easy to prescribe: "Balance survival with your enjoyment." However, it is much more difficult to follow through unless there is a definite

motivation to consider one's priorities, as discussed in Chapter 13, evaluate them, and, if necessary, change them.

Therapeutic

Once one reaches the point of being unable to function or even survive adequately in any setting, then it would stand to reason that, if given preventive and prescriptive interventions have failed, f2f talk-based interventions should lead to the goal of guiding respondents into being able to "Enjoy yourself!" and to laugh. Troubled people as a whole have lost their sense of humor and find it difficult to laugh and enjoy life. Then, would it not be the goal of therapeutic interventions to help them acquire or reacquire the ability to enjoy life?

CONCLUSION

Most intimate relationships develop over time primarily in the home and secondarily in other settings.

Part III

Assumptions of the Theory
Processes and Contents

The purpose of this part is to consider assumptions about two major *processes* of the theory, the ability to love and the ability to negotiate, as well as postulate about the nature of *what* is exchanged among intimates and nonintimates. This postulate deals with the *contents* of what is exchanged during those two processes within intimate and nonintimate relationships. The reason for calling the latter a postulate lies in its being independent from both assumptions, and standing as a model by itself, even though it is connected here to its two assumptions and to foregoing models.

These two assumptions about the ability to love (Ch. 7) and the ability to negotiate (Ch. 8) and one postulate about modalities of exchange (Ch. 9), together with the metatheoretical assumptions, generate an even greater number of models. Moving from assumptions, i.e., abilities and their contents and then to models, is a process based on: (1) levels of abstraction, starting with seemingly very abstract terms, like space and time, to less abstract terms like distance and control, love and negotiation, and to even more concrete models; and (2) levels of generality, starting with very general assumptions, like space and time, to more specific processes, contents, and then to even more specific models. Although assumptions may seem too abstract and too general to appear testable, models, as we shall see, do become somewhat more testable than assumptions. If the models are valid, then the assumptions of the theory may become valid as well.

Thus, this theory follows a hierarchical structure at three levels flowing from two seemingly abstract and general assumptions (space and time) on top of three less abstract and specific modalities (love, negotiation, and contents of exchange) below, to an even more concrete and specific number of models at the bottom. Some models may be more valid than others. Some models are more easily testable than others. Some have not been validated yet. If a few models are wanting, the theory tends to wobble. If most or perhaps all of the models are invalid, the theory will crash of its own weight. If models are valid, the theory will stand on its own feet.

It is crucial for this theory to be evaluated in a variety of ways that are relevant to the laboratory, clinical, and preventive settings, because there are so many competing theories in the marketplace of theory, therapy, and prevention. If a new theory wants to establish its place among already established, competing theories, it has to show that it is "as good as" those theories. "As good as" means being as valid and as encompassing from one setting to another, in short, as verifiable and as accountable as competing theories, if not better, even more verifiable and more accountable.

One cannot enter into the assumptions and models of this theory without considering issues of classification to differentiate between functional and dysfunctional relationships with dimensions derived from the theory of existing classificatory schemes (Stone, 1993; Turner & Hersen, 1997; Widiger, 2001). In this part, for instance, as in most assumptions and models of the theory, prototypes drawn mainly but not solely from personality disorders in Clusters B and C of Axis II in the DSM-IV (Barlow, 1993; Benjamin, 1993; Livesley, 2001). Rather than differentiate between syndromes (Axis I) and symptoms (Axis II) according to the DSM-IV psychiatric classification scheme, personality disorders in Cluster A of Axis II will be will be considered the bases for more extreme disorders to be included with Axis I disorders in Chapter 12.

Benjamin (1993), among many others, proposed a model for personality disorders that consisted of: (1) Cluster B, called a "dramatic, erratic" group, including borderline, narcissistic, histrionic, and antisocial personality disorders—this cluster would be similar to the selfish and externalizing personality propensity (Chs. 8 and 12); (2) Cluster C, called an anxious, fearful group, includes dependent, obsessive compulsive, negativistic or passive-aggressive, and avoidant personality disorders considered in the next chapter; and (3) Cluster A, called an odd, eccentric group, includes paranoid, schizoid, and schizotypal personality disorders (Ch. 12).

As a whole, in spite of various ad hoc attempts to find one (Millon, Blaney, & Davis, 1999; Millon, Meagher, & Grossman, 2001), psychiatric classification, as exemplified by the DSM-IV and its successors, still lacks a satisfactory underlying and encompassing theoretical framework. For some time, even the existence of personality disorders was discounted theoretically, but more recently validated empirically (Arntz, 1999). Nonetheless, by now these disorders are an accepted part of the psychiatric lexicon, even though they may still be viewed as categories rather than dimensions. If these disorders exist, they exist along a continuum of severity as measured by the number of symptoms, ranging from no disorder without any symptoms, personality difficulties, to simple, and to diffuse symptoms (Tyler & Johnson, 1996).

The same issues of continuity and contiguity exist in all categories of psychiatric classification. If a category exists, then it exists in different degrees of severity, with certain types being more contiguous to and more overlapping with some and more discontinuous to and less overlapping with others. For instance, depression may vary from simple, short-lived moods to a severe, chronic, debilitating lifelong condition. In some degrees, it may be close to and overlap with anxiety and internalizing disorders, controlled mostly by fears. By the same token, anger, hostility, and aggression may not overlap and not even be at all contiguous with depression, while overlapping with some externalizing disorders, where fear seems absent.

There may be gender differences among these disorders, with men scoring higher on obsessive-compulsive, antisocial, and narcissistic dimensions. Women, on the other hand, may score higher than men on histrionic, dependent, and avoidant dimensions (Akhtar, 1996; Golomb, Fava, Abraham, & Rosenbaum, 1995; Zimmerman & Coryell, 1990). These gender differences, however, have not been confirmed (Grilo, Becker, Walker, & Edell, 1996). However, they will be revisited within other chapters of this book. There is mounting evidence that these disorders may be due in part to documented physical or sexual childhood abuse or neglect (Johnson, Cohen, Brown, Smailes, & Bernstein, 1999).

Consequently, this theory sees personality disorders and extreme psychopathology in continuity and contiguity with each other as well as with personality propensities described in Chapter 12. Hence, Chapter 7 will include personality disorders of Axis II, Cluster C. Chapter 8 will include personality disorders of Axis II, Cluster B. Chapter 9 will include personality disorders of both Clusters B and C.

Chapter 7

Space and the Ability to Love
Model[4]

"Love makes us who we are, and what we can become (p. viii). Who we are and who we become depends, in part, on whom we love (p. 144). Our culture fawns over the fleetingness of being in love while discounting the importance of loving (p. 206). Loving is limbically distinct from in love. Loving is mutuality; loving is synchronous attunement and modulation. As such, adult love depends critically upon knowing the other. In love demands only the brief acquaintance necessary to establish an emotional genre. Loving derives from intimacy, the prolonged and detailed surveillance of a foreign soul (Lewis, Amini, & Lannon, 2000, p. 207)."
"Relatedness is a physiological process that, like digestion or bone growth, admits no plausible acceleration. And the skill of becoming and remaining attuned to another's emotional rhythms requires a solid investment of years (p. 205). If anyone must jettison a part of life, time with a mate should be last on the list: one needs that connection to live (Lewis, Amini, & Lannon, 2000, p. 206)."

This chapter presents a model about the ability to love as the most fundamental of all abilities. The ability to love develops and is based on Distance in Activity (A) = approach/avoidance and on Emotionality (E), as discussed in Chapter 4. How an infant is born and raised in a loving or nonloving context will determine subsequent personality socialization in future intimate and nonintimate relationships. There is little room at the beginning of life for R, even though eventually it is necessary to include it to take care of how to monitor, control, and regulate approach-avoidance tendencies.

Personality socialization assumes space and time as two basic processes. Space and time, subsume, respectively, primarily distance among, between, and within individuals and secondarily, control among, between, and within individuals. Distance subsumes a dimension defined by extremes in approach-avoidance, approach that leads to closeness, avoidance that leads to distance. Extremes in approach produce symbiotic conditions (Johnson, 1991), which end up in internal (against self rather than others) self-abuse and apathy. Extremes in avoidance lead to abandonment and neglect. Somewhere in the middle of this dimension lies the proper balance of distance, ultimately culminating in closeness and intimacy that are frequent in functional relationships and defective if not absent in dysfunctional ones.

THE ASSUMPTION OF SPACE

The infant is born in a world of space, where surrounding caretaker(s) come and go, some come smiling, some come and go screaming, some come and go slowly, some come and go suddenly. Space may be clean or dirty, orderly or disorderly, attractive or unattractive, and crowded or uncrowded, to the point that excessive crowding may interfere with personal controls (Hayduk, 1978; Schmidt & Keating, 1979). Preferences for personal space may also be related to maladjustment and aggression (Cavallin & Houston, 1980), with proximic distance increasing with neuroticism and gender (DeJulio & Duffy, 1977). Friendships are made and kept, in part on the basis of proximity (Athanasiou & Yoshioka, 1973; Ebbesen, Kjos, & Koneni, 1976). Indeed, proximity may also increase liking (Kahn & McGaughery, 1977) and vary according to culture, class, socialization practices, and gender (Leventhal, Matturro, & Schanerman, 1978). Personal space also increases with age, at least up to the adult years (Hayduk, 1983).

The more maternal affection one received as a child, the closer one may allow even strangers to approach (Hollender, Duke, & Nowicki, 1973). Males and females may start with similar personal space preferences but, by the age of puberty, they start to approximate adult distance patterns (Price & Dabbs, 1974). Furthermore, the more one is liked the greater the chances of others wanting to be close to that one (Schaefer & Higgins, 1976). Stress, of course, may increase or decrease personal space (Hubert, Jay, Saltoun, & Hayes, 1988; Schiavo, Schiffenbauer, & Roberts, 1977). Individual differences seem to determine a great deal how space is used between and among people (Whalen, Flowers, Fuller, & Jernigan, 1975).

Spatial representations may constitute attempts to understand and organize reality and eventually achieve individuation and differentiation. Spatial representations may eventually become important in evaluating the level and extent of psychopathology (Roth & Blatt, 1974). Space, therefore, subsumes a dimension of distance defined by extremes in approach-avoidance functions. We approach who we like and love and we want to be approached by those who like and love us. We avoid those we do not like or love and are avoided by those who do not like or love us. These approach-avoidance functions eventually become socialized into the ability to love and to be intimate, how one behaves with few others who reciprocate the same feelings (Hendrick & Hendrick, 1992).

Without proper socialization, avoidance eventually may lead to estrangement and alienation. Approach may become so extreme to the point of being unable to fend for oneself. Love means wanting to be close physically, emotionally, legally, and practically to another human being, a partner, and to members of one's family of origin and family of procreation. Some people, however, are comfortable in living by themselves and avoiding close and extended contact with others. Hence, there are gradients of approach and of avoidance in how close or how distant one wants to be with others or from others.

These functions stem from E. The ability to love is defined, here, as the attribution and assertion of importance to self and intimate others (parents, partners, children, siblings, relatives, friends, and neighbors), as elaborated in Chapter 12. Intimacy is defined as the sharing of joys as well as of hurts and fears of being hurt with those we like and love and who like and love us (Ch. 16). Distance, measured by emotional involvement, investment, and availability among intimates is one way to evaluate close, committed, interdependent, and prolonged intimate relationships. How much time one spends with intimates means that approaching them and being close to them means more than any other function. Functionalities are found in selective balances of appropriate approach-avoidance tendencies. Dysfunctionalities are found in inappropriate use of extremes in either approach or avoidance tendencies.

Distance and the Ability to Love

Love is expressed through attributing, asserting, and affirming the importance of self and loved ones with the ability to be intimate. This ability is shown by concern for self and intimate others and by being available emotionally to oneself and to intimate others through sharing hurts and fears of being hurt as well as joys and sorrows. This process means being together unconditionally, without demands for performance, perfection, production, or problem solving. The ability to love, therefore, even though it may possess a cognitive component, is based on the ability to experience and accept a wide spectrum of positive feelings (Lee, 1974; Vincent, 1976). Regardless of how love is defined, as already reviewed in previous publications, the bottom line of love remains wanting to be close to those we love and who love us and avoid those who we do not like and who do not like or love us.

The maturational process in the development of love relationships may be represented as crossing a series of boundaries, from childhood to adolescence, on to adulthood, and finally on to maturity. Sexual passion, for instance, may represent one boundary necessary to define a relationship. The most important boundary consists of the identification of self and identification of a beloved. The union of self with a loved one serves as a bond in mature love relationships. Crossing the sexual boundary with the development and enjoyment of full genitality may result in a common social barrier that protects the relationship. Sexual freedom, on the other hand, may threaten the stability of the relationship, especially when pressure develops in other areas, like parenting, work, and leisure activities (Kernberg, 1977).

Hence, Emotionality (E) is at the very bottom of our existence, feelings of love between partners, between parents and children, among intimates, family, and friends. E is the primary component of the first model of the theory (Ch. 4). In E, in its passive, receptive aspects, feelings of hurt and fears of being hurt develop. These feelings are expressed properly and shared in functional relationships. They are avoided, either through internalizations, externalizations, or psychopathologies, in dysfunctional ones (Bradley, 2000). E is the cornerstone of socialization. Infants are born in an emotional context, the marriage or its absence, and are socialized in an emotional network of family or intimate relationships. E is followed developmentally by Rationality (R). Both E and R are the basis for A, Aw, and C, the five components of the ERAAwC model expanded in Chapter 4.

Gradients of Approach-Avoidance

There is no way to summarize here all the past experimental research on gradients of approach-avoidance. They are expanded here to define distance between and among intimates and nonintimates. These gradients have already been considered in Chapter 4 as part of Activity (A). However, here A is made a function of E as well as R, Aw, and C. There are various types and kinds of approach tendencies, just as there are various types and kinds of avoidance tendencies.

Approach-Avoidance—At What Levels of Observation and Interpretation?

Approach and avoidance take place at all four levels of observation and interpretation (Ch. 5), at the presentational, phenotypic, genotypic, and historic/developmental/situational levels, as learned from one's family of origin, intimate relationships, and personal history.

Approach-Avoidance at the Presentational Sublevel. Descriptively, at this level it is pretty easy to observe and even measure who and what one approaches and who and what one avoids publicly or socially, as already suggested in Chapter 6. We approach who and what we need, want, and like and avoid who and what we do not need, do not want, and do not like. Many have to approach a job they do not like but that they need to survive. Some others like their jobs so much that they would pay to keep them. Somewhere in between there are those who enjoy both work and leisure-time activities. Hence, needing to survive, wanting to enjoy, and liking to survive well and enjoy even more, are independent criteria that will be considered in greater detail in Chapter 13.

Approach-Avoidance at the Phenotypic Sublevel. Who and what does one approach away from the public arena of presentation? Does one spend time with one's partner, children, or friends, or does one choose to secret oneself in one's office, tool shed, watching TV, or keeping busy on the Internet, away from loved ones? A gregariously social individual, who spends his or her time outside the home trying to be liked at all costs may become a misanthrope outside the glare of public opinion. Hence, who and what one approaches publicly at the presentational level does not necessarily predict who and what one will approach in the privacy of one's own home.

Approach Avoidance at the Genotypic Sublevel. How one feels about approaching or avoiding who and what depends on how one feels about oneself and intimate others. One may hate the job and would like to quit if one were able to find a better job. Without that possibility, one must consider the welfare of intimate others whose survival would be jeopardized by lack of a job and lowered income. Hence, one would like to approach other job possibilities. However, if there are no jobs available one needs to remain in a hated job. Were one single and without intimate attachments the choice of leaving a hated job would be easier. Need is an objective condition. We all need air, food, clothing, and shelter to survive as comfortably as possible. However, how one chooses to survive depends on who and what one wants and likes. Some people are happy to survive alone. Others are happy to share survival with someone else, with or without enjoyment. Others prefer immediate enjoyment, as in addictions, even at the cost of losing self and intimate others. All these choices are based on how one feels, that is, who and what one wants and who and what one likes. Who and what we do approach represents the promotion of helpful and pleasant relationships. Who and what we do avoid represents the prevention of harmful and unpleasant relationships (Higgins, 2001).

Avoidance of revealing personal information to another person correlates strongly with seeking or not seeking psychological help. Gender and perceived social support predict approach toward seeking psychological help, while fear of disclosure triggers avoidance of seeking help (Vogel & Wester, 2003). Self-disclosure could also be a function of organizational sponsorship, the preferred self-presentational style, and the legitimacy of a request to disclose intimate or painful experiences, even in writing (Finkel & Jacobsen, 1977; Orr, 1976).

Approach-Avoidance at Historic/Developmental/Situational Sublevels. How we feel about who and what we need, want, and like to approach or to avoid is learned from one's family of origin, developed and differentiated in intimate relationships throughout the life cycle. We may learn from our parents to avoid certain ethnic people, for instance, but as we grow up we may see that pattern of avoidance is biased and needs correction to the point that members of that group are now approached. With age, approach and avoidance become selective processes.

Approach-Avoidance Tendencies and Conflict. Clearly the process through which we choose who and what we need, want, or like to approach or to avoid produces internal and external conflicts. This conflict has been called ambivalence in the past and becomes evident externally especially with intimate others who possess divergent views from our own. One may want to go to a movie theater while the other partner might want to watch a special TV show at home. One then needs to consider what to choose and what kind of conflict one would produce inside oneself and outside with intimate others. The conflict between work demands and domestic responsibilities, for instance, looms large in all the choices one needs to make to succeed well in both settings, as discussed in Chapter 6. Prototypes for conflicts in approach-avoidance tendencies could be found in the obsessive-compulsive or passive-aggressive personality disorders (Benjamin, 1993; Stone, 1991). Aggression here is shown by passive avoidance of certain situations or responsibilities and failing to fulfill expectations and requests from others.

Self-defeating personalities are placed here as an example because they tend to support the coexistence of both approach and avoidance tendencies. Individuals with these kinds of personalities seem to avoid success-related choices, choosing instead to approach situations leading to disappointment, failure, and even mistreatment (Skodol, Oldham, Gallaher, & Bezirganian, 1994). Whether these personalities can be distinguished from normal reactions to victimization and abuse remains to be seen (Kass,

Spitzer, Williams, & Widiger, 1989; Mossman & Somoza, 1990; Spitzer & Davies, 1990). Indeed, in spite of insistence as a distinct and clinically useful diagnostic category (Heisler, Lyons, & Goethe, 1995), questions still remain on whether this personality pattern should be included into a psychiatric classification (Fuller, Blashfield, & McElroy, 1995).

Approach-Avoidance of What?

Consistent with has been written earlier, especially in Chapter 4 and what will be written next, as simplisitic as it may seem, the basic processes underlying all human and nonhuman beings consist of the avoidance of pain and hurtful or negative feelings and approach of pleasurable, pleasant, and positive feelings (Stasiewicz & Maisto, 1993). This equation, however, is not always so straightforward. For instance, even though not a formal aspect of Cluster C, a pattern of fear of success and self-defeating personalities is prominent enough to qualify as avoidance of success, by lowering expectations and goals and acting in ways that will lead to failure, either personal or professional defeats, or both. Hence, the approach of failure represents the avoidance of success. Whether this characteristic is more frequent in women remains to be seen (Schecter, 1979). Whether this condition is also related to other personality disorders and even depression remains to be seen. The validity of this construct and consistent ways to measure it are still questionable (Olson & Williamsen, 1978; Singh, 1978). Clearly the pattern of avoidance is not based on a unidimensional contruct. Fear of success may represent test anxiety, sex-role-related attitudes toward success, neurotic insecurity, and questioning the value of success (Sadd, Lenauer, Shaver, & Dunivant, 1978).

The same possibility of multidimensionality could be considered in the approach gradient. Could all these factors stem from "negative feelings"? Its multidimensional characteristics may make it difficult to place it into a distinct niche in the psychiatric lexicon.

Stages of Dependency in Approach-Avoidance

Dependency is one aspect of distance, to the point that one needs to rely on someone else and be physically close for succor, nurturance, and fulfillment of needs, wants, and likes. Hence, dependency represents one aspect of approach at the beginning of life which developmentally becomes integrated into avoidance as one grows older, selective, and more autonomous. Over the life cycle, dependency in childhood represents the need to approach caretakers, this need is extended into adolescence when approach becomes attenuated by the desire for avoidance of caretakers instead of the approach toward peers and others, with a possible denial of dependency and contradictions in approach-avoidance in adolescence.

Mature adulthood is characterized by interdependence where partners have learned to balance and integrate approach-avoidance tendencies in mutually constructive ways. Old age represents a return to dependency, accepting to avoid people and situations that are taxing to oneself and approaching those who are crucial for the survival of the self. Hence, childhood represents extreme dependency and approach toward caretakers, adolescence represents an attempt of integration of approach-avoidance tendencies with sometimes a denial of dependency toward caretakers, while proclaiming one's wanting independence. Adulthood, in its functional aspects represents the acceptance and use of balanced and selective approach-avoidance, interdependence, while old age brings about a restriction of approach-avoidance tendencies.

Functional Aspects of Approach-Avoidance

An alternative model to approach-avoidance suggests that there may be two qualitatively distinct types of negative affective relationships: moving against and moving away (Cronen & Price, 1976). Functionality is found in a consistent balance of positive approach-avoidance tendencies that are age-sex and context appropriate, without extremes in either tendency. This balance is found in an integration of similarities and differences in identity differentiation discussed in Chapter 10, personality propensities in Chapter 12, and priorities in Chapter 13. High approach tendencies at a phenotypic sublevel may be related to low distress at a genotypic sublevel (Hubert et al., 1988).

Dysfunctional Extremes of Approach

Avoidance of painful or threatening situations may be due to a numbing of general responsiveness in posttraumatic stress disorder (Honig, Grace, Lindy, & Newman, 1999). Gradients of avoidance may be steeper than gradients of approach (Depue & Lenzenweger, 2001; Losco & Epstein, 1974). Prototypes for deviant, negative, or extreme approach tendencies are listed from the least to the most severe prototypes of each condition.

Dependent Personalities. Depending on other people for emotional and financial support is not simply a flow or deficit in functioning, but is associated with a variety of healthy, adaptive traits, and behaviors (Bornstein, 1998). The issue here lies in how dependency is reciprocated by intimates.

Without reciprocity, dependency remains a one-way street. With positive reciprocity dependency becomes interdependence.

The etiology of dependency seems to lie in overprotective, authoritarian parents. In social settings, dependency is associated with suggestibility, conformity, compliance, interpersonal yielding, affiliative behavior, and sensitivity to interpersonal cues. Dependency predicts the onset of certain psychological disorders and follows the onset of others. The most fundamental motivation of the dependent person is a strong desire to obtain and maintain nurturant supportive relationships (Bornstein, 1992). Dependency, of course, is closely related to social behavior and to the quality of social networks, where negative and disruptive interpersonal behaviors were also related to feelings of loneliness and depression (Overholser, 1996). As a whole, women tend to be diagnosed (by male professionals?) as dependent (Bornstein, Manning, Krukonis, & Rossner, 1993).

Dependency could be one of two dimensions of depression, i.e., communal needs for closeness/concern with separation (Cluster C) and issues of agentic power, rank, submission, and subordination (feeling inferior to others, subordinate, inhibited) in Cluster B (Gilbert, Allan, & Trent, 1995).

Socioeconomically, male veterans diagnosed with dependent personality disorders tend to come from significantly lower levels and poorer functioning in the family/home sphere. They tend to exhibit more social phobias and borderline and histrionic traits. In relatives, there might have been significantly more generalized anxiety disorder, simple phobias, drug abuse, and dramatic personality disorder Cluster B (Reich, 1996). Individuals with high levels of immature dependency (neediness) tend to be low in agency, while individuals with high levels of mature dependency (connectedness) tend to be high in communion (Zuroff, Moskowitz, & Coté, 1999).

Dependency could be related to a distant relationship with fathers during development and marginally associated with perceptions of increased parental attention and overindulgence. Self-criticism seems related to perceptions of difficulties in the quality of affective bonds with fathers and peers (Rosenfarb, Becker, & Mintz, 1994).

In addition to dependent personalities, one needs to add so-called "co-dependent" personalities, those who are seemingly addicted to the addict, and could also merge with the symbiotic personalities, not contained in Cluster C but described in Chapter 10. Dependent personalities in Cluster C, more likely women, could tend to be attracted to antisocial, addicted men in Cluster B (L'Abate & Harrison, 1992). These personalities, when depressed, seem excessively preoccupied with the lives, feelings, and problems of others, falling in love with chemically dependent individuals (O'Brien & Gaborit, 1992; Prest, Benson, & Protincky, 1998). There is a possibility that this pattern of relating may develop in a family context characterized by parental coercion, control, nonnurturance, and maternal compulsivity (Crothers & Warren, 1996). Indeed, when compared with their addicted spouses, codependent individuals showed little differences between their alcoholic spouses with respect to dysfunctions in their families of origin, current families, or codependency levels. Clinical codependent individuals may differ from their nonclinical counterparts on measures of triangulation, a concept derived from Bowen's (1979) differentiation model, intimacy, and individuation. By the same token, in contrast to clinical populations, codependency in non-clinical populations may have links with favorable characteristics of family functioning (Prest et al., 1998). Dependency under positive conditions, therefore, when reciprocated, could become interdependence. Under negative conditions, when reciprocated, dependency could become symbiosis (Ch. 10).

Symbiotic Personalities. These personalities will be considered in greater detail in Chapter 10, since they constitute the extreme of dependency as well as one extreme in the failure to differentiate.

Dysfunctional Extremes of Avoidance

This gradient is defined by prototypes that increase in dysfunctionality from minimal to maximal avoidance, ranging from perfectionism, shyness, social anxieties, agoraphobias, social phobias and fears, and eventually, more blatantly, avoidant personalities, with autistic children and schizophrenics representing the most severe extreme (Richer, 1976). Avoidance does not necessarily apply only to social situations. There are fears of high places, fear of flying, fear of crowds, and fear of many other objects (snakes, microbes, dogs, heights, etc.). Fears and disgust seem to be the cause of many cases of avoidance (Woody & Teachman, 2000).

The most important aspect of avoidance that is relevant to this theory is the avoidance of painful experiences, hurts, and fears of repeating the occurrence of similar incidents in the present and in the future. This avoidance was already discussed in Chapter 5 and will be discussed again in Chapters 14 and 16. It is usually referred to as "avoidance of negative feelings," which includes past hurts and rejections (Leary, 2001).

School Phobia. This pattern is evident in cultures like Japan, where children find it difficult to disagree with their parents except through phobias. It could also be a precursor to other disorders in adulthood. In our culture, higher rates of depressive and anxiety disorders were found in first-degree relatives of children with school phobia. Twice as many school phobic children with other neuroses seem to show excessive separation anxiety, dependency, and depression. Although a mutually hostile-dependent inter-action seemed apparent in most families of children with school phobia, the development of this phobia may be related to defects in character development in the children as well, in spite of the etiological significance of presumed parental pathology and family malfunctioning (Waldron, Shrier, Stone, & Tobin, 1975).

Even though parents of school-phobic children report more disturbance in family functioning (role performance, communication, affective expression, and control) than comparison parents (Bernstein & Garfinkel, 1988), one needs to ascertain whether this disturbance is the cause or the effect of school phobia. A partial review of the literature on school phobia using manualized treatment and a workbook can be found in Kearney and Alvarez (2004).

Perfectionism. At the lowest level of dysfunctionality, this disorder includes individuals oriented toward high standards and performing well, avoiding mistakes, doubting one's performance, and setting high expectations no matter what the outcome may be on others (Watzlawick, 1977). Its familial antecedents are found in the perception of high parental expectations and criticism, in addition to preference for order and organization, among other characteristics (Frost, Marten, Lahart, & Rosenblate, 1990).

Like Type A personalities, perfectionism is not considered in the DSM-IV. Yet, its existence has produced a great deal of research, especially as two components of depression, an interpersonal factor in the need for approval from others, and perfectionism based on self-criticalness (Blatt, Quinlan, Pilkonis, & Shea, 1995). Perfectionism, therefore, can be considered a risk factor for depression (Hewitt & Dyck, 1986; Hewitt, Flett, & Ediger, 1996; Hewitt & Flett, 1991; Hewitt, Mittelstaedt, & Wollert, 1989). Interpersonally, perfectionism may be comprised of two patterns: self-oriented perfectionism may be associated with assertive, adaptive qualities, and other-oriented perfectionism may be associated with arrogant, dominant, and vindictive qualities (Hill, Zrull, & Turlington, 1997). Perfectionistic undergraduate women, for instance, compared to non-perfectionists, may report higher levels of negative affect and might be more likely to report that they should have done better (Frost & Marten, 1990).

Whether perfectionism is functional or dysfunctional depends on how each aspect is related to compulsive-like behaviors. Functional perfectionists, in comparison to dysfunctional perfectionists, may tend to take significantly less time to complete a precision task and may be more concerned about solving a problem than performing well (Rhéaume, Freeston, Ladouceur, & Bouchard et al., 2000). Extreme perfectionism seems present in eating disorders and beliefs about others' high standards (Minarik & Ahrens, 1996; Shafran & Mansell, 2001; Srinivasagam, Kaye, Plotnicov, Greeno et al., 1995). Only three measures of perfectionism—socially prescribed perfectionism, concern over mistakes, and self-criticism—seem related to depressive symptoms (Ennis, 1999). Some aspects of perfectionism may be related to anxiety, independent of depression. Other aspects may be related to depression independent of anxiety (Kawamura, Hunt, Frost, & DiBartolo, 2001). If anxiety is different from depression on the basis of higher self-esteem, then the level of self-esteem may make the difference on whether different aspects of perfectionism may be mediated or moderated by this variable. Suicide potential may be associated with a dispositional, i.e., perfectionistic tendency to perceive that others are unrealistic in their expectations for the self (Hewitt, Flett, & Turnbull-Donovan, 1992).

This characteristic seems to be present in many disorders of Cluster C, especially in social anxiety (Saboonchi, Lundh, & Ost, 1999), especially when combined with a need for social approval (Blatt et al., 1995). However, it can be separated into two subdimensions, self-oriented perfectionism and socially prescribed perfectionism. Both may predict depression when combined with other personality factors (Hewitt & Flett, 1993). Socially prescribed perfectionism, for instance, may predict maladjustment (Chang & Rand, 1999). Perfectionistic traits may be associated with higher standards for social phobics than for controls. Social phobia, in itself, may be associated with lowered perceptions of social ability (Bieling & Alden, 1997).

Perfectionism may develop from perfectionistic and demanding parents, especially mothers of daughters. The latter rate their fathers as being harsh. Mother's perfectionism may be associated with greater symptoms of psychopathology among daughters, while fathers' perfectionism may lower levels of psychopathology in their daughters (Frost, Lahart, & Rosenblatt, 1991).

Shyness. This type of avoidance is by far the most prevalent, indicating, as in the case of disorders of approach, that as the gradient increases in severity, the smaller the number of signal cases will be. For instance, there are many cases of shyness but fewer cases of the extreme avoidant personality. Shy undergraduates of both genders may be less likely to express interest in interpersonally oriented career fields and to engage in fewer information-seeking activities, being more undecided on how to choose a career. Shy men may be significantly less likely than all other groups to expect that various assertive interview behaviors would lead to favorable evaluations from employers. Both shy men and women compared to nonshy men, seem less likely to expect that they would actually engage in assertive behaviors when interviewing for a job (Phillips & Bruch, 1988).

Interpersonal inhibition, another more technical term for shyness, may be a vulnerability factor for depressive symptoms in the absence but not in the presence of social support, with loneliness mediating the relationship between shyness and depressive symptomatology (Joiner, 1997).

Obsessions. Obsessive disorders could be conceived as worries, phobias, and ruminations, including superstitious beliefs and behaviors directed toward the avoidance of positive action (Frost, Krause, McMahon, & Peppe, et al., 1993). They are considered here, while compulsivity, as observed by actual repetition of rituals and routines, will be considered in the next chapter, as an inconsistent expression of inadequate controls. The decision to place obsessions without compulsions here lies in their differences. By obsessing and worrying, one is bound to avoid doing or approaching anyone or anything. Compulsions, on the other hand, even though they admittedly approach certain objects or even people, are viewed as issues of control, and are, therefore placed in Cluster B, where issues of control are dominant (Ch. 8). Furthermore, obsessions can be distinguished empirically from worries as well as from compulsions (Burns, Keortge, Formea, & Sternberger, 1996; Langlois et al., 2000).

Once the effects of depression and anxiety are removed, obsessional symptoms are significantly associated with passive aggressive traits (Tallis, Rosen, & Shafran, 1996).

Agoraphobias. In spite of fear of leaving one's house being related to cognitive biases (Warren, Zgourides, & Jons, 1989), this debilitating phobia seems quite pronounced in the general population. Individuals with panic disorder but no agoraphobia, panic disorder with agoraphobia, and agoraphobics without a history of panic disorder may show a worst functioning in the latter, best functioning in panic disorder alone, and an intermediate functioning in panic disorder with agoraphobia (Goisman, Warshaw, Peterson, Rogers, et al., 1994). These phobias may be circumscribed to one specific area, like travel, transportation, shopping, meeting people, or to claustrophobia, the fear of closed places (Hamann & Mavissakalian, 1988).

This condition could serve as a paradigm example of avoidance. A great deal of this fear is based on anticipated panic, suggesting that panic and agoraphobia do not share a unique or exclusive relationship. They represent a panic-agoraphobic spectrum with important implications for diagnosis and treatment (Cassano, Michelini, Shear, & Coli, et al., 1997). Panic disorder with various levels of phobic avoidance rather than just agoraphobia would appear to be a more valid diagnostic category (Cox, Endler, & Swinson, 1995). Interpersonal problem-solving deficits for generating alternative solutions and selecting behavioral preferred responses, globality attributions, perceived significance, anticipated outcomes, and performance appraisal seem to differentiate agoraphobic women from nonagoraphobic controls (Brodbeck & Michelson, 1987).

The onset of panic-agoraphobia in a person's late 20s is usually preceded by a long record of neurotic difficulties in relationships with parents as well as with adversaries. Experiences in childhood and conflicts generated by sexuality and aggression within the context of parent-child relationship in the early formative years may be responsible for the etiology of this condition. More specifically, relationship conflicts affect approximately 45% of agoraphobics (Kleiner & Marshall, 1985). Whether gender differences are weighted more toward women than men may be due to traditional sex-role stereotypes that make it difficult for men to openly admit their feelings. Men may cope with their fears through the use of alcohol, a pattern that may confuse the diagnosis of this disorder. Furthermore, avoidance behavior may be related to the sex-specific division of socioeconomic roles (Bekker, 1996).

Dynamically, agoraphobia may be related to separation anxiety as experienced in school phobia, representing a conflict in attachment versus autonomy between the child and parents (Frances & Dunn, 1975) as well as to a regression to unresolved dependency needs, disruption of the symbiotic bond, and separation/individuation (Vandereycken, 1983). A test of the separation hypothesis failed to support its validity (Thyer, Nesse, Cameron, & Curtis, 1985).

Husbands of agoraphobic women tend to choose them on the basis of perceived attributes, some of which may be pathological or at least pathogenic (Hafner, 1977). The inclusion of husbands in the treatment of agoraphobic women may increase the likelihood of a successful outcome (Himadi, 1986).

Significant differences in personality variables between families with agoraphobic parents and their matched controls depend a great deal on whether the agoraphobic parent was female or male (Mlott & Vale, 1986). Specific but moderate aggregation of simple phobia, social phobia, and panic disorder with agoraphobia seems present in families of respondents who had each of these disorders but no other lifetime anxiety disorder comorbidity (Fyer, Mannuzza, Chapman, & Martin, 1995).

The foregoing conclusions suggest that agoraphobias do not develop nor are they maintained in an interpersonal vacuum, but that the family of origin as well as the family of procreation may in some ways contribute to their maintenance.

Social Anxieties. These disorders of avoidance arise from the "prospect or presence of interpersonal evaluation in real and imagined social settings (Leary & Kowalsky, 1995, p. 6)." These settings could be public speaking, taking a test, socializing, talking with authority figures, or anxiety about being watched. Leary and Kowalsky posited a self-presentational theory of social anxiety arising from the desire to make a good impression but also being fearful of having obtained the desired effect. Consequently, this condition illustrates the conflict between needing to approach a social, educational, or professional situation and being fearful of what the results will be to the point that avoidance may be the best way out. Eventually, approach will win out if the payoff is great and avoidance is too costly. Yet, the conflict still remains inside the individual, also producing conflict in intimate relationships. A man who is constantly late because of his fears of making a good impression in a romantic relationship, eventually will find himself without a partner, especially if the partner is concerned about punctuality.

Social anxieties can be distinguished from social phobias by how impaired an individual may be. Most of us do have anxieties about how we present ourselves in social, professional, or educational situations (Mansell & Clark, 1999). Nonetheless, most of us are able to succeed in presenting ourselves in the best possible light. Phobias instead do impair the individual to the point of not being able to fulfill the requirements of a situation.

Social Phobias. Avoidance of social situations is equally distributed between genders and may develop earlier than panic and other disorders (Fredrikson, Annas, Fischer, & Wik, 1996; Turner & Beidel, 1989). It can be differentiated according to severity among discrete, nongeneralized, and generalized social phobia and panic disorder and could be differentiated by fears of negative evaluation and by nonassertiveness. Simple phobias and fears are highly familial disorders that do not seem to transmit an increased risk for other phobic or anxiety disorders (Fyer, Mannuzza, Gallops, & Martin, 1990).

However, a substantial overlap between disorders may exist with regard to anxiety sensitivity and catastrophic beliefs about panic attacks. Comorbid depression may blur the boundaries between social phobias and panic disorder (Alden & Phillips, 1990; Ball, Otto, Pollack, & Uccello, 1995). Furthermore, phobias may be found more likely in dependent personalities, supporting that dependency may be, not without conflict, the root of many avoidant patterns (Reich, Noyes, & Troughton, 1987).

There is some controversy about differentiating social fears and phobias from social anxiety (Dolan-Sewell, Krueger, & Shea, 2001). For the present purposes, phobias and fears will be considered as being somewhat more intense than social anxieties (Heimberg, Liebowitz, Hope, & Schneider, 1995), along a continuum of avoidance. The avoidant personality disorder and generalized social phobia appear to be overlapping constructs that possess only minor differences with respect to age of onset and severity of dysfunction

(Brown, Heimberg, & Juster, 1995; Herbert, Hope, & Bellack, 1992; Holt, Heimberg, & Hope, 1992; Turner, Beidel, & Townsley, 1992; Widiger, 1992).

Why do some individuals with panic disorders become avoidant in various degrees of severity, as in the case of agoraphics? There may be a relationship between cognitive expectations for negative outcomes with an inability to utilize adequate coping strategies and avoidance, with women more likely to develop avoidance than men and avoiders more likely to be depressed (Clum & Knowles, 1991). Anticipation of the occurrence of panic may relate to levels of avoidance of specific situations, whereas anxieties about consequences of panicking, like in physical danger, yield little predictive validity (Craske & Barlow, 1988). The predicted probability of panic seems the most significant variable associated with avoidance (Craske, Rapee, & Barlow, 1988).

Irrational social fears, the components of social phobia, seem related to specific family patterns. Relatives of social phobics may show a greater than threefold increased risk for social phobia as compared to relatives of controls. A significantly higher rate of social phobia may be present among siblings versus parents of social phobics, suggesting the contribution of familial factors to the etiology of this disorder (Fyer, Mannuzza, Chapman, & Liebowitz, 1993). Having an affected family member seems associated with a two- to threefold risk increase for both social phobia and avoidant personality disorder (Tillfors, Furmark, Ekselius, & Fredrikson, 2001).

In spite of theories to the contrary, social phobics and agoraphobics do not seem to differ in separation anxiety experiences, even though social phobics may be more likely to perceive their parents as seeking to isolate them from social experiences (Bruch, 1989). Offspring of parents with DSM-IV social phobia apparently have higher rates of social phobias. Multiple familial factors seem involved in the development of social phobias. Not only parental social phobias, but also other parental psychopathology may contribute to the development of social phobia (Lieb, Wittchen, Höfler, & Fuetsch, 2000). Indeed, individuals with relatives who express a great deal of criticism and negative attributions (expressed emotions) may be more likely to achieve high degrees of panic/fear (Flanagan & Wagner, 1991). Relatives of patients with panic disorder without major depression disorder were at five times the risk for social phobia (Horwath, Wolk, Goldstein, Wickramaratne, et al., 1995). Familial resemblance and transmission of specific phobias could be experiential in origin and mediated by indirect exposure. It could also represent genetically facilitated learning and exemplify imprinting in humans (Fredrikson, Annas, & Wik, 1997).

Avoidant Personalities. In spite of controversies surrounding this personality pattern (Benjamin, 1993), its place in the DSM-IV seems firmly established. This personality is described by a pattern of social discomfort, fear of negative evaluation, and shyness in a variety of social, occupational, and educational contexts. It is represented by an unwillingness to become involved for fear of being rejected, not liked, or disapproved. There are no friends or confidants except for close family members. These and other negative characteristics are fully defined in the DSM-IV as well as by Benjamin (1993) and represent the extreme of avoidance, with the sole exception of schizophrenia, which will be considered in Chapter 12 as an even more severe and extreme prototype of avoidance.

MODELS CONCEPTUALLY SIMILAR BUT INDEPENDENT FROM THIS MODEL

Evidence independent but conceptually similar of this model has already been reviewed in previous publications. Nonetheless, an attempt will be made to update that evidence, especially in light of the attachment model that is conceptually similar to the extent that its underlying dimension relies on how individuals approach or avoid other individuals.

Ethological Theory

Proximity seeking is regarded as the hallmark of attachment in the ethological theory of social development, especially in primates and in infants (Serafica, 1978; Tracy, Lamb, & Ainsworth, 1976). Its many methodological shortcomings bring into question its validity (Lamb, 1976). Nonetheless, this theory was the foundation for the attachment model listed below.

The Attachment Model

There is little doubt whether attachment, viewed as "the need to belong" to frequent, nonaversive interactions within an ongoing relational bond, is powerful, extremely pervasive, and fundamental to the formation of attachments that resist the dissolution of existing bonds. Inadequate or missing attachments are linked to a variety of ill effects on health, adjustment, and well-being (Baumeister & Leary, 1995). The "need to belong" is represented in the attachment model that has been validated across the world with children, adolescents, single adults, and couples and partially reviewed in Chapter 3 (Bartholomew, Kwong, & Hart, 2001). The universal validity of this model has been questioned by Rothbaum, Weisz, Pott, Miyakem, and Morelli (2000), among others (Lamb, 1987; Weinraub, Brooks, & Lewis, 1977). Rothbaum et al. argued that this model is loaded with Western values and meanings. Using Japan as a comparison, for instance, the attachment model stresses a secure base to achieve autonomy and independence. These qualities are not as important in the Japanese culture as they are in ours. Hence, if this argument is correct, one has to question whether the four relational styles developed from this model are "universal" or limited to the Western culture. A great deal of research to support models from the present theory have been validated in the Italian culture, assuming that that culture is somewhat similar to the English-speaking culture. Whether models of this theory are universal or not remains an empirical matter, left to further evaluation. In spite of possible controversy, there is no question that Model[4] bears substantial similarities to the attachment model.

This model considers one functional, secure pattern, and three dysfunctional, insecure styles, avoidant/dismissing, preoccupied/ambivalent, and fearful. For instance, the avoidant style could be related to the avoidant personality, preoccupied could be related to the dependent personality, while fearfulness could be related to borderline personality disorder in Cluster B (Bartholomew et al., 2001). Similarities between the attachment model are stronger with the selfhood model, which will be discussed in Chapter 12.

There are so many primary and secondary sources concerning the attachment model that to attempt another review would be redundant and useless. However, if the links between the selfhood model in Chapter 12 are replicated, then most of the research related to attachment would also be relevant to the validity of that model, and, in part, of this theory.

Exposure Therapy

Exposure therapy is one of the most frequent and powerful techniques to deal and face fearful or painful events or objects and is based on approaching those very traumatic events or objects that have been avoided since their occurrence (L'Abate, 1984). Even writing about painful experiences (Esterling et al., 1999) is another form of approach, just as talk is. The evidence for the usefulness of writing (Ch. 1) is at the basis for the development of workbooks that are relevant to all three Clusters A, B, and C (L'Abate, 1996). However, one should be careful in helping respondents approach, experiencing and expressing, painful emotions without a structure or at least a plan of how this approach is to take place, providing positive alternatives in case of need.

Functions of Model [4]

This model finds its theoretical roots in integrating the humanistic school described in Chapter 4 and stressing the importance of emotional ties in "communal" relationships.

Diagnostically, as discussed at greater length in companion Chapter 16, one would need to ask: "What is the capacity of an individual to be close? Is that individual able to cry and be sad with those one loves and who love reciprocally? How are feelings experienced and expressed in intimate relationships? For instance, in the most common prototype of avoiding feelings, alexithymic individuals (Ch. 4) are not able to feel and therefore are unable to express deep feelings, a condition that produces unwanted negative reactions.

Prescriptively, in keeping with the thesis of this theory, one would simplistically prescribe to: "Share your hurts with those who reciprocate in kind." Unfortunately, this prescription is not as easily applicable as one would like. Nonetheless, a variety of workbooks (L'Abate, 1996) are available to help individuals who do not know how to feel and how to express those feelings. Furthermore, Appendix A contains a list of many workbooks for most personality disorders of both Clusters B and C that heretofore have been resistant to traditional, f2f talk-based, personal contact psychotherapies.

Therapeutically, one needs to establish the intensity of how one approaches or avoids relevant relationships or objects through repetition of heretofore avoided feelings, events, persons, or objects.

CONCLUSION

The ability to love and to be close or distant as one desires is not enough. We need to add the ability to negotiate to give a more complete picture of intimate relationships.

Chapter 8

Time and the Ability
to Negotiate
Model[5,6]

*"... the functioning of an individual in a certain type of situation
changes across time as a result of developmental processes in the
individual and of changes in the person-environment system* (Bergman,
Magnusson, & El-Khouri, 2003, p. 10)."

This chapter expands on a model about the ability to negotiate (bargain
and problem solve) in intimate relationships. This ability in intimate and
nonintimate relationships requires control (Zarit, Pearlin, & Schaie, 2003).
References about control, from both psychological and sociological view-
points, abound. Some were considered in previous publications. There are
too many references to cite here, so only those relevant to this model will
be included.

Time is defined here by a dimension of *control* evaluated by extremes in
discharge-delay functions. A developmental balance and regulation of these
functions eventually would lead to the ability to negotiate and problem
solve in intimate relationships (Ch. 17). These functions are regulated by
R, after E has been experienced and, in ideal situations, expressed and
shared before relying on R. In less than ideal, and usually dysfunctional
relationships, E is expressed without R, leading to destructive expressions
of A. Control should not be equated with the construct of regulation because
that equation is incorrect. Regulation is a supraordinate construct that relates
to balancing both distance and control functions. One needs to balance and
regulate distances as much as one needs to balance and regulate controls.

This balance and regulation would involve the whole person in all his or her qualities, strengths, and weaknesses.

Hence, the two assumptions of the theory postulate that personality socialization is defined by the ability to love and the ability to negotiate. Their two fundamental, underlying dimensions, distance and control, find a great deal of support in studies about the circumplex (not to be confused with David Olson's circumplex) with individuals (Kiesler, 1996; Plutchik & Conte, 1997). However, these studies have not shown, as far as I am aware, how the circumplex can be applied to a typology of intimate relationships. Nor have they lead to preventive or psychotherapeutic interventions. Links between circumplex models of individuals and models of couple and family relationships, based on distance and control functions, have been examined elsewhere (L'Abate & De Giacomo, 2003) and in Chapters 17 and 18.

CONTROL: THE ABILITY TO NEGOTIATE AND TO SOLVE PROBLEMS

Petronio (2000) attributed three meanings to the construct of balance, which is basic to regulation of both distance and control functions. According to her, and in agreement with how this construct is used here, "balance is not an unitary concept (p. xiv)." It consists of:

1. *Polarizations*, which, within this context, encompass the dialectic dimension of balance versus imbalance. For instance, one may be polarized in approaching others while another would be polarized toward avoiding others. One may be polarized toward discharging immediately, while another may be polarized in delaying as much as possible to the point of nonacting.
2. *Equilibrium*, which, within this context, implies oscillations between stasis and status quo on one hand versus change and even conflict, chaos, and confusion on the other. For instance, one may vary contradictorily and inconsistently within approach-avoidance and within discharge-delay, approaching and discharging on some occasions and avoiding and delaying on other, similar occasions.
3. *Weighted proportions*, which, within this context, imply giving greater value and valence to one choice over another. One may value approach over avoidance while another may value avoidance over approach. One may favor discharge over delay, while another may favor delay over discharge. In short, balance means reconciling extremes in polarizations, finding a middle ground that keeps one's

life in equilibrium, after one has weighted pros and cons of certain options and choices over other ones.

The two assumptions of distance and control underlie the concept of competence. This concept implies an interaction of someone with someone else or with something else, be it the presence of someone, a parent, partner, or child to love and to negotiate with, as well as negotiating within oneself on when to discharge and when to delay, or how to discharge or delay. One cannot talk about competence without specifying the context in which such competence is manifested. Ford (1985), for instance, in reviewing past and present definitions of competence, referred to it as: (1) the ability to formulate and produce persistent goal-directed activity, (2) one's behavioral repertoire of specified and specifiable skills and abilities, and (3) effectiveness in relevant contexts. Most dysfunctionalities are the outcome of deficits or excesses in either of these three abilities.

The ability to negotiate, problem solve, brainstorm, and bargain, develops from the ability to regulate self in relationship with intimate and non-intimates (Bazerman, Curhan, Moore, & Velley, 2000). This ability is based on a balance of discharge-delay tendencies that is present in functional relationships but defective or even absent in dysfunctional ones (Bradley, 2000; Shapiro, 2000). It means being able to regulate oneself and, in so doing, allowing others to express themselves, giving them the freedom to discharge, i.e., express oneself and be heard. This ability is shown in helpful and creative ways, without delays, distractions, or procrastination. If there is no balance in control regulation, then severe, abusive, neglectful, and hurtful discharge would bring about similar extremes, either in rebellion and retaliation, or in extreme delays and withdrawals. As a result the process of negotiation will be derailed and become ineffective.

Negotiation and problem solving take place successfully and effectively within functional democratic relationships where the singular importance of all participants is not only acknowledged but valued. In dysfunctional relations, there is either immediate discharge (name calling, blaming, etc.) reaching abusive proportions, or procrastinating delays. There is no possibility of reaching an agreement and consensus about how to solve even the smallest, irrelevant issue.

Time and Controls

Consequently, in this model, time subsumes a dimension of control, defined by extremes in discharge (fast/strong responding) and impulsivity at one end and delay (slow/weak responding) and passivity at the other. Corresponding terms in the literature have been dysregulation or dysinhibition and inhibition respectively (Bradley, 2000; Watson, 2000), or reflection-impulsivity (Finch & Nelson, 1976). Extremes in discharge (dysregulation, dysinhibition) tend to produce reactive and overreactive hyperactivity, attention deficits, impulsivity, and acting out in relationships. Extremes in delay (inhibition) tend to produce overtly underreacting obsessive, ruminative thinking and compulsively repetitive behavior as well as seemingly nonreactivity at the observational level, but evident reactivity at physiological levels.

Functionalities in relationships are found in balances and regulation of discharge-delay tendencies. Dysfunctionalities in relationships are found when there is no balance within extremes but overreliance on extremes. Discharge as well as delay can be expressed in a variety of forms and intensities, all along the ERAAwC Model[1], either consistent or inconsistent among themselves. Discharge in itself means action and talk. However, both actions and talk may be impetuous or deliberate, impulsive or controlled, discharged immediately, or delayed *sine die*, as shown in slowness of E, R, A, and Aw components.

Discharge and weak or inadequate controls is a major characteristic of Cluster B disorders (Barlow, 1993; Benjamin, 1993; Livesley, 2001; Millon et al., 1999). Two major differences between Clusters B and C disorders are speed or slowness of responding and the direction of the disorder. Cluster C disorders are usually slow in responding, characterized by medium to extreme delay, while disorders of Cluster B are characterized by medium to extreme discharge. In Cluster C the direction is oriented toward or even against the self, a so-called autoplasticity, while disorders in Cluster B are oriented outside of the self toward the immediate context, a so-called alloplasticity. Although extremes in inward directions of Cluster C eventually become internalizations, as in anxiety, depression, and fears, extremes in outward directions of Cluster B eventually become externalizations, as in anger, hostility, and aggression. This view is shared by a position that there are two types of psychiatric disorders, those characterized by excessive impulsivity, as in Cluster B, and those characterized by excessive control, as in Cluster C (Lopez-Ibor, 1997). This issue will be revisited in Chapter 12, where Axis I and Cluster A disorders will be considered in relation to a selfhood model.

Discharge in Cluster B disorders may take place with or without anger, hostility, or aggression. For instance, narcissistic, histrionic, or hysterical personalities tend to discharge, but their discharge usually does not contain aggression, which may be verbal but not physical. In borderline and antisocial personalities, on the other hand, discharge, more often than not, will also contain some form of direct or indirect anger, hostility, and aggression. This cluster has been characterized by Benjamin (1993) as "the dramatic erratic group," because the main issue with individuals in this cluster is either minimal or inadequate self-control.

The Measurement of Control

Control, as defined by extremes in inhibition (delay) and dysinhibition (discharge), can be measured by:

- *Reaction time*: This is the time elapsed between introduction or presence of an internal or external stimulus experience or event and reaction to that event as measured by speed (fast/slow) of reacting to that experience. Inhibition, that is, delay in responding to a stimulus event, is present in the development of internalizations (anxiety, depression, and fears). The prototype for high discharge, i.e., low control, is impulsivity and criminal acting out. Prototypes for high delay, i.e., high control, could contribute to obsessive and ruminative personalities (reviewed in the previous chapter) and schizophrenic individuals, which will be reviewed in Chapter 12.

  Dysinhibition and development of externalizations (anger, hostility, and aggression) represent the immediate discharge in responding to a stimulus event. Inhibition and development of internalizations (anxiety, depression, and fears) represent delay, with the exceptions of panic disorders, where discharge takes place as an explosion after a period of delay. Pathology is evident with extreme, contradictory, and inconsistent vacillations between delay and discharge, with permanence of one pattern over the other. Criminals as a whole rely on discharge, while schizophrenics as a whole rely on delay.

- *Duration*: This measure refers to how much time is spent in activities and settings, as measured objectively and subjectively in Chapter 6. Activities and settings include people as well as objects. An addict may spend more time using alcohol or drugs than being with loved ones.

- *Frequency*: This is another measure of how much time one spends with someone or something. A cigarette may take a few minutes to smoke. However, when the number of cigarettes increases, the time spent on smoking increases as well.

- *Rate*: This is another measure of how time is used. One might not be able to smoke in a work environment. However, one may make up for this inability by smoking at a faster rate once at home. The number of total cigarettes smoked at the end of the day may compare in frequency, but the rate of smoking may be different.

- *Intensity*: The response may vary between weak and strong, mild or forceful, pleasurable or unpleasant.

- *Direction*: As already mentioned above, the response can be toward or against self or others, as well as toward or away from settings and/or objects.

- *Temporal perspective*: This measure refers to how one views self and others according to a perspective that includes past, present, and future. Some people are archaeologists and historians, oriented toward ruminating and rambling about the past, trying to relate the present to its historical roots. Depressed individuals, for example, are mostly oriented toward the past, collecting and remembering past hurts and traumas and letting them determine their present behavior. Some people are completely present-oriented and pay little if any attention to either the past or the future. Addicts are the best prototype of this temporal orientation. Some people are oriented toward the future, as in the lives of some tycoons, who are interested in increasing money and possessions for the sake of acquisition. Gamblers and some Type A personalities are another expression of the same perspective, waiting to score big in spite of losses.

Since birth the temporal perspective of life is inevitably totally oriented toward the future. As we age, the future decreases and the past increases. Living in the present means not allowing the past or the future to overwhelm the present (McFadden & Atchley, 2001; Roeckelein, 2000). Some people, for instance, such as the depressed, allow the past to intrude and control the present. Some people live only or mainly in the present, as in the case of economically and educationally deprived people whose only concern is daily survival. Some people allow the future to control the present, as in the case of those with personality disorders like gamblers and driven individuals, who strive for the "big hit."

Prototypes Defining the Model

As discussed in the previous chapter, prototypes for this model will be derived from Cluster B: narcissistic, histrionic (hysterical), borderline, and antisocial, and as representing the inability to control and regulate self in relationships. In addition to these disorders, a developmental attention deficit hyperactivity disorder, and another personality disorder characterized by driven discharge, the Type A personality will be included. Those with these disorders find it difficult to negotiate and problem solve with intimates as well as nonintimates (Mattia & Zimmerman, 2001).

Most prototypes defining the dimension of control are found in Cluster B, where controls are weak, inadequate, or incomplete. Most prototypes in this cluster are characterized by discharge rather than delay. Obsessions, may well belong in Cluster C, where there are conflicts about who and what to approach and avoid. Yet, the action side of obsessions, that is, compulsivity, is in itself a form of discharge, usually with objects rather than people. Hence, its inclusion in this model. Obsessions, if present without compulsions, would belong in Cluster C.

Too Much Control Equals Delay

There is a continuum of delaying, ranging from normal procrastination to fantasies, obsessions, and ruminations.

Procrastination. Although not included in the official DSM-IV classification, procrastination represents avoidance for assuming responsibilities or completing assigned chores or tasks on time. Procrastination has been linked to passive-aggressive personality disorders and to obsessive-compulsive tendencies (Ferrari, Johnson, & McCown, 1995). The latter source is the best compendium to date for all that is known about this characteristic. By the same token, passive-aggressive or negativistic (Millon et al., 1999) personalities may lack validity as a psychiatric diagnosis. However, when the passive-aggressive personality is defined by the interaction of extremes in rigidity, resentment, resistance, reactance, and reversed reinforcement, it may acquire status as a formal diagnosis (Fine, Overholser, & Berkoff, 1992).

Obsessive Compulsive Personalities. Although obsessions per se imply ruminations with avoidance, absence, or delay of action and a medium level of discharge, except in thinking, compulsivity implies external repetition of routines and rituals, actions that represent discharge rather than delay, such as cleaning and/or checking, excessive concerns with cleanliness, eating and food, exactness, counting, hoarding, or slowness rituals (Ball, Baer, & Otto, 1996; Gibbs, 1996). Indeed, female undergraduate compulsives seem to be slower than noncompulsive controls (Frost, Lahart, Dugas, & Sher, 1988), supporting placement of this disorder among disorders of control, i.e., Cluster B in this chapter.

Different kinds of obsessive-compulsive behavior, as distinguished from obsessive-compulsive thoughts, can be reliably measured by the Padua Inventory (Sanavio, 1988; van Oppen, Hoekstra, & Emmelcamp, 1995). Even though obsessions are considered separately from compulsions, there is no denying that obsessional thoughts and compulsive behavior are interrelated (Hoogduin, 1986).

This disorder seems to be the outcome of certain family characteristics (Frost, Steketee, Cohn, & Griess, 1994) as well as having definable effects on family members, including depression, obsessive ruminating, performing rituals, and poor task performance (Cooper, 1996). Whether the reported effects are consequences, concomitants, or determinants of this disorder remains to be seen. About 11% of relatives of severely obsessive-compulsive patients had been hospitalized for other psychiatric conditions. These rather isolated families had cultures that emphasized cleanliness and perfection. However, other family members did not develop rituals or obsessive rationales as had the patients. Apparently, one or both parents, in a seemingly unfulfilled marriage, directed symbiotic needs toward the patients. Parents and offspring seemed trapped in an increasingly powerless struggle against symptoms that acted as a barrier to closeness but that also prevented the patients from developing an autonomous existence. It is possible that parental symbiotic needs combined with perfectionistic family styles, including a constitutional vulnerability to psychiatric disturbance, may make a major contribution to obsessive-compulsive disorder (Hoover & Insel, 1984).

Weak or Inadequate Controls Equals Discharge

There are many prototypes of this extreme, which will be first seen from a developmental viewpoint.

Attention Deficit/Hyperactivity Disorders. Developmentally, this is the major prototype for discharge that supposedly has genetic, temperamental, or hereditary bases (Barkley, 1990), in contrast to a contextual basis (L'Abate, Smith, & Smith, 1985). The latter explained hyperactivity as the outcome of contradictory and inconsistent parental practices within each individual parent and between both parents, with neither parent being aware of these personal and dyadic contradictions and inconsistencies. Since the latter explanation was strictly impressionistic and based on few cases, it remains to be validated by further study and observations. Nonetheless, certain temperamental characteristics seem correlated to behavior problems in children and the quality of the mother-child interactions (Webster-Stratton & Eyberg, 1982).

In contrast to reflective children, who would lie in the middle of this dimension, impulsive children may be more likely to talk of others blaming them unfairly, threaten to harm themselves, hit and bully other children, and be excessively rough in play. On the other hand, reflective children seem more unwilling to talk with adults outside the family (Finch & Nelson, 1976), suggesting that these children may think before acting.

Parents of children with severe symptoms of this disorder seem to demonstrate greater impairment on social and psychological functioning (Murphy & Barkley, 1996). Indeed, risks are higher for hyperactive children if one of their parents suffered from the same disorder in childhood (Biederman, Faraone, Mick, Spencer, et al., 1995). Hence, the possibility of a genetic link seems possible, even though a modeling process between parents and children could account for these results as well. More specifically, fathers of children with this disorder seem to show similarities in child-rearing views, traditional role identification, and some symptoms of the same disorder. Parenting practices seem clearly related to symptoms of this disorder (Arnold, O'Leary, & Edwards, 1997).

A major area of controversy lies in the overlap between these disorders and conduct disorders, especially in children. Supposedly, the latter would be characterized by callous-unemotional traits. Indeed, children high on these traits showed features typically associated with psychopathy, such as a lack of fearfulness, a reward-dominant response style, and little distress by their behavior problems (Barry, Frick, DeShazo, & McCoy, 2000). This possibility is reinforced by the fact that hyperactive children might be more than seven times more likely than controls to have an antisocial personality disorder in adulthood or a drug abuse problem (Mannuzza, Klein, Bessler, & Malroy, 1993).

Type A Personalities.   Placement of this disorder within the rubric of inadequate or weak control is supported by measures of speech speed, rapid motor pace (Anderson & Waldron, 1983), verbal problem solving (Blumenthal, McKee, Haney, & Williams, 1980), and task failure (Lovallo & Pishkin, 1980). The possibility of sex differences in control functions may exist, with Type A women showing better controls than Type B women, while Type A men may display poorer self-control than Type B (Heilbrun & Friedberg, 1988), as also found in Type A adolescents (Johnson, Hunter, Amos, Elder, et al., 1989). Sex-role orientation combined with Type A style may be associated with low social self-esteem, high social anxiety, and depression (Batlis & Small, 1982; De Gregorio & Carver, 1980). This overall Type A personality characteristic seems stable over time (Keltikangas-Jarvinen, 1989), with hostility, competitiveness, and exactingness representing some of the major characteristics of this personality type (Carmelli, Dame, & Swan, 1992; Carmelli, Dame, Swan, & Rosenman, 1991). With increasing age, however, there may be a tendency to perceive oneself less as Type A (Blumenthal & Herman, 1985).

Even though Type A behavior may not be related to impulsivity, the tendency to discharge quickly, driven risk taking, and nonplanning seem more related to it than impulsivity (Innes, 1980). Time urgency seems also a characteristic of this type, at least as measured by respondents with this pattern who arrived earlier to class than those who did not exhibit such a pattern (Gastorf, 1980; Strahan, 1981). More reliable identification of this type may occur once a reliable state measure is developed (Bennett, Gallacher, & Johnston, 1990; Friedman & Booth-Kewley, 1988) with "contextually sensitive multimodal assessments" (Thorensen & Powell, 1992; Yarnold & Bryant, 1988). In children, competitiveness, impatience, anger, and aggression seem to be characteristics of Type A personality that can be reliably assessed through tasks, test scores, and teacher ratings (Matthews & Angulo, 1980).

These personalities would be the best example of compulsive personalities, being more extroverted and neurotic than non-Type A (Lobel, 1988; Smith, O'Keefe, & Allred, 1989), even though they may not be included formally in Cluster B classifications. Many Type A individuals are productive members of society even though they may lose in the arena of intimate relationships. Cognitively, hardy Type A individuals may experience significantly less burnout and psychological distress than less hardy Type B counterparts (Nowack, 1986). Vigilant coping seems to be related to suppressed anger, which in itself may be responsible for coronary heart disease (Evans & Moran, 1987).

Whether these types are more susceptible to coronary heart disease is still a hypothesis that has been subjected to a variety of studies, too many to cite here (Matthews, 1988; Ortega & Weinstein, 1988), at least in predominantly white, middle-class males in the United States, but increasingly recognized in other countries like Italy and Poland (Wrzesniewski, Forgays, & Bonaiuto, 1990) and Japan (Nakano, 1990). Harassment and hostility may be additional contributing factors to the disease (Carmody, Crossen, & Wiens, 1989; Diamond et al., 1984), just as sleep disturbances are (Hicks et al., 1979). The same conclusion applies to headaches as physiological concomitants or determinants of the disease (Pittner & Houston, 1980; Rappaport, McNulty, & Brantley, 1988; Woods et al., 1984).

Type A personality has been made synonymous with coronary-prone disease versus Type B, which is not coronary-prone (Salmon, Pearce, Smith, Manyande et al., 1989). There are some doubts about whether symptoms reported by Type A and Type B personalities are any different from each other (Offitt & Lacroix, 1988; Suls & Sanders, 1988). On the other hand, there are passively dependent individuals at risk for coronary heart disease who do not show Type A characteristics (Rimé, & Bonami, 1979). Differentiation between Type A and Type B personalities may be based on blood pressure alone (Harrell, 1980). Physicians who have divorced more than once may be characterized by greater nonconformity, impulsivity, and risk-taking tendencies than never or once-divorced physicians. The former also reported relying on several negative health practices, like cigarette smoking and drinking. Here is where distinct personality characteristics demonstrate definite outcomes in intimate relationships.

Many of the foregoing references mention the need for social approval, suggesting that Type A personalities may present a "nice" social facade to make a good impression possibly in exchange for relationships but not in friendships (Burke & Weir, 1980). They may also be more dominant interpersonally (Yarnold, Mueser, & Grimm, 1985). However, it remains to be seen whether this social facade is consistent with how Type A personalities behave in intimate relationships (Burke & Weir, 1980a, b). It seems as if mothers may be more responsible for Type A behavior in girls of elementary school age (Sweda, Sines, Lauer, & Clarke, 1986). In school, Type A men spend more time studying, have higher GPAs, recall their fathers as being more severe and punishing them physically more often, making them feel resentful rather than guilty when punished. Type A women recall their mothers as being more punitive physically. These parental practices may have contributed to the anger and hostility that seems more common in this personality type (Waldron et al., 1980).

Histrionic/Hysterical Personalities. These personalities are high in discharge by attempting to control others through seductive, manipulative, and indirect tactics. Nonetheless, they may be low on acting out, and hostility may be expressed more indirectly than in other personality disorders. Borstein (1999) summarized contemporary theoretical perspectives (psychoanalytic, cognitive-dynamic, and biosocial learning), concluding that "inconsistent, early reinforcement patterns" in family dynamics "are central" to the specific interpersonal style found in this disorder. Nonetheless, he failed to produce evidence that would support any of the theories he reviewed about the etiology of this disorder. Overlap of these disorders with narcissistic personality disorders and lack of information about family background and intimate relationships need further attention and research.

Narcissistic Personalities. These personalities may be relatively low in acting out, even though one could argue that most Cluster B personality disorders suffer in one way or another from narcissism and self-centeredness. However, there are distinguishing characteristics that are specific to this disorder, in the sense of: (1) superiority; (2) uniqueness; (3) exaggeration of talents; (4) boastful and pretentious behavior; (5) grandiose fantasies, self-centered and self-referential behavior; (6) need for attention and admiration; (7) arrogant and haughty behavior; and (8) high achievement (Ronningstam, 1999). In addition to these visible characteristics, less visible ones may be underlying feelings of inadequacy, unhappiness, and worry, disturbances in interpersonal relationships, and sensitivity to criticism and defeat (Mullins & Kipelman, 1988). Less empirically based than previous descriptions, there could be a division of strengths in reality testing, thought processes, interpersonal relations, and adaptation to reality. Weaknesses would lie in poor impulse control and frustration tolerance, use of primitive ego-defenses, identity diffusion, and affective instability (Goldstein, 1985). There is the possibility that certain paranoid conditions may develop within a context of narcissistic personality disorders (Garfield & Havens, 1991; Meissnér, 1979).

According to Ronningstam (1999): "...inconsistent attunement between caregiver and child, and the caregiver's failure to help the child to moderate positive and negative hyperarousal states...as well as low arousal states lead to a failure to develop adequate affect regulation (p. 685)." Ronningstam quotes Schore's (1994) identification of two types of caregiver-child interactions that may lead to two different types of narcissism, arrogance and shyness. An insecure-resistant attachment pattern in the caregiver may contribute to states of hyperarousal, while a depressed-preoccupied attachment pattern my contribute to hypoarousal in the offspring. Ronningstam also cites theorists like Kernberg and Kohut as suggesting various family constellations that may be responsible for the development of this personality disorder. In addition to those two theorists, she also included the biosocial-learning perspective of Theodore Millon and T. Beck's cognitive perspective as possible explanations for the etiology of this disorder. Unfortunately, this theorizing does not seem to have produced, as far as I know, empirical evidence to support it.

Borderline Personalities. There has been an increase in the frequencies of this disorder in the psychiatric literature, to the point that children and adolescents have received this diagnosis at an increasing rate. Their families have significantly greater rates of psychopathology, particularly in the areas of depressive, substance abuse, and antisocial disorders (Goldman, D'Angelo, & DeMaso, 1993; Trull, Sher, Minks-Brown, Durbin, et al., 2000). Reported histories of sexual and physical abuse (Ogata, Silk, Goodrich, Lohr, et al., 1990; Silk, Lee, Hill, & Lohr, 1995) and witnessing violence were the main predictors of such a condition. The control dimension, however, significantly predicted this condition even after the influence of sexual abuse was accounted for (Weaver & Clum, 1993).

When women are diagnosed with this disorder, they reported sexual abuse together with suspected seizure, eating, and drug abuse disorders. Physical abuse seemed also related to early family disruption, more frequent hospital admissions, and concomitant antisocial personality disorder (Shearer, Peters, Quaytman, & Ogden, 1990). According to the recollections of individuals with this diagnosis, their parents were viewed as being less caring and more controlling than nonborderline respondents, suggesting a biparental failure in their lives (Paris & Frank, 1989; Zweig-Frank & Paris, 1991). There is a possibility that parents of borderlines could be distinguished by the rigid tightness of the marital bond to the exclusion of attention, support, or protection of their children (Gunderson & Englund, 1980).

Varying from 21% to 57%, a certain percentage of individuals diagnosed with this disorder may be homosexual, 5% may be bisexual, and 11% were diagnoses as paraphiliacs. Fifty-three percent from a sample of 19 men diagnosed with this disorder were homosexual in comparison with 11% of 61 women with the same diagnosis. Apparently homosexuality was 10 times more common among borderline personality disorder (BPD) men than six times more common among BPD women in comparison with the general population or with a controlled group of depressed respondents of either sex (Zubenko, George, Soloff, & Schultz, 1987). Identity disturbances in borderlines may consist of role absorption, painful incoherence, inconsistency, and lack of commitment (Wilkinson-Ryan & Westen, 2000).

A great many borderline personalities have suffered severe sexual, physical, and emotional abuse in childhood (Silk & Lohr, 1996; Westen, Ludolph, Misle, & Ruffins, 1990), especially in women, even though the diagnosis might not correlate with a history of sexual abuse, the severity of symptoms may (Salzman, 1996). In some cases where no sexual abuse occurred, a great percentage of borderline individuals reported being neglected before the age of 18. They reported that caretakers withdrew from them emotionally, treated them inconsistently, denied their thoughts and feelings, placed them in the role of confidant and parent, and failed to provide them with needed protection.

Four risk factors for the development of borderline disorders may be: (1) female gender, (2) sexual abuse by a male noncaretaker, (3) emotional denial by a male caretaker, and (4) inconsistent treatment by a female caretaker (Zanarini, Williams, Lewis, & Reich, 1997).

Antisocial Personalities. This disorder is high on discharge and also on impulsivity (Tremblay, Pihl, Vitaro, & Dobkin, 1994). It is comprised of a variety of patterns of externalization (anger, hostility, and aggression) that, in addition to being reviewed here, will also be considered in Chapters 10, 11, and 12. Many antisocial personalities end up alcoholics (Waldman & Slutske, 2000) or substance abusers (Cacciola, Rutherford, Alterman, & Snider, 1994). An antisocial and unstable lifestyle needs to be differentiated from psychopathy. The latter is characterized by core personality traits that include superficiality, habitual lying and manipulation, callousness, lack of affect, guilt, remorse, and empathy (Harpur, Hakstian, & Hare, 1988).

Antisocial personalities may develop from early age conduct disorders that are marked by family conflict and aggression (Dadds, Sanders, Morrison, & Rebgetz, 1992). Early indications of aggression, one characteristic of antisocial personalities, need to be compared in their familial antecedents with well functioning and anxious children. Aggressive children, for instance, may make regular use of coercive control with their mothers, who may respond indiscriminately by failing to oppose more extreme forms of coercion. In comparison to aggressive children, the mother-child interactions of anxious children seem generally aversive, with mothers attempting to control their children by wavering between coercion and unresponsiveness. These children may try to manage their mothers by being resistant and coercive. Competent children and their mothers, on the other hand, seem to influence each other positively and reciprocally, making prudent use of control exchanges and setting firm limits to coersive attempts. These patterns suggest that children are active agents who influence and are influenced by their relationship with their mother and who behave—across contexts and with different social partners—in ways that reflect that relationship (Dumas, LaFreniere, & Serketich, 1995). It is unfortunate that a similar study has not been replicated with father-child dyads, and with both parents present in interaction with the child.

This disorder is common among the parents of children with conduct disorders, with divorce frequently the result for adults with this disorder. Among boys with divorced parents, more than twice as many boys with an antisocial personality parent might receive a diagnosis of conduct disorder than boys without a parent with the same disorder. Parental divorce does not seem a significant factor in the etiology of conduct disorders in children, but having antisocially disordered parents is (Lahey, Hartdagen, Frick, & McBurnett, 1988).

There may be significant sex differences in early onset conduct problems that may be the harbingers of antisocial personalities in adults (Webster-Stratton, 1996). The possibility that paternal alcoholism or childhood victimization might not tend to increase the risk of antisocial behavior (Pollock, Briere, Schneider, & Knopp, 1990) has been contradicted by following up into adulthood those children who had been substantially abused or neglected at an early age. Childhood victimization seems a significant predictor of the number of lifetime symptoms and a diagnosis of this disorder (Luntz & Widom, 1994). Whether there is a genetic component to the genesis of this disorder is a matter of speculation rather then evidence (Frick & Jackson, 1993). External, situational characteristics account for the development better than any genetic hypothesis. For instance, after controlling for SES, family status, stress level, and parental satisfaction, conduct disorders may be lower in family cohesion and active-recreational orientation but higher in conflict than other control groups (Haddad, Barocas, & Hollenbeck, 1991).

Male adoptees may be at higher risk for antisocial behavior than females due to the adverse effects of a psychiatrically ill adoptive family member or divorce in the adoptive parents. Another so-called genetic variable that predicted antisocial behavior in adoptees was the presence of an antisocial or alcoholic biologic relative (Cadoret & Cain, 1980). Even though heritability may be a factor in the genesis of antisocial behavior, the presence of just another family member is not sufficient to justify such an explanation. One would have to find more than one, and even then, a family climate and interacting parental practices may be sufficient to explain this disorder.

At the very least, antisocial behavior can be distinguished among sociopathic and psychopathic personalities. The latter are characterized by lack of positive emotions and a sense of guilt or regret for negative actions, insight into the nature of the disturbance, and presence of shallow thinking, inability to establish personal relations, and a narcissistic self-concept. Sometimes these characteristics seem related to psychotic behavior since no rationale is found for the behavior itself. Sociopaths, on the other hand, lack a sense of belonging to any community, social judgment, or capacity for enjoyment. Causes of sociopathy can be found in an unhappy home situation characterized by inconsistent discipline, conflicting filial identification, a weak, indulgent mother, and an authoritarian, domineering father (Begun, 1976). Substantial generativity for relations between socialization and antisocial behavior, particularly in men, seems acceptable (Kosson, Steuerwald, Newman, & Widom, 1994).

COMBINING MODELS [4] AND [5]–ORTHOGONALITY OF SPACE AND TIME: MODEL[6]

By considering dimensions of both space and time, that is, distance and control, using Models[4] and [5] as orthogonal dimensions, an additional model is produced by the resulting four quadrants: (1) high love/high negotiation, (2) high love/low negotiation, (3) low love/high negotiation, and (4) low love/ low negotiation. As expanded in the next three chapters, this model allows us to differentiate among four levels of functionality. Quadrant 1 represents the highest, optimal level of functionality in intimate relationships. Quadrants 2 and 3 represent intermediate levels of functionality, while Quadrant 4 represents the lowest level of functionality. Expansions of this model will take place in models covered in Part IV.

Even more specifically, another way to combine both models would be to consider approach-avoidance on a horizontal axis and discharge-delay on a vertical axis. This model would allow placement of personality disorders into the resulting four quadrants. Disorders of high approach and consequently low avoidance, with low discharge and high delay in Cluster

C of Axis II, like dependent personalities, for instance, would fit into that quadrant. Disorders of high avoidance-low approach with low discharge-high delay, like avoidance disorders, would fit into that quadrant. By the same token, Cluster B disorders in Axis II would tend to gravitate into the high discharge-low delay and high approach-low avoidance, like histrionic and narcissistic disorders, would fit into that quadrant. Antisocial and borderline disorders would fit into the high discharge-low delay and high avoidance and low approach quadrant.

Research Supporting Models [4] and [5]

Independent but related support for the validity of both distance and control dimensions has been reviewed in previous publications. Evidence to support both models is found in many independent but conceptually similar dimensions, as, for instance, Bakan's (1968) community and agency; Harter et al.'s (1997) autonomy and connectedness; and Olson's (1996) cohesion and adaptability, among many others. N. E. Aron (2004) has also considered in detail the implication of temperament, how slow or fast one responds, and closeness, how near or far one wants to be from others in ways that support both dimensions of love and intimacy presented here.

A Similar Model: Relational Models Theory

Relational models (RM) theory, developed by Alan P. Fiske (L'Abate, 1997) and expanded into Haslam's (2004) edited work contends that there are four basic types of relationships: (1) communal sharing (CS), which implies giving without expectations of specific reciprocity; (2) authority ranking (AR), where superiors and subordinates look out for each other; (3) equality matching (EM), where distribution of goods and resources is balanced to take care of those participating in the exchange; and (4) market pricing (MP), where competition and economic survival of the fittest are the norm.

When this theory (really a model!) is considered by combining Models[4] and [5], one obtains a 2 × 2 matrix where EM would be high on both love and negotiation, MP would be high on negotiation but low on love, CS would be low on negotiation but high on love, while AR would be low on both love and negotiation. This fit seemed "reasonable" to Haslam (personal communication, November 30, 2003), but he added;

"However...Alan (Fiske and me) would not agree that this (or any other) 2x2 system fully 'encompasses' the 4 RMs. He'd say that each model is distinct and incommensurable, and hence not reducible to simpler dichotomies. That doesn't mean that useful distinctions like yours don't map onto the RMs or help to illuminate them, of course, just that they maybe don't exhaust or define the models (in theory). I'm afraid I forget exactly what 'negotiation' implies in your model. On the face of it your 2 × 2 fits ok with the RMs. CS and EM dyadic relationships are certainly usually warmer than AR and MP. However, most people who fit the models into a 2 × 2 would put EM and MP together as an exchange-like pair and CS and AR together as a more communal one. So maybe you're picking up a different dimension of similarity."

These differences in perspective indicate that clearly objective and measurable definitions of love and negotiation will be needed before reaching a definite conclusion of possible similarity between the two models. At best, the claimed similarity is intriguing and interesting as a hypothesis to be evaluated further.

Practical Implications

Diagnostically one would need to ask how close or how distant and how fast or how slow one is moving; toward whom and what and away from whom and what; and how fast and how slow; and from whom and from what. A complete intergenerational, generational, and developmental history would allow deviant relationships to be placed in the four quadrants of the model. Rather than relying solely on time-consuming interviews, one could rely on a structured, 84-item information form with weights for deviations from the norm and subscores for self, marriage, and family (L'Abate, 1992).

Prescriptively, one would recommend a balance of love and negotiation appropriately and flexibly according to life-cycle demands; aa balance of appropriate distance and appropriate controls according to each specific situation and temporal perspective. Various workbooks (Appendix A) would help a professional deal with the personality disorders classified in this chapter. Instead of relying on talk, motivation to change could be evaluated by a respondent's willingness to complete written homework assignments.

Therapeutically, talk and personal contact with relationships dominated by these disorders should be kept at a minimum unless respondents can demonstrate through completion of written homework assignments that they really want to change and are willing to work for it.

CONCLUSION

Both assumptions of love and negotiation are necessary but not sufficient to "describe" intimate relationships. They are processual, too general, and nonspecific. Nonetheless, their combination allows us to classify Cluster B and C disorders of Axis II into a model that considers both love and negotiation as orthogonal dimensions. However, we need more specific models to cover the whole range of possible intimate relationships, functional and dysfunctional, to indicate especially *what* is exchanged in relationships and the *content* of what is really exchanged and shared between intimates and non-intimates.

Chapter 9

Modalities of Exchange
The Triangle of Living, Model[7]

"The current individual focus on power as a personal attribute can be replaced by a more dynamic, reciprocal, interactive process. Instead of specific or stable power patterns, power interactions should be fluid and time- or situation-specific (Beckman-Brindley & Tavormina, 1978, p. 423)."

This chapter serves as a corollary postulate for the two theoretical assumptions about the ability to love and to negotiate. Those processes describe developmental processes, but the theory needs a postulate about contents of *what* is exchanged and shared among intimates and non-intimates. Contents are composed of six resources classes (Foa et al., 1993; Foa & Foa, 1974): status or importance (Ch. 12), love or intimacy (Ch. 16), services, information, goods or possessions, and money.

From these six resources can be derived three modalities. By combining importance and intimacy we obtain a modality of presence or being, being emotionally available to self and to important others, intimates. The latter is defined as the ability to share joys and pleasures as well as hurts and fears of being hurt (Ch. 16). By combining services and information we obtain a modality of performance or doing. By combining possessions and money we obtain a modality of production or having. Combining performance and production defines the construct of power. Whomever controls all or part of performance and production has power to a degree or another.

Being or presence is relevant to intimate relationships. Doing is relevant to educational and teaching institutions, newspapers, media, welfare, and professional settings. Having is relevant to industry, agriculture, banks, and savings institutions. Developmentally, resources and their modalities change a great deal over the individual and family life cycles, going from being for the first 5 years of life to doing from elementary school years to the end of high school or college to having to work to acquire enough money to buy goods and possessions.

PRESENCE AND POWER

Hence, personality can be defined relationally through competences in being, doing, and having, since these three modalities modulate what we exchange (give and take) with others and with things. The two major dimensions of living, therefore, would be *presence* and *power*. Presence implies the ability to love. It is nonnegotiable in its receptive aspects, but it can be negotiated in its expressive ones. We do not need to argue about our subjectively receptive feelings of love for someone. However, we may need to negotiate how those feelings are expressed to accommodate someone else's needs and wishes. Power, on the other hand, is negotiated in functional relationships and nonnegotiable or poorly negotiated in dysfunctional ones. Thus, all three modalities, in their reduction to two major contents of exchange, are directly related to the theory's major assumptions to the ability to love and the ability to negotiate power. Both elaborate on what it means to love (Ch. 7) and to negotitiate (Ch. 8). Both abilities are lacking in one way or another in semifunctional and dysfunctional relationships, while they are effective in functional ones.

Presence, in the sense of emotional availability to oneself and to significant others, can only be shared. In functionalities, presence is kept separate from performance and production and is negotiated successfully, i.e., positively and effectively. In dysfunctionalities, of course, power and presence become confused, diffused, and fused to the point that issues of power (performance and production) are mixed up with issues of presence. In dysfunctionalities, presence is not shared appropriately, while power is either not negotiated or is negotiated negatively and unsuccessfully. When importance and intimacy become conditional on performance or production or both, oftentimes they become substitute expressions for being ("If you loved me you would do ... If you loved me, you would buy me ... !). Therefore, being deals with the ability to attribute importance to self (status) and to others (partners, family members or friends, Ch. 12) and the ability to be intimate—sharing hurts and fears of being hurt (Ch. 16).

This distinction allows one to relate developmental theory of interpersonal competence to communal psychotherapeutic practice—being emotionally available to respondents, i.e., relationship skills (Lazar, 2000)—and to agentic practice—structuring therapy through homework assignments (Kazantzis et al., in press) or workbooks (Ch. 1). However, as discussed in previous chapters, this context does not need to be f2f and verbal to be helpful.

Conceptual and independent support for this seemingly abstract distinction between modalities of exchange, love and negotiation, in addition to the early work of Foa and Foa (1974), can be found in Bakan's (1968) important and influential distinction between communal and agentic relationships, already introduced in Chapter 3, as applied to psychotherapy, distinguishing between style and structuring skills. However, it is applicable to the assumptions and modalities of this theory as well, relating presence and being to community and power (doing and having) to agency. This distinction has been expanded and supported by Clark and her coworkers (Clark, 1986; Clark & Mills, 1979; Clark, Mills, & Powell, 1986; Clark & Reis, 1989; Clark & Wassell, 1985).

There may be pervasive sex differences in psychological and physical well-being, which may be linked to differential socialization for men and women, especially when these differences are defined by masculinity and femininity. Consequently, agency may mean focus on self and forming separations, possibly reflecting a masculine orientation, while communion may mean focus on others and forming connections, possibly reflecting a feminine orientation. When one occurs in the absence of the other, negative health outcomes may occur. Agency may be more related to control, while communion may be more related to social support (Helgeson, 1994). Agency and communion could be related to depression vulnerabilities as autonomy and sociotropy respectively. Agency seems unrelated to autonomy but inversely related to sociotropy, while communion may be positively related to sociotropy and inversely related to autonomy. After controlling for vulnerabilities, agency may be inversely related to measures of dysphoria and negative affect, while both agency and communion may be related to positive affect (Bruch, 2002).

The distinction between being with intimates through either performance or production or dealing with goods and possessions finds its philosophical roots in differences between "P-predicates" dealing with people and "M-predicates" applying exclusively to material objects (Solomon, 1976). This distinction, person-versus-thing orientation finds support where the former is linked to intimacy, while the latter is not related to any intimate relationship factor (Little & Kane, 1974). Another ready-made source to review this triangle are greeting cards, some stressing sharing and loving unconditionally, some stressing what the beloved has done, some coupled with monetary gifts.

As in the two previous chapters, all three modalities will be illustrated by extreme prototypes.

BEING AND ITS IMPLICATIONS

The ability to love is not enough, we also need to be able to be intimate, that is, being able to share hurts and fears of being hurt *reciprocally* with loved ones. Maslow (1968) and humanistically oriented theorists (stressed the importance of being at the expense of negotiation and problem solving. Behaviorally oriented theorists and therapists stressed the importance of doing, as shown in problem-solving behaviors at the expense of being (Ch. 4).

Support for the former is found in studying the emotional availability in the mother, for instance, as defined by sensitivity, involvement, nonintrusiveness, and child responsiveness, which in return makes the difference in producing positive health outcomes in the child, while its absence or inadequacy may produce negative consequences (Biringen & Robinson, 1991). Support for the latter can be found in examples of problem solving and negatiation reviewed in Chapter 17.

"Being together" in couples and families can be obtained by stressing the importance of hugging, holding, huddling, and cuddling (3HC) as an expression of caring for each other nonverbally, without demands for perfection, productions, performance, or problem solving (L'Abate, 2001, 2003a; L'Abate & De Giacomo, 2003). In addition to 3HC, Omer (2001) recently presented another application of "being present." Although 3HC is directly derived from the modality of presence, Omer's application is independent of but still highly related to it. He applied the principles of nonviolence to deal with difficult parent-child disciplinary problems without escalation. That is a very concrete application of the importance of "being present."

Conceptually relevant models to being present can be found in factors characterized by valuing of relationships and sensitivity to the effects of one's actions on others (connectedness) and by anxious concerns regarding possible rejection (neediness) (Rude & Burnham, 1995). In addition to neediness, one would add vulnerability to hurts from loved ones and fallibility in hurting loved ones without meaning or intending to do it (Ch. 16). Hence, connectedness with loved ones implies also acceptance and acknowledgment of our inherent neediness for intimate others, vulnerability to them, and fallibility in hurting them without intending to do it (L'Abate, 1999a).

There is the possibility of gender differences in belongingness. Women's sociality may be oriented toward dyadically close relationships. Men sociality may be oriented toward a larger group. Gender differences in aggression, helping behavior, desire for power, uniqueness, self-representations, interpersonal behavior, and intimacy may tend to support the validity of this distinction in gender differences (Baumeister & Sommer, 1997).

Importance

This resource, originally called "status" by Foa and Foa (1974), will be considered in greater detail in Chapter 12, where extreme prototypes of how importance is attributed, expressed, and shared will be described.

Intimacy

This resource, originally called "love" by Foa and Foa (1974) will be considered in greater detail in Chapter 16, where examples of how intimacy is expressed and shared will be described.

DOING AND ITS IMPLICATIONS

Included in this category, as prototypes of extreme doing, are Type A and obsessive compulsives personalities, already described in Chapter 8. Extremes in compulsive exercise can be found in certain athletes. Extremes in doing can be found in coronary-prone, driven Type A personalities, continuously or compulsively busy, driven individuals who cannot stop lest they become depressed (workaholics), at the expense of being close and committed to prolonged relationships, as described in Chapter 8 (Newmann, 1975; Nielson & Dobson, 1980; Ottenberg, 1975). The workaholic tendency may also be found in mental health professionals who suffer from a compulsion to work, allowing the immediate needs of their clients to dominate their lives. Symptoms of workaholic tendencies may include excessive gastrointestinal sensitivity, abnormal blood pressure, health problems, sleep difficulties, nervousness, lack of vitality, and inability to relax. The inability to set limits to one's work schedule may be the greatest handicap to this condition (Overbeek, 1976). Workaholics with high work involvement and drive with low enjoyment of work are different from work enthusiasts with high work involvement, low work drive, and enjoyment. "Real" workaholics tend to be more perfectionistic, more unwilling or unable to delegate responsibility, and experience greater work stress than work enthusiasts (Spence & Robbins, 1992). The work ethic of an industrial society like ours may be connected to self-esteem, while the loss or inability to work may result in decrease sex interest or even impotence (Racy, 1974).

Prototypes at the other extreme of nondoing would be procrastinating and passive-aggressive personalities (Ch. 7).

Information

Included in this resource class is education, both formal and informal, the acquisition of everyday information though the media, reading, and listening. Information and knowledge have been considered a source of power, to the point that those who control information, through distortion, suppression, or propaganda, can control the minds and opinions of those who receive it. Extremes in this resource could be found in intellectualizers who soak up information for the sake of information, or puzzle addicts, or, even more to the point Internet addicts who spend a great deal of their time "surfing the net." At the other extreme, there are individuals who do not read, even though they may have this ability, do not listen to the news, and are oblivious to any source of information. Unfortunately, these extremes are impressionistic and need to be bolstered by evidence.

Services

This resource includes all the different work types that encompass the whole range of possible activities available to humans, as reviewed already in Chapter 5. Extremes in this resource may be found in altruistically charitable individuals who give up personal comfort and welfare to attend to the needs of others. On the other extreme, there are individuals who do nothing for others, only for themselves.

HAVING AND ITS IMPLICATIONS

Extremes in having can be seen in tycoons whose major if not sole aim in life is to accumulate more and more money and acquire more and more goods. Extremes in not having can be found in homeless individuals or those who refuse to accumulate money or goods as an act of rebellion against what they perceive an all too materialistic society. Examples can be found in self-sacrificing individuals who give of themselves with little or no stress on worldly goods or money (saints?) at the expense of not being able to protect themselves and eventually becoming dependent on the charity of others.

Basing his conclusions on empirical data, Kasser (2002) examined what happens when we organize our lives around materialistic pursuits. Emphasis on money and possessions, at the expense of the other two modalities, being and doing, affects our internal experience and interpersonal relationships, as well as our communities and the world at large. Materialistic values actually undermine our well-being, as they perpetuate feelings of insecurity, weaken the ties that bind us, and make us feel less free. What is the solution for this misguided emphasis? The answer is found in our priorities, as discussed in Chapter 13.

Having or production will be divided since there are clear prototypes for each resource.

Money

More recently, the importance of money as a source of power has been stressed by Doyle (1999), who developed a very interesting classification of personality in ways similar to those made here. Tycoons whose life ambition is to make and accumulate fortunes are prototypes for the extremes of too much money. On the other extreme, one would find charitable, religious individuals who sacrifice themselves by having or making as little money as possible. In India, such individuals, usually sitting on a bed of nails, are respected as saintly and deserving of some goods and money. By the same token, many tycoons give a great portion of their fortunes away to avoid paying higher taxes to the government. Hence, there are altruistic uses of money as well as self-centered uses with little or no altruism.

In marriage, money is very important primarily in terms of its symbolic meaning. When partners argue about money, it is because they are competitive or because they are engaged in a power struggle for control and dominance. This battle may not have anything to do with money per se. Competency and stability in earning and handling money are among the major criteria for assessing the social and psychological adequacy of a wage earner. Money can be used as an expression of love, and its withholding may indicate a withdrawal of love (Weiner, 1978).

Possessions/Goods/Objects

Possessions, goods, and objects need to be distinguished from each other. By possession is meant usually fixed household items, like heavy appliances and furniture. By goods is meant whatever is imported and is usually movable within and out of the household, like clothes, CD disks, money, or nonedible items. Objects here are referred to as edible substances, like alcohol, food, and substances like drugs. On the positive side of collecting possessions/goods, prototypes can be found in collectors of nonedible goods and possessions whose intent is positive and often aesthetic, versus hoarders on the negative side, who collect objects compulsively. Possessions bought together and displayed in the home have a special meaning for couples, giving those special objects a value that transcends their cost (Lohmann, Arriaga, & Goodfriend, 2003). In other words, possessions and goods may have an emotional meaning to the point that they satisfy aesthetic or selfish needs.

Possessions may be related to two basic components: effectance or competence motivation, and a sense of self. Both components in the control of possessions may become important aspects of dominance and power relations (Furby, 1980). Couples who receive gifts of property or possessions as a wedding gift or as a gift may have to pay back to their parents in terms of loyalty and obligation. This "emotional mortgage" may put the receiving couple in a position of servitude in regard to those parents. By accepting gifts, some couples may give up freedom of choice and decision making, by having to consider what their parents gave to them as gifts instead of the security of unconditional love (Sauer, 1979).

Emotional attachment to objects, as found in hoarders or packrats, indicates extreme concern for maintaining control over one's reality through possessions. Possessions represent the needed emotional comfort that cannot be obtained in any other way (Frost, Hart, Christian, & Williams, 1995). Hoarding seems associated with indeciveness, perfectionism, and obsessive-compulsive symptoms. Hoarders tend to have more first-degree relatives who engaged in excessive savings than nonhoarders. Hoarders may be less likely to be married (Frost & Gross, 1993), supporting the position that inordinate stress on having may be the outcome of deficits in being.

Edible Objects

We need to distinguish among alcohol, drugs, and food as edible objects. Prototypes abound in each category. There are many prototypes for compulsive acquisition of edible objects that include compulsive usage of alcohol, food, substances, and other objects in general. On the positive side there may be gourmands who eat selectively for taste and discernment. On the negative side there are all the addictions to the categories reviewed below.

Alcohol. Extremes of this kind are covered in Chapters 11 and 12.

Alimentary Food and Eating Disorders. Anorexia nervosa, binge eating, and bulimia nervosa are three obvious prototypes of eating disorders along a dimension of severity (Bulik, Sullivan, & Kendler (2000). One disorder that has reached epidemic proportions, in spite of negative societal attitudes in this country is obesity (Friedman & Brownell, 1995), supposedly with behaviorally distinct subsets and differing patterns of disordered eating and elevated rates of psychopathology (Devlin, Yanovski, & Wilson, 2000). These differences may be responsible for differential treatment outcomes (Epstein, Nudelman, & Wing, 1987).

Bulimic patients perceive their families as being low in cohesiveness, lacking in emphasis on independent and assertive behavior, with a high level of conflict coupled with low emphasis on open expression of feelings. High disorganization of families of bulimics seems associated with the severity of the symptoms (Johnson & Flach, 1985).

Substance Abuse. Addictions represent the prototype for the use of objects to satisfy the inability to deal with hurt feelings, i.e., being present to oneself and intimate others. They are covered in Chapters 11 and 12.

Kleptomania. Most individuals affected by this disorder have had life-time diagnoses of major mood, anxiety, and eating disorders. High risk of major mood disorder may be found in their first-degree relatives. Hence, this condition can be considered along with those reviewed in Chapter 12.

This model allows us to classify settings (Ch. 5) according to what resource is exchanged. For instance, being present and other resources are found in the home, where all resources are exchanged. Information is found in media, schools, and libraries. Services are found in transit and transitory settings, as defined in Chapter 5. Goods and possessions are found in industries and retail stores. Money is found in banks, savings and loan associations, and credit unions.

DOING AND HAVING EQUALS POWER: MODEL[7]

The construct of power has been accompanied by a great deal of controversy since its conceptual inception, in terms of rewards, coercive punishment, legitimate expertise, and attributional reference (Podsakoff & Schriescheim, 1985). Steil (1997), for instance, differentiates among six types of power: rewards, coercive, legitimate, expert, referent, and informational. Being powerful could mean the ability to convert resources into influence within a system. Hence, three general aspects of this definition can be distinguished. *Bases* of power are converted into *manifestations* of power through the *processes* of power. Hence, properties of power are power as control of valuable resources through possession versus power as control of valuable resources through possession and constraint (Burt, 1977). Possession of resources forms the basis of power. How these resources are expressed represents their manifestations of power. How those resources are shared or not shared, democratically, authoritatively, or dictatorially represents the processes of power.

Controversies could not be settled because of failure to define the components of power. Combination of both doing and having, on the other hand, allows us to define power in terms of very specific exchanges of four resources defined by doing and having. No power can be exerted on being, no matter how many despots and tyrants may have tried. However, this combination does not include influence, a factor that may reside in personal presence but that is more related to controls and the ability to negotiate (Ch. 8). Power can be dispersed, shared, and delegated reciprocally in democratic relationships (Beckman-Brindley & Tavormina, 1978; Osmond, 1978), or can be kept autocratically by dominant but possibly depressed individuals (Hooper, Vaughan, Hinchliffe, & Roberts, 1978).

The ability to negotiate also requires the skill to separate being from doing and having, in five different settings (residence, work, surplus time, transit, and transitory). Power is negotiated effectively and successfully in functional relationships but is negotiated ineffectively or unsuccessfully, or not negotiated at all, in dysfunctional ones. The greater the level of competence, the greater the possibility of successful negotiation, as shown in Chapter 17. Unwillingness or inadequate ability to negotiate power is the basis for conflicts and struggles. We negotiate about what kind of information should be allowed in the home, who would provide what services within and without the home, and what could or should be bought with the money earned.

Toward a Classification of Sex and Sexuality

L'Abate and Hewitt (1988) applied the distinction of power (performance and production) and presence (importance and intimacy, i.e., being present) to a classification of sex and sexuality. Other classifications of sex relate to its functions, reproductive, relational or romantic, and recreational (Weiner & Rosen, 1999). However, conflicts among partners relate to different emphases allocated to these functions (Morris, 1978). Gender differences in sexual plasticity may occur (Baumeister, 2000), but such a position may not be acceptable to some women (Andersen, Cyranowski, & Aarestad, 2000).

Instead, L'Abate and Hewitt argued that most sexual dysfunctions are based on the inability to be present emotionally to self and to partner. Functional sex and sexuality imply an ability to be available emotionally to self and to partner before one can be available sexually. Sex as performance is represented by one-night stands and short-lived sexual encounters, the physical act of intercourse at the expense of emotional presence, or glorifying the number of partners. Sex as production is found in frequency as well as use of money or "things" to achieve sexual pleasure (pornography, prostitutes, sexual "toys," vibrators, etc.), including fetishes, sex for money, and an industry dedicated to the production of sex objects.

Stress on performance or production with minimal or no presence is bound to produce deviations and disturbances that affect the subsequent development of sexuality in the individual and his or her partners (Andersen et al., 2000; Weiner & Rosen, 1999). Perhaps, our American culture puts too much stress on sexual performance or production at the expense of sexual presence?

This model needs support from the extant literature to show how sexual deviancies or excesses are based on performance or production without presence. In sex and sexuality, production in addition to being based on money and objects, means also repetition of the sex act in a compulsive, obsessive, and ultimately destructive fashion.

Support for a Classification of Sex and Sexuality

Sex as being together and connecting emotionally is more important than "doing" it. Presence in sex and sexuality is more important than performance or production (Abramson & Pinkerton, 2002). As in previous chapters, examples will be listed from the least dysfunctional to the most dysfunctional.

Sexual Dysfunctions. While the deviances reviewed above represent the extreme of strong sexual performance, sexual dysfunctions seem to represent the other extreme of weak sexual performance. For instance, among disorders of sexual desire, weak erection, orgasm, and premature ejaculation, sexual desire and weak erection seem to be related to emotional disturbance (Safir & Almagor, 1991).

When the personality profiles Neuroticism-Extraversion-Openness Personality Inventory (NEO-PI) of individuals with sexual dysfunction are compared with those of individuals diagnosed with paraphelias, the former were close to the profiles of a normative group. The profiles of the latter, on the other hand, were characterized by high neuroticism, low agreeableness, and low conscientiousness. This comparison, if valid, would support the position that sexual dysfunctions are at the low end of performance (i.e., hypoactive), while paraphilias would be at the high end of performance (i.e., hyperactive) (Fagan, Wise, Schmidt, Ponticas et al., 1991).

Risky Sexual Behavior. This behavior is seen as a product of the same peer and family factors that influence a wide range of problem behaviors. Adolescents whose peers were reported to engage in diverse problem behaviors were also likely to engage in risky sexual behavior. Poor parental monitoring, less availability of parental figures in the family, and parent-child coercive interactions were associated with deviant peers and with risky sexual behavior (Metzler, Noell, Biglan, Ary et al., 1994).

Incest. Incest may take place between a parent and a child, as will be reviewed in Chapter 11, or between siblings. Approximately, 15% undergraduate women and 10% undergraduate men admit to some sexual experience involving a sibling, with touching of the genitals being the most common. Most experiences of this kind were viewed as exploitive but having long-term effects on sexual development. Women who reported these experiences may have higher levels of current sexual activity. Experiences with much older siblings taking place before age 9 may be associated with lower levels of self-esteem, with no increase in current sexual activity (Finkelhor, 1980).

Sexual Offenders. Circa 60% of juvenile sexual offenders tend to sexually victimize a child under 12 years of age, one-third victimized a family member, and about 12% committed offenses against peer acquaintances, with less than 10% consisting of rape. Hands-on offenses against peer-aged or older victims most often involved the use of physical force or threats. With children, the misuse of authority or power might be involved more often (Davis & Leitenberg, 1987; Fehrenbach, Smith, Monastersky, & Dersher, 1986).

Significant parts of the risk assessment model proposed by Beech, Fisher, and Thornton (2003), combining contributions by Beech (1998), Hanson and Harris (2000), and Thornton (2002) for sex offenders tend to support the model proposed here. Sex offenders' inability to regulate their sexual preoccupations/obsessions, resulting in illegal sexual preferences for children, is correlated with distorted attitudes and "intimacy deficits." These distortions result in impulsive actions without regard to consequences to their victims or themselves. These observations would support the inability of sex offenders to be in touch with their feelings (intimacy) as well as the feelings of their victims (empathy). This inability in being escalates into exaggerated and illegal performance and, unfortunately, in some cases, continuous production of sexual offenses, as seen in the recidivism of sexual offenders (Furby, Weinrott, & Blackshaw, 1989), which supports the view that abusive-apathetic and to some extent reactive relationships tend to repeat themselves.

Recidivism is high in child molesters, who as a whole have never been married (Rice, Quinsey, & Harris, 1991), supporting the position that these individuals are not able to express openly and directly whatever hurt feelings they may have accumulated from the past. This inability does not allow them to form and forge lasting intimate relationships.

Pedophilias. Homosexual and bi-sexual pedophiles seem to have a later birth order then heterosexual pedophiles or heterosexual men. This effect may be due to the former's being born later among brothers. If valid, these results could be interpreted according to whether homosexual and bisexual pedophiles exert power over children in a way that their older brothers did not allow them to have (Bogaert, Bezeau, Kuban, & Blanchard, 1997). However, one is still left with how to interpret the behavior of heterosexual pedophiles. Why and how are they different from the two other kinds? An overall explanation would be found in their inability to be emotionally available to themselves and others, with little empathy on what will happen to their victims in the long run.

Erotic or Violent Fantasies. Ruminative and intrusive sexual fantasies may be the cause of repetitive acts of sexual violence and even paraphilia (Prentky, Burgess, Rokous, Lee et al., 1989). This pattern could be interpreted as the outcome of an inability to use emotionality and resorting to excessive rationality as ruminations that eventually explode into sexual acting out (as discussed in Ch. 4). In this case, emotionality would consist of hurt feelings, including rejections that have not been allowed into awareness and that instead find an avenue of expression in R and eventually violent A. Indeed, erotic obsessions, as instances of dysregulation in sexual motivation, could be viewed as the outcome of unrequited love (Kaplan, 1996). This possibility suggests that sexual ruminations may stem from the inability to express constructively hurt feelings that have been accumulated from the past. Erotic obsessions can be found in paraphilias in the sense that both disorders are eroticization of childhood trauma or of past, painful relationships with intimates (Kaplan, 1996).

These disorders all have one characteristic in common: perpetrators fail to show any compassion or empathy for their victims. They seem to lack empathy and compassion, without any understanding of the long-term damage they are inflicting on their victims. They simply are unable to be present to themselves and to victimized others, preferring doing to being because they do not know how to be.

CONCLUSION

Personal and interpersonal competence is defined by what an individual *is, does,* and *has* in different settings. From the two sets of abilities and six resource classes are derived various skills and testable models. Presence needs to be balanced with power according to settings and task demands. A classification of sex and sexuality finds support in a culture that apparently makes performance and production more important than presence.

Part IV

Models of the Theory
Back to Processes

This theory has many testable and not-yet tested models that derive in some way or another from its metatheoretical (Chapters 4, 5, and 6) and theoretical assumptions and postulates (Chapters 7, 8, and 9). Chapters 10, 11, and 12 will include severe psychopathology from Axis I and Cluster A of Axis II, as viewed in continuity with personality disorders (Dolan-Sewell et al., 2001; L'Abate, 2003a; L'Abate, Lambert, & Schenck, 2001; Mattia & Zimmerman, 2001). Chapter 13 will deal with priorities, with some indirect links to psychopathology. The remaining models Chapters 14 through 17 in Part V will elaborate and expand on applications from preceding models. Consequently, this could also be called "a relational theory for the DSM-IV and its future revisions," because in many aspects it seems isomorphic with psychiatric classification as we know it.

Chapter 10

Developmental Identity-Differentiation Model[8]

"...formation of personal self-categories is not a matter of differences, but a matter of relative similarities and differences [emphasis in original]. Personal identity is made possible because of self-other differentiation in terms of some shared higher order identity that provides a context for social comparison. This implies quite clearly that similarity and difference go hand in hand in defining the personal self. Thus, even at the personal level, self-definition is inherently social, contextual, and relational. This emphasis represents an important point of departure from dominant social-cognitive models of the personal self, which treats self-schemata as absolute, rather than as relative properties of the perceiver (Onorato and Turner, 2002, p. 151)."

"Similarity in classification is fundamental and functionally many faceted....Once identity is abandoned, similarity changes its nature from being a binary-valued characteristic to a multivalued one, and in some sense continuous (Bergman, Magnusson, & El-Khouri, 2003, p. 54)."

"Attraction is maximized when these two dimensions are in balance—a partner who is similar enough to 'get along' with you, yet different enough to 'be exciting' (and expanding). (Agnew, Loving, Le, & Goodfriend, 2004, p. 114)."

"Thus identity.... provides a potential conceptual link between the psychology of the individual and social structures, including gender (Stewart & McDermott, 2004, p. 526)."

The eighth model of this theory consists of a continuum of likeness that underlies the development of intimate relationships, following the suggestion given above by Bergman et al. In spite of their insistence on a multivalued continuum, these authors still kept to a binary dichotomy of similarity-dissimilarity, as done in most instances by the relevant literature reviewed in previous presentations of the same continuum. This continuum deals with the sense of identity we acquire developmentally in relationship with intimate others, especially our mothers (Ostrauskas, 1977).

This dialectical continuum follows a bell-shaped distribution, where, from the viewpoint of functionality and positive change, the two center ranges, similarity and differentness, are the most functional; the two extreme ranges, symbiosis and autism/alienation are the most dysfunctional, with the two other ranges, sameness and oppositeness, being intermediate between the two other levels in extent of functionality. These ranges are dialectical in the sense that they coexist (Baxter & West, 2003). One range cannot exist without its dialectical counterpart. Each range is needed to help define the corresponding range that would not have any meaning without it. Furthermore, dialectical implies also that these ranges may be difficult to evaluate experimentally, unless one relies on the vast research on similarity. Consequently, symbiosis is coupled with autism/alienation. Sameness is coupled with oppositeness because individuals who are oppositional to their parents, or to authority figures, or to accepted social norms, are also very conforming to and similar with equally oppositional individuals. The range of similarity has no meaning without differentness. This latter pair is the basis for positively creative intimate relationships, while the other two pairs do not possess such a quality.

Up to the present, this model has differentiated how this continuum is expanded and applied to a variety of areas. Most functional individuals behave in the middle in most ranges of this distribution. A few functional individuals may function in either the same-opposite ranges in one or two areas. A smaller number of semifunctional individuals may function well just in few areas but may be unable to behave in most other areas. Very dysfunctional individuals are unable to function in the middle of most areas. Hospitalized or incarcerated individuals are dysfunctional in all areas because they function in the extremes of most areas. The full relevance of these areas to a continuum of likeness will be expanded in Chapter 11.

IDENTITY DIFFERENTIATION OVER THE LIFE CYCLE

Breaking an entity into parts and the greater specificity that each part acquires over time relates to the process of differentiation in a sense of self-identity. This is the image of oneself that is refined into greater parts as we grow older. The child may start with knowing about being a male or female at a certain age. From this definition are added a host of other identities that grow as the individual expands into the various stages of the life cycle. The child's body-image, for instance, may play a major role in the differentiation of an identity (Van der Velde, 1985). A developmental sequence of stages in the development of a child's sense of personal identity seems to follow from externals, relying on others to develop such a sense, to behavioral, by acting on such a sense, to an internal use of that sense (Mohr, 1978). An early autistic stage in the first months of life apparently is followed by a symbiotic stage until the end of the third year, a projective-omnipotent stage between 4 and 6 years, and an autonomous-homonymous stage thereafter (Nichol, 1977).

A child's self-concept, i.e., identity, seems closely related to parental perceptions of the child (mirroring) rather than to parental self-perceptions (modeling), especially on the activity dimension rather than on a self-worth dimension. The father seems perceived as being a more powerful figure than the mother in the development of identity (Gecas, Calonico, & Thomas, 1974).

From being a "child" of a certain gender, the child becomes a teenager of a certain gender with various identities added on according to life experiences and the influence of caretakers, siblings, school mates, peers, teachers, etc. (Lacy & Hendricks, 1980). The child becomes a teenager who likes to dance, date, attend football games, play certain sports, watch specific TV programs, develop crushes, become involved in friendships, etc. This stage has been called "anticipatory socialization" (Mortimer & Simmons, 1978) and is one of many "sensitive periods" in the life cycle (Bornstein, 1989).

Especially in heterosexual development, there may be stages defined initially by sexual awakening (13–15), practicing/dating (14–17), acceptance/rejection of sexual roles (16–19), and eventually, permanence of sexual choices (18–25). This is the stage when the teenager begins to separate emotionally, if not physically or financially, from parents, sometimes with and sometimes without conflict (Feinstein & Ardon, 1973). When reaching 16 years of age the adolescent begins to reorganize self-identity boundaries in terms of sexual and interpersonal choices (Ellis, Gehman, & Katzenmeyer, 1980).

Emotional separation from mother in childhood and from parents later on in adolescence may lead to a process of individuation, that is, a sense of personal identity. Through this process, the individual struggles to develop a sense of identity separate from one's parents. Indeed, the adolescent may achieve a sense of identity when he or she is able to give up dependency on early relationships and recognizes parents as real people (Brandt, 1977). Family structure and psychological separation from the family may effect differentially the adjustment of male or female college students (Lopez, Campbell, & Watkins, 1988).

Once the teenager reaches college or starts working, additional identities in terms of education, work descriptions, marital status, income level, etc. are added until, after completing an educational process, the now adult individual joins the workforce, develops certain leisure-time activities, becomes engaged, marries, has children, and goes through the various stages of the life cycle. Each stage adds a new identity until retirement and old age, which in themselves are also new identities. Successful aging is predicated on the basis of parental social class, family cohesion, ancestral longevity, childhood temperament, and physical health (Gordon, 1976; Vaillant & Mukamal, 2001; Whitbourne & Waterman, 1979). With age, individuals tend to reveal increasing differentiation in categories of personal characteristics when evaluating themselves (Fry, 1974; Lachman, 2004).

Those who feel insecure in relation to their parents early in childhood may have greater difficulty in developing a firm sense of identity than those whose early experiences were relatively more secure. Resolution of crises of separation, real or fantasized, may be dealt with by identification with the lost person, a process that may lead to identity problems. Crises of being uncertain about who to be and how to relate to others become apparent whenever one is faced with having to make choices and decisions. A genuine sense of identity could include the capacity to acknowledge and tolerate conflict and uncertainty when they exist, both within oneself and in one's relationship to others (Wolff, 1972).

Adolescents from consensus-sensitive families may show a higher level of psychological differentiation, a higher self-concept (i.e., identity), and more mature interpersonal choices than adolescents from distance-sensitive families. These differences suggest that the relationship between the family and the adjustment of its children can be better understood and predicted on the basis of family type (Shulman & Klein, 1983).

The self-image of the individual becomes an important factor in adopting to old age. If this image or self-identity is inadequate or incomplete, possible psychopathological outcomes may occur (Weinberg, 1979). This self-image is often referred to as the "self-concept" (Edwins, Small, & Gross, 1980). Here, self-concept refers to "self-identity," because one's identity becomes formed by how one is perceived by others, how one's qualities and abilities compare with those of others, how one's concept of self compares with one's concept of ideal self, and one's experiences that mold a particular identity. A sense of identity can be positive or negative and may underlie whether one develops balanced, age-appropriate emotional stability and needs, and an overall sense of worth and competence (Howe, 1980).

A pathological fear of death, with flight and repression of events related to death, may originate in a disturbed and incomplete development of identity in the family group. People who have not achieved a full sense of identity may live in constant fear of loss of self by death because their self has never become complete. This fear of nonexistence may result in a sense of an "unlived life." Evasion and denial of the fact of death takes many forms in today's society. Communication about death seems to still occur under restrictive taboos. People who are able to live are also able to die. People who have not lived fully cannot cease to live either; they seem filled by an anxiety of uncompleted tasks and still having something to do compulsively. Thus, death often may reflect one's life in some detail, where the dynamics of the family and other groups in which person has lived are clearly shown for the last time (Ammon, 1975). The fear of death seems particularly present in addicts (at least in my clinical experience). Addicts, incidentally, need to restructure their identities completely in the process of becoming nonaddicts, including identity reversion, extension, and emergence of a new identity (Kellogg, 1993).

The outcome of processes described as identification and/or modeling is called identity here, considering the answer to the question of: "Who am I?" This process does not take place in a vacuum. It occurs within a continuous interplay of transactions with caretakers, siblings, peers, teachers, coworkers, bosses, friends, lovers, and even enemies. This interplay shapes how one sees oneself and how one chooses to integrate various identities that are continuously considered in the course of a lifetime. How one sees oneself is the outcome of a process of comparison with intimates and nonintimates. This process occurs according to a comparison of similarities and differences along a continuum, and not just solely in terms of a binary similar-different process that still dominates the relevant literature.

This limited and limiting binary combination of similarities and differences has been instead expanded into a continuum of likeness since the outset of this theory. Very likely, this process occurs below levels of awareness and needs differentiation from a relational, fully visible selfhood model expanded in Chapter 12. Self-differentiation continuously underlies the latter at a genotypic sublevel (Ch. 5).

THE CONTINUUM OF LIKENESS IN INTIMATE RELATIONSHIPS

This continuum derives from the ability to love (Ch. 7), the ability to negotiate (Ch. 8), and sharing of the three modalities (Ch. 9) exchanged between and among intimates. The more functional one is the ability to love and to negotiate, balancing how being is considered appropriately in relationship to doing and having along the life cycle, the more differentiated one will become. By the same token, the more one is defective in the ability to love and negotiate, with imbalances in how being is considered in relationship to doing and having, the less differentiated one will become in one's identity.

This model indicates that we develop a sense of identity by differentiating with and from relevant others according to a curvilinear, dialectical continuum of likeness composed of six ranges. The purpose of this developmental continuum is to describe how people learn to relate with each other and become socialized in intimate and nonintimate relationships, an aspect not covered by previous or subsequent models. This continuum postulates a bell-shaped, dialectical distribution consisting of six ranges: symbiosis, sameness, similarity, differentness, oppositeness, and alienation.

No single range can conceivably describe identity in intimate relationships by itself, isolated from other ranges. Each range needs a counterpart to define itself according to a combination of two ranges dialectically related with each other. Vertically, a dimension of psychopathology lies at the bottom two extremes of the distribution, symbiosis and alienation, where extreme psychopathology is found. At an intermediate level of emotional and mental health are sameness and oppositeness. Creativity lies in the center and peak of the distribution, as defined by similarity and differentness. In the middle of the distribution (similarity-differentness) the likelihood of functionality in most relationships would be high, where differences are reconciled with a minimum of conflict (Aiken, 1999). By the same token, in the two intermediate ranges (sameness-oppositeness) a semifunctional level would be predicted. In the two extremes of the distribution (symbiosis-alienation), dysfunctionality would be the highest. Hence, a sense of identity based on an integration of similarity and differentness will be more functional and "healthier" than a sense of identity developed from sameness and oppositeness in intimate relationships. By the same token, a sense of identity based on symbiosis and alienation would be incomplete, defective, and dysfunctional.

This continuum was first proposed since this theory was still in its *status nascendi* (L'Abate, 1976, p. 179) and expanded progressively over the many revisions of this theory with a maximum of secondary sources and a minimum of supporting primary sources. Here, primary sources, some albeit outdated, will be introduced to support the validity of this model. Hopefully, others will update these primary sources to dispute or support the validity of this and other models of the theory.

The Need for a Developmental Continuum of Likeness

This continuum is needed to account for how we become differentiated developmentally and develop a sense of identity as individuals-in-relationships-with-intimate-others. Hence, the developmental nature of this model makes it basic to the models to follow. Differentiation is a process of relating with intimate others and through this process, whether by modeling, identification, or even a process akin to osmosis in physical processes, without awareness, one learns how to relate with oneself and with intimates. Differentiation, therefore, can be described according to three levels. At the highest level individuals learn to define themselves and develop a healthy sense of identity according to how similar/different they are from intimates. At the intermediate level, individuals learn to differentiate and develop a borderline sense of self from intimates through a process of sameness-oppositeness. At the lowest level, individuals learn to differentiate themselves and develop a defective sense of identity according to symbiotic and alienated process with intimates.

Symbiosis

"You are me, I cannot live without you!" This requirement of coexistence is basic to symbiotic processes (Bryant-Tucker & Silverman, 1984; Geller, 1975). In healthy parent-child relationships, symbiosis becomes increasingly partial as the child grows and learns to take care of him- or herself. In contrast, a premature breakdown of healthy symbiosis may be present in emotional disturbances. Such a breakdown may be initiated by the mother in response to infant demands, which she may perceive as excessive or grandiose, because she is unable to fulfill them. For the breakdown to be maintained, a mother must actively and repeatedly discount the solvability of problems or personal abilities. The premature breakdown of a healthy parent-child symbiosis can produce or reinforce sensory-perceptual or sensory-motor difficulties and impede development of a mature adulthood (Grim, 1977).

Normal dependency occurs when the child is allowed to grow and eventually to leave the dependency relationship, whereas in symbiosis both parties want to maintain the relationship as it is. In normal dependency, it is important to acknowledge and use all the resources available in reciprocal fashion with intimates (Woollams & Hulge, 1977). Symbiosis not only refers to an excessively dependent relationship between two persons, but it can also refer to a connection between the psychic representation of the self and the other (Taylor, 1975).

For instance, schizophrenics and their mothers may show more evidence of being more enmeshed in a symbiotic relationship than did the mothers of other groups. This evidence supports the difference between functional overprotectiveness found in most parent-child relationships and a symbiotic relationship characterized by overdependency, disapproval of other relationships, separation difficulties, intrusiveness, and injunctions against achieving personal autonomy (Summers, 1978; Summers & Walsh, 1977).

In childbirth psychoses, for instance, the mother might be a young woman involved in a symbiotic relationship with her husband and/or mother. The baby's presence, apparently, may threaten the symbiotic equilibrium of these relationships and release the dominant partner's overt or covert aggression against the woman, an outcome that seems to precipitate a psychotic episode (Ficker, 1977; Ketal & Brandwin, 1979). The fear of re-establishing a symbiotic relationship with the mother may prompt a counter-symbiotic suicide (Rachlin, Milton, & Pam, 1977). Symbiosis and autism seem to coexist in most schizophreniacs (Bleger, 1974), a contention that supports the dialectical nature of symbiosis with the other extreme of the likeness continuum, alienation.

There are various types and degrees of symbiosis, going from psychotic *folie a deux* to extremely dependent personalities (Horner, 1986). Johnson (1991) described the symbiotic character as one who is afraid of separating from important individuals, parents, partners, own children, and siblings. The etiology of this character starts in a family constellation where parents squelch personal initiative, self-identity, and individual responsibility through a variety of fearful, threatening, and punitive control methods, producing an individual who cannot feel, think, or act on his or her own. According to Johnson, there are various types of symbiotic characters, ranging from the narcissist, masochist, oedipal/histrionic, to the obsessive-compulsive. There is no need here to go into details about all variations from the same theme. Suffice to say that this is an extreme of a continuum where its dialectical counterpart is alienation. Within this range there are also extremes of dysfunctionality, going from the out-and-out psychotic to the borderline or barely functional.

Shifting symbiosis in families may be a major factor in child abuse. Disturbances in the original symbiotic relationship between the child and the mother could result in an unrealistic fear of independence in the child, which may lead the mother to enter into and struggle to maintain a symbiotic relationship in marriage. Coexistent with the belief in symbiotic relationships, there may be a belief that only one person in a relationship can have his or her needs met. The latter belief leads to a continuous and frantic struggle between the parents to take and maintain a dependent child role, or wanting to be "taken care of" position. Interlocking scripts may underlie the symbiosis of abusive parents. What differentiates abusive families from the many nonabusive families, in which symbiosis is also common, is that abusive parents seemingly attempt to take the child's role in a symbiotic relationship with their own children. Violent behavior is often the outcome when their children fail in their symbiosis (Justice & Justice, 1976).

Families with enchopretic children may represent one type of symbiotic relationship between parents and children. There may be a mutual, possibly pathological advantage in the maintenance of the symptom and its associ- ation with its seemingly provocative aspects. The family is able to displace a great deal of hostility onto the child for having a symptom. By keeping their attention on the child for having this symptom, they can avoid looking at their own pathological relationships. The child, by keeping the symp- tom, keeps their attention on the self rather than on themselves. Parents of enchopretic children tend to exhibit the following interaction patterns: (1) withholding of vital information from the child; (2) infantilization of the child; (3) mishandled anger; and (4) communication distortions (Baird, 1974).

Sameness

"Keep things as they are!" This range includes three major characteristics in rank from most to less severe in intensity: (1) authoritarianism; (2) dogma- tism; and (3) conservativism. "Be like me and do what I tell you," represents a requirement for conformity found in rigid and authoritarian family relations with dogmatic and conservative leanings: how to deal with children, how to deal with economic and political issues, how to eat, how to drink, how to dress, how to vote, and how to shop or perform chores. Parental ideology and family relations, for instance, seem to be important determinants of a student's political ideology. Leftist, i.e., liberal, parental ideology and high family conflict each seem to lead toward a leftist student ideology, at least as reported by students themselves. Apparently, nonpolitical interpersonal relations from one's family of origin may be translated into political ide- ologies (Kraut & Lewis, 1975). Authoritarian parental child-rearing practices may produce within a child a personality that shapes attitudes toward the use of drugs, which in turn may affect the child's use of marijuana, alcohol, and tobacco (Mercer & Kohn, 1980).

Authoritarianism. Authoritarianism may constitute a valuable explana- tory variable in political research (Hanson, 1975). It might be conceived as aggressive dominance or at least some types of assertiveness as non- aggressive dominance (Ray, 1981). Authoritarians might be more likely to believe their preferred media sources than would nonauthoritarians. Addi- tionally, an authoritarian's position on political issues would be closer to the position represented by positively evaluated media but farther from the position of negatively evaluated media.

Coercive force may also be strongly related to authoritarianism when media were described as disagreeing with the views of important political leaders (Levy, 1979). Indeed, religious sons of religious families seem more authoritarian than nonreligious sons of religious families, even though they may not be significantly more authoritarian than religious sons of nonreligious families, supporting the conclusion that authoritarian individuals may be attracted to an orthodox doctrine, showing a strong association between religiosity and authoritarianism. Parents of individuals favoring war seem to demand more obedience and compliance than parents of individuals who resist war. The latter seem to offer rational explanations for actions and views. The former seem to adopt their parents' views without critical appraisal, while the latter seem to consider carefully their commitments. These correlations tend to support the conclusion that the willingness to use violence may be the product of an authoritarian home life in childhood (Mantell, 1974).

The authority complex may be a ubiquitous problem that assumes diverse forms in conjunction with different types of deviations and illnesses. The authoritarian personality structure expresses itself chiefly in oversubmissiveness to superiors and possibly a latent sadism against inferiors. In its fully developed form, the authority image may be both masculine and feminine, father and mother, with an androgynous parent "dragon" in the background. Individuals with an authority complex may tend to experience all powers outside oneself and all weakness and inferiority inside oneself (Wilke, 1977). This conclusion is supported by the finding that high authoritarian men clearly tend to express a personal preference for a traditional view of marital power, devaluing "female" instrumental values. Among women the opposite could be found. Low authoritarian men and women may tend to express a personal preference for an equalitarian view (Craddock, 1977). Authoritarians, therefore, may manifest intolerance of ambiguity. Things are perceived in black or white with no gray areas in between (Zacker, 1973).

Apparently authoritarianism in one parent seems associated with authoritarianism in the other, with their children finding greater difficulty in problemsolving than children of parents low in authoritarianism. Opposite sex correlations between sons and mothers and between daughters and fathers may be stronger than same sex correlations. These results suggest that rigid problem-solving may mediate the transmission of authoritarianism from parent to child (Lesser & Hlavacek, 1977).

The dialectical relationship between authoritarianism and oppositeness is found in various sources, including British undergraduates (Kohn, 1974), while tendencies toward change versus a tendency toward sameness may represent two different stages in personality development (Haan & Day, 1974).

Dogmatism. Low dogmatic individuals seem more self-revealing, more attentive to the here-and-now, less apt to give negative feedback, and less likely to reject others, while dogmatic individuals may tend to be less self-revealing, less attentive to the here-and-now, more apt to give negative feedback, and more likely to reject others (Davis, Frye, & Joure, 1975). Dogmatism tends to be negatively correlated with a concrete/abstract dimension of creativity (Faschingbauer & Eglevsky, 1977). This negative correlation may also be explained by the possibility that authoritarians of the political left and right may tend to be equally dogmatic. There appears to be a tendency, however, for rightists to be slightly, but consistently, more close minded than leftists (Hanson, 1970).

Distinct differences between inpatient adolescents and their parents in aspects of fantasy, empathy, dogmatism, and self-esteem seem apparent, while nonhospitalized adolescents seem very similar in fantasy with their parents. The latter may show higher levels of self-esteem than the former. These results support the process of identification and modeling in socialization that accounts for sameness and oppositeness in intimate relationships (Mlott, Lira, & Campbell, 1978). The more dogmatic a parent may be, the more dogmatic the child might be. However, parents seem more dogmatic than their offspring, suggesting that family experiences may be only one of the sources of children's dogmatism (Lesser & Steininger, 1975).

Conservativism. Conservatives would stress values concerned with attachment to rules and authority, as well as security, cleanliness, and obedience, while downgrading values concerned with equality, freedom, love, pleasure, and open-minded, intellectual, and imaginative modes of thought. This trait may be a function of social class (Stacey, 1977). Older people and women tend to be more conservative than younger people and men (Feather, 1977, 1979). Legal sanctions or threats may be one variable that produces conformity in addition to extralegal factors, with the latter being even more important than legal controls (Meier & Johnson, 1977). In spite of these conclusions, authoritarianism and conformity seem negatively correlated (Singh & Prasad, 1974). Apparently, respondents low in conservatism seem to assign more traits to others than respondents high in conservatism, failing to support the hypothesis that high conservatives make more extreme judgments than low conservatives (Innes, 1978). There may be a curvilinear relationship between moral judgment level and overall frequency of conformity, suggesting a relationship between traditional personality traits like moral judgment and cognitive development (Saltzstein & Diamond, 1972).

Conformity seems to follow a curvilinear age trend, with peer conformity peaking between 11 and 14 years of age and conformity to parents decreasing steadily with age, with possible negative correlations between conformity to parents and conformity to peers (Berndt, 1979).

Similarity

"You can be somewhat like me, but you have room to be different from me without sanctions," seems to be the requirement for freedom to be oneself. Under this range one can find an extremely large number of studies. Only those relevant to this range and that seem related to intimate relationships will be included. This range has been the hobby-horse of social, marital, and family theorists and researchers for decades, sometimes without distinction about the possibility that similarity may be a perceived rather than an actual characteristic that can be assessed in a variety of domains, varying in degrees from very similar to very dissimilar. Hence, the available references on this range of a continuum of likeness will be divided into the domains that were assessed.

Adolescence and Parent Similarity. Adolescents who perceive conjugal relations as equalitarian seem to identify highly with their parents, while adolescents who perceive their mothers as dominant may be the lowest in identification. Sex differences in identification with a parent, however, may occur no less in equalitarian as opposed to other families (Bowerman & Bahr, 1973).

Interest test profiles of biological families of adolescents apparently are more similar than profiles of adoptive families of adolescents. Same-sex biological siblings may be more similar to each other than either opposite-sex sibling pairs or parent-child pairs. Pairs of unrelated children in adoptive families do not seem too similar (Grotevant, Scarr, & Weinberg, 1977). Interests and orientation in parents of adolescent children show similarities, especially father-daughter pairs (Grotevant, 1976). However, offspring between 11 and 42 years of age may resemble their peer group more often than either parent or a composite of both parents (Peck & Everson, 1975).

Family members of adolescents may be more similar in the number of symptoms they report in a health survey, with father-child concordance being the strongest, followed by father-mother. Mother-child pairs may not seem alike in either the level of symptoms reported or doctor visits (Gorton, Doerfler, Hulka, & Tyroler, 1979).

The more traditional the mother's ideology the less the adolescent's involvement in problematic relationships may be, with this effect being especially stronger for daughters than for sons (Jessor & Jessor, 1974). Indeed, the self-concept of mothers seems strongly related to the self-concept of their children (Tocco & Bridges, 1973). By the same token, the role of the mother should receive greater emphasis in socialization theory as far as her emphasis on political and religious orientations (Acock & Bengtson, 1978).

Father and Son Similarity. Profiles of sons from families with imprisoned fathers may be more similar to those of juvenile delinquents and less similar to group norms than profiles of sons from divorced families. Consequently, the conclusion is not justified that father absence or imprisonment per se is the cause of negative reactions in the offspring. Family relationships themselves, before the father left the family, could have been the primary cause of disturbances in their children (Moerk, 1973).

Undergraduates and Their Parents. Jealous undergraduates may be more similar to their parent than nonjealous ones, especially in women undergraduates (Bringle & Williams, 1979). The hypothesis that parents' personality type may foster similar personality development in the offspring may be valid for paternal but not maternal personality types. Apparently, paternal personality type may carry more weight in the development of offspring types than the maternal (DeWinne, Overton, & Schneider, 1978).

Offspring may assume greater similarity of attitudes between themselves and their parents than is actually present, and the degree of assumed similarity may correlate positively with the amount of communication and understanding offspring perceive to have with their parents (Good, Good, & Nelson, 1973).

Cognitive and Academic Achievement. Cognitive and academic dimensions in two generations of parents, both Black and White, their children, and grandchildren, at age 8 in Baltimore were followed over a period of a year. This sample was large enough ($N = 237$) to allow generalizations to other samples. Levels of cognitive development were "virtually similar (p. 347)" in the two generations. However, achievement scores were higher in the current generation compared to their parents (Schley, Brooks-Gunn, & Hardy, 2001).

Similarity and Depression. Identification processes with one parent may be a factor in the etiology of depression because low similarity with one parent may tend in general to be associated with depression. However, this conclusion seems to interact with the sex of respondents. The process of similarity may be gender-linked, identification with father may be more important for men, while identification with mother may be more important for women (Sohlberg, Stahlheuer, & Tell, 1997).

Conjugal Similarity. Both husbands and wives in a similar personality group may tend to score higher on the marriage role factor of male dominance than couples in random or opposite similarity groups. Wives in the similar group may also score higher than wives in the other two groups on marital factors like sexual gratification, togetherness, and role sharing (Barton, 1976). Value similarity in couples may be only peripherally related to level of marital adjustment. However, spouse value similarity may have a significant impact on adjustment in the later years of marriage (Medling & McCarrey, 1981). Wives of middle-aged executives who are most similar to their husbands seem the happiest. Husbands who are somewhat similar to their wives also seem the happiest (Harrison, 1993).

Differentness

"I am or want to be different from you!" This requirement allows one to be as creative as one wants to be. People may organize their personal judgments in such a way that perceived differences between themselves and others, considered as a whole, will stand out maximally as a "figure" against a general background of similarities (Adams-Webber & Davidson, 1979). Clearly, there is a tendency to strive toward diversity in order to express one's uniqueness (Jarymowicz & Codol, 1979), including in the political arena (Sidanius & Ekehammar, 1977). Relationships reflecting the extent of differentiation may be interrelated, resulting in self-consistency in individual functioning across domains, such as cognitive restructuring, interpersonal competencies, and cerebral lateralization (Witkin, Goodenough, & Oltman, 1979). Perhaps cognitive differentiation may need to be distinguished from "cognitive integration" (Miller & Wilson, 1979).

Within this range one needs to consider a variety of variables:

Culture. Of course this variable is an important one (Witkin & Berry, 1975). Consequently, the model being expanded here may be limited to the American and Western culture and not to other cultures.

Social Class and Socioeconomic Differences. This is an important source of differentness and to fully review its importance would take away space needed for other sources of differentness. For instance, middle-class socioeconomic status (SES) and nuclear family system, which interact with each other, and entrepreneurial occupations seem associated with high achievement motivation. Upper and lower SES, joint family system, and bureaucratic occupations may be associated with low achievement motivation (Ojha & Jha, 1979).

Clearly, lower-class mothers interact with their children using more authoritative, coercive, and physically assertive practices, while middle-class mothers interact using more equalitarian, guiding, and verbally orienting techniques. These stylistic differences may be rooted in middle-class emphasis on responsiveness and reciprocation in interaction. Social motivation of children's behavior may be more affected by responsiveness-reciprocation than more one-sided practices (Wandersman, 1973).

Significant associations may exist between lower social class and psychiatric disorders (Gift, Strauss, Ritzler, & Kokes, 1988). Middle-class, white-collar parents may stress the development of internal standards of conduct in their children and are more likely to discipline on the basis of their interpretation of the child's motives, whether accidental or intentional. Lower-class, blue-collar parents may be more likely to react on the basis of the consequences of the child's actual behavior (Gecas & Nye, 1974).

In some cultures, lower classes in comparison to middle classes may disproportionately show parental rejection, perceive greater punitiveness in parents, and feel greater distance from parents, recalling a less consistent and predictable emotional climate in the home, as well as recalling less satisfactory relations with siblings. Personal adjustment may also be more problematic in lower classes in such areas as isolation, self-control, paranoid projections, obsessive-compulsive tendencies, and schizoid symptoms (Williamson, 1976).

Whether social class is related to self-esteem remains to be seen. Relationships between these two factors may increase as a function of age (Rosenberg & Pearlin, 1978). Differences between one's own and a friend's SES might be better predictors of psychological differentiation than either variable separately (Filsinger, 1980).

Ethnicity. It is difficult to separate ethnicity without consideration of socioeconomic differences. Both variables and gender may influence cognitive performance in children (Humphreys, Fleishman, & Lin, 1977) and may be related to personality and family characteristics (Osmond & Grigg, 1978). Furthermore, traditional measures of SES may be impressionistic or outdated (Mueller & Parcel, 1981). Ethnic differences among Black, Latino, and White students contribute to self-definition (self-worth and efficacy) and to interpersonal relatedness with parents and peers (Kuperminc, Blatt, Shahar, Henrich, & Leadbeater, 2004).

Sex and Gender-Role Identification. In addition to obvious anatomical differences between sex as a biological given and gender as a sociocultural construct (Baker, 1980; Unger, 1979), gender role orientation may be a strong factor in perceived differences between the sexes, in spite of objections about its use (McDonald, 1978). Both sex and gender may require a specific taxonomy for sexual anatomy, sexual orientation, sexual behavior, gender assignment, sexual orientation, and gender role (Rosen & Rekers, 1980).

Children may learn which behavior is appropriate to each sex by observing differences in the frequencies with which male and female models perform in various situations. Furthermore, children could employ abstractions of what constitutes male-appropriate and female-appropriate behaviors as models for their imitative performance, according to same-sex norms (Perry & Bussey, 1979). Interest in sex differences may begin with the recognition of limits. Both sexes may envy the sex and gender attributes of the other sex and may perceive not having those attributes as a loss or as incompleteness. For both sexes, success may consist of coming to terms with limits and accepting their actual sexual identity (Fast, 1978).

Sex-role orientation may include such factors as: traditional sex-based division of labor in marriage, traditional sex-based power structure, traditional and nontraditional employment of men and women, appropriate sex role socialization of children, and existing stereotypes of other sex-appropriate behaviors in manners, dress, and morals (Brogan & Kutner, 1976; Worell, 1978). For instance, in adolescents who play sports, gender role orientation seems a more important factor in self-esteem than gender (Bowker & Cornock, 2003). Here, masculine and feminine orientation seems important. Undergraduates who rate themselves low in both masculine and feminine attributes may show significantly poorer self-concepts (i.e., identity) than both androgynous and masculine undergraduates. These and other results support the contention that the presence of masculine attributes, rather than a balance of masculinity and femininity, might be crucial to personal adjustment (Edwins, Small, & Gross, 1980).

Hence, once this dichotomy is accepted as a dimension, at least four categories could occur: androgyny, male-typed, female-typed, and undifferentiated sex roles. The consistency and strength of the masculine effect relative to the femininity effect suggests that masculinity rather than main effects androgyny may predict psychological well-being. This conclusion does not seem to support the traditional model that masculinity is best for men and femininity is best for women (Taylor & Hall, 1982).

Sex typing may derive in part, from gender-based schematic processing—a generalized readiness to process information on the basis of sex-linked associations that constitute the gender schema. Sex typing may result from the fact that the self-concept (i.e., identity) itself is assimilated into the gender schema. Such gender-based schematic processing derives, in part from society's ubiquitous insistence on the functional importance of the gender dichotomy (Bem, 1981). Factors that influence a society toward greater conformity may affect women in that society more strongly than men (Van Leeuwen, 1978). In some societies, women may contribute appreciably to their respective subsistence economies, failing to provide support for sex-role specialization or tasks (Aronoff & Crano, 1975).

Masculinity and femininity research seems dominated traditionally by three unexamined assumptions: (1) masculinity and femininity are bipolar opposites; (2) various classes of masculine and feminine attributes are highly interrelated; and (3) individuals whose behaviors and characteristics correspond to those normatively expected of their sex are psychologically healthier and more socially effective than those who do not. In contrast to those three assumptions, three counter-assumptions could be possible: (1) masculine and feminine trait dimensions of socially desirable personality characteristics are largely independent of each other; (2) correlations among classes of gender-related phenomena are more likely to be weak than strong; and (3) masculine and feminine personality characteristics contribute positively to adjustment and social effectiveness, without regard to the gender of the possessor. The evidence seems to support these counter-assumptions (Spence, 1980). In addition, androgynous individuals are more behaviorally flexible than others, manifesting both masculine and feminine role behaviors. Sex-role androgyny may also correlate highly with self-esteem. Instrumentality and expressiveness seem much more important dimensions than sex-role attitudes or sex-role behaviors (Spence & Helmreich, 1980).

Women's concepts of self and others may be dissimilar and ranked least-to-most sex typed. They may hold inaccurate perceptions of the other sex ideal, while sex-typing may be associated with poor adjustment, contrary to predictions, men sex-typing may be associated with good adjustment (Deutsch & Gilbert, 1976).

Patterns of correlations to assess family resemblances in masculine or feminine preferences seem to reject strongly simple genetic models of identity acquisition. Nonetheless, family correlations seem quite consistent with a same-sex theory of gender identification, even though social class could affect sex-role identification just as well (Munsinger & Rabin, 1978).

Maternal attitudes toward fostering or limiting autonomy and the extent to which the mother expects sex differences in the preschool child may be related to the child's psychological differentiation. Boys seem to demonstrate a significantly higher degree of sex-role preference than girls. Mothers with high expectation of sex differences apparently have daughters with lower levels of psychological differentiation. These high expectations seemed associated with authoritarianism (Domash & Balter, 1976).

Creativity in male adolescents seems related to parental identification as a function of a less conventional sex-role stereotype and paternal masculinity-femininity (Grant & Domino, 1976).

Sexual Identification. Three fourths of children diagnosed with gender identity disorder with cross-gender behavior grew up to be bi- or homosexual (Green, 1985). Whether homosexuality is hereditary is questionable when considering cultures where repeated pleasurable homosexual and homoerotic activities are coercively required at a prepubertal age. Boys raised in such a culture grow up, "almost always" to be heterosexual (Stoller & Herdt, 1985). Hence, such an identity is based on learned behavior rather than on assumed temperamental or hereditary factors. Indeed, a combination of maternal protective overconcernedness, as well as detachment and hypercriticism of the father, may push the boy into avoidance of masculine behavior that in turn may lead to a feeling of inferiority for the boy sensing a lack of masculinity. Hence, the homosexual urge could be considered as an expression of an infantile longing for acceptance to counteract loneliness and self-pity of not belonging (Van den Aardweg, 1984).

Self-Other Differentiation. Regardless of culture or types of family roles (husband, wife, daughter, son), schizophrenics seem to differentiate least between self and other, a normal individual would differentiate most, and mildly disturbed individuals seem to occupy an intermediate position in their degree of differentiation (Foa & Chatterjee, 1974).

Siblings. "Sibling deidentification" refers to a commonplace phenomenon, that is, judgments of being different from one's sibling, especially for first pairs, first-born sib judging second-born sib or second-born sib judging first-born sib (Schachter, 1976). Sibling dissimilarity may be: (1) overstated because of methodological limitations; (2) developmental psychology conceptualizes the family as involving interactions between the person and the environment; (3) objective and subjective family experiences vary for siblings because of birth order, age differences, gender, genetics, and idiosyncratic experiences; and (4) sibling differences and similarities may be tied to whether particular outcomes are influenced by specific, varying environments or general family styles (Hoffman, 1991).

Space limitations make it impossible to review or even cite representative studies on differentness in health and handicap, religion, nationality, urban-rural or region, and, a major source, education. There is no doubt that all these variables help create a sense of differentness in most relationships.

Oppositeness

"In being the opposite of you, I become the same with others like me." This is a requirement of rebellion on one hand and blind conformity to the norms of the rebellious group on the other, supporting the dialectical relationship between sameness and oppositeness. Support for this range comes from a variety of sources, going from near functionality to dysfunctionality: (1) undergraduates; (2) oppositional defiant disorders; and (3) conduct disorders.

Undergraduates. Students who express very positive perceptions of alternate lifestyles may have significantly more negative perceptions of their parent-child relationships than those who express unfavorable perceptions of such lifestyles (Stinnett & Taylor, 1976). Self-defined adolescent rebellion seems associated with perceived parental marital unhappiness, restrictive-permissiveness of child-rearing practices, and division of authority. Apparently, adolescent rebellion may be the product of a home thought to be patriarchal and unhappy, patriarchal and very restrictive, or patriarchal and very permissive (Balswick & Macrides, 1975). The seemingly contradiction between very restrictive and very permissive home atmosphere seems to support the dialectical nature of sameness and oppositeness predicted by the model.

Oppositional Defiant Disorders (ODD). Most of the evidence supports a distinction between conduct disorder (CD) and ODD (Rey, 1993). However, even ODD could be divided into passive noncompliance and active defiance. CD is clearly heterogeneous, with some sex differences. More serious symptoms atypical for the child's sex and age may be prognostic of serious dysfunction. A proportion of children with ODD later develop CD, while a proportion of children with CD later meet criteria for antisocial personality disorders (Loeber, Burke, Lahey, & Winters, 2000). Children with ODD may be at risk for low-grade depressive illness, and to a lesser extent, to specific developmental disorders (Wenning, Nathan, & King, 1993). This "diagnostic conundrum" may be solved by the presence or absence of mild aggression and lying as well as age of onset, which is earlier for ODD than most CD symptoms. Among youth with a history of ODD, not all cases progress to CD. Both disorders demonstrate the same forms of parental psychopathology and family adversity, but in greater degree in CD than in ODD (Frick, Lahey, Loeber, & Stouthamer-Loeber, 1991; Loeber, Lahey, & Thomas, 1991; Rey, 1993).

ODD with or without CD may show higher rates of comorbid psychiatric disorders and significantly greater family and social dysfunctions relative to controls when compared to psychiatric partients, especially mood disorder and social impairment, in multiple domains of functioning (Greene, Biederman, Zerwas, & Monuteaux, 2002). When CDs are conceptualize according to two orthogonal dimensions of overt/covert and destructive/ nondestructive, the resulting four quadrants seem to correspond well to distinctions among norm-violating behaviors and previous diagnostic conceptualizations (Frick, Lahey, Loeber, & Tannenbaum, 1992).

Where is the dividing line between attention deficit hyperactivity disorder (ADHD) and ODD? An ODD diagnosis with or without comorbid ADHD may not be associated with an increased likelihood of a history of trauma exposure. Traumatic victimization may contribute uniquely to the prediction of ODD but not of ADHD diagnoses (Ford, Racusin, Daviss, & Ellis, 1999).

Supposedly, ODD may serve as a prime survival strategy in children, aimed at navigating and regulating the progression, through time, of the family life cycle (Mones, 1998), perhaps due to the possibility that oppositional children and their mothers seem to engage in higher levels of aversive interchanges compared to control mother-child pairs (Sanders, Dadds, & Bor, 1989).

Conduct Disorders (CD). Even though there may not be gender differences in oppositional behavior, aggression, property, and status offenses may be more common among boys, with different offenses perpetuated at different ages (Lahey, Schwab-Stone, Goodman, & Waldman, 2000). Mothers of children diagnosed with CD seem to show characteristics associated with psychopathic, hypomanic, and histrionic disorders. Mothers of children diagnosed with ADHD, on the other hand, may fail to show any of these characteristics (Lahey, Russo, Walker, & Piacentini, 1989), supporting the overall possibility that noncompliance in children might be highly related to maternal depression (Forehand & Furey, 1985).

A diagnosis of CD seems related to several aspects of family functioning: maternal parenting (supervision and persistence in discipline) and parental adjustment (paternal antisocial personality disorder and paternal substance abuse). Children with ODD may be intermediate to families with CD and control children only in having a higher rate of paternal substance abuse and paternal antisocial personality disorder. When both parental antisocial personality disorders and maternal parenting are considered, only parental antisocial personality disorder may be significantly associated with CD (Frick, Lahey, Loeber, & Stouthamer-Loeber, 1992). Juvenile fire setting could be prodromal of conduct disorder later in adolescence (Kolko, 1985).

Another characteristic of oppositional individuals, as in juvenile gangs, anticulture groups, and the like, including motorcycle gangs, which are impressionistically visible, lies in the strenuous and uncritical conformity to group norms exhibited by gang and group members in manners, clothing, appearance, and beliefs. This conformity in rebellion supports the dialectical nature of sameness and oppositeness. One cannot seemingly exist without the other.

Alienation

"I do not want to be like you or like anyone else." This is a requirement of isolation from others (Mijuskovic, 1977, 1979). Past personality and psychopathology theorists have been concerned with this condition (Banerji, 1978; Chakravarti, 1978; Kanungo, 1979). There are various types and degrees of alienation, such as aloneness, loneliness, solitude, and isolation (Kubistant, 1981). Some are possibly imposed by genetic factors (Cantwell, Baker, & Rutter, 1979, some by family factors, some by a combinations of both. Some types are chosen, as in solitude and loneliness. Some are developed from an early age, some develop later on in life. Some forms are exhibited at work, some at home, and some in both or other settings. The most severe instances of prototypes of alienation are found in autism and schizophrenia. Autism consists of a failure or inability to understand self and others' emotions with a parallel handicap in the development and establishment of prolonged intimate relationships (Harris, 1989; Victor, 1983). Schizophrenia may be the outcome of childhood autism or may develop later on in life, usually during adolescence (Walker, Kestler, Bollini, & Hochman, 2004).

At mild levels, when alienation is defined as powerlessness, normlessness, and social isolation, these three characteristics seem to be negatively correlated with emotional maturity (Dean & Lewis, 1978). Couple estrangement and the generation gap may be crucial in disentangling the structure of alienation in both husbands and wives (Neal, Ivoska, & Groat, 1976).

Although alienation can be viewed and evaluated relatively easy, loneliness, on the other hand, may consist of subjective, low levels of satisfaction with casual and close friendships (Cuffel & Akamatsu, 1989). Other possibilities at classification may include: existential loneliness, reactive loneliness, pervasive, nonspecific loneliness, and psychotic loneliness (Applebaum, 1978). Dysfunctional attitudes seem strongly associated with loneliness. Lonely individuals' thinking seems dominated by doubts about their ability to find satisfying romantic relationships and fears of being rejected and hurt in an intimate pairing. These individuals seem to experience a great deal of anxiety about interpersonal encounters and may regard themselves as undesirable to others, within an overall personal context of negative self-evaluation, especially in the social realm (Wilbert & Rupert, 1986).

Feeling lonely may derive from early disrupted attachments and social-emotional isolation (Hecht & Baum, 1984). More specifically, self-reported loneliness seems associated with parental neglect and a failure to provide a social-network support. This association suggests that loneliness may be related to depression, deriving in part from a wide number of experienced stressful life events (Gaudin, Polansky, Kilpatrick, & Shilton, 1993).

APPLICATIONS OF A CONTINUUM OF LIKENESS

In this section, three different applications of this continuum will be considered briefly: (1) likeness and hurt feelings; (2) functions of this model, and (3) Cusinato's, Maino's, and Scilletta's (CMS) development and validation of a Likeness Questionnaire (Appendix C).

Likeness and Hurt Feelings

Feelings, how one perceives and experiences emotionally tinged situations, and how these feelings are expressed as emotions, develop along a continuum of likeness. Feelings can be kept inwardly or can be expressed outwardly verbally, motorically, or manually. How feelings are experienced and expressed is a process related to how differentiated an individual's identity is, as defined by the Likeness Continuum. The direction of these feelings can be internalized and kept inside in symbiosis and sameness, or it can be externalized and directed outwardly in oppositeness and alienation. These two processes reach maximum dysfunctionality when they both coexist, as shown dialectically by this continuum, producing extreme, inconsistent, and contradictory expressions of internalization and externalization, as shown in severe psychopathology. In integrating both similarities and differences, one may be able to express and share hurt feelings with intimates in more creative and constructive fashion than would be possible under the two previous ranges. This issue will be discussed at length in Chapter 16.

Functions of This Model

Theoretically this model allows integration of disparate developmental sequences present in the literature without an overarching connecting model. Diagnostically one needs to ask: "How conforming, rebellious, or creative are you?" "How similar or different are you from your parents? Your partner? Your siblings? Your friends?" Prescriptively, one would simple-mindedly suggest to "Integrate positively similarity and differentness without conforming blindly or rebelling for its own sake." One workbook relates to the construct of identity, "Who Am I?" (L'Abate, 1996), while another includes this model in planned parenting practices (L'Abate, 1996).

Cusinato's, Maino's, and Scilletta's Likeness Questionnaire

To develop this questionnaire (L'Abate, 1996) and evaluate its psychometric qualities, Scilletta (2002), under the mentorship of Mario Cusinato, revalidated the factorial nature of the Self-Other Profile Chart, already mentioned in previous chapters and reviewed also in Chapters 12 and 19. She replicated the same factor structure already reported by Cusinato and Pastore (L'Abate & De Giacomo, 2003) using a stratified sample of juniors and seniors in high school and beginning freshmen in a university ($N = 308$). Attributed self-importance is comprised of two factors. The first includes academic achievement, work success, intelligence, creativity, morality, and self-esteem. The second factor includes physical appearance, physical activity, and sense of humor.

Attribution of importance from others is also comprised of two factors: partner, mother, father, siblings, and children, that is, the nuclear family, and friends, school-mates, colleagues, and others. Furthermore, among many other analyses, she correlated personal attributions of self importance with persons contributing to that sense of self-importance, finding significant correlations between ratings of attributed self-importance and persons who were more significantly responsible for those ratings. Unfortunately, limitations of space do not allow giving Scilletta's work the full attention it deserves.

Maino (Eleonora Maino, personal communication, April 1, 2004) added to the development of this questionnaire by stressing and discriminating between the importance of two variables. The first variable deals with the relationship with one particular, specific person considered in the model, the person who is the most important in our whole being, that is, our attitudes, thoughts, ideas, and feelings that allow our growth and, therefore, the expansion of our being and our personality. Hence, we need not only identify which person is more important, but also identify how one feels in being with that particular person, i.e., the second variable. Quantitatively, this variable deals with the duration or intensity in which the attitudes that more or less favor one's growth are verified in the relationship with that particular person, that is, our being with the person who is most responsible for our growth.

Consequently, one needs to enter the frequency and duration to rate in this way what "being with" that person means. On one hand, we can understand how one sees himself or herself like someone else. On the other hand, it is also important to evaluate *how often* one happens to "be like" that particular person. Hence, this last point is accounted for in the CMS Likeness Questionnaire by adding an additional scoring related to the frequency and duration of how much one rates oneself in relationship to the person rated.

The title of this questionnaire is abbreviated using the initials of the three collaborators who have significantly added to its development.

CONCLUSION

How does the process of developmental identity differentiation take place over the life cycle of individuals and their intimate relationships? It looks like most of the evidence, some of it already admittedly quite outdated, would support the model in the sense that major dysfunctions were present inside the two extreme ranges of the continuum, symbiosis-alienation and sameness-oppositeness. The next chapter will deal with applications of these ranges to styles in intimate relationships.

Chapter 11

Styles in Intimate Relationships
Model[9]

"Although we sometimes talk of ourselves as the authors of our actions, we hardly ever act independently. When a second person responds to the act of a first, and thus acts in a way that depends on the first person's act, the activities of the second person cannot be counted as wholly his own. Important in all of this is the idea that many individual actions are best characterized in collective, rather than purely individual, terms (Gibbs, 2001, p. 113)."

This chapter expands from previous chapters and especially Model[8] (Ch. 10), into a model that classifies intimate relationships into three distinct styles of how individuals relate under the stress of prolonged, close, interdependent, and committed relationships. These styles may not be immediately visible in superficial, short-lived, and contrived situations, in settings where one can put up a "happy" or "nice" facade to make a good impression (Ch. 5). These styles occur in the privacy of one's home, where one does not escape unless he or she leaves the premises, as in moving, abandonment, breakdown, divorce, psychosis, or suicide. Hence, these styles are not visible unless they are extreme and become public because the police or an ambulance is present. These styles become evident when pushed to their extremes, as for instance, when a child's behavior, either depression, isolation, bullying, etc., comes to the attention of school authorities and parents or caretakers are called in to be informed about the severity of the behavior. When abuses, of whatever kind or intensity, occur in the privacy of one's home, they are shielded from public scrutiny. When scrutiny is inevitable, as in cases of child abuse, the abuse is kept hidden either through deception or denial.

Conflicts in intimate relationships focus on or derive from the basic assumptions of the theory: *processes* in the ability to love or distance (Ch. 7), the ability to negotiate or power (Ch. 8), and *contents* of *what* is being exchanged (Ch. 9). To recap, issues of *being* or presence relate to *distance*, how close or how distant one wants or needs to be from other intimates, partners or family members, friends, etc. This area involves *how* emotionally available one can or wishes to be with self and with intimate others. The second area relates to issues of power, dealing with *control*, influence, decision making, authority and responsibility, *what* is to be exchanged. Issues of distance will be covered in greater detail in Chapters 14 and 16. Issues of power will be covered in greater detail in Chapters 15 and 17.

These are issues that stem from dyadic or multiperson relationships. However, they also involve deeper individual conflicts, below the self-presentation facade of individuals, couples, or families (Ch. 5) and involve and require all of the resources available to cope with conflict (Ch. 4). How fearfully, anxiously, depressingly, angrily, etc. one deals with internal conflicts adds to the level of functionality and the styles that will be invoked under stressful situations. Hence, issues of relational conflicts and styles to deal with conflicts involve a pyramid of resources horizontally (Ch. 4), levels of observation and interpretation vertically (Ch. 5), settings, where does the conflict take place (Ch. 6), how issues of love (Ch. 7) and negotiation (Ch. 8) are shared and dealt with, and what style is recruited to deal with the inevitable stress of conflict.

DERIVATION OF STYLES FROM THE LIKENESS CONTINUUM

Three styles are derived directly from the continuum of likeness (Ch. 10). From that continuum it is possible to derive an Abusive-Apathetic, Reactive-Repetitive, & Creative-Conductive ARC model of styles in intimate relationships. This derivation and transition occurs from one "internal" model of identity differentiation (Ch. 10) to "external" and visible styles in intimate relationships. Perhaps the continuum of likeness may be the most tenuous part of the theory, since, with the sole exception of the CMS Likeness Questionnaire and two other measures of likeness (L'Abate & Wagner, 1985, 1988), there is as yet no accurate or reliable way to measure identity differentiation except conceptually and impressionistically. An instrument to evaluate these three styles, however, the Problems-In-Relationships Scale (PIRS) has been developed and validated, albeit once (Ch. 19).

The three styles comprising this model are obtained by combining dialectical, admittedly hypothetical, relationships between the six ranges of identity differentiation. By combining relationships characterized by symbiosis and alienation one obtains the most dysfunctional abusive-apathetic (neglectful) style. By combining relationships that range within the sameness-oppositeness ranges one obtains a reactive-repetitive, competitive/conflictual, semifunctional style. By combining relationships that range within the similarity-differentness ranges, one obtains the most functional creative conductive (CC) style. An attempt will be made to find evidence to support all three styles.

Hence, the ARC Model[9] describes the functionality of behavior, ranging from most functional (CC), to semifunctional/dysfunctional (RR), to most dysfunctional (AA) styles in intimate relationships. One may behave perfectly well and appropriately at the presentational level at work, or in short-lived, superficial situations that do not tax phenotypic relationships. What counts is not how one relates in such transient and superficial situations, but how one relates in the privacy of the home. One may relate in a completely different manner phenotypically from how one presents himself or herself in non-taxing, brief, and short-lived social situations. Hence, one cannot consider this continuum without including the preceding metaassumption of levels of analysis and interpretation (Ch. 5).

One important aspect of these three styles pertains to their ability to change. The AA style, because of its intensity and strength, is the most difficult to change. It needs multimodal interventions based on all three media of intervention, verbal, written, and nonverbal, i.e., medication. The RR style is relatively more amenable to change, provided the intervention matches the particular problem. For instance, internalizations (anxiety, depression, and fears) might improve by whatever positive intervention may occur. Externalizations (anger, hostility, and aggression), on the other hand, are more resistant to change unless mandated and planned carefully under controlled conditions. The CC style, by definition, may welcome and use well almost any type of positive intervention.

INTERGENERATIONAL TRANSMISSION OF RELATIONAL STYLES

This transmission has already been reviewed briefly in Chapter 5, as the ultimate, bottom-line sublevel that "explains" intimate relationships descriptively at presentational, phenotypic, and genotypic sublevels. That this transmission does occur will be seen in parent-child interactions, and the outcome of parental relationships on their children. This transmission can also be observed relatively easy and measured objectively (Carpenter, 1984).

The AA level should be easy to detect in spite of attempts by perpetrators to hide or deny any abuse. The RR is distinguishable from the AA style in terms of intensity and absence or presence of physical, verbal, substance, or alcohol abuse. RR may not be as immediate and extreme as AA. However, it does contain characteristics that do possess abusive and apathetic qualities. It may be more a matter of a large number of RR reaching the AA level when there is frequent physical and verbal violence. For instance, these are verbal characteristics of RR style that may not reach AA proportions: blaming, reading one's mind, distracting from the issue at hand, bringing up the past, ultimatums, use of the pronoun "you" instead of speaking for oneself ("I"), or talking about the relationship ("we"). Nonetheless both styles have one characteristic in common: their repetitiveness.

Practically, differences among the three styles reviewed below will be made on the basis of their origins: AA from studies with clinical populations, RR from studies from nonclinical populations that evidenced some degree or type of distress, and CC from control populations in the same studies that include normal and functional, children, adolescents, and parents. For instance, children and parents seen in clinical settings differ from nonreferred children and their parents. There is greater psychiatric morbidity in clinic mothers, with disciplinary techniques being more punitive than in nonclinic parents, and attitudes toward their children and the marital relationship being more negative in clinic than nonclinic parents (Chawia & Gupt, 1979). Hence, any control group of a normative nature would include a CC style.

ABUSIVE-APATHETIC NEGLECTFUL STYLE

The abusive-apathetic (AA) style can be responsible for many traumas, provoking in some cases dissociative disorders (Hechtman, 1996; Thomas, 2003). At issue here lies the differentiation among abuse, maltreatment, and neglect. Although both abuse and maltreatment imply an active, negatively punitive behavior, as in battering, neglect, on the other hand, implies a failure to pay attention to the child, allowing the child to do whatever the child wants with few if any consequences. Hence, various degrees of AA style can be reliably differentiated: physical or sexual abuse, emotional cruelty, and neglect, from severe but not abusive discipline to mild and nonabusive discipline. The latter may well be placed among the RR style.

Of course, a more possible and serious pattern would consist of inconsistent and even contradictory oscillations between out-and-out abuse, which would be mainly physical, maltreatment, which might imply punitive and aversive verbal punishment, versus out-and-out neglect, ignoring the child completely and not paying attention to his or her needs. Whether low SES is a major factor in this style (Banyard, 1999) seems to be the prevailing view on the basis of evidence (Pelton, 1978).

As a whole, physical abuse may tend to be associated with deviant child behavior, emotional cruelty may be associated with adult conflict that enlarged and involved the child, while neglect may represent a parental failure to assume responsibilities (Herrenkohl, Herrenkohl, & Egolf, 1983). Perceived parental abuse and neglect in adolescent inpatients seem related to self-mutilation and high risk of suicide (Lipschitz, Winegar, Nicolaou, Hartnick et al., 1999). Children of battered mothers tend to show below-average self-concept scores in preschool, more aggressive behavior in school-age than girls, with a pervasive tendency for mothers to rate their children more negatively than did other observers (Hughes & Barad, 1983).

The intergenerational transmission of relationship violence and physical punishment, that is, both physical and verbal aggression in the AA style, is well documented (Deater-Deckard, Lansford, Dodge, Pettit, & Bates, 2003; Kwong, Bartholomew, Henderson, & Trinke, 2003, p. 301). Even alcoholism in youth can be traced directly to family background where excessive drinking was the norm (Abrams & Niaura, 1987; Sadava, 1987). Alcohol and drug additions do not develop in a relational vacuum, as some theories would like one to believe (Blane & Leonard, 1987), but may develop directly as learned behavior based on modeling of important intimates in one's life, initially parents and siblings, and later on, peers. In spite of this background, there are resilient individuals who are able to rise above their early traumas and go on to develop more positive lifestyles (Bonanno, 2004).

Family Dysfunction

Affective characteristics in children's personalities seem related to level of family functioning, the higher the family functioning the more functional the affective characteristics will be (Marjoribanks, 1978). Greater levels of perceived peer rejection and lower levels of close friendship support may be associated with suicidal ideation as a result of family dysfunction (Prinstein, Boergers, Spirito, Little, et al., 2000). The strongest positive correlation may be found between family conflict and lack of positive interactional patterns that are related to abuse potential (Mollerstrom, Patchner, & Milner, 1992). A family emotional climate characterized by parental depression, conflict, and marital unhappiness may have negative implications for the affective quality of the relationships between mothers and daughters (Stoneman, Brody, & Burke, 1989). Although there may be an association between childhood sexual abuse and later symptoms of anxiety and depression, this relationship may not be one of direct causation. It is likely that there are other processes that mediate that relationship. High family conflict, low control (less emphasis on rules and procedures), and high cohesiveness, all in combination with a history of sexual abuse, may place victims at greater risk for subsequent depressive symptoms (Yama, Tovey, & Fogas, 1993).

Families of maladjusted children with conduct disorders might be characterized by single-parent status, increased maternal depression, lower SES, and family history of alcoholism and drug abuse (Webster-Stratton, 1990). Self-report scales measuring skill deficits and beliefs may be sensitive indicators of level of distress in parent-adolescent relations (Robin, Koepke, & Moye, 1990). Substance abuse and psychiatric disorders seemingly produce significantly lower family satisfaction and a greater desire for family treatment than in a family with psychiatric disorders but no substance abuse (Dixon, McNary, & Lehman, 1995).

Protective factors for high-risk children in adulthood may relate to dispositional attributes of the individual, affectionate ties within the family that provide emotional support in times of stress, and external support systems, like close friends and peers (Werner, 1989). Growing up in a harsh family climate, where affiliative needs might not have been met, could produce psychological and physical symptoms in old age, especially in men (Patterson, Smith, Smith, Yager, et al., 1992).

The verbal and physical harassment toward gays, lesbian, and bisexual adolescents by significant others is often associated with several problematic outcomes, including: school-related problems, running away from home, conflicts with the law, substance abuse, prostitution, and suicide (Savin-Williams, 1994), suggesting that a great deal of abusive behavior may be even societally condoned or, at least, sanctioned. There are still a great many cultural and even religious views that condone physical and verbally abusive parental practices.

Parental Practices

In considering child abuse and neglect, one must be mindful of balancing the needs of children with the rights of the parents (Derdeyn, 1978). Abusive parents tend to offer more positive explanations in situations where their child broke an object and would not stop crying, but tend to feel significantly more doubt and anger if the child was disobedient and kept on crying (Rosenberg & Reppucci, 1983). Parental lack of knowledge and excessive or unrealistic expectations may lead parents to interpret their children's behavior as deviant (Rickard, Graziano, & Forehand, 1984).

Parental practices may be associated with the type and profile of a child's disruptive behavior problems, for example, oppositional, aggressive, or hyperactive. Punitive parental practices may tend to be associated with elevated rates of most child disruptive behavior problems. Low levels of warm involvement may be particularly characteristic of parents of children who showed elevated levels of oppositional behavior. Physically aggressive parenting may be linked more specifically with child aggression. These practices contributed more to the prediction of oppositional and aggressive behavior problems than to hyperactive behavior problems (Stormshak, Bierman, McMahon, Lengua, et al., 2000).

Parental practices of neglectful, abusive, mentally retarded, low income, deaf mothers, and middle-class mothers suggest that different types of parental risk may exert different types of impact on maternal sensitivity to her children. Deaf and low SES mothers may tend to show the least reduction in sensitivity in comparison to wide-ranging practices of middle-class mothers. Retarded mothers tend to perform in the middle range of sensitivity, while abusive and neglectful mothers tend to show the least sensitivity to their infants' cues. Neglectful mothers tend to be predictably more uninvolved and passive than abusive mothers who tend to be more active and interfering (Crittenden & Bonvillian, 1984).

Childhood Physical Abuse

Child batterers, as a whole, display a "sick but slick syndrome," presenting a picture of themselves as healthy and unlikely to abuse their children, even though most of them may be characterized by psychopathic tendencies (Wright, 1976). Adolescents suffering from a high degree of abuse could be characterized with significantly higher levels of dependency, suicidality, violence, impulsivity, substance abuse problems, and borderline tendencies (Grilo, Sanislow, Febon, Martino, et al., 1999). Physically abused children tend to display a significantly greater number of behavior problems and lower social competencies than normals (Conway & Hansen, 1989; Wolfe & Mosk, 1983). Abusive mothers may tend to have more negative expectations for their children than nonabusive mothers according to situational factors (Larrance & Twentyman, 1983).

Sexual Abuse

Reports of suspected father-child sexual abuse from practicing psychologists tend to be affected by whether the accused father is willing to admit or a denies the abuse (Kalichman, Craig, & Follingstad, 1989). Incestuous families include a dysfunctional parental coalition, incongruous beliefs about themselves and their families, inability to solve problem constructively, and inability to nurture autonomy in family members (Madonna, Van Scoyk, Jones,

1991). When sexual abuse is coupled with physical abuse, the outcome may result in greater alcoholic consumption, with diagnoses of borderline personality disorders and high risk for suicide (Brown & Anderson, 1991).

The trauma of this experience lasts a lifetime, producing a variety of destructive outcomes in adulthood, including depression and self-destructive behavior, anxiety, feelings of isolation and stigma, poor self-esteem, difficulty in trusting others, a tendency toward revictimization, social isolation, poor social adjustment, substance abuse, and sexual maladjustment, including posttraumatic stress disorder (Browne & Finkelhor, 1986; Cahill, Llewelyn & Pearson, 1991; Harter, Alexander, & Neimeyer, 1988; Lange, de Beurs, Dolan, Lachnit, et al., 1999; Wolfe, Gentile, & Wolfe, 1989).

Respondents with a history of sexual abuse are more likely than nonabused respondents to experience suicidal ideation, reporting histories of drug abuse, suicide attempts, sexual problems, and self-mutilation. Psychiatric diagnoses may be more frequent than in nonabused respondents (Biere & Zaidi, 1989). Sexually abused women from dysfunctional families tend to report the highest level of psychological distress. Conversely, level of psychological distress by abused women from functional families might not differ from that of nonabused functional or nonabused-dysfunctional families (Brock, Mintz, & Good, 1997). Sexually abused girls may experience sexually inappropriate behaviors, sleep disturbances, depressed mood, running away, and delinquent acts. Since these disturbances cannot be traced directly to the original abuse, and occur also in disturbed, nonsexually abused girls, there seems to be few reliable markers for sexual abuse (Goldston, Turnquist, & Knutson, 1989).

If these results are reliable, they indicate how important positive intimate relationships are in mitigating or ameliorating the outcome of traumatic experiences. By the same token, negative family climate may exacerbate past traumas as well.

Parental Alcoholism

When in addition to childhood abuse and a dysfunctional family environment one also considers parental alcoholism, the results are even more deleterious, producing long-term distress and negative assumptions about the self and the benevolence of the world (Harter & Vanecek, 2000). Alcoholic males may subordinate sex for the use of alcohol and to the satisfaction of their wives' neurotic needs (Parades, 1973). If that is the case, children raised under those conditions might, very likely, show sexual disturbances later in life. There is a significant overrepresentation of alcoholism in parents where physical and sexual abuse or neglect required court-ordered removal of the child from the home (Famularo, Stone, Barnum, & Wharton, 1986).

Children of alcoholics, with few exceptions, fail to show clear signs of maladjustment (Calder & Kostyniuk, 1989). Perhaps these children may not show these signs. However, how about when they reach adulthood and become involved in new intimate relationships? Indeed, in college students, clear signs of maladjustment become evident, as in self-deprecation, especially in women, particularly if the father was the alcoholic parent (Berkowitz & Perkins, 1988). This pattern, related to self-esteem, is found in undergraduate children of alcoholics, mentally ill, and substance-abusing parents (Williams & Corrigan, 1992). In comparisons among adolescents of alcoholic, depressed or nondistressed, fathers, the latter showed higher rates of congeniality and problem solving, perhaps supporting the notion that functionality in intimate relationships is shown by the ability to laugh.

Parental Psychopathology

Abusive parents may have been abused as children, lacking accurate parenting knowledge, and may be characterologically impulsive. Maltreating parents, on the other hand, may not lack parenting knowledge but may use different, often aversive, parenting techniques (Friedrich & Wheeler, 1982). Depression in one parent, usually in the mother, which has been studied more often than depression in fathers, is usually associated with undesirable parenting practices, such as: unresponsiveness, inattentiveness, intrusiveness, inept discipline, and negative perceptions of children (Gelfand & Teti, 1990). The greater the level of depression in the mother the greater the likelihood of child noncompliance (Brody & Forehand, 1993).

Children from unipolar or bipolar mothers tend to have a higher rate of diagnosed conditions (82%) than children from medically ill (43%) or normal mothers (32%). Children of bipolar mothers tend to have milder disorders than children of unipolar mothers (Hammen, Burge, Burney, & Adrain, 1990). Unipolar depressed mothers tend to display more negative, less positive, and less task-focused behavior toward their children than nondepressed mothers (Gordon, Burge, Hammen, Adrian, et al., 1989).

Depressed mothers also tend to make more negative comments about their children than nondepressed mothers (Conrad & Hammen, 1989; Krech & Johnston, 1992) and tend to report more cases of child behavior problems than do their mentally healthy counterparts (Najman, Williams, Nikles, Spence et al., 2000). Whether children's adjustment difficulties are specific to maternal depression is questionable. There may be other factors, like low SES and intellectual level of the parents, present (Lee & Gotlib, 1989a). Children of depressed mothers may be at risk for a full range of adjustment problems and at specific risk for clinical depression (Downey & Coyne,

1990). The vast majority of mothers of children with separation anxiety disorder and/or overanxious disorder may have had a lifetime history of an anxiety disorder (Last, Hersen, Kazdin, Francis et al., 1987).

The interaction of maternal and adolescent depression might be a better predictor of adolescent social and cognitive functioning than either variable alone (Dumas & Gibson, 1990; Forehand, Brody, Long, & Fauber, 1988; Forehand & McCombs, 1988). This outcome would be predicted by analyses of parent-infant interaction considered to be the joint outcome of parent and child characteristics (Thomas & Martin, 1976). The child's adjustment may be more strongly related to the presence of maternal psychopathology than just to the mother's diagnostic status (Lee & Gotlib, 1989b). Maternal neglect, rather than abuse, may be more related to delinquency than any other type of abuse (Henggeler, McKee, & Borduin, 1989). Attentional problems in dysfunctional mother-child interactions due to stress level may be relevant to their specific treatment (Wahler & Dumas, 1989).

Children of parents with panic disorder may themselves be at high risk for panic disorders, while children of depressed parents may be at high risk for social phobias, major depression, disruptive behavior disorders, and poorer social functioning. Combination of panic disorder and depression in parents may produce children who are at increased risk for separation anxiety disorder and multiple anxiety disorders (Biederman, Faraone, Hirshfeld-Becker, Friedman et al., 2001).

The level of functionality in the father or at least in one caretaker, may serve as a buffer in cases of teenagers with a depressed mother (Tannenbaum & Forehand, 1994). When maternal depression is expressed in mother-to-child aggression, moderately depressed mothers may be at increased risk for child abuse and physical aggression compared to non-depressed mothers (Zuravin, 1989). Lower levels of personality pathology in the depressed parent, higher levels of parent conscientiousness, and less psychological distress in the spouse may be associated with healthier family functioning (Miller, McDermut, Gordon, Keitner et al., 2000).

Boys born from adolescent mothers tend to be diagnosed as conduct disorders. In teenage motherhood, parental antisocial personality and low each contribute uniquely to the prediction of childhood conduct disorder. Teenage motherhood may be spuriously related with child conduct problems because of common associations with SES and parental antisocial personality (Christ, Lahey, Frick, Russo et al., 1990). Sons of aggressive adolescent mothers and both sons and daughters of aggressive-withdrawn mothers may show elevated and distinctive diagnostic profiles in comparison with children from nondeviant mothers.

When both parents are depressed the likelihood of major depression and other problems in their offspring is high compared with the children of normal parents (Weissman, Gammon, John, Merikangas et al., 1987). Children who grew up away from psychotic parents, compared with children raised by nonpsychotic parents, tend to develop more stable personalities and could probably benefit by free schooling. Adequate, stable surroundings appear to have a mitigating influence on a handicapping genetic heritage (Landau, Daphne, Iuchtman, & Aveneri, 1975).

Marital Conflict

Marital conflict has dire consequences on children who witness it (Goeke-Morey, Harold, Cummings, & Shelton, 2003). Level of marital satisfaction is inversely correlated with antisocial personality in boys (Frick, Lahey, Hartdagen, & Hynd, 1989). Mild marital and individual stress reported by fathers may predict both inconsistent fathering and lack of parental agreement concerning discipline. Correlations between parents' reports of marital adjustment and child conduct problems seem significantly stronger in families of clinic-referred children compared with families of nonclinic children and in families of lower SES compared with families of higher SES (Jouriles, Bourg, & Farris, 1991).

Mothers who might be depressed or stressed due to marital problems perceived more child deviant behaviors and interacted with their children with more commands and criticisms, while the fathers' perceptions were relatively unaffected by personal adjustment measures (Webster-Stratton, 1988). Perhaps these differences between fathers and mothers could be explained by the latter's greater involvement with their children than fathers. Fathers also tend to deny that there are any problems both in the marriage and in their children.

REACTIVE-REPETITIVE STYLE

The reactive-repetitive (RR) style is distinguished from the AA style on the basis of immediate or delayed reactions without physical, sexual, or verbal abuse. Reactivity need not always be immediate. It can be delayed, repressed, or suppressed. One could experience a very painful event and not react to it for days, weeks, months, years, or forever. Furthermore, the reaction could be direct or indirect, with displacement against people or objects that were not part of the original provocation. As already noted, the major characteristic of RR, which is also shared in greater intensity by the AA style, is its repetitiveness. Reactant individuals may be related to "reactive" individuals in the sense that the former may be characterized by a lack of interest in making a good impression on others, being somewhat

careless about meeting obligations, being less tolerant of others' beliefs, re-
sisting rules and regulations, being more concerned about problems and
worried about the future, and being more inclined to express strong feelings and emotions. Reactant women may be different from reactant men by
having a personality style that seemed more decisive, more sociable, and
more self-assured than nonreactant women (Dowd, Wallbrown, Sanders, &
Yesenosky, 1994). How reactance is related with reactivity remains to be
seen.

There exists a substantial number of husbands and wives experiencing
role attitude/behavior incongruence, a possibility that may lead to greater
reactivity. More women than men in the incongruent role attitude/behavior
group tend to express egalitarian attitudes toward the performance of family
roles. Both genders tend to express egalitarian or role sharing attitudes, but
women enact the majority of duties related to all roles with the exception
of the provider role, which, at least in the past, might have been performed
mainly by men. Thus, where a role attitude/behavior incongruence exists,
both married men and women express equalitarian role attitudes, but this
egalitarianism may not be generally reflected in role behaviors (Araji, 1977).
The discrepancy between attitudes and behavior suggests that, over time,
partners will eventually react to it in a variety of ways. Partners without a
clearly differentiated sense of identity would tend to react negatively, while
partners with a differentiated sense of identity may react positively.

Distressed couples, for instance, may be more reactive to recent, high-
valence events than nondistressed counterparts. Distressed couples tend to
report lower rates of positive and higher rates of negative events than nondistressed couples. Subjective satisfaction with the relationship may depend to
a greater degree on the frequency of recent positive or negative events than
might be the case for happily married couples. These differences in reactivity may not be simply a function of differences in behavioral frequencies.
The process of reactivity apparently is separable—both experimentally and
statistically—from the frequency of positive and negative exchanges (Jacobson, Follette, & McDonald, 1982). Overt marital hostility may tend to
correlate significantly more with behavior problems of men than of women
(Porter & O'Leary, 1980). Cardiovascular reactivity in married couples may
be related to psychological reactivity in the sense that cynical hostility may
be associated with greater systolic blood pressure reactivity among husbands' attempts to influence their wives. The latter may not show the same
pattern (Smith & Brown, 1991).

Adolescents from recently divorced parents tend to perceive more interparental conflict and have higher rates of teacher-reported externalizing
and internalizing problems than adolescents from intact parents (Forehand,
Wierson, McCombs, Brody et al., 1989). Indeed, the RR style can be found

in internalizations as in Cluster C (Ch. 7) and externalizations, as in Cluster B (Ch. 8). Extremes in both internalizations and externalizations, as well as inconsistent and contradictory alternations of internalizations and externalizations, found in Cluster A of Axis II and Axis I disorders, will be discussed in Chapter 12.

CONDUCTIVE-CREATIVE STYLE

The conductive-creative (CC) style includes relationships characterized by positively cooperative, nurturing, supportive, and even joyful interactions among intimates. It includes individuals, couples, and families who are happy to be with each other and who are creative in how they relate with one another. Conductivity implies being in charge of oneself and of how one deals with intimate and nonintimate others, without becoming over-charged, or overheated, so to speak, following a score that would produce win-win outcomes. Creativity implies originality in how one deals with self emotionally and practically, showing direct involvement and investment in taking care of self and intimates in ways that improve the welfare of self and intimates. As described in Chapters 6 and 12, there may be various degrees of CC style, varying from superior to adequate, spilling from the home to other settings. One characteristic of CC style, at both the individual and multidyadic levels, may well be laughter and humor (Chapman & Foot, 1976).

Family Climate

Scales from the Family Environment Scale, measuring cohesion, conflict, and active-recreational orientation seem related to adolescent distress in a sample of nonclinical respondents (Kleinman, Handal, Enos, Searight et al., 1989).

Parenting

Positive parental practices are based on decreasing vulnerabilities in the establishment of trustful, supportive relationships between parents and off-spring. They are based on the deliberate nonuse of reproachful and guilt-provoking techniques, with communications geared to reality and rationality, single-minded, and unequivocal in how feelings are related directly to experiences but incongruous with it (Akerley, 1975). Positive parent-child relations seem positively related to a child's cognitive abilities, while negative parent-child relations are negatively related to a child's cognitive abilities (Chu, 1975).

A son's competence is best predicted by parental involvement, socio-economic resources, parental competence, and family cohesion (Kotler, 1975). It seems possible for parents to predict their children responses in middle-class White families, with the exception of predicting negative feelings (Kaufman, Hallahan, & Ball, 1975). Parental assertiveness seems related more to affection than to control, a possibility than runs counter to most published literature in this area (Shilling, 1979). Parents of adolescents seem ill-informed about their children's courtship, sexuality, and marriage, even though they may be more insightful about problems in the home, especially health and physical development in their girls more so than in boys (Collins, Cossel, & Harper, 1975).

Constitutional differences in intrauterine and birth experiences in mono-zygotic twins may form the basis for differential parental perceptions and differential delineations of their roles. This process may create a reciprocal interplay between parents and twins, sometimes reinforcing differences that may lead to different parent-child linkages (Allen, Greenspan, & Pollin, 1976).

Highest degrees of parental acceptance tend to produce greater warmth and flexibility in their adult children. However, stress, as in the case of infant medical risk, may be an important moderator in relations between maternal perceptions of childhood rejection and parental behavior (Hammond, Landry, Swank, & Smith, 2000). Apparently, psychological separation and parental attachment in leaving home for college are areas in need of further research (Schultheiss, Palladino, & Blustein, 1994). High levels of parental monitoring predict lower levels of adolescent deviance (Forehand, Miller, Dutra, & Chance, 1997). Undergraduates with a complex affective style may be more likely to have been disciplined by the opposite-sex parent using a consistent approach. Undergraduates disciplined by the same-sex parent with some disagreement between parents on disciplinary procedures tend to use a more complex analytic style. This style will be elaborated in the next chapter under the rubric of "Healthy Family Relationships," in the section on selffulness.

FUNCTIONS OF THIS MODEL

This model allows us to integrate functionality and dysfunctionality according to styles that might be immediately visible. Diagnostically one needs to find out which style is used most often. The AA style needs multiple reporters from different sources to be reliably identified, since single individuals may tend to report their styles positively and styles of other intimates negatively or deny that certain abusive behaviors are indeed occurring for fear of legal consequences.

Prescriptively is would be very easy to say "Try to be as creative and conductive in your intimate relationships as is humanly possible." One needs to attack directly AA and RR styles. However, relying solely or strictly on f2f talk would make the task impossible in view of the staggering numbers of repeatedly AA and RR relationships. Preventively as well as therapeutically one would be better off, not only cost-wise but also in time and energy saving, to use all the self-help workbooks that abound in these areas (L'Abate, 1998, 2004a).

Therapeutically, it would be extremely difficult to treat reactive or abusive relationships f2f through talk, unless or after respondents involved in those relationships have demonstrated they want to change through completion of homework assignments in workbooks dealing directly with their styles. With externalizing disorders, for instance, talk is cheap. It must be demonstrated that respondents want to change by their efforts to complete written homework assignments in workbooks.

CONCLUSION

Relational styles are not enough. We need additional models to account for the complexity of intimate relationships that overlap in severity with relational styles. Here is where the issue of comorbidity comes into play.

Chapter 12

Selfhood: The Attribution of Importance
Model[10]

"Without sharing there is no happiness in life. Happiness comes from work and discipline and sharing, from using your time in a way that is good for you and for others (Anonymous).*"*

This chapter presents a relational model of selfhood that is based on how a sense of self-importance is attributed to, expressed, and shared with self and intimate others. From where do we receive a sense of self-importance? Some receive it from positive Doing, some receive it from positive Having, some receive it from positive Being. Some get it from doing nothing. Some get it from negative Doing, or Having, or Being. Some receive from the self, some receive it from others, some receive it from neither, some receive it from both. Some get it from owning a gun. Some get it from helping others. Some get it from wearing a uniform. Some get it from dressing in outlandish outfits. Some get it from their looks. Some get it from fooling others. Some get it from the cars they drive. Some get it from criticizing others and feeling superior to them in so doing. Some get it from being Christian. Some get it from being Buddhist. Some get it from being neither. Some get it from their jobs. Some get it from performing and fulfilling their family roles. Some get it from their athletic achievements. Some do not get it from anything.

This model leads to a classification of psychopathologies as stemming from four major personality propensities that include Axis I and Cluster A of Axis II disorders into a meaningful whole. This model delineates personality dysfunctionalities, reviewed in Chapters 7, 8, and 9, as being continuous and contiguous with each other as extensions of those four major personality propensities.

In addition to an underlying Likeness Continuum (Ch. 10) about differentiation in identity, and the three relational styles (Ch. 11) to describe the subtle and not so subtle, or not so obvious development of functionality, internalizations-externalizations, and psychopathology in relationships, it is necessary to introduce a tenth model. This one deals with how intimates interact with each other in fairly visible fashion, if you were allowed in their homes. Here is where the metatheoretical models about levels of analysis, observation, and interpretation (Ch. 5) as well as settings (Ch. 6) come into being. We relate with others in different ways in different settings and at different levels of observation and interpretation. Some relate in ways that are consistent at various levels and sublevels. Some relate in ways that are inconsistent and contradictory at various levels. Some relate in exactly the same way from one setting to another, regardless of setting. Some relate according to the task demands peculiar to each particular setting. How one relates privately and phenotypically at home does not necessarily predict how one is going to relate presentationally in public settings. How one relates in the tennis court does not necessarily predict how one is going to relate at home or at work.

Furthermore, the resource class of importance needs expansion into a full-fledged model. How does the self manifest itself to describe, if not explain, personality propensities that predict how individuals relate with each other in intimate relationships? Hence, this selfhood model assumes that attribution, ascription, and assertion are of importance in the primary, fundamental resource exchanged among intimates and nonintimates, verbally, nonverbally, and in writing.

WHAT DOES SELFHOOD MEAN?

The self and possible selves have received a great deal of attention (Bybee & Wells, 2003) in the literature. However, it is not always clear whether this construct, self, is made synonymous with personality or not. In this theory, self is clearly considered just one aspect, albeit important, of personality as expressed toward oneself and others (Manusov & Harvey, 2001). Selfhood consists of how we show and share care, concern, and compassion for the comfort and welfare of self and intimate others (Wright, 1978). Selfhood is necessary but not sufficient to define a construct like personality. One needs to add all the models of the theory together to achieve an understanding, still tentative, of what is called personality socialization and psychopathology in intimate relationships. Indeed, the self may contain an organized set of identities that are related to self-in-role meanings, defined relationally in terms of self-identities (as dialectical opposites in a continuum of likeness, for instance, as described in Chapter 10). Even though identities may operate indirectly on the self, they might motivate social relationships (Burke, 1980).

This model is called selfhood because it makes self-importance, as conceived and observed by self and others, the centerpiece of exchanges between and among intimates (partners, parent-child, sibling-sibling, friends). The self is shown by how one relates with intimates in close, prolonged, interdependent, and committed relationships, not in superficial, short-lived, artificial, and contrived relationships. Anyone can appear "nice" at first blush. What counts is how that external "niceness" gets transformed under the stress of intimate relationships in the home and not in a bar. Any college sophomore can perform well on an experimental task administered for class credit. What counts is how that college sophomore is going to do when he or she graduates and is eventually going to marry and have children. How will he or she perform at home and how will this performance relate to the work and other settings? This process occurs away from the scrutiny of occasional outsiders, but inside the privacy, and sometimes secrecy, of one's home, where contrived, opportunistic self-presentational facades cannot last very long.

Briefly, to recapitulate, the self is evaluated by how close one comes toward (approach) or comes away (avoidance) from intimates and strangers, i.e., *distance* (Ch. 7), and by how fast or how slow one is in discharging or delaying what needs to be said and done during such exchanges, i.e., *control* (Ch. 8). Developmentally, distance turns into the ability to love, while control turns into the ability to negotiate. Functionality means a balance in distance and control functions, ability to love and to negotiate, while dysfunctionality means imbalances in both functions.

Balances in distance and control functions tend to produce a personality propensity called selffulness that leads toward personal and interpersonal functionality (Fig. 12.1). In this propensity, self-importance is exchanged democratically with intimate others, where "Everybody wins." When approach is greater than avoidance and discharge is greater than delay, a personality propensity called selfishness develops, that, in its extremes, leads toward externalizations and criminalities, including theft, rape, and murder. In this propensity, self-importance is asserted at the expense of others ("I win, you lose"). When avoidance is greater than approach and delay greater than discharge, a personality propensity called selflessness develops that, in its extremes, leads toward internalizations, affective disorders, and suicide. In this propensity, self-importance is denied or negated while the importance of others is asserted and affirmed ("You win, I lose"). When there are extreme imbalances (inconsistencies, contradictions) in distance

```
I                   Selflessness        Selffulness

M     O

P     L    High concern        High concern

O  T  o    for others &         for self &

R  w       low concern for        others

T                   self

A  H       _____

N

C                   No Self              Selfishness

E  E

   H       low concern          high concern

O  i       for self &           for self & low

F  R  g     others              concern for

   h                              others


   S

           _____

           Low                   High

           IMPORTANCE    OF    SELF
```

Figure 12.1. The selfhood model.

and control functions, a personality propensity called no-self develops. This propensity leads toward severe psychopathology, where the importance of self and other is denied and negated ("You and I both lose"). Hence, self-fulness represents the most functional level of personality socialization. No-self represents the most dysfunctional level, with selfishness and selflessness somewhere in between the previous two levels, intermediate as far as levels of functionality/dysfunctionality are concerned.

The selfhood model, thus far has already been related conceptually to and compared with similar models (L'Abate, 1994), among them: self-esteem (p. 123), attachment patterns (p. 137), dependency (p. 138), emotions (p. 139), thinking patterns (p. 141), temporal perspective (p. 143), personality, affective disorders, and psychopathology (p. 144). More recently (L'Abate, 1997), this model has been related to ego-defenses (p. 181), De Giacomo's (L'Abate & De Giacomo, 2003) elementary pragmatic model (pp. 183–187), family defense mechanisms (p. 187), an analytical model of family paradigms (pp. 187–189), Olson's (1996) circumplex model of family relationships (pp. 188–191), and McCubbin et al.'s (1992) model of

Selffulness

Firm, clear &

flexible limit setting

Pushing	Unable to
Selfishness	**Selflessness**
limits	set limits

Inconsistent & contradictory

Extremes in setting limits

No-self

Figure 12.2. Selfhood model and limit setting.

family types and strengths (pp. 190–191). Comparisons among these models were made on the basis of the two assumptions of approach-avoidance and discharge-delay (pp. 193–196).

This model also relates to limit setting, not only intraindividually but also in intimate relationships (Fig. 12.2). Setting limits suggests how personality propensities tend to differ in how personal or relational limits or boundaries are set to protect (or fail to protect) self and intimate others, one of the many applications of this model. The link between selfhood and limit setting is especially relevant to parenting, since this process is basic to how children will be affected by parental practices, as already described in Chapters 8, 10, and 11 (Appendix D).

Selful individuals tend to balance Being, Doing, and Having appropriately and flexibly according to the task demands of a situation (Ch. 9). Selfish individuals will prefer Doing > Having > Being in an internally driven and impulsive sort of way. Selfless individuals will prefer Doing > Being > Having feeling externally "pushed" to Do and Have to save appearances and receive approval from others. No-self individuals may be barely able to Do with little room for Having and practically no Being. These four personality propensities are related to the three styles in intimate relationships derived from a continuum of likeness: abusive-apathetic for no-self, reactive-repetitive for selfishness and selflessness, and conductive-creative for selffulness. As shown in Figure 12.3, this model discriminates among a higher level of functionality, selffulness, two levels intermediate in dysfunctionality—selfishness and externalizations, selflessness in internalizations—and a lower level of psychopathology.

Importance, therefore, not self-esteem, is the primary, fundamental resource exchanged among people, verbally, nonverbally, and in writing.

Importance is exchanged in intimate and nonintimate relationships according to four personality propensities, as derived from the two assumptions of space and time.

Predictions from the Selfhood Model

This model makes some predictions about the links between basic personality propensities and their dysfunctional extremes as laid out on a continuum of intensity or severity. Polarities of dominance-nurturance, assertiveness-passivity, agentic-communal, and empathy-ruthlessness are all individual dimensions that may lead to different types of interactions (Fig. 12.3), democratic and egalitarian in selffulness, autocratic in selfishness, homologous in selflessness, and chaotic in no-self.

Relationships, therefore, can be classified according to two orthogonal axes differing in functionality-dysfunctionality vertically and direction of middle level of functionality horizontally. Moving upward on the left and

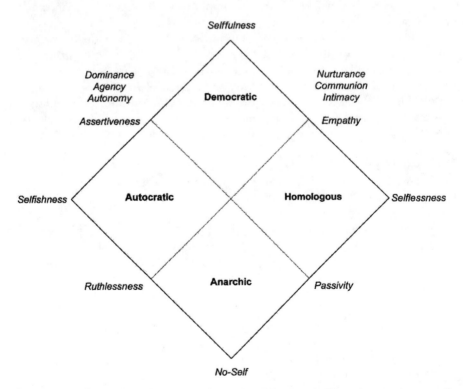

Figure 12.3. The selfhood model, communal and agentic relationships and types of interctions in intimate relationships.

top of Figure 12.3, dominance is used positively with enhancement of self and others, as in democratic relationships. Moving downward on the left, toward selfishness, dominance becomes negative with autocracy, aggressiveness, and even violence designed to enhance self at the expense of others. Its negative extremes are passivity and submissiveness. Community represents how distance is exercised in relationships. On the upper, right side of Figure 12.3, going upward, community means enhancement of self and others. Moving downward toward selflessness, community is used to enhance others at the expense of the self, as in homologous individuals, who agree to abdicate personal control and leave it in the hands of others. Pathological extremes of community are ruthlessness and sadism.

The expansion of the selfhood model more specifically to types of relationships varies from mild adjustment disorders in some selfful individuals, personality disorders in most selfish-selfless relationships (Clusters C and B of Axis II), to severe psychopathologies in no-self relationships (Cluster A and severe psychopathologies of Axis I). These deviant extensions derive from the three basic personality propensities of selfishness/selflessness and no-self (Fig. 12.4).

Selfful individuals expect some degree of reciprocity (i.e., receiving) for giving, as in giving money to charities as a way of reducing tax burden or some degree of recognition, whatever form it may take. Selfless individuals, on the other hand, give without expecting any reciprocity, and some, indeed are loath to receive, no reciprocity, no recognition, no reward: "Giving is more blessed than receiving" is their motto. Selfish individuals are interested in taking more than they can or will give, retaining whatever they can keep, regardless of the outcome on others. In addition, while selffulness relies on interdependence, selfishness abhors and denies dependency, selflessness thrives on dependency, while no-self accepts dependency as a given in spite of contradictorily denying it.

IMPLICATIONS OF THIS MODEL

This model has direct implications for: (1) gender differences; (2) intimacy, how feelings are experienced (E), processed (R) and expressed (A) as emotions; (3) full, creative, and conductive personality functioning; and (4) the classification of psychiatric disorders.

Gender Differences

This model predicts gender differences to the extent that selffulness may contain equal ratios of men and women. Selfishness predicts a higher ratio, up to 5 to 1, depending on the criterion used, of men over women. More men are still socialized for selfishness than women, at least presently in the United States. Selflessness contains a reverse ratio, more women seem socialized for selflessness than men, up to 5 to 1 depending on the criterion used. Some women are still socialized for selflessness, regardless of whether this statement might be denied. Equal gender ratios are predicted in no-self propensities (Gold, 1996). Marital disharmony may be associated with antisocial and emotional disorders in children of both sexes. Divorce may be more strongly associated with disturbances in boys than in girls. However, this difference could be due to social factors rather than to their greater psychological vulnerability (Whitehead, 1979).

Intimacy

Intimacy and negotiation are possible in selffulness, chancy and conflictual in selfishness and selfless, and impossible in no-self. As discussed at greater length in Chapter 16, intimacy is possible and present in selfful (good, successful) relationships that are characterized by cooperative equality, steadfast commitment, and helpful reciprocity. It is sporadic and present only on special occasions (funerals, baptisms, marriages) in selfish/selfless relationships. It is absent in no-self relationships. Selfful relationships are characterized by successful negotiations with a minimum of acrimony and conflict, following a CC style. Selfish/selfless relationships are characterized by a great deal of conflict and questionable ability to negotiate, with an RR style. No-self relationships will be characterized by a failure to be intimate and an inability to negotiate, with an AA style.

The model predicts specific relationships between personality propensities and emotions, especially how to deal with hurts. However, here one has to refer back to the distinction between experiencing feelings and expressing emotions considered in Chapter 4. Feelings are what is experienced (E). Emotions are what is expressed motorically, i.e., nonverbally and/or verbally (A). There is no linear relationship between what is felt and what is expressed in A because of intervening cognitive processing (R), the role of *Aw*areness and of *C*ontext in determining the course and nature of intimate relationships.

Various theories of anger (Wyer & Srull, 1993) seem unable to relate it to personality characteristics. The selfhood model would predict that anger, as a manipulative expression of self-aggrandizement at the expense of others, as usually directed against others, would more likely be found in selfishness, while anger against the self would be more likely to be found in selflessness. By the same token, sadness would be more likely found in selflessness than in selfishness. Neither feelings may be shown in no-self.

Functions of This Model

In addition to proffering a theoretical model for psychiatric classification, which in itself should be an accomplishment, this model allows the development of an arithmetical model for intimate relationships. Referring back to the amplification of five degrees or kinds of relationships among individuals (Ch. 1), one can obtain the following arithmetical outcomes, where individuals have either positive (+) or negative (−) valences. Parentheses mean or include one individual with valences inside parentheses:

a. $(++) + (++) = \mathbf{x}$. Two positive valences in individual in interaction with other similarly valenced individuals would lead to a *multiplication* in the relationship, with maximum growth and change in relationship as seen in superior and intermediate selffulness, characterized by a differentiated, clear sense of identity integrating similarities and differences, a CC style that goes above and beyond one setting but visible in more than one setting, as in superior selffulness, as described in the next section.

b. $(+) + (+) = +$. One positive valence in both individuals with a positive interaction would lead toward an *addition* in relationships with some change and some growth characterized by adequate and appropriate levels of relationships, adequate and appropriate personality functioning, including a sense of identity differentiated by similarities and differences, with a CC style interspersed with some reactivity, and positive outcomes in one to two settings, as in adequate and appropriate selfulness.

c. $(-/+) +/- (+/-) = \mathbf{0}$. A personal imbalance of positive and negative valences in an individual, with positive and negative qualities in his or her interaction would lead to *stasis* with reactively repetitive relationships, little if no change, either upwardly or downwardly, as characterized by a sense of identity based on dichotomous sameness-oppositeness, and an RR style, as found in some individuals with personality disorders described in Clusters B and C (Chapters 7 and 8).

d. $(-) - (-) = -$. Negative individual valences combined with negative dyadic or multirelational interactions would lead to *subtraction*, that is: the individual and/or the relationship or both go slowly downhill but there is no split yet, characterized by a mixture of symbiotic-alienated sense of identity, and a reactive-repetitive (RR) and abusive-apathetic (AA) styles, as found in Clusters B and A (Chapter 9).

e. $(--) - -(--) = /$. When individuals show double negative valences, their interaction would lead to a *division* or split, where there is a break within the individual and/or between and among individuals, characterized by a mixed, confused, and undifferentiated sense of identity, and an out-and-out AA style, hospitalization, incarceration, murder, or suicide (Axis I disorders), as reviewed in the rest of this chapter.

Critique of the Selfhood Model

The only relevant critique so far leveled against this model (that I am aware of) relates to the comment made by one anonymous reviewer that "My boss is important to me, but I do not love him." Clearly, the model refers to intimate, communal relationships and not to adventitious, temporary, and commercially based exchanges, like those occurring in work settings. In those settings negotiation, bargaining, and problem solving are paramount. There is little or no love needed or available, although communal and intimate relationships can be formed there, even between bosses and subordinates. Here is where boundaries between communal and exchange relationships can be found and oftentimes violated. Nonetheless, the comment is relevant to point out that there are important relationships without any love component, as in business exchanges. They are needed to survive and not necessarily for enjoyment.

Selfhood and the Attachment Model

Similarities between the attachment model and the selfhood model have been discussed in previous versions of this theory (L'Abate, 1994, 1997, 2002, 2003a; De Giacomo, L'Abate, et al., 2005). The empirical basis to support the validity of these similarities is found in the research by L'Abate et al. (2000), who found significant correlations between a model-derived measure of selfhood, the Self-Other Profile Chart (SOPC), a measure for the elementary pragmatic model of De Giacomo, and a measure of attachment styles (L'Abate, 2003a). This study, carried out originally with psychiatric patients and normal controls, has been replicated using medical students, and its results are being analyzed (L'Abate, De Giacomo et al., research in progress).

The rest of this chapter will be devoted to expanding the four basic personality propensities in relation to their upward or downward extremes.

EXPANSION OF THIS MODEL TO PSYCHIATRIC CLASSIFICATION

These four personality propensities will be expanded below as parts of a model that includes fully functioning personalities as well as psychiatrically relevant conditions or diagnoses. This model is applicable to a classification of personality functioning, i.e., "normality," and especially criminality, affective disorders, and psychopathology. From the four personality propensities it is possible to extrapolate them at different levels of functionality, to a classification of selffulness and levels of "normal" functioning, selfishness and delinquency (externalizations), selflessness and affective disorders (internalizations), and no-self and psychopathology. The latter is visible through contradictory and inconsistent extremes in both externalizations and internalizations (Fig. 12.4). The process of internalization for depressives, as one prototype for selflessness, and of externalization for paranoia, as one prototype for selfishness, for example, is supported in part by the results of Kinderman and Bentall's (1997) work. They found that: "Depressed patients tended to attribute negative social events to internal (self-blaming) causes. . . . paranoid individuals tended to choose external attributions that located blame in other individuals (p. 341)."

In children, child behavior problems can be classified according to broad-band and narrow-band syndromes, with the former including under- and over-controlled syndromes, matching differentiations already made in Chapters 7 and 8. More efforts are needed to translate syndromes into categories (Achenbach & Edelbrock, 1978). Categories, however, need to be converted into dimensions, because if a category exists, it exists to some degree in its extension and intensity. The continuity of childhood disorders with adult disorders suggests that whatever classification one follows, it should apply to both children and adults. Early onset psychiatric disorders are present in more than three and half million people in the age range between 15 and 54 years, at the time of the National Comorbidity Survey (Kessler, Foster, Saunders, & Stang, 1995) who did not complete high school and close to 4.3 million who did not complete college. Most important were conduct disorders among men and anxiety disorders among women, supporting the model's prediction of greater selfishness at least among men and possibly greater selflessness in women, even though this prediction for women applies to depression and not to anxiety, as discussed later in this chapter.

Once the four personality propensities of the model are related to the DSM-IV, an integrated model is achieved, as shown in Figure 12.4. The cells contained in that figure are filled by syndromes identified in both Axes I and II of DSM-IV. Extremes in either vertical or horizontal directions also represent the extreme prototypes of the model. Personality disorders (Clusters A, B, and C), for instance, would be found in the center of this figure.

Instead of categorical lists of psychiatric syndromes and symptoms, without any rationale behind them, except for a comprehensive description and rational or even empirical classification without a context, this model views psychiatric categories as being integratively contiguous and continuous with each other according to a relational scheme rather than a monadic, nonrelational, and categorical classification. Often, for instance, delinquency has been kept separate from psychiatric classification, while personality functioning was viewed as discontinuous from either criminality and psychopathology. Instead of personality being separate and distinct from delinquency, depression, and psychopathology, this model views these

Selffulness

Superior
Fully Functioning
in all Three
Settings*

Creative Conventional

Intermediate
Fully Functioning
in Two out of
Three Settings

Assertive Empathic

Adequate
Fully Functioning
in One out of
Three Settings

* The three settings are *Family,
School/Work,* and *Surplus Time*

Emotional
Immaturities

Generalized
Anxiety
Disorders

*Without
Agoraphobias*

Inadequate &
Poor Impulse
Control without
Criminal
Acting Out

Attention
Deficit
Disorders

Obsessions
Compulsions Anxieties

Panic Attacks
*With
Agoraphobias*

Oppositional
Defiant
Disorders

Non-
destructive

Attention
Deficits &
Hyperactivity
Disorders

Histrionic

Phobias

Dysthymias

Status
Violation

Property
Violation

Criminalities

Rebellious-
ness

Narcissistic Personality
Disorders

Dependent

Atypical
Depressions

Seasonal   Depressions
Mood
Disorders

Severe,
Recurrent &
Resistant
Depressions

Aggression
&
Violence

Destructive

Delusional

Borderline

Fugues &
Amnesias,
Identity
Disorders

Bipolar
Disorders

Paranoid
Personality

Paranoias Schizophrenic
Paranoid
Type

Depersonal-
ization
Disorders

Dissociative
Disorders

Depersonal-
ization
Neuroses

Acute
Psychotic

Schizophreniform
Disorders

Multiple
Personalities
Disorders

Schizotypal Schizophrenias
Disorders

Schizo-
affective
Disorders

Undifferentiated
Schizophrenias
Disorganized

*Selfishness
Externalizations*

*Selflessness
Internalizations*

No-Self

Figure 12.4. The selfhood model and a classification of personalities, criminalities, and psychopathologies according to the DSM-IV.

conditions orthogonally, according to levels of functionality versus dysfunctionality vertically, and directionality of behavior, internalization versus externalization, horizontally (Figure 12.4).

This relational framework will hopefully improve psychiatric classification from a theoretical model rather than from a strictly descriptive or empirical basis. Relationships between the theoretical model and psychiatric classification can be found in the patterns of intercorrelations among various quadrants and cells of the model (Fig. 12.4). For instance, within each of the four large quadrants, most contiguous conditions, i.e., cells within each quadrant, would correlate positively with each other but would not correlate or correlate negatively with conditions in the other quadrants. Additionally depression would correlate more with measures of introversion and anxiety than with measures of impulsivity and acting out. Codependency would correlate positively with measures of depression than with measures of acting out. By the same token, impulsivity would correlate more with measures of extroversion or externalization than with measures of introversion or internalization.

Support for these predictions is found in correlations and factor analyses suggesting that alcoholism, antisocial personality, and drug dependence form one group of diagnoses, whereas primary depression, primary mania, and secondary affective disorder form another group. Schizophrenia is not associated with any of the other six diagnosis (Wolf, Schubert, Patterson, & Grande, 1988), supporting the position taken here, that schizophrenia would belong in the no-self personality propensity, while the first group would fit into a selfishness propensity, and the second into selflessness.

Selffulness

Developmentally, therefore, an appropriate balance in approach-avoidance, as discussed in Chapter 7, and discharge-delay (Ch. 8) functions eventually leads to a personality propensity named *selffulness*. This balance leads toward personal and interpersonal functionality. In addition, selffulness derives from the integration of similarities and differences in the differentiation of identity (Ch. 10). Attributions and positive relationships that stem from its process result in a positive outcome and synergistic growth in most intimate relationships ("We both win . . . we both must win"). Selffulness tends to balance and regulate appropriately distance (the ability to love) and control (the ability to negotiate) processes. In this personality propensity issues of presence (i.e., being emotionally available to self and intimate others), are kept separate from issues of power, negotiation and problem solving. From this propensity develop mostly functional relationships that include a predominantly conductive-creative (CC) style (Ch. 11). This propensity is somewhat akin to attachment theory's secure style, as shown in the research by L'Abate et al. (2000; L'Abate, 2000, 2003a).

Functionally, selffulness implies a maturational process in its various manifestations and capacities to: (1) differentiate self from family of origin and from significant others; (2) think and to decide by oneself; (3) acknowledge self-value and the value of intimate others through concrete acts and actions of care, concern, and compassion; (4) accept one's self with its strengths and limitations; (5) experience and be aware of one's feelings; (6) communicate, express, and share one's feelings in appropriate and positive ways; (7) establish rapport with and show empathy toward intimate others; (8) undertake useful decisions in a reciprocal fashion with intimate others; and (9) be flexible and adapt oneself to stressful situations without losing a sense of self and to make sense of one's experiences, that is, learning from experience.

In this propensity, importance of self is exchanged democratically with intimate others, where "Everybody wins." Selfful individuals may seek a balance of Being > Doing > Having (Ch. 9), being more comfortable in "doing nothing" than in the other three personality propensities, since their worth is not judged by performance or production but by who they feel and are rather than by what they do or have. They do not receive a sense of self-importance by performing or producing compulsively but by being present and available emotionally to self and intimate others.

Hence, the characteristics of the selfful conductive-creative style most likely found are: (1) commitment to prolonging positively intimate relationships; using (2) predominantly cooperative rather than competitive strategies that value (3) democratically equalitarian and (4) reciprocally mutual actions; (5) emotional articulation, and (6) nonreactivity, by following a score or script that is consistent with their values. If these characteristics are valid, then the outcome of a selfful conductive-creative style would be greater harmony in intimate relationships, greater intimacy, longer life, overall peace and quiet with satisfaction, contentment, and generativity, being able to leave a similar legacy to offspring, rather than superficial, temporary, or counterfeit "happiness."

Levels of Selffulness

There are at least three if not four levels of selffulness according to how fully functioning one is in the settings distinguished by the theory (Ch. 5): home, school/work, survival, and leisure-time activities. This differentiation can take place when one considers the role of settings in contributing to it. A *superior* personality, for instance, would function fully in all settings, achieving success, assuming leadership roles, producing improvements, in each setting, and establishing procedures for growth and change. Superior individuals would show outstanding achievements in at least two or three of the four settings. An *intermediate* personality might function fully in one or two out of four settings, perhaps with superior achievement in one setting and/or adequate achievement in other settings. An *adequate* personality functions fully in one out of three or four settings and normatively in the others. Adequate achievement would also imply mediocre performance in most settings. Perhaps an additional fourth level of functioning should be reserved for people who function *appropriately* in most settings but who tend to follow rather than to lead in any setting. They would conventionally conform and be part of a group or setting without adding substantially to it. Within each level, of course, there are various degrees of functioning, varying from fully adequate to less than adequate. The major issue here would lie in the definition of achievement, functioning, and adequacy, which would require normative comparisons with other individuals in each setting.

Generational and developmental antecedents and family background of most selfful individuals would consist of similarly selfful families, where the major style of relating is conductive and creative. As a result marital relationships would be based on a match with similarly selfful individuals who marry and stay married longer than individuals with less functional propensities. Hence, similar gender ratios would result.

Major indicators of self-importance are visible when individuals match importance of others, through a variety of visible actions: sense of humor, achievement orientation, education, responsible living, paying taxes, and volunteering for extra responsibilities outside of the family. Probably, selfful individuals might live longer than other personality propensities because they take better care of themselves through proper diet, regular exercise, sufficient rest, and relaxing vacations, being able to enjoy life in more responsible ways than other propensities. They should have the lowest indications of dysfunctionalities, divorces, suicides, or homicides, some possible adjustment reactions, or some personality disorders under very stressful circumstances.

Selfful individuals should show a modicum of self-defeating behavior patterns. Nonetheless, depending on close contextual factors, even selfful individuals, perhaps at the lower level of selffulness, may be affected by aversive emotional states and high levels of self-awareness. Counterproductive strategies may exist if they are based on misjudging self or misjudging contingencies. Hence, even some selfful, i.e., "normal" individuals may, under certain circumstances, show that they are human, and subjected to self-defeating relationships based on temporary lapses in judgments, maladaptive reactions, through unforeseen circumstances, and disregarding costs and risks in favor of immediate pleasure or relief (Baumeister & Scher, 1988). The foregoing conclusion, however, is based on lumping together under one catchall term "normal" that which does not differentiate among different levels of functionality. In the present model, by differentiating among at least four levels of selffulness, it is possible to predict that the higher the level of selffulness, the lower the chances of self-defeating relationships.

Selffulness and the ERAAwC Model

In terms of resources (ERAAwC), selfful individuals should be able to use most of them according to the task-requirements of situations in an appropriately balanced fashion that fits age, gender, and stage of life (Ch. 4). Their temporal perspective would include learning from the past, but not being controlled by it, living in the present and enjoying it, preparing responsibly for the future, and being able to achieve intimacy with loved ones through the sharing of joys as well as hurts, leading (Ch. 16) to more effective problem solving than in other propensities (Ch. 17). They would benefit by short-lived f2f crisis interventions for emergencies and unexpected events, like sudden deaths or losses. Of course, they would benefit maximally by self-administered workbooks in selected areas of perceived need or those related to normalization (Appendix A).

Selffulness and Related Constructs

In this section constructs that are in some ways conceptually related to but empirically independent from a selffulness propensity will be reviewed.

Gender Differences. Men usually seem more assertive than women. The latter tend toward being more extroverted than men and more trusting, anxious, and especially more nurturing (Feingold, 1994). In the absence of other gender differences, one wonders whether those found above, when looking at extreme cases, would suggest that assertive men may tend to match and marry nurturing women. In line with the gender difference reported here, self-construal in men and women may be different, with women perceiving themselves as interdependent and men as independent (Cross & Madson, 1997; Martin & Ruble, 1997). On a measure of self-esteem, men may tend to score significantly higher than women on an "inner esteem" dimension composed of terms such as strong, leader, powerful, confident, curious, inventive, sharp, and active, while women may tend to perceive themselves as good, nice, generous, pleasant, dependable, honest, and active (Prescott, 1978).

Autonomy. High ratings of autonomy may be associated with a complex cluster of personological variables, which include achievement orientation, temperamental aggressiveness, moral sensitivity, and, at least for men, masculinity (Kurtines, 1974)

Gifted Children. Parents who perceive their children as gifted seem more proud of their children and tend to describe a closer parent-child relationship. Nongifted siblings of gifted children might be significantly less well-adjusted than other nongifted children. They might be significantly less careful of social rules, less outgoing, more easily upset, more shy, and more frustrated. These differences between gifted and nongifted siblings suggest a powerful positive-labeling effect (Cornell, 1983). Parents of gifted children seem more intelligent, critical, assertive, and likely to stand on their own ideas than people in the general population (Gockenbach, 1989).

Hardiness and Resilience. Resilience seems comprised of at least two factors, the ability to withstand stress and competence (Chandler & Lundahl, 1983; Luthar & Zigler, 1991; Rutter, 1987). Resilience includes considerable self-understanding, deep commitment to relationships, and the ability to think and act separately from parents with serious psychiatric disorders (Beardslee & Podorefsky, 1988). Additionally, self-understanding includes adequate cognitive appraisal, realistic appraisal of the capacity for and consequences of actions, a developmental perspective, and understanding as a protective factor (Beardslee, 1987). Compared with high stress/high illness executives, high stress/low illness executives seem to show more hardiness, that is, have stronger commitment to the self, an attitude of vigorousness toward the environment, a sense of meaningfulness, and internal locus of control (Kobasa, 1979).

Resilient adults with a family history of childhood sexual abuse differed from nonresilient ones on the basis of whether the abuse was coercive or not (Liem, James, O'Toole, & Boudewyn, 1995).

Healthy Adult Adjustment. Warm childhoods seem significantly related to the following traits in middle life: few dependency traits, little psychopathology, capacity to play, and good interpersonal relations. Sustained childhood stresses, on the other hand, seem associated with subsequent poor global mental health (Hightower, 1988; Valliant, 1975, 1977). Individuals from chronically dependent and multiproblem families may be, on the average, indistinguishable by midlife from individuals of more stable, working-class families in terms of mean income, years of employment, criminality, and mental health. Apparently, individuals from multiproblem welfare families do not inevitably perpetuate their initial disadvantages (Long & Vaillant, 1984).

Families of healthy teenagers tend to have more effective parental coalitions and generational boundaries than families of normal controls. The factor found to be the most important to optimal psychological functioning might well be the nature of the parents' interaction with each other (Kleinman, 1981). Healthy families seem to posses the following elements: sharing and understanding feelings, acceptance of individual differences, highly developed sense of caring, cooperation, sense of humor, survival and safety needs met, nonadversary problemsolving, and an overall positive philosophy of life (Ebert, 1978). An optimistic explanatory style may contribute to a prevention of health problems.

Joy of Life. High sensation-seekers seem to assign significantly higher intensity ratings to experiences that produce joy of life than low sensation seekers. Positive emotional events seem related to higher levels of joy (Tolor, 1978).

Self-Actualization. Assertive people may differ from nonassertive ones in terms of personality structure and self-actualizing values, with assertive and more self-actualizing respondents possibly being more gregarious, more present-oriented, inner-directed, existentialistic, spontaneous, adaptable, sensitive, with higher self-regard, social sensitivity, and rational than nonassertives, who may tend to be more subservient, defensive, self-projecting, and approval-seeking. What is more relevant is that assertive respondents may show greater ability than nonassertive respondents to possess "a greater ability to develop intimate relationships" (Ramanaiah, Heerboth, & Jenkerson, 1985). Self-realization also seems associated with rational thinking (Shorkey & Reyes, 1978). One's overall level of psychosocial maturity seems positively related to one's level of self-actualization (Olczak & Goldman, 1975).

Self-Efficacy. One cannot help compare both constructs, selffulness and self-efficacy even though the latter is a perceived construct while selffulness is determined by how one functions visibly in various settings, not just on a self-report, paper-and-pencil test. Clearly, self-efficacy is relevant as a cognitive factor affecting health (O'Leary, 1985). The self-efficacy model originally proposed by Bandura (1978) may also be conceptually problematic because efficacy expectations may not be unambiguously differentiated from outcome expectations (Eastman & Marzillier, 1984; Marzillier & Eastman, 1984). A nurturing parenting style seems related to generalized self-efficacy and mental health (Hoeltje, Zubrick, Silburn, & Garton, 1996).

Self-Regard. Low levels of self-regard seem related to higher and prolonged levels of distress (Horowitz, Sonneborn, Sugahara, & Maercker, 1996).

Sense of Humor. Humor may well be a multidimensional construct intimately related to quality of life. Sense of humor seems associated positively with psychological health, such as optimism and self-esteem and negatively with signs of psychological distress such as depression (Thorson, Powell, Sarmany-Schuller, & Hampes, 1997). Apparently, comprehension of humor and creative thinking, above and beyond intellectual level, may be related to and have a common basis in the ability to link disparities (Rouff, 1975). Given tenuous associations between humor, laughter, and other health and longevity variables, more rigorous and theoretically informed research seems necessary (Martin, 2001).

Social Competence. There may be positive associations between domains of social competene of mothers (social skills, social frames, and network size) and their kindergarten children, with maternal social competence being more related to sons' peer acceptance and daughters' social skills (Prinstein & La Greca, 1999).

Well-Being. Well-being is related to financial, health, and family anxiety and a general factor of happiness (Warr, 1978), to favorable health practices, and to an increase of feelings of well-being with age (Wetzler & Ursano, 1988). "Subjective well-being [seems] a relatively global and stable phenomenon, not simply a momentary judgment based on fleeting influences" (Pavot, Diener, Colvin, Randall, & Sandvik, 1991). This factor may include, among others, happiness, life satisfaction, and positive affect (Diener, 1984).

All these different constructs tend to support the importance of a selfful personality propensity, especially in its intimate relationships.

Selfishness

Developmentally, when approach is greater than avoidance and discharge is greater than delay, a personality propensity named *selfishness* develops. In its extremes, this propensity leads toward externalizations and criminalities, where self-importance is asserted at the expense of others ("I win, you lose"). Selfishness, the positive attribution of importance to self and negative attribution of importance to intimate others, results in a conflictual outcome and no growth in intimate relationships. Individuals characterized by this propensity tend to push limits on their partners, authorities, and anybody else who lets them, as seen in the pathological extremes of this propensity, like addictions and criminalities. Extremes in selfishness are represented by addicts, acting out, impulsiveness, and criminal personalities where the self is asserted at the expense of others, as in theft, rape, and murder (Fishbein, 2000). The level of identity differentiation is shown by a mostly oppositional, even defiant, relational style, mostly in men (Ch. 10). Their relational styles are mainly RR and AA. Of course, there are various degrees of selfishness, from self-centered egoism, to narcissistic self-absorption, and semifunctional selfish behaviors that take place at no cost to anyone else (Cluster B in Axis II). Externalizations, as in acting-out character, antisocial, delinquent, and criminal disorders, are the prototype for selfishness.

Training for Selfishness: Reactive-Alloplastic Externalizations

Some characteristics of selfish individuals, in addition to those already enumerated, are: (1) self-centeredness; (2) denial of others' importance; (3)

immediacy ("I want what I want when I want it."); (4) pushing limits on everybody they come in contact with; (5) grandiose omnipotence and arrogance ("I know better than anybody else"); (6) "spoiled" or self-indulgent, seeking pleasure, even if it is counterfeit, as in additions, or in taking from or harming others; (7) absence of deep feelings, unable to cry or to empathize with or for those who have been hurt by them; and (8) abusive of others to get what is wanted.

It is worth noting, that if many painful and unpleasant experiences, like beatings, scolding, verbal and physical abuse, take place in many toddlers in the preverbal stage, that is, during the first year of life, then it would be practically or humanly impossible for selfish adults to speak about experiences for which they have no words. Consequently, one would hypothesize that many ruthless criminals, those who seem beyond redemption or rehabilitation, would be the outcome of such a process. They cannot share past hurts because they have no way of remembering or even speaking about painful experiences that have taken place during their first year of life. Hence, the presence of deficits and retardation in the use of language and thinking commonly found in delinquents, might be related to an unequal balance of hemispheric functions, with the left hemisphere being relatively less dominant than the right one (Reed, McMahan, & L'Abate, 2001). This propensity is somewhat akin to attachment theory's dismissing style.

The latter style has been submitted to an extensive, cross-cultural evaluation mentioned earlier (Schmitt et al., 2003). Because of its similarity to selfishness, the evaluation of this style is relevant to the predictions that could be made about gender differences in this style. Even though there were extreme cultural variations that supported the greater frequency of this style in men than in women in the 62 cultures studied, these differences were small to moderate.

Would the results of the study by Schmitt et al. (2003) find no gender differences invalidate predictions just made between selfish men and selfless women? Not at all, they would not. Data for that research were obtained from normative samples, not from deviant or acting-out samples of men and depressed women. Indeed, these results support the selfhood model to the extent that, normatively, in the selfful propensity, one expects and predicts equality of gender ratios between selfful and no-self personality propensities. Selfful men would be equal in frequency with selfful women. Gender differences in both selfishness and selflessness are predicted for extreme populations, not for normative samples. Acting out, externalizing criminal behavior, would be found in greater frequency in men than in women. The reverse would be valid for selflessness.

Use of Resources

- *E*: In externalizations *E* is low for fear, anxiety, sadness as well as soft feelings like guilt and shame. It is, however, high for anger, hostility, and perhaps envy.
- *R*: This resource is low except in conning and planning illegal behaviors, cheating, harming, and robbing others.
- *A*: This resource is high in performance with hands, as shown, with exceptions, by a higher performance than verbal IQ, sufficiently high enough to satisfy needs for immediacy and impulsivity, supporting in part the possibility of unequal hemispheric dominance mentioned above.
- *Aw*: This resource is diminished and constricted except for immediate spatial and temporal attentiveness to possibly threatening situations, people, or events.
- *C*: This resource is not considered or considered only in terms of manipulation to get immediate needs satisfied.

Temporal perspective is limited to the satisfaction of immediate needs or goals, while the ability to love is high for self and minimal for others. The ability to negotiate is incomplete or missing except when needed manipulatively to satisfy short-term goals. Modalities exist in performance and production, but presence is limited, as referring to *E* above.

Change Processes. Selfish individuals tend to relate mainly to the present and denying the influence from the past, they won't be able to learn from past experiences, or prepare responsibly for the future, because they cannot see the future consequences of their present actions. They will be more impulsive and act out before thinking about the consequences of their own actions. Therefore, they will tend to act against or approach others at the presentational sublevel, be conflictual with others at the phenotypic sublevel, and avoid any soft or hurtful feelings, using anger and hostility as their preferred modes of interactions with others at the genotypic level. They are not be able to use either *R*, *Aw*, or *C* but will tend to short-circuit them in favor of immediate discharge, little delay, maximum approach, and minimum avoidance. They tend to live shorter lives because of their irresponsible behaviors, car accidents, homicides, drug-overdoses, being killed in fights, or executed.

Because of their need for immediate gratification and without an ability to delay it, one can then understand their greater use of self-medication, substance abuse, alcohol, etc. To obtain what they want, manipulation is used to obtain short-term gains from others. Pathology will tend toward paranoias, psychopathies, or sociopathies, and borderline personalities. If and when intimacy and problem solving are present, these processes are short-lived and sometimes used to obtain manipulatory gains. There is a strong tendency to deny dependency even though they may be in a dependent position, like in jails or prisons. Consequently, they will not need f2f interventions except in dire crises or losses, as in death or unexpected accidents resulting in loss. They cannot profit by f2f talk psychotherapy, because talk is used to manipulate rather than think. They might benefit by workbooks directed specifically toward impulsive, acting-out behaviors, but only under controlled conditions, i.e., confinement in a cell (L'Abate, 1992, 1996; McMahan & Arias, 2004).

Selfishness and Hemispheric Dominance

If externalization implies a weakness in left-hemisphere functioning and thinking, rather than strengthening talk, then thinking (Foglia, 2000; Reed et al., 2001), should be strengthened through the cheapest possible way, and that is: writing and especially programmed writing and workbooks. Strengthening "emotional" talk, that is based mostly on the right hemisphere, would only increase its manipulative qualities rather than thinking, especially in selfish individuals.

Selfishness and Externalizations

The best support for placing selfishness in the delinquency classification and making it a prototype for selfishness comes from the review of Baumeister et al. (1996) about violent and aggressive individuals who tested high in self-esteem rather than low, as expected and predicted from traditional theories. Their results were replicated by Perez, Pettit, David, and Kistner (2001). Inpatient, psychiatric youth with the highest self-esteem reported the fewest interpersonal problems than youth with low or moderate self-esteem. Low and high self-esteem youth, however, were more rejected by their peers than youth with moderate self-esteem. Thus, the high self-esteem group was rejected by their peers in spite of reporting no interpersonal problems, essentially denying them. Self-esteem, as already mentioned in Chapter 5, is viewed by this theory as the internal manifestation of externally visible attribution of importance to self and others. By definition, delinquency represents selfishness at its relative worst, that is: enhancing self at the expense of others. No wonder their self-esteem is unrealistically inflated!

There are different types and intensities of antisocial, externalizing relationships (Lahey, Moffit, & Caspi, 2003), with a variety of hypotheses as to its origin. As already touched in Chapter 10, one can differentiate among antisocial childhood and adolescence, oppositional defiant disorders, conduct disorders, psychopathies, and criminal recidivists among others (Brennan, Grekin, & Mednick, 2003; Fagan & Lira, 1980; Lahey & Waldman, 2003; Moffitt, 2003; Nigg & Huang-Pollock, 2003; Rhee & Waldman, 2003; Rutter, 2003; Snyder. Reid, & Patterson, 2003; Tremblay, 2003). It would be impossible to review all the literature on this subject. Some of the literature related to familial influences and sex differences that support or invalidate the model will be discussed below.

Characteristics of Selfish, Externalizing Individuals

What kind of individuals are included in this personality propensity? The range of personalities included here may vary from simply narcissistic, egocentric individuals, who are dismissing of other people's opinions and ideas, conduct, and antisocial disorders, to out-and-out sociopaths, psychopaths, and hardened criminals. Juvenile inpatients with conduct disorders seem to have an earlier age of first psychiatric contact and may be diagnosed more often with attention deficit hyperactivity disorders. Juvenile inpatients with substance abuse disorders as well as coexisting conduct disorder and substance abuse disorder may be diagnosed more often with borderline personality disorder than inpatients with only conduct disorder. There seems to be a high occurrence of mood disorders in all three groups (Grilo et al., 1996).

Youth and young adult men who commit murder, the ultimate act to discount the importance of another, tend to present a constellation of biopsychosocial characteristics, that may include psychotic symptoms, major neurological impairment, a psychotic first-degree relative, violent acts during childhood, and severe physical abuse (Lewis, 1985). Schizophrenic men may be seven times more likely to commit a homicide, whereas men with a major affective disorder may have about twice the risk. Alcoholic men with a personality disorder may have at least a tenfold higher risk. Antisocial personality disorder (almost always associated with alcoholism) might carry a twentyfold increased risk for homicide (Tiihonen, Eronen, & Hakulo, 1993). These findings were replicated in an Australian sample, where at least 82% of sentenced prisoners had a lifetime diagnosis for at least one mental disorder and 26% more than one disorders. Substance abuse and alcohol were present in 69% of this sample, suggesting that most of these inmates may suffer from largely untreated major depression (Herrman, McGorry, Mills, & Singh, 1991). Consequently, assessment of risk in mentally disordered offenders might be enhanced with more attention given to social psychological criminological literature and less reliance on models of psychopathology (Bonta, Law, & Hanson, 1998).

Not without controversy, impulsivity may well be a hallmark of delinquency, together with lower intellectual level, perhaps as a function of ethnicity (Block, 1995a, b; Hinshaw, 1992; Lynam & Moffitt, 1995; Lynam, Moffitt, & Stouthamer-Loeber, 1993; Stattin & Klackenberg, 1993), supporting the position that impulsivity may be related to an inability to understand or predict future consequences of one's actions. Among children with internalizing psychopathology, increased self-critical awareness about their conduct may be more frequent than in externalizing psychopathology (Han, Weisz, & Weiss, 2001), making the difference for lower acting out but perhaps acting in against the self in the former than in the latter. Temperamental withdrawal, i.e., delay, parental internalizing psychopathology, and early single parenthood (for girls) may correlate with internalizing problems, whereas, temperamental high activity level, i.e., discharge, may be characteristic of externalization in children. Further, parenting stress, poor school results (only for boys), and stressful life events (only for girls) seem associated with psychopathology (Mesman & Koot, 2000).

On a more positive note, delinquency cessation may occur as part of a broader behavioral change and research indicates that cognitive change might be a precursor of behavioral change, as seen by decline in drug use often associated with a change in social networks and improvement in family relationships. Process changes may involve identification of a time period (usually beginning with a particular event or life change) and support from significant others (Mulvey & LaRosa, 1986).

Anger, Hostility, and Aggression. The model also predicts, among others, that anger, hostility, and aggression are more related to selfishness than to the other three personality propensities, even though both anger and masculinity in and by themselves may be strong predictors of many mental health factors (Kopper & Epperson, 1996). It seems that aggression and family size might be related in a linear fashion, with decreasing aggression linked to increasing family size. This outcome may be due to the accelerated development of social skills within children living in large families (Boone & Montare, 1979).

Aggression can be classified in low SES boys according to stability of fighting over time: stable high fighters, high fighters with late onset, desisting high fighters, variable high fighters, and nonfighters. The fighter groups can be differentiated from each other both in family background and parenting behavior. These groups can be significantly associated with delinquency across ages 10 to 14 years. The punishment X fighter group interaction, together with supervision, seems to predict delinquency. Hence, developmental pathways of physical aggression for boys in low SES environments seem related to familial adversity and poor parenting. Both variables tend to predict delinquency (Haapasalo & Tremblay, 1994). The severity of physical discipline, negative quality of the mother's interaction with the child, and the experience of sexual abuse seem related to adolescent assaultive behavior (Herrenkohl, Egolf, & Herrenkohl, 1997).

Adverse home environment factors may result in increased aggressive and conduct disorders in the presence, but not in the absence, of a biological background of antisocial personality disorder. Nonetheless, adverse home environment, independent of biological background, may predict adult antisocial behaviors (Cadoret, Yates, Troughton, & Woodworth, 1995).

Psychiatric inpatients with both self-destructiveness during hospitalization and suicidal behavior before hospitalization seem to engage in the highest frequency of aggression against others (Hillbrand, 1995).

Gender Differences. Out of 32 studies of peer-related aggression, higher male aggression was found in 24 studies, no gender difference in eight, and higher female aggression in none. Differential socialization practices for boys and girls seem to support the view that boys do not receive more reinforcement for aggression than girls, with rates of punishment being similar among boys and girls once the differential base rates for aggression are taken into account. (Barrett, 1979; Eme & Kavanaugh, 1995; Maccoby & Jacklin, 1980; Olweus, 1980). Presumed gender differences may be due to overreliance on self-report measures of general hostility or aggressiveness. Furthermore, what may be anger-provoking for men may be anxiety-provoking in women (Frodi, Macaulay, & Thome, 1977). This possibility might be partially supported by the finding that psychopathic respondents may rate anxiety-related situations as being more anxiety-, fear-, and threat-inducing than nonoffender controls. The reverse, however, might be true for anger-related situations, which psychopathic respondents might see as more anger-inducing (Sterling & Edelmann, 1988). Hence, these conclusions tend to support the model that selfishness, as seen in externalizing disorders, tends to be more present in males than in females.

Family Background of Externalizing Disorders

Superficially, 25% of delinquent boys do not necessarily come from deviant families but rather from working-class intact families and seemingly without serious problems yet they undergo stress as a result of their children acting out. However, a higher percentage (33%) of delinquent boys do come from difficult family circumstances (Power, Ash, Schoenberg, & Sirey, 1974). Delinquency, however, should not be considered as a unitary concept and should be conceptualized instead in terms of configurations of different delinquent behaviors (Hetherington, Stouwic, & Ridberg, 1971). A useful differentiation could be achieved by distinguishing between emotional immaturities and nondestructive and destructive criminalities, as shown in Figure 12.4.

Parents of nondelinquents be can clearly differentiated from parents of delinquents in terms of displaying higher activity levels, less rejection, higher parental adjustment, lower consistency and greater flexibility of controls, but higher consistency of feelings. Within delinquent groups, parents of social delinquents display higher levels of activity and are more restrictive in the area of control than parents of individual delinquents. As a whole, across groups, fathers tend to advocate more authoritarian and more restrictive controls, demanding more conformity, allowing the child more freedom to interact with the environment, and demonstrating less affection to their child than mothers (Duncan, 1971).

Nonetheless, principal predictors of delinquency seem to be inadequate parental family management techniques, poor supervision and discipline, the child's own conduct problems, parental criminality, and the child's poor academic performance. Best predictors of recidivism might be reports of the child's stealing and lying (Loeber & Dishion, 1983). Two marital constellations seem to emerge from parents of delinquents, psychiatrically treated men married to psychiatrically treated women, and criminal men married to psychiatrically treated women (Lewis, Balla, Shanok, & Snell, 1976). Indeed, physical and sexual abuse, family violence, and psychiatric illness endured by juveniles condemned to death, may have led to aggressive crimes (Lewis, Pincus, Bard, & Richardson, 1988). Violent juvenile felons may have suffered poorer relationships with their mothers than did nonviolent felons (Henggeler, 1985).

Neglectful mothers tend to rate their children as having more conduct problems than did comparison mothers (Rohrbeack & Twentyman, 1986). A negative context tends to elicit significantly more negative behaviors in families of delinquent adolescents than a positive context when parents interacted with each other and with their delinquent adolescent. A dissatisfied set seems to produce blaming attributions, while a satisfied set may tend to produce nonblaming, positive attributions (Alexander, Waldron, Barton, & Mas, 1989). Children of distressed mothers tend to be more maladjusted, i.e., and show greater frequency of conduct problems than children of nondistressed mothers. Apparently, maternal distress and maternal indiscriminate responding to the child act as adverse contextual factors that maintain mother-child interactional difficulties by disrupting the attentional and monitoring skills required for contingent responding (Dumas, Gibson, & Albin, 1989). Maternal authoritarian child-rearing practices and mother's parenting stress seem highly related to externalizations (Heller, Baker, Henker, & Hinshaw, 1996). Birth complications, combined with early maternal rejection or inadequate parenting, tend to prodispose children to violent behavior in youth (Hodgins, Kratzer, & McNeil, 2001; Raine, Brennan, & Mednick, 1994).

The departure factor in an attachment-focused structured interview with children of adolescent mothers tends to be associated with externalizing problems (Hubbs-Tait, Hughes, Culp, & Osofsky, 1996). Apparently, externalizations seem more strongly linked to parental caregiving for boys than for girls (Rothbaum & Weisz, 1994).

When adult roles associated with motherhood are activated too early in a woman's life cycle, stress and resultant social pathologies could be generated in families. Early motherhood could be perceived as a form of accelerated role transition and is closely associated with a high incidence of marital dissolution, poverty, and truncated education (Bacon, 1974). This aspect may be also related to lower levels of moral development in delinquent families than in families of nondelinquents (Jurkovic & Prentice, 1974).

There is little doubt that low SES, family adversity, subaverage intellectual functioning, language deficits, and neurodevelopmental delay are possible factors underlying a great deal of delinquency (Hinshaw, 1992), as well as a proportion of mentally ill family members, mother-child discord, and weak activity and school competence (Stiffman, Jung, & Feldman, 1986).

Selflessness

Developmentally, when avoidance is greater than approach and delay is greater than discharge, the personality propensity of *selflessness* develops. In its extremes, this personality propensity leads toward internalizations (anxieties, depressions, and fears), affective disorders, and suicide. Here, self-importance is denied or negated, while the importance of others is asserted and affirmed ("You win, I lose"). Part of this propensity is supported, among others to be reviewed below, by the work of Tomarken and Keener (1998). They suggested that depression, a prototype for the selflessness propensity, was related to an under-activation of the approach system and/or an overactivation of the withdrawal system. Just like selfishness, selflessness is intermediate as far as levels of functionality/dysfunctionality are concerned.

Selflessness results in a conflictual stasis in a relationship. Individuals characterized by this propensity are unable to draw lines to protect themselves ("the condom line"), as in the case of so-called codependent individuals, usually partners or spouses of addicts and criminals (L'Abate & Harrison, 1992). The level of differentiation is mostly blindly conforming, i.e., adhering to sameness, conventionality, and blind obedience to rules and regulations. The normative relational style would be reactive-repetitive (Ch. 11).

Some selfless individuals tend to be gullible, loyal, and responsible, trying to make up complementary qualities not found in selfish individuals. They are attracted to selfish individuals just as the latter are attracted by the former, producing in the long run antagonistic and conflictual relationships, where ultimately divorce, let alone murder or suicide, is the major outcome. The main characteristic of these relationships sometimes lies in the selfless individual's unrealistic optimism, hoping that somehow selfish partners will eventually, by some miracle, change for the better. Extremes in selflessness are represented by depression and affective disorders, leading to suicide, either slow and prolonged as in some addictions, or a sudden, seemingly unexpected, act. This propensity is somewhat akin to attachment theory's preoccupied style.

The major prototypes for selflessness are depression and suicide as found in internalizations. Anxiety disorders, even though a separate aspect of internalizations, cannot be used specifically as prototypes unless linked to depressions, because the self is not as devalued in anxiety disorders as in depressions, as discussed below. However, there is no way that all primary or even a selected number of primary references about depression can be included here. Only those references that tend to support or even invalidate the present definition of selflessness will be considered, as well as family antecedents for depression and even suicide.

Selflessness, Depression, and Internalizations: Anxiety, Sadness, and Fear

Selflessness tends to rely more on avoidance than on approach and on delay more than on discharge. This selfish-selfless dimension has been subjected to a great many theories and theorettes in psychology as well as other disciplines (Sober & Wilson, 1998).

What kind of individuals are included in this personality propensity? Here depressions will be included, ranging from mild anxieties and depressions to extreme, refractory depressions with the highest probability of suicide (Buie & Maltsberger, 1989; Hyman & Arana, 1989; Litman, 1989; Maris, 1989; Perry, 1989; Shneidman, 1989)

Resources

- *E*: This resource is used in terms of specialization in sadness, guilt, shame, and empathy for the feelings of others rather than self. Usually, there is little reliance on anger, hostility, and aggression, which may be suppressed rather than expressed (Riley, Teiber, & Woods, 1989).

- *R*: This resource is dominated by a negative polarity, where all events are viewed in a negative light, as representations of a negative self-view.
- *A*: Activity may vary according to the degree and type of depression, from seemingly normal in masked or subthreshold depressions to extreme passivity and apathy in chronic or severe depression.
- *Aw*: Emphasis in this resource lies in paying attention to the needs of others rather than self. This is done to appear as much as possible as a "good person," even though, if and when this attribution is made, it is usually discounted.
- *C*: Context is limited to those very people who are close but, no matter what they may do or say, they are more important than the self, because the selfless individual needs them to fulfill dependency needs.

The level of functionality may vary from subsyndromal depression to extreme dysfunctionality in severe depression, or worst, bipolar depression.

Temporal Perspective. Temporal perspective is concentrated on the past, with little attention to the present and practically little attention to the future, except to ruminate negatively about past and future events. Depending on the degree and intensity of the depression, ruminations and worries seem to stress the past and the present to the extent that even the present and near future may be negative and even catastrophic.

Ability to Love. Since others, by definition, are important, they deserve to be loved more than self because one has to depend on others for support, as seen in altruism or related selfless acts of charity toward others who are seen as needier, poorer, and more helpless than self. The whole issue of altruism has been covered in previous publications (L'Abate, 1994, 1997; L'Abate & De Giacomo, 2003).

Ability to Negotiate. The level of negotiation and problem solving is handicapped by the severity of the depression. The more depressed one is, the less the chances of reaching a successful outcome, let alone being able to ever initiate the process.

Usage of Modalities. Being present is important in regard to the needs of others rather than self, since this modality consists mostly of ruminations about the past. Performance and production are directly related to the level of depression, that is: the more severe the depression the lower the levels of performance or production.

Change Processes. Selfless individuals may have grown up in families where internalizations were modeled by at least one member of the family, with greater propensities for internalizations, anxiety and depression, denying anger and/or avoiding showing it. They may spend energy and time to ruminate about the past, being unable to live in the present, and even less to prepare for the future (Santor & Zuroff, 1994). They might try to hide their inner feelings of sadness, hopelessness, and hurts, trying to appear normal and functional until the weight of internal feelings increases and even crumbles a weak self-presentational facade and an even weaker phenotype.

Depressed individuals may also come from family backgrounds that stress complete conformity to absolute rules or from oppositional family backgrounds where there were no rules. Consequently, they are unable to enjoy life. Possibly a greater number of women than men may be socialized toward internalizations. Pathology would tend toward depressions, dissociative conditions, and suicides with a minimum of acting out, accepting to be dependent on others. They would benefit by most types of f2f talk psychotherapy with or without workbooks, especially related to depression (Appendix A).

Evidence Supporting or Invalidating This Model

Costs of treating depression are staggering (Simon, VonKorff, & Barlow, 1995), because of the large number of people suffering with this disorder, supporting the need for possibly cost-effective and large-scale distance interventions as found in the administration of workbooks in addition or as an alternative to f2f talk psychotherapy (Appendix A).

One must recognize, however, the presence of a continuum of depressive disorders, rather than just one category, ranging from subthreshold or subsydromal to severe (Behar, Winokur, VanValkenburg, & Lowry, 1980; Flett, Vredenburg, & Krames, 1997; Haslam & Beck, 1993; Lewinsohn, Solomon, Seeley, & Zeiss, 2000; Ruscio & Ruscio, 2001; Santor & Coyne, 2001; Solomon, Haaga, & Arnow, 2001). Three major pathways seem responsible for the development of risk for major depression, at least in women: (1) internalizing symptoms; (2) externalizing symptoms; and (3) psychosocial adversity (Kendler, Gardner, & Prescott, 2002). Within this continuum, one needs to consider introversion and interpersonal dependency as major characteristics of depression (Shea, Leon, Mueller, Solomon, et al., 1996). These sources tend to support a definition of selflessness as avoidance of social situations on one hand, contradicted, on the other hand, by a need for dependency on others.

Six variables may be antecedents, concomitants, and consequences of depression: attributional style, dysfunctional attitudes, personality, social support, marital distress, and coping style. Marital distress and low social integration appear to be involved in the etiology of depression, with introversion and interpersonal dependency as enduring abnormalities in the functioning of remitted depressives (Barnett & Gotlib, 1988). When major depressive disorder is coupled with panic disorder, a more severe and precocious form of illness is possible (Grunhaus, Pande, Brown, & Greden, 1994).

Anxiety and Depression. The reason for not pairing anxiety with depression in selflessness relies on the fact that anxious individuals, unless also depressed (Heimberg, Vermilyea, Dodge, & Becker, 1987) do not devalue the self as depressed individuals do. Depressed patients may show some signs of anxiety. However, seldom do anxious patients show signs of depression unless severely anxious (Coryell, Endicott, & Winokur, 1992). For instance, even though childhood depressive and anxious disorders may be familially related (King, Ollendick, & Gullone, 1991; Livingston, Nugent, Rader, & Smith, 1985), depressive disorders can be distinguished from anxiety disorders in adults on the basis of ratings of cognition, social skills, and family environment (Stark, Humphrey, Laurent, & Livingson, 1993).

Furthermore, anxiety can be distinguished by specific autonomic arousal symptoms, threat-related cognitions, and subjectively described anxiety and tension. Depression, on the other hand, can be distinguished by anhedonia, cognitions of personal loss and failure, and dysphoric mood (Clark, Beck, & Beck, 1994). When anxiety is found in psychiatric patients (not otherwise diagnosed), it may relate to an awareness of unpleasant thoughts about oneself, unpleasant emotions, and even irrational beliefs (Watson, Vassar, Plemel. Herder, et al., 1989). However, no evidence seems present about how many of these patients had been diagnosed with depression, or about the difference between "unpleasant" versus "negative" thoughts that characterize depression.

Empirically anxiety and depression can also be distinguished using A. T. Beck's model described at the end of this section. Excessive concern for others (sociotropy) seems correlated with anxiety, while autonomy, excessive concern for achievement, seems correlated with depression. Sociotropy may moderate the relationship of life stresses to depression symptoms for both negative interpersonal and achievement stress, while autonomy may moderate the relationship of life stress to depression symptoms only for interpersonal events. Finally, sociotropy and autonomy also seem to moderate the relationship between life stress and anxiety symptoms, in a pattern that seems quite different from the pattern with depression symptoms (Fresco, Sampson, Craighead, & Koons, 2001). Additionally, anxiety can be accounted for on the basis of distance, as in social anxieties and avoidance

(Cluster C, Axis II, Ch. 7) as well as low controls (Ch. 8), while depression is accounted for by Axis I disorders not only on the basis of distance, but also on control, identity differentiation (Ch. 10), styles in intimate relationships (Ch. 11), and the selfhood model in this chapter.

Somatization Disorders. Somatization disorders show a distinctive, confused, and negative self-identity that sometimes masks severe depression. Somatic complaints of patients with somatization disorders must not be confused with depression because the complaints serve a more complex and interpersonal function than may be indicated by bodily preoccupations and depression (Oxman, Rosenberg, Schnurr, & Tucker, 1985). Somatization symptoms tend to show strongest associations with anxiety and depressive symptoms, intermediate associations with symptoms of psychotic disorders, and weakest associations with symptoms of substance abuse and antisocial personality (Simon & VonKorff, 1991). These associations lend support to the view that internalization disorders would correlate higher and positively among themselves than with externalization disorders reviewed earlier.

Among children low in social competence, higher levels of subsequent negative life events predicted higher levels of somatic complaints. Among boys in families with high levels of negative life events, those whose mothers were characterized by high levels of somatic complaints also had higher levels of somatic complaints. Children whose fathers were characterized by high levels of somatic symptoms also showed higher levels of somatic complaints, regardless of the level of life events (Walker, Garber, & Greene, 1994).

Self-Criticism. This pattern is so prevalent that only selected references about it can be included briefly, to support the position that selflessness implies a denial of self-importance as shown by self-criticism: (1) continuity of family origins from childhood and adolescent into adulthood (Koestner, Zuroff, & Powers, 1991; Zuroff, Koestner, & Powers, 1994); (2) family antecedents in children (McCranie & Bass, 1984); (3) depression and dependency (Bagby, Schuller, Parker, & Levitt, 1994); (4) interpersonal dependency and depression (Franche & Dobson, 1992); (5) antecedents of negative self-attitudes (a rose by any other name . . .) and defenselessness (Kaplan, 1976); (6) recalled childhood experiences in adulthood (Brewin, Firth-Cozens, Furnham, & McManus, 1992); (7) dependency and depressive attributional style (Brown & Silbershatz, 1989); (8) negative self-perception (another rose by any other name . . .) and adolescent psychopathology (Evans, Noam, Wertlieb, Paget, et al., 1994); (9) dependency and social interaction (Zuroff, Scotland, Sweetman, & Craig, 1995); and (10) dependency and attributional style (Bagby, Segal, & Schuller, 1995).

Worthlessness/Low Self-Esteem. The evidence to support the presence of a "negative self-view" is so overwhelming that only selected references can be cited (Allen, Woolfolk, Gara, & Apter, 1996; Blumberg & Hokanson, 1983; Gara, Woolfolk, Cohen, Goldston, et al., 1993; Haaga, Dyck, & Ernst, 1991). Negative self-complexity (a rose . . .) seems associate with poor recovery from a major depressive episode (Woolfolk, Gara, Ambrose, Williams, et al., 1999). Because of this negative set, depressed individuals tend to evaluate personal feedback in a manner that seems self-derogating (Wenzlaff & Grozier, 1988).

There is a view that depressed individuals, in spite of their feelings of worthlessness, may obtain narcissistic gratification because of their disorder. They may exploit the kindness and attentiveness of others, shirk responsibility, and avoid the demands of interpersonal interactions (Shmagin & Pearlmutter, 1977). Along the same line, the self-verification model predicts that depressed individuals seek and solicit feedback that confirms their negative self-views. This prediction might have been validated since 82% of participants classified as depressed chose unfavorable feedback compared to 64% of low self-esteem and 25% of high self-esteem participants. Depressed individuals may also fail to exploit fully the opportunity to acquire favorable evaluations that were self-verifying (Giesler, Josephs, & Swann, 1998).

Self-esteem may be causally related to depression. However, other factors need to be taken into consideration: (1) structural deficits, such as few, rigid, or externally based sources of self-worth; (2) abnormally low self-esteem may be primed by either mildly depressed mood, stressful events, or schema-congruent experiences; and (3) temporal instability of self-worth (Roberts & Monroe, 1994). Intrusive memories of past sexual or nonsexual abuse are associated with lower levels of self-esteem (Kuyken & Brewin, 1994, 1999).

There seems to be an inverse relation between age and self-esteem and an even stronger inverse relation between depression and self-esteem, but no gender differences in self-esteem in youth (Orvaschel, Beeferman, & Kabakoff, 1997). Whether this characteristic is at the bottom of rejection of depressed individuals remains to be seen (Gurtman, 1986).

Personality Disorders. More specific assessment of personality disorders, particularly of possible underlying dimensions, might be a more fruitful approach than a categorical approach in identifying effective treatments for patients with personality disorders and depression (Shea, Widiger, & Klein, 1992). A vast majority of depressed individuals demonstrate Cluster C personality disorders, such as: avoidant personality (30.4%), compulsive (18.6%), and dependent (15.7%), (Pilkonis & Frank, 1988), or borderline personality disorder (Sullivan, Joyce, & Mulder, 1994). One fourth of individuals diagnosed along the depression spectrum could receive an additional Axis I diagnosis of substance abuse and anxiety disorder, and in Axis II, depressives tend to present a higher frequency of dependent personality disorder and the anxious/fearful Cluster C. Physical illness may also be overrepresented in depression (Mezzich, Favbrera, & Coffman, 1987). Dependency and hysterical personality disorders may also be present in depression (Paykel, Klerman, & Prusoff, 1976). These conclusions seems to support the continuity of depression with personality disorders as shown in Figure 12.4.

Cognitive Style. Three models of negative cognitive style for depression are: (1) a symptom model, in which negative cognitions are a symptom of depression; (2) a vulnerability model, in which a negative life event in combination with cognitive vulnerability lead to depression; and (3) an alternative etiological model in which depression can be precipitated either by stressful life events or by a negative cognitive style. Model 3 seems to be supported more often than the other two models, with Model 1 receiving some support (Parry & Brewin, 1988). According to A. T. Beck's cognitive model of depression, dysfunctional attitudes serve as a cognitive moderator and automatic thoughts as a cognitive mediator in the relationship between negative life events and depressive symptoms. This models seems valid with undergraduates (Kwon & Oel, 1992). However, it also needs validation with really depressed patients.

Gender Differences. According to the attachment model, women may tend to rate themselves as being more preoccupied and fearful than men, who instead may rate themselves as dismissing and selfish. Men seem to have a more positive model of self, while women overall seem to have a more positive model of others. Nevertheless, it is important to see how these gender differences support the possible validity of men being perhaps more assertive than women and women being more nurturing than men (Bartholomew et al., 2001).

Gender differences in depression seem to emerge during adolescence. Three models may account for this emergence: (1) causes for depression are the same for both genders, but these causes become more prevalent in girls than in boys in early adolescence; (2) there are different causes of depression in girls and boys, and these causes become more prevalent in girls then causes of boys' depression in early adolescence; and (3) girls are more likely than boys to carry risk factors for depression even before early adolescence, but these risk factors lead to depression only in the face of challenges that increase in prevalence in early adolescence. Evidence for the variables most commonly thought to contribute to gender differences in depression in children and adolescents seems to support the third model, even though much more research is needed (Nolen-Hoeksema & Girgus, 1994).

There is some evidence to support the increased vulnerability of post-pubertal girls to depression when faced with stressful life events, particularly those events with negative interpersonal consequences (Cyranowski, Frank, Young, & Shear, 2000). Gender roles and gender role ideology may account substantially for sex differences in internally directed psychological distress and in externally directed deviant behavior in adolescence. Masculine instrumental attributes apparently tend to reduce internalized distress, whereas feminine expressive attributes tend to reduce externalized behavior problems. Additionally, conventional gender role attitudes seem positively related to externalizing problems among boys, but seem unrelated to pathology among girls. These associations seemed largely equivalent across Black and White racial groups and across age groups (13–19 years) (Huselid & Cooper, 1994).

Dysthymic young men (18 years old) seemingly may be more negatively evaluated than dysthymic young women and nondysthymic young persons of both genders. These young men were seen as being more disagreeable, aggressive, and antagonistic—a pattern characteristic of externalizations— than young women, who were seen as "ego-brittle," unconventional, and ruminating—a pattern characteristic of internalizations. Both men and women described themselves as aggressive and alienated (Gjerde, Block, & Block, 1988).

Adult women have consistently been found to have higher rates of depression and depressive symptomatology than men. Both sex-role and biological explanations have been suggested to account for these differences. In nontraditional relationships, men may show higher levels of depressive symptoms than women, supporting a sex-role basis for gender differences in depressive symptomatology (Rosenfeld, 1980).

Gender Role Orientation. Greater masculinity seems generally associated with lower levels of different depressive experiences in both men and women. Greater femininity seems related to advantageous outcomes for various depressive experiences in a relatively weaker and gender-specific fashion, but it may also be associated with greater anaclitic depression in men and women. Culturally defined gender-role characteristics, therefore, may be more important than gender itself with respect to different aspects of depressive experiences in young, undergraduate adults (Sanfilipo, 1994).

Loss of Parent. As already presented in Chapter 5, there is almost universal agreement that loss of one parent, usually the mother before 17 years of age, might be a major determinant of depression (Haaga, Dyck, & Ernst,

1991; Lloyd, 1980; O'Neil, Lancee, & Freeman, 1987; Roy, 1978, 1981a). Among males, however, parental loss might not be the only factor associated with depression (Roy, 1981b).

Family Background. The family plays a major role in the development and course of major depression (Keitner & Miller, 1990). Families with a history of affective illness seem more likely to show functional problems, and these problems may differ as a function of the type of diagnosis and number of ill parents (Inoff-Germain, Nottelmann, & Radke-Yarrow, 1997). Differentiating between early versus late onset for depression may be useful to understand the influence of family background on depression. For instance, familial affective disorder might be greater in early rather than late onset, while familial alcoholism and sociopathy might be significantly greater in early versus late onset. Affective disorders in families of early onset seem to be higher in women than in male relatives (Winokur & Coryell, 1991), supporting the position that depression may relate more to the modeling with an important caretaker even earlier than the loss of that caretaker itself. Primary relationships and stresses deriving from them might be one of the major sources of stress in depressed women, in addition to unemployment in low SES (Ilfeld, 1977). Childhood sexual abuse seems associated with adult-onset depression in both men and women, but occurrence of such abuse is more frequent in girls than in boys (Weiss, Longhurst, & Mazure, 1999).

A family history of psychiatric illness, stressful life events, and lack of a confidant seem highly related to depression, even though, in this case, early loss was not associated with depressive symptomatology (O'Neal et al., 1986). The mother-child relationship may reflect mutual themes of depression and loss within families where experience with illness and death may contribute to a hypochondrial concern about body sensations and pain (Hughes, 1984). Decreased relatedness with one's parent is a function of age, however, depressed women tend to report little attachment to their mothers at all ages. This is also the case for attachment to fathers throughout their life span (Rosenfarb, Becker, & Khan, 1994).

Depressed patients with dysfunctional families tend to show a significantly poorer course of illness, as manifested by higher levels of depression, lower levels of overall adjustment, and a lower frequency of recovery (Miller, Keitner, Whisman, & Ryan, 1992). Offspring of unipolar patients might exhibit significantly higher rates of affective disorder, major depression, and dysthymnia than did offspring of medical or normal controls. Parental characteristics associated with dysthymia in offspring may include chronic depression, age of onset of major depression, number of hospitalizations, and multiple family members with major affective illness (Klein, Clark, Dansky, & Margolis, 1988).

Psychosocial outcome variables indicate particular impairment for children of unipolar mothers (Hammen, Gordon, Burge, Adrian, et al., 1987). Children of depressed parents, compared to controls, seem at risk for impaired intellectual competence on selected tasks. Possibly, these specific cognitive deficits may occur through alterations in the quality of parenting and the stresses of familial psychopathology (Kaplan, Beardslee, & Keller, 1987). The widely held assumption that depressed mothers may have distorted perceptions of their children's problems needs to be reevaluated for its validity (Richters, 1992). Maternal interaction with a child may be mediated by task focus and affective quality that may put the child at risk for subsequent depression. Chronic stress could be predictive of more negative, critical maternal behavior, whereas depressed mood may be associated with less task involvement (Burge & Hammen, 1991).

Association between depression and positive maternal behavior seem relatively weak, albeit significant. Residual effects of prior depression seem apparent for all behaviors associated with parenting (Lovejoy, Graczyk. O'Hare. & Neuman, 2000). Predictors of the course, i.e., incidence, recurrence, and recovery, of major depressive disorder in the offspring may vary according to whether or not the parent is depressed and that different factors will predict different types or course of illness (Warner, Weissman, Fendrich, & Wickramaratne, 1992). Depressogenic parenting, at least in college students, seems to include: low care, overprotection, perfectionistic expectations, and criticalness. These four parenting dimensions seem to correlate with dysfunctional attitudes and depression tendencies in offspring (Randolph & Dykman, 1998).

Depression in Children. Principal causes of childhood depression are adverse psychosocial factors resulting mainly from deficient parental nurturing. Aside from separation from the maternal figure, abuse and neglect are the most significant causes of depression in children. Sexual abuse may also create severe emotional difficulties (Lizardi, Klein, Ouimette, & Riso, 1995). When masked in behavioral aberrations and prolonged, depression in children may lead to suicide attempts (Blumberg, 1981). Several consistent patterns of parent-child interactions may be involved in the etiology, maintenance, and/or expression of depressive disorders in children, adolescents, and adults (Burbach & Borduin, 1986).

In light of selective factors on maternal versus paternal psychopathology as a risk factor for child development of either externalizing or internalizing disorders, associations seem stronger between maternal than paternal psychopathology and internalizing (but not externalizing) problems in children. Of course, other variables need to be considered before reaching a definite conclusion about this effect, like age of children, type of parental psychopathology, as well as method of studying (Connell & Goodman, 2002). The possibility of an association between mother-child transmission of depression could be found in the convergence of children's attributional style for negative events and their depressive symptoms with those of their mothers but not of their fathers (Seligman, 1984), just as adjustment difficulties in children of depressed mothers do not abate within the first year after the mothers' recovery (Lee & Gotlib, 1991).

Families of depressed children between 8 and 13 years of age seem to show a more lifetime depressive disorder and recurrent unipolar depressive disorder than did families of controls (Kovacs, Devlin, Pollock, & Richards, 1997). Children of depressed parents are certainly at high risk for depression. Homes of such children indicate a disruptive, hostile, and rejecting environment (Orvaschel, Weissman, & Kidd, 1980). Both children and parents in families with a depressed child seem to perceive their lives as being more stressful and their families' parenting practices more negative than controls. Apparently, family environments of depressed children might be less rewarding, more aversive, and more disengaged than those of controls. Possible bidirectional influences may be operating between depressed children and their families (Messer & Gross, 1995).

Prepubertal children who developed a major depressive disorder seem to come from families with significantly higher prevalence rates for psychiatric disorders and alcoholism than occurred in families of normal children. Families of children with major depressive disorder with no history of concrete suicide plans/conduct disorders may tend to show the highest rates of this disorder among first and second degree relatives (Puig-Antich, Goetz, Davies, & Kaplan, 1989).

Significant risk can be found for children having parents with major affective disorder, and considerable impairment seems evident in these children, such as: neurotic illness, neurotic behavior disturbance, sociopathy, criminal activities, and, most particularly, depression. These children seem more likely than children of healthy parents to have experienced perinatal complications, cognitive impairments in infancy, school and peer problems at ages 6 to 12 years, and adolescent rebellion and withdrawal centering around conflicts with parents (Beardslee, Bemporad, Keller, & Klerman, 1983).

In Australia, maternal and paternal depression may have an additive effect on youth externalizing disorders. Additionally, maternal depression interacted with both paternal depression and paternal substance abuse in predicting youth depression but not youth nondepressive disorders. Chronic family stress and father's expressed emotions may mediate the relation between parental psychopathology and youth depression (Brennan, Hammen, Katz, & LeBroque, 2002).

Depression in Adolescents. There seems to be an aggregation of adolescent major depression disorders with considerable specificity in patterns of familiar transmission. Adolescent anxiety and substance abuse disorders may add to the severity of this disorder (Klein, Lewinsohn, Seeley, & Rohde, 2001). Perceived self-worth tends to predict depressive symptoms in adolescents but not externalizing symptoms (Robinson, Garber, & Hilsman, 1995), supporting the position given by the selfhood model that selflessness and internalizations are related to a negative view of self ("I am not important"). Adolescents' functioning is clearly related to their mothers' depression (Forehand & McCombs, 1988).

The interaction of maternal and adolescent depression might be a better predictor of adolescent social and cognitive functioning than either variable alone (Forehand, Brody et al., 1988). Hypocondrial and psychosomatic symptoms, however, may mask depression in adolescents. Apparently, in typically perfectionistic, overintellectual, and socially withdrawn youngsters, illnesses might be a means of escaping overwhelming responsibilities imposed by critical, superachieving parents, and as means of maintaining parental sympathy. This type of disorder may be precipitated by a combination of: (1) genetic predisposition to depression; (2) childhood ontogenetical trauma; and (3) intolerable adolescent stress (Lesse, 1981).

Couples with a Depressed Spouse. Couples with a depressed spouse tend to rate themselves as experiencing significantly less positive and more negative moods than nondepressed couples. Depressed spouses also may tend to communicate more negatively nonverbally than verbally (Ruscher & Gotlib, 1988). Expressed emotions, marital distress, and perceptions of criticism from nondepressed spouses are all related to relapse rates. The single best predictor of relapse was the patient's response to the question: "How critical is your spouse of you?" Patients who relapsed tend to rate their spouses as significantly more critical than did patients who remained well (Hooley & Teasdale, 1989). The greatest suppression of aggressive behavior in husbands seems present in couples defined as nondepressed-discordant. Length of marital discord seems highly correlated with the magnitude of suppression effects in depressed-discordant and nondepressed-discordant couples. The longer the duration of marital discord, the less the suppression of spousal aggression by depressive behavior (Nelson & Beach, 1990).

Anxiety and Depression. There is no question that depression and anxiety may be related, i.e., comorbid up to a point (Zimmerman, McDermott, & Mattia, 2000). However, there may be differences in goals between depressed and anxious undergraduates (Lecci, Karoly, Briggs, & Kuhn, 1994). This possibility needs replication. The major factor differentiating anxieties from depressions, according to the selfhood model, lies in the sense of self-importance that is low in depressions and higher in anxieties, with depressives being more dependent on others than anxious individuals.

Depression—Learned Helplessness or Just Hopelessness? As introduced in Chapter 5, both learned helplessness and hopelessness were included at the explanatory genotypic level. The reformulated learned helplessness model posits that individuals who make internal, stable, and global attributions for undesired outcomes are more likely than others to become depressed when faced with important life events that are perceived as uncontrollable. When this model was applied to pregnant women, results supporting this model were "negligible" (Manly, McMahon, Bradley, & Davidson, 1982). A refinement of the construct "attributional style" needs to include memory and automatic versus effortful cognitive processing (Hill & Larson, 1992). Thus, there is controversial evidence for learned helplessness being an antecedent or underlying factor in depression, either in favor (Kammer, 1983; Rapps et al., 1982) or in disfavor (Coyne, Aldwin, & Lazarus, 1981; Greer & Calhoun, 1983; Zautra, Guenther, & Chartier, 1985).

Attributional style and dysfunctional attitudes may not be facets of the same underlying dimension, while dysfunctional attitudes and self-esteem may be aspects of the same underlying factor, labeled self-regard, in a way that is consistent with L. Y. Abramson's original hopelessness model (Haaga, Dyck, & Ernst, 1991; Joiner & Rudd, 1996). It may be more useful to ask: "How hopeless is this person when not depressed and how much more hopeless should one be when depressed?" rather than simply ask: "How hopeless is this depressed person?" (Young, Fogg, Scheftner, & Fawcett, 1996).

In support of the hopelessness model, cognitive risk and depressogenic cognitive styles may partially mediate the relation between childhood emotional maltreatment and hopelessness. Reported levels of childhood emotional, but not physical or sexual, maltreatment might be related to levels of hopelessness and episodes of nonendogenous major depression (Alloy, Abramson, Whitehouse, & Hogan, 1999; Gibb, Alloy, Abramson, & Rose, 2001). Three social learning mechanisms in the development of depressogenic cognitive styles consist of: (1) modeling of parents' negative cognitive styles; (2) negative inferential feedback from parents regarding the causes and consequences of stressful events in the child's life; and (3) negative parenting practices. Partial support for the three mechanisms was found, with some support for the presence of hopelessness depression (Alloy, Abramson, Tashman, & Berrebbi, 2001).

Depression, Sociotropy, and Autonomy. Instead of a unitary dimension of depression, a more useful approach has been to differentiate at least two factors, initiated by A. T. Beck—sociotropy, excessive concerns about other people, as in dependency; and autonomy, relying on self-achievement (Robins, Hayes, Block, Kramer, et al., 1995). Sociotropy might be related to interpersonal sensitivity, guilt, and self-blame, and with symptoms suggesting anxious depression or high negative affectivity. Autonomy, on the other hand, might be related to interpersonal distance and hostility, hopelessness/suicidality, feelings of failure, and anhedonia, suggesting low positive affectivity (Robins, Bagby, Rector, & Lynch, 1997).

A similar two-factor model of depression, initiated by S. J. Blatt, stressing originally dependency and self-criticism, seems somewhat closer to the present definition of selflessness, even though there may be personality and gender differences between the four dimensions derived from A. T. Beck's and S. J. Blatt's models (Zuroff, 1994). Alienation and counter-dependency in relation to parents seem associated with self-critical concerns in adolescents. Excessive closeness and dependency seem associated with interpersonal concerns, i.e., dependency, while separation-individuation conflicts seem associated with both types of concerns. Self-critical and interpersonal concerns might be linked to adolescent depression and may account for most of the variance initially explained by difficulties with parents (Frank, Poorman, Van Egeren, & Field, 1997).

Suicide

Suicide is the ultimate prototype of selflessness and self-devaluation. Hence, it tends to support the first part of the selflessness definition: "I am not important," just as murder is the ultimate devaluation of another in selfishness. Suicide can vary along dimensions of intentions, i.e., suicidality, to suicide attempts, and to the ultimate act. Aborted suicide attempts are defined as events in which an individual comes close to attempting suicide but does not complete the act and, therefore, does not sustain any injury. Over half of a sample of adult psychiatric inpatients who reported aborted or actual suicide attempts were diagnosed as borderline personality disorders. Scores for intent versus actual suicidal attempts were comparable, where the first aborted attempt preceded the first actual attempt approximately half the time (Barber, Marzuk, Leon, & Portera, 1998).

Children. Children may evidence psychopathology related to developmental levels. Depression in children, previously rejected, is now accepted as an affective disorder related to both unipolar and bipolar illnesses, with possible potential for suicide (Toolan, 1981). Physically abused children tend to manifest higher levels of depressive symptomatology and suicidality than neglected or nonabused children (Finzi, Ram, Shnit, Har-Even, et al., 2001). Organizational characteristics of families of psychiatrically hospitalized suicidal latency-age children seem based on a lack of self-differentiation and intragenerational guidance, including the following: (1) severely conflicted spouse relationships; (2) parental feelings projected onto the child; and (3) symbiotic parent-child relationships. These patterns may result from negative self-perceptions internalized from the child's negative perceptions of the parents (Pfeffer, 1981).

Adolescents. The increasing incidence of adolescent suicide, close to an epidemic, shows the necessity of developing adequate treatment measures (Toolan, 1981), and one would add, mass-oriented preventative approaches, possibly online. Suicide in adolescents is associated with depression (Chabrol & Moron, 1988), negative self-evaluation, anhedonia, insomnia, poor concentration, indecisiveness, lack of reactivity of mood, psychomotor disturbances, and alcohol and drug abuse (Robbins & Alessi, 1985). Hopelessness does not seem to account for a significant proportion of the variance in adolescent suicide, while depression seem uniquely related to past suicide attempts. Survival-coping beliefs seem associated with self-predicted future suicide and other suicidal attempts (Cole, 1989).

Psychological autopsies of completed suicide in children and adolescents revealed that 85% of the victims and 18% of controls had expressed suicidal ideation. Among the victims, 55% had a history of suicide threats, suicide attempts (40%), drug or alcohol abuse (70%), antisocial behavior (70%), or inhibited personality (65%). Suicide in parents, relatives, or friends and a parental history of emotional problems or abusiveness were also significant factors for the victims (Shafit, Carrigan, Whittinghill, & Derrick, 1985).

Suicide completers and suicidal inpatients show similarly high rates of affective disorder and family histories of affective disorder, antisocial disorder, and suicide, suggesting that in adolescents there is a continuum of suicidality from ideation to completion (Brent, Perper, Goldstein, & Kolko, 1988). Chronic illness or depression in a parent during childhood or latency years may have seriously influenced suicidal adolescents. Perhaps, identification with a depressed parent may lead to a hopeless-helpless view of self and to a suicidal stance, particularly when adaptation to adverse circumstances seems required (Friedman, 1984).

There seems to be a significant degree of individual and family dysfunction among many adolescent suicide attempters. However, strong evidence for the specificity of this dysfunction to suicide attempts, rather than to general emotional disturbance, seems present for hopelessness, family conflict, and contagion (Spirito, Brown, Overholser, & Fritz, 1989). Nonetheless, statistically significant differences in the degree of family normlessness and powerlessness may be present for both suicidal and nonsuicidal adolescents and their families (Wenz, 1978). More specifically, more suicidal adolescents seem to have a history of family disorganization, and may have been exposed to suicide in family members or acquaintances, with feelings of lack of control over their environment, loss of a loved friend, and lack of communication in dealing with parents, than nonsuicidal controls (Corder, Page, & Corder, 1974).

Three characteristics more often exhibited by an adolescent in the year prior to the suicide attempt may be: alcohol, drug use, and rebellion toward authority. Depression, impulsivity, and anger seem the most predominant personality characteristics. The suicide attempt itself seems usually precipitated by conflicts with a significant person, either a parent or an intimate friend, accompanied by drug use (Withers & Kaplan, 1987).

There is consistent evidence that a history of physical or sexual abuse may be a risk factor for adolescent suicide, together with other risk factors, such as poor family or parent-child communication, loss of caregiver to separation or death, and psychopathology in first-degree relatives. This evidence, however, needs further methodological improvements and research (Wagner, 1997). Indeed, only links between early negative life events and cognitive variables and suicide seem supported by research (Yang & Clum, 1996).

Adults. The most frequent diagnosis for suicide in young men is major depression, alcohol or drug dependence, and borderline personality disorder. Among them, 28% had at least two of these disorders, while the rate was 0% in comparison participants (Lesage, Boyer, Grunberg, & Vanier, 1994). Hopelessnes in psychiatric outpatients seems indeed related to eventual suicide, to the point that the Beck Hopelessness Scale may be used as a sensitive indicator of suicide potential (Beck, Brown, Berchick, & Stewart, 1990). However, this scale may be strongly contaminated with social desirability, but results showed that this factor was completely unrelated to suicide attempts, confirming the appropriateness of this scale for suicide assessment (Petrie & Chamberlain, 1983). Other theoretical models predicting suicide failed to predict eventual suicides (Goldstein, Black, Nasrallah, & Winokur, 1991).

The relationship between suicide and personality disorders (at least in Finland) shows that most suicides had been diagnosed with Cluster B in 43 out of 229 victims, and Cluster C in 23 victims, and only one victim in Cluster A. Suicide victims with personality disorders were almost always found to have had current depressed syndromes, substance use disorders, or both (Isometsa, Henrikson, Heikkinen, & Aro, 1996).

Alcoholics. Significantly more alcoholics who had attempted suicide tend to be women compared to alcoholics who had never attempted suicide. Those who attempted suicide seemed to have significantly higher levels of childhood traumas, such as emotional, physical, and sexual abuse, as well as emotional and physical neglect than controls (Roy, 2001).

Parents. Parents who killed themselves, leaving grieving offspring and spouses, may evidence more psychopathology than parents who died from reasons other than suicide. Surviving parents of suicide victims do not seem more impaired than surviving parents of children who died for other causes. Before death, suicide-bereaved families seemed less stable than control families, even though no differences were found between surviving children of both groups (Cerel, Fristad, Weller, & Weller, 2000).

Families. Greater preadolescent suicidality seems associated with both parents' and children's reports of family conflict, disorganization, and lack of achievement orientation, as well as less cohesiveness and less expressiveness (Campbell, Milling, Laughlin, & Bush, 1993). Families of adolescents who had exhibited suicidal behaviors seem to constitute a malfunctioning system that could be differentiated from that of normal controls. The former evidenced family interactions that appeared less effective, with higher rates of conflict and negative reinforcement than the former (Williams & Lyons, 1976).

If some of the above is valid, then the two parts of the definition of selflessness seem supported. "I am not important" is clearly supported, by the extremely large body of evidence indicting self-criticisms and negative self-views. "Others are more important than I am" is also supported by the overwhelming dependency that seems ever present in depressed individuals. The only direct test of this model will take place with depressed patients rather than with functional undergraduates. A beginning in this direction was made by L'Abate et al. (2000; L'Abate, 2003a). However, patients in that study were heterogeneous for diagnosis and cannot be considered as a direct test of the model. Norms for the SOPC, which is the measure directly related to evaluating this model, have been obtained from Italian college students and cannot be compared to norms developed in this country. Some of this research will be presented in Chapter 19.

No-Self

Developmentally, extremely inconsistent, and contradictory imbalances in both distance and control functions tend to produce a personality propensity named no-self, leading to severe psychopathology that includes Cluster A of Axis II and disorders of Axis I. Their prototypes are dissociative identity disorders, paranoias, schizoid, and schizophrenic type disorders. Bipolar disorders, schizophrenias, combined inconsistently and contradictorily with both ruthlessness and apathy with passivity and submission at the two extremes (Fig. 12.3). No-self individuals are dominated by fears, ruminative behavior, irrational thoughts, convoluted thinking, and sudden, unexpected actions. They are called no-self here because they are like a ship without a compass, rudder, motor, or sails. They are unable to enjoy life because of their sometimes complete inability to take care of themselves and to use the many resources available to function in intimate and nonintimate relationships (Ch. 4). Their presentational and phenotypic actions are usually visible to intimates and nonintimates. Their genotypes are chaotic, confused, and extremely limited. Their intergenerational backgrounds are usually replete with illness in intimates, family members, and relatives (Ch. 5). They tend to function minimally in no more than one setting (Ch. 6). They are unable to love, be loved by, or negotiate with intimates and nonintimates (Chs. 7 and 8), or be present emotionally to self and intimates others, performing or producing very little (Ch. 9). The level of identity-differentiation varies between symbiosis and alienation, deriving from similarly symbiotic or alienated family backgrounds (Ch. 10). Their interpersonal style is mainly abusive or apathetic, i.e., neglectful (Ch. 11). They tend to frustrate self and others, exhibiting unpredictable, inconsistent, and contradictory extremes from internalizations to externalizations or in either direction.

No-self, the negative attribution of importance to self and others, results in a negatively nihilistic and ultimately destructively deteriorating breakdown in relationships ("Neither you or I are going to win"). These individuals show extreme resistance to treatment, with prolonged presence of dysfunctionality, intense episodes of actions requiring hospitalization and, in some misdiagnosed cases, incarceration. They probably live shorter than other personality propensities or selfful individuals.

Dissociations

Dissociations represent emotional or cognitive actions usually outside one's usual awareness, operating independently from one's knowledge. Individuals suffering from this disorder seem to function externally to one's self. They seem disconnected or even disengaged from their reality. These disorders cover a full spectrum of functionality-dysfunctionality, ranging from normal dissociation, as seen in complete absorption in a task, dreams, daydreams, or momentary and short-lived lapses of attention or memory, to amnesias, fugues, partial dissociative identity disorders, and full-blown dissociative identity disorders, characterized by multiple selves (Ross, 1997). From the viewpoint of the selfhood model, dissociative disorders would range from attributing importance to both self and others to denying importance for both, depending on the severity of the disorder.

Among no-self prototypes, dissociative disorders are relatively more treatable (Lynn & Rhue, 1994). Most sources relate these disorders to extreme childhood abuse and neglect, factitious factors, and even iatrogenic origins (Lynn & Rhue, 1994; Millon et al., 1999; Ross, 1997). Dissociative symptoms in borderline patients may simply be a lesser form of intrapsychic fragmentation than multiple personalities (Chu & Dill, 1991). Dissociative symptom scores seem highest in psychiatric inpatient women who reported both physical and sexual abuse in childhood. Nearly 25% of respondents scored higher than the established median of patients with posttraumatic stress disorder (Chu & Dill, 1991).

Dissociative symptoms and dissociative identity disorders, with severe abuse during childhood, for instance, seem present in murderers, who are so amnesiac about most of their childhood abuse that they tend to underreport it. Marked changes in their writing style and/or signatures also seem frequent (Lewis, Yeager, Swica, & Pincus, 1997). Dissociative disorders may also be the outcome of excessive stress on specific brain regions and brain chemistry affecting memory and possibly producing alterations in memory functions. Childhood abuse, for instance, may result in long-term alterations in the function of these neuromodulators (Bremner, Krystal, Charney, & Southwick, 1996). Hence, external, painful experiences in childhood, and perhaps throughout the life cycle, may produce changes not only in body-chemestry, but also in physiology (L'Abate, 1998).

Bipolar Disorder

From the viewpoint of the selfhood model, bipolar disorder represents well the contradictory and inconsistent oscillation from selfishness on one hand, in which self-importance is positive during mania, to selflessness during depression, on the other hand, where self-importance is negative. Support for this expansion of the model is found in a study of the self-concept in bipolar disorder (Power, De Jong, & Lloyd, 2002). In a euthymic state, individuals with bipolar disorder, compared to diabetics, may tend to show a "modularized self-concept," in which key aspects of the self tend to be organized as completely positive or completely negative.

Again , it is impossible to review all the relevant literature about this disorder without repeating information that is available in most treatises about abnormal psychology and psychopathology (Millon et al., 1999). Here, the focus will be on the outcome on children of parents with severe psychopathology. Patients with bipolar affective disorder may differ from those with unipolar disorder on many of the variables associated with deterioration of functioning, that is: bipolar disorders tend to deteriorate more often and more severely than unipolar depression (Coryell, Scheftner, Keller, & Endicott, 1993; Vocisano, Klein, Keefe, & Dienst, 1996). There is little doubt that patients with bipolar disorders tend to have first-degree relatives dignosed with the same or recurrent unipolar disorder (McMahon, Stine, Chase, & Meyers, 1994). Modest familial links between Axis I and Axis II disorders exist but with little specificity except for acting out personality disorders from families with nonendogenous types of depression. However, Cluster C disorders seemed more frequent among relatives of bipolar probands (Coryell & Zimmerman, 1989).

Children. By age 2 children with a manic-depressive parent experienced substantial psychiatric problems. Children with a manic-depressive parent seem to have difficulty in sharing with their friends and in handling hostility, showing maladaptive patterns of aggression. The social and emotional problems of these children seem highly similar to the interpersonal problems of their manic-depressive parents (Zahn-Waxler, 1984). Indeed, infants with a manic-depressed parent already show disturbances in the quality of their attachments to their mothers as well as a generalized disturbance in their capacity to regulate their emotions adaptively, with the possibility of an increased severity of disturbance with increasing age (Gaenbauer, Harmon, Cytryn, & McKnew, 1984).

Children's subjective perception of a mentally ill parent's psychiatric symptoms and parenting skills seems significantly related to the child's psychological adjustment. Children perceiving their mothers as manifesting symptoms of mental illness tend to have more serious problems (Scherer, Melloh, Buyck, Anderson, et al., 1996).

A clear tendency to early disturbance in children of parents with affective illness lies in affect regulation and social interaction. There seems to be a gradual coalescence of prodromal symptoms into a clinically diagnosable affective illness with advancing age (Beardslee et al., 1983; Cytryn, 1984). Significant risk and considerable impairment, therefore, exist for children of parents with a major affective disorder.

Mothers in couples with one partner with manic-depressive illness, in contrast to control mothers, seem less attentive to their children's health needs, emphasized performance in some achievement-related areas, seem more overprotective, and tend to report more negative affect toward their children. They also seemed more disorganized, less active with their children, and more unhappy, tense, and ineffective. These parents seem to secure lower scores in areas of family interaction and social adjustment, experiencing situational problems of considerable severity, including clinical depression in the well parent (Davenport, Zahn-Waxler, Adland, & Mayfield, 1984).

Children of parents with bipolar disorder tend to show a range of mal-adjustment problems as infants and toddlers, continuing into the elementary school years (depression, conduct, obsessive-compulsive, and separation anxiety disorders). In addition to internalizing problems, these children tend to show antisocial behavior patterns. Common problems seemed to be difficulties in empathy or role taking and acquiescent patterns of conflict resolution (Zahn-Waxler, Mayfield, Radke-Yarrow, & McKnew, 1988).

Children are at greater risk for being the offspring of psychiatrically ill parents (El-Guebaty & Offord, 1980), where the amount of disqualification in the family is directed against the child from other family members (Wichstrom, Anderson, Holte, & Wynne, 1996). In clearly psychotic families, there seems to be opposition to: (1) extension of the problem to other family members; (2) discussion of family relationships; and (3) often denied opposition to defining such relationships. A paradoxical, that is, inconsistent and contradictory, communication structure seems to derive from rigidity in relational models, roles, and rules. In this kind of family, where psychopathology is preserved and protected, preservation of family myths and secrets is paramount, for fear that these patterns will be discovered to become mere gossip or revenge. This discovery may produce a profound change in the status quo within the family (Vella & Loredo, 1976).

Adolescents. Psychiatrically ill children of lithium-responsive parents tend to show affective disorders remitted when following a recurrent course. Psychiatrically ill children of lithium-nonresponsive parents, however, may manifest a broad range of psychopathology, with high rates of comorbid illnesses, and experience nonremitting affective illnesses. These results suggest that a family history and course of illness are important factors to consider in the diagnosis and pharmacological treatment of affective disorders (Duffy, Alda, Kutchee, & Fusee, 1998).

Adults. Acute depressive episodes and dysthymic-cyclothynic disorders may constitute more common psychopathological features of first degree relatives of known bipolar adults (Akistal et al., 1985), suggesting a generational transmission as well as the modeling of contagious effects among members of extended families. Whether these effects are of genetic origin remains to be seen. The variable of familiar Bipolar I or schizoaffective mania is significantly higher in first degree relatives of patients diagnosed with bipolar or schizoaffective mania than in first degree relatives of patients diagnosed with primary unipolar depressives. This difference suggests that Bipolar I may be an illness independent from primary unipolar depression (Winokur, Coryell, Keller, & Endicott, 1995).

Families. In adult relatives of probands with schizoaffective, Bipolar I, Bipolar II, and unipolar disease and normal controls, lifetime prevalence of major affective disorder were 37%, 24%, 20%, and 7% respectively. Morbidity risk was 74% for offspring of two ill parents, and 27% for offspring of one ill parent (Gershon, 1982). Major depression and personality disorders seem significantly higher in relatives of dysthymic probands than in those of controls (Klein, Riso, Donaldson, & Schwartz, 1995).

Schizotypal and Schizophrenic Disorders

From the viewpoint of the selfhood model, schizophrenia would show greater contradictions in their self-concepts, i.e., identity differentiation, than controls. This seems to be the case (Gruba & Johnson, 1974). One could argue that many schizotypal disorders, Cluster A in Axis II (Fig. 12.4) should be placed with disorders of distance and avoidance of others, as reviewed in Chapter 7. Nonetheless, they are placed here because they represent a range in a continuum of avoidance disorders, as seen in different degrees, types, and severities of schizophrenias. Furthermore, by the same token, paranoias could represent one aspect of externalization disorders and be included either in Chapter 8 or in that section of this chapter, if there are signs of externalization. Without externalization, placement of paranoias in this section could be controversial. However, at this point, this is the best outcome one can reach, awaiting further theoretical and empirical findings and refinements.

Again, a review of all of the relevant literature would be impossible. Here, sources related to these disorders and family and parental origins will be selectively included.

When schizophrenics are separated from schizoaffective, bipolar, and unipolar disorders, for each disorder and for each generation of relatives, relatives tend to show a greater prevalence of the proband's disorder than did relatives of controls. For schizophrenic probands, the prevalence in parents seems substantially lower than that in children or siblings. Familial risk of schizophrenia or schizoaffective disorders seems to increase for families of probands (Maier, Lichtermann, Minges, & Hallmayer, 1993). Personality disorders of nonneurotic type, either alone or in combination with another diagnosis, seem more likely to be biologically related to schizophrenic-spectrum disorders. This association, however, does not seem to fit well with a model of dominant inheritance of schizophrenia and schizoid disease (Stephens, 1975).

Childhood and Adolescence. Children who are both aggressive and withdrawn represent a less mature, less socially skilled group that is potentially at risk for poor adjustment later in life (Ledingham, 1981). This possibility supports the position that no-self propensities may be the outcome of contradictory and inconsistent intimate relationships. For instance, patients with schizophrenia-related psychoses without substance abuse, seem to exhibit significantly more problems as children than adult offspring with affective or anxiety disorders, substance abuse only, or no disorder. These results support the view that schizophrenia-related psychoses can be traced back to early behavioral disturbances (Amminger, Pape, Rock, & Roberts, 1999).

Children of schizophrenic mothers become at risk for developmental deviance because: (1) the mother is the only permanent caregiver; (2) of unstable relations of the mother to her spouse and family; (3) of onset of maternal illness at the time of the child's birth; (4) of chronic damage to the mother's ability to care for herself, and (5) of a maternal system of delusions involving the infant (Grunbaum & Gammeltoft, 1993). High risk male adolescents from a pattern of parental transactional style apparently come from two symptom groups—withdrawn adolescents and adolescents in active family conflict—which are symptom patterns similar to those of premorbid schizophrenia symptoms (Jones, 1977).

Possibly, schizophrenics and schizotypes share a similar genetic dispostion that is more severe than that of high-risk individuals who remain healthy. Schizophenics, rather than schizotypes, may have premorbidly experienced stressful conditions. Early-onset schizophrenics may transmit a more severe diathesis to the offspring, supporting the possibility stated above. Consequences of a disrupted childhood may be more serious in genetically vulnerable offspring (Parnas, Teasdale, & Schulsinger, 1985).

Emotional Experience. There may be a discrepancy between schizophrenics' outward expression of emotions and their reported emotional experience. Schizophrenics seem less facially expressive than controls, experiencing as much positive as negative emotions. Additionally, schizophrenics may exhibit greater skin conductance reactivity than controls. These findings suggest a disjunction among emotional response domains for schizophrenics than for controls (Kring & Neale, 1996).

Communication Deviance and Thought Disorders in Parents. The level of emotions expressed by relatives shortly after a schizophrenic patient is admitted to a hospital seems strongly associated with symptomatic relapse during the 9 months following discharge. The single most important measure contributing to the overall expressed emotion index seems to be the number of critical remarks made about the patient by family members (Vaughn & Leff, 1976).

A measure of communication deviance represents one aspect of expressed emotions, indicating unusual and uncommon use of language. For instance, parents of schizophrenic patients seem to demonstrate levels of language disturbance similar to those of the patients and higher than those of control parents. This disturbance seems positively associated with distractibility and with severity of schizotypy (Docherty, 1993). This inability to focus, coupled with an inability to share feelings, especially in parents of adolescents at risk for schizophrenia, was originally found in high communication deviance parents (Lewis, Rodnick, & Goldstein, 1981).

However, instances of odd word usage seem more frequent among parents of manic patients than among parents of schizophrenics. Also, odd word usage seems more frequent among manic patients, whereas schizophrenics seem to make more ambiguous references, suggesting that high levels of intrafamilial communication deviance may not be unique to schizophrenia (Miklowitz, Velligan, Goldstein, & Nuechterlein, 1991).

Parental communication deviance measured immediately before release from the hospital seems moderately correlated with relapse within a 1-year follow-up period. Hence, this deviance could be conceived of as an environmental stressor after discharge. Whether this deviance is a genetically transmitted cognitive deficit remains to be seen (Velligan, Miller, Eckert, & Vanderburg, 1996). Clearly, there is greater allusive thinking among parents of schizophrenic patients than controls that may be related to another parental risk factor, expressed emotions (Catts, McConaghy, Ward, & Fox, 1993). There is a definite association between being related to a schizophrenic and manifesting a subclinical thought disorder (Romney, 1990).

More specifically, there is substantial evidence that nonschizophrenic parents of schizophrenic patients as a group demonstrate subtle cognitive difficulties in the area of concept formation and maintenance, as well as other cognitive anomalies awaiting further specification (Docherty, 1994).

Absence of a pathologic affective style seems associated with a benign outcome in schizophrenia spectrum disorders. Adolescents whose parents both show a pathologic affective style of communication and a high level of communication deviance could develop schizophrenia-like disorders in young adulthood. Adolescents of parents with both lower levels of communication deviance and a benign affective style seem to have offspring with a healthier outcome (Doane, 1981).

Expressed Emotions (EE). Significant differences in the type of spontaneous fluctuation in skin conductance activity between patients with low and high EE relatives were demonstrated when relatives were present but not when relatives were absent (Sturgeon, 1981). However, relapse seems predicted more effectively by the schizophrenic's previous course of the disorder and by living in a single-parent household than a measure of EE (Parker, Johnston, & Hayward, 1988).

High- and low-EE schizophrenics seem indiscriminable on measures of symptomatology and social adjustment. However, schizophrenics from emotionally overinvolved families were characterized by poorer premorbid adjustment and greater residual symptomatology at discharge than schizophrenics from critical families (Miklowitz, Goldstein, & Falloon, 1983). High EE relatives tend to show higher levels of communication deviance than do low-EE relatives. When high-EE relatives are subdivided according to specific EE attitudes (criticism and/or emotional overinvolvement) those relatives showing emotional overinvolvement seem to exhibit highest levels of communication deviance and were consistently separable from low-EE relatives on the communication deviance measure (Hahlweg, Goldstein, Nuechterlein, & Magana, 1989; Miklowitz, 1986).

High-EE family members may display negative attitudes toward schizophrenics in part because they are exposed to higher levels of unusual or disruptive behavior than low-EE relatives. This explanation suggests a bi-directional, transactional model about the relationship between relatives' EE and patient psychopathology (Rosenfeld, Goldstein, Mintz, & Nuechterlein, 1995).

Some of the above findings have been somewhat contradicted by other research (Brewin, MacCarthy, Duda, & Vaughn, 1991; Mueser, Bellack, Wade, & Sayers, 1993) with variables and inconsistent results that raise questions about the validity of the EE construct, even though schizophrenics tend to recount fewer nonstressful and more stressful memories between high- versus low-EE parents (Cutting & Docherty, 2000).

Substance Abuse. Substance abuse disorders occur in approximately 40% to 50% of schizophrenics. Clinically, these disorders are associated with a variety of negative outcomes in schizophrenia, including incarceration, homelessness, violence, and suicide (Blanchard, Brown, Horan, & Sherwood, 2000).

Families. Risks for schizophrenia and other functional psychoses and schizophrenic-spectrum personality disorders may be significantly higher in relatives of patients with that condition than in relatives of controls (Thaker, Adami, Moran, & Lahti, 1993). Comparison of ages at onset of schizophrenia according to family history reveals that onset is earlier for men than for women (Gorwood, Leboyer, Jay, & Payan, 1995).

Maladaptive parental behavior, above and beyond possible communication deviance, may substantially mediate a significant association between parental and offspring psychiatric symptoms. Parents with psychiatric disorders tend to show higher levels of maladaptive behavior in the household than parents without psychiatric disorders. Maladaptive parental behavior seems, in turn, to be associated with increased offspring risk for psychiatric disorders during adolescence and early adulthood. Most of the youth that experience high levels of maladaptive parental behavior during childhood may have psychiatric disorders during adolescence and early adulthood, whether or not parents had a psychiatric disorder. In contrast, offspring of parents with psychiatric disorders may not be at increased risk for psychiatric disorders unless there was a history of maladaptive behavior in their parents (Johnson, Cohen, Kasen, et al., 2001).

The relationship between a family history of alcoholism and alcoholism in schizophrenics seems significant for women but not for men. Among schizophrenics with alcoholism, a positive family history of alcoholism seems associated with more severe alcoholism and with the use of other drugs. These patients may respond less well to alcholism treatment than patients with a negative family history of alcoholism (Noordsy, Drake, Biesanz, McHugo, et al., 1994).

Siblings. There seems to be some concordance of sibling pairs of schizophrenics for auditory hallucinations, paranoid delusions, formal thought disorder, or presence of positive or negative symptoms. A strong tendency for the presence of an affective component of schizophrenia to segregate in their siblings is possible. This possibility suggests that schizophrenic patients could be subtyped according to the presence or absence of major depressive episodes and/or affective components of illnesses that satisfy criteria for schizoaffective disorder (DeLisi, Goldin, Maxwell, & Kazuba, 1987).

Marital Status. For both sexes, combined drug and alcohol abusers appear more likely to be divorced than to be married when compared to other groups, chronic pain, defendants in competency-to-stand trial, and applicants fo Social Security Disability payments on psychiatric grounds. Both schiziphrenia and drug and alcohol abuse tend to show differential findings by marital status and by sex, with the likelihood of more mentally ill women then men being married. The excess of married women in emotionally ill populations may relate to a fit between emotional assets and social roles available that may not be greatly affected by treatment-seeking actions (Reich & Thompson, 1985).

SELFHOOD AND COMORBIDITY

In the past, comorbidity of psychiatric conditions was considered the exception rather than the rule. Nowadays, comorbidity seems the rule rather than the exception, especially but not exclusively among personality disorders (Chs. 7, 8, and 9), identity-differention (Ch. 10), styles in intimate relationships (Ch. 11), and personality propensities discussed in this chapter.

CONCLUSION

The selfhood model has implications not only for classifications of personality and gender differences but also for classifications of personality, couple, family relationships, criminality, and psychopathology.

Chapter 13

Priorities: What Is Really Important?
Model[11]

*"Americans spur one another to accomplish and acquire before
anything else—our national dream holds that industry leads to a
promised land, and nobody wants to miss out on a share of paradise.
When consummating a career does not bring happiness—as it
cannot—few pause to reconsider their assumptions: most redouble their
efforts. The faster they spin the occupational centrifuge, the more its
high-velocity whine drowns out the wiser whisper of their own hearts*
(Lewis, Amini, & Lannon, 2000, p. 206)."
"Life is a balancing act (Anonymous)."

BEER

A professor stood before his Philosophy 101 class and had some items in front of him.
When the class began, wordlessly, he picked up a very large and empty mayonnaise jar
and proceeded to fill it with golf balls. He then asked the students if the jar was full?
They agreed that it was. So the professor then picked up a box of pebbles and poured
them into the jar. He shook the jar lightly. The pebbles, of course, rolled into the open
spaces between the golf balls. He then asked the students again if the jar was full. They
agreed it was. The professor picked up a box of sand and poured it into the jar. Of
course, the sand filled up everything else. He then asked once more if the jar was full.
The students agreed with a unanimous—yes! The professor then produced two cans
of beer from under the table and proceeded to pour the entire contents in to the jar
effectively filling the empty space between the sand. The students laughed.

"Now," the professor said, as the laughter subsided, "I want you to recognize that
this jar represents your life. The golf balls are the important things—your family, your
partner, your health, your children, your friends, your favorite passions—things that if

305

everything else was lost and only they remained, your life would still be full." "The pebbles are the other things that matter like your job, your house, your car. The sand is everything else—the small stuff!" "If you put the sand into the jar first," he continued, "there is no room for the pebbles or the golf balls. The same goes for your life. If you spend all your time and energy on the small stuff, you will never have room for the things that are important to you. Pay attention to the things that are critical to your happiness. Play with your children. Take time to get medical checkups. Take your partner out dancing. Play another 18 holes. There will always be time to go to work, clean the house, give a dinner party and fix the disposal." "Take care of the golf balls first—the things that really matter. Set your priorities. The rest is just sand." One of the students raised her hand and inquired what the beer represented. The professor smiled. "I'm glad you asked. It just goes to show you that no matter how full your life may seem, there's always room for a couple of beers!!!! (Anonymous)."

This chapter connects most if not all that has been considered in the previous chapters into one single construct of priorities that derives directly from the selfhood model reviewed in the previous chapter. The construct of priorities implies how we balance intimate and nonintimate relationships, as well as the modalities of Being, Doing, and Having (Model[8]) according to how important they are to us. Priorities are part of this theory because they are relevant to how importance is exchanged within individuals themselves, between and among individuals, and between individuals and objects in settings. From the resource of importance, it is possible to differentiate what modalities, individuals, and settings are selectively important.

This model is motivational in nature and similar to "goals" in the work of other theorists (Carver & Scheier, 1999). Priorities pertain to choices we make about who and what is important in our lives. How important is a person, an object, or an activity? How important is one's self in relationship to other selves? In a way, the selfhood model is another way to look at priorities. However, the priorities model goes beyond selfhood. It also includes settings and contexts within each setting. One setting can be enhanced or reduced in importance by increasing or decreasing the importance of other settings. For example, pleasurable activities in the leisure area can become direct antidotes for the negative effects of stresses at work or at home. How one juggles and counterbalances demands and difficulties in maintaining balance in one's life reflects one's priorities. Priorities motivate people to negotiate with themselves and with significant others important issues in their lives. By the same token, narrow and confused or dysfunctional priorities may motivate avoidance of any intimacy and negotiation. Sober and Wilson (1998), in addition to their distinct contribution to the whole dimension of altruism-egotism, distinguished between instrumental and ultimate desires. Instrumental desires are equated here with survival priorities, while ultimate desires are equated with enjoyment priorities (see Table 13.1)

Apparently, the family may seem of limited importance in the ordering of events in the life cycle. However, the manner in which one spends the years of late adolescence and early adulthood is critical to the ordering of those events. For instance, college attendance may delay marriage but not by a sufficient amount of time to prevent substantial numbers of men from marrying prior to completion of their education. Military service may be a disruptive factor but its effects are less deleterious in peace- than in wartimes. Men who order events in a manner deviant from the norm tend to experience higher rates of marital disruption than other men who order events more normatively. These data seem to support the construct of priorities to the extent that the ordering of events in the life course is "a contingency of some importance in the life cycle (Hogan, 1978, p. 573)."

THE NATURE OF PRIORITIES

Priorities can be classified according to at least four dimensions: (1) short versus long term, as would be the case of immediacy versus delay, as reviewed in Chapter 8; (2) realistic versus unrealistic, relating to whether priorities are based on Being, Doing, and Having (Ch. 9) or to fantasies and pipedreams; (3) individual- versus other-centered, as reviewed in Chapter 12; and (4) successful versus unsuccessful priorities, as conceived whether one's priorities were obtained at no cost to anyone or at the expense of someone else.

In addition to this classification, undoubtedly with a great deal of overlap among them, priorities relate first to whether they are necessary to survival versus enjoyment. Survival refers to work and earning a wage to provide for the physical needs of self and intimate others. Enjoyment refers to how much pleasure one gets from whatever activity one may perform, including enjoyment from relaxing and doing nothing with self and intimate others.

Second, vertical priorities refer to how one deals with self, intimates, others, parents, partner, children, relatives, friends, neighbors, acquaintances, and strangers, constituting the breath of one's social network (Reis, Clark, & Homes, 2004), according to love (Ch. 7) and negotiation (Ch. 8).

Third, horizontal priorities refer to settings (Ch. 5): home, school/work, leisure-time activities, transit, and transitory divided into survival versus enjoyment.

Fourth, priorities refer to how one is going to use the component resources included in the ERAAwC Model[1] (Ch. 4), namely: (1) *E*motionality: disclosure versus nondisclosure, expression versus nonexpression, sharing versus. nonsharing, positive versus negative, as discussed further in

Chapter 16; (2) *R*ationality; use versus nonuse, primacy versus nonprimacy, overlap or non-overlap with *E* and *A*; (3) *A*ctivity, that could be disruptive versus non-destructive, helpful versus hurtful, as referred in the classification above; (4) *Aw*areness, referring to its intrusion versus rejection of *Aw*, acceptance versus refusal to deal with *Aw*, with overuse versus underuse of *Aw*; and (5) *C*ontext, which refers to its denial versus its *Aw*, valuing versus dismissal of *C*.

Fifth, refers to practical, reality oriented priorities like grooming (clothes, appearance), shopping, playing versus nonplaying.

Sixth, refers to duties and obligations versus pleasure (Abramson & Pinkerton, 2002), as achieved in at least 15 realms of abilities: aesthetic, physical and kinesthetic, erotic and sexual, spiritual, emotional, cognitive-intellectual, musical-auditory, visual, mathematical, and practical, among others contained in a workbook (Appendix A).

TYPES OF PRIORITIES

These priorities can be measured easily by time analysis. How much time does one spend in each setting? What modality of expression for Being, Doing, or Having is being used in a primary, secondary, and tertiary manner? Of course, Being is much more relevant to the home setting than Doing and Having at work. The latter modelities are more relevant and primary at work and in leisure settings. How important are Being, Doing, and Having? Are other selves more important than ourself? How are these priorities evaluated? If this is the case, why and how are they important? As shown in the selfhood model, individuals choose how self relates with other selves. However, the selfhood model needs to be expanded and specified further. At this point, one can see that, thus far, all models in this theory are sequential expansions of previously presented models. One model builds on a previous one. The leaves of the artichoke are being pealed off, one at a time.

Priorities can be divided into *vertical* and *horizontal*. Vertical priorities can be differentiated into the three modalities of Being, Doing, and Having. Family and interpersonal priorities are ranked according to the relative importance given to self and significant others. Vertical priorities are developmental, horizontal priorities are structural. The latter exist regardless of a person's level of development. One may value Doing more than Having or Being, stressing the work setting at the expense of the home and leisure settings. This emphasis, for instance, could define the great American workaholic man or woman. By the same stereotypic token, of course, a woman may be described by her stress on Being present emotionally in the home.

Work and leisure settings may be considered secondary to her emotional availability. In other words, vertical and horizontal priorities intersect and interact with each other to produce different outcomes.

How successful one is in any of these settings depends a great deal on one's priorities. If one defines oneself primarily in occupational terms, obtaining a sense of importance from one's job ("I am an engineer") rather than domestically ("I am a partner and a parent"), it follows that that person may spend more time and energy at work than at home. By the same token, avocational pursuits may overshadow domestic and occupational roles. There is a need to balance modalities and settings so that no one modality or setting is stressed at the expense of the others.

PRIORITIES AND AWARENESS (*Aw*): A HIERARCHY OF PRIORITIES

Some priorities are automatic, outside the realm of *Aw*. Other priorities are completely conscious and within the realm of *Aw*, including pleasant and unpleasant memories (Bargh & Chartrand, 1999; Gollwitzer, 1999; Kirsch & Lynn, 1999: Wegner & Wheatley, 1999). Within this dimension, defined by automatic/nonconscious *Aw* at one end and by intentional/conscious *Aw* at the other end, there is a whole hierarchy of possible choices or priorities. The choices we make are based on how important the content or process of that choice is to us. Salience and satisfaction derived from each modality and setting remain an individual prerogative that determines how each modality and setting is ranked in respect to how important other modalities are.

Primary priorities are automatic and outside of the realm of individual *Aw*. They are called *primary* because they develop earlier in the life cycle than secondary ones. Consequently, they are more difficult to change, like one's ability to be close or distant and the ability to negotiate or not to negotiate. *Secondary* priorities are semiautomatic and somewhat within the realm of individual *Aw*, depending, of course, on how wide and deep *Aw* is, varying a great deal from one individual to another. *Tertiary* priorities are within the realm of *Aw* and within the conscious regulation of the individual. They become voluntary and intentional. *Quartic* priorities consist of routine, everyday behaviors that are taken for granted, as a matter of course, like brushing one's teeth, taking a shower, etc. This hierarchy of priorities is similar to the one proposed by Carver and Scheier (1999) regarding goals, a notion that is conceptually similar to priorities but more difficult to evaluate.

Ease of change is greater with quartic realities and decreases going up this hierarchy. It is easier to change how one brushes one's teeth or takes a shower than to change developmentally produced, lifelong habits that have been established automatically since early age, as in the case of approach versus avoidance and discharge versus delay processes, Secondary, semiautomatic priorities include the modalities of Being, Doing or Having, where, normatively speaking, Being is balanced with Doing and Having. Dysfunctionalties develop when Doing > Having or Being, or Having > Doing or Being. If economic survival is the major priority, Doing and Having would be the only necessary modalities. However, if enjoyment is an added goal, then Being emotionally present to self and others needs to be added as an additional priority.

Voluntary, intentional, tertiary priorities include the ERAAwC model. Normatively, there are various choices available, each with its pros and cons, as, for instance, in $E > R$ or A; $R > E$ or A; $A > R$ or E; $R > A$ or E. For instance, emphasis on R at the expense of E may lead toward obsessive-compulsive disorders. Emphasis on A at the expense of E or R may lead toward impulsive or driven behavior. Emphasis on E at the expense of R or Aw may lead toward hysteric moods and episodes. Additionally, within each component of this model, there are choices to be made according to which priority is relevant. For instance, within E one must choose between disclosure versus nondisclosure, expression versus nonexpression, processing versus nonprocessing, sharing versus nonsharing, positive versus negative expression. Within R, one can choose whether to use versus nonuse, primacy versus nonprimacy in relationship to E and A. Within A one must choose whether to be destructive versus nondestructive, helpful versus hurtful. Within Aw one needs to choose whether to allow Aw: intrusion versus rejection, acceptance versus refusal; overuse versus underuse or disuse. Within C one can choose between its denial versus its awareness of C, valuing versus dismissing it. Of course, many individuals do not feel they have choices concerning these components. Again, it depends on what is most important to them in terms of their level of differentiation in likeness, interpersonal style, and personality propensity.

Within this level of tertiary conscious choices are *vertical* priorities pertaining to the self, others, parents, partner, children, relatives, friends, and neighbors, and horizontal priorities relevant to settings, pertaining to home, school/work, and leisure-time activities. These priorities are related to the Likeness Continuum by being differentiated and functional within the middle (see Chapter 10), and undifferentiated and dysfunctional toward the two sides of the distribution.

Quartic priorities consist of everyday, routine habits necessary for self-preservation, self-presentation, and self-survival. Attainment of priorities at a higher level begins with completion of priorities at lower levels going up

Table 13.1. Toward a Hierarchy of Priorities: At What Level of Observation and Interpretation?*

1. Processes	
Survival	Enjoyment
Instrumental	Ultimate**/Expressive
Discharge-Delay	Approach-Avoidance
2. Contents	**Experiencing**
Money/Goods/Services/Information	Importance/Intimacy
Having Doing	Being
3. Horizontal (Settings)	**Vertical (Self-Others)**
Power	Presence
Negotiation	Being Together
4. Resources	**ERAAwC**

5. Differentiation: Continuum of likeness and derived styles in intimate relationships.

6. Selfhood: Personality Propensities
7. Distance Regulation'
8. Intimacy

*Adapted from L'Abate & De Giacomo, 2003. Reprinted with permission.
**From Sober & Wilson, 1998.

on the hierarchy. For instance, if the major priority is to advance at work and work is more important than family, then brushing one's teeth, taking a shower, and presenting oneself in acceptable clothes fitting the setting and tasks to be accomplished at work could be the beginning preparation even before going to work. One may not devote too much time and energy at self-presentation if home and family have a different priority. At work, getting along with coworkers and fulfilling well superiors' requests would be another level of attainment. Asking for extra assignments could be another way to enhance oneself, etc. If too much time and energy are expended at work, there may not be sufficient time and energy to devote to one's family, home, and leisure-time activities. A tentative classification of a hierarchy of priorities is summarized in Table 13.1.

The issue of priorities is involved in the next and last models, where one needs to choose whether E is more important than R or other components of the ERAAwC model, and whether reliance on E is made at the expense of the other four components of the model. Functionality is present when there is a balance of all five components. Dysfunctionality is present when just one component is used at the expense of the others.

EVIDENCE SUPPORTING THIS MODEL

There are quite a few constructs that are conceptually similar to this model but that are independent from it. Among the many available, the more relevant are: (1) goals; (2) intentions; (3) values; (4) attitudes; (5) needs or wants; and (6) beliefs.

Goals

There is a great deal of independent evidence that is conceptually similar to the model. For instance, the construct of *goals* has been used repeatedly (Carver & Scheier, 1999; Sanderson, 2004). However, these goals (like self-esteem) are a-theoretical in the sense that they are not part of any specific theory. They form a hierarchical framework where the term "goals" is still identified with the "importance" of an action. Once goals are described, one still needs to prioritize them. How is one going to do that except on the basis of the importance of the goal? Apparently, people seem aware of personal goals and satisfactions to guide their behavior (Wadsworth & Ford, 1983). However, this awareness does not seem related to any other factors.

Intentions

Explanations of intentional actions require teleological characteristics that cannot be explained superficially by past causal theories (Daveney, 1974). Of course, intentions versus nonintentions is a major variable in attributions of responsibility for actions (Anthony, 1978). However, intensions, like goals, lack a connection with theories of personality or of intimate relationships (Malle, Moses, & Baldwin, 2001). According to these authors, social interaction requires social cognition—the ability to perceive, interpret, and explain the actions of others. This ability relies fundamentally on constructs of intention and intentionality. For example, people distinguish sharply between intentional versus unintentional behavior, identifying intentions underlying others' behavior, and explaining completed actions with reference to internal states or traits, intentions, beliefs, and desires. Gibbs (2001), however, differs from other views that intentions reside "inside" individuals. He sees intentions as emerging from interactions between individuals or between individuals and objects in their environment, supporting the position taken here that relationships emerge from and produce other relationships.

If intentions guide behavior and interactions with intimate others, then, like goals, one needs to construct a hierarchy of intentions to guide or to justify one's actions according to their importance, hence, the need to include intentions in an overarching, supraordinate framework.

Values

Values have many similarities with priorities (Lewis, 1990; Schwartz, 1996). Lewis (1990) makes values synonymous with personal evaluation and related beliefs, especially related to the "good," the "just," and the "beautiful." These beliefs propel us to action, to a particular kind of behavior and life (p. 7). They underlie actions and behavior, and, therefore, intimate relationships:

> "There are some basic choices, some uniform options that we are all faced with. The very interesting task that we face as human beings is to identify these options and then to choose among them, not blindly but with a discerning eye, and thus to answer the recurring biblical question 'What manner of men and women shall we be?' (p. 5)."

Lewis identified 74 value systems but differentiated them according to whether they are based on: (1) sense experience, (2) logic, (3) emotion, (4) intuition, (5) authority, or (6) science. There can be two kinds of "basic" values, hedonistic and legalistic (Glasser & Glasser, 1977). Values may be consistent or inconsistent with each other for people who put pleasure before legality, such as with drug addicts. For people who put legality before pleasure, there may not be any conflict.

Patients (hospitalized adolescents and their parent) seemed to score significantly worse than controls on the part of a scale of values (Hartman Value Profile) that relates subjective items to judgments about oneself and one's function in the world. Mothers of both depressed and schizophrenic adolescents tend to score low on self-concepts. All parents apparently may be more consistent and stable than their children in their values and self-concepts. These and other results "... suggest that emotional and mental symptoms and parental attitudes effect the *priorities* [emphasis added] adolescents choose in making value comparisons (Tucker, 1976, p. 549)."

Attitudes

Attitudes are supposed to relate to how we behave. However, there may be a gap between theory and research, with a relative neglect of theoretical formulations (Petersen & Dutton, 1975). Unless considered as part of a larger theoretical framework, attitudes may be another ubiquitous construct that, like self-esteem, hopelessness, helplessness, and other ad hoc constructs or models, lacks an underlying theoretical structure.

Attitudes of parents in regard to high use of punishment and low use of reason may be found in families characterized by high interspouse hostility. A high use of rewards and punishments could be found in parents who scored highly on attitudes of interspousal protectiveness-assertiveness. Promotion of dependent behavior might be found in families where parents are high on general hostility-pugnacity. An emerging pattern in a continuum of attitudes may range from a constellation of early responsible parental child rearing and low authoritarianism, with a concomitant promotion of independence all the way to an authoritarian control pattern with promotion of dependence. The former pattern was shown more by parents who were low in hostile attitudes and high on interspouse gregariousness (Dickman, Barton, & Cattell, 1977). Hence, one cannot separate attitudes from what one considers important in one's life.

Lower-class mothers seem to differ significantly from the general population of mothers on measures of parental attitudes and internality-externality. The former may tend to be more external in the perceived locus of control, more authoritarian, less hostile and reflective, and more democratic in their self-descriptions (Ramey & Campbell, 1976). Hence, attitudes may be a function of SES as well as gender and education.

Needs or Wants

Kasser (2002) classified needs and wants according to: (1) security, safety, and sustenance; (2) self-worth, esteem, and competence; (3) connectedness and belonging; and (4) autonomy, freedom, and authenticity. In spite of their respective similarity to constructs of this theory to serve as possible genotypes for describing relationships, it remains to be seen how these needs and wants are related to priorities as defined here.

Beliefs

Eidelson and Eidelson (2003) identified five dangerous belief domains (selected from a review of the literature and by nomination from "experts") that lead to conflict: superiority, injustice, vulnerability, distrust, and helplessness. How these domains derive from research, rather than expert opinion, remains to be seen.

BALANCING WORK AND FAMILY LIFE

A great deal has been written about the difficulties of balancing work with home, but only one recent reference can be cited. When work, homelife, and purpose are proposed, a person should ask: "Where is the balance?" (Bonebright, Clay, & Ankenman, 2000). This question needs to be addressed not by highly abstract models, like the present one, but by how real people make real choices. Hence, there is little that can be added to that literature except to present a survey that allows us to distinguish between ideal and real priorities. In a way, rankings given above could be considered as ideal. Very few people follow them to the letter. It is much more important to find how real people really rank their priorities.

Demographic Data

Sources for the State of the Family survey included the U.S. Census 2000, data collected by First Things First, which surveyed 1,000 people, and Wirthling Worldwide, which surveyed 600 respondents. The organization also used a report on risky behaviors among Hamilton County teens released in October 2002. A summary of findings in the State of the Family 2003 report provided these data: Children born and raised outside of marriage will spend an average of 51% of their childhood in poverty. In contrast, a child born and raised by both parents in an intact marriage will spend an average of 7% of their childhood in poverty.   In addition, a child living with a single mother is 14 times more likely to suffer serious physical abuse, and a child living with a single mother and man who is not the biological father is 33 times more likely to suffer physical abuse.

Putman (2003), for instance, reported the results of a survey in Hamilton County (Chattanooga, Tennessee) that rated children, faith, and health ahead of spouse. Respondents ranked the most important priorities as part of the State of the Family 2003 report as follows: (1) family; (2) faith; (3) children; (4) career/work; (5) health; (6) money/finance; (7) hobbies/leisure; (8) getting ahead in life; (9) marriage/spouse; and (10) school. Hamilton County residents, therefore, ranked their families as the most important priority in their lives, but placed marriage ninth after getting ahead in life, leisure, and money: (1) 54% of Hamilton County residents believe that if the traditional family unit falls apart, the stability of American society will collapse; (2) 70% believe the typical marriage today is weaker than the typical marriage 30 years ago; (3) 69% agree that, in most cases, children who are raised in a home with both of their natural parents will grow up to be more stable emotionally than children raised by one parent.

A Plan to Identify Priorities in Families

Butchorn (1978) presented a conceptual framework for working with problem-ridden, crisis-prone families. Family structure and interaction processes that attempt to meet the needs of family members are viewed as the key components of this framework. The structure of a family is assessed in four areas: (1) self-concept; (2) roles: (3) rules; and (4) boundaries.

Communicating, parenting, and coping are seen as the essential processes to be evaluated in their effectiveness in meeting the needs of a family. As intuitively appealing as this framework may be it is a first attempt to measure "family priorities." Unfortunately, it lacks empirical or experiential support from sources external to its author.

FUNCTIONS OF THIS MODEL

This model allows an integration of disparate motivational constructs like "goals," "intentions," "values," and "psychological needs" or wants under the rubric of importance. We become involved in what is most important to us first to postpone less important matters. Diagnostically, we need to ask: "What are your priorities?" "What is most important to you and what is less important to you?" Asking to rank-order these priorities is also an important assignment to give as homework. Prescriptively one needs to: "Balance your horizontal and vertical priorities." That is, one needs to balance home with work, survival and enjoyment tasks with leisure-time activities and even no activity.

CONCLUSION

If goal theorists, as well as other theorists of intentions, values, attitudes, beliefs, needs, and wants were to use the construct of importance as underlying their constructs, then their conceptualizations would become much more closely related to the present model of priorities.

Part V

Applications of the Theory

The chapters in this part are natural extensions and expansions of models reviewed earlier, and especially the four previous models. Chapter 14, for instance, is an extension and expansion of Chapter 7. Chapter 15 is an extension and expansion of Chapters 10 and 11. Chapter 16 is an extension and expansion of many previous chapters and especially Chapter 12. Chapter 17 is based on all the models of the theory, with Chapter 18 including an overall general model that includes all the models of the theory, and another model comparing selfhood (Ch. 12) with models extraneous to the theory itself, circumplex, attachment, elementary pragmatic, family paradigms, and family types.

The sequence and numbering of models followed in this part differs somewhat from the sequence and numbering of models presented in a previous publication (L'Abate & De Giacomo, 2003). Chapter 17, on negotiating and problem solving, for instance, is placed at the end of Part V rather than in the middle of these applications.

Chapter 14

Distance Regulation
Model[12]

This chapter presents a model of distance regulation between and among intimate relationships. At first blush, this model would seem to derive directly from the assumption of space (Ch. 7). On the contrary, it is also derived from assumptions of space and time (Ch. 8), because to learn to regulate distance among intimates and nonintimates involves not only approach-avoidance tendencies, but also how fast (discharge) and how slow (delay) those tendencies are expressed.

MODELS OF DISTANCE REGULATION

Supposedly, the therapeutic literature abounds with unidimensional models of pursuer/distancer (Santelli, Bernstein, Zborowski, & Bernstein, 1990), or "demand/withdrawal" (Berns, Jacobson, & Gottman, 1999a, 1999b) or rejection/intrusion (Betchen, 1991). Apparently pursuing and distancing seem to be semi-independent constructs sharing variance with assertiveness, sensation-seeking, introversion-extraversion, and sex roles. Locus of control (internal versus external) and neuroticism may be significantly related to pursuing and distancing in Asians, who seem to pursue less and distance more than American respondents (Santelli et al., 1990).

Early models of "enmeshment" and "cohesion" seemed concerned with self/other differentiation. More recent models favored a "spatial metaphor" that stressed "closeness-distance." According to Green and Werner (1996) self-other differentiation and closeness-distance are different classes of behavior. Instead, they suggested two separate dimensions: (1) intrusiveness, which includes coercive control, separation anxiety, possessiveness/

jealousy, emotional reactivity, and projective identification; and (2) closeness-caregiving, which includes warmth, time together, nurturance, physical intimacy, and consistency. Both dimensions seem extremely similar to those presented here, distance (Ch. 7) for closeness-caregiving, and control (Ch. 8) for intrusiveness. By the same token, closeness/caregiving may relate to being present, while intrusiveness may relate to power (Ch. 9). Bakan's (1968) differentiation of communal and agentic relationships seems to be the foundation of both dimensions.

Demand-withdrawal seems a pattern in couples with a violent husband. Interaction patterns of such couples usually are compared to distressed couples without violence, and to happily married, nonviolent couples. Both batterers and battered women seemingly show less positive and more negative communication than their nonviolent counterparts. Batterers seem to show significantly higher levels of both demanding and withdrawing than did the other men. Battered women demanded more changes than did women in nonviolent marriages. However, they seemed significantly less inclined to withdraw than their husbands (Berns, Jacobson, & Gottman, 1999a, 1999b).

More specifically, wives who pursue and husbands who withdraw during marital conflict do not seem to differ between distressed and nondistressed couples. Distressed husbands seem to show the highest proportion of anxious effects (Turgeon, Julien, & Dion, 1998).

A MODEL OF DISTANCE REGULATION[12]

Instead of a single dimension, as stressed by models reviewed above, however, the model presented in this chapter supports a tripartite perspective composed of three roles: pursuer/distancer/regulator. Although the pursuer wants to approach, and the distancer wants to avoid, there is a third role to consider and that is, individuals who want to approach or want to be approached, but who then either withdraw, or make the partner withdraw. In this fashion, distance regulators control the relationship: "Come here, go away," Help me, I need you, but your help did not help me."

How to Regulate Distance and Create Dysfunctionality

The pursuer wants and needs to approach, asking the partner for sex or just wanting to be emotionally close with the spoken or unspoken but nonverbal injunction to: "Come closer, sexually or emotionally or both," or "I want to be close to you because I love you so much, you are beautiful," etc.

The distancer, instead, uses verbal and nonverbal injunction to: "Go away," "I am not interested (for whatever reason)," "I have a headache," "I am busy," "I am tired," etc.

The regulator, on the other hand, uses both injunctions sequentially, contradictorily, and inconsistently: "Come closer, I want you, I need you, please help me," with "I do not need you, I do not want you, please go away, you did not help me, or you did not give what I want or need," "You are inefficient, lazy, impotent, inept," etc. Hence, one way to discount the original injunction for closeness is contradicted by blaming the one who does want closeness and wants to help. Examples of this particular role abound in Sheffield's (2003) impressionistic account of tactics used with intimate others by depressed individuals.

It should be made clear that the same individual could well play all three roles, depending on the nature of the situation. For instance, a partner may want emotional closeness but deny or reject sexual relationships. By the same token, a partner may be playing the role of regulator in the sexual arena but assume a distancer role emotionally. Once this rotating function is present, one can see how confusing and mystifying this triangle can be in intimate relationships. If and when a partner or family member monopolizes one specific role, greater confusion and mystification could occur in the whole system.

Parties' reactions in this model not only rely on distance but also on control. These reactions could be quick or slow, fast or delayed, but they do occur reactively. Hence, this model is found more often primarily in intimate relationships characterized by latent or overt conflict.

Three Clinical Examples

Since literature on the role of distance regulator is missing, I will rely on clinical experience and written reports of respondents who completed the specifically designed assignment in the original workbook on depression for couples and families (L'Abate, 1986; L'Abate et al., 1992), and who elaborated on these reports in f2f talks with me as therapist. Admittedly, clinical experience to validate this model as an application of the two dimensions subsumed by them, distance and control, is unreliable. However, it is a beginning step toward finding more reliable ways to identify, validate, or invalidate the validity of this model.

A Frigid Housewife

This woman was a responsible and in some ways a responsive, if not some-time intrusive, mother. Premaritally, however, she had been in treatment for depression stemming from her family background. She was born in an immigrant family where her mother, in her native country, had been severely abused and deprived by the family of her husband. He had immigrated to the United States to escape military conscription and to look for more financially secure work. After coming to the United States, once her husband recalled her, and after experiencing the death of her first child in her native country, without any emotional or financial support from her husband's family, the mother gave birth to two daughters. One eventually became severely obese, never marrying, while the second sought escape in reading, listening to music, and eventually being the first one in her generation, from the immigrant community where they lived, to attend and graduate from college.

She reported that her mother was subject to extreme explosions of rage on an almost monthly basis, blaming the husband continuously for having left her in the clutches of his family who had severely abused and deprived her in their native country. These repeated recriminations, among others, was a theme that pervaded the family atmosphere as long as the mother lived. The mother, apparently, never forgave the husband for having abandoned her to the abuse of his family. The father, either ignored these recriminations or discounted them by laughing and immersing himself in working 16-hour days at his business. As a result, the underlying hurts in the mother, which also affected the daughters severely, were never resolved.

The second daughter dated in college but was extremely avoidant of sex until after her 30s, when, while being in therapy, she initiated a brief affair, without love, to experiment with the brother of her best friend in college. After marriage, some of the patterns in the family of origin persisted. She continued to collect alleged, imaginary, or real hurts from her husband, avoiding his frequent requests for sex by using her busyness with the two children as an excuse. Eventually, during therapy, this pattern of monthly recriminations and explosions against her husband were decreased by medication. However, in therapy she remained adamant in not discussing her sexuality, while her husband accused her of faking orgasms throughout their marriage and being essentially frigid, never reporting whether she had reached an orgasm, while she accused her husband of being sexually inept.

The distance regulator role came eventually but clearly to the fore during the last part of the couple's therapy, after her monthly upsets subsided. She usually became angry at the husband the day after they had had a handful of sexual intercourses in so many months. Even though she denied this pattern, the husband was able to produce a calendar where he had monitored and registered when they had had intercourse and when she had become enraged at him the day after. Since she adamantly continued to refuse to talk about sex or sexuality, or to travel with him, continuing to blame the husband for whatever was wrong in their marriage, therapy was discontinued.

Eventually, the husband, left with a no-win situation and with an edict from the wife that there should not be any more sex or travel in the marriage, eventually moved out, divorced her, and married a woman who apparently satisfied him sexually and otherwise. She retaliated by forbidding her two children to have anything to do with the new wife of their father under penalty of excluding them and their children from her will.

The College Professor

This middle-aged man had been divorced twice. The first time, he divorced his supposedly alcoholic wife, and the second time, he was divorced when his second wife was discovered being unfaithful to him. He eventually started to date a former, younger student who had divorced her first husband for his continued emotional distancing and unavailability. In this pair, the distance regulator role was repeated again and again throughout the 1-year relationship with this partner. He would compliment her, bring her flowers, take her gifts with additional offers of financial support and travels, prompting the partner to come very close to him, emotionally and physically.

However, as soon as she got too close for his comfort, he would discount her by either finding something wrong with her ("You are too lazy") or demanding that she change diet to sooth his veritable obsessions with eating "healthy" food. Once she distanced herself by not returning his phone calls or talk to him, and he would try to amend his fault-finding or corrective behavior by offering sincere apologies for what he had said, promising to avoid making negative comments about her or expect her to change her diet to soothe him. He would then use more bribes (flowers, gifts, travel, promises of money) to get her back, only to resume the same pattern of criticisms and diet injunctions as soon as she fell into these seductive but abusive practices. After 1-year of this repeated pattern that produced oppositional-distance-producing, avoidant maneuvers on the partner's part, she severed this relationship completely. She then decided to marry an old college sweetheart who was waiting in the wings for her, and apparently loved her regardless of her "laziness" or culinary excesses.

Both cases illustrate different patterns where either sexuality or intimacy are avoided at various levels of functioning, personal and intimate. In the next case, there may have been an *unwillingness* to become intimate rather than an *inability* to become intimate.

A Millionairess

This woman was not only rich, but she was also beautiful and intelligent. She, her previous husband, and their children had been in therapy intermittedly for about 10-years with various therapists. After divorcing her husband (with a hefty settlement for him), she embarked on a series of affairs with a number of men, whom she found initially attractive enough to sleep, socialize, and travel with, but, who, eventually, were found wanting on a variety of grounds: "boring," "sexually inept," "not matching her annual income," "different social class," or "not belonging to the financial elite," which she was frequently accociated with socially. Most of them she brought into therapy with her to see how they fit into her overall perspective.

Eventually, after the breakup with the last lover, and after administering a Minnesota Multiphasic Personality Inventory-2 (MMPI-2), she demonstrated a psychopathic deviate score in the 90th percentile, talk therapy was discontinued. Treatment consisted solely of administering her weekly assignments from the Social Training workbook that had been developed years earlier for the specific purpose of lowering impulsivity in criminals (L'Abate, 1992, 1996; McMahan & L'Abate, 2001). She completed this workbook in about 6 months at a distance, by mailing completed assignments and receiving feedback on each assignment through the mail once a week. During this time, she avoided almost completely any new sexual encounters. On retest with the MMPI-2, she scored in the 50th percentile in the PD scale. As a result, she wanted her children to follow the same kind of treatment, but they were not interested. At this point therapy was discontinued. She eventually married a successful professional in the same income bracket and similar social circles. A follow-up after a few years found her happy and satisfied with her life.

FUNCTIONS OF THIS MODEL

This model has a somewhat more integrative role in intimate relationships than dichotomous models summarily reviewed at the beginning of this chapter, because it adds a third role not considered in those models. Diagnostically, one needs to find out how close or distant respondents are with intimates and nonintimates. Some respondents are able to get closer with strangers than with loved ones. Some want to be extremely close but for whatever reason select partners who are unable to become close. How entrenched, specialized, or rigid are these roles? How consistently or inconsistently are they played?

Prescriptively, one needs to evaluate the underlying factors involved in the distancing. Are they intergenerational, as in the case of the housewife? Are they personal, being repeated from one relationship to another, as in the case of the college professor? Or are they situational, as in the case of the millionaire woman? If the underlying antecedents, if not causes, can be pinpointed, using either a Depression workbook, an Intimacy workbook, or other workbooks to help respondents deal with dependency and codependency may be appropriate (Appendix A).

Therapeutically, one needs to assess how intrenched and rigid this triangle is in a relationship. Combination of repeated role playing of all three parts in the professional's office with administration of any of the workbooks suggested above or other workbooks more specific to individual and relational dynamics may be appropriate.

CONCLUSION

The model presented here lacks empirical support and is based strictly on my clinical observations of couples and families. It should be evaluated by others impressionistically at first, but, eventually, if found valid in the clinic, a more specific and repeatable way to evaluate it will be necessary to either support or invalidate this model.

Chapter 15

The Drama Triangle
Model[13]

This chapter presents a universal drama triangle that is responsible for the genesis of dysfunctionality in intimate relationships. This triangle is composed of three roles: the victim, the savior, and the persecutor. In some ways, this model is an expansion of Chapters 10 and 11. However, since both of those chapters are also derived from previous ones and additional models followed, this model contains roles that were not considered in those two chapters.

Variations on these three major parts were developed as part of a depression workbook (L'Abate, 1986, 1996). This triangle is found in many religions, where a pure, perfect savior helps poor, helpless sinners from the evil intents of an infernal entity. In fiction, the Grimm's brothers fairytales, for instance, are egregious variations on the same theme. They are based on someone who is helpless, oppressed, or unable to fend for himself or herself and is helped by some miraculous being, a speaking cat with boots on or a fairy godmother from the effects of another, malignant being, a witch or a monster. The same triangle is found in the alter egos of many dissociative identity disorders (Ross, 1997), where the victim develops protector and persecutor alters. Of course, if one were to extend this analysis to works of fiction, the same triangle would be found operating in many. Unfortunately, this triangle is just as universal and operative in intimate relations and is at the genesis of most if not all dysfunctional relationships.

THE DRAMA TRIANGLE AND DEPENDENCY

An aspect of the relationship between intimacy and selfhood at the expressive level is the differentiation among three roles in intimate relationships.

They have been called the Drama Triangle basic to the development of psychopathology (L'Abate, 1986). Given this Triangle, there are four possible interpersonal roles on how to deal with hurt feelings, when they are avoided through the distraction offered by the first three roles:

1. *Rescuer or savior*, trying to make things better for those who are hurting, often at one's own expense, by not valuing one's own feelings, and valuing others' feelings more than one's own instead, leading to *selflessness*. The rescuer accepts that dependent role uncritically and tries to help the victim. Supposedly, this role would seem independent from the other two, but it is not. Rescuers need and depend on victims to make themselves feel and look good. Without victims there would be no rescuers. Many rescuers are killed in trying to end an argument or a conflict between two individuals, for instance. Variations on this role consist of saviors, therapists, nurses, doctors, and wholesalers among others.

2. *Persecutor* denies, rejects, and even ridicules dependency in both self and others. Inflicting hurts on others, making things worst for them, whether intimates or not intimates, to protect one's feelings and avoid being hurt, leading to *selfishness*. In the persecutor role, one denies and berates dependency, magnifying independence as the position to value and stress, berating both victims and rescuers for their respective helplessness and helpfulness. Most persecutors, as seen in character and personality disorders, especially in Cluster B, tend to deny dependency and see themselves as not needed by others, except their victims. Variations on this role consist of individuals who behave as tyrants, detectives, investigators, and eventually as judges, juries, and executioners.

3. *Martyr, saint*, or *victim*, plays the helpless, dependent role, keeping hurt feelings inside without ever expressing them. The victim role represents the epitome of helplessness and dependency, usually provoking the rescuer to accept the dependency and capitalize on it by being helpful. At the other extreme, some victims explode in a destructive manner, assuming three roles all at the same time, i.e., stoic victim, hateful persecutor, and noble, compassionate savior, leading to *no-self*. Variations on this role consist of: "Poor little me," "I am helpless," "I do not know anything," "I am innocent," "I couldn't help it."

Hence, in this triangle, dependency is pronounced in the victim role, denied in the persecutor role, and accepted in the rescuer role.

All three roles are played out in dysfunctional relationships, with each individual switching from one role to another. The fourth alternative is played out in functional relationships. This is the normalizing role of *self-fulness* by *sharing* hurt feelings with loved ones though crying, hugging, and cuddling together, that is, being together physically and emotionally (L'Abate, 2001b, 2003a) without demands for perfection, production, performance, or problem solving, as discussed at greater length in the next chapter. Sharing hurts means not playing these destructive roles and becoming sane and intimate, a process that happens sometimes between individual respondents and therapists when partners or family members are not included in the therapeutic process.

THE DRAMA TRIANGLE AND ITS INTENSITY

This triangle is usually absent in most functional, i.e., conductively creative, relationships where cooperation, care, sharing of feelings, intimacy, and successful negotiation of issues are present no matter the level of stress.

It may be present in functional relationships under stress or only with selected individuals, i.e., present between partners and repeated intergenerationally in family members. However, in functional relationships if and when this triangle takes place, it is usually temporary and forgotten, and, whatever may have been said in the course of its presence, forgiven. In semifunctional relationships, this triangle may be present in selected areas of functioning, but not in others, e.g., absent in sexual intimacy but present in emotional exchanges. In dysfunctional relationships, this triangle is present in most areas of functioning, regardless of stress level, through specialization and rigidity in roles, i.e., a family member plays persecutor most of the time, while another family member plays rescuer most of the time, with a third one plays victim most of the time. In most cases, each member uses all three roles, rotating from one to the other according to the situation.

VICTIMIZATION AND ITS AFTERMATH

Evidence for the presence of this triangle has been presented in the literature covered in Chapter 11. Just exposure to and witnessing violence, even without direct abuse, may produce problems in adjustment similar to those who have been abused (Jaffe, Wolfe, Wilson, & Zak, 1986). Attitudes toward violence in themselves may mediate self-reported aggression toward others but not about self-victimization. There seems to be a clear link between feeling victimized and aggression toward others (Vernberg, Jacobs, & Hershberger, 1999), supporting the position of this model that would predict switching from the role of victim to the role of persecutor.

Indeed, when middle school children are being maltreated at home, they are more likely to behave as bullies in school. Bullying is even more prevalent among children who have experienced direct acts committed at home, like physical and sexual abuse. Emotional dysregulation may make a unique contribution toward differentiating victims and bullies from children who did not experience bully-victim problems (Shields & Cicchetti, 2001).

More recently, popular literature and the media have stressed the widespread seriousness of bullying in schools, where victims of bullying suffer a great deal of distress and deficits in means-end thinking (Biggam & Power, 1999). Victimization produces coping and adaptation that persists over the entire life span, as already reviewed in Chapter 11. Recovery from victimization evolves through a process of interaction along three dimensions: social cognition, environmental sensitivity, and emotional-behavioral functioning. The meaning of the original trauma made at the time of abuse may influence how the experience will affect the victim in the future. Some children might be better able to interpret a traumatic, emotional event as being contained within the victimization itself, rather than inside the individual (Newberger & DeVos, 1988).

Unfortunately, many women who were sexually abused as children tend to repeat being victimized in the form of falling victims as adults to sexual and physical assault, with devastating effects on their subsequent adjustment. Among the many possible theoretical explanations for this re-victimization (Messman & Long, 1996), one is inclined to use the presence and effects of having developed a reactive-repetitive style, as discussed in Chapter 11.

WHO WILL BE THE RESCUERS?

What is missing here is the presence of rescuers, that is, mental health professionals who must intervene with most victims, since by definition, most persecutors deny needing help. How can mental health professionals help victims and bullies without entering this deadly triangle and becoming rescuers and losing therapeutic effectiveness? The dependency of victims may trigger rescuing efforts on the part of would-be helpers. Those efforts may strengthen and prolong the dependency of victimized individuals. Two possible ways to deal with the anger that makes it possible to deal with the underlying hurts (Davenport, 1991) and avoid strengthening the dependency would be groups and workbooks. Both approaches tend to increase the victims' responsibility to take charge of their lives by becoming more involved, active, and interactive in the treatment process.

FUNCTIONS OF THIS MODEL

This model is integrative of psychopathological processes in the intergenerational rise of dysfunctionality in relationships, as seen especially in Chapters 5, 6, 10, 11, and 12. Diagnostically, it is important to ask "Which part of the triangle do you play best or do you play all three parts well?" Prescriptively, one would suggest that respondents let go of this deadly triangle before it increases the level of distress in intimate relationships. However, before giving up this triangle, respondents may need to become aware of its omnipresence in their dysfunctional relationships. To increase this awareness, they need to repeat it, verbally but not physically, until they are sick of its presence and want more positive ways of interacting. This is why a completely written homework assignment was developed to make couples and families practice this triangle at home until they gave it up after a few repetitions. This triangle is too strong and intense to be eliminated through just talk. Nonetheless, therapeutically, victimized respondents need to share the hurts produced by this triangle, with a minimum of structure in therapy and a maximum of structure in homework assignments.

CONCLUSION

This triangle is deadly and difficult to break before respondents can assume a more constructive and conductive role in their intimate relationships. This is why to help break it one needs to rely on more than just words. This triangle needs to be structured and prescribed in writing to ensure that enough repetition will take place before partners or family members become painfully aware of its deleterious consequences on themselves and on each other. Only after they become aware of this triangle can they decide to give up being part of it. Only after they give it up can they learn to relate with each other in more constructive ways.

Chapter 16

Intimacy: Sharing Hurts and Fears of Being Hurt
Model[14]

". . . emotional support is a basic function of human communication and is as ubiquitous in everyday life as the upsets that occasion its use. At one time or another, all of us are seekers and providers of emotional support (Burleson, 2003, p. 557)."

"Emotions determine the quality of our lives. They occur in every relationship we care about—in the workplace, in our friendships, in dealing with family members, and in our most intimate relationships. They can save our lives, but they can also cause real damage. They may lead us to act in ways that we think are realistic, and appropriate, but our emotions can lead us to act in ways we regret terribly afterward (Ekman, 2003, p. xiii)."

The thesis of this theory is that underlying personality socialization, in whatever setting, there are hurt feelings and fears of being hurt, as discussed throughout this work. Hurts include losses of loved ones, bereavement, and grief, rejections from loved ones, put-downs, sexual, verbal, and physical abuse, including "ambiguous losses," or "negative life events" (Golish & Powell, 2003). This thesis is supported strongly by the work of Bradley (2000), Firestone and Catlett (1999) on affect regulation, Hayes, Strosahl, and Wilson (1999) on affect avoidance, Pennebaker (2001) on traumas and expressive emotions, and Watson (2000) on mood regulation.

This definition of intimacy, therefore, is an extension of previous models, but especially Model[10] (Ch. 12), since many of the applications reviewed here will be linked to that model. Yet, all previous models are necessary to make sense of this one. Hence, as already noted, personality, as defined by characteristics reviewed in previous chapters, is like an artichoke. Underneath the external leaves, appearance, presentational and phenotypic levels, and below them, after passing through its prickly choke of anger and even rage, at the very bottom, lies hurt feelings, the genotypic sublevel already considered in Chapter 5 and linked to one's differentiation in identity (Ch. 10).

These feelings are sometimes solved and resolved in functional relationships. However, when unresolved, i.e., not expressed and shared mutually with intimates, they linger on and influence the development of dysfunctionalities throughout the individual and family life cycle. Before getting to those feelings, however, one must deal with the many leaves that cover and protect them, overcoming the anger and rage that makes it difficult, and, in some cases, impossible, to get to those feelings, especially in hardened criminals and in schizophrenics.

Once intimacy is defined as the sharing of joys and hurts and fears of being hurt (Leary, Springer, Negel, Ansell, & Evans, 1998), it brings it within the realm of *E*, which is differentiated between the internal experience of hurts from people or events on the passive, receptive, input side, that is, feelings, what happens to us, and their active, external expression on the output side (*A*), how we expressed those feelings positively or negatively as emotions, as noted repeatedly in Chapter 4 (Hussong, 2000a, b, c). Two synonyms for feelings are moods and affect (Watson, 2000). Hurt feelings and fears of being hurt, therefore, are the root of our socialization. These feelings are fiercely avoided (repressed, suppressed, denied) at all costs in most dysfunctional, no-self (AA) styles, and somewhat avoided at some cost in semifunctional (RR) styles, including selfish and selfless personality propensities. Mainly in selfful, CC styles it is possible to achieve intimacy (Firestone & Catlett, 1999).

This position is supported conceptually by Bradley (2000) who brings an array of empirical evidence to support it:

> "My thesis is that emotional arousal and the failure to regulate this arousal constitute a general factor in the development, recurrence, and maintenance of various forms of psychopathology. In so-called 'internalizing' disorders, such dysregulation occurs most typically when an individual with heightened stress reactivity becomes stressed. In the 'externalizing' disorders, stress reactivity may be less central to affect dysregulation; a genetic vulnerability to anger and aggressive behavior may instead play the pivotal role (p. vi)."

Hurt feelings are still a taboo topic that has been bypassed or even ignored by some personality theorists as well as by some therapists, as demonstrated in previous publications by L'Abate. This bypassing has been achieved through outright avoidance (Cacioppo & Gardner, 1999; Harter, 1990), and/or stress on other generic feelings (i.e., guilt, shame, fear) and emotions (i.e., anger) or through circumlocutions. Indirect references or synonyms, like distress, trauma, grief, bereavement, or simply "negative feelings," have been used instead. Intimacy, the sharing of joys as well as hurts and of fears to being hurt, has not been considered in many theoretical and therapeutic treatises until recently. We cannot share joys unless we share hurts, just as much we cannot experience the full impact and ecstasy of an orgasm with a loved one unless we have also shared tears.

Hurt feelings underlie most so-called negative emotions. For instance, Suinn (2001) has shown how anger and anxiety are detrimental to physical and mental health. However, as discussed in Chapter 12, anger is an emotion more likely to be found in externalizations, while anxiety is an emotion more likely to be found in internalizations. Fears lie beneath many no-self propensities. Those are the leaves of the artichoke. Underneath anger, anxiety, and fears there are avoided (suppressed, repressed, denied) hurt feelings.

Most, if not all, hurt feelings are produced within the context of the family or intimate relationships. Sharing joys is relatively easy. Anyone in a bar will cheer for your victory, especially if you pay the tab. Sharing hurt feelings is much more difficult. Even though other contexts (school/work, surplus leisure time) are important, *how* hurt feelings are experienced and expressed throughout the life cycle depends a great deal on how one learns to experience, express, and share them from and with intimates. We may be hurt by words and actions of strangers, but we are more vulnerable to be hurt by actions and words from those we love and who love us, because they are important to us and to our emotional and physical survival, if not enjoyment. Consequently, one needs to examine and to evaluate the validity and usefulness of looking at hurt feelings as being basic to personality socialization and to functional and dysfunctional relationships.

A more elaborate version of this model includes the following, circular dimensions (Cusinato & L'Abate, 1994): (1) communicating personal values; (2) respect for self-other feelings; (3) accepting limitations in self and other; (4) affirming possibilities, (5) sharing hurts; and (6) forgiving errors. This model has been evaluated by Cusinato and his students using a questionnaire and a workbook developed from this model (Cusinato, Aceti, & L'Abate, 1997).

HURT FEELINGS AND LEVELS OF ANALYSIS/OBSERVATION

Internally, feelings in general and hurt feelings in particular can be approached or avoided. Once they are approached allowing one to become aware of them, one needs to decide on whether to express and share them positively or negatively, recruiting R as the next step toward discharging them externally or delaying their expression for a more appropriate time. Once feelings are avoided and kept inside oneself, with or without awareness, their internal permanence, without expression, can have deleterious effects in internalizations. Once feelings are avoided and externalized, without reliance on *R*, they can discharged through explosions, impulsivity, and acting out. Either direction, as shown repeatedly in previous chapters, involves destructive outcomes to both self and others.

At this juncture, therefore, one needs to invoke and involve the meta-theoretical model of levels of observation and interpretation to expand on how hurt feelings are avoided at the genotypic level and expressed outwardly at self-presentational and phenotypic levels (Model^2, Ch. 5). For instance, acting-out character disorders, i.e., selfish individuals, avoid dealing with hurt feelings internally at the genotypic level. However, the outward, phenotypic, and self-presentational expression of these feelings consists of anger, hostility, and aggression. Hence, these individuals would benefit by workbooks directed toward learning how to express anger in more constructive ways than done in the past (L'Abate, 1966). In addition, it is important to introduce ways of thinking that would reduce impulsivity (acting before thinking) and increase *R* (thinking before acting*)* through cognitive (rational) activities like writing, as discussed in this book (Chs. 1 and 3) and elsewhere.

By the same token, self-defeating, depressed, fearful, and anxiously internalizing personalities, even though they may seem able to experience hurt feelings, may actually express themselves through distancing, distracting, ruminating, and relying on unrelated emotions, like grief, sadness, and guilt, maneuvers designed to withdraw and avoid these deeper feelings. Furthermore, personal hurt feelings and fears of being hurt are avoided by making the feelings of others more important than one's own. These individuals, even though they may appear "emotional," are not able to express their hurts any better than their externalizing counterparts. They may avoid them in different ways, but they nevertheless avoid those feelings through distracting and distancing. Although the latter deal with hurt feelings through externalizations, the former deal with hurt feelings though internalization, as discussed earlier in this chapter. Consequently, they are unable to be as intimate as they would like to be, or as they claim to want to be at the descriptive level, as discussed in Chapter 15. They avoid hurt feelings and fears of being hurt at the genotypic, explanatory sublevel. Hence, selfless internalizers need to learn ways to protect themselves and their bodies in better ways than they have done in the past (L'Abate & Harrison, 1992). They can do it through workbooks designed to draw lines, as in the Co-dependency workbook, or through the many depression and dependency workbooks available (L'Abate, 1966).

In no-self psychopathologies, the problem is even more complex because it is very difficult to access hurt feelings and fears of being hurt without provoking a great deal of agitation and distress, including a psychotic break. Feelings in general, let alone hurts, are almost completely avoided to the point that a resulting psychosis may well be the outcome of any attempt to access and express them. Hence, a workbook approach may be coupled with medication and with crisis intervention. Clearly, this is still an unexplored area for workbook applications.

Emotions and Intimacy

This chapter, therefore, elaborates the relationship between feelings and emotions and the construct of intimacy as defined here. To achieve this purpose it will be necessary to: (1) look at the state of feelings and emotions in the relevant literature, consisting mostly of lists of emotions; (2) suggest an alternative way to evaluate emotions according to their placement in a nomological network, rather than just listing them and comparing numbers of emotions according to one's viewpoint with competing lists; and (3) connect feelings and emotions with hurts according to the selfhood model explained in Chapter 12.

How Many Emotions? List Theories of Emotion and Intimacy

The marketplace of emotion theories is comprised of what has been called "list" theories of emotions (L'Abate, 1997). These theories (really models!) consist essentially of various lists of emotions, anywhere from 4 to 15. One reason these lists cannot be tested comparatively is due to their very nature. These lists are not theories in the sense of what is understood here as theory, i.e., a list does not a theory make. If a theory consists of a hierarchical structure composed of assumptions, postulates, models, and ways to evaluate the models, then these lists do not qualify as theories. They qualify eminently for what they are as just lists, perhaps at best as models, but not as theories.

This is one reason why these lists are unable to find a criterion that will allow comparable evaluation among themselves. Whether there are 4 or 15 emotions, the issue is not how many emotions there are, but how these lists can be evaluated, especially when the commonalities among them are greater than their differences. It is not the number of emotions that counts, but how emotions are located in a nomological network. What is meant by a nomological network? Both terms mean a model that will allow one to order or classify emotions (Blashfield & Livesley, 1999).

Furthermore, a major area of continuing debate in the study of emotions is the differentiation between experiencing emotional stimuli or events on the receptive, input side versus expression of these stimuli or events on the output side. The importance of separating clearly between emotional stimuli on the receptive side, as feelings, affect, or moods, versus the output of such feelings on the expressive side, as emotions, is crucial to personality socialization. Between experiencing of hurt feelings and their expression lies the importance of cognition in the reception, processing, and expression of emotionally tinged stimuli, including self-awareness, and awareness of external, interpersonal, and intimate contexts, as detailed in Chapters 4 and 5.

The number of primary emotions is another competitive attempt to add to the continuing and seemingly futile controversy about how many emotions we should be endowed with. This controversy can go on forever as long as the battle is fought in the arena of numbers, seemingly without a solution, because there is no solution. How can these different theories be evaluated comparatively? If there is no criterion (or model!) to evaluate them, there is no way to find out which list is "better" than all the others, certainly not by the number of emotions. Does the larger number of emotions listed mean a "better" list than a shorter list? To differentiate developmentally between primary or simple feelings (anger, sadness, joy, and fear) on the receptive side and more complex or secondary feelings (contentment, arrogance, humility, misery, guilt, shame, envy, embarrassment) requires a sense of self (Johnson-Laird & Oatley, 2000) in order to become aware and process these emotions cognitively.

Experiencing Feelings and Expressing Emotions

Experiencing feelings, coupled with management and regulation of emotions, can be used as a criterion to differentiate between functionality and dysfunctionality. Functionality can be defined, among other definitions, as the ability to experience a wide range of differentiated feelings, expressing them helpfully without blaming, criticising, or attack self and/or others. In functionality, rationality plays a significant role in how feelings are expressed. Dysfunctionality, in the expression of felt feelings, is defined as overreliance on experience and consequent expression of a restricted emotional repertoire limited at best to one, two, or a few feelings with a subsequent hurtful expression against self or others. Indeed, a limited repertoire of expressed, mostly negative, emotions is one of the marker variables in the etiology of schizophrenia (Nicholson, 1998).

A comprehensive and original model for experiencing has been proposed by two economists (Pine & Gilmore, 1999), and summarized by McLellan (2000). These authors argued that we are globally switching from a service to an experience economy. They proposed a model of passive versus active participation, and external versus internal involvement, producing four types of experiencing: entertainment (movies, theater), education (books), aesthetics (art, music), and escapisms (addictions). Hence, in their own original way, these authors support the importance of experiencing dear to the heart of humanistic theorists as well as to recent affect and emotionality researchers and scholars (Bradley, 2000; Watson, 2000).

This stress on subjective experience is basic to this theory in relation to avoiding painful experiences and approaching pleasurable ones instead. Pine and Gilmore's model, however, is too detailed and important to be summarized briefly. A distinct advance could be reached when various models of experiencing feelings, proposed by Bradley, Thayer, Watson, and other mood researchers, will be related to Pine and Gilmore's model. The former are abstract models constructed in an interpersonal vacuum. No one knows empirically what feelings or moods are associated with what particular external events (Gergen, 1994).

Pine and Gilmore's model, on the other hand, is interactional in nature because it classifies different types of experiencing on the basis of external events. It begs the question about what kind of feelings are elicited during any four classes of experiences they classified. For instance, while most legitimate educational, entertainment, and aesthetic experiences are pleasurable, what kind of feelings are elicited during escapist experiences, like alcohol or drug addictions? One would argue that the temporary and artificial high obtained during the latter experiences may be a temporary approach and a short-lived, superficial respite, but it is also an avoidance of hurt feeling and of fears of being hurt.

First, E, in the passive-receptive sense of just plain experiencing, is the foundation of our ability to be moved by external events and to remember those that are either very pleasurable or very painful. In this sense, E is basic to personality socialization. The inability to feel is deleterious to personality socialization and the beginning of psychopathology, as seen, for instance, in alexithymia, and in other psychopathological conditions (Bradley, 2000). Hence, no theory of personality socialization is complete without a statement about the functions and processes of E.

Second, if E is important to the development of intimacy, then most close, committed, interdependent, and prolonged relationships have to rely on experiencing, i.e., being together, for their existence. The greater the sharing of E, especially hurt feelings, the greater the chances of a positive and constructive relationship. Third, it is important to help people learn to share their hurts and become intimate with those who are bound with them by ties of love, caring, compassion, and concern. This outcome can be achieved therapeutically through the sharing hurts exercise and hugging, holding, huddling, and cuddling for extended periods of time (Ch. 19). Given the immense number of people in need of learning how to share feelings, it becomes crucial to have a variety of workbooks devoted to this topic, as reviewed in the previous chapter, and as stressed elsewhere (L'Abate & Kern, 2002). There are no sufficient personnel, professional or paraprofessional, to teach all who need to learn to express feelings in positive and constructive ways using talk and f2f contacts.

Both distinctions, feelings versus emotions, positive versus negative emotions, therefore, bring about the need to review the nature of emotions (Gergen, 1994), a topic too vast and too important to consider here. It is introduced briefly here to help locate feelings and emotions within the selfhood model. This introduction necessitated a discussion about list theories of emotions that have proliferated in the extant literature, and allows connecting and classifying feelings and emotions according to the selfhood Model[10].

Selfhood and Hurt Feelings

The purpose of this section is to suggest an alternative way to evaluate feelings as well as emotions according to their placement in two nomological networks—one receptive and the other expressive—rather than just listing them and comparing numbers in their respective lists. From both networks it is possible to administer feelings- and emotion-related workbooks in a more specific way than would be otherwise. What does this classification of functionality/dysfunctionality have to do with emotions and their classification (rather than their simple listing)? It has everything to do with it, because in selffulness one is most likely to find happiness/joy, surprise, interest, and desire. In selfishness, one is mostly likely to find anger, disgust, hate, and contempt. In selflessness, one is most likely to find anxiety, sadness, and grief. In no-self, one is most likely to find distress and fear. When most lists of emotions are compared according to this model, very few discrepancies among them appear. This model allows a classification of emotions that will allow greater ease of evaluation than just lists about how many emotions we should have. Now it will be possible to evaluate different list theories of emotions comparatively according to where emotions are likely to be found.

From gender ratios discussed in Chapter 12, the model predicts specific relationships between personality propensities and emotions, especially how to deal with hurts. However, here one has to refer to the initial distinction between experiencing feelings and expressing emotions (Ch. 4). Feelings are what is experienced (E). Emotions are what is expressed

Figure 16.1. A taxonomic tree of emotions and hurts according to the selfhood model (Storm & Storm, 1987).

motorically and/or verbally (*A*). There is no linear relationship between what is felt and what is expressed because of intervening cognitive processing (*R*), Actions, *Aw*areness, and *C*ontext.

The selfhood Model[10] will be used to illustrate what is meant by a nomological network. This model will place and locate feelings and emotions according to some semblance of order and classification. By differentiating between feelings at the receptive end from emotions at the expressive side, it is possible to obtain a framework of emotions around hurts, as shown in Figure 16.1 (Storm & Storm, 1987) and Figure 16.2 to show how a model of emotions, developed by Averill (1997), seems consistent with their placement according to the selfhood model.

In selffulness, one is most likely to find happiness/joy, surprise, interest, and desire (Fig. 16.1). In selfishness, one is most likely to find anger, disgust, hate, and contempt. In selflessness, one is most likely to find anxiety, sadness, and grief. In no-self, one is most likely to find chronic and chaotic distresses and fears. Once feelings are considered separately from emotions, they can be classified according to the approach-avoidance Model[4] presented in Chapter 7, as shown in Figure 16.3. By the same token, emotions can be classified according to the discharge-delay Model[5] presented in Chapter 8 and as shown in Figure 16.4.

Receptive Distance Regulation of Hurt Feelings

Receptive distance regulation of hurt feelings (Fig. 16.3) shows different characteristics according to specific personality propensities.

Selffulness

Positive

Amused   Nostalgic

Proud   Humble

Affectionate   Serene

<u>Positively Aroused</u>   <u>Positively Unaroused</u>

Astonished   Shy

Excited   Solemn

Eager   Sleepy

Selfishness   **Hurts**   **Selflessness**

Aroused-defiant   Dazed

Alarmed   Bored

Incensed   Lethargic

<u>Negatively Aroused</u>   <u>Negative Unaroused</u>

Envious   Miserable

Disgusted   Ashamed

Embarrassed-Disappointed

Negative

No-self

Figure 16.2. Organization of emotional terms and hurts according to the selfhood model (Averill, 1997, p. 518).

S	**Selffulness**	S
e	Positive and balanced	e
l	Approach-avoidance to hurts and self	l
f	Positive approach to self Negative approach to self	f
i	Negative avoidance of hurts **Hurts** Collection of hurts/sadness	l
s	positive approach to others	e
h		s
n	Extreme, negative, and contradictory	s
e	Approach-avoidance to self and others	n
s	**No-self**	e
s		s
s		s

Figure 16.3. The selfhood model and receptive distance regulation of hurt feelings.

Selffulness. This personality propensity would imply a balance in: (1) *E* requiring approach toward pleasant as well as unpleasant (hurt) feelings in self and in intimate others; (2) *R*, that is, positive thinking is more dominant than negative thinking; (3) *A*, that is, positive, helpful, constructive behavior is more predominant than negative, hurtful behavior; (4) wide and articulate *Aw* of self and intimate others; and (5) sensitivity to *C*.

Selfishness. In this personality propensity, one would more likely find: (1) an inability to approach and talk about unpleasant (hurt) feelings; (2) approach toward pleasant feelings in the self through drugs, alcohol, or putting others down, i.e., artificial, or similar, counterfeit approaches to receive and keep pleasant feelings; (3) avoidance of hurt feelings in the self (perhaps because of inadequate *Aw*); (4) approach toward others through manipulation and attribution of external threats and possible attack; (5) avoidance of hurt feelings in others; and (6) self-preservational thinking with negative thinking against others, i.e., "I hurt you before you hurt me"; (7) unrealistically magnified *Aw* of self with limited *Aw* of others; and (8) denial or limited *Aw* of *C*.

Selflessness. Here, one is more likely to find: (1) approach toward unpleasant (hurt) feelings in the self by collecting them inside without resolution; (2) avoidance of pleasant feelings in the self; but (3) approach toward hurt feelings in others; with (4) avoidance of pleasant feelings in others; (5) negative thinking about self and positive, unrealistically magnified, if not idealized, thinking about others; (6) negative *A* toward self, but positive *A* toward others; (7) limited *Aw* of self, magnified *Aw* of others; (8) constricted, biased, or distorted *Aw* of *C*.

No-Self. Here, one is more likely to find: (1) extreme, negative, inconsistent and contradictory avoidance of unpleasant (hurt) feelings in self and others with complete avoidance of pleasant feelings, if one cannot experience hurts one cannot experience joys; (2) exaggerated all-or-none thinking, absolutistic, dogmatic, one-sided thinking with contradictory and inconsistent views; (3) extremes and contradictory *A* toward self and others; (4) extremely limited *Aw* of self and others, and (5) denial of *C*.

Receptively, at the experiencing side, Thayer's (1989, 1996) model of mood management seems to fit into the selfhood model in some tentative fashion (Fig. 16.2). Given his two orthogonal axes of energy versus tiredness and calmness versus tension, Thayer considers the ability to self-regulate optimally as taking place within individuals who are energetic and calm in their moods. Driven individuals, like Type A personality, would be characterized by energy and tension, while anxious and depressed moods would characterize individuals who are tense and tired at the same time. Exhaustion would take place within extremes of calmness and tiredness.

Thayer's model would seem to fit partially with the selfhood model, to the extent that selffulness would indicate self-regulation, and selfishness could be equated with drivenness. However, anxiety and depression would not fit into the no-self propensity any more than exhaustion with selflessness would. This partial isomorphism between moods and selfhood could be attributed to the possibility that no subjects, in Thayer's studies as well as in those cited by him but performed by others, included severely distressed or disturbed patients. Hence, it remains to be seen whether there is a correspondence between moods and personality propensities at the receptive as well as at the expressive side.

Expressive Control Regulation of Hurt Feelings

As far as expressed emotions are concerned, the model would predict that in selffulness there is a preponderance of positive feelings expressed through emotions like joy, surprise, and pleasurable intimate interactions. When hurt feelings are expressed, it is done in conjunctively constructive ways. In selfishness, there is a preponderance of negative feelings that are expressed as anger, followed by envy and hostility. Unpleasant or painful feelings are avoided and usually expressed through externalizations, attacking others, using others as targets, and holding them responsible for the individual's own behavior. In selflessness, the most preponderant feelings are shame, guilt, and sadness, expressed by using the self as an intrapunitive target, excusing others from responsibility. In no-self, the most preponderant feelings are fear, disgust, and despair, expressed through inconsistent and contradictory vacillations between externalizations and internalizations, or simply apathy and withdrawal.

Hence, this model examines emotions according to a framework that raises questions about so-called "list theories of emotions." These traditional theories argue that many emotions exist in their lists with no overarching theory or model to classify them. In selffulness one is more likely to find positive and balanced regulation of discharge-delay of hurt feelings in self and others (Fig. 16.4). Discharge here would be equal to delay in the sense that both are necessary and inevitable in dealing with various people, situations, and objects. However, they are used flexibly, selectively, and appropriately.

In selfishness, discharge is greater than delay as seen in impulsivity, externalizations, acting out, and even murder, with: (1) little if any discharge of hurt feelings toward self and reactive discharge of hurt feelings against

S		Selffulness		S
e		Positive and balanced		e
l		Discharge-delay of hurts		l
f	Self-indulgence/discharge		Attack aganst self	f
i	Anger and attack against	**Hurts**	Indulging others	l
s	others		Negative delay to self	e
h			Positive disharge to others	s
n		Extreme, negative, and contradictory		s
e		Discharge-delay toward self and others		n
s		**No-self**		e
s				s
				s

Figure 16.4. The selfhood model and expressive control regulation of hurt feelings.

others; (2) almost complete delay of unpleasant hurt feelings toward self; and (3) limited, if any, delay of hurt feelings toward or against others.

In selflessness, delay is greater than discharge, as seen in internalizations, acting out, depression, and even suicide, with: (1) negative discharge of hurt feelings toward self; (2) positive discharge of hurt feelings toward others; (3) negative delay of hurt feelings toward self; and (4) delay of hurt feelings toward others ("They did not mean it").

In no-self one is more likely to find an extreme, negative, and contradictory relationship between discharge and delay, from complete withdrawal to complete explosions, including murder or suicide.

As seen in these figures, the selfhood Model[10] allows us to integrate feelings at the receptive side as E, and emotions at the expressive side as A. In these, as well as in other preceding figures, hurt is central but, in most cases, avoided, or handled inadequately or destructively, especially in externalizations, internalizations, and psychopathologies. When most lists of emotions are compared with each other according to this model, very few discrepancies appear among them. This model, therefore, should allow a classification of emotions, allowing greater ease of evaluation than just lists about how many emotions we should have. Now it should be possible to evaluate different list models of emotions comparatively according to where emotions are likely to be found. For instance, using a self-report, paper-and-pencil test used to measure the four personality propensities of selffulness, selfishness, selflessness, and no-self, the SOPC (Chs. 12 and 19), it is possible to use any measure of emotionality developed from each theory to evaluate whether this model is indeed valid.

List theories of emotions, as well as proponents of Figures 16.1 and 16.2, seem to miss that at the bottom of all our feelings and emotions lies feelings of hurt, helplessness, hopelessness, and despair. We all, in one way or another and to some degree or another, are hurt human beings, as Pennebaker (1997) has found in written essays of "functional" undergraduates. If we are not hurt or we deny our ultimate vulnerability to being hurt, we are bound to hurt those who love us. How we deal with our hurt feelings has a great deal to do with how we relate to intimate others. We can avoid those feelings, clutching them inside very carefully, or we can express and share them verbally, nonverbally, or in writing. Their expression can occur in thoughtlessly impulsive and very likely destructive ways, or it can occur caringly and positively. We may not have choices on how we are hurt by others, but we do have choices on how we are going to deal with these hurt feelings and how we are going to express and share them with those we love and who love us.

Why is it theoretically relevant to stress the importance of receptive experiences and not just expressive ones? From the viewpoint of the selfhood model, a model-driven classification of feelings, affect, and moods might show some relationship with a classification of emotions, demonstrating that receptive (in E) and expressive processes (in A) have some lawful relationship with each other. Furthermore, receptive experiences, when positive, like happiness, joy, contentment, and satisfaction, lead to better psychological functioning and even improved negotiation and problem-solving skills (Isen, 2000, pp. 417–435).

If this conclusion is valid, then these positive emotions would be more likely to be present in selfful personality propensities than in the other three, less functional personality propensities. Functional, i.e., selfful individuals, would negotiate and problem solve more efficiently and effectively than dysfunctional ones, as discussed in the next chapter. As Isen (2000) concluded:

> " . . . people in the positive affect condition who bargained face-to-face were significantly less likely to break off negotiation, and more likely to reach agreement, and to reach the original agreement possible in the situation than were face-to-face bargainers in the control condition (p. 421)."

More to the point of the selffulness propensity, Isen added:

> " . . . more positive affect in general promotes not selfishness (sic), but a tendency to be kind to both self and others, social connectedness, responsibility, and the ability to see situations from another's person perspective (p. 424)."

Consequently, through the selfhood model it is possible to link E with personal and interpersonal relationships in a more specific way than it would be possible with equivalent theoretical list models, including attachment.

There is no question that being able to put oneself in another person's position may produce personal and social benefits. However, if and when empathy for another person is exaggerated or extreme, with a loss to the self, it may signify the possibility of selflessness and at least temporarily, a loss of self-importance for the benefit of another.

APPLICATIONS OF THIS MODEL

Sharing hurts as in crying together, that is, being together physically and emotionally, with those we love and who love us would lead to or relate with selfulness. Here is where the importance of hugging and holding in intimate relations (object relations school) come into being, as in the hugging, holding, huddling, and cuddling (3HC) exercise recommended for some couples and families (L'Abate, 2001). A sharing of hurts exercise, especially for couples, may help them share hurt feelings that they were unable to share heretofore (L'Abate, 1986, 1994, 1997, 2003a; L'Abate & De Giacomo, 2003).

The Nonlinearity of E and A

In spite of some theoretical attempts (Plutchik, 1993) to relate feelings (E) with emotions and external behavior (A), the gap between these two aspects of behavior is too wide to expect that given any feeling there is a corresponding, matching emotion. As argued elsewhere (L'Abate, 1994, 1997), given the same feeling, hostility or anger, for example, there myriad ways in which one can express that very same feeling. Hence, this nonlinearity between E and A needs to consider many factors, as in the ERAAwC Model[1] as mentioned in Chapter 4: (1) intensity of E; (2) strength of boundaries among E with R, A, Aw, C, as described in Figures 4.1 and 4.2; (3) amount of overlap among components of the model; (4) strength of R as interposed between E and A; (5) strength of Aw intervening after A as a circular change loop to revert to E, R, A, and C; and (6) Aw of C, as an overarching factor in bridging the gap between E and A.

In spite of this nonlinearity between E and A, through a selfhood model it is possible to make sense and show that there is still some relationship between E and Aw, when Aw is defined as unexpressed emotions. One can feel and be aware of one's anger and hostility. However, as long as

R is present and functioning, various ways, some constructive and some destructive, of expressing this *Aw* outwardly exist. However, if *Aw* is restricted, then feedback to *E* may be limited, inadequate, faulty, and possibly distorted, short-circuiting even more the circularity of *E* to *R* and to *A*.

Intimacy and Personality Socialization

Implications for personality socialization within the context of intimacy and selfhood are twofold. One aspect of intimacy and selfhood relates to how we deal with our hurts at the receptive level: (1) we are all hurt human beings, in some way or another; (2) some are more hurt than others; (3) some are able to deal with their hurts more constructively than others; (4) some are completely unable to deal with their hurts because they are unable to face this fundamental human condition.

Once intimacy is defined according to the presence of hurt feelings, three paradoxes seem related: (1) we need to be separate as individuals in order to be together with intimate others, i.e., we need to be "strong" enough to allow ourselves to be "weak"; (2) we only hurt the ones we love, we are not hurt by strangers except physically; and (3) we need to seek comfort from the very ones we have hurt or who have hurt us. It we are hurt verbally and behaviorally by the very ones we love, we witness the effects of verbal abuse being even more hurtful than physical abuse (Ch. 11).

Once we accept the importance of these feelings, three different possibilities come to mind, our: (1) *neediness* in wanting to be close to someone who will share hurt feelings reciprocally with us, because without this reciprocity there is little if any potential for a harmonious relationship; (2) *vulnerability* in being hurt by the very ones we love and who love us—we are not vulnerable to slights from strangers—we are vulnerable to people who are important to us, because we are more liable to be hurt "unintentionally" from those we love and who love us; and (3) *fallibility* in hurting the very ones we love "unintentionally" without intending to hurt them.

Intimacy and Forgiveness

Acceptance of these existential conditions and forgiveness (Fincham, 2000; McCullough, Pargament, & Thorensen, 2000) may go a long way toward achieving selffulness in personality socialization. Almost 20 years ago (L'Abate, 1986), when it was still professionally questionable to introduce the process of forgiveness in psychotherapy with couples and families, a crucial part of the model of intimacy included forgiveness. Before one can share hurts and fears of being hurt, forgiveness needs to be included. Otherwise, it is difficult, if not impossible, to achieve intimacy. An assignment about forgiveness was included in the Intimacy workbook (L'Abate, 1986, 1996).

Since then, a great deal of attention has been devoted to this topic, to the point that a veritable science of forgiveness has mushroomed into a campaign for forgiveness research that culminated with the 2003 Forgiveness Conference about scientific findings to help people forgive. Among the scores of papers presented at this conference, its highlights included evidence about the physiological correlates of forgiveness (Witvliet, 2003) and the importance of forgiveness for physical and mental health. This campaign reached the point where Fincham and Beach (2002) even proposed a plan for a public health approach to forgiveness in relation to transgressions. The large incidence of needed forgiveness, above and beyond what therapists in private practice can manage, requires a public health model through paraprofessional intermediaries using writing rather than talking. The use of computers, self-administered workbooks, and the Internet, however, may make paraprofessional intermediaries obsolete, costly, if not useless. Perhaps one day Fincham and Beach's proposal may become a reality through the Internet.

Sharing Support Online

More and more hurt people find instant or prolonged and anonymous support through the Internet (Tichon & Shapiro, 2003). This process will make it easier for a larger segment of the population to share their hurts without seeing a professional f2f. This outcome will serve as primary prevention for people who do hurt but who do not need or want a professional to hear their hurts.

Hence, the purpose of most emotion-oriented workbooks, like most other workbooks, is parapreventive as well as paratherapeutic (Appendix A). There are many workbooks specifically targeted for the externalization of emotions, such as anger, hostility, and aggression. Other workbooks have been targeted toward internalization of emotions, like anxiety, fears, intimacy, and depression (L'Abate & Kern, 2002).

Empirically, for instance, the Fear of Intimacy Scale developed by Thelen and associates (Descoutner & Thelen, 1991; Doi & Thelen, 1993) contains many items that deal with hurtful situations that the individual may want to either disclose without fear or keep inside because of fear of closeness. Hence, this test shows face validity in being related to the definition of intimacy as the sharing of joys, hurts, and fear of being hurt. Fear of intimacy would imply avoidance of such disclosure. By the same token, Pennebaker's work (Esterling et al., 1999) demonstrates how writing about one's past traumatic events (hurts) can lead to beneficial physical and emotional results and be interpreted within the definition of intimacy given earlier. Other empirical results, which are independent of the theory but which show conceptual similarities with it, have been reviewed elsewhere.

Hurt Feelings and Gender Differences

Older men seem to react with negative feelings after disclosing their grief and continued to keep those feelings for some time. Older women, on the other hand, may show a steady decrease across disclosure sessions. For them, higher levels of negative feelings and greater decreases in negative thoughts were correlated with greater therapeutic changes. This outcome was not clear for men (Guinther, Segal, & Bogaards, 2003). These results, among others, indicate that women may tend to accept and deal with negative feelings like grief, while men may not be as comfortable in experiencing and expressing them. This possibility derives from possible gender differences in selfhood propensities, as discussed in Chapter 12.

Related Research

This model can be directly evaluated from a test derived from the model, that is: Stevens and L'Abate's (1989) Sharing of Hurts Scale. Indirectly related to the model is the (Fear of Intimacy Scale), which contains mostly fear of hurts items. Independently from the model but conceptually similar to this model is forgiveness (Fincham, 2000; McCullough et al., 2000), a topic which is not usually related to any specific theory or therapeutic approach. Vangelisti (2001) generated and reviewed research supporting the validity of this model.

Obstacles to Intimacy

One the major obstacles to intimacy is helpfulness, because too much of it or too little of it are produced by two different personality propensities. Selfishness produces little helpfulness toward others, while selflessness may produce too much. No-self may waiver between extremes of the two polarities or not being able to be helpful at all. When considering being helpful in creating intimacy in relationships, one needs to decide "When does helpfulness become control and cease to be helpful?" These are the conditions under which helpfulness to reach and obtain intimacy may be useless or irrelevant:

- When intimacy is not asked for or needed.
- When intimacy deprives the helped other of self-determination.

- When intimacy takes away from the self of the supposedly helpful person ("See what I have done for you!").
- When intimacy is a sacrifice to the self rather than a straightforward gift and a way to enhance self and other.
- When intimacy is perceived as control rather than helpfulness from the one who is being helped.
- When intimacy is given and received reciprocally and voluntarily without a hidden or not so hidden agenda on the part of parties involved.

Functions of This Model

This model integrates how hurt feelings are fundamental to our existence. Diagnostically one needs to ask: "Did you ever see your parents cry together?"; "What does your partner do when you cry and when you hurt?" Prescriptively one needs to learn to: "Cry when you are hurting with those you love and who love you." "Forgive your errors if you want to be forgiven." Therapeutically, there are many ways to help hurt people if they want help. The process of change may take place within Rogers's sine qua non requirements of warmth, empathy, and unconditional regards for certain (depressed and anxious) individuals, but these requirement are questionable with character disorders, severe psychopathology, couples, and families. It takes more than these requirements to help people who hurt.

CONCLUSION

"It is better to have loved and lost than to have never loved at all." Love and hurts are intertwined, we only hurt and are hurt by those we love because they are important to us and what they say and do becomes an indication of our and their importance. A specific and concrete definition of intimacy defined as sharing of joys, hurts, and fears of being hurt has been productive, if not successful, in creating distance programmed writing, i.e., workbooks, with f2f approaches to improve intimacy. How we deal with (approach, face, confront, access, process, and express) hurt feelings in the self determines a great deal how we relate in intimate as well as in nonintimate relationships.

Chapter 17

Negotiating How to Solve Problems
Model[15]

"Many personality factors have been studied in relation to the management of conflict. Of those relevant to the skillful management of conflict, the property of personal control *[emphasis added] appears most important* (Canary, 2003)."

"Negotiation, then, is a unique form of social interaction that incorporates argumentation, persuasion, and information exchange into reaching agreements and working out future interdependence. As a mixed endeavor, negotiation can develop though distributive processes aimed at maximizing self-interest, centering on positions, and claiming optimal value, or it can evolve in a 'win-win' manner in which parties pursue common interests, seek creative options, and engage in cooperative problem-solving (Roloff, Putman, & Anastasiou, 2003, p. 804)."

"The basic cognitive processes that appear to be necessary for effective problem-solving are related to inhibition of action [emphasis added] *and memory* (Tremblay, 2003, p. 201)."

Conflict among intimates and nonintimates is inevitable (Canary, 2003). The issue lies in how conflict is managed: poorly, successfully, effectively, ineffectively, constructively, or destructively. This chapter introduces a model of negotiation in intimate relationships that may lead to expand on what was considered in the light of Model[1] and Model[8] and to substantive interventions in prevention and psychotherapy.

Since negotiation requires a certain level of functionality, all of the dimensions reviewed in previous chapters come to bear on the structure and process of negotiation. All the evidence reviewed here indicates that to negotiate and problem solve successfully and effectively, a relational system needs to reach a modicum of individual, dyadic, and multirelational functionality. Those in semifunctional and dysfunctional relationships are unable and sometimes unwilling to even attempt negotiating, let alone problem solve successfully or otherwise. Even if and when the latter try to negotiate, the process is difficult and the outcome questionable. Hence, a relational system needs to have all its ducks in a row, so to speak, to negotiate successfully and effectively. This is the reason why the first workbook on negotiation was suggested as a second step in couple and family psychotherapy, after the initial crisis or reason for referral was first dealt with and tensions lowered (L'Abate, 1986).

Control is a basic requirement for effective negotiation, not just in terms of controlling others, but in terms of controlling oneself, that is, being able to regulate approach-avoidance and discharge-delay tendencies in ways that allow others to express themselves, brainstorm, and come up with solutions that are acceptable to whomever is involved in the negotiation process. Control, therefore, means being able to put limits on oneself and freeing others to function effectively and efficiently. As we have seen from previous chapters, one needs to be able to function relatively well to "be in control" and problem solve successfully

THE NATURE OF NEGOTIATION

The nature of negotiation is comprised of characteristics that go above and beyond the personal characteristics of negotiators and encompass both parties: structure and process. Even though the structure may determine the process, one needs to be mindful that both structure and process, as described here, are strictly ideal. Most people in intimate relationships do not follow them as clearly as described in this model, unless they need and want a formal structure administered to them. However, if professionals do not have a clear model of what is entailed in the structure and process of negotiation, even if ideal, how are they going to impart it to others?

The Structure of Negotiation

It is assumed that whoever wants to negotiate and problem solve is involved in a loving system that needs and wants more than love. Love is not enough. A loving relational system needs to solve problems as well (Ch. 8). Hence, the structure of negotiation is composed of: (1) power sharing and division of labor, consisting of authority in who makes the decisions, and who has the responsibility to carry those decisions out (Ch. 8); (2) task assignments, consisting of decisions concerning *orchestration* of decisions about very important tasks, such as moving or buying a house or a car, and *instrumentation* decisions about small, routine, everyday tasks, like what we will have for dinner and what TV show we will watch; (3) contents for what needs to be negotiated (information, services, goods, and money) (Ch. 9); and (4) the level of functionality of parties involved that will determine whether they want to negotiate and whether the process will be effective in producing a "win-win" outcome for both parties.

What has been learned thus far in this work is that it requires a fairly well-functioning relational system to achieve successful or at least effective negotiation, and problem solving (Spangle & Isenhart, 2002). Indeed, this chapter is toward the end of this book because the process of negotiation requires all the positive skills that individuals in intimate relationships can muster in order to negotiate successfully and effectively.

The potential for the ability to negotiate, therefore, is a multiplicative level of functionality (Ill), the ability to negotiate (Skill), and the motivation to negotiate (Will). These characteristics seem self-explanatory and have been expanded in previous chapters and past publications. Hopefully, they will not require further explanation here since in one way or another they are contained in all the previous chapters of this book.

The Process of Negotiation

Although the process of being present is based mostly on *E*motionality, the process of negotiation requires access, acknowledgment of, and reliance on *E* first, followed by *R*ationality and *R*egulation. Both *E* and *R* determine subsequent *A*ctivities, *A*wareness, and *C*ontext, as elaborated in Chapter 4. Ideally, one should start from *E*, expression and sharing feelings, progressing to *R*, discussing or brainstorming about possible courses of actions—their pros and cons—with agreement or consensus about following one particular course of *A*ction. After trying *A* for a chosen period of time, ideally, there should be feedback, i.e., *A*w, about whatever has been learned during this course of *A*ction. This feedback loop would return to *E*, starting the process all over again. This circular process takes place within the overarching *A*w (feedback, acknowledgment, denial, or ignorance) of *C*. This process, of course, could take place internally, as a dialogue, as well as between and among individuals. These constructs will be elaborated below, applied to the process of negotiation below, and found also in the Planned Parenting workbook (L'Abate, 1996).

ABILITY TO NEGOTIATE

Those in dysfunctional intimate relationships not only have difficulties in exchanging love (Ch. 7), but they show difficulties in problem solving and probably in negotiating problem areas, where power, in one way or another is either shared or kept in one party without hope of sharing it in the process of negotiating problem solving (Chs. 8 and 9).

Developmental Antecedents in the Ability to Negotiate

This section reviews studies of problem solving with functional, nonclinical respondents. The following section reviews studies with dysfunctional respondents. Of course, problem solving cannot be considered as a unitary, factor. It is composed of many personal and interpersonal qualities that need specification (Cassidy & Long, 1996; D'Zurilla & Maydeu-Olivares, 1995). Even though samples from normal populations may contain a certain percentage of depressed respondents on the basis of self-report, paper-and-pencil tests, they do not compare, nor are they included with, hospitalized respondents with clinical diagnoses of depression or other disorders.

Individuals

Children. In kindergarten, children who tend to isolate themselves from their peers apparently show lower skills in social problem solving. Nonassertive, compliant social problem-solving strategies may relate concurrently to isolated play and predictively with isolated play in first grade (Rubin, Daniels-Beirness, & Bream, 1984). Sixth graders with negative peer status tend to generate fewer alternative solutions, propose fewer assertive and mature solutions, generate more intense aggressive solutions, and show less adaptive planning, evaluating physically aggressive responses more positively and positive responses more negatively than positive peer status counterparts. These results would support the notion that boys with social maladjustment problems may well be deficient in cognitive problem-solving skills in generating multiple alternative solutions. Differences in knowledge and/or attitudes concerning normative socially acceptable standards may contribute to the more negative patterns observed in socially maladjusted boys (Asarnow & Callan, 1985).

In elementary school, popular boys tend to generate more solutions than either aggressive or isolated counterparts. This possibly suggests that deviant boys may be deficient in cognitive problem-solving skills in generating alternative solutions, even though they may not be deficient in evaluating solutions presented to them (Richard & Dodge, 1982).

Preadolescents sixth-grade respondents who produce solutions of relatively inconsistent quality seem less competent than their more consistent peers. Both dimensions of prospective taking, social and affective interpersonal problem solving and means-end analytical thinking, may be related to each other. A positive relationship may exist between social-cognitive ability and effective interpersonal relations, and in some yet to be specified ways, with interpersonal problem solving (Marsh, Serafica, & Barenbolm, 1981).

Solutions in social-cognitive problem-solving skills that are interpersonally oriented and active across situations may be associated with lower levels of social withdrawal. Intellectual and demographic variables can play an important part in predicting problem-solving skills and adjustment (Fishler & Kendall, 1988).

Adolescents. Social competence in adolescents may be composed, among other factors, of moral reasoning and interpersonal, cognitive problem solving. However, this conclusion may become questionable when social class is introduced as a variable. Overall interpersonal, cognitive problem solving may be a better predictor of personal and academic outcomes than any single component of that skill. Components of that skill also seem related both to family functioning patterns and the respondents' level of adjustment (Kennedy, Felner, Cauce, & Primavera, 1988).

Interpersonal stress in adolescent girls may affect interpersonal problem solving even though no relationship may be present between depressive symptoms and interpersonal problem solving (Davila, Hammen, Burge, Paley et al., 1995).

College Students. Social problem solving may consist of two general components—problem orientation and problem-solving skills (Maydeu-Olivares & D'Zurilla, 1996). Other components, including social class, educational level, and age may also be important factors to consider in problem solving, where interpersonal sensitivity may be related to problem solving, particularly negative problem orientation. Both interpersonal sensitivity and social problem solving seem to predict levels of self-esteem and depressive symptoms, as well as academic performance. There may be some sex differences in regard to acadmic performance, which might not be related to social problem solving in women. Dysfunctional problem-solving styles may be important components of overall problem solving related to academic performance (McCabe, Blankstein, & Mills, 1999).

Positive problem orientation may contain common characteristics with optimism and positive affectivity, while a negatige problem-solving orientation may share a large amount of variance with pessimism and negative affectivity (Chang & D'Zurilla, 1996). By the same token, hopelessness and negative life stresses may be associated with problem-solving self-appraisal by decreasing it (Bonner & Rich, 1988).

Both a problem-solving deficit and a conservative problem-solving style in depressed college students are apparent when the difficulty of solving a problem increases (Dobson & Dobson, 1981). Dysphoric undergraduates seem to use fewer problem-focused and more emotion-focused statements than nondysforic counterparts. Frequencies of task-inhibiting and emotion-focused self-statements may be associated negatively with solution effectiveness (Mayo & Tanaka-Matsumi, 1996). Depressed students may show a significant lack of action-oriented strategies in problem solving (Marx & Schulze, 1991). When a depression, mood-inducing procedure is administered, it is very likely that it will affect negatively interpersonal problem-solving performance (Mitchell & Madigan, 1984).

Single Adults. Poor problem solving may be associated with both low levels of global self-worth and attachment insecurity. Global self-worth may also mediate the relationship between attachment cognitions and interpersonal problem-solving strategies, suggesting that attachment insecurity may have an indirect association with poor problem solving through low self-worth. Early experience could lead to negative beliefs about self and others, and these beliefs could lead to poor problem solving (Davila, Hammen, Burge, Daley et al., 1996). Depressed patients might be less likely to use problem solving and more likely to use emotion-focused coping skills, possibly associated with a background of fewer and less supportive relationships with friends, family members, and coworkers than nondepressed controls (Billings, Cronkite, & Moos, 1983).

Couples. Apparently, there is a positive relationship between femininity and problem solving and a negative relationship between femininity and aversive problem-solving strategies in couples (Burger & Jacobson, 1979). Marital satisfaction is clearly linked to the ability to negotiate cooperatively. For both complementary as well as husbands and wives separately, their or their spouses' ability to negotiate cooperatively may be significant predictors of marital happiness (Harrison, 1993).

Parents. More competent parents seem to treat their children as being more capable and resourceful, showing generally warm and positive feelings, being more helpful with their children in problem solving (Mondell & Tyler, 1981).

Families. As discussed above, social class may be an important factor in problem solving, where middle-class families may be "better" problem solvers than working-class families because role expectations will account for those differences. Blue-collar families may problem solve better when they are father-led, while white-collar families may problem solve better when they are egalitarian. Perhaps open communication structures and normative role expectations might account in part for the better problem solving of white-collar families (Tallman & Miller, 1974).

When the mother or a sibling helps the child in a problem-solving task, different outcomes may become evident. When the helper is a sibling, older sisters may give more explanations, feedback, and total verbalizations than older brothers. Mothers, on the other hand, may also give more explanations, feedback, and total verbalizations to children with older brothers. Children from large families tend to seek and receive more help than children from smaller families (Cicirelli, 1976).

Dysfunctional Antecedents in the Ability to Negotiate

The previous section summarized results from research with functional, or semifunctional but nonclinical respondents, and this section will summarize the results from clinical research.

Single Adults

Depressed patients may show deficits in problem solving by producing less effective solutions than normal or clinical controls. Depressed as well as anxious individuals may also have difficulties at different stages of the problem solving process (Marx, Williams, & Claridge, 1992). Schizophrenics seem impaired in many problem-solving domains compared with nonpatient controls. However, bipolar patients might equally be impaired and different factors may be operating in clinical patients. Schizophrenics may suffer from cognitive impairment while bipolars may suffer from acute illness (Bellack, Sayers, Mueser, & Bennett, 1994).

Couples

Couples with a depressed wife may or may not suffer marital distress. Predictably, depressed women may exhibit significantly higher rates of depressive behavior than their husbands or either of normal couples. Depressed women may tend to display less problem solving strategies than their husbands, while both husbands and wives in couples with a depressed wife may exhibit less self-disclosure than normal dyads (Biglan et al., 1985).

Families

Although most clinical families with depressed and conduct-disordered children may have lower levels of effective problem solving than nonclinical, control children, their deficiencies in problem solving may be somewhat different. Conduct disordered children may show lower levels of positive problem solving and higher levels of aversive content than nonconduct-disordered children (Sanders, Dadds, Johnston, & Cash, 1992). For instance, mothers of disruptive children tend to take over the task more often and provided fewer close-ended questions about problem solving than mothers of nondisruptive children. The higher the depression level in the mother the greater the likelihood that they may ask fewer closed-ended questions related to problem solving, suggesting a limited problem-solving repertoire (Bloomquist, August, Brombach, Anderson, et al., 1996).

SETTING BOUNDARIES

How is this model related to intervening in intimate relationships? From the assumptions of the theory, it follows that we need to help (teach, coach, demonstrate, model) intimates how to love and negotiate with each other in better ways than they might have done heretofore. A basic issue in negotiation is setting boundaries spatially ("Where shall we negotiate and how shall we be seated?"), temporally ("For how long shall we meet and how often?"), and practically ("Who will chair this meeting? Who will take notes? How are we going to share responsibilities?"). Possibly positive or negative styles, in addition to the ARC model (Ch. 11), relating to setting limits, are contained in Figure 12.2.

Practically, one needs to have helped both parties involved in the process to solve successfully issues of distance regulation (Ch. 14, Model[12]), to eliminate the deleterious effects of the drama triangle (Ch. 15, Model[13]), and to deal with how feelings of joy and hurt are expressed and shared by both parties (Ch. 16, Model[14]). Put another way, both parties need to have reached a certain level of functionality to be able and willing to negotiate effectively.

For this process to run smoothly and eventually end successfully, it might help to have parties involved follow a sequence of resources given by the ERAAwC model (Ch. 4): (1) express how they feel about the issue to be negotiated (E); (2) consider all possible solutions through brainstorming about pros and cons of the issue at hand (R); (3) put into action the best possible solution (A); (4) reach a mutual understanding about a time limit to review the positive or negative outcome of the solution (Aw); (5) agree to review and renegotiate how both parties feel about the chosen solution; and (6) if the previous solution does not seem to work or be acceptable to both parties, consider pros and cons of alternative solutions, thus producing a change in C as well as a change in the whole process and the

Table 17.1. Summary of the Nature of Negotiation

A. The Structure and Process of Negotiation

1. Decision making: Authority versus responsibility: who makes decisions and who carries them out, together or separately.
2. Division of labor: Orchestration (large) versus instrumental (routine) tasks.
3. Motivation to negotiate involves most models of the theory.
4. Contents of what is negotiated (Model[4]).
    a. E = expression and sharing of what and how one feels about the issue.
    b. R = what to do about the issue, brainstorming about pros and cons.
    c. A = applying a solution with the most pros and least cons.
    d. Aw = monitoring and checking whether any change has taken place, and, if necessary, using Plan B if Plan A does not work.
    e. C = going back to *E* and thus changing the *C* of the whole process.
5. Resources available: ERRAwC (Model[1]).

B. Negotiation and Level of Functionality: (Models[9 & 10])

1. Motivation to negotiate: WILL, Models[11&12]
2. There is no "Ideal" process of negotiation, not all negotiations in intimate relationships occur according to an ideal process (Roloff, Putman, & Anastasiou, 2003).
3. Relationship of this model with metatheoretical assumptions and previous models.
4. Functional versus dysfunctional negotiation.
    a. Effective versus ineffective process.
    b. Successful versus unsuccessful outcome.

---

foregoing sequence of resources. A summary of this structure is included in Table 17.1.

Consequently, to achieve a goal of effective negotiation, we need to help intimates learn how to: (1) express feelings (*E*) in more helpful and constructive ways than they have done before to receive help; (2) think (*R*) in more appropriate and flexible ways to negotiate and solve family problems; (3) act (*A*) on the basis of full *Aw*areness of feelings and thinking within the context (*C*) of intimates involved in the process. Furthermore, intimates need to learn to respond to each other in *C*onstructive-*C*reative fashion rather than *A*busively or *A*pathetically, or *R*eactively-*R*epetitively (ARC model, Ch. 11). As one can readily see, this is a very tall order that cannot be achieved solely on the basis of verbal f2f interactions, no matter how prolonged they might be. A great deal of homework needs to be assigned (Kazantzis, Deane et al., in press; Kazantzis & L'Abate, in press; L'Abate, 2004a, 2004b; L'Abate & De Giacomo, 2003).

One important issue that needs to be settled at the outset of negotiation is what is negotiable and what is not. For instance, whether intimates love each other, i.e., presence, in terms of emotional availability might not be negotiable. However, how love is expressed and shared may need clarification whenever there are doubts about its presence. Intimates may want to start any meeting reassuring each other of their mutual love. One could start by asking parties involved to write down issues that need to be negotiated versus issues that do not need negotiation. Once this list is done, parties may be asked to rank these issues according to their importance. Once this task is accomplished, all the issues to be negotiated need to be put into a master list where they are then negotiated according to their importance. If one party's issue is ranked No. 1, then the next two issues of the other party would be ranked Nos. 2 and 3. No. 4 would be occupied by the second issue belonging to the first party, and so on. Detailed instructions for conducting a family conference are contained in the Planned Parenting workbook (L'Abate, 1996).

Functions of This Model

This model integrates both theoretical and therapeutic schools in the sense that structure and process contain almost all the previous models contained in the theory and beyond the theory itself.

Diagnostically one needs to relate how a person negotiates to what the outcome will be. It is doubtful that most clinical relationships in need of help will be negotiable in a time of crisis. Only after the tension of the referral question or crisis has been subsided will one be able to negotiate with loved ones.

Prescriptively, most disturbed intimate relationships need a structure because most respondents do not have an idea of what is involved in negotiating. Hence, the prescription goes like this: "Formalize your process of negotiation so you don't get lost in the process."

Therapeutically, if a therapist does not have a model, however abstract, ideal, or theoretical, of how negotiation should take place, it will be very difficult to impart it to intimate relationships in need of guidance and structure, especially verbally.

CONCLUSION

Life is a continuously negotiated process within the context of intimate and nonintimate relationships. However, as indicated here, the ability to negotiate, although necessary, is not sufficient to achieve intimacy in intimate relationships.

Chapter 18

A Concluding Model[16] and a Comparative Model[17]

This brief chapter presents a concluding model that integrates most if not all of the models of the theory into one large scheme (Table 18.1) and presents a second model for integrating at least one model of the theory, selfhood, with individual approaches stressing "internal" characteristics, shared by both attachment and circumplex models, with "external," and multirelational models (Table 18.2).

INTEGRATING THE MODELS OF THE THEORY: MODEL[16]

This model summarizes and puts together most of the models of the theory, illustrating how complex is the task of understanding intimate relationships. Not much needs to be added, since Table 18.1 is self-explanatory.

INTEGRATING RELATIONSHIP MODELS INTO ONE: MODEL[17]

This section presents an integrative model that allows us to see how selfhood (Ch. 12), as exemplary among the many models of this theory, stands in comparison with models that in some way deal with intimate relationships. The selfhood model stands in the very middle of a continuum defined by internality on the left side (Table 18.2) and externality on the right side, with attachment and circumplex models dealing with internal traits or states, and De Giacomo's Elementary Pragmatic Model, Family Paradigms (Reiss, 1981), and Family Types (McCubbin et al., 1988), dealing with observable and

Table 18.1. Toward a Classification of Relationships: Model[17]

*Priorities	Settings	Contexts	Resources	Situations	Interactions
Survival					
Information	Home	Communal versus, agentic	Emotionality	Intense-relaxed	Parent-child
Services	School/ work	Personal versus impersonal	Rationality	Involved-uninvolved	Partner-partner Sibling-sibling
Money	Leisure	Egalitarian versus dominant/ submissive	Activity	Superficial-profound Short-lived-prolonged	Extended family Friends
Enjoyment					
Importance	Transit	Casual formal/informal	Awareness	Relevant-irrelevant	Neighbors
Intimacy	Transitory	Intimate versus nonintimate Cooperative versus competitive		Friendly-hostile	Acquaintances Employer-employee Employee-employee Stranger-stranger

*Please note that entries in columns do not match with each other horizontally.

Table 18.2. Theoretical Integration of Six Relational Models According to a Continuum of Internality-Externality*

Internality					Externality
		Models			
Attachment	Circumplex	Selfhood	EPM	Family Paradigms	Family Types
Secure	Friendly	Selfful	Sharing	Environmental balanced	Balanced
Dismissing	Dominant	Selfish	Maintaining	Achieving-distancing-limiting	Disconnected
Preoccupied	Submissive	Selfless	Accepting	Consensus-preoccupied	Traditional
Fearful	Hostile	No-self	Antifunction	Emotionally strained	

*See text for references.

measurable family interactions. The selfhood model stands in the middle of both internal and external factors.

This integrative model acknowledges the relevance of internal feelings and cognitions as well as underlying external, intimate, interpersonal, and intergenerational relationships. These relationships are stressed by other models that are independent but conceptually similar with selfhood, especially in stressing just four major dimensions, one functional and three dysfunctional. Comparison of selfhood with attachment and De Giacomo's Elementary Pragmatic model (L'Abate, 2003a; L'Abate & De Giacomo, 2003; L'Abate et al., 2000) showed that all three models deal with similar dimensions defined by one functional and three dysfunctional ones, a characteristic also shared by the two family paradigms and family types.

CONCLUSION

A concluding summary model integrates the various models of the theory. Whether this model is useful remains to be seen. Another model of the theory compares selfhood well conceptually by bridging the gap between models of internal, intrapsychic dimensions with models of how families function or dysfunction.

Part VI

Conclusion

This concluding part indicates where evidence can be found to evaluate models of the theory in Chapter 19. Clearly, a great deal of research will be necessary to evaluate all the models in the laboratory, and in primary, secondary, and tertiary prevention settings. In Chapter 20, I prognosticate what is necessary to keep a theory alive, that is: excellent collaborators in the past as well as colleagues who, hopefully in the future, will disprove the validity of the models in this theory.

Chapter 19

Testing the Theory in the Laboratory and Prevention Settings

This chapter summarizes how models derived from meta-theoretical assumptions, as well as models derived from the theory proper, can be evaluated in the laboratory as well as in primary, secondary, and tertiary prevention settings.

EVALUATING MODELS OF THE THEORY

Evidence to support the validity of methods of evaluation for previous models of the theory has taken place since their creation (L'Abate & Wagner, 1985; L'Abate & Wagner, 1988). All this evidence cannot be summarized here for reasons of redundancy and space. Hence, only sources where this evidence can be found will be given, with the exception of the selfhood Model[10].

ERAAwC: Model[1]

In addition to the evidence reported in Chapter 4, methods of evaluation for this model can be found in the following sources:

- *Laboratory*: Evidence to support the Relational Answers Questionnaire (RAQ) has been presented in Chapter 4 and in L'Abate and De Giacomo (2003). Items and scoring information for this test are available in L'Abate (1996).

- *Primary prevention*: This model can be evaluated interactively through the Helpfulness Enrichment Program (L'Abate & Weinstein, 1987; L'Abate & Young, 1987). Unpublished research supporting the usefulness of this model was reported in Cusinato and L'Abate (2003).
- *Secondary prevention*: Research to support the effectiveness and accountability of the Negotiation workbook has been summarized in L'Abate (1992), and in L'Abate and De Giacomo (2003). An estimated effect size analysis for this workbook is available in L'Abate (2004b).
- *Tertiary prevention*: It is doubtful whether negotiation skills can be imparted directly to respondents using unstructured, f2f talk-based approaches in psychotherapy. It would be very costly and time-consuming to attempt it. Even if taught in the professional's office, skills required for negotiation need to be practiced and rehearsed at home. Some psychotherapists argue that respondents learn to negotiate by emulating the therapist's style. This argument, however, needs to be demonstrated.

Models [2,3,4,5,&6]

- *Laboratory*: Models 2 through 6 have not been evaluated directly, even though suggestions about how to evaluate them have been given. However, evaluation of models in the theory is contained in the still experimental 200-item "What Applies to Me that I Agree With?" questionnaire (L'Abate & De Giacomo, 2003) that has never been administered anywhere.
- *Primary prevention*: Some of these models can be evaluated indirectly through various lessons from enrichment programs for couples and families (L'Abate & Weinstein, 1987; L'Abate & Young, 1987).
- *Secondary prevention*: If not directly, some models can be evaluated indirectly through workbooks independent but conceptually similar to them (L'Abate, 2004a).
- *Tertiary prevention*: Through f2f talk, therapists who become familiar with this theory may be able to see how its models apply to themselves as well as to respondents seen in their offices.

The Triangle of Living: Model [7]

- *Laboratory*: Since this model is derived directly from Foa and Foa's (1974) resource exchange theory (really a model!), instruments derived from that model could be used by combining them according to this model to see whether the original model, revised in combination of two resources for each modality, is still valid.

- *Primary prevention*: This model is contained in a lesson of an enrichment program for couples and families (L'Abate & Weinstein, 1987; L'Abate & Young, 1987).
- *Secondary prevention*: This model is contained as an assignment of the Negotiation workbook (L'Abate, 1986, 1996).
- *Tertiary prevention:* This model can be evaluated easily f2f through talk with prototypes defining this model (Ch. 9).

The Likeness Continuum in Identity-Differentiation: Model [8]

- *Laboratory:* This model can be evaluated through paper and pencil, self-report tests that have been applied only once or not at all: (1) Likeness Scale, which is global and nonspecific (L'Abate, 1994; L'Abate & Wagner, 1985); (2) Likeness Grid, which is also global and nonspecific (L'Abate, 1994; L'Abate & Wagner, 1988); (3) this dimension is contained in the What Applies to Me that I Agree With? Questionnaire (L'Abate & De Giacomo, 2003), which is very specific and evaluates most models of the theory; (4) the CMS Likeness Questionnaire (Cusinato, 1999) has been evaluated in a different format in Italy (L'Abate & De Giacomo, 2003), and is found in L'Abate (1996).
- *Primary prevention*: This model is available as a lesson in the Negotiation Enrichment program (L'Abate & Weinstein, 1987; L'Abate & Young, 1987).
- *Secondary prevention*: This model is available as an assignment in the Negotiation workbook (L'Abate, 1986, 1996) as well as a workbook on Who Am I? (L'Abate, 1996; L'Abate & De Giacomo, 2003).
- *Tertiary prevention:* This continuum can be evaluated impressionistically through specific questions in f2f interviews.

Styles in Intimate Relationships: Model [9]

These styles, as defined in Chapter 11—(1) abusive-apathetic (AA); (2) reactive-repetitive (RR); and (3) conductive-creative (CC)—are readily observable and visible in f2f interviews, except when the abuse is hidden to avoid legal persecution.

- *Laboratory:* These styles can be evaluated in the 240-item Problems-in-Relationships Scale (PIRS), which is described in L'Abate (1992, 1996) and in additional publications. It was used by McMahan and L'Abate (2001) to evaluate the outcome of two workbooks administered to seminarian couples. It correlated significantly with the Spanier Dyadic Adjustment Scale for couples.

- *Primary prevention*: This model is part of an enrichment program (L'Abate & Weinstein, 1987; L'Abate & Young, 1987).
- *Secondary prevention*: This model is contained as an assignment in the Negotiation workbook (L'Abate, 1986, 1996). It is also part of a workbook where written homework assignments match the various conflict scales composing the PIRS (L'Abate, 1992, 1996).
- *Tertiary prevention:* As already mentioned above, these styles are readily available in f2f interviews, except when respondents are aware that reporting abuse is a punishable offense and they try to fake a CC style at least in initial interviews. This presentational facade may crumble when members of the family eventually break the nondisclosing taboo.

Selfhood: Model [10]

This model has been evaluated more often than all the other models even though it still needs further evaluation through a variety of instruments: (1) The Self-Other Profile Chart (SOPC; L'Abate, 1992, 1994, 1997, 2002, 2003a, 2004b; L'Abate & De Giacomo, 2003); and (2) The Dyadic Relations Test (Cusinato & L'Abate, 2003, 2004). Research directed toward evaluating this model has been presented in previous publications. Here, two different sources of support will be considered: indirect and direct.

Indirect Evidence

Evidence that is conceptually similar but independent of this model has been reviewed consistently in previous publications, as in the case of research by Baumeister et al. (1996). Blatt's original model is specific to the nature of depression but is not related to any other personality propensities of selfhood except selflessness and its prototype depression. Therefore, one needs to look at depression where individuals value others more than themselves. Blatt has changed from two factors of dependency versus self-criticism in depression, considered in Chapter 12, to relatedness and self-definition, adding also a third factor of efficacy.

To wit: Blatt and coworkers (Blatt, Zohar et al., 1995; Henrich, Blatt, Kuperminc, Zohar, & Leadbeater, 2001; Zuroff, Moskowitz, & Koestner, 1996), and Rude and Burnham (1993, 1995) have identified subcomponents of the dependency construct—connectedness and neediness—that are even closer to the constructs of self-other importance. Both factors are related to social functioning, especially in pubertal girls (Henrich et al., 2001). What Blatt has called dependency can be thought of as consisting both of "neediness" and a somewhat more mature/adaptive form or concern for relationships and "connections with others." Using the Depressive Experiences Question-naire (DEQ), both relatedness (dependency, helplessness, and feelings of loss and abandonment) and self-definition (self-criticism, self-worth, loss of autonomy, and feelings of failure, and guilt) might be related to internal-izing and externalizing problems, after controlling for levels of depressive symptoms (Kupermink, Blatt, & Leadbetter, 1997).

Gender differences in externalizing and internalizing problems on the QED-A seem to relate to increases in girls' internalizing symptoms and, compared to boys, were partly explained by greater stability in girls' rela-tionships with parents and peers. Boys' greater tendencies toward external-ization might be partly explained by greater vulnerability to self-criticism (Leadbeater, Kuperminc, Hertzog, & Blatt, 1999).

Beck's Model of sociotropy and autonomy has been reviewed in Chap-ter 12, but it relates only to selflessness and depression.

Direct Evidence

The selfhood model can be evaluated through three different tests (Table 1.1). The Self-Other Profile Chart (SOPC; L'Abate, 1992, 1997) consists of ratings of self-characteristics (intelligence, looks, sense of humor, etc.) that make one feel important, and of selected intimates (parents, partner, chil-dren, etc.) that make one feel important. It takes a few minutes to adminis-ter and score and it correlates significantly with two lengthier self-concept scales (L'Abate, 1997), suggesting that this instrument shows sufficient psy-chometric strength to warrant further research. In a sample of 430 high school students, Cusinato (personal communication, June 18, 1997) found an alpha coefficient of .83 for self-ratings ($p < .001$) and of .88 for rat-ings of others ($p < .001$). Considering the results of internal consistency for this instrument with undergraduates, and with psychiatric patients and controls, it would seem that the internal consistency of this instrument is acceptable.

Problems in Relationships Scale (L'Abate, 1992) consists of 240 items on a applicable/nonapplicable format that measures 20 problem areas of couple relationship conflicts that are paralleled by 20 written homework lessons isomorphic to the 20 areas measured by the test. From the 240 items, it is possible to extract scores on the four personality propensities of the model. Some preliminary data from my practice show that clinical couples tend to fall within the no-self propensity.

Cusinato (personal communication, October 17, 1997) has found that most normal couples tend to fall within the selfful propensity range. He has constructed (1997) seven visual versions of the Problems in Relationships Test called the Dyadic Relationships Test. It consists of comic-type visual and verbal vignettes for the seven different stages of the life cycle—close to wedding, young married couple without children, couple with small (preschool) children, couple with school-age children, couple with teenagers, couple with adult children, and empty nest couples. For example, one vignette shows and describes a change of plans for a couple who was going to spend the weekend with friends. At the last minute, the parents of one partner report that a long-lost uncle was coming and the couple was invited to a party to celebrate his return. The four answers to this conflict represent the four personality propensities: selfful. "Let's see how we can combine both parties," selfish, "I have no intention of changing my program!" selfless, "If you like, we can let go of our friends," no-self, "We will end arguing again."

The psychometric properties of this instrument were evaluated in 23 dissertations covering internal consistency (between .33 for no-self to .75 for selfulness), correlations with Parental Locus of Control scale (positive and statistically significant, $p < .05$), correlations with a scale of Couple Negotiation (positive and statistically significant, $p < .05$ level), and correlations with a scale of Couple Communication (positive and statistically significant, $p < .05$). On the basis of the studies that evaluated the concurrent validity of an earlier version of this test, a second version showed acceptable item homogeneity as well as significant inter-correlations ($p < .001$): negative between selfulness and selfishness, positive but not significant between selfulness and selflessness, negative but not significant between selfulness and no-self (Cusinato & L'Abate, 2004). The correlations between selfishness, selflessness, and no-self were all positive and statistically significant. A more complete report of this research has been submitted for publication.

Selfhood and Classification of Psychopathology

This model of psychopathology (Fig. 12.4) was evaluated with the MMPI-2, as well as the Doverspike's Rating Sheets (L'Abate, Lambert, & Schenck, 2001) using four algorithms with over 800 clinical respondents made available from 75 clinical psychologists in Georgia. The results of this study tend to support a relationship between profiles of externalization with ratings of externalization, profiles of internalization with ratings of internalization, and profiles of psychopathology with severe psychopathology. Since this was a sample of clinical respondents, there was no way to measure functionality, since there were very few respondents who ranged in the "normal" category.

When this four-partite model is applied to couple relationships, there are at least three research studies, in addition to evidence summarized elsewhere (L'Abate, 1994, 1997; L'Abate & De Giacomo, 2003), that support a classification of couples according to how importance is attributed and asserted, even though different constructs and measures were used.

Selfhood and Addictions

In Franzoso's (2002) research with 100 drug addicts using the SOPC and the RAQ, correlations among self-importance (SI) and other-importance (OI) were almost all statistically significant in the clinical group: between SI and E ($r = .20$, $p < .05$), SI and R ($r = .45$, $p < .01$), SI and A ($r = .30$, $p < .01$), SI and Aw ($r = .29$, $p < .01$). OI correlated significantly with E ($r = .23$, $p < .05$), R ($r = .36$, $p < .01$), and A ($r = .32$, $p < .01$). In the control group (nonclinical, functional) there were no significant correlations between SI, OI, and the scales of the RAQ. Hence, these correlations tend to suggest that only with extreme scores, certain relationships between personality and relational styles become evident.

The factorial structure of the selfhood and ERAAwC models within the clinical and control groups, obtained through the LISREL analysis, allows us to identify its formal structure though item correlations. In both groups, in the taxonomy of the SI, all the items are significantly correlated and one can identify that in the SI items of clinical cases, there is a high degree of correlation between report of academic success ($r = .92$, $p < .05$), career ($r = .53$, $p < .05$), creativity ($r = .53$, $p < .05$), and sense of humor ($r = .52$, $p < .05$). These correlations suggest unrealistically high scores in self-evaluation that parallel those of Baumeister et al. (1996) with criminals. In the control group, instead, items with the highest values were intelligence ($r = .76$, $p < .05$), morality ($r = .40$, $p < .05$), self-esteem ($r = .63$, $p < .05$), physical appearance ($r = .70$, $p < .05$), and sports ($r = .69$, $p < .05$). In the OI, on the other hand, there was no factorial relevance in the clinical group. In drug addicts, the items with the highest values were: father ($r = .82$, $p < .05$), children ($r = .39$, $p < .05$), coworkers ($r = .71$, $p < .05$), and another significant person ($r = .48$, $p < .05$). In the control group, the only two items with elevated values were partner ($r = .52$, $p < .05$) and mother ($r = .77$, $p < .05$). In the control group, all items were highly significant.

- *Primary prevention*: Some lessons derived from this model are available in enrichment programs for couples and families (L'Abate & Weinstain, 1987; L'Abate & Young, 1987).
- *Secondary prevention*: A workbook developed from the SOPC is available online (L'Abate, 1996).
- *Tertiary prevention*: Patterns of selfhood are easily visible in f2f talk, especially when intergenerational, generational, and developmental histories are taken.

Priorities: Model [11]

- *Laboratory:* The Priorities Grid and the Priorities Scale were reported in early publications (L'Abate, 1994; L'Abate & Wagner, 1985).
- *Primary prevention:* There is one assignment in the Negotiation Enrichment program (L'Abate & Weinstein, 1987; L'Abate & Young, 1987).
- *Secondary prevention:* There is one assignment in the Negotiation workbook (L'Abate, 1986, 1996).
- *Tertiary prevention:* Priorities can be assessed through f2f interviews. However, one must be careful about looking at the consistency between what respondents say and what they actually do, intentions are not always linked to actual behavior ("The road to hell is paved with ... ").

Distance Regulation Model [12]

- *Laboratory:* There is not yet a direct way developed to evaluate this model.
- *Primary prevention:* Ditto.
- *Secondary prevention:* There is an assignment about this triangle in the Depression workbook (L'Abate, 1986, 1996).
- *Tertiary prevention:* This model can be evaluated relatively well in f2f interviews, by how respondents sit, how they talk to each other, and how they indicate their distance through nonverbal movements and acts.

The Drama Triangle Model [13]

- *Laboratory:* There is no direct way yet devised to evaluate this model.
- *Primary prevention:* Ditto.
- *Secondary prevention:* There is an assignment for this triangle in the Depression (L'Abate, 1986, 1996) workbook.
- *Tertiary prevention:* This model in especially evident in seriously handicapped relationships through prolonged f2f interviews.

Intimacy: Model [14]

- *Laboratory:* This model has been evaluated with Sharing of Hurts Scale (Stevens & L'Abate, 1989) and with a revision of that scale by Cusinato (Cusinato et al., 1998).
- *Primary prevention:* This model is found in various exercises from various structured enrichment programs (L'Abate & Weinstein, 1987).

- *Secondary prevention*: Intimacy workbook (L'Abate, 1986, 1992) and research by Cusinato et al. (1998) with undergraduates. An estimated effect size analysis about the outcome from the administration of this workbook is found in L'Abate (2004b).
- *Tertiary prevention*: In psychotherapy, this model can be evaluated and applied through f2f interviews and administration of therapeutic tasks in the professional's office as well as through homework assignments: (1) Sharing of Hurts (L'Abate, 1986, 1994, 1997, 1999a; Vangelisti & Maguire, 2002); and (2) Being Together Task: hugging, holding, huddling, and cuddling (3HC) (Feldman, Weller, Sirota, & Eidelman, 2003; L'Abate, 2003a; L'Abate & De Giacomo, 2003). This prescribed task could be conceived of as a universal vaccine in view of its cost-effectiveness and its possible mass administration.

Negotiating How to Solve Problems: Model [15]

- *Laboratory*: No direct instrument has been devised to evaluate this model directly.
- *Primary prevention*: An enrichment program (helpfullness) is available (L'Abate & Weinstein, 1987; L'Abate & Young, 1987).
- *Secondary prevention*: There is a workbook about this model (L'Abate, 1986) as well as the Planned Parenting workbook (L'Abate, 1996).
- *Tertiary prevention*: It is questionable whether this skill can be imparted to respondents verbally in f2f interviews. It is necessary to help respondents learn this skill through repeated homework assignments.

Classifying Relationships: Model [16]

- *Laboratory*: No available instruments is yet available to test this model.
- *Primary prevention*: Ditto.
- *Secondary prevention*: Ditto.
- *Tertiary prevention*: This model is too encompassing to be evaluated directly in f2f interviewd.

Integrating Various Models of Relationships: Model [17]

- *Laboratory*: A beginning step was taken by L'Abate et al. (2000) by correlating the SOPC, the Self-View Questionnaire by De Giacomo and L'Abate (2003), and the Italian version of an Adult Attachment Questionnaire to four groups of respondents, one control group and three clinical groups with significant correlations among the three

instruments (L'Abate, 2003a), suggesting that even though these instruments were derived from three different theoretical sources, they
were all looking at pretty much the same type of relationships. The
results of a replication of this study are being analyzed (L'Abate et al.,
research in progress).

- *Primary prevention*: Only the selfhood model has developed a lesson in an enrichment program (L'Abate & Weinstein, 1987; L'Abate &
Young, 1987).
- *Secondary prevention*: Only the attachment, elementary pragmatic,
and selfhood models have developed structured approaches to evaluate their respective models. The Circumplex, Family Paradigms, and
Family Types lack such an approach.
- *Tertiary prevention*: It would be very difficult to evaluate these models
in f2f interviews.

CONCLUSION

A beginning step has been made in trying to evaluate the models of this
theory in the laboratory as well as in primary, secondary, and tertiary settings.
However, a great deal of work still needs to be done to evaluate whether
this theory and its models are valid.

Chapter 20

The Future of the Theory

It follows from this theory that the goal of any psychological intervention would be to help people learn to love themselves and intimate others and to negotiate with them and nonintimates in more effective ways than they have done heretofore. How can this goal be achieved? It can be achieved very gradually and in many ways: some independent from the theory, some indirectly related to the theory, and some derived directly from the theory. The process of testing models drawn from this theory in the laboratory has been developed and revised *pari passu* with theory building and theory testing (L'Abate & Wagner, 1985, 1988) (see Table 1.1, Ch. 19).

Admittedly, the scope and range encompassed by this theory and its applications are quite grandiose. The issue, however, is not whether the theory is grandiose or modest. The issue with any theory is whether it is reliably verifiable, valid in the laboratory and other settings, and useful in producing results in clinical situations. Unfortunately, no matter how hard one may try, no criteria of verifiability and accountability can be fulfilled by the author of any theory, and especially this one. Building a theory is a full-time job that leaves little time for its author to verify it. In spite of this limitation, I have attempted to verify bits and pieces of the theory through the provision of instruments and intervention strategies that would allow replicability of operations in the laboratory and other settings.

However, clinical or empirical results claimed by a researcher or his coworkers would very likely be biased, suspect, and, therefore, question-able. Ultimately, any theory needs evaluation by those who have no other aim than to evaluate whether the theory is everything it claims to be. Whether the theory is valid and useful needs to be evaluated by those who did not create it. Hence, the need to provide instruments that are easily and readily replicable.

The rest of this chapter provides some guidelines on how to keep a theory alive and well in spite of the odds against it.

HOW TO KEEP THE THEORY ALIVE

The best way to keep a theory alive is to research it as often and as easily as possible. I and my two major collaborators, Mario Cusinato and Piero De Giacomo, have attempted, as shown in some pages of this work, to do just that. Given the wide range of detailed relationships encompassed by the models of the theory, it is virtually and practically impossible for one author to accomplish this task, no matter how important. The best one can do is provide ways and means whereby others can evaluate models of the theory directly, and by evaluating its models, evaluate also the theory indirectly. More important, the best thing a theoretician can do is find competent collaborators, like Mario Cusinato and Piero De Giacomo, who, with their students, are able to expand and verify parts of the theory piecemeal.

HOW TO KEEP A THEORY FLEXIBLE

Since its inception (L'Abate, 1976), the theory has undergone many revisions, becoming more and more complex, more and more specific, and, with the constructions of ways and means to evaluate it, easier to evaluate it (L'Abate, 2003a). Hence, the way to keep a theory up-to-date is to keep it flexible enough to change it as one goes on the basis of evidence rather than on the basis of wishful thinking or faith.

HOW TO KEEP A THEORY USEFUL

The ways to keep a theory useful are to apply it however and whenever you can in the laboratory, in prevention, psychotherapy, and rehabilitation settings, using methods developed from models of the theory and to evaluate it comparatively with other methods developed from competing theories or interventions.

CONCLUSION

As Lewin (1935) was fond of saying: "There is nothing as practical as a good theory)." However, there are many theories that may not be useful or at least appear to be useful at first blush, but become superseded by newer and more useful theories. Most theories of personality, for instance, except perhaps for psychoanalytic and systems theories, do not show or produce ways to apply them either in the laboratory or in the clinic. By the same token, the personality circumplex model, as another instance, is completely devoid of clinical interventions. It may serve as an outcome measure. However, like many theories in relationship science (Bradbury, 2003), it does not lend itself to clinical interventions.

Consequently, this theory has raised the ante for the evaluation of a theory. A theory must not only be valid in the laboratory but also in the clinic and other settings. Furthermore, while interventions must be empirically based, as the latest requirement is now becoming more and more widespread, according to this theory, interventions must also be theory-derived. If empirically based interventions are not theory-derived, they must at least be theory-related, as the case may be. There may be interventions that are independent from theories. If and when that is the case, no matter how useful they may be, theoretical links will be made on a post hoc basis, since no intervention can survive in an a-theoretical vacuum. Empiricism and theory construction must go hand-in-hand, because one cannot survive without the other.

References

Abela, J. R. Z. (2002). Depressive mood reactions to failure in the achievement domain: A test of the integration of the hopelessness and self-esteem theories of depression. *Cognitive Therapy & Research, 26*, 531–552.

Abidin, R. (1992). The determinants of parenting behavior. *Journal of Clinical Child Psychology, 21*, 407–412.

Abidin, R., Jenkins, C., & McGaughey, M. (1992). The relationship of early family variables to children's subsequent behavioral adjustment. *Journal of Clinical Child Psychology, 21*, 60–69.

Abrams, D. B., & Niaura, R. S. (1987). Social learning theory. In H. T. Blane & K. E. Leonard (Eds.), *Psychological theories of drinking and alcoholism* (pp. 131–178). New York: Guilford.

Abramson, P. R., & Pinkerton, S. D. (2002). *With pleasure: Thoughts on human sexuality*. New York: Oxford University Press.

Achenbach, T. M., & Edelbrock, C. S. (1978). The classification of child psychopathology: A review and analysis of empirical efforts. *Psychological Bulletin, 85*, 1275–1301.

Acock, A. C., & Bengtson, V. L. (1978). On the relative influence of mothers and fathers: A covariance analysis of political and religious socialization. *Journal of Marriage & the Family, 40*, 519–530.

Adam, K., Bouckoms, A., & Streiner, D. (1982). Parental loss and family stability in attempted suicide. *Archives of General Psychiatry, 39*, 1081–1085.

Adams, P. L., Milner, J. R., & Schrepf, N. A. (1984). *Fatherless children*. New York: Wiley-Interscience.

Adams-Webber, J., & Davidson, D. (1979). Maximum contrast between self and others inpersonal judgment: A repertory grid study. *British Journal of Psychology, 70*, 517–518.

Agnew, C. R., & Loving, T. J. (1998). Future time orientation and condom use attitudes, intentions, and behavior. *Journal of Social Behavior & Personality, 13*, 755–764.

Agnew, C. R., Loving, T. J., Le, B., & Goodfriend, W. (2004). Thinking close: Measuring relational closeness as perceived self-other inclusion. In D. J. Mashek & A. Aron (Eds.), *Handbook of closeness and intimacy* (pp. 103–115). Mahwah, NJ: Earlbaum.

Agrawal, G., & Saksena, N. (1977). Emotional development of the child and role of the parents: An overview. *Child Psychiatry Quarterly, 10*, 1–7.

Aiken, L. R. (1999). *Human differences*. Mahwah, NJ: Earlbaum.

Akerley, M. S. (1975). The invulnerable parent. *Journal of Autism & Childhood Schizophrenia, 5*, 275–281.

Akhtar, S. (1996). Further exploration of gender differences in personality disorders. *American Journal of Psychiatry, 153*, 846–847.

Akiskal, H. S., et al. (1985). Affective disorders in referred children and younger siblings of manic depressives: Modes of onset and prospective source. *Archives of General Psychiatry, 42*, 996–1003.

Alden, L. E., & Phillips, N. (1990). An interpersonal analysis of social anxiety and depression. Self perception, social anxiety, social behavior and major depression. *Cognitive Therapy & Research, 14*, 499–512.

Alden, L., Teschuk, M., & Tee, K. (1992). Public self-awareness and withdrawal from social interactions. *Cognitive Therapy & Research, 16*, 249–267.

Alexander, J. F., Waldron, H. B., Barton, C., & Mas, C. H. (1989). The minimizing of blaming attributions and behaviors in delinquent families. *Journal of Consulting & Clinical Psychology, 57*, 19–24.

Allen, M. G., Greenspan, S. I., & Pollin, W. (1976). The effect of parental perceptions on early development in twins. *Psychiatry, 39*, 65–71.

Alley, P. M. (1984). The Family Responsibility Index: A behavioral measure of marital work allocation. *Journal of Personality Assessment, 48*, 3–5.

Alloy, L., Abramson, L., Tashman, N., & Berrebbi, D. (2001). Developmental origins of cognitive vulnerability to depression: Parenting, cognitive, and inferential feedback styles of the parents of individuals at high and low cognitive risk for depression. *Cognitive Therapy & Research, 25*, 397–423.

Alloy, L. B., Abramson, L. Y., Metalsky, G. I., & Hartlage, S. (1988). The hopelessness theory of depression: Attributional aspects. *British Journal of Clinical Psychology, 27*, 335–349.

Alloy, L. B., Abramson, L., Whitehouse, W. G., & Hogan, M. E. (1999). Depressogenic cognitive styles: Predictive validity, information processing and personality characteristics and developmental origin. *Behavior Research & Therapy, 37*, 503–531.

Alloy, L. B., & Clements, C. M. (1998). Hopelessness theory of depression: Tests of the symptom component. *Cognitive Therapy & Research, 22*, 303–335.

American Psychiatric Association. (1994). *Diagnostic criteria from DSM-IV*. Washington, DC: Author.

Amir, N., Freshman, M., Ramsey, B., & Neary, E. (2001). Thought-action fusion in individuals with OCD symptoms. *Behavior Research & Therapy, 39*, 765–776.

Ammerman, R., & Patz, R. (1996). Determinants of child abuse potential: Contribution of parent and child factors. *Journal of Clinical Child Psychology, 25*, 300–307.

Amminger, G. P., Pape, S., Rock, D., & Roberts, S. (1999). Relationship between childhood behavioral disturbance and later schizophrenia in the New York high-risk project. *American Journal of Psychiatry, 156*, 525–530.

Ammon, G. (1975). Death and identity. *Human Context, 7*, 94–102.

Andersen, B. L., Cyranowski, J. M., & Aarestad, S. (2000). Beyond artificial, sex-linked distinctions to conceptualize female sexuality: Comment on Baumeister (2000). *Psychological Bulletin, 126*, 380–384.

Anderson, J. R., & Waldron, I. (1983). Behavioral and content components of the structured interview assessment of the Type A behavior patterns in women. *Journal of Behavioral Medicine, 6*, 123–134.

Angold, A., & Costello, E. J. (1993). Depressive comorbidity in children and adolescents: Empirical, theoretical, and methodological issues. *American Journal of Psychiatry, 150*, 1779–1791.

Anthony, E. J. (1978). Operational thinking at adolescence in relation to psychosomatic disorder. *Journal of Youth & Adolescence, 7*, 307–318.

Applebaum, F. (1978). Loneliness: A taxonomy and psychodynamic view. *Clinical Social Work Journal, 6,* 13–20.

Araji, S. (1977). Husbands' and wives' attitude-behavior congruence on family roles. *Journal of Marriage & the Family, 39,* 309–320.

Arnold, E., O'Leary, S., & Edwards, G. (1997). Father involvement and self-report parenting of children with attention deficit-hyperactivity disorder. *Journal of Consulting & Clinical Psychology, 65,* 337–342.

Arntz, A. (1999). Do personality disorders exist? On the validity of the concept and its cognitive behavioral formulation and treatment. *Behaviour Research & Therapy, 37,* 97–134.

Aron, E. N. (2004). The impact of adult temperament on closeness and intimacy. In D. J. Mashek & A. Aron (Eds.), *Handbook of closeness and intimacy* (pp. 267–283). Mahwah, NJ: Earlbaum.

Aronoff, J., & Crano, W. D. (1975). A re-examination of the cross-cultural principles of task segregation and sex role differentiation in the family. *American Sociological Review, 40,* 12–20.

Asarnow, J., & Callan, J. (1985). Boys with peer adjustment problems: Social cognitive processes. *Journal of Consulting & Clinical Psychology, 53,* 80–87.

Athanasiou, R., & Yoshioka, G. A. (1973). The spatial character of friendship formation. *Environment & Behavior, 5,* 43–65.

Averill, J. R. (1997). The emotions: An integrative approach. In R. Hogan, J. Johnson, & S. Briggs (Eds.), *Handbook of personality psychology* (pp. 513–541). San Diego, CA: Academic Press.

Averill, J. R., & Nunley, E. P. (1992). *Voyages of the heart: Living an emotionally creative life.* New York: Free Press.

Axelrod, S. D. (1999). *Work and the evolving self: Theoretical and clinical considerations.* Hillsdale, NJ: Analytic Press.

Aydin, G. (1988). The remediation of children's helpless explanatory style and related unpopularity. *Cognitive Therapy & Research, 12,* 155–165.

Azar, S. T. (2002). Adult development and parenthood: A social-cognitive perspective. In J. Demick & C. Andreortti (Eds.), *Handbook of adult development* (pp. 391–415). New York: Kluwer Academic.

Bacon, L. (1974). Early motherhood, accelerated role transition, and social pathologies. *Social Forces, 52,* 333–341.

Bagby, R. M., Schuller, D., Parker, J., & Levitt, A. (1994). Major depression and the self-criticism and dependency personality dimensions. *American Journal of Psychiatry, 151,* 597–599.

Bagby, R. M., Segal, Z., & Schuller, D. R. (1995). Dependency, self-criticism and attributional style: A re-examination. *British Journal of Clinical Psychology, 34,* 82–84.

Bahal, M., & Sexena, V. (1978). Effects of family setting upon cognitive development of the children: A review. *Child Psychiatry Quarterly, 11,* 1–5.

Baird, M. (1974). Characteristic interaction patterns in families of encopretic children. *Bulletin of the Menninger Clinic, 38,* 144–153.

Bakan, D. (1968). *Disease, pain and sacrifice: Toward a psychology of suffering.* Boston: Beacon Press.

Baker, L. J., Hastings, J. E., & Hart, J. D. (1984). Enhanced psychological responses of Type A coronary patients during Type A–relevant imagery. *Journal of Behavioral Medicine, 7,* 287–306.

Baker, S. (1980). Biological influences on human sex and gender. *Signs—Cornell University Medical College, 6,* 80–90.

Baldwin, K., & Tinsley, H. E. (1988). An investigation of the validity of Tinsley and Tinsley (1986) theory of leisure experience. *Journal of Counseling Psychology, 35,* 263–267.

Ball, S. G., Baer, L., & Otto, M. W. (1996). Symptoms subtypes of obsessive-compulsive disorder in behavioral treatment studies: A quantitative review. *Behaviour Research & Therapy, 34,* 47–51.

Ball, S. G., Otto, M. W., Pollack, M. H., & Uccello, R. (1995). Differentiating social phobia and panic disorder: A test of core beliefs. *Cognitive Therapy & Research, 19,* 473–481.

Balswick, J. O., & Macrides, C. (1975). Parental stimulus for adolescent rebellion. *Adolescence, 10,* 253–266.

Bandura, A. (1978). The self-system in reciprocal determinism. *American Psychologist, 33,* 344–358.

Bandura, A. (2001). Social cognitive theory: An agentic perspective. *Annual Review of Psychology, 52,* 1–26.

Banerji, S. (1978). On alienation: Psychological point of view. *Samiksa, 32,* 32–43.

Bank, S., & Kahn, M. D. (1976). Sisterhood-brotherhoodis powerful: Sibling subsystems and family therapy. *Annual Progress in Child Psychiatry & Child Development,* 493–519.

Banyard, V. L. (1999). Childhood maltreatment and the mental health of low-income women. *American Journal of Orthopsychiatry, 69,* 161–171.

Barber, M., Marzuk, P., Leon, A., & Portera, L. (1998). Aborted suicide attempt: A new classification of suicidal behavior. *American Journal of Psychiatry, 155,* 385–389.

Bargh, J. A., & Chartrand, T. L. (1999). The unbearable automaticity of being. *American Psychologist, 54,* 462–479.

Barkley, R. A. (1990). *Attention deficit hyperactivity disorder: A handbook for diagnosis and treatment.* New York: Guilford.

Barlow, D. H. (Ed.). (1993). *Clinical handbook of psychological disorders.* New York: Guilford.

Barnes, J., Fisher, J., & Palmer, M. (1979). Family characteristics and intellectual growth: An examination by race. *Educational & Psychological Measurement, 39,* 625–636.

Barnett, P. A., & Gotlib, I. H. (1988). Psychosocial functioning and depression: Distinguishing among antecedents, concomitants, and consequences. *Psychological Bulletin, 104,* 97–126.

Barnett, R. C., & Hyde, J. S. (2001). Women, men, work, and the family: An expansionistic theory. *American Psychologist, 56,* 781–796.

Bar-On, R., & Parker, J. D. A. (Eds.). (2000). *The handbook of emotional intelligence: Theory, development, assessment, and applications at home, school, and the workplace.* San Francisco: Jossey-Bass.

Barone, D. F., Hersen, M., & Van Hasselt, V. B. (Eds.). (1998). *Advanced personality.* New York: Plenum.

Barnett, L. A. (1985). Young childrenís free play and problem-solving ability. *Leisure Sciences, 7,* 25–46.

Barrett, D. E. (1979). A naturalistic study of sex differences in children's aggression. *Merrill-Palmer Quarterly, 25,* 193–203.

Barry, C., Frick, P., DeShazo, T., & McCoy, M. (2000). The importance of callous-unemotional traits for extending the concept of psychopathy to children. *Journal of Abnormal Psychology, 109,* 335–340.

Barsky, A. J., Wool, C., Barnett, M. C., & Cleary, P. D. (1994). Histories of childhood trauma in adult hypochondriacal patients. *American Journal of Psychiatry, 151,* 397–401.

Bartholomew, K., Kwong, M. J., & Hart, S. D. (2001). Attachment. In W. J. Livesley (Ed.), *Handbook of personality disorders: Theory, research, and treatment* (pp. 196–230). New York: Guilford.

Barton, K. (1976). Personality similarity in spouses related to marriage roles. *Multivariate Experimental Clinical Research, 2,* 107–111.

Batlis, N., & Small, A. (1982). Sex roles and Type A behavior. *Journal of Clinical Psychology, 38,* 315–316.

Battle, J. (1978). Relationship between self-esteem and depression. *Psychological Reports, 42,* 745–746.

Baumeister, R. F. (1998). The self. In D. T. Gilbert, S. T. Fiske, & G. Lindzey (Eds.), *Handbook of social psychology* (pp. 680–740). New York: McGraw-Hill.

Baumeister, R. F. (2000). Gender differences in erotic plasticity: The female sex drive as socially flexible and responsive. *Psychological Bulletin, 126,* 347–374.

Baumeister, R. F., & Leary, M. R. (1995). The need to belong: Desire for interpersonal attachments as a fundamental human motivation. *Psychological Bulletin, 117,* 497–529.

Baumeister, R. F., & Scher, S. J. (1988). Self-defeating behavior patterns among normal individuals: Review and analysis of common self-destructive tendencies. *Psychological Bulletin, 104,* 3–22.

Baumeister, R. F., Smart, L., & Boden, J. M. (1996). Relation of threatened egotism to violence and aggression. *Psychological Review, 105,* 5–33.

Baumeister, R. F., & Sommer, K. L. (1997). What do men want? Gender differences and two spheres of belongingness: Comment on Cross and Madson (1997). *Psychological Bulletin, 122,* 38–44.

Baumeister, R. F., Stillwell, A. M., & Heatherton, T. F. (1994). Guilt: An interpersonal approach. *Psychological Bulletin, 115,* 243–267.

Baumeister, R. F., & Tice, D. M. (2001). *The social dimension of sex.* Boston: Allyn & Bacon.

Baumrind, D. (1975). The contributions of the family to the development of competence in children. *Schizophrenia Bulletin, 14,* 12–37.

Baxter, L. A., & West, L. (2003). Couple perception of their similarities and differences: A dialectical perspective. *Journal of Social and Personal Relationships, 20,* 491–514.

Bazerman, M. H., Curhan, J. R., Moore, D. A., & Velley, K. L. (2000). Negotiation. *Annual Review of Psychology, 51,* 279–314.

Beane, J., & Lipka, R. (1980). Self-concept and self-esteem: A construct differentiation. *Child Study Journal, 10,* 1–6.

Beardslee, W. (1987). The role of self-understanding in resilient individuals: The development of a perspective. *American Journal of Orthopsychiatry, 59,* 266–278.

Beardslee, W., Bemporad, J., Keller, M., & Klerman, G. (1983). Children of parents with major affective disorder: A review. *American Journal of Psychiatry, 140,* 825–832.

Beardslee, W., & Podorefsky, D. (1988). Resilient adolescents whose parents have serious affective and other psychiatric disorders: Importance of self-understanding and relationships. *American Journal of Psychiatry, 145,* 63–69.

Beck, A. T. (1976). *Cognitive therapy and the emotional disorders.* New York: International Universities Press.

Beck, A., Brown, G., Berchick, R., & Stewart, B. (1990). Relationship between hopelessness and ultimate suicide: A replication with psychiatric outpatients. *American Journal of Psychiatry, 147,* 190–195.

Beck, J., & Van der Kolk, B. (1987). Reports of childhood incest and current behavior of chronically hospitalized psychotic women. *American Journal of Psychiatry, 144,* 1474–1476.

Beckman-Brindley, S., & Tavormina, J. B. (1978). Power relationship in the families: A social-exchange perspective. *Family Process, 17,* 423–436.

Beech, A. R. (1998). A psychometric typology of sex offenders. *International Journal of Offender Therapy & Comparative Criminology, 42,* 319–339.

Beech, A. R., Fisher, D. D., & Thornton, D. (2003). Rick assessment of sex offenders. *Professional Psychology: Research & Practice, 34,* 339–352.

Begun, J. H. (1976). The sociopathic or psychopathic personality. *International Journal of Social Psychiatry, 22,* 25–46.

Behar, D., Winokur, G., VanValkenburg C., & Lowry M. (1980). Familial subtypes of depression: A clinical view. *Journal of Clinical Psychiatry, 41,* 52–56.

Beirut, L. J., Heath, A. C., Bucholz, K. K., Dinwiddie, S. H. et al. (1999). Major depressive disorder in a community-based twin sample: Are there different genetic and environmental contributions for men and women? *Archives of General Psychiatry, 57,* 557–563.

Bekker, M. H. J. (1996). Agoraphobia and gender: A review. *Clinical Psychology Review, 16,* 129–146.

Bellack, A. S., Sayers, M., Mueser, K., & Bennett, M. (1994). Evaluation of problem solving in schizophrenia. *Journal of Abnormal Psychology, 103,* 371–378.

Belmont, L. (1977). Birth order, intellectual competence, and psychiatric status. *Journal of Individual Psychology, 33,* 97–104.

Belmont, L. (1978). Birth order, intellectual competence, and psychiatric status. *Annual Progress in Child Psychiatry & Child Development,* 51–58.

Belmont, L., Wittes, J., & Stein, Z. (1977). Relation of birth order, family size and social class to psychological functions. *Perceptual & Motor Skills, 5,* 1107–1116.

Belsky, J. (1981). Early human experience: A family perspective. *Developmental Psychology, 17,* 23.

Bem, S. L. (1981). Gender schema theory: A cognitive account of sex typing. *Psychological Review, 88,* 354–364.

Benedict, L., & Zautra, A. (1993). Family environmental characteristics as risk factors for childhood abuse. *Journal of Clinical Psychology, 22,* 365–374.

Benett, P., Gallacher, J., & Johnston, D. (1990). Towards a state measure of Type A behavior. *British Journal of Clinical Psychology, 29,* 155–165.

Benjamin, L. S. (1993). *Interpersonal diagnosis and treatment of personality disorders.* New York: Guilford.

Bennett, L. A., Wolin, S. J., & Reiss, D. (1988). Cognitive, behavioral and emotional problems among school age children of alcoholic parents. *American Journal of Psychiatry, 145,* 185–190.

Berbaum, M., & Moreland, R. (1980). Intellectual development within the family: A new application of the confluence model. *Developmental Psychology, 16,* 506–515.

Berenbaum, H., Raghavan, C., Le, H. N., Vernon, L. L., & Gomez, J. J. (2003). A taxonomy of emotional disturbances. *Clinical Psychology: Science and Practice, 10,* 206–226.

Berger, C. R. (2003). Message production skill in social interaction. In J. O. Green & B. R. Burleson (Eds.), *Handbook of communication and social interaction skills* (pp. 357–389). Mahwah, NJ: Earlbaum.

Bergman, L. R., Magnusson, D., & El-Khouru, B. M. (2003). *Studying individual development in an interindividual context.* Mahwah, NJ: Earlbaum.

Berkovec, T. D., Ray, W. J., & Stober, J. (1998). A cognitive phenomenon intimately linked to affective, phyisiological, and interpersonal behavioral processes. *Cognitive Therapy & Research, 22,* 561–576.

Berkowitz, A., & Perkins, H. W. (1988). Personality characteristics of children of alcoholics. *Journal of Consulting & Clinical Psychology, 56,* 206–209.

Berndt, T. J. (1979). Developmental changes in conformity to peers and parents. *Developmental Psychology, 15,* 608–616.

Berns, S. B., Jacobson, N. S., & Gottman, J. M. (1999a). Demand/withdraw interaction in couples with a violent husband. *Journal of Consulting & Clinical Psychology, 67,* 666–674.

Berns, S. B., Jacobson, N. S., & Gottman, J. M. (1999b). Demand/withdraw interaction patterns between different types of batterers and their spouses. *Journal of Marital & Family Therapy, 25,* 337–347.

Bernstein, G. A., & Garfinkel, B. D. (1988). Pedigrees, functioning and psychopathology in families of school phobic children. *American Journal of Psychiatry, 145,* 70–74.

Berscheid, E. (1999). The greening of relationship science. *American Psychologist, 54,* 260–266.

Betchen, S. J. (1991). Male masturbation as a vehicle for the pursuer/distancer relationship in marriage. *Journal of Sex & Marital Therapy, 17,* 269–278.

Biederman, J., Faraone, S. V., Mick, E., Spencer, T. et al. (1995). High risk for attention deficit hyperactivity disorder among children of parents with childhood onset of the disorder: A pilot study. *American Journal of Psychiatry, 152,* 431–435.

Biederman, J., Faraone, S. V., Hirshfeld-Becker, D. R., Friedman, D. et al. (2001). Patterns of psychopathology and dysfunction in high-risk children of parents with panic disorder and major depression. *American Journal of Psychiatry, 158,* 49–57.

Bieling, P. J., & Alden, L. E. (1997). The consequences of perfectionism for patients with social phobia. *British Journal of Clinical Psychology, 36,* 387–395.

Biggam, F. H., & Power, K. G. (1999). Social problem solving skills and psychological distress among incarcerated young offenders: The issue of bullying and victimization. *Cognitive Therapy & Research, 23,* 307–326.

Biglan, A. et al. (1985). Problem-solving interactions of depressed women and their husbands. *Behavior Therapy, 16,* 431–451.

Biglan, A., Glasgow, R., & Singer, G. (1990). The need for a science of larger social units: A contextual approach. *Behavior Therapy, 21,* 195–215.

Billings, A. G., Cronkite, R. C., & Moos, R. H. (1983). Social-enivronmntal factors in unipolar depression: Comparisons of depressed patients and nondepressed controls. *Journal of Abnormal Psychology, 92,* 119–133.

Biringen, Z. (2000). Emotional availability: Conceptualization and research findings. *American Journal of Orthopsychiatry, 70,* 104–114.

Biringen, Z., & Robinson, J. (1991). Emotional availability in mother-child interactions: A reconceptualization for research. *American Journal of Orthopsychiatry, 61,* 258–271.

Birtchnell, J., & Mayhew, J. (1977). Toman's theory: Tested for mate selection and friendship formation. *Journal of Individual Psychology, 33,* 18–36.

Bishop, S., & Leadbeater, B. (1999). Maternal social support patterns and child maltreatment: Comparison of maltreating and no maltreating mothers. *American Journal of Orthopsychiatry, 69,* 172–181.

Bisnaire, L. M., Firestone, P., & Rynard, D. (1990). Factors associated with academic achievement in children following parental separation. *American Journal of Orthopsychiatry, 60,* 67–76.

Blanchard, J. J., Brown, S. A., Horan, W. P., & Sherwood, A. R. (2000). Substance use disorders in schizophrenia: Review, integration, and a proposed model. *Clinical Psychology Review, 20,* 207–234.

Blane, H. T., & Barry, H. (1973). Birth order and alcoholism: A review. *Quarterly Journal of Studies on Alcohol, 34,* 837–852.

Blane, H. T., & Leonard, K. E. (Eds.). (1987). *Psychological theories of drinking and alcoholism.* New York: Guilford.

Blashfield, R. K., & Livesley, J. W. (1999). Classification. In T. Millon, P. H. Blaney, & R. D. Davis (Eds.), *Oxford textbook of psychopathology* (pp. 3–28). New York: Oxford University Press.

Blashfield, R. K., & Livesley, W. J. (1999). Classification. In T. Millon, P. H. Blaney, & R. D. Davis (Eds.), *Oxford textbook of psychopathology* (pp. 3–28). New York: Oxford University Press.

Blatt, S. J., Quinlan, D. M., Pilkonis, P. A., & Shea, M. T. (1995). Impact of perfectionism and need for approval on the brief treatment of depression: The National Institute of Mental Health Treatment of Depression Collaborative Research Program revisited: Correction. *Journal of Consulting & Clinical Psychology, 63,* 494.

Blatt, S. J., Zohar, A. H., Quinlan, D. M., Zuroff, D. C., & Mongrain, M. (1995). Subscales within the dependency factor of the Depressive Experiences Questionnaire. *Journal of Personality Assessment, 64*, 319–339.

Blazer, D. G., Kessler, R. C., McGonagle, K. A., & Swartz, M. S. (1994). The prevalence and distribution of major depression in a national community sample: The National Comorbidity Survey. *American Journal of Psychiatry, 151*, 979–986.

Bleger, J. (1974). Schizophrenia, autism and symbiosis. *Contemporary Psychoanalysis, 10*, 19–26.

Bless, H., & Forgas, J. P. (Eds.). (2000). *The message within: The role of subjective experience in social cognition and behavior.* Philadelphia: Psychology Press.

Blieszner, R., & Adams, R. G. (1992). *Adult friendship.* Newbury Park, CA: Sage.

Block, J. (1995a). A contrarian view of the five-factor approach to personality description. *Psychological Bulletin, 117*, 187–215.

Block, J. (1995b). Going beyond the five factors given: Rejoinder to Costa and McCrae (1995) and Goldberg and Saucier (1995). *Psychological Bulletin, 117*, 226–229.

Bloomquist, M. L., August, G. J., Brombach, A. M., Anderson, D. L., et al. (1996). Maternal facilitation of children's problem solving: Relation to disruptive child behavior and maternal characteristics. *Journal of Clinical Child Psychology, 25*, 308–316.

Blumberg, M. (1981). Depression in abused and neglected children. *American Journal of Psychotherapy, 35*, 342–355.

Blumberg, S. R., & Hokanson, J. E. (1983). The effects of another person's response style on interpersonal behavior in depression. *Journal of Abnormal Psychology, 92*, 196–209.

Blumenthal, J. A., & Herman, S. (1985). Age differences in self-perception of Type A traits. *Journal of Consulting & Clinical Psychology, 53*, 264–266.

Blumenthal, J. A., McKee, D. C., Haney, T., & Williams, R. B. (1980). Task incentive, Type A behavior pattern, and verbal problem solving performance. *Journal of Applied Social Psychology, 10*, 101–114.

Blustein, D., Walbridge, M., Friedlander, M., & Palladino, D. (1991). Contributions of psychological separation and parental attachment to the career development process. *Journal of Counseling Psychology, 38*, 39–50.

Bodiford, C. A., Eisenstadt, T. H., Johnson, J. H., & Bradlyn, A. S. (1988). Comparison of learned helpless cognitions and behavior in children with high and low scores on the Children's Depression Inventory. *Journal of Clinical Child Psychology, 17*, 152–158.

Bogaert, A. F., Bezeau, S., Kuban, M., & Blanchard, R. (1997). Pedophilia, sexual orientation, and birth order. *Journal of Abnormal Psychology, 106*, 331–335.

Bogels, S., Van Oosten, A., Muris, P., & Smulders, D. (2001). Familial correlates of social anxiety in children and adolescents. *Behaviour Research & Therapy, 39*, 273–287.

Bohart, A. C., & Tallman, K. (1999). *How clients make therapy work: The process of active self-healing.* Washington, DC: American Psychological Association.

Bohen, H. H., & Viveros-Long, A. (1981). *Balancing jobs and family life: Do flexible work schedules help?* Philadelphia: Temple University Press.

Bonanno, G. A. (2004). Loss, trauma, and human resilience: Have we underestimated the human capacity to thrive after extremely adverse events? *American Psychologist, 59*, 20–28.

Bond, C., & McMahon, R. (1984). Relationships between marital distress and child behavior problems, maternal personal adjustment, maternal personality, and maternal parenting behavior. *Journal of Abnormal Psychology, 93*, 348–351.

Bond, T. G., & Fox, C. M. (2001). *Applying the Rasch model: Fundamental measurement in the human sciences.* Mahwah, NJ: LEA.

Bonebright, C. A., Clay, D. L., & Ankenman, R. D. (2000). The relationship of workolism with work-life conflict, life satisfaction, and purpose in life. *Journal of Counseling Psychology, 67*, 469–474.

Bonner, R. L., & Rich, A. R. (1988). Negative life stress, social problem-solving, self-appraisal, and hopelessness: Implications for suicide research. *Cognitive Therapy & Research, 12*, 549–556.

Bonta, J., Law, M., & Hanson, K. (1998). The prediction of criminal and violent recidivism among mentally disordered offenders: A meta-analysis. *Psychological Bulletin, 123*, 123–142.

Boone, S., & Montare, A. (1979). Aggression and family size. *Journal of Psychology, 103*, 67–70.

Borkovec, T. D., Ray, W. J., & Stober, J. (1998). Worry: A cognitive phenomenon intimately linked to affective, physiological and interpersonal behavioral processes. *Cognitive Therapy & Research, 22*, 561–576.

Bornstein, M. (1989). Sensitive periods in development: Structural characteristics and causal interpretations. *Psychological Bulletin, 105*, 179–197.

Bornstein, R. F. (1992). The dependent personality: Developmental, social, and clinical perspectives. *Psychological Bulletin, 112*, 3–23.

Bornstein, R. F. (1998). Depathologizing dependency. *Journal of Nervous & Mental Disease, 186*, 67–73.

Bornstein, R. F. (1999). Dependent and histrionic personality disorders. In T. Millon, P. H. Blaney, & R. D., Davis (Eds.), *Oxford textbook of psychopathology* (pp. 535–554). New York: Oxford University Press.

Bornstein, R. F., Manning, K. A., Krukonis, A. B., & Rossner, S. C. (1993). Sex differences in dependency: A comparison of objective and projective measures. *Journal of Personality Assessment, 61*, 169–181.

Borrine, M., Handal, P., Brown, N., & Searight, J. (1991). Family conflict and adolescent adjustment in intact, divorced, and blended families. *Journal of Consulting & Clinical Psychology, 59*, 753–755.

Boss, P. (1977). A clarification of the concept of psychological father presence in families experiencing ambiguity of boundary. *Journal of Marriage & the Family, 39*, 141–151.

Bouffard, T., & Vezeau, (1998). The developing self-system and self-regulation of primary school children. In M. Ferrari & R. J. Sternberg (Eds.), *Self-awareness: Its nature and development* (pp. 246–272). New York: Guilford.

Bowen, M. (1979). *Family therapy in clinical practice.* New York: Jason Aronson.

Bowerman, C., & Bahr, S. (1973). Conjugal power and adolescent identification with parents. *Sociometry, 36*, 366–377.

Bowker, G. S., & Cornock, B. (2003). Sports participation self-esteem: Variations as a function of gender and gender role orientation. *Sex Roles, 49*, 47–58.

Boyd, G. H., & Forehand, R. (1986). Maternal perception of child maladjustment as a function of the combined influence of child behavior and maternal depression. *Journal of Consulting & Clinical Psychology, 54*, 237–240.

Bradbury, T. N. (2003). Invited program overview: Research on relationships as a prelude to action. *Journal of Social and Personal Relationships, 19*, 571–599.

Bradley, S. J. (2000). *Affect regulation and the development of psychopathology.* New York: Guilford.

Brandt, D. E. (1977). Separation and identity in adolescence: Erikson and Mahler—some similarities. *Contemporary Psychoanalysis, 13*, 507–518.

Breier, A., Kelsoe, J. P., Kirwin, P. D., Beller, S. A., et al. (1988). Early parental loss and development of adult psychopathology. *Archives of General Psychiatry, 45*, 987–993.

Breland, H. (1977). Family configuration and intellectual development. *Journal of Individual Psychology, 33*, 86–89.

Bremner, J. D., Krystal, J. H., Charney, D. S., & Southwick, S. M. (1996). Neural mechanisms in dissociative amnesia for child abuse: Relevance in the current controversy surrounding the "false memory syndrome." *American Journal of Psychiatry, 153*, 71–82.

Brennan, P. A., Grekin, E. R., & Mednick, S. A. (2003). Prenatal and perinatal influences on conduct disorder and serious delinquency. In B. B. Lahey, T. E. Moffitt, & A. Caspi (Eds.), *Causes of conduct disorder and juvenile delinquency* (pp. 319–341). New York: Guilford.

Brennan, P. A., Hammen, C., Katz, A. R., & LeBrocque, R. M. (2002). Maternal depression, paternal psychopathology and adolescent diagnostic outcomes. *Journal of Consulting & Clinical Psychology, 70*, 1075–1085.

Brennan, P. A., & Harvey, P. D. (2001). Vulnerability to schizophrenia across the lifespan. In R. E. Ingram & J. M. Price (Eds.), *Vulnerability to psychopathology: Risks across the life span* (pp. 382–386). New York: Guilford.

Brent, D., Perper, J., Goldstein, C., & Kolko, D. (1988). Risk factors for adolescent suicide: A comparison of adolescent suicide victims with suicidal inpatients. *Archives of General Psychiatry, 45*, 581–588.

Breslau, N., Chilcoat, H. D., Kessler, R. C., & Davis, G. C. (1999). Previous exposure to trauma and PTSD effects of subsequent trauma: Results from the Detroit Area Survey of Trauma. *American Journal of Psychiatry, 156*, 902–907.

Breslau, N., & Prabucki, K. (1987). Siblings of disabled children: Effects of chronic stress in the family. *Archives of General Psychiatry, 44*, 1040–1046.

Bretherton, I., Ridgeway, D., & Cassidy, J. (1990). Assessing internal working models of the attachment relationship. In M. T. Greenberg, D. Cicchetti, & M. Cummings (Eds.), *Attachment in the preschool years: Theory, research and intervention* (pp. 273–308). Chicago: University of Chicago Press.

Brewin, C. R., Andrews, B., & Gorlib, I. (1993). Psychopathology and early experience: A reappraisal of retrospective reports. *Psychological Bulletin, 113*, 82–98.

Brewin, C. R., Firth-Cozens, J., Furnham, A., & McManus, C. (1992). Self-criticism in adulthood and recalled childhood experience. *Journal of Abnormal Psychiatry, 101*, 561–566.

Brewin, C. R., MacCarthy, B., Duda, K., & Vaughn, C. E. (1991). Attribution and expressed emotion in the relatives of patients with schizophrenia. *Journal of Abnormal Psychology, 100*, 546–554.

Briere, J., & Zaidi, L. Y. (1989). Sexual abuse histories and sequelae in female psychiatric emergency room patients. *American Journal of Psychiatry, 146*, 1602–1606.

Bringle, R. G., & Williams, L. J. (1979). Parental offspring similarity on jealousy and related personality dimensions. *Motivation & Emotion, 3*, 265–286.

Brock, K. J., Mintz, L. B., & Good, G. E. (1997). Differences among sexually abused and nonabused women from functional and dysfunctional families. *Journal of Counseling Psychology, 44*, 425–432.

Brodbeck, C., & Michelson, L. (1987). Problem solving skills and attributional styles of agoraphobics. Agoraphobia, attribution, anagram problem solving and task complexity. *Cognitive Therapy & Research, 11*, 593–610.

Brody, G. H., & Forehand, R. (1993). Prospective associations among family form, family processes and adolescents' alcohol and drug use. Family relations, family structure, drug usage and peer relations. *Behaviour Research & Therapy, 31*, 587–593.

Brody, G. H., Stoneman, Z., & Burke, M. (1988). Child temperament and parental perceptions of individual child adjustment: An interfamilial analysis. *American Journal of Orthopsychiatry, 58*, 532–542.

Brody, G. H., Stoneman, Z., Millar, M., & McCoy, J. K. (1990). Assessing individual differences: Effects of responding to prior questionnaires on the substantive and psychometric properties of self-esteem and depression assessments. *Journal of Personality, 54*, 401–411.

Brogan, D., & Kutner, N. G. (1976). Measuring sex role orientation: A normative approach. *Journal of Marriage & the Family, 38*, 31–40.

Bronfenbrenner, U. (1979). *The ecology of human development*. Cambridge, MA: Harvard University Press.

Brooks, B. (1985). Sexually abused children and adolescent identity development. *American Journal of Psychotherapy, 39*, 401–410.

Brown, C. C., & Gottfried, A. W. (Eds). (1985). *Play interactions: The role of toys and parental involvement in child's development*. Skillman, NJ: Johnson & Johnson.

Brown, E. J., Heimberg, R. G., & Juster, H. R. (1995). Social phobia subtype and avoidant personality disorder: Effect on severity of social phobia, impairment and outcome of cognitive behavioral treatment. *Behavior Therapy, 26*, 467–486.

Brown, G. R., & Anderson, B. (1991). Psychiatric morbidity in adult inpatients with childhood histories of sexual and physical abuse. *American Journal of Psychiatry, 148*, 55–61.

Brown, J., Cohen, P., Johnson, J. G., & Salzinger, S. (1998). A longitudinal analysis of risk factors for child maltreatment: Findings of a 17-year prospective study of officially recorded and self-reported child abuse and neglect. *Child Abuse & Neglect, 22*, 1065–1078.

Brown, J., Cohen, P., Johnson, J. G., & Smailes, E. M. (1999). Childhood abuse and neglect: Specificity and effects on adolescent and young adult depression and suicidality. *Journal of the American Academy of Child & Adolescent Psychiatry, 38*, 1490–1496.

Brown, J., Cohen, P., Johnson, J. G., & Smailes, E. M. (2000). Assessing child maltreatment: Reply. *Journal of the American Academy of Child and Adolescent Psychiatry, 39*, 11–13.

Brown, J., & Silberschatz, G. (1989). Dependency, self-criticism and depressive attributional style. *Journal of Abnormal Psychology, 98*, 187–188.

Browne, A., & Finkelhor, D. (1986). Impact of child sexual abuse: A review of the research. *Psychology Bulletin, 99*, 66–76.

Bruch, M. A. (1989). Familial and developmental antecedents of social phobia: Issues and findings. *Clinical Psychology Review, 9*, 37–47.

Bruch, M. A. (2002). The relevance of mitigated and unmitigated agency and communion for depression vulnerabilities and dysphoria. *Journal of Counseling Psychology, 49*, 449–459.

Bryant-Tucker, R., & Silverman, L. H. (1984). Effects of the subliminal stimulation of symbiotic fantasies on the academic performance of emotionally handicapped students. *Journal of Counseling Psychology, 31*, 295–305.

Buchanan, G. M., & Seligman, M. E. P. (Eds.). (1995). *Explanatory style*. Hillsdale, NJ: Earlbaum.

Buie, D. H., & Maltsberger, J. T. (1989). The psychological vulnerability to suicide. In D. Jacobs & H. N. Brown (Eds.), *Suicide: Understanding and responding: Harvard Medical School perspectives*. Madison, CT: International Universities Press.

Bulik, C. M., Sullivan, P. F., & Kendler, K. S. (2000). An empirical study of the classification of eating disorders. *American Journal of Psychiatry, 157*, 886–895.

Burbach, D., & Borduin, C. (1986). Parent-child relations and the etiology of depression: A review of methods and findings. *Clinical Psychology Review, 6*, 133–153.

Burge, D., & Hammen, C. (1991). Maternal communication: Predictors of outcome at follow-up in a sample of children at high and low risk for depression. *Journal of Abnormal Psychology, 100*, 174–180.

Burge, D., Hammen, C., Davila, J., & Daley, S. E. (1997). The relationship between attachment cognitions and psychological adjustment in late adolescent women. *Development & Psychopathology, 9*, 151–167.

Burge, D., Hammen, C., Davila, J., Daley, S. E., et al. (1997). Attachment cognitions and college and work functioning two years later in late adolescent women. *Journal of Youth & Adolescence, 26*, 285–301.

Burger, A. L., & Jacobson, N. S. (1979). The relationship between sex role characteristics, couple satisfaction and couple problem-solving skills. *American Journal of Family Therapy, 7,* 52–60.

Burgoon, J. K., & Bacue, A. E. (2003). Nonverbal communication skills. In J. O. Green & B. R. Burleson (Eds.), *Handbook of communication and social interaction skills* (pp. 179–219). Mahwah, NJ: Earlbaum.

Burk, J. P., & Sher, K. J. (1988). The "forgotten children" revisited: Neglected areas of COA research. *Clinical Psychology Review, 8,* 285–302.

Burke, P. J. (1980). The self: Measurement requirements from an interactionist perspective. *Social Psychology Quarterly, 43,* 18–25.

Burke, R. J., & Weir, T. (1980a). Personality, value and behavioral correlates of the Type A individual. *Psychology Reports, 46,* 171–181.

Burke, R. J., & Weir, T. (1980b). The Type A experience: Occupational and life demands, satisfaction and well-being. *Journal of Human Stress, 6,* 28–38.

Burleson, B. R. (2003). Emotional support skill. In J. O. Green & B. R. Burleson (Eds.), *Handbook of communication and social interaction skills* (pp. 551–594). Mahwah, NJ: Earlbaum.

Burns, D., Sayers, S., & Moras, K. (1994). Intimate relationships and depression: Is there a casual connection? *Journal of Consulting & Clinical Psychology, 62,* 1033–1043.

Burns, G., Keortge, S., Formea, G., & Sternberger, L. (1996). Revision of the Padua Inventory of obsessive-compulsive disorder symptoms: Distinctions between worry, obsessions and compulsions. *Behavior Research & Therapy, 34,* 163–173.

Burt, R.S. (1977). Power in a social topology. *Social Science Research, 6,* 1–83.

Buss, D. (1981). Predicting parent-child interactions from children's activity level. *Developmental Psychology, 17,* 59–65.

Bybee, J. A., & Wells, Y. V. (2003). The development of possible selves during adulthood. In J. Demick & G. Andreotti (Eds.), *Handbook of adult development* (pp. 257–270). New York: Kluwer Academic.

Cacciola, J. S., Rutherford, M. J., Alterman, A. I., & Snider, E. C. (1994). An examination of the diagnostic criteria for antisocial personality disorder in substance abusers. *Journal of Nervous & Mental Disease, 182,* 517–523.

Cacioppo, J. T., & Gardner, W. L. (1999). Emotion. *Annual Review of Psychology, 50,* 191–214.

Cadoret, R. J., & Cain, C. (1980). Sex differences in predictors of antisocial behavior in adoptee. *Archives of General Psychiatry, 37,* 1171–1175.

Cadoret, R. J., Winokur, G., Langbehn, D., Troughton, E., et al. (1996). Depression spectrum disease, I: The role of gene-environment interaction. *American Journal of Psychiatry, 153,* 892–899.

Cadoret, R., Yates, W., Troughton, E., & Woodworth, G. (1995). Genetic-environmental interaction in the genesis of aggressivity and conduct disorders. *Archives of General Psychiatry, 52,* 916–924.

Cahill, C., Llewelyn, S. P., & Pearson, C. (1991). Long-tern effects of sexual abuse which occurred in childhood: A review. *British Journal of Clinical Psychology, 30,* 117–130.

Calder, P., & Kostyniuk, A. (1989). Personality profiles of children of alcoholics. *Professional Psychology: Research & Practice, 20,* 417–418.

Campbell, N., Milling, L. Laughlin, A., & Bush, E. (1993). The psychosocial climate of families with suicidal pre-adolescent children. *American Journal of Orthopsychiatry, 63,* 142–145.

Canary, D. J. (2003). Managing interpersonal conflict: A model of events related to strategic choices. In J. O. Green & B. R. Burleson (Eds.), *Handbook of communication and social interaction skills* (pp. 515–549). Mahwah, NJ: Earlbaum.

Canary, D. J., Emmers-Sommer, T. M., & Faulkner, S. (1997). *Sex and gender differences in personal relationships.* New York: Guilford.

Cantor, N., & Kihlstrom, J. F. (1987). *Personality and social intelligence*. Englewood Cliffs, NJ: Prentice-Hall.

Cantwell, D. P., Baker, L., & Rutter, M. (1979). Families of autistic and dysphasic children: 1. Family life and interaction patterns. *Archives of General Psychiatry, 36*, 682–687.

Capaldi, E., J., & Proctor, R. W. (1999). *Contextualism in psychological research? A critical review*. Thousand Oaks, CA: Sage.

Carmelli, D., Dame, A., & Swan, G. E. (1992). Age-related changes in behavioral components in relation to changes in global Type A behavior. *Journal of Behavioral Medicine, 15*, 143–154.

Carmelli, D., Dame, A., Swan, G. E., & Rosenman, R. H. (1991). Long-term changes in Type A behavior: A 27-year follow-up of the Western Collaborative Group Study. *Journal of Behavioral Medicine, 14*, 593–606.

Carmody, T. P., Crossen, J. R., & Wiens, A. N. (1989). Hostility as a health factor: Relationships with neuroticism, Type A behavior, attentional focus, and interpersonal style. *Journal of Clinical Psychology, 45*, 754–762.

Carpenter, P. J. (1984). The use of intergenerational family ratings: Methodological and interpretive considerations. *Journal of Clinical Psychology, 40*, 505–512.

Carroll, J. S., & Payne, J. W. (Eds.). (1976). *Cognition and social behavior*. Hillsdale, NJ: Earlbaum.

Carroll, K. M., & Nuro, K. E. (2002). One size cannot fit all: A stage model for psychotherapy manual development. *Clinical Psychology: Science & Practice, 9*, 396–406.

Carver, C. S., & Scheier, M. E. (1999). Stress, coping, and self-regulatory processses. In L. A. Pervin & O. P. John (Eds.), *Handbook of personality: Theory and research* (pp. 553–575). New York: Guilford.

Cassano, G. B., Michelini, S., Shear, M. K., Coli, E., et al. (1997). The panic-agoraphobic spectrum: A descriptive approach to the assessment and treatment of subtle symptoms. *American Journal of Psychiatry, 154*, 27–38.

Cassidy, T., & Long, C. (1996). Problem-solving style, stress and psychological illness: Development of a multifactorial measure. *British Journal of Clinical Psychology, 35*, 265–277.

Cath, S. H., Gurwitt, A., & Gunsberg, L. (Eds.). (1989). *Fathers & their families*. Hillsdale, NJ: Analytic Press.

Catts, S., McConaghy, N., Ward, P., & Fox, A. (1993). Allusive thinking in parents of schizophrenics: Meta-analysis. *Journal of Nervous & Mental Disease, 181*, 298–302.

Cavallin, B. A., & Houston, B. K. (1980). Aggressiveness, maladjustment, body experience and the protective function of personal space. *Journal of Clinical Psychology, 36*, 170–176.

Cantor, N., & Kihlstrom, J. F. (1987). *Personality and social intelligence*. Englewood Cliffs, NJ: Prentice-Hall.

Cerel, J., Fristad, M. A., Weller, E. B., & Weller, R. A. (2000). Suicide-bereaved children and adolescents: II. Parental and family functioning. *Journal of the American Academy of Child & Adolescent Psychiatry, 39*, 437–444.

Cervone, D., & Mischel, W. (2002). *Advances in personality science*. New York: Guilford.

Chabrol, H., & Moron, P. (1988). Depressive disorders in 100 adolescents who attempted suicide. *American Journal of Psychiatry, 145*, 379.

Chafetz, J. S. (Ed.). (1999). *Handbook of the sociology of gender*. New York: Kluwer Academic.

Chaiken, S., & Trope, Y. (Eds.). (1999). *Dual-process theories in social psychology*. New York: Guilford.

Chakravarti, S. (1978). Alienation in existentialism. *Samiksa, 32*, 23–31.

Chandler, L., & Lundahl, W. (1983). Empirical classification of emotional adjustment reaction. *American Journal of Orthopsychiatry, 53*, 460–467.

Chang, E. C., & Rand, K. L. (1999). Perfectionism as a predictor of subsequent adjustment: Evidence for a specific diathesis-stress mechanism among college students. *Journal of Counseling Psychology, 46,* 515–523.

Chang, E. C., & D'Zurilla, T. J. (1996). Relations between problem orientation and optimism, pessimism, and trait affectivity: A construct validation study. *Behavior Research & Therapy, 34,* 185–194.

Chapman, T., & Foot, H. (Eds.). (1976). *Humour and laughter: Theory, research and applications.* New York: Wiley.

Chassin, L., Collins, R. L., Ritter, J., & Shirley, M. C. (2001). Vulnerability to substance use disorders across the lifespan. In R. E. Ingram & J. M. Price (Eds.), *Vulnerability to psychopathology: Risks across the life span* (pp. 165–172). New York: Guilford.

Chassin, L., Mann, L., & Sher, K. (1988). Self-awareness theory, family history of alcoholism, and adolescent alcohol involvement. *Journal of Abnormal Psychology, Special Issue: Models of Addiction, 97,* 206–217.

Chassin, L., Pillow, D., Curran, P., & Molina, B. (1993). Relation of parental alcoholism to early adolescent substance use: A test of three mediating mechanisms. *Journal of Abnormal Psychology, 102,* 3–119.

Chassin, L., Rogosch, F., & Barrera, M. (1991). Substance use and symptomatology among adolescent children of alcoholics. *Journal of Abnormal Psychology, 100,* 449–463.

Chawa, R. L., & Gupt, K. (1979). A comparative study of parents of emotionally disturbed and normal children. *British Journal of Psychiatry, 134,* 406–411.

Chorpita, B., Albano, A., & Barlow, D. (1996). Cognitive processing in children: Relation to anxiety and family influences. *Journal of Clinical Child Psychology, 25,* 170–176.

Christie, K., Burke, J., Regier, D., & Rae, D. (1988). Epidemiologic evidence for early onset of mental disorders and higher risk of drug abuse in young adults. *American Journal of Psychiatry, 145,* 971–975.

Christ, M. A., Lahey, B. B., Frick, P. J., Russo, M. F., et al. (1990). Serious conduct problems in the children of adolescent mothers: Disentangling confounded correlations. *Journal of Consulting & Clinical Psychology, 58,* 840–844.

Christian, K. W. (1978). Aspects of the self-concept related to level of self-esteem. *Journal of Consulting & Clinical Psychology, 46,* 1151–1152.

Chu, C. (1975). The development of differential cognitive abilities in relation to children's perceptions of their parents. *Cortex, 17,* 41–61.

Chu, J. A., & Dill, D. L. (1990). Dissociative symptoms in relation to childhood physical and sexual abuse. *American Journal of Psychiatry, 147,* 887–892.

Chusid, H., & Cochran, L. (1989). Meaning of career change from the perspective of family roles and dramas. *Journal of Counseling Psychology, 36,* 34–41.

Cicchetti, D. (1987). Developmental psychopathology in infancy: Illustration from the study of maltreated youngsters. *Journal of Consulting & Clinical Psychology, 55,* 837–845.

Cicirelli, V. G. (1976). Mother-child and sibling-sibling interactions on a problem-solving task. *Child Development, 47,* 588–596.

Clance, P., Mitchell, M., & Engelman, S. (1980). Body cathexis in children as a function of awareness training and yoga. *Journal of Clinical Child Psychology, 9,* 82–85.

Clark, D. (1988). The validity of measures of cognition: A review of the literature. *Cognitive Therapy & Research, 12,* 1–20.

Clark, D., Beck, A., & Beck, J. (1994). Symptoms differences in major depression, dysthymia, panic disorder, and generalized disorder. *American Journal of Psychology, 151,* 205–209.

Clark, L. A. (1990). Toward a consensual set of symptom clusters for assessment of personality disorders. In J. H. Butcher & C. D. Splielberger (Eds.), *Advances in personality assessment* (pp. 243–266). Hillsdale, NJ: Earlbaum.

Clark, M. S. (Ed.). (1992). *Emotion and social behavior*. Newbury Park, CA: Sage.

Clark M. S., & Fiske, S. T. (Eds.). (1992). *Affect and cognition*. Hillsdale, NJ: Earlbaum.

Clark, M. S., & Mills, J. (1979). Interpersonal attraction in exchange and communal relationships. *Journal of Personality & Social Psychology, 37,* 12–24.

Clark, M. S., Mills, J., & Powell, M. C. (1986). Keeping track of needs in communal and exchange relationships. *Journal of Personality and Social Psychology, 51,* 333–338.

Clark, M. S., & Reis, H. (1988). Interpersonal processes in close relationships. *Annual Review of Psychology, 39,* 609–672.

Clark, M. S., Pataki, S. P., & Carver, V. H. (1996). Some thoughts and findings on self-presentation of emotions in relationships. In G. J. O. Fletcher & J. Fitness (Eds.), *Knowledge structures in close relationships: A social psychological approach* (pp. 247–324). New York: Guilford.

Clark, M. S., & Wassell, B. (1985). Perceptions of exploitation in communal and exchange relationships. *Journal of Social and Personal Relationships, 2,* 403–418.

Cleyman, R. B. (1992). The procedural organization of emotions: A contribution from cognitive science to the psychoanalytic theory of therapeutic action. In T. Shapiro & R. N. Emde (Eds.), *Affect: Psycho-analytic perspectives* (pp. 349–382). Madison, CT: International Universities Press.

Climent, C., Plutchik, R., Ervin, F., & Rollins, A. (1977). Parental loss, depression and violence: III. Epidemiological studies of female prisoners. *Acta Psychiatric Scandinavia, 55,* 261–268.

Clum, G. A., & Knowles, S. L. (1991). Why do some people with panic disorders become avoidant? A review. *Clinical Psychology Review, 11,* 295–313.

Cohen, R., & Siegel, A. W. (Eds.). (1991). *Context and development*. Hillsdale, NJ: Earlbaum.

Cole, D. (1989). Psychopathology of adolescent suicide: Hopelessness, coping beliefs, and depression. *Journal of Abnormal Psychology, 98,* 248–255.

Collins, J. K., Cassel, A. J., & Harper, J. F. (1975). The perception of adolescent problems by their parents. *British Journal of Educational Psychology, 45,* 77–79.

Colombi, F. (2002, April). Relationship answer competence in teenager, young adult, and adult people (males and females). Poster presented at the International Congress of Family Psychology. Heidelberg, Germany.

Connell, A. M., & Goodman, S. H. (2002). The association between psychopathology in fathers versus mothers and children's internalizing and externalizing behavior problems: A meta-analysis. *Psychological Bulletin, 128,* 746–773.

Commons, M. L., & Richards, F. A. (2002). Four postformal stages. In J. Demick & C. Andreotti (Eds.), *Handbook of adult development* (pp. 199–219). New York: Kluwer Academic.

Connell, A. M., & Goodman, S. H. (2002). The association between psychopathology in fathers versus mothers and children's internalizing and externalizing behavior problems: A meta-analysis. *Psychological Bulletin, 128,* 746–773.

Conrad, M., & Hammen, C. (1989). Role of maternal depression in perceptions of child maladjustment. *Journal of Consulting & Clinical Psychology, 57,* 663–667.

Consumer Reports. (1995, November). Mental health: Does therapy help? *Consumer Reports,* 734–739.

Conway, L. P., & Hansen, D. J. (1989). Social behavior of physically abused and neglected children: A critical review. *Clinical Psychology Review, 9,* 627–652.

Cook, W., Kenny, D., & Goldstein, M. (1991). Parental affective style risk and the family system: A social relations model analysis. *Journal of Abnormal Psychology, 100,* 492–501.

Cooper, M. (1996). Obsessive-compulsive disorder: Effects on family members. *American Journal of Orthopsychiatry, 66,* 296–304.

Corder, B., Page, P., & Corder, R. (1974). Parental history, family communication and interaction patterns in adolescent suicide. *Family Therapy, 1,* 285–290.

Cornell, D. G. (1983). Gifted children: The impact of positive labeling on the family system. *American Journal of Orthopsychiatry, 53*, 322–335.

Corsi, M. (2002). *Le risposte relazionali dall'adolescenza all'eta' adulta* (Relational answers from adolescence to adult age). Doctoral thesis, University of Padua.

Coryell, W. H., Endicott, J., & Winakur, G. (1992). Anxiety syndromes as epiphenomenona of primary major depression? Outcome and familial psychopathology. *American Journal of Psychiatry, 149*, 100–107.

Coryell, W. H., Scheftner, W., Keller, M., & Endicott, J. (1993). The enduring psychosocial consequences of mania and depression. *American Journal of Psychiatry, 150*, 720–727.

Coryell, W. H., & Zimmerman, M. (1989). Personality disorder in the families of depressed, schizophrenic, and never-ill probands. *American Journal of Psychiatry, 146*, 496–502.

Costa, P., & McCrae, R. (1995). Solid ground in the wetlands of personality: A reply to Block. *Psychological Bulletin, 117*, 216–220.

Costa, P., & McCrae, R. (1997). Age differences in personality structure revisited: Studies in validity, stability, and change. *International Journal of Aging & Human Development, 8*, 261–275.

Coyne, J. C. (1994). Self-reported distress: Analog or ersatz depression? *Psychological Bulletin, 116*, 29–45.

Coyne, J. C., Aldwin, C., & Lazarus, R. S. (1981). Depression and coping in stressful episodes. *Journal of Abnormal Psychology, 90*, 439–447.

Coyne, J. C., & Gotlib, I. (1983). The role of cognition in depression: A critical appraisal. *Psychological Bulletin, 94*, 472–505.

Cox, B. J., Endler, N. S., & Swinson, R. P. (1995). An examination of levels of agoraphobic severity in panic disorder. *Behaviour Research & Therapy, 33*, 57–62.

Craddock, A. E. (1977). Relationships between authoritarianism, marital power expectations and marital value systems. *Australian Journal of Psychology, 29*, 211–221.

Craske, M. G., & Barlow, D. H. (1988). A review of the relationship between panic and avoidance. *Clinical Psychology Review, 8*, 667–685.

Craske, M. G., Rapee, R. M., & Barlow, D. H. (1988). The significance of panic expectancy for individual patterns of avoidance. Panic disorder and avoidance. *Behaviour Therapy, 19*, 577–592.

Craske, M. G., & Tsao, J. C. I. (1999). Self-monitoring with panic and anxiety disorders. *Psychological Assessment, 11*, 466–479.

Crittenden, P. M., & Bonvillian, J. D. (1984). The relationship between maternal risk status and maternal sensitivity. *American Journal of Orthopsychiatry, 54*, 250–262.

Cromer, G. (1978). A comparison of intergenerational relations in Jewish and non-Jewish family. *Adolescence, 13*, 297–309.

Cronen, V. E., & Price, W. K. (1976). Affective relationship between the speaker and listener: An alternative to the approach-avoidance model. *Speech Monographs, 43*, 51–59.

Cross, S. E., & Madson, L. (1997). Elaboration of models of the self: Reply to Baumeister and Sommer (1997) and Martin and Ruble (1991). *Psychological Bulletin, 122*, 51–55.

Crothers, M., & Warren, L. (1996). Parental antecedents of adult codependency. *Journal of Clinical Psychology, 52*, 231–239.

Cuffel, B., & Akamatsu, T. (1989). The structure of loneliness: A factor-analytic investigation. *Cognitive Therapy & Research, 13*, 459–474.

Cummings, E. M., Davies, P. T., & Campbell, S. B. (2000). *Developmental psychopathology and family process: Theory, research, and clinical implications.* New York: Guilford.

Cupach, W. R., & Metts, S. (1994). *Facework.* Thousand Oaks, CA: Sage.

Cusinato, M. (1998). Parenting styles and psycho-pathology. In L. L'Abate (Ed.). *Family psychopathology: The relational roots of dysfunctional behavior* (pp. 158–184). New York: Guilford.

Cusinato, M., Aceti, G., & L'Abate, L. (1997). Condivisione del dolore e intimita' di coppia (Hurt sharing and couple intimacy). *Famigla, Interdisciplinarita', Ricerca, 2,* 31–49.

Cusinato, M., & L'Abate, L. (1994). A spiral model of intimacy. In S. M. Johnson & L. S. Greenberg (Eds.), *The heart of the matter: Perspectives on emotion in marital therapy* (pp. 108–123). New York: Brunner/Mazel.

Cusinato, M., & L'Abate, L. (2003). The Dyadic Relationships Test: Creation and validation of a model-derived, visual-verbal instrument to evaluate couple relationships. *American Journal of Family Therapy, 31,* 79–89.

Cusinato, M., & L'Abate, L. (2004). The Dyadic Relations Test: A decade of research (submitted for publication).

Cusinato, M., & Pastore, M. (2001). Uno strumento di valutazione dell'importanza di se' e di altri: Analisi delle strutture tassonomiche in prospettiva evolutiva (An instrument to evaluate self-importance: Analysis of taxonomic structures in an developmental perspective). *Eta' Evolutiva: Rivista di Scienze dello Sviluppo, 69,* 5–18.

Cutting, L., & Docherty, N. (2000). Schizophrenia outpatients' perceptions of their parents: Is expressed emotion a factor? *Journal of Abnormal Psychology, 109,* 266–272.

Cyranowski, J. M., Frank, E., Young, E., & Shear, K. (2000). Adolescent on-set of the gender difference in lifetime rates of major depression. *Archives of General Psychiatry, 57,* 21–27.

Cytryn, L. (1984). A developmental view of affective disturbances in the children of affectively ill parents. *American Journal of Psychiatry, 141,* 219–222.

Dadds, M. R., Sanders, M. R., Morrison, M., & Rebgetz, M., (1992). Childhood depression and conduct disorder: II. An analysis of family interaction patterns in the home. *Journal of Abnormal Psychology, 101,* 505–513.

Dahlstrom, W. G. (1995). Pigeons, people and pigeonholes. *Journal of Personality Assessment, 64,* 3–20.

Darling, N., & Steinberg, L. (1993). Parenting style as context: An integrative model. *Psychological Bulletin, 113,* 487–496.

Daveney, T. K. (1974). Intentional behavior. *Journal for the Theory of Social Behaviour, 4,* 111–129.

Davenport, D. (1991). The function of anger and forgiveness: Guidelines for psychotherapy with victims. *Special Issue: Psychotherapy With Victims, 28,* 140–144.

Davenport, Y., Zahn-Waxler, C., Adland, M., & Mayfield, A. (1984). Early child-rearing practices in families with a manic-depressive parent. *American Journal of Psychiatry, 141,* 230–235.

Davies, P., & Cummings, E. (1994). Marital conflict and child adjustment: An emotional security hypothesis. *Psychological Bulletin, 116,* 387–411.

Davila, J., Hammen, C., & Burge, D. (1996). Cognitive/interpersonal correlates of adult interpersonal problem-solving strategies. *Cognitive Therapy & Research, 20,* 465–480.

Davila, J., Hammen, C., Burge, D., Daley, S. E., et al. (1996). Cognitive-interpersonal correlates of adult interpersonal problem-solving strategies. *Cognitive Therapy & Research, 20,* 465–480.

Davila, J., Hammen, C., Burge, D., Paley, B., et al. (1995). Poor interpersonal problem solving as a mechanism of stress generation in depression among adolescent women. *Journal of Abnormal Psychology, 104,* 592–600.

Davis, G. E., & Leitenberg, H. (1987). Adolescent sex offenders. *Psychology Bulletin, 101,* 417–427.

Davis, T., Frye, R., & Joure, S. (1975). Perceptions and behaviors of dogmatic subjects in a T-group setting. *Perceptual & Motor Skills, 41,* 375–381.

Dawis, R. V. (1995). For the love of working on play: Comment on Tinsley and Eldredge (1995). *Journal of Counseling Psychology, 42*, 136–137.

Dean, D., & Lewis, A. (1978). Alienation and emotional maturity: A preliminary investigation. *Psychological Reports, 42*, 1006.

Deater-Deckard, K. (1998). Parenting stress and child adjustment: Some old hypotheses and new questions. *Clinical Psychology: Science and Practice, 5*, 315–332.

Deater-Deckard, K., Lansford, J. E., Dodge, K. A., Pettit, G. S., & Bates, J. E. (2003). The development of attitudes about physical punishment: An 8-year longitudinal study. *Journal of Family Psychology, 17*, 351–360.

Decker, P., & Borgen, F. (1993). Dimensions of work appraisal: Stress, strains, coping, job satisfaction, and negative affectivity. *Journal of Counseling Psychology, 40*, 470–478.

de Figueiredo, J., Boerstler, H., & O'Connell, L. (1991). Conditions not attributable to a mental disorder: An epidemiological study of family problems. *American Journal of Psychiatry, 148*, 780–783.

De Giacomo, L'Abate, et al. (2005). "Compass" sentences with strong psychological impact: Preliminary investigations (research in progress).

De Gregorio, E., & Carver, C. S. (1980). Type A behavior pattern, sex role orientation, and psychological adjustment. *Journal of Personality & Social Psychology, 39*, 286–293.

DeJulio, S., & Duffy, K. (1977). Neuroticism and proximic behavior. *Perceptual & Motor Skills, 45*, 51–55.

DeLisi, L. E., Goldin, L. R., Maxwell, M. E., & Kazuba, D. M. (1987). Clinical features of illness in siblings with schizophrenia or schizoaffective disorder. *Archives of General Psychiatry, 44*, 891–896.

De Maria, R. (2003). Psycho-education and enrichment: Clinical considerations for couple and family therapy. In L. Sexton, G. Weeks, M. Robbins (Eds.), *Handbook of family therapy* (pp. 411–430). New York: Brunner-Rutledge.

Demick, J., & Andreotti, C. (Eds). (2002). *Handbook of adult development*. New York: Kluwer Academic.

Denoff, M. S. (1987). Irrational beliefs as predictors of adolescent drug abuse and running away. *Journal of Clinical Psychology, 43*, 412–423.

DePaulo, B. (1992). Nonverbal behavior and self-presentation. *Psychological Bulletin, 111*, 203–243.

Depue, R. A., & Lenzenweger, M. F. (2001). A neurobehavioral dimensional model. In W. J. Livesley (Ed.), *Handbook of personality disorders: Theory, research, and treatment* (pp. 136–176). New York: Guilford.

Derdeyn, A. R. (1978). Child abuse and neglect: The rights of parents and the needs of their children. *Annual Progress in Child Psychiatry & Child Development*, 556–569.

Derlega, V. J., & Winstead, B. A. (Eds.). (1986). *Friendship and social interaction*. New York: Springer-Verlag.

Descoutner, C. J., & Thelen, M. H. (1991). Development and validation of a fear-of-intimacy scale. *Psychological Assessment, 3*, 218–225.

Deutsch, C. J., & Gilbert, L. A. (1976). Sex role stereotypes: Effect on perceptions of self and others, and on personal adjustment. *Journal of Counseling Psychology, 23*, 373–379.

Devlin, M. J., Yanovski, S. Z., & Wilson, G. T. (2000). Obesity: What mental health professionals need to know. *American Journal of Psychiatry, 157*, 854–866.

DeWinne, R., Overton, T., & Schneider, L. (1978). Types produce types—especially fathers. *Journal of Vocational Behavior, 12*, 140–144.

Diamond, E. L., et al. (1984). Harassment, hostility, and Type A as determinants of cardiovascular reactivity during competition. *Journal of Behavioral Medicine, 7*, 171–189.

Dickman, T., Barton, K., & Cattell. T. (1977). Relationships among family attitudes and child rearing practices. *Journal of Genetic Psychology, 130*, 105–112.

Diener, E. (1984). Subjective well-being: Mental health, satisfaction and literature review. *Psychological Bulletin, 95*, 542–575.

Diener, E. (1999). Introduction of the special section on the structure of emotion. *Journal of Personality and Social Psychology, 76*, 803–804.

Dix, T. (1991). The affective organization of parenting: Adoptive and maladaptive processes. *Psychological Bulletin, 110*, 3–25.

Dixon, L., McNary, S., & Lehman, A. (1995). Substance abuse and family relationships of persons with severe mental illness. *American Journal of Psychiatry, 152*, 456–458.

Doane, J. (1981). Parental communication deviance and affective style: Predictors of subsequent schizophrenia spectrum disorders in vulnerable adolescents. *Archives of General Psychiatry, 38*, 679–685.

Dobson, D. J., & Dobson, K. S. (1981). Problem-solving strategies in depressed and nondepressed college students. *Cognitive Therapy & Research, 5*, 237–249.

Docherty, N. (1993). Communication deviance, attention, and schizotypy in parents of schizophrenic patients. *Journal of Nervous & Mental Disease, 181*, 750–756.

Docherty, N. (1994). Cognitive characteristics of the parents of schizophrenic patients. *Journal of Nervous & Mental Disease, 182*, 443–451.

Doi, S. C., & Thelen, M. H. (1993). Fear-Of-Intimacy Scale: Replication and extention. *Psychological Assessment, 5*, 377–383.

Dolan-Sewell, R. T., Krueger, R. F., & Shea, M. T. (2001). Co-occurrence with symdrome disorders. In W. J. Livesley (Ed.), *Handbook of personality disorders: Theory, research, and treatment* (pp. 84–104). New York: Guilford.

Domash, L., & Balter, L. (1976). Sex and psychological differentiation in preschoolers. *Journal of Genetic Psychology, 128*, 77–84.

Donnenwerth, G., Teichman, M., & Foa, U. (1973). Cognitive differentiation of self and parents in delinquent and non-delinquent girls. *British Journal of Social & Clinical Psychology, 12*, 144–152.

Dowd, E. T., Wallbrown, F., Sanders, D., & Yesenosky, J. M. (1994). Psychological reactance and its relationship to normal personality variables. *Cognitive Therapy & Research, 18*, 601–612.

Downey, G., & Coyne, J. C. (1990). Children of depressed parents: An integrative review. *Psychology Bulletin, 108*, 50–76.

Doyle, K. O. (1999). *The social meanings of money and property: In search of a talisman.* Thousand Oaks, CA: Sage.

Drum, D. J., & Hall, J. E. (1993). Psychology's self-regulation and the setting of professional standards. *Applied & Preventive Psychology, 2*, 151–161.

Duck, S. (Ed.). (1988). *Handbook of personal relationships: Theory, research, and interventions.* New York: Wiley.

Duffy, A., Alda, M., Kutchee, S., & Fusee, C. (1998). Psychiatric symptoms and syndromes among adolescent children of parents with lithium-responsive or lithium-nonresponsive bipolar disorder. *American Journal of Psychiatry, 155*, 431–433.

Dumas, J. E., & Gibson, J. A. (1990). Behavioral correlates maternal depressive symptomatology conduct–disorder children: II. Systemic effects involving fathers and siblings. *Journal of Consulting & Clinical Psychology, 58*, 877–881.

Dumas, J. E., & Gibson, J. A., & Albin, J. B. (1989). Behavioral correlates of maternal depressive symptomatology in conduct-disorder children. *Journal of Consulting & Clinical Psychology, 57*, 516–521.

Dumas, J. E., LaFreniere, P. J., & Serketich, S. J. (1995). Balance of power: A transactional analysis of control in mother-child dyads involving socially competent, aggressive and anxious children. *Journal of Abnormal Psychology, 104*, 104–113.

Duncan, P. (1971). Parental attitudes and interactions in delinquency. *Child Development, 42*, 1751–1765.

Duncan, R., Saunders, B., Kilpatrick, D., & Hanson, R. (1996). Childhood physical assault as a risk factor for PTSD, depression, and substance abuse: Findings from a national survey. *American Journal of Ortho-Psychology, 66*, 437–448.

Dunn, M. G., Tarter, R. E., Mezzich, A. C., & Vanyukov, M. (2002). Origins and consequences of child neglect in substance abuse families. *Clinical Psychology Review, 22*, 1063–1090.

D'Zurilla, T. J., & Maydeu-Olivares, A. (1995). Conceptual and methodological issues in social problem-solving assessment. *Behavior Therapy, 26*, 409–432.

East, M., & Watts, F. (1994). Worry and the suppression of imagery. *Behavior Research & Therapy, 32*, 851–855.

Eastman, C., & Marzillier, J. S. (1984). Theoretical and methodological difficulties in Bandura's self-efficacy theory. *Cognitive Therapy & Research, 8*, 213–229.

Ebbesen, E. B., Kjos, G. L., & Koneni, V. J. (1976). Spatial ecology: Its effects on the choice of friends and enemies. *Journal of Experimental Social Psychology, 12*, 505–518.

Ebert, B. (1978). The healthy family. *Family Therapy, 5*, 227–232.

Edwins, C., Small, A., & Gross, R. (1980). The relationship of sex role to self-concept. *Journal of Clinical Psychology, 36*, 111–115.

Egami, Y., Ford, D., Greenfield, S., & Crum, R. (1996). Psychiatric profile and sociodemographic characteristics of adults who report physically abusing and neglecting children. *American Journal of Psychiatry, 153*, 921–928.

Ehrensaft, M. K., Cohen, P., Brown, J., Smailes, E., Chen, H., & Johnson, J. G. (2003). Inter-generational transmission of partner violence: A 20-year prospective study. *Journal of Consulting & Clinical Psychology, 71*, 741–753.

Ehrenwald, J. (Ed.). (1991). *The history of psychotherapy*. Northvale, NJ: Aronson.

Eidelson, R. J., & Eidelson, J. I. (2003). Dangerous ideas: Five beliefs that propel groups toward conflict. *American Psychologist, 58*, 182–192.

Einbender, A., & Friedrich, W. (1989). Psychological functioning and behavior of sexually abused girls. *Journal of Consulting & Clinical Psychology, 57*, 155–157.

Ekman, P. (2003). *Emotions revealed*. New York: Henry Holt.

El-Guebaly, N., & Offord, D. (1980). The competent offspring of psychiatrically ill parents: A search for behavioural variables. *Journal of Psychiatry, 25*, 464–467.

Elliott, A. J. (1997). Integrating the "classic" and the "contemporary" approaches to achievement motivation: A hierarchical model of approach and avoidance achievement motivation. *Advances in Motivation and Achievement, 10*, 143–179.

Ellis, D., Gehman, W., & Katzenmeyer, W. (1980). The boundary organization of self-concept across the 13- through 18-year age span. *Educational & Psychological Measurement, 40*, 9–17.

Eme, R. F., & Kavanaugh, L. (1995). Sex differences in conduct disorder. *Journal of Clinical Child Psychology, 24*, 406–426.

Englander, S. W. (1984). Some self-reported correlates of runaway behavior in adolescent females. *Journal of Consulting & Clinical Psychology, 52*, 484–485.

Enns, M. W. (1999). Perfectionism and depression symptoms severity in major depressive disorder. *Behaviour Research & Therapy, 37*, 783–794.

Epstein, A. S., & Radin, N. (1976). Motivational components related to father behavior and cognitive functioning in preschoolers. *Child Development, 46*, 831–839.

Epstein, L. H., Nudelman, S., & Wing, R. R. (1987). Long-term effects of family-based treatment for obesity on nontreated family members. *Behavior Therapy, 18*, 147–152.

Erdman, P., & Caffery, T. (Eds.). (2003). *Attachment and family systems: Conceptual, empirical, and therapeutic relatedness*. New York: Brunner/Rutledge.

Erel, O., & Burman, B. (1995). Interrelatedness of marital relations and parent-child relations: A meta-analytic review. *Psychological Bulletin, 118*, 108–132.

Esterling, B. A., L'Abate, L., Murray, E., & Pennebaker, J. M. (1999). Empirical foundations for writing in prevention and psychotherapy: Mental and physical outcomes. *Clinical Psychology Review, 19*, 79–96.

Evans, D., Pellizzari, J., Culbert, B., & Metzen, M. (1993). Personality, marital, and occupational factors associated with quality of life. *Journal of Clinical Psychology, 49*, 477–485.

Evans, D. W., Noam, G. G., Wertlieb, D., Paget, K. F., et al. (1994). Self-perception and adolescent psychopathology: A clinical-developmental perspective. *American Journal of Orthopsychiatry, 64*, 293–300.

Evans, P. D., & Moran, P. (1987). The Framingham Type A scale, vigilant coping, and heart-rate reactivity. *Journal of Behavioral Medicine, 10*, 311–321.

Everson, M. D., Hunter, W. M., Runyon, D. K., & Edelsohn, G. A. (1989). Maternal support following disclosure of incest. *American Journal of Orthopsychiatry, 59*, 197–207.

Fagan, T. J., & Lira, F. T. (1980). The primary and secondary sociopathic personality: Differences in frequency and severity of antisocial behavior. *Journal of Abnormal Psychology, 89*, 493–496.

Fagan, P. J., Wise, T. N., Schmidt, C. W., Ponticas, Y., et al. (1991). A comparison of five-factor personality dimensions in males with sexual dysfunction and males with paraphilia. *Journal of Personality Assessment, 57*, 434–448.

Famularo, R., Stone, K., Barnum, R., & Wharton, R. (1986). Alcoholism and severe child maltreatment. *American Journal of Orthopsychiatry, 56*, 481–484.

Faschingbauer, T., & Eglevsky, D. (1977). Relation of dogmatism to creativity: Origence and intellectence. *Psychological Reports, 40*, 391–394.

Fast, I. (1978). Developments in gender identity: The original matrix. *International Review of Psychoanalysis, 5*, 265–273.

Feather, N. T. (1977). Generational and sex differences in conservativism. *Australian Psychologist, 12*, 76–82.

Feather, N. T. (1979). Value correlates of conservativism. *Journal of Personality & Social Psychology, 37*, 1617–1630.

Featherstone, J. (1979). Family matters. *Harvard Educational Review, 49*, 20–52.

Feehan, M., McGee, R., Stanton, W., & Silva, P. (1991). Strict and inconsistent discipline in childhood: Consequences for adolescent mental health. *Journal of Clinical Psychology, 30*, 325–331.

Fehr, B. (1996). *Friendship processes*. Thousand Oaks, CA: Sage.

Fehrenbach, P. A., Smith, W., Monastersky, C., & Dersher, R. W. (1986). Adolescent sexual offenders: Offender and offense characteristics. *American Journal of Orthopsychiatry, 56*, 225–233.

Feingold, A. (1994). Gender differences in personality: A meta-analysis. *Psychological Bulletin, 116*, 429–456.

Feinstein, S. C., & Ardon, M. S. (1973). Trends in dating patterns and adolescent development. *Journal of Youth & Adolescence, 2*, 157–166.

Feist, J., & Feist, G. J. (2002). *Theories of personality*. New York: McGraw-Hill.

Feldman, L. B., & Rivas-Vazquez, R. A. (2003). Assessment and treatment of social anxiety disorder. *Professional Psychology: Research & Practice, 34*, 396–405.

Feldman, R., Weller, A., Sirota, L., & Eidelman, A. I. (2003). Testing a family intervention hypothesis: The contribution of mother-infant skin-to-skin contact (kangaroo care) to family interaction, proximity, and touch. *Journal of Family Psychology, 17,* 94–107.

Ferrari, J. R., Johnson, J. L., & McCown, W. G. (1995). *Procrastination and task avoidance: Theory, research, and treatment.* New York: Plenum.

Ferrari, M. (1998). Being and becoming self-aware. In M. Ferrari & R. J. Sternberg (Eds.), *Self-awareness: Its nature and development* (pp. 387–422). New York: Guilford.

Ferrari, M., & Sternberg, R. J. (Eds.). (1998). *Self-awareness: Its nature and development.* New York: Guilford.

Ficker, F. (1977). The path dynamic of symbiotic psychoses. *Psychiatria Clinica, 10,* 199–213.

Filsinger, E. E. (1980). Difference between own and friend's socioeconomic status as a predictor of psychological differentiation. *Psychological Reports, 46,* 613–614.

Finch, A., & Nelson, W. (1976). Reflection-impulsivity and behavioral problems in emotionally disturbed boys. *Journal of Genetic Psychology, 128,* 271–274.

Fincham F. D. (2000). The kiss of the porcupines: From attributing responsibility to forgiving. *Personal Relationships, 7,* 1–23.

Fincham, F. D., & Beach, S. R. H. (2002). Forgiveness: Toward a public health approach to intervention. In J. H. Harvey & A. Wenzel (Eds.), *A clinician's guide to maintaining and enhancing close relationships* (pp. 277–300). Mahwah, NJ: Earlbaum.

Fincham, F. D., Beach, S. R., & Bradbury, T. N. (1989). Marital distress, depression, and attributions: Is the marital distress-attribution association an artifact of depression? *Journal of Consulting & Clinical Psychology, 57,* 768–771.

Fincham, F., & Osborne, L. (1993). Marital conflict and children: Retrospect and prospect. *Clinical Psychology Review, 13,* 75–88.

Fine, M. A., Overholser, J. C., & Berkoff, K. (1992). Diagnostic validity of a passive-aggressive personality disorder: Suggestions for reform. *American Journal of Psychotherapy, 46,* 470–484.

Finkel, N. J., & Jacobsen, C. A. (1977). Significant life experiences in an adult sample. *American Journal of Community Psychology, 5,* 165–175.

Finkelhor, D. (1980). Sex among siblings: A survey on prevalence, variety, and effects. *Archives of Sexual Behavior, 9,* 171–194.

Finn, P. R., Kleinman, I., & Pihl, R. O. (1990). The lifetime prevalence of psychopathology in men with multigenerational family histories of alcoholism. *Journal of Nervous & Mental Disease, 178,* 500–504.

Finn, P. R., Sharkansky, E., Viken, R., & West, T. (1997). Heterogeneity in the families of sons of alcoholics: The impact of family's vulnerability type on offspring characteristics. *Journal of Abnormal Psychology, 106,* 26–36.

Finzi, R., Ram, A., Shnit, D., Har-Even, D., et al. (2001). Depressive symptoms and suicidality in physically abused children. *American Journal of Orthopsychiatry, 71,* 98–107.

Firestone, R. W., & Catlett, J. (1999). *Fear of intimacy.* Washington, DC: American Psychological Association.

Fischer, A., & Good, G. (1997). Men and psychotherapy: An investigation of alexithymia, intimacy, and masculine gender roles. *Psychotherapy, 34,* 160–170.

Fischer, K. W., & Pruyne, E. (2003). Reflective thinking in adulthood emergence. In J. Demick & C. Andreotti (Eds.), *Handbook of adult development* (pp. 169–198). New York: Kluwer Academic.

Fischler, G. L., & Kendall, P. C. (1988). Social cognitive problem-solving and childhood adjustment: Qualitative and topological analyses. *Cognitive Therapy & Research, 12,* 133–153.

Fishbein, D. H. (Ed.). (2000). *The science, treatment, and prevention of antisocial behaviors: Applications to the criminal justice system.* Kinston, NJ: Civic Research Institute.

Fisher, L., Kokes, R. F., Ransom, D. C., Phillips, S. L., & Rudd, P. (1985). Alternative strategies for creating "relational" family data. *Family Process, 24*, 213–224.

Fisher, L., & Ransom, D. C. (1995). An empirically derived typology of families: Relationships with adult health. *Family Process, 34*, 161–182.

Fiske, A. P., & Haslam, N. (1996). Social cognition is thinking about relationships. *Current Directions. Psychological Science, 5*, 143–148.

Fitzgibbons, R. (1986). The cognitive and emotive uses of forgiveness in the treatment of anger. *Psychotherapy, 23*, 629–633.

Flack, W. F. Jr., & Laird, J. D. (Eds.). (1998). *Emotions and psychopathology: Theory and research.* New York: Oxford University Press.

Flanagan, D., & Wagner, H. (1991). Expressed emotion and panic-fear in the prediction of diet treatment compliance. *British Journal of Clinical Psychology, 30*, 231–240.

Flett, G. L., Vredenburg, K., & Krames, L. (1997). The continuity of depression in clinical and nonclinical samples. *Psychological Bulletin, 121*, 395–416.

Foa, E. B., & Chatterjee, B. (1974). Self-other differentiation: A cross-culturally invariant characteristic of mental patients. *Social Psychiatry, 9*, 119–122.

Foa, U. G., & Foa, E. B. (1974). *Societal structures of the mind.* Springfield, IL: Thomas.

Foa, U. G., Converse, J. Jr., Tornblom, K. J., & Foa, E. B. (Eds.). (1993). *Resource theory: Explorations and applications.* San Diego, CA: Academic Press.

Fogg, B. J. (2003). *Persuasive technology: Using computers to change what we think and do.* San Francisco: Morgan Kaufmann.

Foglia, W. D. (2000). Adding an explicit focus on cognition to criminological theory. In D. H. Fishbein (Ed.), *The science, treatment, and prevention of antisocial behaviors: Application to the criminal justice system* (pp. 10.1–10.25). Kinston, NJ: Civic Research Institute.

Fonagy, P., Target, M., Cottrell, D., Phillips, K., & Kurtz, Z. (2002). *What works for whom? A critical review of treatments for children and adolescents.* New York: Guilford.

Ford, J. D., Racusin, R., Daviss, W. B., & Ellis, C. G. (1999). Trauma exposure among children with oppositional defiant disorder and attention deficit-hyperactivity disorder. *Journal of Consulting & Clinical Psychology, 67*, 786–789.

Forehand, R., Brody, G. H., Long, N., & Fauber, R. (1988). The interactive influence of adolescent and maternal depression on adolescent social and cognitive functioning. *Cognitive Therapy & Research, 12*, 341–350.

Forehand, R., & Furey, W. (1985). Predictors of depressive mood in mothers of clinic-referred children. *Behaviour Research & Therapy, 23*, 415–421.

Forehand, R., & McCombs, A. (1988). Unraveling the antecedent-consequence condition in maternal depression and adolescent functioning. *Behaviour Research & Therapy, 26*, 399–405.

Forehand, R., McCombs, A., Long, N., Brody, G. H., et al. (1988). Early adolescent adjustment to recent parental divorce: The role of interparental conflict and adolescent sex as mediating variables. *Journal of Consulting & Clinical Psychology, 56*, 624–627.

Forehand, R., Miller, K. S., Dutra, R., & Chance, M. W. (1997). Role of parenting in adolescent deviant behavior: Replication across and within two ethnic group. *Journal of Consulting and Clinical Psychology, 65*, 1036–1041.

Forehand, R., Wierson, M., McCombs, A., Brody, G., et al. (1989). Interparental conflict and adolescent problem behavior: An examination of mechanisms. *Behaviour Research & Therapy, 27*, 365–371.

Ford, M. E. (1985). The concept of competence: Themes and variations. In H. A. Marlowe & R. B. Weinberg (Eds.), *Competence development: Theory and practice in special populations* (pp. 3–49). Springfield, IL: C. C. Thomas.

Forgas, J. P. (Ed.). (2001). *Handbook of affect and social cognition.* Mahwah, NJ: Earlbaum.

Forsyth, D. R. (1980). The functions of attributions. *Social Psychology Quarterly, 43*, 184–189.

Frances, A., & Dunn, P. (1975). The attachment autonomy conflict in agoraphobia. *International Journal of Psycho-Analysis, 56*, 435–439.

Frances, A., Clarkin, J., & Perry, S. (1984). DSM-III and family therapy. *American Journal of Psychiatry, 141*, 406–409.

Franche, R., & Dobson, K. S. (1992). Self-criticism and interpersonal dependency as vulnerability factors to depression. *Cognitive Therapy & Research, 16*, 419–435.

Frank, S. J., Poorman, M. O., Van Egeren, L. A., & Field, D. T. (1997). Perceived relationship with parents among adolescent in-patients with depressive preoccupations and depressed mood. *Journal of Clinical Child Psychology, 26*, 205–215.

Franko, D., Powers, T., Zuroff, D., & Moskowitz, D. (1985). Children and affect: Strategies of self-regulation and sex differences in sadness. *American Journal of Orthopsychiatry, 55*, 210–219.

Franzoso, T. (2002). *La competenza relazionale nei tossico-dipendenti* (Relational competence in drug addicts). Ph.D. thesis. University of Padua, Italy.

Fredrikson, M., Annas, P., Håkan, L., & Wilk, G. (1996). Gender and age differences in the prevalence of specific fears and phobias. *Behaviour Research & Therapy, 34*, 33–39.

Fredrikson, M., Annas, P., & Wik, G. (1997). Parental history, aversive exposure and the development of snake and spider phobia women. *Behaviour Research & Therapy, 35*, 23–28.

Freedheim, D. K. (1992). *History of psychotherapy: A century of change*. Washington, DC: American Psychological Association.

Freeman, D. S. (1976). The family as a system: Fact or fantasy? *Comprehensive Psychiatry, 17*, 735–747.

Freeston, M., Dugas, M., & Ladouceur, R. (1996). Thoughts, images, worry and anxiety. *Therapy & Research, 20*, 256–273.

Fresco, D. M., Sampson, W. S., Craighead, L. W., & Koons, A. N. (2001). The relationship of sociotropy and autonomy to symptoms of depression and anxiety. *Journal of Cognitive Psychotherapy, 15*, 17–31.

Frick, P. J., & Jackson, Y. (1993). Family functioning and childhood antisocial behavior: Yet another reinterpretation. *Journal of Clinical Child Psychology, 22*, 410–419.

Frick, P. J., Lahey, B. B., Hartdagen, S., & Hynd, G. W. (1989). Conduct problems in boys: Relations to maternal personality, martial satisfaction, and socioeconomic status. *Journal of Clinical Child Psychology, 18*, 114–120.

Frick, P. J., Lahey, B. B., Loeber, R., & Stouthamer-Loeber, M. (1992). Oppositional defiant disorder and conduct disorder in boys: Patterns of behavioral co-variation. *Journal of Clinical Child Psychology, 20*, 202–208.

Frick, P. J., Lahey, B. B., Loeber, R., & Stouthamer-Loeber, M. (1992). Familial risk factors to oppositional defiant disorder and conduct disorder: Parental psychopathology and maternal parenting. *Journal of Consulting & Clinical Psychology, 60*, 49–55.

Frick, P. J., Lahey, B. B., Loeber, R., & Tannenbaum, L. (1993). Oppositional defiant disorder and conduct disorder: A meta-analytic review of factor analyses and cross-validation in a clinic sample. *Clinical Psychology Review, 13*, 319–340.

Friedlander, M. L., & Schwartz, G. S. (1985). Toward a theory of strategic self-presentation in counseling and psychotherapy. *Journal of Counseling Psychology, 32*, 483–501.

Friedman, H. S., & Booth-Kewley, S. (1988). Validity of the Type A construct: A reprise. *Psychology Bulletin, 104*, 381–384.

Friedman, M. A., & Brownell, K. D. (1995). Psychological correlates of obesity: Moving to the next research generation. *Psychological Bulletin, 117*, 3–20.

Friedman, R. (1984). Family history in the seriously suicidal adolescent: A life-cycle approach. *American Journal of Orthopsychiatry, 54*, 390–397.

Friedrich, W. N., Tyler, J. D., & Clark, J. A. (1985). Personality and psycho-physiological variables in abusive, neglectful and low income control mothers. *Journal of Nervous & Mental Disease, 8*, 449–460.

Friedrich, W. N., & Wheeler, K. K. (1982). The abusing parent revisited: A decade of psychological research. *Journal of Nervous & Mental Disease, 170*, 577–587.

Frodi, A., Macaulay, J., & Thome, P. R. (1977). Are women always less aggressive than men? A review of the experimental literature. *Psychological Bulletin, 84*, 634–660.

Frost, R., Lahart, C., & Rosenblate, R. (1991). The development of perfectionism: A study of daughters and their parents. *Cognitive Therapy & Research, 15*, 469–489.

Frost, R. O., & Gross, R. C. (1993). The hoarding of possessions. *Behaviour Research & Therapy, 31*, 367–381.

Frost, R. O., Hart, T. L., Christian, R., & Williams, N. (1995). The value of possessions in compulsive hoarding: Patterns of use and attachment. *Behaviour Research & Therapy, 33*, 897–902.

Frost, R. O., Krause, M. S., McMahon, M. J., Peppe, J. et al. (1993). Compulsivity and superstitiousness. *Behaviour Research & Therapy, 31*, 423–425.

Frost, R. O., Lahart, C. M., Dugas, K. M., & Sher, K. J. (1988). Information processing among non-clinical compulsives. *Behaviour Research & Therapy, 26*, 275–277.

Frost, R. O., & Marten, P. A. (1990). Perfectionism and evaluative threat. *Cognitive Therapy & Research, 14*, 559–572.

Frost, R. O., Marten, P., Lahart, C., & Rosenblate, R. (1990). The dimensions of perfectionism. *Cognitive Therapy & Research, 14*, 449–468.

Frost, R. O., Steketee, G., Cohn, L., & Griess, K. (1994). Personality traits in subclinical and non-obsessive-compulsive volunteers and their parents. *Behaviour Research & Therapy, 32*, 47–56.

Fry, P. (1974). The development of differentiation in self-evaluations: A cross-cultural study. *Journal of Psychology, 87*, 193–202.

Fuller, A. K., Blashfield, R. K., & McElroy, R. A. (1995). Self defeating personality disorder and the infancy of psychiatric classification. *Journal of Nervous & Mental Disease, 183*, 222–223.

Funder, D. C. (2001). Personality. *Annual Review of Psychology, 52*, 197–221.

Furby, L. (1980). The origins and early development of possessive behavior. *Political Psychology, 2*, 30–42.

Furby, L., Weinrott, M. R., & Blackshaw, L. (1989). Sex offender recidivism: A review. *Psychological Bulletin, 105*, 3–30.

Furnham, A. (1981). Personality and activity preference. *British Journal of Social Psychiatry, 20*, 57–68.

Fyer, A., Mannuzza, S., Chapman, T., & Liebowitz, M. (1993). A direct interview family study of social phobia. *Archives of General Psychiatry, 50*, 286–293.

Fyer, A. J., Mannuzza, S., Chapman, T. F., & Martin, L. Y. (1995). Specificity in familial aggregation of phobic disorders. *Archives of General Psychiatry, 52*, 564–573.

Fyer, A. J., Mannuzza, S., Gallops, M. S., & Martin, L. Y. (1990). Familial transmission of simple phobias and fears: A preliminary report. *Archives of General Psychiatry, 47*, 252–256.

Gaddy, C., Glass, C., & Arnkoff, D. (1983). Career involvement of women in dual-career families: The influence of sex role identity. *Journal of Counseling Psychology, 30*, 388–394.

Gaensbauer, T., Harmon, R., Cytryn, L., & McKnew, D. (1984). Social and affective development in infants with a manic depressive parent. *American Journal of Psychiatry, 141*, 223–229.

Gara, M. A., Woolfolk, R. L., Cohen, B. D., Goldston, R. B., et al. (1993). Perceptions of self and other in major depression. *Journal of Abnormal Psychology, 102*, 93–100.

Garbarino, J., & Sherman, D. (1980). High-risk neighborhoods and high-risk families: The human ecology of child maltreatment. *Child Development, 51*, 188–198.

Gardner, P., & Oei, T. P. (1981). Depression and self-esteem: An investigation that used behavioral and cognitive approaches to the treatment of clinically depressed clients. *Journal of Clinical Psychology, 37*, 128–135.

Garfield, D., & Havens, L. (1991). Paranoid phenomena and pathological narcissism. *American Journal of Psychotherapy, 45*, 160–172.

Gastorf, J. W. (1980). Time urgency of the Type A behavior pattern. *Journal of Consulting & Clinical Psychology, 48*, 299.

Gaudin, J. M., Polansky, N. A., Kilpatrick, A., & Shilton, P. (1993). Loneliness, depression, stress and social supports in neglectful families. *American Journal of Orthopsychiatry, 63*, 597–605.

Gecas, V., & Nye, F. (1974). Sex and class differences in parent-child interaction: A test of Kohn's hypothesis. *Journal of Marriage & the Family, 36*, 742–749.

Gecas, V., Calonico, J. M., & Thomas, D. L. (1974). The development of self-concept in the child: Mirror theory versus model theory. *Journal of Social Psychology, 92*, 67–76.

Geiger, T. C., & Crick, N. R. (2001). In R. E. Ingram & J. M. Price (Eds.), *Vulnerability to psychopathology: Risks across the life span* (pp. 57–102). New York: Guilford.

Gelfand, D. M., & Teti, D. M. (1990). The effects of maternal depression on children. *Clinical Psychology Review, 10*, 329–353.

Geller, J. J. (1975). Developmental symbiosis. *Perspectives in Psychiatric Care, 8*, 10–12.

Geller, V., & Shaver, P. (1976). Cognitive consequences of self-awareness. *Experimental Social Psychology, 12*, 99–108.

Gelso, C. J. (1978). Intergenerational relationships in the development of child rearing attitudes. *Journal of Genetic Psychology, 133*, 31–41.

Gelso, C. J., Birk, J. M., & Powers, R. (1978). Intergenerational relationships in the development of child rearing attitudes. *Journal of Genetic Psychology, 133*, 31–41.

George, L. K., & Maddox, G. L. (1977). Subjective adaptation to loss of the work role: A longitudinal study. *Journal of Gerontology, 32*, 456–462.

Gershon, E. (1982). A family study of schizoaffective bipolar I, bipolar II, unipolar and normal control probands. *Archives of General Psychiatry, 39*, 1157–1167.

Gergen, K. J. (1994a). Exploring the postmodern: Perils or potentials? *American Psychologist, 49*, 412–416.

Gergen, K. J. (1994b). *Realities and relationships: Soundings in social construction.* Cambridge, MA: Harvard University Press.

Gibb, B., Alloy, L., Abramson, L., & Rose, D. (2001). History of childhood maltreatment, negative cognitive styles, and episodes of depression in adulthood. *Cognitive Therapy & Research, 25*, 425–446.

Gibbons, F. (1987). Mild depression and self-disclosure intimacy: Self and others' perceptions. *Cognitive Therapy & Research, 11*, 361–380.

Gibbs, N. A. (1996). Nonclinical populations in research on obsessive-compulsive disorder: A critical review. *Clinical Psychology Review, 16*, 729–773.

Gibbs, R. W., Jr. (2001). Intentions as emergent products of social interactions. In B. F. Malle, L. J. Moses, & D. A. Baldwin (Eds.), *Intentions and intentionality: Foundations of social cognition* (pp. 105–122). Cambridge, MA: MIT Press.

Giesler, R. B., Josephs, R. A., & Swann, W. B. Jr. (1998). Self-verification in clinical depression: The desire for negative evaluation. *Journal of Abnormal Psychology, 105*, 358–368.

Gift, T., Strauss, J., Ritzler, B., & Kokes, R. (1988). Social class and psychiatric disorder: The examination of an extreme. *Journal of Nervous & Mental Disease, 176*, 593–597.

Gilbert, P., Allan, S., & Trent, D. R. (1995). Involuntary subordination or dependency as key dimensions of depressive vulnerability? *Journal of Clinical Psychology, 51*, 740–752.

Gilford, R., & Bengston, V. (1979). Measuring marital satisfaction in three generations: Positive and negative dimensions. *Journal of Marriage & the Family, 41*, 387–398.

Gjerde, P. F., Block, J., & Block, J. H. (1988). Depressive symptoms and personality during late adolescence: Gender differences in the externalization-internalization of symptom expression. *Journal of Abnormal Psychology, 97*, 475–486.

Gladstone, G., Parker, G., Wilhelm, K., & Mitchell, P. (1999). Characteristics of depressed patients who report childhood sexual abuse. *American Journal of Psychiatry, 156*, 431–437.

Glasser, L. N., & Glasser, P. H. (1977). Hedonism and the family: Conflict in values? *Journal of Marriage & Family Counseling, 3*, 11–18.

Godin, G., Valois, P., Shephard, R., & Desharnais, R. (1987). Prediction of leisure-time exercise behavior: A path analysis (LISREL V) model. *Journal of Behavioral Medicine, 10*, 145–158.

Gockenbach, L. (1989). A review of personality factors in parents of gifted children and their families: Implications for research. *Journal of Clinical Psychology, 45*, 210–213.

Goeke-Morey, M. C., Harold, G. T., Cummings, E. M., & Shelton, K. H. (2003). Categories and continua of destructive and constructive marital conflict tactics from the perspective of U.S. and Welsh children. *Journal of Family Psychology, 17*, 327–338.

Goisman, R. M., Warshaw, M. G., Peterson, L. G., & Malcolm P. (1994). Panic, agoraphobia and panic disorder with agoraphobia: Data from a multi-center anxiety disorders study. *Journal of Nervous & Mental Disease, 182*, 72–79.

Gold, J. (1996). Intolerance of aloneness. *American Journal of Psychiatry, 153*, 749–750.

Goldfried, M. R., & Robins, C. (1982). On the facilitation of self-efficacy. *Cognitive Therapy & Research, 6*, 361–379.

Goldman, S. J., D'Angelo, E. J., & DeMaso, D. R. (1993). Psychopathology in the families of children and adolescents with borderline personality disorder. *American Journal of Psychiatry, 150*, 1832–1835.

Goldstein, R., Black, D., Nasrallah, A., & Winokur, G. (1991). The prediction of suicide: Sensitivity, specificity, and predictive value of a multivariate model applied to suicide among 1906 patient with affective disorders. *Archives of General Psychiatry, 48*, 418–422.

Goldstein, W. N. (1985). DSM-III and the narcissistic personality. *American Journal of Psychotherapy, 39*, 2–16.

Goldston, D. B., Turnquist, D. C., & Knutson, J. F. (1989). Presenting problems of sexually abused girls receiving psychiatric services. *Journal of Abnormal Psychology, 98*, 314–317.

Goldston, R. B., Gara, M. A., & Woolfolk, R. L. (1992). Emotion differentiation: A correlate of symptom severity in major depression. *Journal of Nervous & Mental Disease, 180*, 712–718.

Golish, T. D., & Powell, K. A. (2003). Ambiguous loss: Managing the dialectics of grief associated with premature birth. *Journal of Social and Personal Relationships, 20*, 309–334.

Gollwitzer, P. M. (1999). Implementation effects: Strong effects of simple plans. *American Psychologist, 54*, 493–503.

Gollwitzer, P., & Bargh, J. (Eds.). (1996). *The psychology of action.* New York: Guilford.

Golomb, M., Fava, M., Abraham, M., & Rosenbaum, J. F. (1995). Gender differences in personality disorders. *American Journal of Psychiatry, 152*, 579–582.

Good, L. R., Good, K. C., & Nelson, D. A. (1973). Assumed attitude similarity and perceived intra-familial communication and understanding. *Psychological Reports, 31*, 3–11.

Goodman, M., Brown, J., & Deitz, P. (1992). *Managing managed care: A mental health practitioner's survival guide.* Washington, DC: American Psychiatric Association.

Goodnow, J. J. (1988). Children's household work: Its nature and functions. *Psychological Bulletin, 103*, 5–26.

Gorall, D. M., & Olson, D. H. (1995). Circumplex model of family systems: Integrating ethnic diversity and other social systems. In R. H. Mikesell, D. D. Lusterman, & S. H. McDaniel (Eds.), *Integrating family therapy: Handbook of family psychology and systems theory* (pp. 217–233). Washington, DC: American Psychological Associaton.

Gordon, C. (1976). Development of evaluated role identities. *Annual Review of Sociology, 2,* 405–433.

Gordon, D., Burge, D., Hammen, C., Adrian, C., et al. (1989). Observations of interactions of depressed women with their children. *American Journal of Psychiatry, 146,* 50–55.

Gorton, T. A., Doerfler, D. L., Hulka, B. S., & Tyroler, H. A. (1979). Intra-familial patterns of illness reports and physician visits in a community sample. *Journal of Health & Social Behavior, 20,* 37–44.

Gorwood, P., Leboyer, M., Jay, M., & Payan, C. (1995). Gender and age at onset in schizophrenia: Impact of family history. *American Journal of Psychiatry, 152,* 208–212.

Gottfredson, G., Jones, E., & Holland, J. (1993). Personality and vocational interests: The relation of Holland's six interest dimensions to five robust dimensions of personality. *Journal of Counseling Psychology, 40,* 518–524.

Gottman, J. M. (1979). *Marital interaction: Experimental investigations.* New York: Academic Press.

Gottman, J. M. (1993). The roles of conflict engagement, escalation, and avoidance in marital interaction: A longitudinal view of five types of couples. *Journal of Consulting & Clinical Psychology, 61,* 6–15.

Gottschalk, L., & Keatinge, C. (1993). Influence of patient caregivers on course of patient illness: "Expressed emotion" and alternative measures. *Journal of Clinical Psychology, 49,* 898–912.

Gould, R. L. (2001). A feedback-driven computer program for outpatient training. In L. L'Abate (Ed.), *Distance writing and computer-assisted interventions in psychiatry and mental health* (pp. 93–111). Westport, CT: Ablex.

Grams, A. (2001). Learning, aging, and other predicaments. In S. H. McFadden & R. C. Atchley (Eds.), *Aging and the meaning of time* (pp. 99–111). New York: Springer.

Grant, I., Patterson, T., & Yager, J. (1988). Social supports in relation to physical health and symptoms of depression in the elderly. *American Journal of Psychiatry, 145,* 1254–1258.

Grant, T., & Domino, G. (1976). Masculinity-femininity in fathers of creative male adolescents. *Journal of Genetic Psychology, 129,* 19–27.

Green, R. (1985). Gender identity in childhood and later sexual orientation: Follow-up of 78 males. *American Journal of Psychiatry, 142,* 339–341.

Green, R. J., & Werner, P. D. (1996). Intrusiveness and closeness-caregiving: Rethinking the concept of family enmeshment. *Family Process, 35,* 115–136.

Greene, R. W., Biederman, J., Zerwas, S., & Monuteaux, M. (2002). Psychiatric comorbidity, family dysfunction and social impairment in referred youth with oppositional defiant disorder. *American Journal of Psychiatry, 159,* 1214–1224.

Greenfield, S. (2000). *The private life of the brain: Emotions, consciousness, and the secret of the self.* New York: Wiley.

Greenfield, S., Swartz, M., Landerman, L., & George, L. (1993). Long-term psychosocial effects of childhood exposure to parental problem drinking. *American Journal of Psychiatry, 150,* 608–613.

Greer, S., & Calhoun, J. (1983). Learned helplessness and depression in acutely distressed community residents. *Cognitive Therapy & Research, 7,* 205–222.

Grieger, R., & Grieger, I. Z. (Eds.). (1982). *Cognition and emotional disturbance.* New York: Human Sciences Press.

Grilo, C. M., Becker, D. F., Walker, M. L., & Edell, W. S. (1996). Gender differences in personality disorders in psychiatrically hospitalized young adults. *Journal of Nervous & Mental Disease, 184*, 754–757.

Grilo, C. M., Sanislow, C., Fehon, D. C., Martino, S., et al. (1999). Psychological and behavioral functioning in adolescent psychiatric inpatients who report histories of childhood abuse. *American Journal of Psychiatry, 156*, 538–543.

Grim, D. (1977). Disturbances of symbiosis in infancy and early childhood. *Transactional Analysis Journal, 7*, 231–234.

Grimm, L. G., & Yarnold, P. R. (1984). Performance standards and the Type A behavior pattern. *Cognitive Therapy & Research, 8*, 59–66.

Gross, J., & Levenson, R. (1997). Hiding feelings: The acute effects of inhibiting negative and positive emotion. *Journal of Abnormal Psychology, 106*, 95–103.

Grotevant, H. D. (1976). Family similarities in interests and orientation. *Merrill-Palmer Quarterly, 22*, 61–72.

Grotevant, H. D. (1977). Patterns of interest similarity in adoptive and biological families. *Journal of Personality & Social Psychology, 35*, 667–676.

Grotevant, H. D., Scarr, S., & Weinberg, R. A. (1977). Patterns of interest similarity in adoptive and biological families. *Journal of Personality & Social Psychology, 35*, 667–676.

Grown, G. (1980). Parental behavior and self-esteem in children. *Psychological Reports, 47*, 499–502.

Gruba, F. P., & Johnson, J. E. (1974). Contradictions within the self-concepts of schizophrenics. *Journal of Clinical Psychology, 30*, 253–254.

Grunbaum, L., & Gammeltoft, M. (1993). Young children of schizophrenic mothers: Difficulties of intervention. *American Journal of Orthopsychiatry, 63*, 16–27.

Grunhaus, L., Pande, A., Brown, M., & Greden, J. (1994). Clinical characteristics of patients with concurrent major depressive disorder and panic disorder. *American Journal of Psychiatry, 151*, 541–546.

Grych, J., & Fincham, F. (1990). Marital conflict and children's adjustment: A cognitive-contextual framework. *Psychological Bulletin, 108*, 267–290.

Guinther, P. M., Segal, D. L., & Bogaards, J. A. (2003). Gender differences in emotional processing among bereaved older adults. *Journal of Loss & Trauma, 8*, 15–33.

Gunderson, J., & Englund, D. (1980). The families of borderlines: A comparative study. *Archives of General Psychiatry, 37*, 27–33.

Gurman, A. S. (1997, Spring). Soft-hard methodology X traditional-modern perspective grid. *AFTA Newsletter, 62*.

Gurtman, M. B. (1986). Depression and the response of others: Reevaluating the reevaluation. *Journal of Abnormal Psychology, 95*, 99–101.

Haaga, D. A., Dyck, M. J., & Ernst, D. (1991). Empirical status of cognitive theory of depression. *Psychological Bulletin, 110*, 215–236.

Haan, N., & Day, D. (1974). A longitudinal study of change and sameness in personality development: Adolescence to later adulthood. *International Journal of Aging & Human Development, 5*, 11–39.

Haapasalo, J., & Tremblay, R. E. (1994). Physically aggressive boys from ages 6 to 12: Family background, parenting behavior and prediction of delinquency. *Journal of Consulting & Clinical Psychology, 62*, 1044–1052.

Haddad, J., Barocas, R., & Hallenbeck, A. (1991). Family organization and parent attitudes of children with conduct disorder. *Journal of Clinical Child Psychology, 20*, 152–161.

Hafner, J. (1977). The husbands of agoraphobic women: Assortative mating or pathogenic interaction? *British Journal of Psychiatry, 130*, 233–239.

Hafner, J. L., Fakouri, M. E., & Chesney, S. M. (1988). Early recollections of alcoholic women. *Journal of Clinical Psychology, 44*, 302–306.

Hahlweg, K., Goldstein, M., Nuechterlein, K., & Magana, A. (1989). Expressed emotion and patient-relative interaction in families of recent onset schizophrenics. *Journal of Consulting & Clinical Psychology, 57*, 11–18.

Halberstadt, A. G., Cassidy, J., Stifter, C. A., & Parke, R. D. (1995). Self-expressiveness within the family context: Psychometric support for a new measure. *Psychological Assessment, 7*, 93–103.

Hall, J. (1981). A self-awareness model of the causes and effects of alcohol consumption. *Journal of Abnormal Psychology, 90*, 586–600.

Hamann, M. S., & Mavissakalian, M. (1988). Discrete dimensions in agoraphobia: A factor analytic study. *British Journal of Clinical Psychology, 27*, 137–144.

Hammen, C., Adrian, C., & Hiroto, D. (1988). A longitudinal test of the attributional vulnerability model in children at risk for depression. *British Journal of Clinical Psychology, 27*, 37–46.

Hammen, C., Burge, D., Burney, E., & Adrian, C. (1990). Longitudinal study of diagnoses in children of women with unipolar and bipolar affective disorder. *Archives of General Psychiatry, 47*, 1112–1117.

Hammen, C., & Garber, J. (2001). Vulnerability to depression across the lifespan. In R. E. Ingram & J. M. Price (Eds.), *Vulnerability to psychopathology: Risks across the life span* (pp. 258–267). New York: Guilford.

Hammen, C., Gordon, D., Burge, D., Adrian, C., et al. (1987). Maternal affective disorders, illness, and stress: Risk for children's psychopathology. *American Journal of Psychiatry, 144*, 736–741.

Hammond, M. V., Landry, S. H., Swank, P. R., & Smith, K. E. (2000). Relation of mothers' affective development history and parenting behavior: Effects on infant medical risk. *American Journal of Orthopsychiatry, 70*, 95–103.

Han, S., Weisz, J., & Weiss, B. (2001). Specificity of relations between children's control-related beliefs and internalizing and externalizing psychopathology. *Journal of Consulting & Clinical Psychology, 69*, 240–251.

Hansen, J. C., & L'Abate, L. (1982). *Approaches to family therapy*. New York: Macmillan.

Hanson, D. (1970). Dogmatism and political ideology. *Journal of Human Relations, 18*, 995–1002.

Hanson, D. (1975). Authoritarianism as a variable in political research. *Politico, 40*, 700–705.

Hanson, R. K., & Harris, A. J. R. (2000). Where should we intervene? Dynamic predictors of sexual offense recidivism. *Criminal Justice and Behavior, 27*, 6–35.

Harder, D., Cutler, L., & Rockart, L. (1992). Assessment of shame and guilt and their relationship to psychopathology. *Journal of Personality Assessment, 59*, 584–604.

Hardesty, S. A., & Betz, N. E. (1980). The relationships of career salience, attitudes toward women, and demographic and family characteristics to marital adjustment in dual career couples. *Journal of Vocational Behavior, 17*, 242–250.

Harpur, T. J., Hakstian, A. R., & Hare, R. D. (1988). Factor structure of the Psychopathy Checklist. *Journal of Consulting & Clinical Psychology, 56*, 741–747.

Harrell, J. P. (1980). Psychological factors and hypertension: A status report. *Psychological Bulletin, 87*, 482–501.

Harrington, C., & Metzler, A. (1997). Are adult children of dysfunctional families with alcoholism different from adult children of dysfunctional families without alcoholism? A look at committed, intimate relationships. *Journal of Counseling Psychology, 44*, 102–107.

Harrington, D., Dubowitz, H., Black, M., & Binder, A. (1995). Maternal substance use and neglectful parenting: Relations with children's development. *Journal of Clinical Child Psychology, 24*, 258–263.

Harris, P. L. (2000). Understanding emotion. In M. Lewis & J. M. Haviland-Jones (Eds.), *Handbook of emotions* (pp. 281–292). New York: Guilford.

Harrison, M. G (1993). *The relationship among Adlerian lifestyle themes, gender roles, cooperative negotiation, and marital satisfaction.* Unpublished Ph.D. dissertation. Georgia State University.

Hart, C. H., Newell, L. D., & Frost-Olsen, S. (2003). Parenting skills and social communicative competence in childhood. In J. O. Green & B. R. Burleson (Eds.), *Handbook of communication and social interaction skills* (pp. 753–797). Mahwah, NJ: Earlbaum.

Harter, S. (1990). Developmental differences in the nature of self-representations: Implications for the understanding, assessment, and treatment of maladaptive behavior. *Cognitive Therapy & Research, 14*, 113–142.

Harter, S., Alexander, P. C., & Neimeyer, R. A. (1988). Long-term effects of incestuous child abuse in college women: Social adjustment, social cognition, and family characteristics. *Journal of Consulting & Clinical Psychology, 56*, 5–8.

Harter, S., Waters, P. I., Pettitt, L. M., Whitesell, J. K., & Jordan, J. (1997). Autonomy and connectedness as dimensions of relationship styles in men and women. *Journal of Social and Personal Relationships, 14*, 147–164.

Harter, S. L., & Vanecek, R. J. (2000). Cognitive assumptions and long-term distress in survivors of childhood abuse, parental alcoholism, and dysfunctional family environments. *Cognitive Therapy & Research, 24*, 445–472.

Harvey, J. H., & Galvin, K. S. (1984). Clinical implications of attribution theory and research. *Clinical Psychology Review, 4*, 15–33.

Harvey, J. H., & Weber, A. L. (2002). *Odyssey of the heart: Close relationships in the 21st century.* Mahwah, NJ: Earlbaum.

Haskett, M., Myers, L., Pirrello, V., & Dombalis, A. (1995). Parenting style as a mediating link between parental emotional health and adjustment of maltreated children. *Behavior Therapy, 26*, 625–642.

Haslam, N. (Ed.). (2004). *Relational models theory: A contemporary overview.* Mahwah, NJ: Earlbaum.

Haslam, J., & Beck, A. T. (1993). Categorization of major depression in an outpatient sample. *Journal of Nervous & Mental Disease, 181*, 725–731.

Haslam, N., & Beck, A. T. (1994). Subtyping major depression: A taxometric analysis. *Journal of Abnormal Psychology, 103*, 686–692.

Haviland, M., Hendryx, M., Cummings, M., & Shaw, D. (1991). Multidimensionality and state dependency of alexithymia in recently sober alcoholics. *Journal of Nervous & Mental Disease, 179*, 284–290.

Hayano, J., Takeuchi, S., Yoshida, S., Jozuka, H., et al. (1989). Type A behavior pattern in Japanese employees: Cross-cultural comparison of major factors in Jenkins Activity Survey (JAS) responses. *Journal of Behavioral Medicine, 12*, 219–231.

Hayduk, L. A. (1978). Personal space: An evaluative and orienting overview. *Psychological Bulletin, 85*, 117–134.

Hayduk, L. A. (1983). Personal space: Where we now stand. *Psychological Bulletin, 94*, 293–335.

Hayes, S. C., Strosahl, K. D., & Wilson, K. G. (1999). *Acceptance and commitment therapy: An experiential approach to behavior change.* New York: Guilford.

Haynes, S. N. (1992). Models of causality in psychopathology: Toward dynamic, synthetic, and nonlinear models of behavior disorders. New York: Macmillan.

Hecht, D. T., & Baum, S. K. (1984). Loneliness and attachment patterns in young adults. *Journal of Clinical Psychology, 40*, 193–197.

Hechtman, L. (Ed.). (1996). *Do they grow out of it? Long term outcomes of childhood disorders.* Washington, DC: American Psychiatric Association.

Heilbrun, A. B., & Friedberg, E. B. (1988). Type A personality, self-control, and vulnerability to stress. *Personality Assessment, 52,* 420–433.

Heimberg, R. G., Liebowitz, M. R., Hope, D. A., Schneider, F. R. (Eds.). (1995). *Social phobia: Diagnosis, assessment, and treatment.* New York: Guilford.

Heimberg, R. G., Vermiyea, J., Dodge, C., & Becker, R. (1987). Attributional style, depression, and anxiety: An evaluation of the specificity of depressive attributions. *Cognitive Therapy & Research, 11,* 537–550.

Heisler, L. K., Lyons, M. J., & Goethe, J. W. (1995). Self defeating personality disorder: A cross-national study of clinical utility. *Journal of Nervous & Mental Disease, 183,* 214–221.

Helgeson, V. S. (1994). Relation of agency and communion to well-being: Evidence and potential explanations. *Psychological Bulletin, 116,* 412–428.

Heller, T. L., Baker, B. L., Henker, B., & Hinshaw, S. P. (1996). Externalizing behavior and cognitive functioning from preschool to first grade: Stability and predictors. *Journal of Clinical Child Psychology, 25,* 376–387.

Henderson, J. (1980). On fathering: The nature and functions of the father role: II. Conceptualization of fathering. *Canadian Journal of Psychiatry, 25,* 413–431.

Hendrick, C. (2002). A new age of prevention? *Journal of Social and Personal Relationships, 19,* 621–628.

Hendrick, S. S., & Hendrick, C. (1992). *Romantic love.* Thousand Oaks, CA: Sage.

Hendriks-Jansen, H. (1996). *Catching ourselves in the act: Situated activity, interactive emergence, evolution, and human thought.* Cambridge, MA: MIT Press.

Henggeler, S. W. (1985). Mother–son relationships of juvenile felons. *Journal of Consulting & Clinical Psychology, 53,* 942–943.

Henggeler, S. W., McKee, E., & Borduin, C. M. (1989). Is there a link between maternal neglect and adolescent delinquency? *Journal of Clinical Child Psychology, 18,* 242–246.

Heniksson, M., Aro, H., Martunen, J., & Heikkien, M. (1993). Mental disorders and comorbidity in suicide. *American Journal of Psychiatry, 150,* 935–940.

Henrich, C. C., Blatt, S. J., Kuperminc, G. P., Zohar, A., & Leadbeater, B. J. (2001). Levels of interpersonal concerns and social functioning in early adolescent boys and girls. *Journal of Personality Assessment, 76,* 48–67.

Herbert, J. D., Hope, D. A., & Bellack, A. S. (1992). Validity of the distinction between generalized social phobia and avoidant personality disorder. *Journal of Abnormal Psychology, 101,* 332–339.

Herman, J., Perry, C., & Van der Kolk, B. (1989). Childhood trauma in borderline personality disorder. *American Journal of Psychiatry, 146,* 490–495.

Herrenkohl, R. C., Egolf, B., & Herrenkohl, E. (1997). Preschool antecedents assaultive behavior: A longitudinal study. *American Journal of Orthopsychiatry, 67,* 422–432.

Herrenkohl, R. C., Herrenkohl, E. C., & Egolf, B. P. (1983). Circumstances surrounding the occurrence of child maltreatment. *Journal of Consulting & Clinical Psychology, 51,* 424–431.

Herrman, H., McGorry, P. D., Mills, J., & Singh, B. (1991). Hidden severe psychiatric morbidity in sentenced prisoners: An Australian study. *American Journal of Psychiatry, 148,* 236–239.

Hetherington, E. M., Stouwie, R. J., & Ridberg, E. H. (1971). Patterns of family interaction and child-rearing attitudes related to three dimensions of juvenile delinquency. *Journal of Abnormal Psychology, 78,* 160–176.

Hewitt, P. L., & Dyck, D. G. (1986). Perfectionism, stress, and vulnerability to depression. *Cognitive Therapy & Research, 10,* 137–142.

Hewitt, P. L., & Flett, G. L. (1991). Dimensions of perfectionism in unipolar depression. *Journal of Abnormal Psychology, 100,* 98–101.

Hewitt, P. L., & Flett, G. L. (1993). Dimensions of perfectionism, daily stress and depression: A test of the specific vulnerability hypothesis. *Journal of Abnormal Psychology, 102,* 58–65.

Hewitt, P. L., Flett, G. L., & Ediger, E. (1996). Perfectionism and depression: Longitudinal assessment of a specific vulnerability hypothesis. *Journal of Abnormal Psychology, 105,* 276–280.

Hewitt, P. L., Flett, G. L., & Turnball-Donovan, W. (1992). *British Journal of Clinical Psychology, 31,* 181–190.

Hewitt, P. L., Mittelstaedt, W., & Wollert, R. (1989). Validation of a measure of perfectionism. *Journal of Personality Assessment, 53,* 133–144.

Hibbs, E. D., Hamburger, S. D., Kruesi, M. J., & Lenane, M. (1993). Factors affecting expressed emotion in parents of ill and normal children. *American Journal of Orthopsychiatry, 63,* 103–112.

Hicks, R. A., et al. (1979). Type A behavior and normal habitual sleep duration. *Bulletin of the Psychonomic Society, 14,* 185–186.

Higgins, E. T. (2001). Promotion and prevention experiences: Relating emotions to nonemotional motivational states. In J. P. Forgas (Ed.), *Handbook of affect and social cognition* (pp. 186–211). Mahwah, NJ: Earlbaum.

Higgins, E. T. (1997). Beyond pleasure and pain. *American Psychologist, 52,* 1280–1300.

Higgins., E. T., & Kruglanski, A. W. (Eds.). (1996). *Social psychology: Handbook of basic principles.* New York: Guilford.

Hightower, E. (1988). Four illustrations of healthy personality: A prescription for living the good life. *Journal of Clinical Psychology, 44,* 527–535.

Hill, K., & Larson L. (1992). Attributional style in the reformulated learned helplessness model of depression: Cognitive processes and measurement implications. *Cognitive Therapy & Research, 16,* 83–94.

Hill, M. K., & Lando, H. A. (1976). Physical attractiveness and sex-role stereotypes in impression formation. *Perceptual & Motor Skills, 43,* 1251–1255.

Hill, R. W., Zrull, M. C., & Turlington, S. (1997). Perfectionism and interpersonal problems. *Journal of Personality Assessment, 69,* 81–103.

Hillbrand, M. (1995). Aggression against self and aggression against others in violent psychiatric patients. *Journal of Consulting & Clinical Psychology, 63,* 668–671.

Hilsenroth, M. J., Handler, L., & Blais, M. A. (1996). Assessment of narcissistic personality disorder: A multi-method review. *Clinical Psychology Review, 16,* 655–683.

Himadi, W. G. (1986). The relationship of marital adjustment to agoraphobia treatment outcome. *Behaviour Research & Therapy, 24,* 107–115.

Himmelfarb, S. (1972). Integration and attribution theories in personality impression formation. *Journal of Personality & Social Psychology, 23,* 309–313.

Hinrichsen, G. A., & Pollack, S. (1997). Expressed emotion and the course of late-life depression. *Journal of Abnormal Psychology, 106,* 336–340.

Hinshaw, S. (1992). Externalizing behavior problems and academic underachievement in childhood and adolescence: Cause relationships and underlying mechanisms. *Psychological Bulletin, 111,* 127–155.

Hirsch, B. (1980). Natural support systems and coping with major life changes. *American Journal of Community Psychology, 8,* 159–172.

Hodgins, S., Kratzer, L., & McNeil, T. E. (2001). Obstetric complications, parenting and risk of criminal behavior. *Archives of General Psychology, 58,* 746–752.

Hoeltje, C. O., Zubrick, S. R., Silburn, S. R., & Garton, A. F. (1996). Generalized self-efficacy: Family and adjustment correlates. *Journal of Clinical Child Psychology, 25,* 446–453.

Hoffman, L. (1991). The influence of the family environment on personality: Accounting for sibling differences. *Psychological Bulletin, 110,* 187–203.

Hogan, D. (1978). The variable order of events in the life course. *American Sociological Review, 43,* 573–586.

Hogan, R., Johnson, J., & Briggs, S. (Eds.). (1997). *Handbook of personality theory*. San Diego, CA: Academic Press.

Hogg, J. A., & Deffenbacher, J. L. (1988). A comparison of cognitive and interpersonal-process group therapies in the treatment of depression among college students. *Journal of Counseling Psychology, 35*, 304–310.

Hogg, M. A. (2000). Identity and social comparison. In J. Suls & L. Wheeler, L. (Eds.), *Handbook of social comparison: Theory and research* (pp. 401–421). New York: Kluwer Academic.

Holden, E., Willis, D., & Flotz, L. (1989). Child abuse potential and parenting stress: Relationships in maltreating parents. *Psychological Assessment, 1*, 64–67.

Holden, R. R., Mendonca, J. D., & Serin, R. C. (1989). Suicide, hopelessness, and social desirability: A test of an interactive model. *Journal of Consulting & Clinical Psychology, 57*, 500–504.

Holland, J., & Gottfredson, G. (1975). Using a typology of persons and environments to explain careers: Some extensions and clarifications. *Center for Social Organization of Schools Report, Johns Hopkins University, 204*, 43.

Hollender, J. W., Duke, M. P., & Nowicki, S. (1973). Interpersonal distance: Sibling structure and parental affection antecedents. *Journal of Genetic Psychology, 123*, 35–45.

Holt, C. S., Heimberg, R. G., & Hope, D. A. (1992). Avoidant personality disorder and the generalized subtype of social phobia. *Journal of Abnormal Psychology, 101*, 318–325.

Honig, R. G., Grace, M. C., Lindy, J. D., & Newman, C. J. (1999). Assessing long term effects of trauma: Diagnosing symptoms of avoidance and numbering. *American Journal of Psychiatry, 156*, 483–485.

Hoogduin, K. (1986). On the diagnosis of obsessive-compulsive disorder. *American Journal of Psychotherapy, 40*, 36–51.

Hooley, J., & Hiller, J. (2000). Personality and expressed emotion. *Journal of Abnormal Psychology, 109*, 40–44.

Hooley, J., & Richters, J. (1991). Alternative measures of expressed emotion: A methodological and cautionary note. *Journal of Abnormal Psychology, 100*, 94–97.

Hooley, J., & Teasdale, J. (1989). Predictors of relapse in unipolar depressives: Expressed emotion, martial distress, and perceived criticism. *Journal of Abnormal Psychology, 98*, 229–235.

Hooper, D., Vaughan, P. W., Hinchliffe, M. K., & Roberts, F. J. (1978). Expressed emotions in families of schizophrenics. *British Journal of Medical Psychology, 51*, 387–398.

Hooveer, C. F., & Insel, T. R. (1984). Families of origin in the obsessive-compulsive disorder. *Journal of Nervous & Mental Disease, 172*, 207–215.

Horner, T. M. (1986). On symbiosis and infantile omnipotence: Reply. *American Journal of Orthopsychiatry, 56*, 167–168.

Hornung, C. A., & McCullough, B. C. (1981). Status relationships in dual-employment marriages: Consequences for psychological well-being. *Journal of Marriage & the Family, 43*, 125–141.

Horowitz, M. (1984). Reactions to the death of a parent: Results from patients and field subjects. *Journal of Nervous & Mental Disease, 172*, 383–392.

Horowitz, M., Sonneborn, D., Sugahara, C., & Maercker, A. (1996). Self-Regard: A new measure. *American Journal of Psychiatry, 153*, 382–385.

Horwath, E., Wolk, S. I., Goldstein, R. R., & Wickramaratne, P., et al. (1995). Is the co-morbidity between social phobia and panic disorder due to familial co-transmission or other factors? *Archives of General Psychiatry, 52*, 574–582.

Howe, F. C. (1980). Self-concept. *Child Study Journal, 1*, 51.

Hoyt, L. A., Cowen, E. L., Pedro-Carroll, J. L., & Alpert-Gillis, L. J. (1990). Anxiety and depression in young children of divorce. *Journal of Clinical Child Psychology, 19*, 26–32.

Huang, M., & Alessi, N. (1996). The Internet and the future of psychiatry. *American Journal of Psychiatry, 153*, 861–869.

Hubbs-Tait, L., Hughes, K., Culp, A., & Osofsky, J. (1996). Children of adolescent mothers: Attachment representation, maternal depression, and later behavior problems. *American Journal of Orthopsychiatry, 66,* 416–426.

Hubert, N. C., Jay, S. M., Saltoun, M., & Hayes, M. (1988). Approach–avoidance and distress in children undergoing preparation for painful medical procedures. *Journal of Clinical Child Psychology, 17,* 194–202.

Hughes, H. M., & Barad, S. J. (1983). Psychological functioning of children in a battered women's shelter: A preliminary investigation. *American Journal of Orthopsychiatry, 53,* 525–531.

Hughes, M. C. (1984). Recurrent abdominal pain and childhood depression: Clinical observations of 23 children and their families. *American Journal of Orthopsychiatry, 54,* 146–155.

Humphreys, L., Fleishman, A., & Lin, P. (1977). Causes of racial and socioeconomic differences in cognitive tests. *Journal of Research in Personality, 11,* 191–208.

Hunsley, J. (1989). Vulnerability to depressive mood: An examination of the temporal consistency of the reformulated learned helplessness model. *Cognitive Therapy & Research, 13,* 599–608.

Hurtug, J., Audy, J. R., & Cohen, Y. A. (Eds.). (1998). *The anatomy of loneliness.* New York: International Universities Press.

Huselid, R. F., & Cooper, M. L. (1994). Gender roles as mediators of sex differences in expressions of pathology. *Journal of Abnormal Psychology, 103,* 595–603.

Hussong, A. M. (2000a). Distinguishing mean and structural sex differences in adolescent friendship quality. *Journal of Social & Personal Relationships, 17,* 223–243.

Hussong, A. H. (2000b). The settings of adolescent alcohol and drug use. *Journal of Youth on Adolescence, 29,* 107–119.

Hussong, A. M. (2000c). Perceived peer context and adolescent adjustment. *Journal of Research on Adolescence, 10,* 391–415.

Huth, C. (1978). Married women's work status: The influence of parents and husbands. *Journal of Vocational Behavior, 13,* 272–286.

Hyman, S., & Arana, G. W. (1989). Suicide and affective disorders. In D. Jacobs & H. N. Brown (Eds.), *Suicide: Understanding and responding: Harvard Medical School perspectives* (pp. 171–181). Madison, CT: International Universities Press.

Ickes, W., Layden, M., & Barnes, R. (1978). Objective self-awareness and individuation: An empirical link. *Journal of Personality, 46,* 146–161.

Ihinger-Tallman, M., Pasley, K., & Buehler, C. (1995). Developing a middle-range theory of father involvement post-divorce. In W. Marsilio (Ed.), *Fatherhood: Contemporary theory, research, and social policy* (pp. 57–77). Thousand Oaks, CA: Sage.

Ilfeld, F. W. (1977). Current social stressors and symptom of depression. *American Journal of Psychiatry, 134,* 161–166.

Ingram, R. E., & Price, J. M. (Eds.). (2001). *Vulnerability to psychopathology: Risks across the life span.* New York: Guilford.

Innes, J. M. (1978). Conservatism and the perception of self and others. *Social Behavior & Personality, 6,* 17–20.

Innes, J. M. (1980). Impulsivity and the coronary-prone behavior pattern. *Psychological Reports, 47,* 976–978.

Inoff-Germain, G., Nottelmann, E., & Radke-Yarrow, M. (1997). Relation of parental affective illness to family, dyadic, and individual functioning: An observational study of family interaction. *American Journal of Orthopsychiatry, 67,* 433–483.

Irwin, H. J. (1998). Affective predictors of dissociaiton II: Shame and guilt. *Journal of Clinical Psychology, 54,* 237–245.

Isometsa, E., Henrikson, M., Heikkinen, M., & Aro, H. (1996). Suicide among subjects with personality disorder. *American Journal of Psychiatry, 153,* 667–673.

Izard, C. E., Kagan, J. R., & Zajonc, R. B. (Eds.). (1984). *Emotions, cognition, and behavior.* New York: Cambridge University Press.

Isen, A. M. (2000). Positive affect and decision making. In M. Lewis & J. M. Haviland-Jones (Ed.), *Handbook of emotions* (pp. 417–435). New York: Guilford.

Jackson, R. M., Meara, N. M., & Arora, M. (1974). Father identification, achievement, and occupational behavior of rural youth. *Journal of Vocational Behavior, 4,* 85–96.

Jacob, T., Krahn, G. L., & Leonard, K. (1991). Parent-child interactions in families with alcoholic fathers. *Journal of Consulting & Clinical Psychology, 59,* 176–181.

Jacobson, D. S. (1978). The impact of marital separation/divorce on children: III. Parent-child communication and child adjustment, and regression analysis of findings from overall study. *Journal of Divorce, 2,* 175–194.

Jacobson, N. S., Follette, W. C., & McDonald, D. W. (1982). Reactivity to positive and negative behavior in distressed and nondistressed married couples. *Journal of Consulting & Clinical Psychology, 50,* 706–714.

Jaffe, P., Wolfe, D., Wilson, S., & Zak, L. (1986). Similarities in behavioral and social maladjustment among child victims and witnesses to family violence. *American Journal of Orthopsychiatry, 56,* 142–146.

Jarmas, A., & Kazak, A. (1992). Young adult children of alcoholic fathers: Depressive experiences, coping styles, and family systems. *Journal of Consulting & Clinical Psychology, 60,* 244–251.

Jarymowicz, M., & Codol, J. P. (1979). Self-others similarity perception: Striving for diversity from other people. *Polish Psychological Bulletin, 10,* 41–48.

Jellison, J., & Gentry, K. (1978). A self-presentation interpretation of the seeking of social approval. *Personality & Social Psychology Bulletin, 4,* 227–230.

Jenkins, J., & Karno, M. (1992). The meaning of expressed emotion: Theoretical issues raised by cross-cultural research. *American Journal of Psychiatry, 149,* 9–21.

Jensen, L. C., & Kingston, M. (1986). *Parenting.* New York: Holt, Rinehart, & Winston.

Jensen, P. S. (1999). Links among theory, research, and practice: Cornerstones of clinical scientific progress. *Journal of Clinical Child Psychology, 28,* 553–557.

Jessor, S. L., & Jessor, R. (1974). Maternal ideology and adolescent problem behavior. *Developmental Psychology, 10,* 246–254.

Johnson, C., & Flach, A. (1985). Family characteristics of 105 patients with bulimia. *American Journal of Psychiatry, 142,* 1321–1324.

Johnson, C. C., Hunter, S. M., Amos, C. I., Elder, S. T., et al. (1989). Cigarette smoking, alcohol, and oral contraceptive use by Type A adolescents: The Bogalusa Heart Study. *Journal of Behavioral Medicine, 12,* 13–24.

Johnson, J. G., Cohen, P., Brown, J., Smailes, E. M., & Bernstein, D. P. (1999). Childhood maltreat-ment increases risk for personality disorders during early adulthood. *Archives of General Psychiatry, 56,* 600–606.

Johnson, J. G., Cohen, P., Kasen, S., & Smailes, E., et al. (2001). Association of maladaptive parental behavior with psychiatric disorder among parents and their offspring. *Archives of General Psychiatry, 58,* 453–460.

Johnson, J. G., Cohen, P., Smailes, E. M., Skodol, A. E., Brown, J., & Oldham, J. M. (2001). Childhood verbal abuse and risk for personality disorders during adolescence and early adulthood. *Comprehensive Psychiatry, 42,* 16–23.

Johnson, J. G., Smailes, E. M., Cohen, P., Brown, J., & Bernstein, D. P. (2000). Associations between four types of childhood neglect and personality disorder symptoms during adolescence and early adulthood: Findings of a community-based longitudinal study. *Journal of Personality Disorders, 14,* 171–187.

Johnson, S. M. (1991). *The symbiotic character.* New York: Norton.

Johnson-Laird, P. N., & Oatley, K. (2000). Cognitive and social construction of emotions. In M. Lewis & J. M. Haviland-Jones (Eds.), *Handbook of emotions* (pp. 458–475). New York: Guilford.

Joiner, T. E. Jr. (1993). Discrimination between anxiety and depression. *Journal of Nervous & Mental Disease, 181,* 708–709.

Joiner, T. E. Jr. (1996). A confirmatory factor-analytic investigation of the tripartite model of depression and anxiety in college students. *Cognitive Therapy & Research, 20,* 521–539.

Joiner, T. E. Jr. (1997). Shyness and low social support as interactive diatheses, with loneliness as a mediator: Testing an interpersonal-personality view of vulnerability to depressive symptoms. *Journal of Abnormal Psychology, 106,* 386–394.

Joiner, T. E. Jr., & Rudd, D. M. (1996). Toward a categorization of depression-related psychological constructs. *Cognitive Therapy & Research, 20,* 51–68.

Jones, J. (1977). Parental transactional style deviance as a possible indicator of risk for schizophrenia. *Archives of General Psychiatry, 34,* 71–74.

Jordan, K. B., & L'Abate, L. (1995). The Tape-of-the Mind workbook: A single case study. *Journal of Family Psychotherapy, 10,* 13–25.

Jöreskog, K. G., & Sörbom, D. (1996), *Lisrel 8: User's reference guide.* Chicago: Scientific Software International.

Joseph, R. (1992). *The right brain and the unconscious: Discovering the stranger within.* Cambridge, MA: Perseus Books.

Jouriles, E. N., Bourg, W. J., & Farris, A. M. (1991). Marital adjustment and child conduct problems: A comparison of the correlation across subsamples. *Journal of Consulting & Clinical Psychology, 59,* 354–357.

Jouriles, E., & Farris, A. (1992). Effects of marital conflict on subsequent parent-son interaction. *Behavior Therapy, 23,* 355–374.

Jouriles, E., Mehta, P., McDonald, R., & Francis, D. (1997). Psychometric properties of family members reports of parental physical aggression toward clinic-referred children. *Journal of Consulting & Clinical Psychology, 65,* 309–318.

Jurkovic, G., & Prentice, N. (1974). Dimensions of moral interaction and moral judgment in delinquent and nondelinquent families. *Journal of Consulting & Clinical Psychology, 42,* 256–262.

Justice, B., & Duncan, D. (1977). Child abuse as a work-related problem. *Corrective & Social Psychiatry & Journal of Behavior Technology, Methods & Therapy, 23,* 53–55.

Justice, R., & Justice, B. (1976). Shifting symbiosis in abusive families. *Transactional Analysis Journal, 6,* 423–427.

Kahn, A., & McGaughery, T. A. (1977). Distance and liking: When moving close produces increased liking. *Sociometry, 40,* 138–144.

Kalichman, S. C., Craig, M. E., & Follingstad, D. R. (1989). Factors influencing the reporting of father-child sexual abuse: Study of licensed practicing psychologists. *Professional Psychology: Research & Practice, 20,* 84–89.

Kammer, D. (1983). Depression, attributional style, and failure generalization. *Cognitive Therapy & Research, 7,* 413–423.

Kanungo, R. (1979). The concepts of alienation and involvement revisited. *Psychological Bulletin, 86,* 119–138.

Kaplan, B., Beardslee, W., & Keller, M. (1987). Intellectual competence in children of depressed parents. *Journal of Clinical Child Psychology, 16,* 158–163.

Kaplan, H. B. (1976). Antecedents of negative self-attitudes: Membership group devaluation and defenselessness. *Social Psychiatry, 11,* 15–25.

Kaplan, H. S. (1996). Erotic obsession: Relationship to hypoactive sexual desire disorder and paraphilia. *American Journal of Psychiatry, 153,* 30–41.

Karpman, B. (1996). Insecurity in search of security. Emotional security and human development. *American Journal of Psychotherapy, 50*, 437–457.

Karson, S., & Markenson, D. (1973). Some relations between parental personality factors and childhood symptomatology. *Journal of Personality Assessment, 37*, 249–254.

Kashani, J. H., Reid, J. C., & Rosenberg, T. K. (1989). Levels of hopelessness in children and adolescents: A developmental perspective. *Journal of Consulting & Clinical Psychology, 18*, 351–359.

Kass, F., Spitzer, R. L., Williams, J. B., & Widiger, T. (1989). Self defeating personality disorder and DSM-III-R: Development of the diagnostic criteria. *American Journal of Psychiatry, 146*, 1022–1026.

Kasser, T. (2002). *The high price of materialism.* Cambridge, MA: MIT Press.

Kassinove, H., & Tafrate, R. C. (2002). *Anger management: The complete treatment guidebook for practitioners.* Atascadero, CA: Impact Publishers.

Kataoka, S. H., Zhang, L., & Wells, K. B. (2002). Unmet need for mental health care among U.S. children: Variation by ethnicity and insurance status. *American Journal of Psychiatry, 159*, 1548–1555.

Kaufman, J. M., Hallahan, D. P., & Ball, D. W. (1975). Parents' predictions of their children's perception of family relations. *Journal of Personality Assessment, 39*, 228–235.

Kawamura, K. Y., Hunt, S. L., Frost, R. O., & DiBartolo, P. M. (2001). Perfectionism, anxiety, and depression: Are the relationships independent? *Cognitive Therapy & Research, 25*, 291–301.

Kazantzis, N., Deane, F. P., Ronan, K. R., & L'Abate, L. (Eds.). (in press). *Homework assignments in cognitive-behavioral therapy.* New York: Brunner-Routledge.

Kazantzis, N., & L'Abate, L. (Eds.). (in press). *Handbook of homework assignments in psychotherapy: Theory, research, and prevention.* New York: Kluwer Academic.

Kazdin, A. (1983). Hopelessness, depression, and suicidal intent among psychiatrically disturbed inpatient children. *Journal of Consulting & Clinical Psychology, 51*, 504–510.

Kearney, C. A., & Alvarez, K. A. (2004). Manualized treatment for school refusal behavior in youth. In L. L'Abate (Ed.), *Using workbooks in mental health: A resources for clinicians and researchers* (pp. 283–299). Binghamton, NY: Haworth.

Keenan, K., & Shaw, D. S. (2003). Starting at the beginning: Exploring the etiology of antisocial behavior in the first years of life. In B. B. Lahey, T. E. Moffitt, & A. Caspi (Eds.), *Causes of conduct disorder and juvenile delinquency* (pp. 153–181). New York: Guilford.

Keitner, G., & Miller, I. (1990). Family functioning and major depression: An overview. *American Journal of Psychiatry, 147*, 1128–1137.

Keitner, G., Ryan, C., Miller, I., & Kohn, R. (1995). Role of the family in recovery and major depression. *American Journal of Psychiatry, 152*, 1002–1008.

Kellam, S., Ensminger, M., & Turner, J. (1978). Family structure and the mental health of children. *Annual Progress in Child Psychiatry & Child Development, 61*, 264–291.

Kellogg, S. (1993). Identity and recovery. *Psychotherapy, 30*, 235–244.

Kelly, A. B., Fincham, F. D., & Beach, S. R. H. (2003). Communication skills in couples: A review and discussion of emerging perspectives. In J. O. Green & B. R. Burleson (Eds.), *Handbook of communication and social interaction skills* (pp. 723–751). Mahwah, NJ: Earlbaum.

Kelly, J. B. (2000). Children's adjustment in conflicted marriage and divorce: A decade review of research. *Journal of the American Academy of Child & Adolescent Psychiatry, 39*, 963–973.

Keltikangas-Jarvinen, L. (1989). Stability of Type A behavior during adolescent, young adulthood, and adulthood. *Journal of Behavioral Medicine, 12*, 387–396.

Kemper, T., & Reichler, M. (1976). Work integration, marital satisfaction, and conjugal power. *Human Relations, 29*, 929–944.

Kendler, K. S. (1996). Parenting: A genetic-epidemiologic perspective. *American Journal of Psychiatry, 153*, 11–20.

Kendler, K. S., Gardner, C. O., & Prescott, C. A. (2002). Toward a comprehensive developmental model for major depression in women. *American Journal of Psychiatry, 159*, 1133–1145.

Kendler, K. S., Neale, K., Kessler, R., & Heath, A. (1992). Childhood parental loss and adult psycho-pathology in women: A twin study perspective. *Archives of General Psychiatry, 49*, 109–116.

Kennedy, M. G., Felner, R. D., Cauce, A., & Primavera, J. (1988). Social problem solving and adjustment in adolescence: The influence of moral reasoning level, scoring alternatives, and family climate. *Journal of Clinical Child Psychology, 17*, 73–83.

Kennedy-Moore, E., & Watson, J. C. (1999). *Expressing emotion: Myths, realities, and therapeutic strategies*. New York: Guilford.

Kenny, M. E., & Barton, C. E. (2002). Attachment theory and research: Contributions for understanding late adolescent and young adult development. In J. Demick & C. Andreortti Eds.), *Handbook of adult development* (pp. 371–389). New York: Kluwer Academic.

Kernberg, O. (1977). Boundaries and structure in love relations. *Journal of the American Psychoanalytic Association, 25*, 81–114.

Kessler, R., Foster, C., Saunders, W., & Stang, P. (1995). Social consequences of psychiatric disorders I: Educational attainment. *American Journal of Psychiatry, 152*, 1026–1032.

Ketai, R. M., & Brandwin, M. A. (1979). Childbirth related psychosis and familial symbiotic conflict. *American Journal of Psychiatry, 136*, 190–193.

Ketring, S. A., & Feinauer, L. L. (1999). Perpetrator-victim relationship: Long term effects of sexual abuse for men and women. *American Journal of Family Therapy, 27*, 109–120.

Kiesler, D. J. (Ed.). (1996). *Contemporary interpersonal theory and research: Personality, psychopathology, and psychotherapy*. New York: Wiley.

Kinderman, P., & Bentall, R. P. (1997). Causal attributions in paranoia and depression: Internal, personal, and situational attributions for negative events. *Journal of Abnormal Psychology, 106*, 341–345.

Kinderman T. A., & Valsiner, J. (Eds.). (1995). *Development of person-context relations*. Mahwah, NJ: Earlbaum.

King, N., Ollendick, T., & Gullone, E. (1991). Negative affectivity in children and adolescents: Relations between anxiety and depression. *Clinical Psychology Review, 11*, 441–459.

Kinzl, J., Traweger, C., Guenther, V., & Biebl, W. (1994). Family background and sexual abuse associated with eating disorders. *American Journal of Psychiatry, 151*, 1127–1131.

Kirmayer, L. J., & Young, A. (1999). Culture and context in the evoluationary concept of mental disorder. *Journal of Abnormal Psychology, 108*, 446–452.

Kirsch, I., & Lynn, S. J. (1999). Automaticity in clinical psychology. *American Psychologist, 54*, 504–515.

Kleiman, J. I. (1981). Optimal and normal family functioning. *American Journal of Family Therapy, 9*, 37–44.

Klein, D., Clark, D., Dansky, L., & Margolis, E. (1988). Dysthymis in the offspring of parents with primary unipolar affective disorder. *Journal of Abnormal Psychology, 97*, 265–274.

Klein, D., Lewinsohn, P., Seeley J., & Rohde, P. (2001). A family study of major depression disorder in a community sample of adolescents. *Archives of General Psychiatry, 58*, 13–20.

Klein, D., Riso, L., Donaldson, S., & Schwartz, J. (1995). Family study of early-onset dysthymia: Mood and personality disorder in relatives of outpatients with dysthymia and episodic major depression and normal controls. *Archives of General Psychiatry, 52*, 487–496.

Klein, D. M., & White, J. M. (1996). *Family theories: An introduction*. Thousand Oaks, CA: Sage.

Klein, M., & Shulman, S. (1980). Behavior problems of children in relation to parental instrumentality-expressivity and marital adjustment. *Psychological Reports, 47*, 11–14.

Kleiner, L., & Marshall, W. L. (1985). Relationship difficulties and agoraphobia. Interpersonal Interaction, Assertiveness, Dependency (Personality) and agoraphobia. *Clinical Psychology Review, 5*, 581–595.

Kleinman, S. L., Handal, P. J., Enos, D., Searight, H. R., et al. (1989). Relationship between perceived family climate and adolescent adjustment. *Journal of Clinical Child Psychology, 18*, 351–359.

Kling, K. C., Hyde, J. S., Showers, C. J., & Buswell, B. N. (1999). Gender differences in self-esteem: A meta-analysis. *Psychological Bulletin, 125*, 470–500.

Kobasa, S. C. (1979). Stressful life events, personality, and health: An inquiry into hardness. *Journal of Personality & Social Psychology, 37*, 1–11.

Kobasa, S. C., Maddi, S. R., & Zola, M. A. (1983). Type A and hardiness. *Journal of Behavioral Medicine, 6*, 41–51.

Koenigsberg, H., Klausner, E., Pelino, D., & Rosnick, P. (1993). Expressed emotion and glucose control in insulin dependent diabetes mellitus. *American Journal of Psychiatry, 150*, 1114–1115.

Koestner, R., Zuroff, D., & Power, T. (1991). Family origins of adolescent self-criticism and its continuity into adulthood. *Journal of Abnormal Psychology, 100*, 191–197.

Kohn, P. M. (1974). Authoritarianism, rebelliousness and their correlates among British undergraduates. *British Journal of Social & Clinical Psychology, 13*, 245–255.

Kolko, D. J. (1985). Juvenile firesetting: A review and methological critique. *Clinical Psychology Review, 5*, 345–376.

Kopper, B., & Epperson, D. (1996). The experience and expression of anger: Relationships with gender, gender role socialization, depression, and mental health functioning. *Journal of Counseling Psychology, 43*, 158–165.

Korzybski, A. (1949). *Science and sanity: An introduction to non-aristotelian systems and general semantics.* Lakewille, CT: International Non-Aristotelian Library Publishing House.

Kosson, D. S., Steurwald, B. L., Newman, J. P., & Widom, C. S. (1994). The relation between socialization and antisocial behavior, substance abuse, and family conflict in college students. *Journal of Personality Assessment, 63*, 473–488.

Kotler, T. (1975). Characteristics and correlates of parent-son interactions. *Psychology Monographs, 91*, 121–168.

Kovacs, M., Devlin B., Pollock, M., & Richards, C. (1997). A controlled family history study of childhood onset depressive disorder. *Archives of General Psychiatry, 54*, 613–623.

Krain, A. L., & Kendall, P. C. (2000). The role of parental emotional distress in parent report of child anxiety. *Journal of Clinical Child Psychology, 29*, 328–335.

Kraut, R., & Lewis, S. (1975). Alternate models of family influence on student political ideology. *Journal of Personality & Social Psychology, 31*, 791–800.

Krech, K. H., & Johnston, C. (1992). The relationship of depressed mood and life stress to maternal perceptions of child behavior. *Journal of Clinical Child Psychology, 21*, 115–122.

Kring, A., & Neale, J. (1996). Do schizophrenic patients show a disjunctive relationship among expressive, experiential and psycho-physiological components of emotion? *Journal of Abnormal Psychology, 105*, 249–257.

Krueger, D. (1983). Childhood parent loss: Developmental impact and adult psychopathology. *American Journal of Psychotherapy, 37*, 582–592.

Krueger, R. F. (1999). The structure of common mental disorders. *Archives of General Psychiatry, 56*, 921–926.

Krueger, R. F., Caspi, A., Moffitt, T., & Silva, P. (1996). Personality traits are differentially linked to mental disorders: A multitrait-multidiagnosis study of an adolescent birth cohort. *Journal of Abnormal Psychology, 105*, 299–312.

Kubistant, T. (1981). Resolutions of aloneliness. *Personnel & Guidance Journal, 59*, 461–465.

Kuipers, L., Sturgeon, D., Berkowitz, R., & Leff, J. (1983). Characteristics of expressed emotion: Its relationship to speech and looking in schizophrenic patients, and their relatives. *British Journal of Clinical Psychology, 22,* 257–264.

Kukla, A. (2001). *Methods of theoretical psyhology.* Cambridge, MA: MIT Press.

Kuperminc, G. P., Blatt, S. J., & Leadbeater, B. J. (1997). Relatedness, self-definition, and early adolescent adjustment. *Cognitive Therapy and Research, 21,* 301–320.

Kuperminc, G. P., Blatt, S. J., Shahar, G., Henrich, C., & Leadbeater, B. J. (2004). *Journal of Youth and Adolescence, 33,* 13–30.

Kuperminc, G. P., Leadbeater, B. J., & Blatt, S. J. (2001). School social climate and individual differences in vulnerability to psychopathology among middle school students. *Journal of School Psychology, 39,* 141–159.

Kuperminc, G. P., Leadbeater, B. J., Emmons, C., & Blatt, S. J. (1997). Perceived school climate and difficulties in the social adjustment of middle school students. *Applied Developmental Science, 1,* 76–88.

Kurdek, L. A., Blisk, D., & Siesky, A. E. (1981). Correlates of children's long-term adjustment to their parents' divorce. *Developmental Psychology, 17,* 565–579.

Kurtines, W. (1974). Autonomy: A concept reconsidered. *Journal of Personality Assessment, 38,* 243–246.

Kuyken, W., & Brewin, C. R. (1994). Intrusive memories of childhood abuse during depressive episodes. *Behaviour Research & Therapy, 32,* 525–528.

Kuyken, W., & Brewin, C. R. (1999). The relation of early abuse to cognition and coping in depression. *Cognitive Therapy & Research, 23,* 665–677.

Kwon, S., & Oei, T. P. (1992). Differential causal roles of dysfunctional attitude and automatic thoughts in depression. *Cognitive Therapy & Research, 16,* 309–328.

Kwong, M. J., Bartholomew, K., Henderson, A. J. Z., & Trinke, S. J. (2003). Intergenerational transmission of relationship violence. *Journal of Family Psychology, 17,* 288–301.

L'Abate, L. (1976). *Understanding and helping the individual in the family.* New York: Grune & Stratton.

L'Abate, L. (1983). *Family psychology: Theory, therapy, and training.* Washington, DC: University Press of America.

L'Abate, L. (1984). Beyond paradox: Issues of control. *American Journal of Family Therapy, 12,* 12–20.

L'Abate, L. (1986). *Systematic family therapy.* New York: Brunner/Mazel.

L'Abate, L. (1987). *Family psychology II: Theory, therapy, enrichment, and training.* Latham, MD. University Press of America.

L'Abate, L. (1990). *Building family competence: Primary and secondary prevention strategies.* Newbury Park, CA: Sage.

L'Abate, L. (1992). *Programmed writing: Self-administered interventions for individuals, couples, and families.* Pacific Grove, CA: Brooks-Cole.

L'Abate, L. (1994). *A theory of personality development.* New York: Wiley.

L'Abate, L. (1996). *Workbooks for better living.* Available at www.mentalhealthhelp.com.

L'Abate, L. (1997). *The self in the family: A classification of personality, psychopathology, and criminality.* New York: Wiley.

L'Abate, L. (Ed.). (1998). *Family psychopathology: The interpersonal roots of dysfunctional behavior.* New York: Guilford.

L'Abate, L. (1999a). Being human: Loving and hurting. In A. C. Richards & T. Schumrum, (Eds.), *Invitations to dialogue: The legacy of Sidney Jourard* (pp. 81–90). Dubuque, IA: Kent/Kendall.

L'Abate, L. (1999b). Taking the bull by the horns: Beyond talk in psychological interventions. *Family Journal: Therapy and Counseling for Couples and Families, 7,* 206–220.

L'Abate, L. (Ed.). (2001). *Distance writing and computer-assisted interventions in psychiatry and mental health.* Westport, CT: Ablex.

L'Abate, L. (2002). *Beyond psychotherapy: Programmed writing and structured computer-assisted interventions.* Westport, CT: Ablex.

L'Abate, L. (2003a). *Family psychology III: Theory-building, theory-testing, and psychological interventions.* Lanham, MD: University Press of America.

L'Abate, L. (2003b). Treatment through writing: A unique new direction. In T. L. Sexton, G. Weeks, & M. Robbins (Eds.), *The handbook of family therapy* (pp. 397–409). New York: Brunner-Routledge.

L'Abate, L. (2004a). *A guide to self-help workbooks for mental health clinicians and researchers.* Binghamton, NY: Haworth.

L'Abate, L. (2004b). Commentary: Current and future prospects. In L. Sperry (Ed.), *The handbook of stress, trauma, and the family* (pp. 247–269). New York Brunner/Routledge.

L'Abate, L. (2004c). Family psychology as laboratory science. *Family Psychologist, 20,* 21–22.

L'Abate, L. (Ed.). (2004d). *Using workbooks in prevention, psychotherapy, and rehabilitation: Resources for clinicians and researchers.* Binghamton, NY: Haworth.

L'Abate, L., & Bagarozzi, D. A. (1993). *Sourcebook of marriage and family evaluation.* New York: Brunner/Mazel.

L'Abate, L., Boyce, J., Fraizer, L., & Russ, D. A. (1992). Programmed writing: Research in progress. *Comprehensive Mental Health Care, 2,* 45–62.

L'Abate, L., & De Giacomo, P. (2003). *Intimate relationships and how to improve them: Integration of theoretical models with prevention and psychotherapy interventions.* Westport, CT. Praeger.

L'Abate, L., De Giacomo, P., McCarty, F., De Giacomo, A., & Verrastro, G. (2000). Testing three models of intimate relationships. *Contemporary Family Therapy: An International Journal, 22,* 103–122.

L'Abate, L., & Dunne, E. E. (1978). The family taboo in psychology textbooks. *Teaching of Psychology, 5,* 115–117.

L'Abate, L., Embry, D. D., & Baggett, M. S. (Eds.). (in press). *Handbook of low-cost interventions to promote physical and mental health.* Mahwah, NJ: Earlbaum.

L'Abate, L., Frey, J., & Wagner, V. (1982). Toward a classification of family therapy theories: Further elaborations and implications of the E-R-A-Aw-C model. *Family Therapy, 9,* 251–262.

L'Abate, L., & Harrison, M. G. (1992). Treating codependency. In L. L'Abate, J. E. Farrar, & D. A. Serritella (Eds.), *Handbook of differential treatments for addictions* (pp. 286–306). Boston: Allyn & Bacon.

L'Abate, L., & Hewitt, D. (1988). Toward a classification of sex and sexual behavior. *Journal of Sex and Marital Therapy, 14,* 29–39.

L'Abate, L., & Kern, R. (2002). Emotionality, technology, and workbooks. In S. Lepore and J. Smyth (Eds.), *The writing cure* (pp. 239–255). Washington, DC: American Psychological Association.

L'Abate, L., L'Abate, B. L., & Maino, E. (2005). A review of 25 years of part-time professional practice: Workbooks and length of psychotherapy. *American Journal of Family Therapy, 33,* 1–13.

L'Abate, L., Lambert, R. G., & Schenck, P. (2001). Testing a relational model of psycho-pathology with the MMPI-2. *American Journal of Family Therapy, 29,* 221–238.

L'Abate, L., Smith, M. T., & Smith, M. P. (1985). Systems interventions with hyperactive children: An interdisciplinary perspective. In L. L'Abate (Ed.), *Handbook of family psychology and therapy* (pp. 1152–1177). Pacific Grove, CA: Brooks/Cole.

L'Abate, L., & Wagner, V. (1985). Theory-derived, family-oriented test batteries. In L. L'Abate (Ed.), *Handbook of family psychology and therapy* (pp. 1006–1032), Pacific Grove, CA: Brooks/Cole.

L'Abate, L., & Wagner, V. (1988). Testing a theory of developmental competence in the family. *American Journal of Family Psychology, 16*, 23–35.

L'Abate, L., & Weinstein, S. E. (1987). *Structured enrichment programs for couples and families.* New York: Brunner/Mazel.

L'Abate, L., & Young, L. (1987). *Casebook of structured enrichment programs for couples and families.* New York: Brunner/Mazel.

Labouvie, E. W. (1975). The dialectical nature of measurement activities in the behavioral sciences. *Human Development, 18*, 396–403.

Lachman, M. E. (2004). Development in midlife. *Annual Review of Psychology, 55*, 305–331.

Lacy, W., & Hendricks, J. (1980). Developmental models of adult life: Myth or reality. *International Journal of Aging & Human Development, 11*, 89–110.

Lahey, B. B., Moffitt, T. E., & Caspi, A. (Eds.). (2003). *Causes of conduct disorder and juvenile delinquency.* New York: Guilford.

Lahey, B., Russo, M. F., Walker, L., & Piacentini, J. C. (1989). Personality characteristics of the mothers of children with disruptive behavior disorders. *Journal of Consulting & Clinical Psychology, 57*, 512–515.

Lahey, B. B., Hartdagen, S. E., Frick, P. J., & McBurnett, K. (1988). Conduct disorder: Parsing the confounded relation to parental divorce and antisocial personality. *Journal of Abnormal Psychology, 97*, 334–337.

Lahey, B. B., Schwab-Stone, M., Goodman, S., & Waldman, I. (2000). Age and gender differences in oppositional behavior and conduct problems: A cross-sectional household study of middle childhood and adolescence. *Journal of Abnormal Psychology, 109*, 488–503.

Lahey, B. B., & Waldman, I. D. (2003). A developmental propensity model of the origins of conduct problems during childhood and adolescence. In B. B. Lahey, T. E. Moffitt, & A. Caspi (Eds.), *Causes of conduct disorder and juvenile delinquency* (pp. 76–117). New York: Guilford.

Lamb, M. E. (1976). Proximity seeking attachment behaviors: A critical review of the literature. *Genetic Psychology Monographs, 93*, 63–89.

Lamb, M. E. (1987). Predictive implications of individual differences in attachment. *Journal of Consulting & Clinical Psychology, 55*, 817–824.

Landau, R., Daphne, Y., Iuchtman, C., & Aveneri, V. (1975). The development of children of psychotic parents reared away from home. *Israel Annals of Psychiatry & Related Disciplines, 13*, 48–57.

Lane, R. D. (2000). Levels of emotional awareness: Neurological, psychological, and social perspectives. In R. Bar-On & J. D. A. Parker (Eds.), *The handbook of emotional intelligence: Theory, development, assessment and applications at home, school, and the workplace* (pp. 171–191). San Francisco: Jossey-Bass.

Lange, A., de Beurs, E., Dolan, C., Lachnit, T., et al. (1999). Long-term effects of childhood sexual abuse: Objective and subjective characteristics of the abuse and psychopathology in later life. *Journal of Nervous & Mental Disease, 187*, 150–158.

Langford, J., & Clance, P. (1993). The imposter phenomenon: Recent research finding regarding dynamics, personality and family patterns and their implications for treatment. *Psychotherapy, 30*, 495–501.

Langlois, F., Freeston, M. H., & Ladouceur, R. (2000). Differences and similarities between obsessive intrusive thoughts and worry in non-clinical population: Study 1. *Behavior Research & Therapy, 38*, 157–173.

Larrance, D. T., & Twentyman, C. T. (1983). Maternal attributions and child abuse. *Journal of Abnormal Psychology, 92*, 449–457.

Last, C. G., Hersen, M., Kazdin, A. E., Francis, G., et al. (1987). Psychiatric illness in the mothers of anxious children. *American Journal of Psychiatry, 144*, 1580–1583.

Lazar, R. (2000). Presentness: An intersubjective dimension of the therapeutic act. *American Journal of Psychotherapy, 54*, 340–354.

Lazarus, R., & Folkman, S. (1984). *Stress, appraisal, and coping.* New York: Springer.

Le, B., & Agnew, C. R. (2003). Commitment and its theoretical determinants: A meta-analysis of the Investment Model. *Personal Relationships, 10*, 37–57.

Leadbeater, B. J., Kuperminc, G. P., Hertzog, C., & Blatt, S. J. (1999). A multivariate model of gender differences in adolescents' internalizing and externalizing problems. *Developmental Psychology, 15*, 1268–1282.

Leary, M. R. (1979). Interpersonal orientation and self-presentation style. *Psychology Reports, 45*, 451–456.

Leary, M. R. (2001). *Interpersonal rejection.* New York: Oxford University Press.

Leary, M. R., & Kowalski, R. M. (1990). Impression management: A literature review and two-component model. *Psychology Bulletin, 107*, 34–47.

Leary, M. R., & Kowalski, R. M. (1995). *Social anxiety.* New York: Guilford.

Leary, M. R., Springer, C., Negel, L., Ansell, E., & Evans, K. (1998). The causes, phenomenology, and consequences of hurt feelings. *Journal of Personality & Social Psychology, 74*, 1225–1237.

Lebow, J. (2001, Winter–Spring). The changing face of models of marital and family therapy. *Supervision Bulletin, AAMFT, 3–4.*

Lecci, L., Karoly, P., Briggs, C., & Kuhn, K. (1994). Specificity and generality of motivational components in depression: A personal projects analysis. *Journal of Abnormal Psychology, 103*, 404–408.

Ledingham, J. (1981). Developmental patterns of aggressive and withdrawn behavior in childhood: A possible method for identifying pre-schizophrenics. *Journal of Abnormal Child Psychology, 9*, 1–22.

Lee, C. M., & Gotlib, I. (1991). Adjustment of children of depressed mothers: A 10-month follow-up. *Journal of Abnormal Psychology, 100*, 473–477.

Lee, C. M., & Gotlib, I. H. (1989a). Clinical status and emotional adjustment of children of depressed mothers. *American Journal of Psychiatry, 146*, 478–483.

Lee, C. M., & Gotlib, I. H. (1989b). Maternal depression and child adjustment: A longitudinal analysis. *Journal of Abnormal Psychology, 98*, 78–85.

Lee, J. A. (1974). The styles of loving. *Psychology Today, 8*, 43–50.

Lepore, S. J., & Smyth, J. M. (Eds.). (2002). *The writing cure: How expressive writing promotes health amd emotional well-being.* Washington, DC: American Psychological Association.

Lesage, A., Boyer, R., Grunberg, F., & Vanier, C. (1994). Suicide and mental disorders: A case-control study of young men. *American Journal of Psychiatry, 151*, 1063–1068.

Lesse, S. (1981). Hypochondriacal and psychosomatic disorders masking depression in adolescents. *American Journal of Psychotherapy, 35*, 356–367.

Lesser, H., & Hlavacek, P. (1977). Problem-solving rigidity of children on perceptual tasks as a function of parental authoritarianism. *Journal of Genetic Psychology, 131*, 97–106.

Lesser, H., & Steininger, M. (1975). Family patterns in dogmatism. *Journal of Genetic Psychology, 126*, 155–156.

Levenson, M., Aldwin, C., Bossé, R., & Spiro, A. (1988). Emotionality and mental health: Longitudinal findings from the normative aging study. *Journal of Abnormal Psychology, 97*, 94–96.

Leventhal, G., Matturro, M., & Schanerman, J. (1978). Effects of attitude, sex and approach on nonverbal and projective measures of personal space. *Perceptual & Motor Skills, 47*, 107–118.

Levis, D. (1980). The learned helplessness effect: An expectancy, discrimination deficit, or motivational-induced persistence? *Journal of Research in Personality, 14*, 158–169.

Levy, C. M., & Randsdell, S. (Eds.). (1996). *The science of writing: Theories, methods, individual differences and applications.* Mahwah, NJ: Earlbaum.

Levy, S. (1979). Authoritarianism and information processing. *Bulletin of the Psychonomic Society, 13*, 240–242.

Lewin, K. (1935). *A dynamic theory of personality.* New York: McGraw-Hill.

Lewinsohn, P. M., Gotlib, I. H., Lewinsohn, M., Seeley, J. R., et al. (1998). Development of depression from preadolescence to young adulthood: Emerging gender differences in a 10-year longitudinal study. *Journal of Abnormal Psychology, 107*, 109–117.

Lewinsohn, P. M., Solomon, A., Seeley, J. R., & Zeiss, A. (2000). Clinical implications of "subthreshold" depressive symptoms. *Journal of Abnormal Psychology, 109*, 345–351.

Lewis, C. (1981). The effects of parental firm control: A reinterpretation of findings. *Psychological Bulletin, 90*, 547–563.

Lewis, D. (1985). Biopsychosocial characteristics of children who later murder: A prospective study. *American Journal of Psychiatry, 142*, 1161–1167.

Lewis, D., Pincus, J., Bard, B., & Richardson, E. (1988). Neuropsychiatric, psychoeducational, and family characteristics of 14 juveniles sentenced to death in the United States. *American Journal of Psychiatry, 145*, 584–589.

Lewis, D., Yeager, C., Swica, Y., & Pincus, J. (1997). Objective documentation of child abuse and dissociation in 12 murderers with dissociated identity disorder. *American Journal of Psychiatry, 154*, 1703–1710.

Lewis, D. O., Balla, D., Shanok, S., & Snell, L. (1976). Delinquency, parental psychopathology and parental criminality: Clinical and epidemiological findings. *Journal of the American Academy of Child Psychiatry, 15*, 665–678.

Lewis, H. (1990). *A question of values.* New York: Harper & Row.

Lewis, J. M., Rodnick, E. H., & Goldstein, M. J. (1981). Intra-familial interactive behavior, parental communication defiance, and risk for schizophrenia. *Journal of Abnormal Psychology, 90*, 448–457.

Lewis, M. (2000). The emergence of human emotions. In M. Lewis & J. M. Haviland-Jones, (Eds.), *Handbook of emotions* (pp. 265–280). New York: Guilford.

Lewis, M., & Haviland-Jones, J. M. (Eds.).(2000). *Handbook of emotions.* New York: Guilford.

Lewis, M., & Michalson, L. (1983). *Children's emotions and moods: Developmental theory and measurement.* New York: Plenum.

Lewis, T., Amini, F., & Lannon, R. (2000). *A general theory of love.* New York: Vintage Books.

Lieb, R., Wittchen, H. U., Höfler, M., & Fuetsch, M. (2000). Parental psychopathology, parenting styles and the risk of social phobia in offspring: A prospective longitudinal community study. *Archives of General Psychiatry, 57*, 859–866.

Lieberman, A. F., & Zeanah, C. H. (1999). Contributions of attachment theory to infant-parent psychotherapy and other interventions with infants and young children. In J. Cassidy & P. K. Shaver (Eds.), *Handbook of attachment: Theory, research, and clinical applications* (pp. 555–574). New York: Guilford.

Liem, J., James, J., O'Toole, J., & Boudewyn, A. (1995). Assessing resilience in adults with histories of childhood sexual abuse. *American Journal of Orthopsychiatry, 67*, 594–606.

Liddle, H. A. (1992). Family psychology: Progress and prospects of a maturing discipline. *Journal of Family Psychology, 5*, 249–263.

Liddle, H. A., Santisteban, D. A., Levant, R. F., & Bray, J. H. (Eds.). (2002). *Family psychology: Science-based interventions.* Washington, DC: American Psychological Association.

Lipschitz, D. S., Winegar, R. K., Nicolaou, A., L., Hartnick, E., et al. (1999). Perceived abuse and neglect as risk factors for suicidal behavior in adolescent inpatients. *Journal of Nervous & Mental Disease, 187,* 32–39.

Lipsitz, J., Martin, L., Mannuzza, S., & Chapman, T. (1994). Childhood separation anxiety disorder in patients with adult anxiety disorders. *American Journal of Psychiatry, 151,* 927–929.

Litman, R. E. (1989). Suicides: What do they have in mind? In D. Jacobs & H. N. Brown (Eds.), *Suicide: Understanding and responding* (pp. 143–154). Madison, CT: International Universities Press.

Little, B. R., & Kane, M. (1974). Person-thing orientation and privacy. *Man-Environment Systems, 4,* 361–364.

Livesley, W. J. (Ed.). (2001). *Handbook of personality disorders: Theory, research, and treatment.* New York: Guilford.

Livingston, R., Nugent, H., Rader, L., & Smith, G. (1985). Family histories of depressed and severely anxious children. *American Journal of Psychiatry, 142,* 1497–1499.

Lizardi, H., Klein, D., Ouimette, P., & Riso, L. (1995). Reports of the childhood home environment in early-onset dysthymia and episodic major depression. *Journal of Abnormal Psychology, 104,* 132–139.

Lloyd, C. (1980a). Life events and depressive disorder reviewed: I. Events as predisposing factors. *Archives of General Psychiatry, 37,* 529–539.

Lloyd, C. (1980b). Life events and depressive disorder reviewed: II. Events as precipitating factors. *Archives of General Psychiatry, 37,* 541–548.

Lobel, T. E. (1988). Personality correlates of Type A coronary-prone behavior. *Journal of Personality Assessment, 52,* 434–440.

Locke, L. M., & Prinz, R. J. (2002). Measurement of parental discipline and nurturance. Reviews of the measurement of parental discipline and nurturance over past 20 years. *Clinical Psychology Review, 22,* 895–930.

Loeber, F., Burke, J. D., Lahey, B. B., & Winters, A. (2000). Oppositional defiant and conduct disorder: A review of the past 10 years, Part I. *Journal of the American Academy of Child & Adolescent Psychiatry, 39,* 1468–1484.

Loeber, R., & Dishion, T. (1983). Early predictors of male delinquency: A review. *Psychological Bulletin, 94,* 68–99.

Loeber, R., Lahey, B. B., & Thomas, C. (1991). Diagnostic conundrum of oppositional defiant disorder and conduct disorder. *Journal of Abnormal Psychology, 100,* 379–390.

Lohmann, A., Arriaga, X. B., & Goodfriend, W. (2003). Close relationships and placemaking: Do objects in a couple's home reflect couplehood? *Personal Relationships, 10,* 437–449.

Long, J. V., & Vaillant, G. E. (1984). Natural history of male psychological health: XI. Escape from the underclass. *American Journal of Psychiatry, 141,* 341–346.

Long, N., Slater, E., Forehand, R., & Fauber, R. (1988). Continued high or reduced interparental conflict following divorce: Relation to young adolescent. *Journal of Consulting & Clinical Psychology, 56,* 467–469.

Lopez, F. G., Campbell, V. L., & Watkins, C. E. (1988). Family structure, psychological separation and college adjustment: A canonical analysis and cross-validation. *Journal of Counseling Psychology, 35,* 402–409.

Lopez-Ibor, J. J. (1997). The concept and boundaries of personality disorders. *American Journal of Psychiatry, 154,* 21–25.

Lorr, M., & Wunderlich, R. A. (1988). Self-esteem and neglect affect. *Journal of Clinical Psychology, 44,* 36–39.

Losco, J., & Epstein, S. (1974). Relative steepness of approach and avoidance gradients in humans. *Personality & Social Psychology Bulletin, 1*, 203–206.

Loukas, A., Twitchell, G. R., Piejak, L. A., Fitzgerald, H. E., & Zuckder, R. A. (1998). The family as a unity of interacting personalities. In L. L'Abate (Ed.), *Family psychopathology: The relational roots of dysfunctional behavior* (pp. 35–59). New York: Guildford.

Lovallo, W. R., & Pishkin, V. (1980). Performance of Type A (coronary-prone) men during and after exposure to uncontrollable noise and task failure. *Journal of Personality & Social Psychology, 38*, 963–971.

Lovejoy, M. C., Graczyk, P. A., O'Hare, E., & Neuman, G. (2000). Maternal depression and parenting behavior: A meta-analytic review. *Clinical Psychology Review, 20*, 561–592.

Luntz, B., & Widom, C. (1994). Antisocial personality disorder in abused and children grown up. *American Journal of Psychiatry, 151*, 670–674.

Luthar, S., Merikangas, K., & Rounsaville, B. (1993). Parental psychopathology and disorders in offspring: A study of relatives of drug abusers. *Journal of Nervous & Mental Disease, 181*, 351–357.

Luthar, S., & Zigler, E. (1991). Vulnerability and competence: A review of research on resilience in childhood. *American Journal of Orthopsychiatry, 61*, 6–22.

Lynam, D. R., & Moffitt, T. E. (1995). Delinquency *and* impulsivity *and* IQ: A reply to Block (1995). *Journal of Abnormal Psychology, 104*, 399–401.

Lynam, D. R., Moffitt, T. E., & Stouthamer-Loeber, M. (1993). Explaining the relation between IQ and delinquency: Class, race, test motivation, school failure, or self-control? Correction. *Journal of Abnormal Psychology, 102*, 552.

Lynn, S. J., & Rhue, J. W. (Eds.). (1994). *Dissociation: Clinical and theoretical perspectives*. New York: Guilford.

Lyon, J. B., & Vandenberg, B. R. (1989). Father death, family relationships, and subsequent psychological functioning in women. *Journal of Clinical Psychology, 18*, 327–335.

Lyons, R. F. (1997). An interview with Ellen Berscheid: "From Madison to Banff safely, but miles to go." *ISSPR Bulletin, 13*, 4–6.

Lytton, H., & Romney, D. (1991). Parents differential socialization of boys and girls: A meta-analysis. *Psychological Bulletin, 109*, 267–296.

Maccoby, E. E., & Jacklin, C. N. (1980). Sex differences in aggression: A rejoinder and reprise. *Child Development, 52*, 964–980.

Madonna, P. G., Van Scoyk, S., & Jones, D. (1991). Family interactions within incest and non-incest families. *American Journal of Psychiatry, 148*, 46–49.

Magai, C., & McFadden, S. H. (1995). *The role of emotions in social and personality development: History, theory, and research*. New York: Plenum.

Magnusson, D. (1999). Holistic interactionism: A perspective for research on personality development. In L. A. Pervin & O. P. John (Eds.), *Handbook of personality: Theory and research* (pp. 219–247). New York: Guilford.

Mahoney, A., Boggio, R., & Jouriles, E. (1996). Effects of verbal marital conflict on subsequent mother-son interactions in a child clinical sample. *Journal of Clinical Child Psychology, 25*, 262–271.

Maier, W., Lichtermann, D., Minges, J., & Hallmayer, J. (1993). Continuity and discontinuity of affective disorders and schizophrenia: Results of a controlled family study. *Archives of General Psychiatry, 50*, 871–883.

Maino, E. Personal communication, July 20, 2003.

Majoribanks, K. (1976). Birth order, family environment, and mental abilities: A regression surface analysis. *Psychological Reports, 39*, 759–765.

Majoribanks, K. (1978). Personality and environmental correlates of cognitive performance and school related affective characteristics: A regression surface analysis. *Alberta Journal of Educational Research, 24*, 230–243.

Majoribanks, K. (1981). Sibling correlates of family environment dimensions: Ethnic group differences. *Journal of Psychology, 107*, 29–40.

Majoribanks, K., & Walberg, H. (1975). Ordinal position, family environment, and mental abilities. *Journal of Social Psychology, 95*, 77–84.

Malle, B. F., Moses, L. J., & Baldwin, D. A. (2001). *Intentions and intentionality: Foundations of social cognition*. Cambridge, MA: MIT Press.

Mallinckrodt, B. (1992). Childhood emotional bonds with parents, development of adult social competencies and availability of social support. *Journal of Counseling Psychology, 39*, 453–461.

Manly, P., McManhon, R., Bradley, C., & Davidson, P. (1982). Depressive attributional style and depression following childbirth. *Journal of Abnormal Psychology, 91*, 245–254.

Mann, B. J., & Mackenzie, E. P. (1996). Pathways among marital functioning, parental behaviors and child behavior problems in school age boys. *Journal of Clinical Child Psychology, 25*, 183–191.

Manne, S., Taylor, K., Dougherty, J., & Kemeny, N. (1997). Supportive and negative responses in the partner relationship: Their association with psychological adjustment among individuals with cancer. *Journal of Behavioral Medicine, 20*, 101–125.

Mannuzza, S., Klein, R. G., Bessler, A., & Malroy, P. (1993). Adult outcome of hyperactive boys: Educational achievement, occupational rank and psychiatric status. *Archives of General Psychiatry, 50*, 565–576.

Mansell, W., & Clark, D. M. (1999). How do I appear to others? Social anxiety and processing of the observable self. *Behaviour Research & Therapy, 37*, 419–434.

Mantell, D. M. (1974). Doves vs. Hawks: Guess who had the authoritarian parents? *Psychology Today, 8*, 56–62.

Mantovani, G. (2000). *Exploring borders: Understanding culture and psychology*. New York: Routledge.

Manusov, V., & Harvey, J. H. (Eds.). (2001). *Attribution, communication behavior, and close relationships*. Cambridge, UK: Cambridge University Press.

Maris, R. W. (1989). The social relations of suicide. In D. Jacobs & H. N. Brown (Eds.), *Suicide: Understanding and responding: Harvard Medical School perspectives* (pp. 87–125). Madison, CT: International Universities Press.

Markus, G., & Zajonc, R. (1977). Family configuration and intellectual development: A simulation. *Behavioral Science, 22*, 137–142.

Marsh, D. T., Serafica, F., & Barenboim, C. (1981). Interrelationships among perspective taking, interpersonal problem solving, and interpersonal functioning. *Journal of Genetic Psychology, 138*, 37–48.

Marshall, W. L. (1989). Intimacy, loneliness and sexual offenders. *Behavior Research & Therapy, 27*, 491–503.

Marsilio, W. (Ed.). (1995). *Fatherhood: Contemporary theory, research, and social policy*. Thousand Oaks, CA: Sage.

Martin, C. L., & Ruble, D. N. (1997). A developmental perspective of self-construal and sex differences: Comment on Cross and Madson (1997). *Psychological Bulletin, 122*, 45–50.

Martin, R. A. (2001). Humor, laughter, and physical health: Methodological issues and research findings. *Psychological Bulletin, 127*, 504–519.

Martin, R. A., Puhlik-Doris, P., Larsen, G., Gray, J., & Weir, K. (2003). Individual differences in uses of humor and their relation to psychological well-being: Development of the Humor Styles Questionnaire. *Journal of Research in Personality, 37*, 48–75.

Marx, E. M., & Schulze, C. C. (1991). Interpersonal problem-solving in depressed students. *Journal of Clinical Psychology, 47*, 361–367.

Marx, E. M., Williams, J. M., & Claridge, G. C. (1992). Depression and social problem-solving. *Journal of Abnormal Psychology, 101*, 78–86.

Marzillier, J., & Eastman, C. (1984). Continuing problems with self-efficacy theory: A reply to Bandura. *Cognitive Therapy & Research, 8*, 257–262.

Mascolo, M. F., & Fischer, K. W. (1998). The development of self through the coordination of component systems. In M. Ferrari & R. J. Sternberg (Eds.), *Self-awareness: Its nature and development* (pp. 332–384). New York: Guilford.

Mascolo, M. F., & Griffin, S. (Eds.). (1998). *What develops in emotional development?* New York: Plenum.

Maslow, A. H. (1968). *Toward a psychology of being*. Princeton, NJ: Norstrand.

Masters, J., Barden, C., & Ford, M. (1979). Affective states, expressive behavior, and learning in children. *Journal of Personality & Social Psychology, 37*, 380–390.

Mathews, A., & Milroy, R. (1994). Effects of priming and suppression of worry. *Behavior Research & Therapy, 32*, 843–850.

Matteson, R. (1974). Adolescent self-esteem, family communication, and marital satisfaction. *Journal of Psychology, 86*, 35–47.

Matthews, G., Zeidner, M., & Roberts, R. D. (2002). *Emotional intelligence: Science & myth*. Cambridge, MA: MIT Press.

Matthews, K. A. (1988). Coronary heart disease and Type A behaviors: Update on and alternative to the Booth-Kewley and Friedman (1987) quantitative review. *Psychological Bulletin, 104*, 373–380.

Matthews, K. A., & Angulo, J. (1980). Measurement of the Type A behavior pattern in children: Assessment of children's competitiveness, inpatient-anger, and aggression. *Child Development, 51*, 466–475.

Mattia, J. I., & Zimmerman, M. (2001). Epidemiology. In W. J. Livesley (Ed.), *Handbook of personality disorders: Theory, research, and treatment* (pp. 107–123). New York: Guilford.

Maydeu-Olivares, A., & D'Zurilla, T. J. (1996). A factor-analytic study of the social problem-solving inventory: An integration of theory and data. *Cognitive Therapy & Research, 20*, 115–133.

Mayer, J. D. (2003). Structural divisions of personality and the classification of traits. *Review of General Psychology, 7*, 381–401.

Mayne, T. J., & Bonanno, G. A. (Eds.). (2001). *Emotions: Current issues and future directions*. New York: Guilford.

Mayo, V. D., & Tanaka-Matsumi, J. (1996). Think aloud statements and solutions in dysphoric persons on a social problem-solving task. *Cognitive Therapy & Research, 20*, 97–113.

McCabe, R. E., Blankstein, K., & Mills, J. S. (1999). Interpersonal sensitivity and social problem-solving: Relations with academic and social self-esteem, depressive symptoms, and academic performance. *Cognitive Therapy & Research, 23*, 587–604.

McCrae, R. R., & Costa, P. T. Jr. (1995). Trait explanations in personality psychology. *European Journal of Personality, 9*, 231–252.

McCrae, R. R., & Costa, P. T. Jr. (1997). Personality trait structure as a human universal. *American Psychologist, 52*, 509–516.

McCranie, E., & Bass, J. (1984). Childhood family antecedents of dependency and self-criticism: Implications for depression. *Journal of Abnormal Psychology, 93*, 3–8.

McCranie, E., Hyer, L., Boudewyns, P., & Woods, M. (1992). Negative parenting behavior, combat exposure, and PTSD symptom severity: Test of a person-event interaction model. *Journal of Nervous & Mental Disease, 180*, 431–438.

McCranie, E. W., & Kahan, J. (1986). Personality and multiple divorce: A prospective study. *Journal of Nervous & Mental Disease, 174*, 161–164.

McCubbin, H. I., Thompson, A. I., Kretzschmar, H. O., Smith, F. A., et al. (1992). Family systems and work environment predictors of employee health risk: A discriminant function analysis. *American Journal of Family Therapy, 20*, 123–144.

McCullough, M. E., Pargament, K. I., & Thoresen, C. E. (Eds.). (2000). *Forgiveness, research, and practice.* New York: Guilford.

McDonald, G. W. (1978). A reconsideration of the concept sex-role identification in adolescent and family research. *Adolescence, 13*, 215–220.

McElroy, S. L., Pope, H. G., Hudson, J. I., Keck, P. E., et al. (1991). Kleptomania: A report of 20 cases. *American Journal of Psychiatry, 148*, 652–657.

McFadden, S. H., & Atchley, R. C. (Eds.). (2001). *Aging and the meaning of time.* New York: Springer.

McFarlane, W. R., Dixon, L., Lukens, E., & Lucksted, A. (2003). Family psychoeducation and schizophrenia: A review of the literature. *Journal of Marital & Family Therapy, 29*, 223–245.

McGuire, W. J. (1997). Creative hypotheses generating in psychology: Some useful heuristics. *Annual Review of Psychology, 48*, 1–30.

McLellan, H. (2000). Experience design. *CyberPsychology & Behavior, 3*, 59–69.

McLaughlin, M., Cormier, L., & Cormier, W. (1988). Relation between coping strategies and distress, stress, and marital adjustment of multiple-role women. *Journal of Counseling Psychology, 35*, 187–193.

McMahon, F., Stine, O., Chase, G., & Meyers, D. (1994). Influence of clinical subtype, sex, and lineality on age at onset of major affective disorder in a family sample. *American Journal of Psychiatry, 151*, 210–215.

McMahan, O., & Arias, J. (2004). Workbooks and psychotherapy with incarcerated felons: Replication of research in progress. In L. L'Abate (Ed.), *Using workbooks in mental health: A resource for clinicians and researchers* (pp. 205–213). Binghamton, NY: Haworth.

McMahan, O., & L'Abate, L. (2001). Programmed distance writing with seminarian couples. In L. L'Abate (Ed.), *Distance writing and computer-assisted interventions in psychiatry and mental heath* (pp. 137–156). Westport, CT: Ablex.

McNally, R. J., & Malcarne, V. I., & Hansdottir, I. (2001). Vulnerability to anxiety disorders across the lifespan. In R. E. Ingram & J. M. Price (Eds.), *Vulnerability to psychopathology: Risks across the life span* (pp. 322–325). New York: Guilford.

McReynolds, W. (1980). Theories, research, and evidence of learned helplessness: A reply to Lewis and Maier. *Journal of Research in Personality, 14*, 187–195.

Medling, J., & McCarrey, M. (1981). Marital adjustment over segments of the family life cycle: The issue of spouses' value similarity. *Journal of Marriage & the Family, 43*, 195–203.

Mednick, B. R. (1973). Breakdown in high-risk subjects: Familial and early environmental factors. *Journal of Abnormal Psychology, 82*, 469–475.

Mehrabian, A. (1976). *Public places and private spaces: The psychology of work, play, and living environments.* Oxford, UK: Basic Books.

Meier, R., & Johnson, W. (1977). Deterrence as social control: The legal and extralegal production of conformity. *American Sociological Review, 42*, 292–304.

Meissnér, W. W. (1979). Narcissism and paranoia: A comment on "Paranoid Psychodynamics." *Contemporary Psychoanalysis, 15*, 527–538.

Mercer, G., & Kohn, P. (1980). Child-rearing factors, authoritarianism, drug use attitudes, and adolescent drug use: A model. *Journal of Genetic Psychology, 136*, 159–171.

Mesman, J., & Koot, H. (2000). Common and specific correlates of preadolescents internalizing and externalizing psychopathology. *Journal of Abnormal Psychology, 109*, 428–437.

Messer, S. C., & Gross, A. M. (1995). Childhood depression and family interaction: A naturalistic observation study. *Journal of Clinical Child Psychology, 24*, 77–88.

Messman, T., & Long, P. (1996). Child sexual abuse and its relationship in adult women: A review. *Clinical Psychology Review, 16*, 397–420.

Metalsky, G. I., & Joiner, T. E. Jr. (1997). The Hopelessness Depression Symptoms Questionnaire. *Cognitive Therapy & Research, 21*, 359–384.

Metts, S., & Grohskopf, E. (2003). Impression management: Goals, strategies, and skills. In J. O. Green & B. R. Burleson (Eds.), *Handbook of communication and social interaction skills* (pp. 357–399). Mahwah, NJ: Earlbaum.

Metzler, C. W., Noell, J., Biglan, A., Ary, D., et al. (1994). The social context for risky sexual behavior among adolescents. *Journal of Behavioral Medicine, 17*, 419–438.

Meyers, J. K., Lindenthal, J. J., & Pepper, M. P. (1975). Life events, social integration and psychiatric symptomatology. *Journal of Health & Social Behavior, 16*, 421–429.

Mezzich, J. E., Fabrega, H., & Coffman, G. A. (1987). Multiaxial characterization of depressed patients. *Journal of Nervous & Mental Disease, 175*, 339–346.

Miere, S., McCarthy, P., & Schmeck, R. (1984). Validity of self-efficacy as a predictor of writing performance. *Cognitive Therapy & Research, 8*, 107–120.

Mijuskovic, B. (1977). Types of loneliness. *Psychology, 14*, 24–29.

Mijuskovic, B. (1979). Loneliness and personal identity. *Psychology: A Quarterly Journal of Human Behavior, 16*, 11–20.

Miklowitz, D. (1986). Expressed emotion and communication deviance in the families of schizophrenics. *Journal of Abnormal Psychology, 95*, 60–66.

Miklowitz, D., Goldstein, M., & Falloon, I. (1983). Pre-morbid and symptomatic characteristics of schizophrenics from families with high and low levels of expressed emotion. *Journal of Abnormal Psychology, 92*, 359–367.

Miklowitz, D., Velligan, D., Goldstein, M., & Nuechterlein, K. (1991). Communication deviance in families of schizophrenic and manic patients. *Journal of Abnormal Psychology, 101*, 163–173.

Mikulincer, M. (1989). Causal attribution, coping strategies, and learned helplessness. *Cognitive Therapy & Research, 13*, 565–582.

Miller, A., & Wilson, P. (1979). Cognitive differentiation and integration: A conceptual analysis. *Genetic Psychology Monographs, 99*, 3–40.

Miller, I., & Norman, W. (1979). Learned helplessness in humans: A review and attribution-theory model. *Psychological Bulletin, 86*, 93–118.

Miller, I., Keitner, G., Whisman, M., & Ryan, C. (1992). Depressed patients with dysfunctional families: Description and course of illness. *Journal of Abnormal Psychology, 101*, 637–646.

Miller, I. W., McDermut, W., Gordon, K. C., Keitner, G. I., et al. (2000). Personality and family functioning in families of depressed patients. *Journal of Abnormal Psychology, 109*, 539–545.

Miller, M. W. (2003). Personality and the etiology and expression of PTSD: A three factor model perspective. *Clinical Psychology: Science and Practice, 10*, 373–393.

Miller, W. R., & Baca, J. C. (2001). *Quantum change: When epiphanies and sudden insights transform ordinary lives.* Washington, DC: American Psychological Association.

Millon, T. (2003). It's time to rework the blueprint: Building a science for clinical psychology. *American Psychologist, 58*, 949–961.

Millon, T., Blaney, P. H., & Davis, R. D. (Eds.). (1999). *Oxford textbook of psycho-pathology.* New York: Oxford University Press.

Millon, T., & Klerman, G. L. (Eds.). (1986). *Contemporary directions in psychopathology: Toward the DSM-IV.* New York: Gilford.

Millon, T., Meagher, S. E., & Grossman, S. D. (2001). Theoretical perspectives. In W. J. Livesley (Ed.), *Handbook of personality disorders: Theory, research, and treatment* (pp. 39–59). New York: Guilford.

Minarik, M. L., & Ahrens, A. H. (1996). Relations of eating and symptoms of depression and anxiety to the dimensions of perfectionism among undergraduate women. *Cognitive Therapy & Research, 20,* 155–169.

Mischel, W. (2004). Toward an integative science of the person. *Annual Review of Psychology, 55,* 1–22.

Mitchell, J., & Madigan, R. J. (1984). The effects of induced elation and depression on interpersonal problem solving. *Cognitive Therapy & Research, 8,* 277–285.

Mlott, S. R., Lira, F. T., & Campbell, P. L. (1978). A comparison of self esteem, dogmatism and fantasy in psychiatric inpatient adolescents and their parents with non-hospitalized adolescents and their parents. *Adolescence, 13,* 201–207.

Mlott, S. R., & Vale, W. H. (1986). Performance of agoraphobic families vs. non-agoraphobic families of the Sixteen Personality Factor Questionnaire (16PF). *Journal of Clinical Psychology, 42,* 244–250.

Moen, P., Elder. G. H., Jr., & Luscher, K. (Eds.). (1995). *Examining lives in context: Perspectives on the ecology of human development.* Washington, DC: American Psychological Association.

Moerk, E. (1973). Like father like son: Imprisonment of fathers and the psychological adjustment of sons. *Journal of Youth & Adolescence, 2,* 303–312.

Moffitt, T. E. (2003). Life-course-persistent and adolescence-limited antisocial behavior. In B. B. Lahey, T. E. Moffitt, & A. Caspi (Eds.), *Causes of conduct disorder and juvenile delinquency* (pp. 49–75). New York: Guilford.

Moffitt, T. E., Caspi, A., Rutter, M., & Silva, P. A. (2001). *Sex differences in antisocial behavior: Conduct disorders, deliquency, and violence in the Dunedin Longitudinal Study.* New York: Cambridge University Press.

Mogg, K., Bradley, B. P., & Williams, R. (1995). Attentional bias in anxiety and depression: The role of awareness. *British Journal of Clinical Psychology, 34,* 17–36.

Mogul, K. (1979). Women in midlife: Decisions, rewards, and conflicts related to work and careers. *American Journal of Psychiatry, 136,* 1139–1143.

Mohr, D. M. (1978). Development of attributes of personal identity. *Developmental Psychology, 14,* 427–428.

Molinari, G. (2000). *Exploring borders: Understanding culture and psychology.* London, UK: Routledge.

Mollerstrom, W. W., Patchner, M. A., & Milner, J. S. (1992). Family functioning and child abuse potential. *Journal of Clinical Psychology, 48,* 445–454.

Mondell, S., & Tyler, F. B. (1981). Parental competence and styles of problem-solving/play behavior with children. *Developmental Psychology, 17,* 73–78.

Mones, A. (1998). Oppositional children and their families: An adaptational dance in space and time. *American Journal of Orthopsychiatry, 68,* 147–153.

Moos, R. H. (1974). *The family environment scale: Preliminary manual.* Palo Alto, CA: Consulting Psycologists Press.

Morris, M. H. (1978). The three Rs of sex. *Journal of Religion & Health, 17,* 48–56.

Mortimer, J., & Simmons, R. (1978). Adult socialization. *Annual Review of Sociology, 4,* 421–454.

Mortimer, J. T., & Lorence, J. (1979). Occupational experience and the self-concept: A longitudinal study. *Social Psychology Quarterly, 42,* 307–323.

Mossman, D., & Somoza, E. (1990). Criteria of self defeating personality disorder. Psychodiagnostic typologies, self defeating behavior and personality disorders. *American Journal of Psychiatry, 147,* 1107.

Muehlhoff, T. M., & Wood, J. T. (2002). Speaking of magical communication: The marriage between theory and practice. *Journal of Social and Personal Relationships, 19,* 613–620.

Mueller, C., & Parcel, T. (1981). Measures of socioeconomic status: Alternatives and recommendations. *Child Development, 52,* 13–20.

Mueser, K., Bellack, A., Wade, J., & Sayers, S. (1993). Expressed emotion, social skills and response to negative affect in schizophrenia. *Journal of Abnormal Psychology, 102,* 339–351.

Mulinski, P. (1989). Male alcoholics perceptions of their fathers. *Journal of Nervous & Mental Disease, 177,* 101–104.

Mullins, L. S., & Kipelman, R. E. (1988). Toward an assessment of the construct validity of four measures of narcissism. Construct validity, personality measures and narcissism. *Journal of Personality Assessment, 52,* 610–625.

Mulvey, E. P., & LaRosa, J. F. (1986). Delinquency cessation and adolescent development: Preliminary data. *American Journal of Orthopsychiatry, 56,* 212–224.

Munroe, R. H., & Munroe, R. L. (1980). Household structure and socialization practices. *Journal of Social Psychology, 111,* 293–294.

Munsinger, H., & Rablin, A. (1978). Family study of gender identification. *Child Development, 49,* 537–539.

Muris, P., Meesters, C., Rassin, E., & Merckelbach, H. (2001). Thought-action fusion and anxiety disorders symptoms in normal adolescents. *Behaviour Research & Therapy, 39,* 843–852.

Muris, P., Steerneman, P., Merckelbach, H., & Meesters, C. (1996). The role of parental fearfulness and modeling in children's fear. *Behaviour Research & Therapy, 34,* 265–268.

Murphy, J. M., Laird, N. M., Monson, R. R., Sobol, A. M., et al. (2000). A 40 year perspective on the prevalence of depression: The Stirling County Study. *Archives of General Psychiatry, 57,* 200–215.

Murphy, K., & Barkley, R. (1996). Parents of children with attention-deficit/hyperactivity disorders: Psychological and attentional impairment. *American Journal of Orthopsychiatry, 66,* 93–102.

Myhill, J. E., & Lorr, M. (1988). The place of self-esteem in interpersonal behavior. *Journal of Clinical Psychology, 44,* 206–209.

Najman, J. M., Williams, G. M., Nikles, J., Spence, S., et al. (2000). Mothers, mental illness and child behavior problems: Cause-effect association or observation bias? *Journal of the American Academy of Child & Adolescent Psychiatry, 39,* 592–602.

Nakano, K. (1990). Hardiness, Type A behavior, and physical symptoms in a Japanese sample. *Journal of Nervous & Mental Disease, 178,* 52–56.

Nash, M., Hulsey, T., Sexton, M., & Harralson, T. (1993). Long-term sequel of childhood sexual abuse: Perceived family environment, psychopathology, and dissociation. *Journal of Consulting & Clinical Psychology, 61,* 276–283.

Nation, M., Crusto, V., Wandersman, A., Kumpfer, K. L., Seybolt, D., Morrissey-Kane, E. et al. (2003). What works in prevention: Principles of effective prevention programs. *American Psychologist, 58,* 449–456.

Neal, A. G., Ivosk, W. J., & Groat, H. T. (1976). Dimensions of family alienation in the marital dyad. *Sociometry, 39,* 396–405.

Nelson, G., & Beach, S. (1990). Sequential interaction in depression: Effects of depressive behavior on spousal aggression. *Behavior Therapy, 2,* 167–182.

Neumann, C. P. (1975). Success today: Achievement without happiness. *Psychosomatics, 16,* 103–106.

Newberger, C., & DeVos, E. (1988). Abuse and victimization: A life-span developmental perspective. *American Journal of Orthopsychiatry, 58,* 505–511.

Nichol, H. (1977). A developmental hierarchy of dyadic relationships. *Canadian Psychiatric Association Journal, 22*, 3–9.

Nicholson, I. R. (1998). Schizophrenia and the family. In L. L'Abate (Ed.), *Handbook of family psychopathology* (pp. 280–210). New York: Guilford.

Nielson, W. R., & Dobson, K. S. (1980). The coronary-prone behavior pattern and trait anxiety: Evidence for discriminant validity. *Journal of Consulting and Clinical Psychology, 48*, 546–549.

Nigg, J. T., & Huang-Pollock, C. L. (2003). An early-onset model of executive functions and intelligence in conduct disorder/delinquency. In B. B. Lahey, T. E. Moffitt, & A. Caspi (Eds.), *Causes of conduct disorder and juvenile delinquency* (pp. 227–253). New York: Guilford.

Nolen-Hoeksema, S., & Girgus, J. S. (1994). The emergence of gender differences in depression during adolescence. *Psychological Bulletin, 115*, 424–443.

Noorsdsy, D. L., Drake, R. E., Biesanz, J. C., McHugo, G. J., et al. (1994). Family history of alcoholism in schizophrenia. *Journal of Nervous & Mental Disease, 182*, 651–655.

Norton, N. (1989). Three scales of alexithymia: Do they measure the same thing? *Journal of Personality Assessment, 53*, 621–637.

Nover, A., Shore, M. F., Timberlake, E. M., & Greenspan, S. I. (1984). The relationship of maternal perception and maternal behavior: A study of normal mothers and their infants. *American Journal of Orthopsychiatry, 54*, 210–223.

Nowack, K. M. (1986). Type A, hardiness, and psychological distress. *Journal of Behavioral Medicine, 9*, 537–548.

O'Brien, M., Bahadur, M., Gee, C., & Balto, K. (1997). Child exposure to marital conflict and child coping responses as predictors of child adjustment. *Cognitive Therapy & Research, 21*, 39–59.

O'Brien, M., Margolin, G., & John, R. (1995). Relation among marital conflict, child coping, and child adjustment. *Journal of Clinical Psychology, 24*, 346–361.

O'Brien, P. E., & Gaborit, M. (1992). Co-dependency: A disorder separate from chemical dependency. *Journal of Clinical Psychology, 48*, 129–136.

O'Donnell, W. (1979). Affectional patterns of adolescents. *Adolescence, 14*, 681–686.

Offutt, C., & Lacroix, J. M. (1988). Type A behavior pattern and symptom reports: A prospective investigation. *Journal of Behavioral Medicine, 11*, 227–237.

Ogata, S. N., Silk, K. R., Goodrich, S., Lohr, N. E., et al. (1990). Childhood sexual and physical abuse in adult patients with borderline personality disorder. *American Journal of Psychiatry, 147*, 1008–1013.

Ohnnessain, C., Lerner, R., Lerner, J., & VonEye, A. (1998). Perceived parental acceptace and early adolescent self-competence. *American Journal of Orthopsychiatry, 68*, 621–629.

Ojha, H., & Jha, P. (1979). A study of achievement motivation as a function of social class, family system and family occupation. *Psychologia: An International Journal of Psychology in the Orient, 22*, 57–63.

O'Keffe, J. L., & Allred, K. D. (1989). Neuroticism, symptom reports, and Type A behavior: Interpretive cautions for the Framingham scale. *Journal of Behavioral Medicine, 12*, 1–11.

Olczak, P. V., & Goldman, J. A. (1975). The relationship between self-actualization and psychosocial maturity. *Journal of Clinical Psychology, 31*, 415–419.

O'Leary, A. (1985). Self-efficacy and health. *Behavior Research & Therapy, 23*, 437–451.

Oliver, J. E. (1993). Intergenerational transmission of child abuse: Rates, research, and clinical implications. *American Journal of Psychiatry, 150*, 1315–1324.

Olsen, N.J., & Willemsen, E.W. (1978). Fear of success—fact or artifact? *Journal of Psychology, 98*, 65–70.

Olson, D. (1996). Clinical assessment and treatment interventions using the Family Circumplex Model. In F. W. Kaslow (Ed.), *Handbook of relational diagnosis and dysfunctional family patterns* (pp. 59–77). New York: Wiley.

Olweus, D. (1980). The consistency issue in personality psychology revisited—with special reference to aggression. *British Journal of Social & Clinical Psychology, 19*, 377–390.

O'Malley, S. S., Foley, S. H., Rounsaville, B. J., Watkins, J. T., et al. (1988). Therapist competence and patient outcome in interpersonal psychotherapy of depression. *Journal of Consulting & Clinical Psychology, 56*, 496–501.

Omer, H. (1985). Fulfillment of therapeutic tasks as a precondition for acceptance in therapy. *American Journal of Psychotherapy, 39*, 175–186.

Omer, H. (2001). Helping parents deal with children's acute disciplinary problems without escalation: The principle of nonviolent resistance. *Family Process, 40*, 53–66.

Omer, H., & Dar, R. (1992). Changing trends in three decades of psychotherapy research: The flight from theory into pragmatics. *Journal of Consulting & Clinical Psychology, 60*, 88–93.

O'Neil, M. K. (1987). Loss and depression: A controversial link. *Journal of Nervous & Mental Disease, 175*, 354–359.

O'Neil, M. K., Lancee, W. J., & Freeman, S. J. (1986). Psychosocial factors and depressive symptoms. *Journal of Nervous & Mental Disease, 174*, 15–23.

Onorato, R. S., & Turner, J. C. (2002). Challenging the primacy of the personal self: The case for depersonalized self-conception. In Y. Kashima, M. Foddy, & M. Platow (Eds.), *Self and identity: Personal, social, and symbolic* (pp. 145–178). Mahwah, NJ: Earlbaum.

Orr, C. J. (1976). Sponsorship, self-presentation, and legitimacy. *Speech Monographs, 43*, 80–90.

Ortega, D. F., & Weinstein, K. (1988). Cognitive simplicity in the Type A "coronary-prone" pattern. *Cognitive Therapy & Research, 12*, 81–87.

Orvaschel, H., Beeferman, D., & Kabacoff, R. (1997). Depression, self-esteem, sex, and age in a child and adolescent clinical sample. *Journal of Clinical Child Psychology, 26*, 285–289.

Orvaschel, H., Weissman, M., & Kidd, K. (1980). Children and depression: The children of depressed parents; depression in children. *Journal of Affective Disorders, 2*, 1–16.

Oshman, H. P., & Manosevitz, M. (1976). Father absence: Effects of stepfathers upon psychosocial development in males. *Developmental Psychology, 12*, 479–480.

Osmond, M. W. (1978). Reciprocity: A dynamic model and a method to study family power. *Journal of Marriage & the Family, 40*, 49–61.

Osmond, M., & Grigg, C. (1978). Correlates of poverty: The interaction of individual and family characteristics. *Social Forces, 56*, 1099–1120.

Ostrauskas, D. V. (1977). The integration of self and significant others. *Psychiatry, 40*, 352–362.

Ottenberg, P. (1975). The physician's disease: Success and work addition. *Psychiatric Opinion, 12*, 6–11.

Overbeek, T. J. (1976). The workaholic. *Psychology, 13*, 36–42.

Overholser, J. (1996). The dependent personality and interpersonal problems. *Journal of Nervous & Mental Disease, 18*, 8–16.

Oxman, T. E., Rosenberg, S. D., Schnurr, P., & Tucker, G. (1985). Linguistic dimensions of affect and thought in somatization disorder. *American Journal of Psychiatry, 142*, 1150–1155.

Pachman, J. S., & Foy, D. W. (1978). A correlational investigation of anxiety, self-esteem and depression: New findings with behavioral measures of assertiveness. *Journal of Behavior Therapy & Experimental Psychiatry, 9*, 97–101.

Page, E., & Grandon, G. (1979). Family configuration and mental ability: Two theories contrasted with U.S. data. *American Educational Research Journal, 16*, 257–272.

Pallanti, S., Quercioli, L., Pazzagli, A., & Rossi, A., (1999). Awareness of illness and subjective experience of cognitive complaints in patients with bipolar II disorders. *American Journal of Psychiatry, 156*, 1094–1096.

Pangler, D., Simons, A., Monroe, S., & Thase, M. (1993). Evaluating the hopelessness model of depression: Diathesis-stress and symptom components. *Journal of Abnormal Psychology, 102,* 592–600.

Papageorgiou, C., & Wells, A. (2003). Rumination and depression: Advances in theory and research. *Cognitive Therapy and Research, 27,* 243–245.

Paredes, A. (1973). Marital-sexual factors in alcoholism. *Medical Aspects of Human Sexuality, 7,* 98–115.

Paris, J. (2001). Psychosocial adversity. In W. J. Livesley (Ed.), *Handbook of personality disorders: Theory, research, and treatment* (pp. 231–241). New York: Guilford.

Paris, J., & Frank, H. (1989). Perceptions of parental bonding in borderline patients. *American Journal of Psychiatry, 146,* 1498–1499.

Parke, R. D. (2004). Development in the family. *Annual Review of Psychology, 55,* 365–399.

Parker, G., & Barnett, B. (1988). Perceptions of parenting in childhood and social support in adulthood. *American Journal of Psychiatry, 145,* 479–482.

Parker, G., Barrett, E., & Hickie, I. (1992). From nurture to network: Examining links between perceptions of parenting received in childhood and social bonds in adulthood. *American Journal of Psychiatry, 149,* 877–885.

Parker, G., Johnston, P., & Hayward, L. (1988). Parental "expressed emotion" as a predictor of schizophrenic relapse. *Archives of General Psychiatry, 45,* 806–813.

Parnas, J., Teasdale, T., & Schulsinger, H. (1985). Institutional rearing and diagnostic outcome in children of schizophrenic mothers: A prospective high-risk study. *Archives of General Psychiatry, 42,* 762–769.

Parrott, W., & Sabini, J. (1989). On the "emotional" qualities of certain types of cognition: A reply to arguments for the independence of cognition and affect. *Cognitive Therapy & Research, 13,* 49–65.

Parry, G., & Brewin, C. (1988). Cognitive style and depression: Symptom-related, event-related or independent provoking factor? *British Journal of Clinical Psychology, 27,* 23–35.

Patterson, T. L., Smith, L. W., Smith, T. L., Yager, J., et al. (1992). Symptoms of illness in late adulthood are related to childhood social deprivation and misfortune in men but not in women. *Journal of Behavioral Medicine, 15,* 113–125.

Pavot, W., Diener, E., Colvin C., Randall, L., & Sandvik, E. (1991). Further validation of the Satisfaction With Life Scale: Evidence for the cross-method convergence of well-being measures. *Journal of Personality Assessment, 57,* 149–161.

Paykel, E. S., Klerman, G. L., & Prusoff, B. A. (1976). Personality and symptom pattern in depression. *British Journal of Psychiatry, 129,* 327–334.

Paznanski, E., Krahenbuhl, V., & Zrull, J. (1976). Childhood depression: A longitudinal perspective. *Child Psychiatry, 15,* 491–501.

Peck, R., & Everson, J. (1975). Similarities between parents and offspring on a personality inventory. *American Journal of Psychiatry, 132,* 453–454.

Pelham, W., & Lang, A. (1993). Parental alcohol consumption and deviant child behavior: Laboratory studies of reciprocal effects. *Clinical Psychology Review, 13,* 763–784.

Pelton, L. H. (1978). Child abuse and neglect: The myth of classlessness. *American Journal of Orthopsychiatry, 48,* 608–617.

Pennebaker, J. W. (2001). Explorations into health benefits of disclosure: Inhibitory, cognitive, and social processes. In L. L'Abate (Ed.), *Distance writing and computer-assisted interventions in psychiatry and mental health* (pp. 33–44). Westport, CT: Ablex.

Pennebaker, J. W. (1997). *Opening up: The healing power of confiding in others.* New York: Guilford.

Pennington, B. F. (2002). *The development of psychopathology: Nature and nurture.* New York: Guilford.

Perez, M., Pettit, J., David, C., & Kistner, J. (2001). The interpersonal consequences of inflated self-esteem in an inpatient psychiatric youth sample. *Journal of Consulting & Clinical Psychology, 69,* 712–716.

Perons, J., Burns, D., Perloff, J. M., & Mironda, J. (1993). Relationship between symptoms of depression and anxiety and dysfunctional about achievement and attachment. *Journal of Abnormal Psychology, 102,* 51–52.

Perry, J. C. (1989). Personality disorders, suicide and self-destructive behavior. In D. Jacobs & H. N. Brown (Eds.). *Suicide: Understanding and responding: Harvard Medical School Perspectives* (pp. 157–169). Madison, CT: International Universities Press.

Perry, D. G., & Bussey, K. (1979). The social learning theory of sex differences: Imitation is alive and well. *Journal of Personality & Social Psychology, 37,* 1699–1712.

Pervin, L. A., & John, O. P. (Eds.). (1999). *Handbook of personality: Theory and research.* New York: Guilford.

Petersen, K. K., & Dutton, J. E. (1975). Centrality, extremity, intensity: Neglected variables in research on attitude-behavior consistency. *Social Forces, 54,* 393–414.

Peterson, C., & De Avila, M. E. (1995). Optimistic explanatory style and the perception of health problems. *Journal of Clinical Psychology, 51,* 128–132.

Petrie, K., & Chamberlain, K. (1983). Hopelessness and social desirability as moderator variables in predicting suicidal behavior. *Journal of Consulting & Clinical Psychology, 51,* 485–487.

Petronio, S. (2000). Preface: The meaning of balance. In S. Petronio (Ed.), *Balancing the secrets of private disclosures* (pp. xiii–xvi). Mahwah, NJ: Earlbaum.

Pfeffer, C. (1981). The family system of suicidal children. *American Journal of Psychotherapy, 35,* 330–341.

Phares, V. (1996). *Fathers and developmental psychopathology.* New York: Wiley.

Phillips, S. D., & Bruch, M. A. (1988). Shyness and dysfunction in career development. Timidity, occupational interests and vocational maturity, information seeking and job applicant interviews. *Journal of Counseling Psychology, 35,* 159–165.

Pickett, S., Cook, J., Cohler, B., & Solomon, M. (1997). Positive parent/adult child relationships: Impact of severe mental illness and care giving burden. *American Journal of Orthopsychiatry, 67,* 220–230.

Pilkonis, P. A., & Frank, E. (1988). Personality pathology in recurrent depression: Nature, prevalence, and relationship to treatment response. *American Journal of Psychiatry, 145,* 435–441.

Pine, B. J., III, & Gilmore, J. H. (1999). *The experince economy: Work is theater and every business a stage.* Cambridge, MA: Harvard Business School.

Pittner, M. S., & Houston, B. K. (1980). Response to stress, cognitive coping strategies, and the Type A behavior pattern. *Journal of Personality & Social Psychology, 39,* 147–157.

Plas, J. M., & Hoover-Dempsey, K. V. (1988). *Working up a storm: Anger, anxiety, joy, and tears on the job-and how to handle them.* New York: Norton.

Plutchik, R. (1993). Emotions and their vicissitudes: Emotions and psychopathology. In M. Lewis & J. M. Haviland (Eds.), *Handbook of emotions* (pp. 53–66). New York: Guilford.

Plutchik, R., & Conte, H. R. (Eds.). (1997). *Circumplex models of personality and emotions.* Washington, DC: American Psychological Association.

Podsakoff, P. M., & Schriescheim, C. A. (1985). Field studies of French and Raven's bases of power: Critiques, reanalysis, and suggestions for future research. *Psychology Bulletin, 97,* 387–411.

Pollack, W., Briere, J., Schneider, L., & Knopp, J. (1990). Childhood antecedents of antisocial behavior: Parent alcoholism and physical abusiveness. *American Journal of Psychiatry, 147,* 1290–1293.

Porter, B., & O'Leary, K. D. (1980). Marital discord and childhood behavior problems. *Journal of Abnormal Child Psychology, 8*, 287–295.

Power, M., & Dalgleish, T. (1997). *Cognition and emotion: From order to disorder.* East Sussex, UK: Psychology Press.

Power, M. J., Ash, P. M., Shoenberg, E., & Sirey, E. C. (1974). Delinquency and the family. *British Journal of Social Work, 4*, 13–38.

Power, M. J., De Jong, F., & Lloyd, A. (2002). The organization of the self-concept in bipolar disorders: An empirical study and replication. *Cognitive Therapy & Research, 26*, 553–561.

Prentky, R. A., Burgess, A. W., Rokous, F., Lee, A., et al. (1989). The presumption role of fantasy in serial sexual homicide. *American Journal of Psychiatry, 146*, 887–891.

Prescott, P. (1978). Sex differences on a measure of self-esteem: Theoretical implications. *Journal of Genetic Psychology, 132*, 67–85.

Prest, L. A., Benson, M. J., & Protinsky, H. O. (1998). Family of origin and current relationship influence on codependency. *Family Process, 37*, 513–528.

Price, G. H., & Dabbs, J. M. (1974). Sex, Setting and Personal Space: Changes as children grow older. *Personality & Social Psychology Bulletin, 1*, 362–363.

Price, J. A. (1975). Sharing: The integration of intimate economies. *Anthropologica, 71*, 3–27.

Prinstein, M. J., Boerger, J., Spirto, A., Little, T. D., et al. (2000). Peer functioning, family dysfunction, and psychological symptoms in a risk factor model for adolescent inpatients' suicidal ideation severity. *Journal of Clinical Child Psychology, 29*, 392–405.

Prinstein, M. J., & La Greca, A. M. (1999). Links between mothers' and children's social competence and association with maternal adjustment. *Journal of Clinical Child Psychology, 28*, 197–210.

Prochaska, J. O., DiClemente, C. C., & Norcross, J. C. (1992). In search of how people change: Applications to addictive behaviors. *American Psychologist, 47*, 1102–1114.

Pruitt, J. A., Kappius, R. E., & Gorman, P. W. (1992). Bulimia and fear of intimacy. *Journal of Clinical Psychology, 48*, 472–476.

Puig-Antich, J., Goetz, D., Davies, M., & Kaplan, T. (1989). A controlled family history study of prepubertal major depressive disorder. *Archives of General Psychiatry, 46*, 406–418.

Pulakos, J. (1996). Family environment and shame: Is there a relationship? *Journal of Clinical Psychology, 52*, 617–623.

Purdon, C. (1999). Thought suppression and psychopathology. *Behavior Research & Therapy, 37*, 1029–1054.

Puryear-Keita, G., & Sauter, S. L. (Eds.). (1992). *Work and well-being: An agenda for the 1990s.* Washington, DC: American Psychological Association.

Putman, Y. (2003, November, 25). Families important, marriage is not. *Chattanooga Times Free Press*, Front Page.

Rachlin, S., Milton, J., & Pam, A. (1977). Counter-symbiotic suicide. *Archives of General Psychiatry, 34*, 965–967.

Racy, J. (1974). How the "work ethic" influences sexuality. *Medical Aspects of Human Sexuality, 8*, 84–119.

Radziszewska, B., Richardson, J., Dent, C., & Flay, B. (1996). Parenting style and adolescent depressive symptoms, smoking, and academic achievement: Ethnic, gender, and SES differences. *Journal of Behavioural Medicine, 19*, 289–305.

Ragan, P., & McGlashan, T. (1986). Childhood parental death and adult psychopathology. *American Journal of Psychiatry, 143*, 153–157.

Raine, A., Brennan, P., & Mednick, S. A. (1994). Birth complications combined with early maternal rejection at age 1 year predispose to violent crime at age 18 years. *Archives of General Psychiatry, 51*, 984–988.

Raine, A., Brennan, P., Mednick, B., & Mednick, S. A. (1994). High rates of violence, crime, academic problems, and behavioral problems in males with both early neuromotor deficits and unstable environments. *Archives of General Psychology, 53*, 544–549.

Ramanaiah, N. V., Heerboth, J. R., & Jinkerson, D. L. (1985). Personality and self-actualizing profiles of assertive people. *Journal of Personality Assessment, 49*, 440–443.

Ramey, C., & Campbell, F. (1976). Parental attitudes and poverty. *Journal of Genetic Psychology, 128*, 3–6.

Randolph, J., & Dykman, B. (1998). Perceptions of parenting and depression-proneness in the offspring: Dysfunctional attitudes as a mediating mechanism. *Cognitive Therapy & Research, 22*, 377–400.

Rappaport, N. B., McAnulty, D. P., & Brantley, P. J. (1988). Exploration of the Type A behavior pattern in chronic headache suffers. *Journal of Consulting and Clinical Psychology, 56*, 621–623.

Rapps, C. C., et al. (1982). Attributional style among depressed patients. *Journal of Abnormal Psychology, 91*, 102–108.

Rasch, J. (1960–1980). *Probabilistic model for some intelligence and attainment tests.* Chicago: University of Chicago Press.

Raschke, R. (1979). Family conflict and children's self-concept: A comparison of intact and single-parent families. *Journal of Marriage & the Family, 41*, 367–374.

Rassin, E., Diepstraten, P., Merckelbach, H., & Muris, P. (2001). Thought-action fusion and thought suppression in obsessive-compulsive disorder. *Behaviour Research & Therapy, 39*, 757–764.

Ray, J. (1981). Authoritarianism, dominance and assertiveness. *Journal of Personality Assessment, 45*, 390–397.

Ray, O. (2004). How the mind hurts and heals the body. *American Psychologist, 59*, 29–40.

Reed, R., McMahan, O., & L'Abate, L. (2001). Workbooks and psychotherapy with incarcerated felons: Research in progress. In L. L'Abate (Ed.), *Distance writing and computer-assisted interventions in psychiatry and mental health* (pp. 157–167). Westport, CT: Ablex.

Reich, J. (1996). The morbility of DSM-III-R dependent personality disorder. *Journal of Nervous & Mental Disease, 184*, 22–26.

Reich, J., Noyes, R., & Troughton, E. (1987). Dependent personality disorder associated with phobic avoidance in patents with panic disorder. *American Journal of Psychiatry, 144*, 323–326.

Reich, J., & Thomson, W. D. (1985). Marital status of schizophrenic and alcoholic patients *Journal of Nervous & Mental Disease, 173*, 499–502.

Reis, H. T. (2002). Action matters, but relationship science is basic. *Journal of Social and Personal Relationships, 19*, 601–612.

Reis, H. T., Clark, M. S., & Holmes, J. G. (2004). Perceived partner responsiveness as an organizing construct in the study of intimacy and closeness. In D. J. Mashek & A. Aron (Eds.), *Handbook of closeness and intimacy* (pp. 201–245). Mahwah, NJ: Earlbaum

Reis, H. T., Collins, W., & Berscheid, E. (2000). The relationship context of human behavior and development. *Psychological Bulletin, 126*, 844–872.

Reis, H. T., & Gruzen, J. (1976). On mediating equity, equality, and self-interest: The role of self-presentation in social exchange. *Journal of Experimental Social Psychology, 12*, 487–503.

Reiss, D. (1981). *The family's construction of reality.* Cambridge, MA: Harvard University Press.

Rende, R., Wickramaratne, P., Warner, V., & Weissman, M. M. (1995). Sibling resemblance for psychiatric disorders in offspring at high and low risk for depression. *Journal of Child Psychology & Psychiatry & Allied Disciplines, 36*, 1353–1363.

Rennie, D. L. (1998). Grounded theory methodology: The pressing need for a coherent logic of justification. *Theory and Psychology, 8*, 101–109.

Rey, J. (1993). Oppositional defiant disorder. *American Journal of Psychiatry, 150,* 1769–1778.

Rhéaume, J., Freeston, M. H., Ladouceur, R., Bouchard, C., et al. (2000). Functional and dysfunctional perfectionists: Are they different on compulsive-like behaviors? *Behaviour Research & Therapy, 38,* 119–128.

Rhee, S. H., & Waldman, I. D. (2003). Testing alternative hypothesis regarding the role of development on genetic and environmental influences underlying antisocial behavior. In B. B. Lahey, T. E. Moffitt, & A. Caspi (Eds.), *Causes of conduct disorder and juvenile delinquency* (pp. 305–318). New York: Guilford.

Rice, M. E., Quinsey, V. L., & Harris, G. T. (1991). Sexual recidivism among child molesters released from a maximum security psychiatric institution. *Journal of Consulting & Clinical Psychology, 59,* 381–386.

Richard, B. A., & Dodge, K. E. (1982). Social maladjustment and problem-solving in school-age children. *Journal of Consulting & Clinical Psychology, 50,* 226–233.

Richard, K., Graziano, W., & Forehand, R. (1984). Parental expectations and childhood deviance in clinic-referred and non-clinic children. *Journal of Clinical Child Psychology, 13,* 179–186.

Richer, J. (1976). The social-avoidance behaviour of autistic children. *American Behaviour, 24,* 898–906.

Richters, J. (1992). Depressed mothers as informants about their children: A critical review of the evidence for distortion. *Psychological Bulletin, 112,* 485–499.

Rickard, K. M., Graziano, W., & Forehand, R. (1984). Parental expectations and childhood deviance in clinic-referred and non-clinic children. *Journal of Clinical Child Psychology, 13,* 179–186.

Ridgewood Financial Institute, Inc. (1993). *Psychotherapy finances: Managed care handbook.* Jupiter, FL: Author.

Riley, W. T., & Treiber, F. A. (1989). The validity of multidimensional self-report anger and hostility measures. *Journal of Clinical Psychology, 45,* 397–404.

Riley, W. T., Treiber, F. A., & Woods, M. G. (1989). Anger and hostility in depression. *Journal of Nervous & Mental Disease, 177,* 668–674.

Rimé, B., & Bonami, M. (1979). Overt and covert personality traits associated with coronary heart disease. *British Journal of Medical Psychology, 52,* 77–84.

Ritterband, L. M., Gonder-Frederick, L. A., Cox, D. J., Clifton, A. D., West, R. W., & Borowitz, S. M. (2003). Internet interventions: In review, in use, and into the future. *Professional Psychology: Research and Practice, 34,* 527–534.

Robbins, D., & Alessi, N. (1985). Depressive symptoms and suicidal behavior in adolescents. *American Journal of Psychiatry, 142,* 588–592.

Roberts, J., & Monroe, S. (1994). A multidimensional model of self-esteem in depression. *Clinical Psychology Review, 14,* 161–181.

Robin, A. L., Koepke, T., & Moye, A. (1990). Multidimensional assessment of parent-adolescent relations. *Psychological Assessment, 2,* 451–459.

Robins, C., Bagby R., Rector, N., & Lynch, T. (1997). Sociotropy, autonomy, and patterns of symptoms I in patients with major depression: A comparison of dimensional and categorical approaches. *Cognitive Therapy & Research, 21,* 285–300.

Robins, C. J., Hayes, A. M., Block, P., Kramer, R. J. et al. (1995). Interpersonal and achievement concerns and the depressive vulnerability and symptom specificity hypotheses: A prospective study. *Cognitive Therapy & Research, 19,* 1–20.

Robinson, B. E., Carroll, J. E., & Flowers, C. (2001). Marital estrangement, positive affect, and locus of control among spouses of workaholics and spouses of nonworkaholics. *American Journal of Family Therapy, 29,* 397–410.

Robinson, B. E., & Kelley, L. (1998). Adult children of workaholics: Self-concept, anxiety, depression, and locus of control. *American Journal of Family Therapy, 26,* 223–238.

Robinson, N., Garber, J., & Hilsman, R. (1995). Cognitions and stress: Direct and moderating effects on depressive versus externalizing symptoms during the junior high school transition. *Journal of Abnormal Psychology, 104,* 453–463.

Roeckelein, J. E. (2000). *The concept of time in psychology: A resource book and annotated bibliography.* Westport, CT: Greenwood.

Roesler, T. A., & McKenzie, N. (1994). Effects of childhood trauma on psychological functioning in adults sexually abused as children. *Journal of Nervous & Mental Disease, 182,* 145–150.

Rogers, C. R. (1957). The necessary and sufficient conditions of therapeutic personality change. *Journal of Consulting Psychology, 21,* 95–103.

Rogers, R. (1976). The emotional contamination between parents and children. *American Journal of Psychoanalysis, 36,* 267–271.

Rohrbeck, C. A., & Twentyman, C. T. (1986). Multimodal assessment of impulsiveness in abusing, neglecting, and nonmaltreating mothers and their preschool children. *Journal of Consulting & Clinical Psychology, 54,* 231–236.

Roloff, M. E., Putman, L. L., & Anastasiou, L. (2003). Negotiation skills. In J. O. Green & B. R. Burleson (Eds.), *Handbook of communication and social interaction skills* (pp. 801–833). Mahwah, NJ: Earlbaum.

Romans, S., Martin, J., Anderson, J., & Herbison, G. (1995). Sexual abuse in childhood and deliberate self-harm. *American Journal of Psychiatry, 152,* 1336–1342.

Romney, D. (1991). Thought disorder in the relatives of schizophrenics: A meta-analytic review of selected published studies. *Journal of Nervous & Mental Disease, 178,* 481–486.

Ronins, S., & Novaco, R. (1999). Systems conceptualization and treatment of anger. *Journal of Clinical Psychology, 55,* 325–337.

Ronningstam, E. (1999). Narcissistic personality disorder. In T. Millon, P. H. Blaney, & R. D. Davis (Eds.), *Oxford textbook of psychopathology* (pp. 674–693). New York: Oxford University Press.

Rosefield, L. B., & Plax, T. G. (1975). Personality determinants of autocratic and democratic leadership. *Speech Monographs, 42,* 203–208.

Rosen, A., & Rekers, G. (1980). Toward a taxonomic framework for variables of sex and gender. *Genetic Psychology Monographs, 102,* 191–218.

Rosenberg, M., & Pearlin, L. L. (1978). Social class and self-esteem among children and adults. *American Journal of Sociology, 84,* 53–77.

Rosenberg, M. S., & Reppucci, N. D. (1983). Abusive mothers: Perceptions of their own and their children's behavior. *Journal of Consulting & Clinical Psychology, 51,* 674–682.

Rosenfarb, I., Becker, J., & Khan, A. (1994). Perceptions of parental and peer attachments by women with mood disorders. *Journal of Abnormal Psychology, 103,* 637–644.

Rosenfarb, I., Becker, J., & Mintz, J. (1994). Dependency, self-criticism, and perceptions of socialization experiences. *Journal of Abnormal Psychology, 103,* 669–675.

Rosenfarb, I. S., Goldstein, M. J., Mintz, J., & Nuechterlein, K. H. (1995). Expressed emotion and subclinical psychopathology observable within the transactions between schizophrenic patients and their family members. *Journal of Abnormal Psychology, 104,* 259–267.

Rosenfield, S. (1980). Sex differences in depression: Do women always have higher rates? *Journal of Health & Social Behavior, 21,* 33–42.

Rosenthal, T., Montgomery, L., Shadish, W., & Lichstein, K. (1989). Leisure interest patterns and subjective stress in college students. *Behaviour Research & Therapy, 27,* 59–64.

Ross, C. A. (1997). *Dissociative identity disorder: Diagnosis, clinical features, and treatment of multiple personality.* New York: Wiley.

Roth, D., & Blatt, S. J. (1974). Spatial representations and psychopathology. *Journal of the American Psychoanalytic Association, 22,* 854–872.

Rothbaum, F., Weisz, J., Pott, M., Miyakem K., & Morelli, G. (2000). Attachment and culture: Security in the United States and Japan. *American Psychologist, 55,* 1093–1104.

Rothbaum, F., & Weisz, J. (1994). Parental care giving and child externalizing behavior in nonclinical samples: A meta-analysis. *Psychological Bulletin, 116,* 55–74.

Rotheram-Borus, M., Mahler, K., Koopman, C., & Langabeer, K. (1996). Sexual abuse history and associated multiple risk behavior in adolescent runaways. *American Journal of Orthopsychiatry, 66,* 390–400.

Rouff, L. (1975). Creativity and sense of humor. *Psychological Reports, 37,* 1022.

Roy, A. (1978). Vulnerability factors and depression in women. *British Journal of Psychiatry, 133,* 106–110.

Roy, A. (1981a). Role of past loss in depression. *Archives of General Psychiatry, 38,* 301–302.

Roy, A. (1981b). Specificity of risk factors for depression. *American Journal of Psychiatry, 138,* 959–961.

Roy, A. (1985). Early parental separation and adult depression. *Archives of General Psychiatry, 42,* 987–991.

Roy, A. (2001). Childhood trauma and attempted suicide in alcoholics. *Journal of Nervous & Mental Disease, 189,* 120–121.

Rubin, K. H., Daniels-Beirness, T., & Bream, L. (1984). *Journal of Consulting & Clinical Psychology, 52,* 17–25.

Rude, S. S., & Burnham, B. L. (1993). Do interpersonal and achievement vulnerabilities interact with congruent events to predict depression? Comparison of DEQ, SAS, DAS, and combined scales. *Cognitive Therapy & Research, 17,* 531–548.

Rude, S. S., & Burnham, B. L. (1995). Connectedness and neediness: Factors of the DEQ and SAS dependency scales. *Cognitive Therapy & Research, 19,* 323–340.

Rumstein-McKean, O., & Hunsley, J. (2001). Interpersonal and family functioning of female survivors of childhood sexual abuse. *Clinical Psychology Review, 21,* 471–490.

Ruscher, S., & Gotlib, I. (1988). Marital interaction patterns of couples with and without a depressed partner. *Behavior Therapy, 19,* 455–470.

Ruscio, J., & Ruscio, A. M. (2000). Informing the continuity controversy: A taxometric analysis of depression. *Journal of Abnormal Psychology, 109,* 473–487.

Russek, L., & Scheartz, G. (1997). Feelings of parental caring predict health status in midlife: A 35-year follow-up of the Harvard Mastery of Stress Study. *Journal of Behavioral Medicine, 20,* 1–13.

Russell, J., & Pratt, G. (1980). A description of the affective quality attributed to environments. *Journal of Personality & Social Psychology, 38,* 311–322.

Rutter, M. (1979). Maternal deprivation, 1972–1978: New finding, new concept, new approaches. *Child Development, 50,* 283–305.

Rutter, M. (1987). Psychosocial resilience and protective mechanisms. *American Journal of Orthopsychiatry, 57,* 316–331.

Rutter, M. (2003). Crucial paths from risk indicator to causal mechanism. In B. B. Lahey, T. E. Moffitt, & A. Caspi (Eds.), *Causes of conduct disorder and juvenile delinquency* (pp. 3–24). New York: Guilford.

Ryan, N. E., Solberg, V. S., & Brown, S. D. (1996). Family dysfunction, parental attachment and career search self-efficacy among community college students. *Journal of Counseling Psychology, 43,* 84–89.

Saarni, C. (1999). *The development of emotional competence.* New York: Guilford.

Saboonchi, F., Lundh, L. G., & Ost, L. G. (1999). Perfectionism and self-consciousness in social phobia and panic disorder with agoraphobia. *Behaviour Research & Therapy, 37,* 799–808.

Sacco, W., Dumont, C., & Dow, M. (1993). Attributional, perceptual, and affective response to depressed and non-depressed martial partners. *Journal of Consulting & Clinical Psychology, 61,* 1076–1082.

Sabourin, S., Bourgeois, L., Gendreau, P., & Morval, M. (1989). Self-deception, impression management, and consumer satisfaction with mental health treatment. *Psychological Assessment, 1,* 126–129.

Sadava, S. W. (1987). Interactional theory. In H. T. Blane, & K. E. Leonard (Eds.), *Psychological theories of drinking and alcoholism* (pp. 90–130). New York: Guilford.

Sadd, S., Lenauer, M., Shaver, P., & Dunivant, N. (1978). Objective measurement of fear of success and fear of failure: A factor analytic approach. *Journal of Consulting & Clinical Psychology, 46,* 405–416.

Safir, M. P., & Almagor, M. (1991). Psychopathology associated with sexual dysfunction. *Journal of Clinical Psychology, 47,* 17–27.

Safran, J. D., Segal, Z. V., Hill, C., & Whiffen, V. (1990). Refining strategies for research on self-representations in emotional disorders. *Cognitive Therapy & Research, 14,* 143–160.

Salmon, P. (2001). Effects of physical exercise on anxiety, depression and sensitivity to stress: A unifying theory. *Clinical Psychology Review, 21,* 33–61.

Salmon, P., Pearce, S., Smith, C. C., Manyande, A., et al. (1989). Anxiety, Type A personality and endocrine responses to surgery. *British Journal of Clinical Psychology, 28,* 279–280.

Saltzstein, H., & Diamond, R. (1972). Moral Judgment level and conformity behavior. *Developmental Psychology, 7,* 327–336.

Salzman, C. (1996). Sexual abuse and borderline personality disorder. *American Journal of Psychiatry, 153,* 848.

Sameroff, A. J., Lewis, M., & Miller, S. M. (Eds.). (2000). *Handbook of developmental psychopathology.* New York: Kluwer Academic/Plenum.

Sanavio, E. (1988). Obsessions and compulsions: The Padua Inventory. *Behavior Research & Therapy, 26,* 169–177.

Sanders, M. R., Dadds, M. R., & Bor, W. (1989). Contextual analysis of child oppositional and maternal aversive behaviors in families of conduct-disordered and non-problem children. *Journal of Clinical Child Psychology, 18,* 72–83.

Sanders, M. R., Dadds, M. R., Johnson, B. M., & Cash, R. (1992). Childhood depression and conduct disorder: I. Behavioral, affective, and cognitive aspects of family problem-solving interactions. *Journal of Abnormal Psychology, 101,* 495–504.

Sanderson, C. A. (2004). The link between the pursuit of intimacy goals and satisfaction in close relationships: : An examination of the underlying processes. In D. J. Mashek & A. Aron (Eds.), *Handbook of closeness and intimacy* (pp. 247–266). Mahwah, NJ: Earlbaum.

Sanderson, W. C. (2002). Comment on Hansen et al.: Would the results be the same if patients were receiving an evidence based treatment? *Clinical Psychology: Science & Practice, 9,* 350–352.

Sanfilipo, M. (1994). Masculinity, femininity, and subjective experiences of depression. *Journal of Clinical Psychology, 50,* 144–157.

Santelli, J., Bernstein, D., Zborowski, L., & Bernstein, J. (1990). Pursuing and distancing, and related traits: A cross cultural assessment. *Journal of Personality Assessment, 55,* 663–672.

Santor, D. A., & Coyne, J. C. (2001). Evaluating the continuity of symptomatology between depressed and non-depressed individuals. *Journal of Abnormal Psychology, 110,* 216–225.

Santor, D. A., & Zuroff, D. C. (1994). Depressive symptoms: Effects of negative affectivity and failing to accept the past. *Journal of Personality Assessment, 63,* 294–312.

Santostefano, S., & Rieder, C. (1984). Cognitive controls and aggression in children: The concept of cognitive-affective balance. *Journal of Consulting & Clinical Psychology, 52,* 46–56.

Santrock, J. W. (1977). Effects of father absence on sex-typed behaviors in male children: Reason for the absence and age of onset of the absence. *Journal of Genetic Psychology, 130,* 3–10.

Sauer, R. J. (1979). Emotional mortgage. *American Journal of Family Therapy, 7,* 49–51.

Sauter, S. L., Murphy, L. R., & Hurrell, J. J. Jr. (1992). Prevention of work-related psychological disorders. In G. Puryear Keita & S. L. Sauter (Eds.), *Work and well-being: An agenda for the 1990s* (pp. 17–40). Washington, DC: American Psychological Association.

Savin-Williams, R. C. (1994). Verbal and physical abuse as stressors in the lives of lesbian, gay male, and bisexual youths: Associations with school problems, running away, substance abuse, prostitution, and suicide. *Journal of Consulting & Clinical Psychology, 62*, 261–269.

Scales, P. C., & Leffert, N. (1999). *Developmental assets: A synthesis of the scientific research on adolescent development*. Minneapolis: Search Institute.

Schachter, F. (1976). Sibling de-identification. *Developmental Psychology, 12*, 418–427.

Schaefer, C. E. (Ed.). (1993). *The therapeutic power of play*. Northvale, NJ: Aronson.

Schaefer, C. E., & Higgins, J. (1976). A note on the relationship between the Comfortable Interpersonal Distance Scale and the sociometric status of emotionally disturbed children. *Journal of Genetic Psychology, 128*, 91–93.

Schecter, D. E. (1979). Fear of success in women: A psychodynamic reconstruction. *Journal of the American Academy of Psychoanalysis, 7*, 33–43.

Scherer, D. G., Melloh, T., Buyck, D., Anderson, C. et al. (1996). Relation between children's perceptions of maternal mental illness and children's psychological adjustment. *Journal of Clinical Child Psychology, 25*, 156–169.

Schiavo, R. S., Schiffenbauer, A., & Roberts, J. (1977). Methodological factors affecting interpersonal distance in dyads. *Perceptual & Motor Skills, 44*, 903–906.

Schlenker, B., & Leary, M. R. (1982). Social anxiety and self-presentation: A conceptualization model. *Psychological Bulletin, 92*, 641–669.

Schley, S., Brooks-Gunn, J., & Hardy, J. (2001). *Intergenerational similarities in achievement.* In J. R. M. Gerris (Ed.), *Dynamics of parenting* (pp. 346–362). Kessel-Lo, Belgium: Garant.

Schmidt, D. E., & Keating, J. P. (1979). Human crowding and personal control: An integration of the research. *Psychological Bulletin, 86*, 680–700.

Schmidt, N., & Mellon, P. (1980). Life and job satisfaction: Is the job central? *Journal of Vocational Behavior, 16*, 51–58.

Schmitt, D. O., et al. (2003). Are men universally more dismissing than women? Gender differences in romantic attachment across 62 cultural regions. *Personal Relationships, 10*, 307–331.

Schore, A. N. (1994). *Affect regulation and the origin of the self: The neurobiology of emotional development*. Hillsdale, NJ: Erlbaum.

Schoedel, J., Frederickson, W. A., & Knight, J. M. (1975). An extrapolation of the physical attractiveness and sex variables within the Byrne attraction paradigm. *Memory & Cognition, 3*, 527–530.

Schofield, L., & Abbuhl, S. (1975). The stimulation of insight and self-awareness through body-movement exercise. *Journal of Clinical Psychology, 31*, 745–746.

Schore, A. N. (2003). *Affect dysregulations and disorders of the self*. New York: Norton.

Schuckit, M., & Smith, T. (1996). An 8-year follow-up of 450 sons of alcoholic and control subjects. *Archives of General Psychiatry, 53*, 202–210.

Schulman, D. G., & Ferguson, G. R. (1988). An experimental investigation of Kernberg's and Kohut's theories of narcissism. *Journal of Clinical Psychology, 44*, 445–451.

Schultheiss, D. E. P., & Blustein, D. L. (1994). Role of adolescent-parent relationships in college student development and adjustment. *Journal of Counseling Psychology, 41*, 248–255.

Schwartz, R. C. (2001). Self-Awareness in schizophrenia: Its relationship to depressive symptomatology and broad psychiatric impairments. *Journal of Nervous & Mental Disease, 189*, 401–403.

Schwartz, S. H. (1996). Value priorities and behavior: Applying a theory of integrated value systems. In C. Seligman, J. M. Olson, & M. P. Zanna (Eds.), *The psychology of values: The Ontario Symposium* (pp. 1–24). Hillsdale, NJ: Earlbaum.

Schwartzman, H. B. (1978). *Transformations: The anthropology of children's play.* New York: Plenum.

Scilletta, C. (2002). *Versione computerizzara della prova di competenza relazionale; Esplorazione delle opportunita' teoriche e pratiche* (Conpurized version of relational competence: Exploration of the theoriecal and practical opportunities). Ph.D. dissertation. University of Padua, Italy.

Seeman, M. V. (Ed.). (1995). *Gender and psychopathology.* Washington, DC: American Psychiatric Association.

Segerstrom, S., Tsao, J., Alden, L., & Craske, M. (2000). Worry and rumination: Repetitive thought as a concomitant and predictor of negative mood. *Cognitive Therapy & Research, 24,* 671–688.

Seifer, R., Sameroff, A., Dickstein, S., & Keitner, G. (1996). Parental Psychopathology, multiple contextual risks, and one-year outcomes in children. *Journal of Clinical Child Psychology, 25,* 423–435.

Seigman, A., & Snow, S. (1997). The outward expression of anger, the inward experience of anger and CVR: The role of vocal expression. *Journal of Behavioral Medicine, 20,* 29–45.

Seligman, M. E. (1984). Attributional style and depressive symptoms among children. *Journal of Abnormal Psychology, 93,* 235–238.

Seligman, M. E. P., & Csikszentmihalyi, M. (2000). Positive psychology: An introduction. *American Psychologist, 55,* 5–14.

Selman, R., Jaquette, D., & Lavin, D. (1977). Interpersonal awareness in children: Toward an integration of developmental and clinical child psychology. *American Journal of Orthopsychiatry, 47,* 264–274.

Selvini-Palazzoli, M., Cirillo, S., Selvini, M., & Sorrentino, A. M. (1989). *Family games: General models of psychotic processes in the family.* New York: Norton.

Serafica, F. C. (1978). The development of attachment behaviors: An organismic—developmental perspective. *Human Development, 21,* 119–140.

Serbin, L. A., & Karp, J. (2004). The intergenerational transfer of psychological risk: Mediators of vulnerability and resilience. *Annual Review of Psychology, 55,* 333–363.

Sexton, T. L., Robbins, M. S., Hollison, A. S., Mease, A. L., & Mayorgia, C. C. (2003). Efficacy, effectiveness, and change mechanisms in couple and family therapy. In T. L. Sexton, G. R. Weeks, & M. S. Robbins (Eds.), *Handbook of family therapy* (pp. 229–261). New York: Brunner/Routledge.

Shahani, C., Dipboye, R., & Phillips, A. (1990). Global self-esteem as a correlate of work-related attitudes: A question of dimensionality. *Journal of Personality Assessment, 54,* 276–288.

Shafii, M., Carringan, S., Whittinghill, J., Russell, J., & Derrick, A. (1985). Psychological autopsy of completed suicide in children and adolescents. *American Journal of Psychiatry, 142,* 1061–1064.

Shafran, R., & Mansell, W. (2001). Perfectionism and psychopathology: A review of research and treatment. *Clinical Psychology Review, 21,* 879–906.

Shane, M., Shane, E., & Gales, M. (1997). *Intimate attachments: Toward a new self-psychology.* New York: Guilford.

Shankman, S. A., & Klein, D. N. (2003). The relation between depression and anxiety: An evaluation of the tripartite, approach-withdrawal, and valence-arousal models. *Clinical Psychology Review, 23,* 605–637.

Shapiro, D. (2000). *Dynamics of character: Self-regulation in psychopathology.* New York: Basic Books.

Shaver, P. (Ed.). (1984). *Emotions, relationships, and health.* Beverly Hills, CA: Sage.

Shea, M. T., Leon, A. C., Mueller, T. I., Solomon, D. A., et al. (1996). Does major depression result in lasting personality change? *American Journal of Psychiatry, 153,* 1404–1410.

Shea, M. T., Widiger, T. A., & Klein, M. H. (1992). Comorbidity of personality disorders and depression: Implications for treatment. *Journal of Consulting & Clinical Psychology, 60,* 857–868.

Shearer, S. L., Peters, C. P., Quaytman, M. S., & Ogden, R. L. (1990). Frequency and correlates of childhood sexual and physical abuse histories in adult female borderline inpatients. *American Journal of Psychiatry, 147,* 214–216.

Shedlock, D. J., & Cornelius, S. W. (2002). Psychological approaches to wisdom and its development. In J. Demick & C. Andreotti (Eds.), *Handbook of adult development* (pp. 153–167). New York: Kluwer Academic.

Sheffield, A. (2003). *Depression fallout: The impact of depression on couples and what you can do to preserve the bond.* New York: Quill.

Shelton, R. C., Hollon, S. D., Purdon, S. E., & Loosen, P. T. (1991). Biological and psychological aspects of depression. *Behavior Therapy, 22,* 201–228.

Sher, K., Walitzer, K., Wood P., & Brent, E. (1991). Characteristics of children of alcoholics: Putative risk factors, substance use and abuse, and psychopathology. *Journal of Abnormal Psychology, 100,* 427–448.

Sherer, D., Melloh, T., Buyck, D., & Anderson, C. (1996). Relation between children's perception of maternal mental illness and children's psychological adjustment. *Journal of Clinical Child Psychology, 25,* 156–169.

Shields, A., & Ciccetti, D. (2001). Parental maltreatment and emotional dysregulation as risk factors for bullying and victimization in middle childhood. *Journal of Clinical Child Psychology, 30,* 349–363.

Shilling, C. S. (1979). The relationship between the assertive behavior of parents and the behavior of their children. *American Journal of Family Therapy, 7,* 59–64.

Shmagin, B. G., & Pearlmutter, D. R. (1977). The pursuit of unhappiness: The secondary gains of depression. *Perspectives in Psychiatric Care, 15,* 63–65.

Shneidman, E. S. (1989). Overview: A multidimensional approach to suicide. In D. Jacobs & H. N. Brown (Eds.), *Suicide: Understanding and responding* (pp. 1–30). Madison, CT: International Universities Press.

Shorkey, C. T., & Reyes, E. (1978). Relationship between self-actualization and rational thinking. *Psychological Reports, 42,* 842.

Shrout, P. E., Link, B. G., Dohrenwend, B. P., Skodol, A. E., et al. (1989). Characterizing life events as risk factors for depression: The role of fateful loss events. *Journal of Abnormal Psychology, 98,* 460–467.

Shulman, S., & Klein, M. (1983). Psychological differentiation, self-concept, and object relations of adolescents as a function of family consensual types. *Journal of Nervous & Mental Disease, 171,* 734–741.

Sidanius, J., & Ekehammar, B. (1977). Cognitive differentiation and socio-politico ideology: An exploratory study. *Psychological Reports, 41,* 203–211.

Sifneos, P. (1996). Alexithymia: Past and present. *American Journal of Psychiatry, 153,* 137–142.

Silk, K. R., Lee, S., Hill, E. M., & Lohr, N. E. (1995). The borderline personality disorders symptoms and severity of sexual abuse. *American Journal of Psychiatry, 152,* 1059–1064.

Silk, K., & Lohr, N. (1996). Sexual abuse and borderline personality disorder: Reply. *American Journal of Psychiatry, 153,* 848–849.

Silver, D., & Rosenbluth, M. (Eds.). (1992). *Handbook of borderline disorders.* Madison, CT: International Universities Press.

Silverstone, P. H. (1991). Low self-esteem in different psychiatric conditions. *British Journal of Clinical Psychology, 30,* 185–188.

Simkin, D. K., Lederer, J. P., & Seligman, M. E. (1983). Learned helplessness in groups. *Behaviour Research & Therapy,* 21, 613–622.

Simon, G. E., & VonKorff, M. (1991). Somatization and psychiatric disorder in the NIMH Epidemiologic Catchment Area study. *American Journal of Psychiatry, 148,* 1494–1500.

Singer, M. (1974). Family structure, disciplinary configurations, and adolescent psychopathology. *Adolescent Psychiatry, 3,* 373–386.

Singh, S. (1978). Motive to avoid success. *Asian Journal of Psychology & Education, 3,* 39–45.

Singh, U. P., & Prasad, T. (1974). Authoritarianism and conformity behaviour. *Journal of Psychological Researches, 18,* 67–71.

Simon, G. E., VonKorff, M., & Barlow, W. (1995). Health care costs of primary care patients with recognized depression. *Archives of General Psychiatry, 52,* 850–856.

Sinnott, J. D. (2002). Postformal thought and adult development. In J. Demick & C. Andreotti (Eds.), *Handbook of adult development* (pp. 221–238). New York: Kluwer Academic.

Skodol, A. E., Oldham, J. M., Gallaher, P. E., & Bezirganian, S. (1994). Validity of self-defeating personality disorder. *American Journal of Psychiatry, 151,* 560–567.

Slade, A. (1999). Attachment theory and research: Implications for the theory and practice of individual psychotherapy with adults. In J. Cassidy & P. K. Shaver (Eds.), *Handbook of attachment: Theory, research, and clinical applications* (pp. 575–594). New York: Guilford.

Sloman, S. A. (1996). The empirical case for two systems of reasoning. *Psychological Bulletin, 119,* 3–22.

Smith, A., & O'Leary, S. (1995). Attributions and arousal as predictors of maternal discipline. *Cognitive Therapy & Research, 19,* 459–471.

Smith, S., & Hanson, R. (1975). Interpersonal relationships and childrearing practices in 214 parents of battered children. *British Journal of Psychiatry, 127,* 513–525.

Smith, T. W., & Brown, P. C. (1991). Cynical hostility, attempts to assert social control, and cardiovascular reactivity in married couples. *Journal of Behavioral Medicine, 14,* 581–592.

Smith, T. W., O'Keffe, J. L., & Allred, K. D. (1989). Neuroticism, symptom reports, and Type A behavior: Interpretive cautions for the Framingham scale. *Journal of Behavioral Medicine, 12,* 1–11.

Smyth, J. M., & L'Abate, L. (2001). A meta-analytic evaluation of workbook effectiveness in physical and mental health. In L. L'Abate (Ed.), *Distance writing and computer-assisted interventions in psychiatry and mental health* (pp. 77–90). Westport, CT: Ablex.

Snoek, D., & Rothblum, E. (1979). Self-disclosure among adolescents in relation to parental affection and control patterns. *Adolescence, 14,* 333–340.

Snyder, J., Reid, J., & Patterson, G. (2003). A social learning model of child and adolescent antisocial behavior. In B. B. Lahey, T. E. Moffitt, & A. Caspi (Eds.), *Causes of conduct disorder and juvenile delinquency* (pp. 27–48). New York: Guilford.

Sober, E., & Wilson, D. S. (1998). *Unto others: The evolution and psychology of unselfish behavior.* Cambridge, MA: Harvard University Press.

Sohlberg, S., Stahlheuer, P., & Tell, P. (1997). Depression, gender and identification: Replication and extension. *British Journal of Clinical Psychology, 36,* 453–455.

Solman, S. (1996). The empirical case for two systems of reasoning. *Psychological Bulletin, 119,* 3–22.

Solomon, A., Haaga, D. A. F., & Arnow, B. A. (2001). *Journal of Nervous & Mental Disease, 189,* 498–506.

Solomon, R. C. (1976). Psychological predicates. *Philosophy & Phenomenological Research, 36,* 472–493.

Spangle, M. L., & Isenhart, M. W. (2002). *Negotiation: Communication for diverse settings.* Thousand Oaks, CA: Sage.

Spangler, D. L., Simons, A. D., Monroe, S. M., & Thase, M. E. (1993). Evaluating the hopelessness model of depression: Diathesis-stress and symptom components. *Journal of Abnormal Psychology, 102,* 592–600.

Spence, J. T. (1980). The psychological dimensions of masculinity and femininity and achievement motivation. *Annals of the New York Academy of Sciences, 340*, 88–101.

Spence, J. T., & Helmerick, R. L. (1980). Masculine instrumentality and feminine expressiveness: Their relationships with sex role attitudes and behaviors. *Psychology of Women Quarterly, 5*, 147–163.

Spence, J. T., & Robbins, A. S. (1992). Workaholism: Definition, measurement, and preliminary research. *Journal of Personality Assessment, 58*, 160–178.

Sperry, L. (Ed.). (2004). Assessment of couples and families: Contemporary and cutting-edge strategies. New York: Brunner/Routledge.

Spigelman, A., & Spigelman, G. (1991). The relationship between parental divorce and the child's body boundary definiteness. *Journal of Personality Assessment, 56*, 96–105.

Spirito, A., Brown, L., Overholser, J., & Fritz, G. (1989). Attempted suicide in adolescence: A review and critique of the literature. *Clinical Psychology Review, 9*, 335–363.

Spitzer, R. L., & Davies, M. (1990). Criteria for self defeating personality disorder: Reply. *American Journal of Psychiatry, 147*, 1107–1108.

Srinivasagam, N. M., Kaye, W. H., Plotnicov, K. H., Greeno, C., et al. (1995). Persistent perfectionism, symmetry, and exactness alter long-term recovery from anorexia nervosa. *American Journal of Psychiatry, 152*, 1630–1634.

Srofe, L., & Waters, E. (1976). The ontogenesis of smiling and laughter: A perspective on the organization of development in infancy. *Psychological Review, 83*, 173–189.

Stacey, B. (1977). The psychology of conservatism. II: Wilson's theory and general trends in the study of conservatism. *New Zealand Psychologist, 6*, 109–123.

Stallard, P. (1996). Validity and reliability of the Parent Satisfaction Questionnaire. *British Journal of Clinical Psychology, 35*, 311–318.

Stark, K., Humphrey, J., Laurent, J., & Livingston, R. (1993). Cognitive, behavioral, and family factors in the differentiation of depressive and anxiety disorders during childhood. *Journal of Consulting & Clinical Psychology, 61*, 878–886.

Stasiewicz, P. R., & Maisto, S. A. (1993). Two-factor avoidance theory: The role of negative affect in the maintenance of substance use and substance use disorder. *Behavior Therapy, 24*, 337–356

Stanton, J. (1999). Generational transmission of child maltreatment. *Journal of the American Academy of Child & Adolescent Psychiatry, 38*, 14–19.

Stastny, P., et al. (1984). Early parental absence as an indicator of course and outcome in chronic schizophrenia. *American Journal of Psychiatry, 141*, 294–296.

Stattin, H., & Klackenberg-Larsson, I. (1993). Early language and intelligence development and their relationship to future criminal behavior. *Journal of Abnormal Psychology, 102*, 369–378.

Steinberg, R. J., & Ben-Zeev, T. (2001). *The psychology of human thought*. London, UK: Oxford University Press.

Steinhauer, P. D. (1983). Assessing for parental capacity. *American Journal of Orthopsychiatry, 53*, 468–481.

Stephens, D. A. (1975). Psychiatric morbidity in parents and sibs of schizophrenics and nonschizophrenics. *Journal of Psychiatry, 127*, 97–108.

Sterling, S., & Edelmann, R. J. (1988). Reactions to anger and anxiety-provoking events: Psychopathic and nonpsychopathic groups compared. *Journal of Clinical Psychology, 44*, 96–100.

Stevens, F. E., & L'Abate, L. (1989). Validity and reliability of a theory-derived measure of intimacy. *American Journal of Family Therapy, 17*, 359–368.

Stevenson, C. S., Stevenson, R. J., & Whitmont, S. (2003). A self-directed psychosocial intervention with minimal therapist contact for adults with attention deficit hyperactivity disorder. *Clinical Psychology and Psychotherapy, 10,* 93–101.

Stewart, A. J., & McDermott, C. (2004). Gender in psychology. *Annual Review of Psychology, 55,* 519–544.

Stiffman, A. R., Jung, K. G., & Feldman, R. A. (1986). A multivariate risk model for childhood behavior problems. *American Journal of Orthopsychiatry, 56,* 204–211.

Stinnett, N., & Taylor, S. (1976). Parent-child relationships and perceptions of alternate life styles. *Journal of Genetic Psychology, 129,* 105–112.

Stoller, R. J., & Herdt, G. H. (1985). Theories of origins of male homosexuality: A cross-cultural look. *Archives of General Psychiatry, 42,* 399–404.

Stoltz, R. F., & Galassi, J. P. (1989). Internal attributions and types of depression in college students: The learned helplessness model revisited. *Journal of Counseling Psychology, 36,* 316–321.

Stone, M. H. (1993). *Abnormalities of personality: Within and beyond the realm of treatment.* New York: Norton.

Stoneman, Z., Brody, G. H., & Burke, M. (1989). Marital quality, depression, and inconsistent parenting: Relationship with observed mother-child conflict. *American Journal of Orthopsychiatry, 59,* 105–117.

Storm, C., & Storm, T. (1987). A taxonomic study of the vocabulary of emotions. *Journal of Personality and Social Psychology, 53,* 805–816.

Stormshak, E. A., Bierman, K. L., McMahon, R. J., Lengua, L. J., et al. (2000). Parenting practices and child disruptive behavior problems in early elementary school. *Journal of Clinical Child Psychology, 29,* 17–29.

Stosney, S. (1995). *Treating attachment abuse: A compassionate approach.* New York: Springer.

Stout, M. (2001). *The myth of sanity: Divided consciousness and the promise of awareness.* New York: Viking.

Stout, M., & Mintz, L. (1996). Differences among non-clinical college women with alcoholic mothers, alcoholic fathers, and nonalcoholic parents. *Journal of Counseling Psychology, 43,* 466–472.

Strahan, R. F. (1981). Time urgency, Type A behavior, and effect strength. *Journal of Consulting & Clinical Psychology, 49,* 134.

Stranger, C., & Lewis, M. (1993). Agreement among parents, teachers, and children on internalizing and externalizing behavior problems. *Journal of Clinical Child Psychology, 22,* 107–115.

Stricker, G. (1992). The relationship of research to clinical practice. *American Psychologist, 47,* 543–549.

Stricker, G. (1997). Are science and practice commensurable? *American Psychologist, 52,* 442–448.

Sturgeon, D. (1981). Psychophysiological responses of schizophrenic patients to high and low expressed emotion relatives. *British Journal of Psychiatry, 138,* 40–45.

Sudstrom, E., & Altman, I. (1976). Interpersonal relationships and personal space: Research review and theoretical model. *Human Ecology, 4,* 47–67.

Suinn, R. M. (2001). The terrible twos—Anger and anxiety: Hazardous to your health. *American Psychologist, 56,* 27–36.

Sullivan, P. F., Joyce, P. R., & Mulder, R. T. (1994). Borderline personality disorder in major depression. *Journal of Nervous & Mental Disease, 182,* 508–516.

Suls, J., & Sanders, G. S. (1988). Type A behavior as a general risk factor for physical disorder. *Journal of Behavioral Medicine, 11,* 201–226.

Summers, F. (1978). Manual for the measurement of symbiosis in human relationships. *Psychological Reports, 43*, 663–670.

Summers, F., & Walsh, F. (1977). The nature of the symbiotic bond between mother and schizophrenic. *American Journal of Orthopsychiatry, 47*, 484–494.

Susser, E., Struening, E. L., & Conover, S. (1987). Childhood experiences of homeless men. *American Journal of Psychiatry, 144*, 1599–1601.

Swann, W. B., Wenzlaff, R., & Tafarodi, R. (1992). Depression and the search for negative evaluation: More evidence of the role of self-verification strivings. *Journal of Abnormal Psychology, 101*, 314–317.

Swart, C., Ickes, W., & Morgenthaler, E. (1978). The effect of objective self-awareness on compliance in a reactance situation. *Social Behavior & Personality, 6*, 135–139.

Sweda, M. G., Sines, J. O., Lauer, R. M., & Clarke, W. R. (1986). Familial aggression of Type A behavior. *Journal of Behavioral Medicine, 9*, 23–32.

Tafarodi, R. W., & Swann, W. B. (1995). Self-liking and self-competence as dimensions of global self-esteem: Initial validation of a measure. *Journal of Personality Assessment, 65*, 322–342.

Tallis, F., & DeSilva, P. (1992). Worry and obsessional symptoms: A co-relational analysis. *Behavior Research & Therapy, 30*, 103–105.

Tallis, F., Tosen, K., & Shafran, R. (1996). Investigation into the relationship between personality traits and OCD: A replication employing a clinical population. *Behaviour Research Therapy, 34*, 649–653.

Tallman, I., & Miller, G. (1974). Class differences in family problem solving: The effects of verbal ability, hierarchical structure, and role expectations. *Sociometry, 37*, 13–37.

Tangney, J., Wagner, P., & Gramzow, R. (1992). Proneness to shame, proneness to guilt, and psychopathology. *Journal of Abnormal Psychiatry, 101*, 469–478.

Tannenbaum, L., & Forehand, R. (1994). Maternal depressive mood: The role of the father in preventing adolescent problem behaviors. *Behaviour Research & Therapy, 32*, 321–325.

Taylor, A., Brannigan, G., & Murphy, V. (1970). Psychological distance, future time perceptive and internal-external expectancy. *Journal of Projective Techniques & Personality Assessment, 34*, 283–294.

Taylor, G. (1975). Separation-individuation in the psychotherapy of symbiotic states. *Canadian Psychiatric Association Journal, 20*, 521–526.

Taylor, G. (1984). Alexithymia: Concept, measurement, and implications for treatment. *American Journal of Psychiatry, 141*, 725–732.

Taylor, G. J., Bagby, R. M., & Luminet, O. (2000). Assessment of alexithymia: Self-report and observer-rated measures. In R. Bar-On & J. D. A. Parker (Eds.), *The handbook of emotional intelligence: Theory, development, assessment, and applications at home, school, and the workplace* (pp. 299–319). San Francisco, CA: Jossey-Bass.

Taylor, M. C., & Hall, J. A. (1983). Psychological androgyny: Theories, methods and conclusions. *Psychological Bulletin, 92*, 347–366.

Taylor, S. (1991). Asymmetrical effects of positive and negative events: The mobilization-minimization hypothesis. *Psychological Bulletin, 110*, 67–85.

Tennant, C. (1988). Parental loss in childhood: Its effect in adult life. *Archives of General Psychiatry, 45*, 1045–1050.

Terr, L. C. (1991). Childhood traumas: An outline and overview. *American Journal of Psychiatry, 148*, 10–20.

Thaker, G., Adami, H., Moran, M., & Lahti, A. (1993). Psychiatric illness in families of subjects with schizophrenia-spectrum personality disorders: High morbidity risks for unspecified functional psychoses and schizophrenia. *American Journal of Psychiatry, 150*, 66–71.

Thayer, R. F. (1989). *The biopsychology of mood and arousal*. London, UK: Oxford University Press.

Thayer, J., Rossy, I. A., Ruiz-Padial, E., & Johnsen, B. H. (2003). Gender differences in the relationship between emotional regulation and depressive symptoms. *Cognitive Therapy and Research, 27*, 349–364.

Thayer, R. E. (1996). *The origin of every day moods: Managing energy, tension, and stress.* New York: Oxford University Press.

Thomas, A., & Forehand, R. (1993). The role of parental variables in divorced and married families: Predictability of adolescent adjustment. *American Journal of Orthopsychiatry, 63*, 126–135.

Thomas, E. A., & Martin, J. A. (1976). Analyses of parent-infant interaction. *Psychological Review, 83*, 141–156.

Thomas, P. M. (2003). Protection, dissociation, and internal roles: Modeling and treating the effects of child abuse. *Review of General Psychology, 7*, 364–380.

Thoresen, C. E., & Powell, L. H. (1992). Type A behavior pattern: New perspectives on theory, assessment, and intervention. *Journal of Consulting & Clinical Psychology, 60*, 595–604.

Thornton, D. (2002). Constructing and testing a framework for dynamic risk assessment. *Sexual Abuse: A Journal for Research and Treatment, 14*, 139–154.

Thorson, J. A., Powell, F. C., Sarmany-Schuller, I., & Hampes W. P. (1997). Psychological health and sense of humor. *Journal of Clinical Psychology, 53*, 605–619.

Thyer, B. A., Nesse, R. M., Cameron, O. G., & Curtis, G. C. (1985). Agoraphobia: A test of the separation anxiety hypothesis. *Behaviour Reasearch & Therapy, 23*, 75–78.

Thayer, R. F. (1989). *The biopsychology of mood and arousal.* London, UK: Oxford University Press.

Tichon, J. G., & Shapiro, M. (2003). The process of sharing social support in cyberspace. *CyberPsychology & Behavior, 6*, 161–170.

Tiihonen, J., Eronen, M., & Hakola, P. (1993). Criminality associated with mental disorders and intellectual deficiency. *Archives of General Psychiatry, 50*, 917–918.

Tillfors, M., Furmark, T., Ekselius, L., & Fredrikson, M. (2001). Social phobia and avoidant personality disorder as related to parental history of social anxiety: A general population study. *Behaviour Research & Therapy, 39*, 289–298.

Timmons-Mitchell, J., Chandler-Holts, D., & Semple, W. (1996). Post-traumatic stress symptoms in mothers following children's reports of sexual abuse: An exploratory study. *American Journal of Orthopsychiatry, 66*, 463–467.

Tinsley, H., Hinson, J., Tinsley, D., & Holt, M. (1993). Attributes of leisure and work experiences. *Journal of Counseling Psychology, 40*, 447–455.

Tinsley, H. E. (1995). I am wanting to tell you: Reply to Borgen (1995) and Dawis (1995): Needs, taxonomies and leisure time. *Journal of Counseling Psychology, 42*, 138–140.

Tinsley, H. E., & Eldredge, B. D. (1995). Psychological benefits of leisure participation: A taxonomy of leisure activities based on their need/gratifying properties. *Journal of Counseling Psychology, 42*, 123–132.

Tobin, P. L. (1975). Perceived contribution of children to marriage and its effects on family planning behavior. *Social Biology, 22*, 75–85.

Tocco, T. S., & Bridges, C. M. (1973). The relationship between the self-concepts of mothers and their children. *Child Study Journal, 3*, 161–179.

Tolor, A. (1978). Personality correlates of the joy of life. *Journal of Clinical Psychology, 34*, 671–676.

Tomarken, A. J., & Keener, A. D. (1998). Frontal lobe asymmetry and depression: A self-regulatory perspective. *Cognition and Emotion, 12*, 387–420.

Toolan, J. (1981). Depression and suicide in children: An overview. *American Journal of Psychotherapy, 35*, 311–322.

Touhey, J. (1975). Interpersonal congruency, attitude similarity and interpersonal attraction. *Journal of Research in Personality, 9*, 66–73.

Tracy, R. L., Lamb, M. F., & Ainsworth, M. D. (1976). Infant approach behavior as related to attachment. *Child Development, 47*, 571–578.

Travis, L. L., & Sigman, M. D. (2000). A developmental approach to autism. In A. J. Sameroff, M. Lewis, & S. M. Miller (Eds.), *Handbook of developmental psychopathology* (pp. 641–655). New York: Kluwer Academic Publishers.

Trembley, R. E. (2003). Why socialization fails: The case of chronic physical aggression. In B. B. Lahey, T. E. Moffitt, & A. Caspi (Eds.), *Causes of conduct disorder and juvenile delinquency* (pp. 182–224). New York: Guilford.

Trembley, R. E., Pihl, R. O., Vitaro, F., & Dobkin, P. L. (1994). Predicting early onset of male antisocial behavior from pre-school behavior. *Archives of General Psychiatry, 51*, 732–739.

Treynor, W., Gonzales, R., & Nolen-Hoeksema, S. (2003). Rumination reconsidered: A psychometric analysis. *Cognitive Theory & Research, 27*, 247–259.

Troisi, A., D'Argenio, A., Peracchio, F., & Petti, P. (2001). Insecure attachment and alexithymia in young men with mood symptoms. *Journal of Nervous & Mental Disease, 189*, 311–316.

Troisi, A., Delle Chiaie, R., Russo, F., & Russo, M. (1996). Nonverbal behavior and alexithymic traits in normal subjects: Individual differences in encoding emotions. *Journal of Nervous & Mental Disease, 184*, 561–566.

Trull, T. J., Sher, K. J., Minks-Brown, C., Durbin, J., et al. (2000). Borderline personality disorder and substance use disorders: A review and integration. *Clinical Psychology Review, 20*, 235–255.

Tucker, L. (1976). A comparison of the value preferences of emotional disturbed adolescents and their parents with normal adolescents and their parents. *Adolescence, 11*, 549–567.

Tudge, J., Shanahan, M. J., & Valsiner, J. (Eds.). (1997). *Comparisons in human development: Understanding time and context*. New York: Cambridge University Press.

Turgeon, L., Julien, D., & Dion, E. (1998). Temporal linkages between wives' pursuit and husbands' withdrawal during marital conflict. *Family Process, 37*, 323–334.

Turner, S. M., & Beidel, D. C. (1989). Social phobia: Clinical syndrome, diagnosis, and comorbidity. *Clinical Psychology Review, 9*, 3–18.

Turner, S. M., Beidel, D. C., & Townsley, R. M. (1992). Social phobia: A comparison of specific and generalized sub-types and avoidant personality disorder. *Journal of Abnormal Psychology, 101*, 326–331.

Turner, S. M., & Hersen, M. (Eds.). (1997). *Adult psychopathology and diagnosis*. New York: Wiley.

Twenge, J. M., & Baumeister, R. F. (2002). Self-control: A limited yet renewable resource. In Y. Kashima, M. Foddy, & M. Platow (Eds.), *Self and identity: Personal, social, and symbolic* (pp. 57–70). Mahwah, NJ: Earlbaum.

Tyrer, P., & Johnson, T. (1996). Establishing the severity of personality disorder. *American Journal of Psychiatry, 153*, 1593–1597.

Uddenberg, N., Englesson, I., & Nettelbladt, P. (1979). Experience of father and later relations to men: A systematic study of women's relation to their father, their partner and their son. *Acta Psychiatrica Scandinavia, 59*, 87–96.

Unger, R. (1979). Toward a redefinition of sex and gender. *American Psychologist, 34*, 1085–1094.

U.S. Department of Health and Human Services (1999). *Mental health: A report of the Surgeon General*. Washington, DC: Office of Public Health and Science.

Ussher, J., & Dewberry, C. (1995). The nature and long-term effects of childhood sexual abuse: A survey of adult women survivors in Britain. *British Journal of Clinical Psychology, 34*, 177–192.

Uzoka, A. F. (1979). The myth of the nuclear family: Historical background and clinical implications. *American Psychologist, 34,* 1095–1106.

Vaillant, G., & Mukamal, K. (2001). Successful aging. *American Journal of Psychiatry, 158,* 839–847.

Vaillant, G. E. (1975). Natural history of male psychological health: III. Empirical dimensions of mental health. *Archives of General Psychiatry, 32,* 420–426.

Vaillant, G. E. (1977). Natural history of male psychological health: VI. Correlates of successful marriage and fatherhood. *American Journal of Psychiatry, 134,* 653–659.

Vaillant, G. E., & Vaillant, C. O. (1981). Natural history of male psychological health: X. Work as a predictor of positive mental health. *American Journal of Psychiatry, 138,* 1433–1440.

Valone, K., Norton, J., Goldstein, M., & Doane, J. (1983). Parental expressed emotion and affective style in an adolescent sample at risk of schizophrenia spectrum disorders. *Journal of Abnormal Psychology, 92,* 399–407.

Van den Aardweg, G. J. (1984). Parents of homosexuals—not guilty? Interpretation of childhood psychological data. *American Journal of Psychotherapy, 38,* 180–189.

Vandereycken, W. (1983). Agoraphobia and marital relationship: Theory, treatment and research. *Clinical Psychology Review, 3,* 317–338.

Van der Velde, C. D. (1985). Body images of one's self and of others: Developmental and clinical significance. *American Journal of Psychiatry, 142,* 527–537.

Vangelisti, A. L., & McGuire, K. (2002). Hurtful messages in family relationships: When the pain lingers: In J. H. Harvey & A. Wenzel (Eds.), *A clinician's guide to maintaining and enhancing close relationships* (pp. 43–62). Mahwah, NJ: Earlbaum.

Vangelisti, A. L. (2001). Making sense of hurtful interactions in close relationships: When hurt feelings create distance. In V. Manuson & J. H. Hanvey (Eds.), *Attribution, communication behavior, and close relationships* (pp. 38–58). New York: Cambridge University Press.

Van Leeuwen, M. S. (1978). A cross-cultural examination of psychological differentiation in males and females. *International Journal of Psychology, 13,* 87–122.

van Oppen, P., Hoeskstra, R. J., & Emmelkamp, P. M. G. (1995). The structure of obsessive-compulsive symptoms. *Behaviour Research & Therapy, 33,* 15–23.

Vasiljeva, O. A., Kornetov, N. A., Zhankov, A. I., & Reshetnikov, V. I. (1989). Immune function in psychogenic depression. *American Journal of Psychiatry, 146,* 284–285.

Vaughan, S. C. (2000). *Half empty half full: Understanding the psychological roots of optimism.* New York: Harcourt.

Vaughn, C., & Leff, J. (1976). The measurement of expressed emotion in the families of psychiatric patients. *British Journal of Social & Clinical Psychology, 15,* 157–165.

Veiel, H. (1993) Detrimental effects of kin support networks on the course of depression. *Journal of Abnormal Psychology, 102,* 419–429.

Vella, G., & Loredo, C. (1976). The psychotic family. *Archivio di Psicologia, Neurologia e Psichiatria, 37,* 417–433.

Velligan, D., Miller, A., Eckert, S., & Funderburg, L. (1996). The relationship between parental communication deviance and relapse in schizophrenic patients in the 1-year period after hospital discharge. *Journal of Nervous & Mental Disease, 184,* 490–496.

Vernberg, E., Jacobs, A., & Hershberger, S. (1999). Peer victimization and attitudes about violence during early adolescence. *Journal of Clinical Child Psychology, 28,* 386–395.

Victor, G. (1983). *The riddle of autism.* Lexington, MA: Lexington Books.

Vincent, C. E. (1976). Historical and theoretical perspectives: Sex, love and commitment revisited. *Journal of Sex & Marital Therapy, 2,* 265–272.

Vocisano, C., Klein, D., Keefe, R., & Dienst, E. (1996). Demographics, family history, premorbid functioning, developmental characteristics, and course of patients with deteriorated affective disorder. *American Journal of Psychiatry, 153,* 248–255.

Vogel, D. L., & Wester, S. R. (2003). To seek help or not to seek help: The risks of self-disclosure. *Journal of Counseling Psychology, 50,* 351–361.

Wadsworth, M., & Ford, D. H. (1983). Assessment for personal goal hierarchies. *Journal of Counseling Psychology, 30,* 514–526.

Wagner, B. (1997). Family risk factors for child and adolescent suicidal behavior. *Psychological Bulletin, 121,* 246–298.

Wahler, R. G., & Dumas, J. E. (1989). Attentional problems in dysfunctional mother-child interactions: An interbehavioral model. *Psychological Bulletin, 105,* 116–130.

Walberg, H., & Marjoribanks, K. (1976). Family environment and cognitive development: Twelve analytic models. *Review of Educational Research, 46,* 527–551.

Waldman, I. D., & Slutske, W. S. (2000). Antisocial behavior and alcoholism: A behavioral genetic perspective on comorbidity. *Clinical Psychology Review, 20,* 255–287.

Waldron, I., et al. (1980). Type A behavior pattern: Relationship to variation in blood pressure, parental characteristics, and academic and social activities of students. *Journal of Human Stress, 6,* 16–27.

Waldron, S., Shier, D. K., Stone, B., & Tobin, F. (1975). School phobia and other childhood neuroses: A systematic study of the children and their families. *American Journal of Psychiatry, 132,* 802–808.

Walker, E., Kestler, L., Bollini, A., & Hochman, K. M. (2004). Schizophrenia: Etiology and course. *Annual Review of Psychology, 55,* 401–430.

Walker, L., Garber, J., & Greene, J. (1994). Somatic complaints in pediatric patients: A prospective study of the role of negative life events, child social and academic competence, and parental somatic symptoms. *Journal of Consulting & Clinical Psychology, 62,* 1213–1221.

Walker, L., & Greene, J. (1987). Negative life events, psychosocial resources, and psychophysiological symptoms in adolescents. *Journal of Clinical Child Psychology, 16,* 29–36.

Walsh, F. W. (1979). Breaching of family generation boundaries by schizophrenics, disturbed, and normals. *International Journal of Family Therapy, 1,* 254–275.

Wamboldt, M., & Wamboldt, F. (2000). Role of the family in the onset and outcome of childhood disorders: Selected research findings. *Journal of the American Academy of Child & Adolescent Psychiatry, 39,* 1212–1219.

Wandersman, A., & Florin, P. (2003). Community interventions and effective prevention. *American Psychologist, 58,* 441–448.

Wandersman, L. P. (1973). Stylistic differences in mother-child interaction: A review and re-evaluation of the social class and socialization research. *Cornell Journal of Social Relations, 8,* 197–218.

Warner, V., Weissman, M., Fendrich, M., & Wickramaratne, P. (1992). The course of major depression in the offspring of depressed parents: Incidence, recurrence, and recovery. *Journal of Clinical Psychology, 25,* 356–358.

Warr, P. (1978). A study of psychological well-being. *British Journal of Psychology, 69,* 111–121.

Warren, R., Zgourides, G., & Jons, A. (1989). Cognitive bias and irrational belief as predictors of avoidance. *Behaviour Research & Therapy, 27,* 181–188.

Wasserstein, S., & La Greca, A. (1996). Can peer support buffer against behavioral consequences of parental discord? *Journal of Clinical Child Psychology, 25,* 177–182.

Watson, D. (2000). *Mood and temperament.* New York: Guilford.

Watson, D., & Tellegen, A. (1985). Toward a consensual structure of mood. *Psychological Bulletin, 98,* 219–235.

Watson, C. G., Vassar, P., Plemel, D., Herder, J. et al. (1990). A factor analysis of Ellis's irrational beliefs. *Journal of Clinical Psychology, 46,* 412–415.

Watts, F. (1983). Affective cognition: A sequel to Zajonc and Rachman. *Behavior Research & Therapy, 21*, 89–90.

Watzlawick, P. (1977). The pathologies of perfectionism. *Etc., 34*, 12–18.

Wearden, A., Tarrier, N., Barrowclough, C., & Zastowny, T. (2000). A review of expressed emotion research in health care. *Clinical Psychology Review, 20*, 633–666.

Weaver, T. L., & Clum, G. A. (1993). Early family environments and traumatic experience associated with borderline personality disorder. *Journal of Consulting & Clinical Psychology, 61*, 1068–1075.

Webster-Stratton, C. (1988). Mothers' and fathers' perceptions of child deviance: Roles of parent and child behaviors and parent adjustment. *Journal of Consulting & Clinical Psychology, 56*, 909–915.

Webster-Stratton, C. (1990a). Long-term follow-up of families with young conduct problem children: From preschool to grade school. *Journal of Clinical Child Psychology, 19*, 144–149.

Webster-Stratton, C. (1990b). Stress: A potential disruptor of parent perceptions and family interactions. *Journal of Clinical Child Psychology, 19*, 302–312.

Webster-Stratton, C. (1996). Early onset conduct problems: Does gender make a difference? *Journal of Consulting & Clinical Psychology, 64*, 540–551.

Webster-Stratton, C., & Eyberg, S. M. (1982). Child temperament: Relationship with child behavior problems and parent-child interactions. *Journal of Clinical Child Psychology, 11*, 123–129.

Weeks, G., & L'Abate, L. (1982). *Paradoxical psychotherapy: Theory and practice with individuals, couples, and families.* New York: Brunner/Mazel.

Wegner, D. M., & Wheatley, T. (1999). Apparent mental causation: Sources of the experience of will. *American Psychologist, 54*, 480–492.

Weinberg, J. (1979). Of slings and arrows and outrageous fortune. *American Journal of Psychoanalysis, 39*, 195–210.

Weinberg, R. P., Kumpfer, K. I., & Seligman, M. E. P. (2003). Prevention that works for children and youth. *American Psychologist, 58*, 425–432.

Weiner, D. N., & Rosen, R. C. (1999). Sexual dysfunctions and disorders. In T. Millon, P. H. Blaney, & R. D. Davis (Eds.), *Oxford textbook of psychopathology* (pp. 410–443). New York: Oxford University Press.

Weiner, M. (1978). Money myths in marriage. *Clinical Social Work Journal, 6*, 53–56.

Weinraub, M., Brooks, J., & Lewis, M. (1977). The social network: A reconsideration of the concept of attachment. *Human Development, 20*, 31–47.

Weiss, E. L., Longhurst, J. G., & Mazure, C. M. (1999). Childhood sexual abuse as a risk for depression in women: Psychosocial and neurobiological correlates. *American Journal of Psychiatry, 156*, 816–828.

Weissman, M. M., Gammon, G. D., John, K., Merikangas, K. R., et al. (1987). Children of depressed parents: Increased psychopathology and early onset of major depression. *Archives of General Psychiatry, 44*, 847–853.

Weller, L., Levinbok, S., Maimon, R., & Shaham, A. (1975). Religiosity and authoritarianism. *Journal of Social Psychology, 95*, 11–18.

Wells, A., & Morrison, A. (1994). Qualitative dimensions of normal worry and normal obsessions: A comparative study. *Behavior Research & Therapy, 32*, 867–870.

Welner, A., et al. (1976). Obsessive-compulsive neurosis: Record, follow-up, and family studies: I. Inpatient record study. *Comprehensive Psychiatry, 17*, 527–539.

Wenning, K., Nathan, P., & King, S. (1993). Mood disorders in children with oppositional defiant disorder: A pilot study. *American Journal of Orthopsychiatry, 63*, 295–299.

Wenz, F. (1978). Economic status, family anomie, and adolescent suicide potential. *Journal of Psychology, 98*, 45–47.

Wenzlaff, R., & Grozier, S. (1988). Depression and the magnification of failure. *Journal of Abnormal Psychology, 97*, 90–93.

Werner, E. E. (1989). High-risk children in young adulthood: A longitudinal study from birth to 32 years. *American Journal of Orthopsychiatry, 59*, 72–81.

Westen, D. (2000). Manualizing manual development. *Clinical Psychology: Science & Practice, 9*, 416–418.

Westen, D., Ludolph, P., Misle, B., & Ruffins, S. (1990). Physical and sexual abuse in adolescent girls with borderline personality disorder. *American Journal of Orthopsychiatry, 60*, 55–60.

Westen, D., Muderrisoglu, S., Fowler, C., Shedler, J., & Koren, D. (1997). Affect regulation and affective experience: Individual differences, group differences, and measurement using a Q-sort methodology. *Journal of Consulting and Clinical Psychology, 65*, 429–439.

Wetzler, H. P., & Ursano, R. J. (1988). A positive association between physical health practices and psychological well-being. *Journal of Nervous & Mental Disease, 176*, 280–283.

Wetzel, R. D., Margulies, T., Davis, R., & Karam, E. (1980). Hopelessness, depression, and suicide intent. *Journal of Clinical Psychiatry, 41*, 159–160.

Whalen, C. K., Flowers, J. V., Fuller, M. J., & Jernigan, T. (1975). Behavioral studies of personal space during early adolescence. *Man Environment Systems, 5*, 289–297.

Whisman, M. A., & Pinto, A. (1997). Hopelessness depression in depressed inpatient adolescents. *Cognitive Therapy & Research, 21*, 345–358.

Whitbourne, S., & Waterman, A. (1979). Psychosocial development during the adult years: Age and cohort comparisons. *Developmental Psychology, 15*, 373–378.

Whitehead, L. (1979). Sex differences in children's responses to family stress: A re-evaluation. *Journal of Child Psychology & Psychiatry, 20*, 247–254.

Whiteside, M. (1977). Self-concept differences among high and low creative college students. *Journal of College Student Personnel, 18*, 224–227.

Wichstrom, L., Anderson, A., Holte, A., & Wynne, L. (1996). Disqualifying family communication and childhood social competence as predictors of offspring's mental health and hospitalization: A 10 to14 year longitudinal study of children at risk of psychopathology. *Journal of Nervous & Mental Disease, 184*, 581–588.

Wicklund, R. (1979). The influence of self-awareness on human behavior. *American Scientist, 67*, 187–193.

Widiger, T. A. (1992). Generalized social phobia versus avoidant personality dosorder: A commentary on three studies. *Journal of Abnormal Psychology, 101*, 340–343.

Widiger, T. A. (2001). Official classification systems. In W. J. Livesley (Ed.), *Handbook of personality disorders: Theory, research, and treatment* (pp. 60–83). New York: Guilford.

Wikstrom, P. H., & Sampson, R. J. (2003). Social mechanisms of community influences on crime and pathways to criminality. In B. B. Lahey, T. E. Moffitt, & A. Caspi (Eds.), *Causes of conduct disorder and juvenile delinquency* (pp. 118–148). New York: Guilford.

Wilbert, J. R., & Rupert, P. A. (1986). Dysfunctional attitudes, loneliness and depression in college students. *Cognitive Therapy & Research, 10*, 71–77.

Wilke, H. (1977). The authority complex and the authoritarian personality. *Journal of Analytical Psychology, 22*, 243–249.

Wilkinson-Ryan, T., & Westen, D. (2000). Identity disturbance in borderline personality disorder: An empirical investigation. *American Journal of Psychiatry, 157*, 528–541.

Williams, C., & Lyons, C. M. (1976). Family interaction and adolescent suicidal behavior: A preliminary investigation. *Australian & New Zealand Journal of Psychiatry, 10*, 243–252.

Williams, E., & Radin, N. (1993). Paternal involvement, maternal employment and adolescent academic achievement: An 11 year follow-up. *American Journal of Orthopsychiatry, 63,* 306–312.

Williams, O. B., & Corrigan, P. W. (1992). The differential effects of parental alcoholism and mental illness on their adult children. *Journal of Clinical Psychology, 48,* 406–414.

Williamson, J., Bordin, C., & Howe, B. (1991). The ecology of adolescent maltreatment: A multilevel examination of adolescent physical abuse, sexual abuse, and neglect. *Journal of Consulting & Clinical Psychology, 59,* 449–457.

Williamson, R. (1976). Socialization, mental health, and social class: A Santiago sample. *Social Psychiatry, 11,* 69–74.

Willis, D. (1995). Psychological impact of child abuse and neglect. *Journal of Clinical Child Psychology, 24,* 2–4.

Wilson, J. P., & Wilson, S. B. (1976). Sources of self-esteem and the person X situation controversy. *Psychological Reports, 38,* 355–358.

Wilson, T. D., & Dunn, E. W. (2004). Self-knowledge: Its limits, value, and potential for improvement. *Annual Review of Psychology, 55,* 493–518.

Winegar, N. (1992). *The clinician's guide to managed mental health care.* New York: Haworth.

Winokur, G., & Coryell, W. H. (1991). Familial alcoholism in primary unipolar major depressive disorder. *American Journal of Psychiatry, 148,* 184–188.

Winokur, G., Coryell, W. H., Keller, M., & Endicott, J. (1995). A family study of manic-depressive (bipolar I) disease: Is it a distinct illness separable from primary unipolar depression? *Archives of General Psychiatry, 52,* 367–373.

Winters, K. C., & Neale, J. M. (1985). Mania and low self-esteem. *Journal of Abnormal Psychology, 94,* 282–290.

Wirsching, M., & Stierlin, H. (1979). Family dynamics and family psychotherapy of psychosomatic disorders. *Psychotherapy & Psychosomatics, 32,* 128–133.

Wiseman, M. A., & Pinto, A. (1997). Hopelessness and depression in depressed inpatient adolescents. *Cognitive Therapy & Research, 21,* 345–358.

Wisom, C. (1999). Posttraumatic stress disorder in abused and neglected children grown up. *American Journal of Psychiatry, 156,* 1223–1229.

Withers, L., & Kaplan, D. (1987). Adolescents who attempt suicide: A retrospective clinical chart review of hospitalized patients. *Professional Psychology: Research & Practice, 18,* 391–393.

Witkin, H. A., & Berry, J.W. (1975). Psychological differentiation in cross-cultural perspective. *Journal of Cross-Cultural Psychology, 6,* 4–87.

Witkin, H. A., Goodenough, D., & Oltman, P. (1979). Psychological differentiation: Current status. *Journal of Personality & Social Psychology, 37,* 1127–1145.

Witvliet, C. V. O. (2003, October 24). *Forgiveness, emotion, and psychophysiology: Four experiments.* Paper presented at the Scientific Findings about Forgiveness Conference, Atlanta.

Wolf, A., Schubert, D., Patterson, M., & Grande, T. P. (1988). Associations among major psychiatric diagnoses. Psycho-diagnosis, epidemiology and mental disorders. *Journal of Consulting & Clinical Psychology, 56,* 292–294.

Wolfe, D. A., & Mosk, M. D. (1983). Behavioral comparisons of children from abusive and distressed families. *Journal of Consulting & Clinical Psychology, 51,* 702–708.

Wolfe, V. V., Gentile, C., & Wolfe, D. A. (1989). The impact of sexual abuse on children: A PTSD formulation. *Behavior Therapy, 20,* 215–228.

Wolff, H. (1972). Crisis points and problems of identity. *Journal of Psychosomatic Research, 16,* 229–234.

Woods, P. J., et al. (1984). Findings on a relationship between Type A behavior and headaches. *Journal of Behavioral Medicine, 7,* 277–286.

Woody, S. R., & Teachman, B. A. (2000). Intersection of disgust and fear: Normal and pathological views. *Clinical Psychology: Science & Practice, 7*, 291–311.

Woolfolk, R. L., Gara, M. A., Ambrose, T. K., Williams, J. E., et al. (1999). Self-complexity and the persistence of depression. *Journal of Nervous & Mental Disease, 187*, 393–399.

Woollams, S. J., & Huige, K. A. (1977). Normal dependency and symbiosis. *Transactional Analysis Journal, 7*, 217–220.

Worell, J. (1978). Sex roles and psychological well-being: Perspectives on methodology. *Journal of Consulting & Clinical Psychology, 46*, 777–791.

Wortman, C. B., & Silver, R. C. (1989). The myths if coping with loss. *Journal of Consulting & Clinical Psychology, 57*, 349–357.

Wright, L. (1976). The "sick but slick" syndrome as a personality component of parents of battered children. *Journal of Clinical Psychology, 32*, 41–45.

Wright, P. H. (1978). Toward a theory of friendship based on a conception of self. *Human Communication Research, 4*, 196–207.

Wrzeniewski, K., Forgays, D. G., & Bonaiuto, P. (1990). Measurement of the Type A behavior pattern in adolescent and young adults: Cross-culture development of AATAB. *Journal of Behavioral Medicine, 13*, 111–135.

Wyer, R. S., Jr., & Srull, T. K. (Eds.). (1993). *Perspectives on anger and emotion*. Mahwah, NJ: Earlbaum.

X Day, D., & Schneider, P. L. (2002). Psychotherapy using distance technology: A comparison of face-to-face, video, and audio treatment. *Journal of Counseling Psychology, 49*, 499–503.

Yama, M. F., Fogas, B. S., Teegarden, L., & Hastings, B. (1993). Childhood sexual abuse and parental alcoholism: Interactive effects in adult women. *American Journal of Orthopsychiatry, 63*, 300–305.

Yama, M. F., Tovey, S. L., & Fogas, B. S. (1993). Childhood family environment and sexual abuse as predictors of anxiety and depression in adult women. *American Journal of Orthopsychiatry, 63*, 136–141.

Yang, B., & Clum, G. (1996). Effects of early negative life experiences on cognitive functioning and risk of suicide: A review. *Clinical Psychology Review, 16*, 77–195.

Yarnold, P. R., & Bryant, F. B. (1988). A note on measurement issues in Type A research: Let's not throw out the baby with the bath water. *Journal of Personality Assessment, 52*, 410–419.

Yarnold, P. R., Bryant, F. B., & Grimm, L. G. (1987). Comparing the long and short forms of the student version of the Jenkins Activity Survey. *Journal of Behavioral Medicine, 10*, 75–90.

Yarnold, P. R., Mueser, K. T., & Grimm, L. G. (1985). Interpersonal dominance of Type As in group discussions. *Journal of Abnormal Psychology, 94*, 233–236.

Yates, A. (1991). *Compulsive exercise and the eating disorders: Toward an integrated theory of activity*. New York: Brunner/Mazel.

Yates, B. T., Fullerton, C. S., Goodrich, W., Heinssen, R. K., et al. (1989). Grandparent deaths and severe maternal reaction in the etiology of adolescent psychopathology. *Journal of Nervous & Mental Disease, 177*, 675–680.

Young, M., Fogg, L., Scheftner, W., & Fawcett, W. (1996). Stable trait components of hopelessness: Baseline and sensitivity to depression. *Journal of Abnormal Psychology, 105*, 155–156.

Zacker, J. (1973). Authoritarian avoidance of ambiguity. *Psychological Reports, 33*, 901–902.

Zahn-Waxler, C. (1984). Problem behavior and peer interactions of young children with a manic-depressive parent. *American Journal of Psychiatry, 141*, 236–240.

Zahn-Waxler, C., Mayfield, A., Radke-Yarrow, M., & McKnew, D. (1988). A follow-up investigation of offspring of parents with bipolar disorder. *American Journal of Psychiatry, 145*, 506–509.

Zajonc, R. (1976). Family configuration and intelligence: Variations in scholastic aptitude scores parallel trends in family size and the spacing of children. *Science, 192,* 227–236.

Zajonc, R., & Markus, G. (1975). Birth order and intellectual development. *Psychological Review, 82,* 74–88.

Zajonc, R., Markus, H., & Markus, G. (1979). The birth order puzzle. *Journal of Personality & Social Psychology, 37,* 1325–1341.

Zanarini, M., Williams, A., Lewis, R., & Reich, R. (1997). Reported pathological childhood experiences associated with the development of borderline personality disorder. *American Journal of Psychiatry, 154,* 1101–1106.

Zappert, L. T., & Weinstein, H. M. (1985). Sex differences in the impact of work on physical and psychological health. *American Journal of Psychiatry, 142,* 1174–1178.

Zarit, S. H., Pearlin, L. I., & Schaie, K. W. (Eds.). (2003). *Personal control in social and life course contexts.* New York: Springer.

Zaslow, M. J. (1988). Sex differences in children's response to parental divorce: I. Research methodology and post-divorce family forms. *American Journal of Orthopsychiatry, 58,* 355–378.

Zaslow, M. J. (1989). Sex differences in children's response to parental divorce: II. Samples, variables, ages, and sources. *American Journal of Orthopsychiatry, 59,* 118–141.

Zautra, A., Guenther, R., & Chartier, G. (1985). Attributions for real and hypothetical events: Their relation to self-esteem and depression. *Journal of Abnormal Psychology, 94,* 530–540.

Zeitlin, S., & McNally, R. (1990). Alexithymia and anxiety sensitivity in panic disorder and obsessive compulsive disorder. *American Journal of Psychiatry, 150,* 658–660.

Zeitlin, S., McNally, R., & Cassidy, K. (1993). Alexithymia in victims of sexual assault: An effect of repeated traumatization? *American Journal of Psychiatry, 150,* 661–663.

Zimmerman, M., & Coryell, W. H. (1990). DSM-III personality disorder dimensions. *Journal of Nervous & Mental Disease, 178,* 686–692.

Zimmerman, M., McDermott, W., & Mattia, J. I. (2000). Frequency of anxiety disorders in psychiatric outpatients with major depressive disorder. *American Journal of Psychiatry, 157,* 1337–1340.

Zubenko, G. S., George, A. W., Soloff, P. H., & Schulz, P. (1987). Sexual practices among patients with borderline personality disorder. *American Journal of Psychiatry, 144,* 748–752.

Zuravin, S. J. (1989). Severity of maternal depression and three types of mother-to-child aggression. *American Journal of Orthopsychiatry, 59,* 377–389.

Zuroff, D. C. (1994). Depressive personality styles and the five-factor model of personality. *Journal of Personality Assessment, 63,* 453–472.

Zuroff, D. C., Koestner, R., & Powers, T. (1994). Self-criticism at age 12: A longitudinal study of adjustment. *Cognitive Therapy & Research, 18,* 367–385.

Zuroff, D. C., Moskowitz, D. S., & Coté, S. (1999). Dependency, self-criticism, interpersonal behaviour and affect: Evolutionary perspectives. *British Journal of Clinical Psychology, 38,* 231–250.

Zuroff, D. C., Moskowitz, D. S., & Koestner, R. (1996, August). *Differentiating the construct of dependency: Rude and Burnham's neediness and connectedness factors.* Paper presented at the American Psychological Association, Toronto, Canada.

Zuroff, D., Scotland, S., Sweetman, E., & Craig, J. (1995). Dependency, self-criticism and social interactions. *British Journal of Clinical Psychology, 34,* 543–553.

Zweig-Frank, H., & Paris, J. (1991). Parents emotional neglect and overprotection according to the recollections of patients with borderline personality disorder: Correction. *American Journal of Psychiatry, 148,* 1282.

Index

463